The Letters of
William Cullen Bryant

I

Printed in the United States of America

Contents

Illustrations   between pages 248 and 249

Key to Manuscript Sources Often Cited in Footnotes

BCHS   Bryant Family Association Papers, Bureau County Historical Society, Princeton, Illinois.

BPL   Boston Public Library.

HCL   Harvard College Library.

HEHL   Henry E. Huntington Library and Art Gallery.

Homestead Collection. The William Cullen Bryant Homestead Collection of the Trustees of Reservations, Cummington, Massachusetts.

LH   Longfellow House, Cambridge, Massachusetts.

MHS   Massachusetts Historical Society.

NYHS   New-York Historical Society.

NYPL–Berg   Henry W. and Albert A. Berg Collection, The New York Public Library, Astor, Lenox and Tilden Foundations.

NYPL–BFP   Bryant Family Papers, Manuscript Division, The New York Public Library, Astor, Lenox and Tilden Foundations.

NYPL–BG   Bryant–Godwin Collection, Manuscript Division, The New York Public Library, Astor, Lenox and Tilden Foundations.

NYPL–Flagg   Flagg Collection, Manuscript Division, The New York Public Library, Astor, Lenox and Tilden Foundations.

NYPL–GR   Goddard–Roslyn Collection, Manuscript Division, The New York Public Library, Astor, Lenox and Tilden Foundations.

NYPL–Miscellaneous Bryant Papers   Miscellaneous Bryant Papers, Manuscript Division, The New York Public Library, Astor, Lenox and Tilden Foundations.

Sheldon Museum. Manuscript letters from the estate of Charity Bryant, in the Sheldon Museum at Middlebury, Vermont.

UVa   The Clifton Waller Barrett Library of the University of Virginia Library.

Weston Family Papers. Letters in the possession of the descendants of the late Byron Weston, of Dalton, Massachusetts.

ACKNOWLEDGMENTS

In their wish to express sincere appreciation to the many institutions and individuals who have aided in the preparation of this first general collection of the letters of William Cullen Bryant, its editors face a formidable task.

Facsimiles of manuscript letters written by Bryant, and others written to or about him, have been acquired from more than 135 institutional and private collections, in this country and abroad. Several of these are very large: five libraries hold an average of one hundred letters each, and Bryant's descendants, direct or collateral, possess many hundreds more which have been in the family since his death nearly a century ago. The wide dispersal of even a larger number is made evident in forty-seven collections containing five or more letters each. The following institutions own an average of more than forty Bryant letters: Amherst College; the Boston Public Library; Brown University; The Bryant Library at Roslyn, New York; the Bureau County Historical Society, Princeton, Illinois; the Chicago Historical Society; Columbia University; Duke University; Harvard University; the Henry E. Huntington Library and Art Gallery; Johns Hopkins University; The Library of Congress; The Longfellow House, Cambridge, Massachusetts; the Massachusetts Historical Society; The New-York Historical Society; The New York Public Library; The New York State Library; New York University; The Historical Society of Pennsylvania; The Pierpont Morgan Library; Princeton University; Queens Borough Public Library, New York City; The University of Texas at Austin; the University of Virginia; Williams College; and Yale University. These institutions and all others providing the editors with letter facsimiles have kindly agreed to permit their publication in this edition. Acknowledgment has been made, immediately following the text of each letter printed in the present volume, of its ownership, and similar acknowledgments will be made in each succeeding volume. The editors hope that the responsible officers of each institution named will understand the gratitude implicit in such acknowledgment.

There are many persons now, or lately, associated with these institutions for whose services we should like to express our thanks. Because of the passage of time and the mobility of professional careers, we do not try to identify by title and affiliation those who gave their time to answer our questions, and shared with us their specialized knowledge. We simply list their names in appreciation. They are Robert Balay, Roy P. Basler, Kathleen Boyd, Dorothy W. Bridgewater, Adele Capps, Winifred V. Collins, Florence Connolly, Elizabeth Daly, Pat Drechsler, Elizabeth S. Duvall, Janet M. Edwards, Lynne Easter, Nicholas Falco, Gerritt E. Fielstra, Anne Freudenberg, Mary Isabel Fry, Donald Gallup, John D. Gordan, J. Owen Grundy, Mihai H. Handrea, Jacquelin K. Haring, Elinor S. Hearn, James J. Heslin, Edith G. Henderson, James W. Henderson, Robert W. Hill, Alan Jutzi, Dorothy King, Sharon E. Knapp, Mildred M. Ledden, Kenneth A. Lohf, Kathleen Luhrs, Glenise A. Matheson, Charles W. Mixer, James E. Mooney, Mrs. Richard Mudge, Robert G. Newman, Joseph M. O'Donnell, William A. Pease, Cynthia D. Perlis, Julia C. Peters, Polly Pierce, John E. Powers, John E. Pomfret, Paul Rugin, J. Thomas Russell, Patricia J. Sarro, Jean Saunders, J. C. Sharp, Barbara Shepherd, Lee Stanton, Lola L. Szladits, H. S. Tallamy, Joshua C. Taylor, W. A. Taylor, Maude C. Trimble, Thomas H. de Valcourt, Egon Weiss, Earle Whitmore, Lawrence E. Wikander, and Wyllis H. Wright.

Between the accumulation of Bryant's letters and their assembly in a coherent whole, there have been many occasions when the editors have, of necessity, asked the help of scholarly friends and acquaintances. Their assistance, freely accorded, has taken many forms—advice, information, guidance, correction, admonition, and, above all, interest and encouragement. We are indebted particularly, for their many unselfish services, to Dimmes McDowell Bishop, Julian P. Boyd, Donald C. Bryant, Solena V. Bryant, Lyman H. Butterfield, James T. Callow, Rose M. Cascio, Harry George Fletcher III, David C. Gordon, Giovanni Giovannini, Oliver W. Holmes, David Horne, Herbert L. Kleinfield, Andrew Breen Myers, James Kerby Neill, Allan Nevins, Harry Oster, Norman Holmes Pearson, DeWolf Perry, Ralph Leslie Rusk, Mary Beatrice Schulte, Jane C. Voss, and Richard Wilbur. We have also been favored with the knowledge and insights of several scholars who have, during the past several decades, clarified many matters relating to Bryant's varied career. We are most in debt to the writing of James T. Callow, Tremaine McDowell, Allan Nevins, Herman E. Spivey, and Stanley T. Williams.

The recent publication (1974) of an exhaustively researched and documented history of the Town of Cummington, Massachusetts, has facilitated the preparation of Bryant's letters for publication. This admirable account of the town where he was born, and to which he returned in old age to become its almost legendary citizen, was initiated by the Cummington Historical Commission. Written by the Commission's co-chairman, William W. Streeter (whose ancestral farm embraces the site of the one-room school where Bryant began his lessons at the age of three), and narrated with a warmth of insight by Helen H. Foster, this account will remain a remarkable testimonial to the lives of a dozen of its citizens, Bryant among them, who rose to national prominence. And we should like to express our gratitude to other Cummingtonites who have made their various contributions to the publication of the Bryant letters: Peggy and Philip Dater, Barbara D. Goldsmith, the late Martin K. Howes, Evelyn Seely Jackson, Alice C. Steele, Olive and Leon Thayer, and Josephine and Harold Whitford.

Several organizations and individuals have given monetary support to our research and writing: the National Historical Publications Commission, the National Endowment for the Humanities, and two members of the Bryant family. A number of the Bryant descendants either have given their approval to the publication of letters in their possession, or have supported our project in other effective ways. They include Mrs. Winthrop Murray Crane III, Miss Elizabeth Love Godwin, Mrs. Mildred Bryant Kussmaul, Mrs. Donald Weston, and the late Conrad Godwin Goddard, great-grandson of the poet, who lived for much of his lifetime on Bryant's estates at Roslyn and Cummington. Mr. Goddard, who was for a great many years the custodian both of Bryant's properties and his papers, was the possessor of irreplaceable knowledge about Bryant's life as a man, distinct from that as a poet. But his sympathy with literary and historical scholars who came to him time and again with probing questions about his ancestor, and insistent requests to reproduce Bryant's writings, proved him a literary executor of extraordinary perspicacity as well as generosity. Without his cooperation and encouragement from the outset, this work could not have been accomplished. The present editors regret, profoundly, that Conrad Goddard did not live to see the publication of *The Letters of William Cullen Bryant.*

Introduction

ADDRESSING A WOULD-BE BIOGRAPHER near the close of his incomparable career, Thomas Jefferson wrote, "The letters of a person, . . . form the only full and genuine journal of his life; and few can let them go out of their own hands while they live. A life written after these hoards become open to investigation must supercede any previous one."

Like Jefferson, whose many-sided public life his own resembled significantly, William Cullen Bryant began in old age a narrative of his early years. But, unlike his great democratic precursor, whom he had lampooned in youth and grown in maturity to admire greatly, he refused to undertake an autobiography. When, nearing eighty, he was urged by William Dean Howells to compose an account of his life, he replied, "I have thought a good deal of the reminiscences which you ask me to dish up for the Atlantic [*Monthly*], and the more I have thought the less am I inclined to the task. I cannot set them down without running into egotism. I remember more of my own experiences than of my associations with other men and the part they took in what fell under my observation."

In the absence of a skillful and uniquely informed biographer, the record of Bryant's versatile career has become "thin and shadowy," wrote Vernon Parrington, since his death nearly a century ago. The unusual length of his public life (just seventy years), his extraordinarily various professional and civic activities, and his insatiable habit of travel, both at home and abroad, pose a stiff challenge to the best of chroniclers. Thus, while it might be supposed that the biography written by his editorial associate and son-in-law, Parke Godwin, five years after Bryant's death in 1878, must be both thorough and authoritative, its imbalance becomes more apparent as its subject's scattered correspondence is brought together for the first time.

Bryant was a publishing poet for almost seventy years, from "The Embargo" in 1808 to "The Flood of Years" in 1876. For half a century he was an influential political journalist. Throughout that period—which spanned the tenures of fourteen presidents—his leading editorials in the New York *Evening Post* expressed opinions often implemented afterward in public policy. His friendships with artists and writers were more numerous than those of any of his contemporary Americans. Landscape painters rendered his themes in half a hundred works, and he sat for nearly that many portraits in his lifetime. His memorial discourses on a dozen of his fellows, notably Thomas Cole, Fenimore Cooper, Washington Irving, and Fitz-Greene Halleck, remain in some instances the best existing brief accounts of their lives. In upwards of a hundred public addresses Bryant showed his informed concern with a great variety of subjects, from Greek Independence to Municipal Reform, from Public Health to Music in the Public Schools, from Mythology to Pomology. Yet, despite his many preoccupations, he wrote nearly twenty-five hundred identifiable letters, of which more than two thousand have been recovered for the present collection.

No previous compilation of Bryant's correspondence has ever been attempted. His first important biographer, Godwin, printed numerous "extracts" from such letters as he managed to retrieve; but even of these many were taken from rough drafts without comparison with later final copies, and few were reproduced in their entirety. Bryant himself gathered together three volumes of the travel letters he had previously published in the *Evening Post*. Since his death, letters have appeared from time to time in various periodicals—all too often transcribed and edited inaccurately. In such ephemeral form they have added little to his epistolary reputation.

Although Godwin managed to keep the overt expression of animosity out of his family-authorized biography, there is little doubt that he felt an imperfect sympathy for the father-in-law upon whom he had long been financially dependent, and whom he once characterized as a "cold, irritable and selfish man" who "wants human every day sympathies and is a little malignant." This covert bias inevitably led him to ignore or to slight activities central to his subject's career and essential to a rounded image of the man. Among these were Bryant's role in forming cultural organizations and civic institutions such as the National Academy of Design, Sketch Club, American Art Union, Century Association, Central Park, and the Metropolitan Museum of Art, and his powerful aesthetic influence on the painting of the Hudson River School, both now freely credited by historians; his intimacy with such artists as John James Audubon, Edwin Booth, George Catlin, Thomas Cole, Lorenzo Da Ponte, Andrew Jackson Downing, Asher Durand, Edwin Forrest, Horatio Greenough, Henry Inman, Samuel F. B. Morse, Frederick Law Olmsted, and Robert Weir; his seminal writing as a literary critic, also now generally recognized; his long concern with public health, culminating in his ten-year presidency of the New York Medical College; and the countless personal services he performed for friends and even casual acquaintances which led his longtime partner, John Bigelow, to remark that Bryant "treated every neighbor as if he were an angel in disguise sent to test his loyalty to the golden rule."

Godwin's biography was vitiated by its author's failure to recover more than a relative handful of Bryant's letters—so few, indeed, that he could suppose Bryant had not "maintained any extensive correspondence," seldom finding it possible to "engage in discussions of opinions or of the events of the day." Yet, by themselves, more than thirty letters addressed to Abraham Lincoln during his short presidency evidence the contrary. Except for some letters to a few close friends who outlived Bryant and made them available to his biographer, and others to members of his immediate family, Godwin relied on initial drafts (though never so designating them), and on copies provided by his sister-in-law Julia Bryant of such letters "as she supposed might be useful in the preparation of a memoir of [her father's] life." Barely a third of the nearly two hundred surviving letters from Bryant to his wife, Frances, during their fifty years of courtship and marriage found a place, even in fragmentary form, in Godwin's account. During Bryant's first visit to the British Isles in 1845, for instance, he sent Frances, almost daily, intimate accounts of his experiences, and of meetings with and impressions of prominent persons such as Charles Babbage, Joanna Baillie, Sir John Bowring, John Bright, Francis Buckland, Rev. Robert Candlish, Richard Cobden, Dr. John Conolly, Sir Charles Fellows, Edwin Field, Rev. William Johnson Fox, Henry Hallam, William and Mary Howitt, Leigh Hunt, Harriet Martineau, Rev. James Martineau, Richard Monckton Milnes, first Baron Houghton, James Montgomery, Sir Roderick Murchison, Spencer Joshua Alwyne Compton, second Marquis of Northampton, John O'Connell, John Poole, Henry Crabb Robinson, Samuel Rogers, Adam Sedgwick, William Guy Wall, William Whewell, and the Wordsworth family. These accounts do not appear in Godwin's biography; we are told instead that Bryant's "brief pocket-Diary . . . save a few notes to his newspaper, is all the record we have of his movements." More regrettably, recent biographers seem to have been unaware of the easy availability of such letters, apparently accepting Godwin's statement without question.

Many of Bryant's correspondents in public life do not figure in Godwin's pages. Of one hundred letters to a random list of fifteen statesmen and prominent educators, none is quoted therein: Charles Francis Adams, Salmon P. Chase, Cyrus W. Field, Hamilton Fish, Daniel C. Gilman, Mark Hopkins, William L. Marcy, James McCosh, Edwin D. Morgan, Theophilus Parsons, Jared Sparks, Charles Sumner, Samuel J. Tilden, Gideon Welles, and Silas Wright. Letters to Bryant's literary friends and acquaintances were most numerous; yet, of nearly five hundred he wrote to sixty such persons, relatively few appear in Godwin's work. In some cases recipients were reluctant to make them available; the historian–statesman George Bancroft, to whom Bryant wrote more than fifty letters during a long friendship, admitted to finding but one—a brief invitation to a meeting!

Bryant corresponded with almost every president from Jackson to Hayes, and with members of their cabinets, key senators and representatives, state and local officials, and civic leaders throughout the country. His concern with religious matters in the United States and Europe is reflected in dozens of letters addressed to his newspaper and to prominent clergymen among his friends, including Orville Dewey, Andrews Norton, Samuel Osgood, Henry Ware, Sr., William Ware, and Robert Waterston. His analyses of events and personalities in the news provide insights into the positions he took concurrently in *Evening Post* editorials. These are further illuminated by frank comments to such intimates as his brother John, John Bigelow, Richard Henry Dana, John Durand, Ferdinand Field, John Gourlie, Isaac Henderson, William Leggett, Charles Nordhoff, James Kirke Paulding, Charles and Theodore Sedgwick, and William Gilmore Simms.

While there is much which is fresh and enlightening in Bryant's letters to close associates and public men, his personality is more intimately projected in those to a number of women to whom he addressed some of his most exuberant communications. Early letters to his sister Sally, his mother, and his intended bride show Bryant at times playful, at others prim or moralistic, occasionally sardonic, and frequently lively. As the years went on, and particularly after his wife's death in 1866, he found sympathetic understanding in a number of talented women, several of whom were popular authors—Carolina Coronado, Julia Ward Howe, Caroline Kirkland, Catharine Sedgwick; some, the relatives of men friends—Charlotte Dana, Jerusha Dewey, Julia Sands, Anna Waterston; and others—the English widow Susan Renner, the educational writer Eliza Robbins, the Scottish schoolteacher Christiana Gibson, his Roslyn neighbor Leonice Moulton—stimulating conversationalists and warm friends.

The bringing together in sequence of over two thousand letters written by Bryant between the ages of fourteen and eighty-four provides the closest possible approximation of an autobiography—the one which he might have been persuaded to undertake, but declined to do so, during his lifetime. It makes more convincing a remark made by Benjamin F. Butler to Martin Van Buren when Bryant had angered the former President by supporting the new Republican party in 1856: "I regard him as one of the brightest luminaries of the age—not only in the department of letters but in that also of politics. Posterity, I think, will place him on the same roll with Miltons, Hampdens and Jeffersons of the last two centuries."

Editorial Plan

THE TEXTS OF THE 314 available letters written by Bryant between April 1809 and April 1836 are included in this first volume. Wherever possible, they are printed from the original manuscripts. In some instances they are reproduced from authenticated holograph or typewritten copies. In others, only the published texts have been preserved, and are used here.

Bryant's frequent practice of drafting and then revising letters before making final copies provides a number of preliminary texts not known to have survived in another form. Where final copies of such letters have been recovered they are reproduced, with occasional marked differences from the preliminary drafts indicated in footnotes.

The letters are arranged chronologically, and grouped to reflect significant periods in Bryant's life. Each period is prefaced by a brief account of its principal events. Letters of uncertain date are placed conjecturally. When both month and day can be assigned with reason, they appear in the chronological sequence. If only the month can be determined, they are put at its end; where they can be placed with assurance only within a longer period, a like procedure is followed.

Bryant's frequent use of foreign languages in the letters suggests that their translation in footnotes, or occasionally between square brackets in the text, will be a welcome accommodation to many readers. The inclusion of an introductory sketch of frequent correspondents relieves the textual footnotes of much biographical material, and provides a summary of other background detail. This device is useful in acquainting readers with the several members of the Bryant family, about whom little coherent information is elsewhere available. Wherever applicable, reference is made in the footnotes to this essay, "Bryant's Correspondents." Cross-reference by letter, or by letter number and footnote ("see Letter 37," or "see 74.5"), provides a means of identifying recurrent names and topics. The names of persons mentioned in the letters, footnotes, and introductory matter are listed in the Index. Canceled matter in Bryant's letter drafts has been silently removed, except in a few instances where its inclusion reveals significant revision, in which case it appears within ⟨angle brackets⟩ immediately before the later version. Where manuscripts are so badly worn that textual content can only be conjectured, it is placed between [square brackets].

Usually in firm control of his syntax, Bryant was sparing in punctuation. In his letter drafts, a dash often stands for other medial and terminal marks, and is retained. Final copies are usually punctuated with care, and only occasionally require additional marks for clarity. Their insertion has been made silently. Bryant's orthography needs little correction. He was, it is true, lax in spelling proper names: even his close friends Robert Weir, William Leggett, and Horatio Greenough, appear for some time after he meets them as "Wier," "Legget," and "Greenhow." And certain aberrational forms persist, such as his use of "birth" for "berth," and his preference for "i" before "e" even after "c," as in "recieve" for "receive," to which he invariably clung. Since their retention would be both tedious and pointless, these forms are noted on their first appearance and silently corrected thereafter. Occasional misspellings and departures from conventional usage are indicated in footnotes, as are misdatings, but obvious inadvertencies are usually corrected silently. Spellings and usages now considered archaic, but current in Bryant's day—or at least acceptable then—are retained without comment. Such inconsistencies in spelling and punctuation as are evident between manuscript and printed sources will be recognized as unavoidable.

In the *descriptive notes*, addresses of recipients are given in run-on style as they appear on address leaves or envelopes. Postmarks and postal annotations are included, as are docketing entries and longer endorsements. The source and ownership of each letter, as well as its location if previously published, are added.

In the *explanatory footnotes*, recipients are identified with the first letter addressed to each, either by brief biographical notes or by reference to earlier identification in footnotes or in the sketch, "Bryant's Correspondents." Persons, places, publications, and events referred to in the letters are identified, if known, and the sources of quotations and allusions given insofar as they have been located. Published and manuscript sources of information are acknowledged closely following the matter derived from them. If the sources appear more than twice in the volume, they are given in brief form at each appearance, and in full in the List of Abbreviations and Short Titles in a single alphabetical roll. Omitted from this list, however, are such commonly available reference works as the *Dictionary of American Biography* and foreign national biographical dictionaries, and standard encyclopedias containing generally accepted historical and other factual information.

The introductory "Bryant Chronology" provides a succinct outline of significant dates and events in the first forty-two years of Bryant's life.

Bryant Chronology
1794–1836

1794. William Cullen Bryant born November 3 to Dr. Peter and Sarah Snell Bryant at Cummington, Massachusetts.

1798. June, enters district school.

1802. Begins to compose verses.

1807. March 18, first published poem in *Hampshire Gazette*.

1808. June, "The Embargo; or Sketches of the Times: A Satire. By a Youth of Thirteen," published in Boston. November, begins college preparation in Latin under uncle, Rev. Thomas Snell, at North Brookfield, Massachusetts.

1809. February, "The Embargo," second edition with other poems, Boston. July, returns to Cummington. August to October, studies Greek with Rev. Moses Hallock at Plainfield, Massachusetts.

1810. Spring, studies mathematics with Hallock. October, enters sophomore class at Williams College.

1811. May, returns to Cummington. July 9, receives honorable dismissal from Williams. December, begins law study with Samuel Howe at Worthington, Massachusetts. Composes verses on love and death, 1811–1815.

1814. June, continues law study with Congressman William Baylies at West Bridgewater, Massachusetts. November–December, ill at Cummington.

1815. July, completes "To a Waterfowl." August, admitted to practice law in Massachusetts Court of Common Pleas; returns to Cummington. Autumn, writes first, incomplete draft of "Thanatopsis." December, begins law practice at Plainfield.

1816. July, appointed lieutenant in Massachusetts militia. August, leaves law practice at Plainfield. October, enters partnership at Great Barrington, Massachusetts, with George Ives. December, meets Frances Fairchild.

1817. February, resigns lieutenancy in militia. May, Bryant–Ives partnership dissolved; enters solitary practice. September, "Thanatopsis" and other verses published anonymously in *North American Review*. Admitted to practice in Massachusetts Supreme Judicial Court.

1818. March, "To a Waterfowl" in *NAR*. June, visits New York City. July, publishes criticism of Solyman Brown's verse *Essay on American Poetry* in *NAR*.

1819. June, essay "On the Happy Temperament" in *NAR*. September, given honorary M.A. by Williams; essay "On the Use of Trisyllabic Feet in Iambic Verse" in *NAR*.

1820. February, elected town clerk of Great Barrington. March, death of Dr. Peter Bryant. May, appointed justice of the peace. July 4, gives oration at Stockbridge, Massachusetts, on Missouri Compromise. August, contributes five hymns to Unitarian hymnal to be published in New York. October, notice of James Hillhouse's *Percy's Masque* in *NAR*. December, appointed to seven-year term as justice of the peace, Berkshire County.

1821. January 11, marries Frances Fairchild at Great Barrington. April, appointed clerk of center school district, Great Barrington. August, reads Phi Beta Kappa poem, "The Ages," at Harvard commencement. September, *Poems* published at Cambridge. Contributes poems to Richard Dana's periodical, *The Idle Man*.

1822. January 2, daughter Frances (Fanny) born. cFebruary–March, Bryant's 1821 *Poems* reprinted at London in William Roscoe's *Specimens of the American*

Poets, and reviewed in *Blackwood's Edinburgh Magazine* for June. October–November, literary and political criticisms printed in Massachusetts newspapers.

1823. March, serves as Secretary of the Federal Republican Convention at Lenox, Massachusetts. December, gives address at Great Barrington in support of Greek revolutionaries.

1824. April, composes first of twenty-three poems for *United States Literary Gazette*. Visits New York, meeting Cooper, Halleck, Sands, and Verplanck. July, notice of Henry Pickering's *The Ruins of Paestum* in *NAR*. September, verdict favorable to Bryant's client in *Bloss vs. Tobey* reversed by judges on appeal. December, death of Sarah (Sally) Bryant Shaw.

1825. April, notice of Catharine Sedgwick's *Redwood* in *NAR*. May, moves to New York City. June, first number of *New-York Review*, edited by Bryant and Henry Anderson. November, elected to Bread and Cheese Lunch Club.

1826. January, *Miscellaneous Poems Selected from the United States Literary Gazette*, with Bryant's contributions. March–April, four Lectures on Poetry before New York Athenaeum. July, becomes editorial assistant on New York *Evening Post*. October, first number of *United States Review*, edited by Bryant and Charles Folsom.

1827. September, *USR* ceases publication. December, made joint editor of *EP*. *The Talisman for MDCCCXXVIII* published.

1828. February, gives first annual series of five lectures on mythology at National Academy of Design. December, *The Talisman for MDCCCXXIX*.

1829. February, first recorded attendance at Sketch Club. July 13, becomes editor-in-chief of *EP*. December, *The Talisman for MDCCCXXX*. Edwin Forrest performs *Metamora*, selected by prize committee led by Bryant.

1830. November, Bryant's committee gives prize offered by James Hackett to Paulding's *Lion of the West*. December, *The American Landscape*, with introduction and letterpress by Bryant.

1831. April 20, horsewhips editor Stone of *Commercial Advertiser*. June 29, daughter Julia Sands Bryant born at Cummington.

1832. January, *Poems* published at New York; London edition "edited" by Washington Irving. Visits Washington, meeting President Jackson and cabinet members. May, moves to Hoboken, New Jersey. May–July, visits John Bryant at Jacksonville, Illinois, and tours prairie; buys first parcel of Illinois land. June, *Tales of Glauber-Spa* with two stories by Bryant published. December, death of Robert Sands.

1833. July–August, visits northern New England and Canada.

1834. January, *Poems*, second edition, published at Boston. June, contracts to furnish twenty poems to *New-York Mirror*. June 24, sails on packet boat *Poland* with wife and daughters for indefinite stay in Europe. July 15, lands at Le Havre; travels by steamboat to Rouen, by diligence to Paris, arriving July 18 at Hôtel des Étrangers. August 21, leaves by diligence for Châlons, steamboat to Lyons, diligence to Marseilles, carriage to Nice, diligence to Genoa, carriage to Florence, reaching Hôtel de l'Europe September 12. September 17, takes lodgings on Lung' Arno near Ponte alla Carraia. November 19, departs for Pisa, lodging on Lung' Arno at 700 Casa Genoni.

1835. March 18, by carriage to Rome, through Volterra, Siena, Ronciglione, reaching Hôtel Frantz March 26. cApril 2 to lodgings at Palazzo Corca, 57 Via Pontifici. April 28, by diligence to Naples, arriving May 1 and lodging at 267 Strada Chiaga. Visits Pompeii, Herculaneum; climbs Vesuvius. cMay 22 leaves Naples; May 26–June 2 at Rome; June 9–16 at Florence. Passes through Bologna, Ferrara, Padua, and Mestre to Venice, reaching Albergo dell'Europa June 20. June

24, takes carriage through Italian and Austrian Tyrol, via Cenada, Serravalle, Venas, Landro, Bruneck, Sterzing, and Innsbruck to Munich, arriving June 30. Lodges at 31 The Bazaar, at the southeastern corner of Ludwigstrasse. October 2, departs for Heidelberg, staying at King of Portugal Hotel from October 6 to November 1, then engaging house for six months at 266 Friedrichstrasse. December 8, learns of William Leggett's illness and of substitute editors on *EP*. December 11, Henry Longfellow and Clara Crowninshield settle at Heidelberg for winter. December 14–January 24, Bryants see Longfellow and Miss Crowninshield almost daily.

1836.   January 25, Bryant departs for New York, leaving wife and daughters at Heidelberg. Travels by diligence, in company with Philip Zimmern, through Karlsruhe, Strasbourg, Metz, Verdun, Châlons, and Meaux, reaching Paris January 29 and Le Havre February 1. Sails *c*February 7; becalmed in Plymouth Harbor *c*February 12–17; arrives at New York March 26.

Bryant's Correspondents
1809–1836

OF 424 LETTERS BRYANT is known to have written between April 1809 and April 1836, 314 to 76 correspondents have been recovered, and are included in this volume. In addition, a brief journal entry and two contracts in his hand-writing provide additional insights into Bryant's first European visit. Most of the letters to principal correspondents—his father, mother, wife, sister Sally, Richard Henry Dana, Charles Folsom, and Gulian Verplanck—survive in final form. For other, occasional letters to fellow-students and tutors, professional acquaintances, and travel companions, the editors have often depended on pre-liminary drafts Bryant made and then corrected, a habit gained in the careful revision of his poems.

Although their correspondence ended with Peter Bryant's early death in 1820, Cullen's letters to his father comprise a record of youthful hopes and the concerns of early manhood, showing great respect for his father's judgment in matters of literature as well as of practical living. All but one of the eighteen known letters he wrote to Dr. Bryant have been recovered.

Born in 1767 at North Bridgewater, Massachusetts, to Dr. Philip (1732–1817) and Silence Howard Bryant (1738–1777), the fifth of nine children whose mother died when Peter was nine years old, Cullen's father was raised by a dour, dominating stepmother who kept him at farm labor until he rebelled. He managed through self-study to qualify himself, at the age of twenty, for entrance to Harvard College, but, lacking means of support, he withdrew almost at once, and went home to study medicine with his father. During two years as a self-styled "drudge" in his father's office, Peter audited a few medical lectures at Harvard, and spent some time with an unusually competent French surgeon, Louis Le Prilette, at nearby Norton. In 1792 he set out to practice medicine at Cummington, a newly settled hill town in western Massachusetts. Here he mar-ried Sarah Snell (1768–1847), daughter of one of the town's founders, Deacon Ebenezer Snell (1738–1813), a prosperous farmer and a justice of the peace.

Young Dr. Bryant soon met bitter opposition from an established practi-tioner, James Bradish, who was determined, Peter wrote his father, "to root me out if possible." There followed three precarious years, at the end of which Peter, by now the father of two infant boys, escaped debtors' prison only by signing on as a ship's doctor on a voyage to the Indian Ocean. During nearly two years there, for a part of which time his vessel was interned at Mauritius by the French revolutionary Directory, Peter Bryant gained much practical ex-perience in hospitals on shore.

Home again in 1797, and freed from the rancor of his competitor, Dr. Bry-ant took up a practice which soon made him the leading physician and surgeon of his district. He was called away from Cummington to treat patients and to operate, first in neighboring towns, then at Northampton, the Hampshire County seat, and later at Worcester and Boston. Once, he traveled by sleigh in mid-winter three hundred miles westward to Palmyra, New York, to be consulted in a difficult case. At the office he added to his father-in-law's house in 1801, the doctor trained as many as ten medical students at a time, giving them the use of the largest medical library in western Massachusetts.

Wider recognition came to Peter Bryant in 1806, with his election to the Massachusetts Medical Society in Boston, and the award of an honorary Master of Arts degree by Williams College. In 1812 he became a Councilor to the Medical Society; that year, and again in 1818, he was invited to deliver its annual discourse. In the last-named year, his friend Dr. John Collins Warren, dean of the Harvard Medical School, secured for him the honorary degree of Doctor of Physic from Harvard University.

Chronically ill with consumption, Peter Bryant nevertheless served his district in the state legislature during a period of twelve years. From 1806 to 1814 he represented Cummington in the lower house—with the exception of one year when, he told his father, his neighbors refused to send him to Boston "on account of their alarm, and apprehensions about the prevailing fever." And from 1816 to 1818, when he became seriously ill, he was a member of the state senate.

Mrs. Bryant remarked to Cullen that her husband rarely sat down without a book in hand, for then, he said, he was never sleepy. Buying medical books he could ill afford, he constantly added as well to a large collection of history and literature for his own enjoyment and his children's instruction. His pride in the education of his five sons and two daughters was a recurrent theme in his letters; but a special concern for the development of his second child, Cullen, reflected his faith in the boy's literary promise, and his determination to give him an education he himself had been denied. It was Cullen's application to study and composition to which he referred most often. At the age of nine Cullen was a "very distinct accurate reader." When he was thirteen, his poem "The Embargo" was "very much admired at Boston," where the doctor's literary friends credited the boy with being a "very extraordinary genius." At fourteen, Cullen was making "surprising progress" through Vergil's *Aeneid*, *Eclogues*, and a part of the *Georgics*. He was also showing "great proficiency in drawing," and good judges thought that "if he had suitable instruction he would make an eminent painter."

Cullen's aptitude for classical studies made him, rather than his older brother, Austin, his father's choice to receive a college education. Entering him as a sophomore at Williams College in his sixteenth year, Dr. Bryant worried lest the expense be unfair to his other children; yet, he wrote Dr. Philip Bryant, "I thought, as he had exhibited a genius, and a taste for literature, rather above the ordinary level, it would be almost criminal not to gratify him as far as I could."

Peter Bryant did not live to hear his son read the Phi Beta Kappa poem at the Harvard commencement in 1821, or to see Cullen's first slim volume of poems published that fall at Cambridge. But before his death in 1820, at the age of fifty-three, he had secured publication in the *North American Review* of Cullen's first memorable verses—"Inscription for the Entrance to a Wood," "Thanatopsis," and "To a Waterfowl"—thus setting his son on the path toward lasting fame.

Of thirteen known letters Cullen wrote his mother before 1836, eight have been recovered. The first of these came after Peter Bryant died, for Cullen's channel of communication with his family during early absences from home had nearly always been through his father. Sarah Snell Bryant epitomized the pioneer woman. She was, in truth, an emigrant twice within her lifetime. At six she came with her parents from Bridgewater to an uncleared hillside farm at Cummington; sixty-one years later she settled with four sons and her younger daughter on the Illinois prairie. With little formal schooling herself, she guided the secular and religious instruction of seven children in turn, meanwhile spinning, weaving, washing, ironing, and making most of the clothes for a family of nine, in addition to cooking for family, medical students, and farm laborers. Beyond these homely chores, Sarah Bryant made a distinctive imprint on family and community. She worked for the improvement of public roads and schools, as well as public morals. She persuaded her boys to plant shade trees along the highways, setting a pattern for Cummington and nearby towns, where her vision was later realized in widespread beauty. For fifty-three years she kept a daily diary, an extraordinary family-record and the witness to a remarkable life. Begun before the birth of her first child, it contains a succinct entry for November 3, 1794: "Stormy; wind N. E.; churned; unwell; seven at night a son born." This was her second son, William Cullen.

Cullen's letters to his brothers and sister other than Sally were infrequent before their migration to Illinois between 1830 and 1835. All the boys but one were too young to offer him companionship before Cullen left home at fourteen to begin college-preparatory study. Austin (1793–1866), Cullen's early companion in play and study, had only grade schooling before he was old enough to care for his father's farm. Married in 1819 to Adeline Plummer (1801–1882) of Pittsfield, Austin continued for fifteen years after his father's death to run the homestead, until in 1835 he sold it and took his family and his mother west to join three younger brothers at Princeton, Illinois. By 1836 Cullen had written Austin five known letters, of which four have been recovered.

Cyrus (1798–1865) shared some of Cullen's scholarly interests. After early schooling and several years of summer farming and winter teaching, Cyrus spent four years in South Carolina as a store clerk. Returning to Cummington, he organized its lyceum and agricultural association, attended Rensselaer Polytechnic School, and was for two years an itinerant lecturer on chemistry and mineralogy, teaching one winter at George Bancroft's and Joseph Cogswell's Round Hill School at Northampton. In 1832 he emigrated by way of Michigan to Illinois, homesteaded there with his brother John, and in 1834 married Julia Everett (1808–1875) of Worthington, Massachusetts. A farmer with one of the finest orchards in the area, he organized the first library, printing press, and agricultural exhibition at Princeton, Illinois; served as county clerk and master in chancery; and lectured on botany and chemistry. Of Cullen's ten known letters to Cyrus during this period, four have been recovered.

John Howard Bryant (1807–1902), youngest and longest-lived of the five boys, was not yet a year old when Cullen's "The Embargo" was published at Boston. There are no surviving letters to John before he went west in 1831. Thereafter he was Cullen's agent in Illinois land investment and his close confidant, the recipient of at least one hundred letters. With his older brothers,

John learned farming at home. He attended the Cummington Academy, taught district school, and passed brief periods in college at Rensselaer and Williams, before leaving for Illinois. There, in 1833, he married Harriett Wiswall (c1803–1883), once of Cummington. He developed a six-hundred-acre farm, helped organize Bureau County, and as a legislator and a founder of the state's Republican Party knew Owen Lovejoy, Stephen A. Douglas, and Abraham Lincoln. His older brother's example led him to write his own verses, printed at first in newspapers and magazines, then in Rufus Griswold's *The Poets and Poetry of America*, and ultimately in a volume from the press of Cullen's newspaper, the New York *Evening Post*. During the period covered by this volume, John was the recipient of ten known letters, of which six have been recovered.

A number of Cullen's early letters went to his sister Sally, a slender, auburn-haired girl with whom he shared their father's susceptibility to lung trouble. Sarah Snell Bryant (1802–1824) was the favorite of all her brothers. With a sweet soprano voice which they recalled in old age, and prone to tease, without tormenting, those she loved, Sally responded eagerly when Cullen offered her, soon after her fifteenth birthday, the guidance of "a friend whose affections even misconduct can hardly alienate," and begged for a "transcript" of her "sentiments and feelings." Though Sally's letters to Cullen have not survived, those to others reflect her affection for him. Thwarted in her hope to enter Emma Willard's school at Middlebury, Vermont, Sally passed two terms at Miss Bancroft's school in Northampton and taught briefly at Plainfield, near home, before marrying in 1821 her father's former pupil and successor to his practice, Dr. Samuel Shaw (1790–1870), who had been treating her for the lung infection of which she died three years later. Her death inspired one of Cullen's most poignant poems, "The Death of the Flowers," in which he mourned "The fair meek blossom that grew up and faded by my side." Eight of the nine known letters he wrote to Sally have been recovered.

There are only two known letters to Cullen's fourth brother during this period, neither of which is recovered, and none to the younger of his two sisters, but both left insights into their older brother's life. Peter Rush Bryant (1803–1883), later known as "Arthur," was, until he went west in 1830, the most restless of the brothers. After failing to get Peter a scholarship at Harvard, Cullen prevailed upon friends in Congress to appoint him to the United States Military Academy at West Point. But Peter was miserable there, and persuaded his mother to allow his resignation after only six months as a cadet. Then he audited classes at Williams, and taught school briefly in New York, before finally settling in Illinois. Married in 1832 to Henrietta Plummer (1812–1895) of Richmond, Massachusetts, Arthur Bryant later became a skillful nursery gardener and the author of a manual on the cultivation of forest trees. Charity Louisa (1805–1868), small, homely, and overshadowed by her pretty older sister, had a shrewd and at times caustic wit which enlivened her reports of visits to Cullen and Frances. In 1835 she went to Illinois with her mother and Austin's family. There, in 1837, she married Justin H. Olds (1806–1879) and provided a home for Sarah Bryant.

Frances Fairchild (1797–1866), who became Cullen's wife in 1821, was the daughter of Zachariah (c1749–1814) and Hannah Pope Fairchild (c1757–1814). Orphaned at seventeen, she was living with a married sister when she met

Cullen at a village "ball" soon after he came to Great Barrington in October 1816 to practice law. Within a few months Frances left for a long visit with relatives in western New York, leaving with Cullen the image, he later recalled, of a "pretty blonde with light brown hair, . . . gray eyes of a remarkably frank expression, an agreeable figure, a dainty foot, and pretty hands, and the sweetest smile I had ever seen." His letters to her during this separation, and those to his mother and Sally just after his marriage, mirror the growth of his love and respect for this unassuming farmer's-daughter, and his estimate of her high qualities which grew steadily thereafter. With no evident artistic talent, Frances soon became, nevertheless, her husband's closest literary confidante. In a private reminiscence after her death forty-five years later Cullen said, "I never wrote a poem that I did not repeat it to her, and take her judgment upon it. I found its success with the public to be precisely in proportion to the impression it made upon her."

Correspondence between husband and wife was necessarily infrequent until they moved to New York City in 1825, and Frances began to make summer visits to Cummington and Great Barrington, and to resorts nearer New York where Cullen could join her only on weekends. In 1843 they bought a home at Hempstead Harbor, Long Island, where Frances usually spent all but the winter months, while her husband boarded in the city during the week and wrote her almost daily. And Cullen was a tireless traveler. Though Frances went with him to Europe for two long visits, and to Canada, South Carolina, and Illinois, he visited Europe three times with other companions, and traveled to Cuba and the West without her. As a result, Cullen's letters to his wife are more numerous than those to anyone else. Of over 200 letters he is known to have sent Frances, 191 have been recovered. Thirty-four are included in this volume.

Of Bryant's friendships outside his family, the longest was with Richard Henry Dana (1787–1879, Harvard 1808). For fifty-seven years, from the publication of Bryant's 1821 *Poems* under Dana's eye, the friends exchanged frank and constructive comments on each other's writings. At the Dana homes in 1821 Bryant met Edmund Dana, the Channings, Washington Allston, and other members of the Cambridge literary group who had published his first magazine verses. In turn, Bryant's appreciative criticism of Dana's essays and stories in *The Idle Man*, publication of his verses in the *New-York Review*, and defense of Dana's first volume of poetry, literally established his friend's literary reputation. On the surface, these two poets would seem to have had little else in common; Dana was a monarchist, an Anglophile, a Trinitarian, and an anti-reformer, while Bryant was a radical democrat, a frequent critic of British manners and institutions, an avowed Unitarian, and a vigorous advocate of social and political reforms. Yet they maintained a lifelong correspondence in which they found much to stimulate and little to strain their friendship. All but one of the 108 known letters to Dana have been recovered. Twenty-eight appear herein.

Among unrelated correspondents Bryant's earliest acquaintance was Willard Phillips (1784–1873, Harvard 1810), Dana's friend and associate on the *North American Review*. Phillips lived as a boy in Cummington, and later prepared for Harvard at the Bryant home with one of Dr. Bryant's pupils. Publishing Cullen's early verses in 1817–1818, Phillips wrote him, "I recollect the epitome of your present self, and with pleasure renew the acquaintance." After Peter Bryant's death Phillips took his place for a time as literary mentor, coaching Cullen on the delivery of his Phi Beta Kappa poem at Cambridge in 1821, arranging publication of his first volume and reviewing it in the *North American Review*, and acting as agent for its sale. Although their correspondence was thereafter only occasional, they remained friends and infrequent companions for over half a century. Of Bryant's eight known letters to Phillips in the early period, five have been recovered.

As a young law student Bryant was most fortunate in his tutors, both men of legal acumen and integrity as well as cultural breadth. The first of these was Samuel Howe (1785–1828, Williams 1804), Dr. Bryant's close friend and near neighbor at Worthington, only four miles away. Howe had attended the pioneering law school of Judge Tapping Reeve at Litchfield, Connecticut, then studied with Judge Theodore Sedgwick at Stockbridge, Massachusetts, before taking his own pupils into his home. Made an associate justice of the new Court of Common Pleas in 1821 at the age of thirty-six, Howe was the principal founder two years later of the Northampton Law School which, before his early death in 1828, introduced significant innovations in legal instruction, notably the moot court. The high regard for Howe outside his home district was evidenced in tributes to his memory by George Bancroft, Ralph Waldo Emerson, and Chief Justice Isaac Parker of Massachusetts.

After Bryant left Worthington to continue law study at West Bridgewater near his father's home town, Howe sent him advice designed to quiet his fear of arguing cases in open court. Though only two of Cullen's letters to his first law tutor have reappeared, they met during the young attorney's visits at home and later at the Berkshire County courthouse in Lenox, where they were sometimes associated or opposed in the same cases.

Bryant wrote more frequently to his second tutor, Congressman William Baylies (1776–1865, Brown 1795), who was in Washington during nearly half the time Cullen was reading law in his West Bridgewater office. Like Howe and Peter Bryant a veteran of the Massachusetts legislature and a Federalist opponent of the War of 1812, Baylies was nevertheless instrumental in liberalizing his student's inherited political conservatism. To Cullen's complaints about the bigoted farmers who were his first clients in the little village of Plainfield adjoining Cummington, Baylies replied, "Experience will teach you that it is from that class of society sometimes denominated—previously denominated—the lower—as *much*—probably *more* than from any other, you are to expect zealous support, & disinterested friendship." Half a century later Bryant wrote, "For Mr. Baylies's character I have always entertained the profoundest respect; . . . few lawyers ever exercised their profession so exempt from complaint and criticism." Ten of the thirteen letters he wrote Baylies before 1836 have been recovered.

Of the friendships Bryant made during his Massachusetts years, those with the Sedgwick family of Stockbridge most influenced his later career. Meeting Charles (1791–1856) in court soon after moving to Great Barrington, he became acquainted in turn with Theodore II (1781–1839, Yale 1798), Henry Dwight (1785–1831) and Robert (1787–1841), both 1804 classmates of Samuel Howe's at Williams, and Catharine Maria (1789–1867). All four brothers, like their father, Judge Theodore Sedgwick (1746–1813, Yale 1765), were attorneys; Catharine was starting a career as a novelist. She led Cullen in 1820 to compose several hymns for a Unitarian collection to be published in New York. Bryant's most intimate associations were with Charles, a warm and lively companion during court sessions at Lenox, where he was clerk of the court for many years, and with Henry, a New York lawyer active in humanitarian causes. Henry and Robert were largely instrumental in bringing Bryant to New York City in 1825 and establishing him as editor and critic. But it was Theodore who most influenced the future journalist's political and economic thought. A state legislator who quit the dominant conservatism of his district to support Andrew Jackson, he was a student of economics who wrote popular books in support of free trade, and opposed slavery even as he deplored both coercive reform and reaction. Bryant called him a "politician without party vices." During the period covered by this volume Bryant wrote fifteen known letters to members of the Sedgwick family, ten of which are included here.

A close collaborator of Bryant's during his early years in New York was the essayist, satirist, historian, and legislator Gulian Crommelin Verplanck (1786–1870, Columbia 1801). Verplanck's notice of Bryant's 1821 *Poems* in the New York *American* was, except for Willard Phillips' in the *North American Review*, the only notable criticism of that work in the year of its publication. Bryant's wry acknowledgment of the blank pages the critic sent him, thinking they contained his notice, was the first of fifty known letters to Verplanck during a long friendship. The grandson of one Columbia College president and great-grandson of another, Verplanck gained notoriety as a young lawyer by heading a raucous protest at the 1811 college commencement in Trinity Church against the "oppressive" acts of his alma mater's administrators. Convicted of inciting to riot, and charged by the presiding judge at his trial, Mayor DeWitt Clinton, with "obtuseness of moral perception," Verplanck led a long pamphlet-war of verse satire, joined at times by the Irvings, Paulding, Halleck, and Drake, against the political faction led by Clinton. Later, after three years in the legislature, Verplanck served from 1825 to 1833 as a leading Jackson-congressman. For several years during that period he joined Bryant and Robert Sands in writing an annual gift book, *The Talisman*, and in organizing the Sketch Club, composed of artists and writers, which succeeded Fenimore Cooper's earlier Bread and Cheese. While in Washington Verplanck sent Bryant confidential information for the *Evening Post*, and passed on to con gressional committees the journalist's private views on proposed legislation. Their most active correspondence came between 1827 and 1833, when Bryant wrote Verplanck forty-four known letters, of which thirty-nine appear herein.

Another of Bryant's lifelong friends, George Bancroft (1800–1891, Harvard 1817), is represented in this volume by only three letters. These concern his contribution to the *New-York Review* of translations from Goethe and Schiller, and a notice of Edward Everett's *Orations*. An early acquaintance grew gradually into the intimacy reflected in Bancroft's characterization of Bryant in 1868 as "the oldest friend I have now alive."

About a fifth of the letters Bryant wrote during the first period concern his own contributions to magazines, or his editorial work on the *New-York Review* and its successor, the *United States Review and Literary Gazette*. Principal recipients were Edward Tyrell Channing (1790–1856, M.A. Harvard 1819), editor of the *North American Review*, three letters; Jared Sparks (1789–1866, Harvard 1815), a later editor of the same review, nine letters; Theophilus Parsons (1797–1882, Harvard 1815), conductor of the *United States Literary Gazette*, thirteen letters, one of which is unrecovered; James G. Carter (1795–1849), briefly Parsons' successor, eight letters (all apparently lost); Charles Folsom (1794–1872, Harvard 1813), Carter's successor, and Bryant's co-editor of the *United States Review and Literary Gazette* in 1826–1827, twenty-five letters, all recovered; and Edward Wigglesworth (1804–1876, Harvard 1822), Folsom's and Bryant's assistant, two letters. Biographical information about these correspondents will be provided as they are first addressed in the letters.

About a score of letters and notes about legal matters of the period 1816–1825 have been preserved, but only a handful are included in this volume as bearing upon Bryant's life apart from routine law practice. Most important of these is the one concerning the case of *Bloss vs. Tobey*, Letter 92, which was the crucial factor in alienating Bryant from the law. Three others are printed because they represent the kind of legal business conducted by a village lawyer at that period, and provide insight into Bryant's practice of the profession which gave him a living for nearly a decade.

Three-quarters of the addressees in this volume received at most two or three letters, and will be identified as they are introduced. Some were early companions and fellow-students, such as John Avery, George Downes, John Howard, Elisha Hubbard, and Jacob Porter. Others were editors or publishers who asked contributions from Bryant, or to whose journals he sent unsolicited literary or political articles. A few were statesmen and politicians of whom he asked favors, for himself or others: Andrew Jackson, Lewis Cass, Azariah Flagg, Caleb Strong, and Campbell White. Some had paid him some sort of honor— Amos Eaton, Maria Edgeworth, Philip Hone and David Hosack, Sarah Howe, Cornelius Lawrence, John Pierpont, and William Spooner. A related group, which included several distinguished Unitarians—Andrews Norton, Nathaniel Preston, Henry Sewall, Henry Ware, Sr., and William Ware—drew from Bryant observations on the condition of religion in American and European society, and revelations of his own religious beliefs. A few of his letters went to casual business or travel acquaintances, and his experiences abroad and insights into foreign cultures are recounted in the first five of more than one hundred letters he sent to the *Evening Post* over a period of forty years. Finally, other recipients, such as Thomas Cole, Horatio Greenough, Washington Irving, William Leggett, George Pope Morris, Thatcher Payne, John Rand, and Julia Sands, were friends with whom Bryant enjoyed a degree of intimacy, then or later, not reflected in the few letters he wrote them during this early period.

I

Student of Life and the Law
1809–1815
(LETTERS 1 TO 33)

WHEN, IN APRIL 1809, CULLEN BRYANT posted the first letter we can be sure he wrote, he was already a poet of seven years' experience with thirteen hundred lines of verse to his credit. He had recited his couplets in the district school at Cummington at the age of nine, and later seen them printed in the *Hampshire Gazette* at Northampton. His juvenile masterpiece, a satire scoring the bugbear of his community, Democratic President Thomas Jefferson, had been published anonymously in 1808 at Boston as "By a Youth of Thirteen." It had been reviewed in the *Monthly Anthology* as an "extraordinary performance," and praised so highly by his father's Federalist friends in the legislature that within eight months it reappeared under the resounding title, "The Embargo; or Sketches of the Times. A Satire. The Second Edition, Corrected and Enlarged. Together with The Spanish Revolution, and Other Poems. By William Cullen Bryant."

Bryant's precocity, and the strain such praise must have put on the boy's modesty, might suggest that his deprecatory words to Dr. Peter Bryant in submitting his translation of verses from the *Aeneid* were written with tongue in cheek. But the evidence of a lifetime of publication, during which Bryant never reprinted a poem he had composed before the age of twenty, attests rather an early impulse toward the high degree of self-criticism he practiced in after years.

The talents which his Grandfather Snell encouraged in Cullen's tenth year, by setting him to versifying Old Testament stories, and which his father later directed toward translation of classical epic and neo-classical satire, Cullen applied—when left to himself—to lampooning schoolmates and companions. His sharp sallies have not been preserved, but they were evidently early attempts at epistolary communication. That they were barbed we know from the replies of an older friend, Jacob Porter, who quailed under the verbal lashings of his nimble antagonist. Cullen's "boyish ire," so hot that it "like fury smok'd, like fury blaz'd," flung its "pointless satyre" at Porter until this Yale graduate cried,

> I'd rather yield up, as they all did,
> Than be by such hot water scalded;
> I once had courage, but I say now,
> I will take shelter in a haymow!

Perhaps Porter, whose friendship for his tormentor somehow survived, became proud a few months later of the company he kept when, in "The Embargo," the young satirist turned on his country's President:

And thou, the scorn of every patriot name,
Thy country's ruin, and her council's shame! . . .
Go, wretch, resign the presidential chair,
Disclose thy secret features foul or fair,
Go, search, with curious eyes, for hornèd frogs,
'Mongst the wild wastes of Louisianian bogs;
Or where Ohio rolls his turbid stream,
Dig for huge bones, thy glory and thy theme; . . .
But quit to abler hands, the helm of state,
Nor image ruin on thy country's fate!

When he dispatched to his father his "crude efforts of puerility" in the spring of 1809, Cullen had been studying Latin for five months under his mother's brother, Rev. Thomas Snell, in the parsonage at North Brookfield, fifty miles east of his birthplace. After three months more of construing the Latin of Vergil, Horace, Cicero, and the New Testament under the stern regimen of his Uncle Thomas, Cullen returned to Cummington to join his brothers in the dreaded chore of summer haymaking, which, under his grandfather's prodding, often brought on sick headaches. But within a few weeks he was off again to continue preparation for college, this time in the nearby village of Plainfield, to be tutored in Greek at the locally renowned "Bread and Milk College" of Rev. Moses Hallock, who was notable for getting his graduates into Williams. Here too Cullen applied himself intensively; in two months he knew the New Testament in Greek, he later recalled, "from end to end almost as if it had been English." Home again for the winter of 1809–1810, he went on preparing himself for the sophomore class at Williams College which, it had been decided for economy's sake, he should enter directly. After another two-month tutorial with Hallock in the spring, this time in mathematics, he entered Williams in October 1810.

Bryant's brief stay in college seems, from his point of view, to have been largely unproductive. He found the entrance examination no challenge, the faculty and curriculum dull, and the students addicted to indolence and mischief. He did, indeed, enjoy the literary exercises of the Philotechnian Society, and his discovery of the Greek poets Anacreon, Simonides of Ceos, and Sophocles, some of whose verses he translated. His reputation as a published poet had preceded him to Williamstown, and it awed some of his classmates, while others speculated whether he or his father had really written "The Embargo." But his marked modesty spared him from open criticism. And when, in March, he offered the Philotechnian Society the fruits of his college experience in the verse satire, *Descriptio Gulielmopolis*, the doubters were quieted and his clubmates delighted. This sharp indictment of faculty, physical plant, and the conditions of health and sanitation as he saw them is the only contemporary record he left of his seven-months' residence at Williams.

Before the third quarter of his sophomore year was over, Cullen withdrew from college with his father's permission, in the hope that he might transfer to Yale as his roommate John Avery and classmate Theodore Clapp were planning to do. But the chief virtue of Williams in Dr. Peter Bryant's mind had been its modest cost, and it was soon decided instead that Cullen should read law with his father's friend Samuel Howe in neighboring Worthington. Here the boy spent the period from December 1811 to May 1814 living in the Howe household and enjoying an association with a tutor who was learned in both the law and literature. Here, too, Cullen had his first contact with a young woman of wit and charm. Mrs. Howe had been Sarah Lydia Robbins, daughter of the lieutenant governor of Massachusetts. She read poetry beautifully and passionately, for she had been equally at home in the social circles of Boston and the literary society of New York. Though Cullen's natural shyness seems to have been made more acute by her presence, his letters to fellow-students soon after leaving Worthington suggest that his emotional interest in the opposite sex had first been aroused under the Howe roof, and a letter to his sister Sally several years later seems to confirm this.

In June 1814 Cullen moved on to West Bridgewater, which adjoined his parents' birthplace, North Bridgewater, to continue preparation for admission to the bar. Here, in the office of Congressman William Baylies, he read legal decisions, corresponded about politics with his tutor when Baylies was in Washington, and wrote his young friends of his real or fancied flirtations and amorous conquests. Here he agonized over his health and his legal prospects, and fancied ways he might postpone the assumption of professional responsibilities. And as he read the poetry of Henry Kirke White and Byron, of Southey and Cowper, the composition of his own verses, patterned on those of his romantic contemporaries, became first his diversion and then his solace. Before his admission to law practice in August 1815 he had completed one of the two poems by which he is now best remembered, "To a Waterfowl," and by the time he entered his own law office at Plainfield in December he had written the first version of "Thanatopsis."

1. *To* Peter Bryant

Brookfield   April 4th— 1809—

Respected Father

You will doubtless find in the preceding lines[1] much that needs emendation and much that characterizes the crude efforts of puerility. They have received[2] some correction from my hands, but you are sensible that the partiality of an Author for his own compositions, and an immature judgment, may have prevented me from perceiving the most of its defects however prominent. I will endeavour to the utmost of my ability, to follow the excellent instructions which you gave me in your last.[3] I have now proceeded in my studies as far as the Seventh book of the Aeneid— The federal party here, is now strengthened by the addition of a considerable number— The family are still favoured with their usual degree of health—[4] But I must conclude

Your dutiful Son
W. C. B.—

MANUSCRIPT: Iowa State Department of History and Archives ADDRESS: Doct Peter Bryant / Cummington / To be left / at the Post / office in / Worthington POST-MARK (*in script*): BROOKFIELD APRIL 4th— 1809— POSTAL ANNOTATION: 10 PUBLISHED: *Life*, I, 77.

1. With this letter Bryant enclosed to his father two English translations from Vergil's *Aeneid*, totaling 116 lines, in heroic couplets. These were titled "Description of a Storm," from Book I and "Polyphemus," from Book III. The greater part of the first of these appears, with numerous minor textual changes, in *Life*, I, 77–78.

2. Here Bryant wrote "recieved," as he did consistently elsewhere in the letters. His misspelling of this and of other words with the combination -*cei* will be silently corrected hereafter.

3. Peter Bryant's careful guidance of Cullen's early versification is amply documented. See "Autobiography," p. 28; Donald M. Murray, "Dr. Peter Bryant: Preceptor in Poetry to William Cullen Bryant," *New England Quarterly*, 33 (December 1960), 513–522.

4. Rev. Thomas Snell (1774–1862, Dartmouth 1795), the younger of Sarah Snell Bryant's two brothers, had been pastor of the Second Congregational Church in North Brookfield, Massachusetts, since 1798. His son, Ebenezer Strong Snell (1801–1876), was later a member of the Amherst College faculty. See "Autobiography," p. 28.

2. *To* Austin Bryant[1]

[Brookfield, April? 1809][2]

Once more the Bard, with eager eye, reviews
The flowery paths of fancy, and the Muse
Once more essays to trill forgotten strains,
The loved amusement of his native plains.
Late you beheld me treading labor's round,
To guide slow oxen o'er the furrowed ground;
The sturdy hoe or slender rake to ply,
'Midst dust and sweat, beneath a summer sky.

But now I pore o'er Virgil's glowing lines,
Where, famed in war, the great Æneas shines;
Where novel scenes around me seem to stand,
Lo! grim Alecto whirls the flaming brand.
Dire jarring tumult, death and battle rage,
Fierce armies close, and daring chiefs engage;
Mars thunders furious from his flying car,
And hoarse-toned clarions stir the raging war.
Nor with less splendor does his master-hand
Paint the blue skies, the ocean, and the land;
Majestic mountains rear their awful head,
Fair plains extend, and bloomy vales are spread.
The rugged cliff in threatening grandeur towers,
And joy sports smiling in Arcadian bowers;
In silent calm the expanded ocean sleeps,
Or boisterous whirlwinds toss the rising deeps;
Triumphant vessels o'er his rolling tide,
With painted prows and gaudy streamers, glide.

1. Originally containing 180 lines, this verse letter to Cullen's elder brother, Austin, was once in the possession of his youngest brother, John. The original manuscript is unrecovered. The portion printed here was first published in *The Bryant Celebration by the Chicago Literary Club. November 3, 1874* (Chicago, 1875), pp. 18–19, and reprinted in *Life*, I, 79, from which source the present text is taken.

2. Dated conjecturally, as written "a little while after the foregoing letter [Letter 1] was sent to his father." *Life*, I, 78–79.

3. *To* The Philotechnian Society of Williams College[1]

[Williamstown, March 1811]

No more the brumal tempest sheds
Its gathered stores in sleety showers,
Nor yet the vernal season spreads
Its verdant mantle gemmed with flowers,
But fettered stands the naked year,
And shivers in the chilling air,
And lingers, dubious, on the wing,
And often struggles to unclasp
Reluctant Winter's icy grasp
And greet the arms of spring—

Hemmed in with hills whose heads aspire,
Abrupt and rude and hung with woods,
Amid these vales, I touch the lyre
Where devious Hoosic rolls his flood—[2]
Dear vales! where every pleasure meets,

Fain would I paint thy slimy streets,
Extended views and wholesome air,
Thy soil with churlish guardians blest
And horrors of the bleak Northwest
Pour'd through thy chasm afar.

Safe from the morning's golden eye,
And sheltered from the western breeze,
These happy regions, bosomed lie,
The seats of bliss and bowers of ease,
Thrice favord spot! whose fertile breast
Now, droughts, with lengthnd blaze infest,
Now, tempests drench with copious flood;
Alternate heat and cold surprise,
A frozen desert, now, it lies,
And now, a sea of mud.—[3]

While rising on the tainted gale
The morbid exhalations ride,
And hover oer the unconscious vale
Or sleep upon the mountain side.
There, on her misty throne reclined
Her aching brows with nightshade twined,
Disease, unseen, directs her sway,
Wields the black sceptre of her reign
And dips her shafts in keenest pain
And singles out her prey.

Why should I sing these reverend domes
Where science rests, in grave repose,
Ah me! their terrors and their glooms
Only the wretched inmate knows—
When through the horror breathing hall
The pale faced, moping students crawl
Like spectral monuments of woe;
Or drooping, seek the unwholesome cell
Where shade and dust and cobwebs dwell
Dark, dirty, dank and low—

But on the picture, dark with shade—
Let not the eye forever gaze
Where ruthless power, his nest has made
And stern suspicion treads her maze—
The storm, that oer the midnight waste
Rides, howling on the Northern blast,
In time, shall cease its furious sway.

But that, oer Hoosic's vale, which lowers
Will never know serener hours
Nor open to the day—

MANUSCRIPT: NYPL–GR PUBLISHED (*in part*): *Life*, I, 92–93.

1. At least five versions of these verses have been recorded, one in Bryant's hand—though he seems never to have published or referred to them. See "Youth," p. 95. The present text is from a copy made by Bryant's classmate Charles F. Sedgwick from one given him by Arthur Bryant. Sedgwick to Parke Godwin, January 21, 1880, NYPL–GR.

2. The Hoosic River rises in the Hoosac Range near Adams, Massachusetts, and flows past North Adams and Williamstown, crossing the southwest corner of Vermont and entering the Hudson River above Troy, New York. Its short course is indeed devious.

3. "The mud of Williamstown was long notorious. General Samuel Sloan[e], who built a home in the village in 1801, was accustomed, whenever his daughters went abroad in the spring, to send with them a man-servant bearing two long boards as portable sidewalks." "Youth," p. 111n.

4.   *To* John Avery[1]

Worthington   January 9th [1812]

Friend Avery,

I write to tell you that it is very problematical whether I shall go to Yale, unless I can enter at the beginning of or middle of next term rather than at the end of this vacation— I would therefore wish you to write up immediately to inform me whether this be the case. Supposing I should put it off two or three weeks next term, would I be refused admission? I wrote my other letter to get an answer to this question, but amidst my other matters forgot it.[2] I wish you would make particular inquiry into this subject & not let "ill health" prevent your writing back immediately so that I may know before the end of the vacation.[3] I presume that your not mentioning Euclid in your catalogue of Mathematics was an oversight. If so, let me know. I have studied more Greek than was necessary and am sorry for spending so much of my time on it.

However, if I should not enter *this time* I shall quit study and go to farming or turn mechanic. Would not blacksmithing be as good a trade as any for the display of one's abilities? Vulcan though the son of Jupiter and *sleeping partner* of Cytherea, gloried in his skill in *hot iron* and forging the thunderbolts of Eternal Jove. If, after you have passed through the [. . .][4] of academic honor & [. . .] the diploma [. . .] sweating over the anvil and wielding the hammer "with an air of majesty." "Much study" says Solomon "is a weariness to the flesh,"[5] and I think Solomon perfectly in the right. Yet, without this "weariness of the flesh," I conjecture that Solomon would never have attained to that reputation for learning and wisdom that he possessed. You may perhaps smile at my gravity when I add that all the learning and wisdom of

Solomon did not prevent him from going "after strange women and idols in his old age."[6] —Bacon notwithstanding he was the wisest & the brightest, yet the "meanest of mankind."[7] The government of passion rather than the acquisition of science ought to be the study of man. Of what benefit is it that the understanding and imagination should be cultivated when the heart, the fountain of all noble or infamous actions, lies, like a garden covered with weeds whose rank luxuriance choaks ever the plants that are natural to the soil? —Learning only points to the easier gratification of our sensualities & teaches us to conceal our passions, only to give them vent when the shackles of law and disgrace are removed. All the dark, deliberate, and subtle machinations of iniquity, every plan that has ever been formed against the peace and prosperity of the human race, by confederated art and villany, have been organized and directed chiefly by men of learning. The illuminated society of France & Germany was a vortex which drew into its periphery and involved the most wise and learned men of all Europe.— The bloody and ignorant tools of the French Revolution were not the men by whom it was planned— [. . .] learning, necessary to civilization [. . .] the comforts, all [. . .] more *dear* in the proper sense of the word, the higher & more [. . .] All the foregoing *propositions* are I conceive very clear— It now remains for you to let me know whether I can enter, supposing two or three weeks of the next term should elapse before I come down. If not I will go to cleaning cowstables.

W. C. BRYANT.

P. S. Write me a good long letter this time & tell me what your cogitations about matters may be.

MANUSCRIPT: Mrs. Inge Selden, Greensboro, Alabama PUBLISHED: Tremaine McDowell, "William Cullen Bryant and Yale," *New England Quarterly*, 3 (October 1930), 709–710.

1. Cullen's roommate at Williams, John Avery (1786–1837), of Conway, Massachusetts, had transferred in the spring of 1811 to Yale College, from which he graduated in 1813. Ordained to the Episcopal ministry in 1818, he later held pastorates in North Carolina and Alabama. "Autobiography," pp. 34–35; Dexter, *Graduates of Yale*, VI, 518–520.

2. Letter unrecovered.

3. Avery replied on February 29, "If you present yourself any time within a year from *this last vacation* nothing will hinder you from entering, if, upon examination, you are found qualified— And on this head I am not at all apprehensive." NYPL–GR.

4. Here, and further on, the manuscript is mutilated.

5. Eccles. 12:12.

6. 1 Kings 11:1–8.

7. Cf. Pope, *Essay on Man*, Ep. IV.281–282:

> "If parts allure thee, think how Bacon shined,
> The wisest, brightest, meanest of mankind!"

5. *To* John Avery[1]

Worthington   March 27, 1813.

Friend Avery

Notwithstanding my utter amazement at receiving a letter from you[2] I am very glad to find you so well contented with your literary prison. As I presume you are to have the valedictory I take this opportunity to inform you that if I do not attend the commencement at Williams College next fall, I shall most likely do myself the pleasure of hearing you spout at Yale. On the profession of law I am happy to hear you express so favourable an opinion, —and the more so because it was something different from what I expected. You will forgive me, if I confess that I thought you a little prejudiced in that particular. With your remarks on the study of mineralogy, I readily concur. Though I cannot scarcely boast of a smattering of it, yet it has always been a subject of interest to me from its connection with chemistry. The banished Duke in Shakespeare's *As you like it*

> "Finds tongues in trees, books in the running brooks
> Sermons in stones, and good in every thing."[3]

Indeed all the departments of natural history, so far from deserving neglect, afford an inexhaustible source of information to the most eager inquiry after knowledge and of gratification to the most unwearied curiosity.

You will easily believe me when I tell you that I like *natural history* better than *natural philosophy*, —not forgetting Botany to which I slightly attended last summer, as a sauce to my Blackstone.[4]

I am not sorry that Clapp has resumed his collegiate studies but I am sorry that he has found it necessary to enter the Junior class.[5] Remember me to him, and likewise to my witty friend Clark who I hear has become a member of your class, —or college (which is it?).[6]

You mention the speakers at the bar. I hope you will fulfill your intimation which I consider almost a promise of giving me a few sketches of their different merits as a specimen of your skill in drawing characters as well as for my information. I should here close my letter had I not remarked at the conclusion a request to "tell you whether you ought to study law or not." What you ought to do is a question which you must [settle?] with your own conscience. Yet of all studies I cannot help thinking that of the law would most interest you. It has been called dry, but you are doubtless acquainted with a class of people to whom drudgery and labour are synonymous. The study requires diligence of research which you eminently possess; —accuracy of reasoning and nicety of discrimination in which you excel; —its connection with the History of our *grandmother-country* England is intimate, and I may add inseparable;

—and to me the necessity of being a dabbler in antiquarianism is not the least of its attractions. Should you therefore coincide in opinion with the eloquent Lecturer Sullivan that "The character of an honest and upright lawyer is one of the most glorious, because one of the most useful to mankind"[7] and with Montesquieu (whose name needs no epithet of eloquent, or celebrated, or any thing else), that a multiplicity of laws are the evidences and the intrenchments of liberty;[8] and lastly should you prefer it, before any other profession or plan of life I would then *advise* you to become an inquirer into what my Lord Coke calleth "the amiable and admirable secrets of the law."[9]

A circumstance which I did not think to mention in my last[10] has made our situation in this part of the country very melancholy. A strange species of the typhus accompanied in most [tho?] not all cases with an infection of the lungs whether symptomatic of the disease or arising from the sudden changes of the weather I cannot determine,— has visited us with the most alarming ravages. Three or four die in a week nor does the disorder seem much to abate. It is the same fever that has swept off so many of our soldiers in the camp where it originated—[11]

Amidst the awful concussions and changes which are taking place in the moral, political and physical world I much doubt whether the good man can find any better consolation than that the hand of an over-ruling and all-directing Providence will prescribe the course of revolutions, mark the bounds of war and slaughter and recall from the hot pursuit his ministers of vengeance.—

William C. Bryant

MANUSCRIPT: Mrs. Inge Selden, Greensboro, Alabama PUBLISHED: Tremaine McDowell, "William Cullen Bryant and Yale," *New England Quarterly*, 3 (October 1930), 713–715.

1. This manuscript, like that of Letter 4, is worn.

2. Letter unrecovered.

3. II.i.16–17.

4. Sir William Blackstone, *Commentaries on the Laws of England*, 1765–1769.

5. Their classmate Theodore Clapp (1792–1866), of Easthampton, Massachusetts, lost a year between his leaving Williams in the spring of 1811 and his transfer to Yale, from which he graduated in 1814 to enter the Unitarian ministry. Dexter, *Graduates of Yale*, VI, 632–634.

6. Probably the "Eber-Liscom Clark," member of the Williams College class of 1811, who was granted an M.A. degree by Yale in 1816. See *Catalogus Collegii Gulielmensis MDCCCLXXIV*, p. 18.

7. Probably Francis Stoughton Sullivan (1719–1776), the first American edition of whose *Lectures on the Constitution and Laws of England* was published at Portland, Maine, in 1805. The quotation is unidentified.

8. Charles Louis de Secondat, Baron de Montesquieu (1689–1755), *De l'esprit des lois* (1748; English trans., *The Spirit of Laws*, 1750).

9. Sir Edward Coke (1552–1634), *The Institutes of the Laws of England* (1628–1644); an American edition was published at Philadelphia in 1812. The quotation has not been located.

10. Letter unrecovered.

11. This epidemic, from which several of Cullen's young friends died that season, apparently led to the composition of his earliest verses concerned with death. See *Vital Records of Worthington, Massachusetts, to the Year 1850* (Boston: New England Historical and Genealogical Society, 1911), p. 124; Bryant II, "Thanatopsis," pp. 169–172.

6. *To* Jacob Porter[1]

[Worthington, April 26, 1813]

To Jacob Porter, on his Marriage to
Miss Betsey Mayhew of Williamsburg

While now the tepid skies and gentle rains
Of April bid the gushing brooks o'erflow;
While scarce their earliest verdure tints the plains
And cold in hollows lurks the lingering snow;—
Love, sauntering in the sunny glade to know
If yet upon the moss banks of the Grove
That little flower of golden vesture blow
Which first the spring receives of Flora's love;
I hum this careless strain as deviously I rove.

Yet not unlovely, nor with song uncheer'd
Is this pale month, and still I love to greet,
At misty dawn, the bluebird's carol heard,
And red breast, from the orchard warbling sweet;
The fogs, that, as the sun arises, meet
In snowy folds along the channell'd flood;
The squirrel issuing from his warm retreat,
The purple glow that tints the budding wood,
The sound of bursting streams by gathered mounds withstood.

And now the heaving breast, and glances meek,
The unbidden warmth in beauty's veins declare;
The gale that lifts the tresses from her cheek,
Can witness to the fires that kindle there;
Now is the time to woo the yielding fair;—
But thou, my friend, may'st woo the fair no more;
Thine are connubial joys and wedded care,
And scarce the hymenean moon is o'er,
Since first, in bridal hour, thy name Eliza bore.

And if thy poet's prayer be not denied,
The hymenean moon shall ever last;
The golden chain, indissolubly tied,
Shall heighten as the winged hours glide past;
And whereso'er in life thy lot be cast,
For life at best is bitterness and guile—

Still may thy own Eliza cheer the waste,
Soften its weary ruggedness the while,
And gild thy dreams of peace, and make thy sorrows smile.

Such be thy days. —O'er Coke's black letter page,
Trimming the lamp at eve, 't is mine to pore;
Well pleased to see the venerable sage
Unlock his treasur'd wealth of legal lore;
And I, that lov'd to trace the woods before,
And climb the hill a play mate of the breeze,
Have vow'd to tune the rural lay no more,
Have bid my useless classics sleep at ease,
And left the race of bards to scribble, starve and freeze.

Farewell. —When mildly through the naked wood,
The clear warm sun effus'd a mellow ray;
And livelier health propell'd the vital flood,
Loitering at large, I poured the incondite lay,
Forgot the quirks of Littleton[2] and Coke,
Forgot the publick storms, and party fray;
And, as the inspiring flame across me broke,
To thee the lowly harp, neglected long, I woke.[3]

MANUSCRIPT: Unrecovered TEXT: *To the Memory of Mrs. Betsey Porter* (Cambridge, 1813), pp. 5–6; also published in *NAR*, 6 (March 1818), 384–385.

1. Dr. Jacob Porter (1783–1846, Yale 1803), of Plainfield, Massachusetts, had been Dr. Peter Bryant's medical student, and an early antagonist of young Cullen's in an exchange of verse lampoons. See the introduction to this section, "Student of Life and the Law."

2. Coke's commentaries, in his *Institutes* (see 5.9), on the *Tenures* of Sir Thomas Littleton (1422–1481) had long been a basic text for students of real estate law.

3. Bryant's letter accompanying these verses is unrecovered. See Porter to Bryant, May 24, 1813, NYPL–BG.

7. *To* Jacob Porter

[Worthington, July 23, 1813]
[Not Often, From These Faultering Wires]

Not often, from these faultering wires,
    The pensive strain is wont to flow.
Yet when a weeping friend requires,[1]
    I steep them in the stream of woe.
Alas! When late for thee I twined,
    And thy lost love, the bridal wreath;—
I little thought so soon to bind
    The cypress round the urn of death.

No sage, cold precepts not to feel,
   I bring; no stoic rules are mine;
The kindred tear alone can heal
   The mind that bleeds at sorrow's shrine.
The heart, when fierce afflictions urge,
   Must melt or break;—nor thou believe
That he, who holds the chastening scourge,
   Will frown to see his children grieve.

There came a vision to thy sight,
   Such as to tranced saint appears;
A heavenly form—a sylph of light,—
   That told of love, and happy years.
'Tis fled, and thou to life and woe
   Hast waked, a heart-dejected one,
The weary journey doomed to go,
   Through the wide world, a *wretch alone*!

O'er the low graves where brambles peer
   And yellow blooms invest the sands,[2]
There is a spot to thee more dear
   Than Ind or Asia's loveliest lands.[2]
For all that gladdened life's dull maze
   The mutual wish, the mutual care
And fondly cherished hopes, and days
   Of promised peace lie buried there.

Three little months—a transient space
   Didst thou in hymen's bands consume
Three anxious months twas thine to trace
   Eliza's progress to the tomb.
With thee her destined hours to pass
   When late she vowed with blushes meek
Consumption gave the rose, alas!
   That blossomed on her maiden cheek.

I cannot think when life retires
   From this frail pulse of doubt and fear
The soul forgets its wonted fires
   And all it loved and cherished here.
It soothes me to believe that still
   The spirits of each dear lost friend
With forms of peace my dreams to fill
   And watch my lonely walks attend.

Perhaps the one whose righteous hand
   Gives and resumes the blessing given

To thee thy parted bride may send
  A minister of love from heaven.
Each wandering thought the *Attendant Shade*
  To truth and virtue shall restore
And when the thorns of woe invade
  Shall bid thy bosom bleed no more.

Yes! o'er thy steps where'er they tread
  A silent guardian, watch shall keep
And to thy solitary bed
  Lead the soft balm of anguish, sleep.
And oft, with warbled airs of dove,
  The hovering spirit shall delight
Thy sunset walk by the still grove
  Thy musing wakefulness at night.

To think that life is quickly past
  Is solace to the mind opprest
That on the couch of death at last
  The weary frame shall welcome rest.
And let the thought thy breast console
  That thou no more with anguish tossed
Ere many years shall o'er thee roll
  Shalt be with her whom thou hast lost.[3]

MANUSCRIPT: NYPL–GR (draft) PUBLISHED: *To the Memory of Mrs. Betsey Porter* (Cambridge, 1813), pp. 7–8.

1. Two months after Cullen sent Porter his congratulatory verses, Betsey Porter died. Her husband had feared this; thanking Bryant on May 24 for his "wedding hymn," he added, "I fear [your hopes] will not long be realized, my partner being very much out of health. . . . Should she fall I hope your lyre will not be silent on the occasion." NYPL–BG. Later in the year the widower published both poems in a memorial volume, *To the Memory of Mrs. Betsey Porter.* Porter later turned from medical practice to the study of natural history, publishing the first accounts of his neighborhood in "Some Account of Cummington, in Hampshire County, Massachusetts," *Collections of the Massachusetts Historical Society*, Second Series, 10 (1823), 41–45; and *Topographical Description and Historical Sketch of Plainfield* (Greenfield, 1834). It was Porter who first identified and described the rare mineral Cummingtonite.

2. These two lines, canceled in the draft manuscript, were restored in the printed version.

3. These verses, the first Bryant wrote which were seriously concerned with death, expressed in rudimentary form (especially the sixth and last stanzas) the theme of "Thanatopsis," written two years later. See Bryant II, "Thanatopsis," pp. 169–173.

8. *To* Peter Bryant

                                     Worthington   Oct. 2, 1813
Dear Sir,

    Mr. Howe, who set out for Boston today,[1] wished me to send over, the first opportunity, for the execution on the action against Sears, defaulted last Monday.[2] I am told that my uncle[3] is coming over tomorrow —if you will have the goodness to send by him you will much oblige

Your devoted son,
W. C. BRYANT

My regards to my uncle and aunt.

MANUSCRIPT: Mrs. Mildred Bryant Kussmaul, Brockton, Massachusetts ADDRESS: Dr. Peter Bryant.

1. Bryant's law tutor, Samuel Howe, a widower when Cullen entered his home in December 1811, was probably then on his way to bring back his new bride, Sarah Lydia Robbins (c1788–1852), of Milton, Massachusetts. They were married on October 13 at the Northampton home of Howe's cousin Judge Joseph Lyman, whose wife, Anne Jean, was Sarah's younger sister. Lesley, *Recollections of My Mother*, pp. 97–100.

2. Dr. Bryant was then a justice of the peace in Cummington, as well as the town's representative in the state legislature.

3. Probably Rev. Thomas Snell of Brookfield, Cullen's early Latin tutor. See 1.4.

9. *To* Peter Bryant

[Bridgewater] Aug 20 1814

Dear Sir

You will recollect that something was said last Spring about my reading law next winter in Boston. As Mr. Baylies will probably be soon on his way to the seat of Government it will be proper perhaps if any such plan should be thought expedient to inform him of it before he goes.[1] I take this early opportunity to write to you on this subject because the mails between this place and Boston are very irregular and a letter may be ten or a dozen days in getting from here to Worthington and vice-versa. —I went to Plymouth last week where I staid four days and might perhaps have been obliged to stay a week had it not been for good luck in finding a Bridgewater man there with a vacant seat in his chaise. I there received a certificate in the handwriting of A[braham] Holmes Esquire & sprinkled with his snuff instead of sand for which I paid six dollars according to the tenor and substance following— "These certify that William C. Bryant a student at Law in Brother Baylies's office has been examined by us and we do agree that he be recommended by the bar to be admitted an attorney at August Term, 1815 he continuing his studies regularly till that time—

Joshua Thomas ⎤ Committee of the bar for
August 9, 1814—Impress Abm Holmes⎦ Examining candidates—"

By the bye I ought to have mentioned, and perhaps I did mention in my last that there is a bar rule providing that all students at law who have not had the happiness and honour of an academick degree should be examined by a committee of three any two of whom will do who were to decide how long such person should study— Now you will see by that the time fixed to admit me to the bar is before I emerge from my minority—whether this will be any objection or not I cannot tell— I have not been able to find any law which makes it so—and the examiners inquired my age at the time—but if there should be any impropriety in being [admitted next August]—nothing is more easy you know than to postpone it till November—

When I was at Plymouth I went on to the Gurnet—[2] There are rather more than sixty men at the place all stowed into about a dozen or fifteen small tents. Their accommodations are not very comfortable— There are seven guns in the fort—two twelves, two twenty fours, and three eighteen pounders.[3]

[unsigned]

MANUSCRIPT: NYPL–GR (draft) PUBLISHED (in part): Life, I, 122–123.

1. On June 1, 1814, Bryant left Worthington to continue his legal studies with Congressman William Baylies (see "Bryant's Correspondents") at West Bridgewater, twenty-five miles from Plymouth—apparently in the hope of moving on soon to nearby Boston. To Cullen's inquiry about this possibility, his father replied, "You have cost me already four hundred dollars at Mr. Howe's, and I have other children entitled to my care. Besides, my health is imperfect; I have suffered much from the fatigues of the last season, and, as I may not long be with you, I must do what I can for you all while I am still here." Undated letter in Life, I, 119.

2. The Gurnet, a fortified promontory at the mouth of Plymouth harbor, was later renamed for the Civil War governor of Massachusetts, John Andrew.

3. By the spring of 1814 the British fleet had extended its blockade of American ports to the New England coast, making occasional raids on shore towns, including Plymouth. Soon after this letter was written Governor Strong called out the Massachusetts militia without federal sanction. Morison, History of the American People, pp. 386–387, 396.

10.   To Elisha Hubbard[1]

Bridgewater   August 30, 18[14]

My dear friend—

I have waited for you to write to me, long enough to weary the patience of the man of Uz,[2] and I assure you I should really have been angry at your conduct had I not suspected that the fascinations of some fair Northampton belle might have caused you to forget the existence of your old friends. If you will honestly own this to be the fact I will lay aside my resentment for you know I am partial to those errors which owe their origin to the tender passion. My situation here is perfectly agreeable —books enough—a convenient office and for their owner a good lawyer and an amiable man. The testimony which all classes of men and I might perhaps say every individual bear to the uprightness of Mr. Baylies's character is truly wonderful. Every body—even those who entertain the greatest dislike to lawyers in general concur in ascribing to him the merit of an Honest Lawyer— You, who know how much calumny is heaped upon the members of our profession even the most uncorrupt can esti-

mate the strict and scrupulous integrity necessary to acquire this reputation— Mr. Baylies is a man of no ostentation— He has that about him
which was formerly diffidence but is now refined and softened down into
modesty. —As for old Worthington—not the wealth of the Indies could
tempt me back to my former situation— I am here much in my old way,
very lazy—but something different in being very contented— Were you
not so near the end of your law studies I would recommend this place to
you, as of all others likely to please you.

Bye the bye—in compliance with a bar-rule I went to Plymouth last
month and was examined that the term of study might be prescribed to
me, and the good-natured creatures told me that I might be admitted to
the bar next August.

In about ten days I shall be alone as Mr. Baylies sets out to join the
Legislature Nationale and if you and the rest of my friends neglect to
write to me I shall be *Melancholy*.— Send me a diary of your cogitations
and tell me what you are thinking of and what you are doing, and what
you are going to do.

It is said that you Hampshire folks mean to make Mills your representative in Congress, next fall—[3] What will his brethren of the long robe
say? I suspect there will be a little envy excited by his elevation— However their business will not be the less for it— This however may be
balanced in some measure by the addition his absence will make to their
business.

[unsigned]

MANUSCRIPT: NYPL–GR (draft) ADDRESS: Mr. Elisha Hubbard / Northampton PUB-
LISHED (*in part*): *Life*, I, 123–124.

1. Elisha Hubbard (1790–1853, Williams 1811) had been Bryant's fellow-student
under Samuel Howe at Worthington. After his admission to the bar, Hubbard practiced law at Williamsburg, Massachusetts. Calvin Durfee, *History of Williams College*
(Boston, 1860), p. 324.
2. Job 1:1.
3. Elijah Hunt Mills (1776–1829, Williams 1797), a friend of Peter Bryant's, and
in 1823 a founder with Samuel Howe of the Northampton Law School, was then district attorney for Hampshire County. Elected as a Federalist to the United States House
of Representatives in 1814, he served two terms there and later one in the Senate,
where he was succeeded in 1827 by Daniel Webster.

11. To George Downes[1]

Bridgewater   Sept. 19, 1814

My dear George—

You are mistaken. I did not write to my father for his permission to
go to Boston. The plan in the first place was proposed by him and I
wrote merely to enquire his wishes, mentioning next winter, because I
thought it the only eligible time to reside there. —This is all— My con-

duct in this instance I would not have you suppose arose from that restlessness and desire of change which perhaps I have naturally too much of. I am certainly as well contented with this place as I could be with any, and I would not exchange it for Worthington if the wealth of the Indies was thrown into that side of the balance— Yet I must acknowledge that when I think of Ward's Store and Mills's tavern and Taylor's grog-shop and Sears's, [J?] Daniels's and Briggs's (&c. &c. &c.—) such cool comfortable lounging places[2] it makes me rather melancholy, for by the bye there is not a tavern in this parish. A store with a hall, however, —close to my door, supplies the place of one. Here we had a ball last Friday, and it rained like the devil. —We had been putting it off for about a week, from day to day, on account of the wet weather, and at last despairing of ever having a clear sky, we got together in a most tremendous thunderstorm, and a very good scrape we had of it. —I however was NOT manager. The next morning we set out, six couple of us, to go to a great pond in Middleborough about 12 miles from this place on a sailing party, which we had likewise been procrastinating a number of days on account of the weather. When we commenced our journey there was every sign of rain— the clouds were thick and dark and there was a devil of a mist—but the sun came out about ten o'clock and we had one of the most delightful days I ever saw. Mine Host and Hostess were very accommodating, they gave us some fine grapes and peaches, a good dinner and some tolerable wine—we had a charming sail on the lake, and our ladies were wonderfully sociable and awake, considering that they were up till three o'clock the night before, and about eight in the evening we got back safe to the West Parish of Bridgewater. —You talk in your last of my owing you a letter. Have you not received the one I wrote you last month?[3] It was written before the one to my father. I bragged largely in it of the beauty of our Bridgewater girls compared with those of Worthington. I mentioned that there was a whole army of them who were under my almost sole protection and I promised you Downes if you would come and read law with Mr. Baylies that I would make a liberal assignment of some half-dozen to your share, —more especially as I wanted to operate on one only at a time. —Now seriously, Downes, think of coming to reside at Bridgewater, and write me your opinion on the subject. Have a little compassion upon a fellow who is entirely alone in his office. By the bye I thank you most sincerely for your advice on the subject of my going to Boston— I am happy to receive such a manifestation of your good-will and friendship—As far as you understand my intentions your opinion was perhaps correct.[4] But I know no reason why you should not have filled up the blank parts of your letter with a few of your every day cogitations, and let me know what you and the rest of the people were doing. Yesterday we received orders from the Major General of this division to detach 800 men from this Brigade to march to the defence of Plymouth. This takes all our militia from this quarter. They marched this morning— The streets were full of them a little while ago, but now the place is as solitary and silent as a desert.[5]

[unsigned]

MANUSCRIPT: NYPL–GR (draft) PUBLISHED (*in part*): *Life*, I, 124–125.

1. A former fellow-student of Bryant's under Samuel Howe, Downes is otherwise unidentified.

2. Worthington was a station on the Boston–Albany stage line, as well as the post town for the extreme western part of Hampshire County. It then contained three distilleries, in addition to the five taverns and "grog-shops" Bryant lists—an unusual number even then for so small a community. *Town of Worthington, Massachusetts Bicentennial 1768–1968* (n. p., 1968), pp. 17, 151, and map laid in.

3. Letter unrecovered.

4. In a letter dated at Worthington on August 30, Downes had reported hearing from Dr. Bryant of Cullen's wish to study in Boston, adding, "What for mercy sake can have happened to induce you to this course? I . . . have no hesitation in saying you will not be pleased with Boston nor its inhabitants and believe me when I say that after staying in the metropolis three months you would be pleased with a retreat even in W[orthington]." NYPL–BG.

5. See 9.3.

12.   *To* William Baylies

Bridgewater   Sept. 26, 1814.

Dear Sir.—

We are in rather an unpleasant pickle in this part of the country. Gen. Goodwin,[1] having read Cochrane's Letter in which he communicated to Mr. Monroe his intention of destroying all the towns on the seacoast,[2] posted off to Governor S[trong][3] and after giving him some idea of the dangers which threatened the goodly and important town of Plymouth got permission to call out as many men from his division to the defense of the place as he thought proper. A detachment was accordingly made of 890—men from this brigade [who?] received the orders last Sunday week & the next Tuesday our people marched— Thirty from this brigade were called for, *from* Captain Lothrop's company besides 2 serjeants—2 corporals 2 drummers & Lt Leonard—Thirty seven from Captain Edson's—besides a like number of serjeants &c—&c a Captain and [Ensign?]. This draft takes all the militia from this parish without being full—the companies being very small some having got certificates and some being sick—and excused by the Captains— Our streets are now very solitary—this place is a perfect desert— You would hardly recognize the country around your office if you were to see it now. Briggs & Ben Howard & Charles and Allen have gone—Eaton only is left to sell a little of something to drink—[. . .].[4] It is understood to be the intention of said Goodwin to keep these men at Plymouth till winter as a scarecrow to the British fleet— The people here grumble heartily at the affair, and seem angry that the General should think the safety of his [pitiful?] village of more consequence than that of their corn & potatoes— Those however who stay at home are the more discontented— The soldiers are said to enjoy themselves wonderfully & some of them swear that they would not come back if they could have an opportunity— They have been attentively supplied with every comfort & convenience which their situation could possibly admit of— They are established at the rope-walks— We are very anxious to hear from Congress—our paper of today in which we expected the President's message failed.[5] I believe everybody knows what kind of talk to expect from the mouth of His Imbecility, if he may be so titled—but the eyes of an attentive nation are fixed upon their Legislature to see what steps they will take upon this momentous occasion.

How does a southern autumn agree with your constitution? I hope it has not given you the fever & ague which we who dwell on the salubrious sands of the *Old Colony* dread so much. It is *bitter cold* today with us, and I have several times regretted that you were not here to enjoy it— The Judge and his family are I believe, well—[6]

[unsigned]

MANUSCRIPT: NYPL–GR (draft) PUBLISHED (*in part*): *Life*, I, 125–126.

1. State militia general Nathaniel Goodwin of Plymouth. See "A Description of Bridgewater, 1818," *Collections of the Massachusetts Historical Society*, Second Series, 7 (1818), 165.
2. Admiral Sir Alexander Cochrane, commander of the British fleet, had reported to Secretary of State James Monroe his order to Gen. Robert Ross, commander of the invading land forces, to "destroy and lay waste such towns and districts upon the coast" as he might find vulnerable. Morison, *History of the American People*, pp. 392–396, *passim*.
3. Caleb Strong (1745–1819, Harvard 1764), then governor of Massachusetts.
4. Illegible. Of the militiamen Bryant names, only his cousin Ben Howard has been identified. Cullen does not mention other cousins, Oliver Bryant and Oliver Snell, then also in the militia. See Bradford Kingman, *History of North Bridgewater* (Boston, 1886), pp. 247–248.
5. President Madison's message to a special session of Congress on September 20 urged the need for money and men to fight another campaign. See James B. Richardson, *A Compilation of the Messages and Papers of the Presidents 1789–1897, Published by Authority of Congress* (Washington, 1899), I, 547–551.
6. Probably Judge Daniel Howard of West Bridgewater, a neighbor of Baylies' and cousin of Dr. Peter Bryant's. "Youth," p. 159.

13. *To* Peter Bryant

Bridgewater   September 30   1814

Dear Sir

Yours of August 30 I received the eighth of this month.[1] Your determination was what I expected. Yet I am rather of opinion that if I do not go to Boston this winter I shall hardly go at all. If I am admitted next

August, although a Minor has not in the eye of the law every capacity which is enjoyed after arriving at what is technically called *lawful age*, yet there is no rule that I know of human or divine which prohibits him from appearing in court in the character of an attorney— Mr. Baylies however recommends to me to wait till November court before I apply to be admitted to the bar and I think myself that this would be the most proper course— As for Mr. Baylies being much in the way of collection— you will perhaps recollect that he told you at the time you was here he had little business of that sort and I find this to be the case, even more than I at that time anticipated. —He has intrusted me *to be sure* with his business in his absence, but while *I have been with him* he has not had a single Justice trial, and it is morally impossible then that I should do any thing in that way, when there are two lawyers in town—besides Mr. Baylies. The most eminent lawyers in Boston it is true are never troubled with these small matters and this is the reason that a clerk or a pettifogger would have more of them, and you will recollect what Mr. Holmes said of procuring business for me.[2] I do not say these things because I am dissatisfied but because I wish to put the subject in its proper light— With regard to my situation and the place and people here if I had disliked them I should have written about it. My situation in the office is agreeable enough—of the character of Mr. Baylies, I think you have my opinion— and Captain Ames is an honest, blunt, hospitable loquacious man and his wife a very good sort of woman.[3] —The rest of the people, from my secluded habits I know little about—but in the main they seem to be tolerably civil— I should like however if there were more apples in this country. There are orchards plenty but hardly apples enough to eat. The corn too is rather poor this year.— My Grandfather I believe is well & his family— I have been once to see him.[4]

—You inquire when I am coming home— Why, if you want me to bring your sleigh I must wait till providence pleases to send sleighing— I should like to come the first of December or thereabouts. As for cash I think I shall perhaps want more. Mr. Baylies recommended it to me, when he went away, to attend the Supreme court at Taunton this month and familiarize myself to the *arena*. By the bye Mr. Baylies set out for Washington the tenth of this month—I conveyed him to Taunton—

[unsigned]

MANUSCRIPT: NYPL–GR (draft).

1. Bryant mistakenly wrote "Sept." Dr. Bryant's letter is unrecovered.

2. Probably Abraham Holmes, a member of the examining committee for the bar before whom Bryant appeared in August, at Plymouth. See Letter 9.

3. Cullen had boarded with Capt. Ellis Ames in West Bridgewater since June 10, soon after reaching Bridgewater.

4. Dr. Philip Bryant lived in North Bridgewater, three miles from West Bridgewater. His house still stands at 815 Belmont Street, in what is now Brockton.

14. *To* William Baylies

Bridgewater   October 9, 1814—

Dear Sir

I enclose you an Examiner[1] which I suppose came to this place by mistake. I thought you might like to read it, if you did not meet with another copy, although you should get it rather late. I received, last mail, a goodly number of papers which shall be taken care of— I received the other day a letter from a young man of my acquaintance, inquiring if there was any opening for a young lawyer in this quarter, as he expects to be admitted this fall. What is your opinion? If, from the affairs of state you can

"steal

"An hour, and not defraud the public weal,"[2]

will you be good enough to let me know what prospect the Old Colony affords to the new-fledged babe of the law, and whether you can recommend any particular situations? I am really anxious that this young man, who possesses much talent and merit should not be induced by his diffident and desponding cast of character to rest upon his haunches, without making any exertion—[3] Some of our Soldiers have now returned upon furloughs—which makes the place seem less solitary than heretofore— By the bye, the sixteen companies required from Hampshire County were principally filled up by voluntary enlistment— They were not called for by single companies, but in the usual mode of drafting— Twenty-six were called for from Cummington, who volunteered to a man— Such is the spirit of patriotism that animates these *children of the Hills*.— We are all well here. Judge Howard is at Boston—

I am, Sir,—

to use the diplomatic phrases

with much consideration,

Yours &c.

W. C BRYANT

MANUSCRIPT: NYPL–GR ADDRESS: Hon. William Baylies / Member of Congress / Washington City.

1. Bryant probably refers to the Richmond *Enquirer*, a powerful Democratic organ which had absorbed the earlier Richmond *Examiner*. Mott, *American Journalism*, pp. 150–151, 188–189.

2. This quotation is unidentified.

3. Elisha Hubbard had written Bryant from Northampton on September 13, "As for myself where to turn or go or to rest still, I cannot determine. The prospect to me is a forbidding one; if in your quarter there is an opening, please to give me information in your next letter." NYPL–BG. See Letter 16.

15. *To* Peter Bryant

Bridgewater, Oct 10, 1814—

Dear Father—

I send this by Mr. E. Richards[1] who has been on a visit to his friends here. The Militia are now about to return from Plymouth and New-Bedford except 200 from the latter— The number at the former of these places was about 1000—at the latter very considerably less although much the most important place and much the most exposed. I have not however been able to learn the exact number. They were called out upon a representation of Gen. Goodwin of this division—an inhabitant of Plymouth—to the Governor who gave him permission accordingly to order out as many of the militia from his division as he saw fit. The Legislature have now taken the subject into consideration and an order is issued for their recall. It is rumoured today that they will not return to their homes but will be marched to New-Bedford as thirteen sail of vessels were said to have been seen there the latter part of last week, and a large party of the enemy on shore [on] some of the islands exercising, under arms. How this is I do not know. I was not called upon to go to Plymouth, but I was almost ashamed to stay at home when every body else was gone. I was however not a little comforted by the reflection in which I believe most people concurred with me that the place was in no danger, and that the detachment was entirely unnecessary, and therefore I might as well stay as go.— Politics begin to effervesce here a little. People are afraid of paper money—afraid of exorbitant taxes &c. &c.— Democracy is still as obstinate, and inclined to justify its Leaders as ever. I suppose you in Hampshire County begin to wax warm by this time— The fact is, there is more party-feeling—more party union in your part of the country than here. You are more a newspaper-reading people—and let the Hampshire Gazette but give the word—which is generally a faithful echo of some leading federal print—and every federalist in the county has his cue, and knows what to think. It is like the polypus taking its colour from every thing it devours, and imparting the same tinge to its young.[2] Here (if this parish affords a fair specimen of the habits and feelings of the people in this part of the state) the case is different—one takes the Centinel, one the Messenger, one the Boston Gazette, while by far the greater part take no paper at all—[3] The consequence is, that one is very warm another very moderate, and another is in doubt how to be— I heard the other day from my Grandfather and his family—they are well— I have not seen Mr. Porter nor any body else from your quarter except Miss D Lazell—[4] It is but once in a century that I get an apple here and that is such as you would not give to your hogs.— I have been obliged to speak for a pair of shoes— It does not require a longer time for my shoes to get their eyes open than it does a kitten. Remember me to the family & all my friends. Your affectionate Son

W C B[5]

MANUSCRIPT: NYPL–GR ADDRESS: Dr. Peter Bryant / Cummington / By the politeness / of Mr. Richards PUBLISHED (*in part*, from preliminary draft): *Life*, I, 128–130.

1. Probably Ezra Richards of Cummington, a near neighbor of the Bryants'. See *Only One Cummington*, p. 260.

2. The weekly *Hampshire Gazette* of Northampton was then, as it is today, read widely in the hill towns of western Hampshire County. Cullen here suggests that his own conservatism was losing its parental coloring in the less rigid political climate of the eastern seaboard.

3. The *Columbian Centinel* of Boston, founded in 1784, was a Federalist organ, while the Boston *Weekly Messenger* was a short-lived paper only three years old, and the Boston *Gazette*, distinguished as a patriot journal during the Revolution, had by now little influence. Mott, *American Journalism*, pp. 14–15, 131–133, 81, 174; Clarence Saunders Brigham, *History and Bibliography of American Newspapers: 1690–1820* (Worcester: American Antiquarian Society, 1947), II, 385.

4. Adam Porter, near neighbor of the Bryants', was town treasurer of Cummington. Deborah Lazell, daughter of Nathan Lazell of Bridgewater, apparently lived with her uncle, Capt. Edmund Lazell, in Cummington. Loren H. Everts, *History of the Connecticut Valley in Massachusetts, . . .* (Philadelphia, 1879), I, 442; *Vital Records of Bridgewater, Massachusetts, to the Year 1850* (Boston: New England Historical and Genealogical Society, 1916), I, 204.

5. In a preliminary draft not incorporated in the final copy of this letter, Cullen presented to his father a detailed argument in favor of his joining the militia. Since this is probably a fair summary of his remarks during a visit to Cummington the next month, which led to his applying for a commission (see Letter 20), it is printed here from the manuscript in NYPL–GR.

"I have a question for you—Whether it would be proper for me to have any thing to do with the army which is to be raised by voluntary enlistment for the defence of the State. Attached as you are to your native soil, to its rights and safety you could not surely be unwilling that your son should proffer his best exertions, and even his life, to preserve them from violation— The force now to be organized may not be altogether employed against a foreign enemy—it may become necessary to wield it against an intestine foe in the defence of dearer rights than those which are endangered in a contest with Great Britain— If we create a standing army of our own, if we take into our hands the publick revenue (for these things are contemplated in the answer to the Governor's message) we so far throw off our allegiance to the general government, we disclaim its control and revert to an independent empire— The posture therefore which is now taken by the State Legislature if followed up by correspondent measures is not without hazard— If we proceed in the manner in which we have begun and escape a civil war it will probably be because the administration is awed by our strength from attempting our subjugation. By increasing that strength therefore we shall lessen the probability of bloodshed. Every individual therefore who helps forward the work of collecting this army takes the most effectual means in his power to bring the present state of things to a happy conclusion— A general spirit of devotion to the cause of the state, and of attachment to the measures into which we have been driven by the weakness and wickedness of our rulers ought to pervade all ranks of men—no one should be induced to shrink from the contest on account of petty personal sacrifices— That even these would not be made in case I should enter into the service I am inclined to think from the following reasons—

"1st. If I enter upon my profession next year I shall come into the world raw & rustic to a degree uncommon even in most persons of my age & situation, in all the greenness of a secluded education—without that respect which greater maturity of years and more acquaintance with the world would give me— Now as I understand the matter the objection which is made to my spending five years in the study of the law is not upon the grounds that I shall not come soon enough into business but that the expenses attending my education would be greater than you could meet without injuring the interest of the family— In this reason I have always concurred and this it is that has led me to endeavour to shorten the term of my studies as much as possible— If I should enter into the service of the state I should procure the means of present support and perhaps with prudence, might enable myself to complete my studies without further assistance— I should come into the world likewise with my excessive bashfulness and rusticity rubbed off by a military life which is said to polish and improve the manners more than any other method in the world— It is not probable that the contest in which we are to be engaged will be a long one— The War with Britain certainly will not. The people cannot exist under it and if the government will not make peace Massachusetts must— Whether there may be an intestine contest or not admits of doubt, and if there should be, the entire hopelessness of the southern states succeeding against us will probably terminate it after the first paroxysm of anger and malignity is over— If these ideas should meet your approbation you will make some interest for me at Headquarters. The army you will perceive is to be officered by the Governor.

"Nor do I think that the fatigues of a military life would have any unfavourable effect upon my constitution— I am rather of opinion that they would tend to confirm it— It is such as to corroborate; it needs only exercise and hardship. I have no particular predisposition to disease that I know of.—

"With regard to my coming home, would not it be better that some of the family should come down on horseback for me, and return in the sleigh, than for me to hire a horse here to carry up the sleigh and return on horseback— It certainly would be more convenient; I am of opinion it would be cheaper— My Grandfather called upon me last Tuesday— He was well with his family— Last Wednesday was very warm more so than most days in summer—."

16.   *To* Elisha Hubbard

[Bridgewater, cOctober 12, 1814]

Mr. Hubbard—

Yours of the 13 I received on the 20th ult. If you please, Sir I will set out in my letter with correcting what I apprehend to be a mistake of yours respecting which of us was to begin the correspondence— I believe you mentioned the subject and asked me to write first— I then told you that I was going to a place that neither you nor I knew any thing about and said you had better write first as it was not very probable that I should write any thing which you wanted to know, and I should like to hear from my friends— You then inquired to which parish you should direct your letters, and I replied, the West. —From this conversation I concluded that you agreed to commence the correspondence and under this impression I delayed writing so long— You inquire if there is any opening in this vicinity, for a young lawyer. —I believe Sir, there are; Sir, openings enough—not, however to let lawyers in, but to let them out— There are three lawyers in Bridgewater— As, however, I have some compassion upon your situation I have written to Mr. Baylies upon the subject—[1] who knows much more about it than I; —and I will communicate to you his ideas upon it as soon as I receive his answer— I hope however that you will not be discouraged by the forbidding prospect which is presented to the new-fledged adventurer—*pedlar of law*—from pursuing a profession in which you may arrive at eminence— When shall you be admitted—next Nov. or next March? Almost every one of the Militia are taken from this town & went to Plymouth— They have been gone about 3 weeks— This makes the place very solitary— We had a ball however before they went—in a most tremendous thunderstorm—and the next day a sailing-party or water-party on a great pond in Middleborough. They did not call upon me to go to Plymouth—I have been however almost ashamed of myself for staying at home alone— Should not you advise me to *volunteer* my services? In that case I should have to tear myself from my fair protegées— Politics begin to rage here. The democrats themselves begin to grumble at the Administration— How are politics with you? do the people begin to feel like rebellion in old Hampshire again?[2] I wish you would give me all the information on this subject in your power.

[unsigned]

MANUSCRIPT: NYPL–GR (draft).

 1. See Letter 14.
 2. An allusion to Daniel Shays' Rebellion in 1786–1787 against court judgments for delinquency in debts and taxes, which had centered in Hampshire and Berkshire counties.

17. *To* William Baylies

Bridgewater Oct 18 1814

Yours of the 4th I received on the 12th— We too had some very warm weather last week—for one or two days there was what might be called comfortable summer heat— Today is as cold as the devil— The action of Howard vs. Howard and Williams terminated in favour of the plaintiff. Sproat, it is said, came off with flying colours— The trial began last Saturday about eleven o'clock in the forenoon and was not ended till eight in the evening—Sproat exerted himself to get it continued but Dewey who only of the Judges was present would not suffer it— It is suspected and I believe with reason that on the very night the case was decided an attachment was laid on the land of Snell by Howard & Williams to the amount of their respective claims—[1]

People talk to me about redeeming land taken in execution, by the defendant within one year after it is levied— I am unable to find any such law. Will you inform me how the case is?

You have probably before you receive this heard of the great doings of our Legislature— I have great hopes, notwithstanding there are no great pecuniary temptations held out, that the project of a standing army will succeed— (You will recollect that only eight dollars a month are allowed the soldier if his arms and uniform are provided by the Commonwealth and [twelve?] dollars & fifty cents if he procures them himself—)

Will you be good enough to tell me something about this new Secretary of the Treasury—what sort of character he is &c— Is he a foreigner?[2] —I have felt very sensibly since your absence the want of some Living Encyclopaedia to instruct me upon these subjects. The delegates from our state to meet those from the other New England States were to be chosen today—[3]

[unsigned]

MANUSCRIPT: NYPL–GR (draft).

1. Of those persons named in this paragraph, the only one who can be identified with reasonable certainty is Daniel Dewey (c1766–1815, M.A. Yale 1792) of Williamstown, who served for the last year of his life as a justice of the Supreme Judicial Court of Massachusetts. [Beers] *Berkshire County*, I, 335–336.

2. Alexander James Dallas (1759–1817), a Pennsylvania lawyer and state official, who was born in Jamaica, British West Indies, and educated in London, had succeeded George W. Campbell on October 6 as President Madison's Secretary of the Treasury.

3. On October 17 the Massachusetts legislature had invited the New England states to send delegates to a convention at Hartford, Connecticut, on December 15 to protest President Madison's war policy. Henry Adams, *History of the United States During the Administrations of Jefferson and Madison.* II. *Madison.* Abr. with Introduction by George Dangerfield and Otey M. Scruggs (Englewood Cliffs: Prentice–Hall, 1963), pp. 134–137.

18. *To* William Baylies

Bridgewater   Oct— [c20] 1814

I forgot to tell you in my last that the decision of Judge Thomas[1] in favour of the will of Daniel Sampson was affirmed in the Supreme Court—Parker, Jackson & Dewey on the bench—*Dewey dissentiente*—[2] Since my last I have seen the documents from our ministers at Ghent—of a nature to most I believe unexpected, and unwelcome I am sure to all—[3] Our politicians in this quarter as far as I am acquainted with their opinions upon the subject hardly know what to do with them—but perhaps we are too apt to forget that the great question is whether the conditions proposed are such as the heads of the republick can honourably accede to, and to consider the demands made merely as they affect the Eastern States. We should be much gratified with hearing something from you in the way of political speculation—I have looked to receive something of this kind from you— You send us the news regularly in the publick prints—but we want a little prophesy. It is thought the *people* have some claim for information of this kind from one who makes these matters his study—a professed statesman—one whose situation and high office give him every opportunity for examining these subjects—

What are the views of administration and the prospects of the nation? Is all probability of peace cut off? Is the war to be interminable? I earnestly wish you would tell me something about these things not only for my sake but that of others and you would save me much of such dialogue as the following— "Any letters from Mr. Baylies lately?" "Yes." —"Well, what does he write?" —"That it is very hot weather at Washington." You may tell the administration that if the system of taxation proposed by the committee of ways and means goes into effect the people of the Old Colony will not like them any better for it. [If Mr. Madison wants to make us sick of his war let him lay upon our shoulders those "burdens" which are so cheerfully and proudly borne; let him increase those "taxes" which are paid with so much "promptness and alacrity."][4] Many are very boisterous about it but then become calm by the time the taxes are to be paid.

I cannot tell how mature the publick feelings are—but the subject of a separation of the states is more boldly and frequently discussed—and the measures of our State Legislature are received amongst our party as far as I can judge with universal approbation—while the democrats regard them with considerable alarm.

[unsigned]

MANUSCRIPT: NYPL–GR (draft) PUBLISHED (in part): Life, I, 126–127.

1. Probably Joshua Thomas; see Letter 9.
2. Isaac Parker (1768–1830, Harvard 1786) was Chief Justice, from 1814 to 1830, of the Supreme Judicial Court of Massachusetts; Charles Jackson (1775–1855) and Daniel Dewey were associate justices.
3. In August 1814 the American peace commissioners at Ghent—John Quincy Adams, James Asheton Bayard, Henry Clay, Albert Gallatin, and Jonathan Russell— were confronted by their British counterparts with what amounted to conqueror's terms. Only after American victories on Lake Champlain and at Baltimore in October did Britain so modify her demands that Gallatin could lead his colleagues, on Christmas Eve, to an advantageous treaty. Bailey, Diplomatic History, pp. 149–154.
4. The quotations are from Madison's message to Congress on September 20; see 12.5. The brackets are Bryant's. (This draft letter has been rearranged by the editors in accordance with what seem to have been the writer's intentions.)

19. To William Baylies

[Bridgewater, October c29, 1814]

My Dear Sir

Yours of the 12th and 18th I received on the 26th of this month, and thank you for the solicitude you express concerning my studies—[1] Although you may not *doubt* my *diligence* yet perhaps you may justly fear my indolence— I go on much after my old way making very good resolutions to be industrious and never fulfilling them— To prevent however too many objects from interfering with the studies I ought to pursue I have given up reading much else but law books and newspapers— I could not go on with Comyns. His book is absolutely the dullest reading I ever knew.[2] I quitted him in about a week after you went away—and am now hovering on the last pages of Selwyn—[3] As you express so high an opinion of Saunders Reports perhaps I had better read them next.[4] What is your opinion? I am not good at reading half a dozen books at once. It is only by giving my undivided attention to a work of this kind that I can make it interesting— I do not at present think of any particular enquiry that I want to make which concerns my profession— I have had a thousand of them in my head since your absence—& some of them I have found means to satisfy myself about—the rest I have forgotten— You inquire what our people think of the new system of taxation—[5] I believe that I said something upon the subject in my last and I can now still more confidently say that if the taxes proposed are laid they will be in my opinion the cause of violent and unstifled discontent— Perhaps we *shall not* agree to pay them— This will however, depend upon the determinations of our State Legislature of which you have all the means of forming an opinion which we have here— I regret that I cannot give you a more particular account of the state of publick feeling in these parts, but as far as I am acquainted with it—there seems to be a deep presentiment of an approaching dissolution of the Union—

[unsigned]

MANUSCRIPT: NYPL–GR (draft) PUBLISHED (*in part*): *Life*, I, 130.

1. Baylies' letters are unrecovered.
2. Sir John Comyns (d. 1740), *A Digest of the Laws of England*, the fourth edition of which was published at Dublin in 1793.
3. William Selwyn (1775–1855), *An Abridgement of the Law of Nisi Prius*. Perhaps Bryant had the edition published at Philadelphia in 1808.
4. Sir Edmund Saunders (d. 1683), *The Reports . . . of Several Pleadings and Cases in the Court of King's Bench. . . .* There was a Philadelphia edition in 1807.
5. Secretary of the Treasury Dallas was pressing Congress to levy heavier federal taxes than had heretofore been imposed, an inordinate share of which would be borne by Massachusetts.

20. *To* Caleb Strong

Cummington, November 16, 1814.

To His Excellency Caleb Strong, Governor and Commander-in-Chief of the Commonwealth of Massachusetts:

Humbly represents that William C. Bryant, of Cummington, in the County of Hampshire, your petitioner, being desirous to enter the service of the State, in the present struggle with a powerful enemy, respectfully solicits your Excellency for a lieutenancy in the army about to be raised for the protection and defense of Massachusetts. Your petitioner presumes not to choose his station, but were he permitted to express a preference, he would request the place of first lieutenant in the First Regiment of Infantry, but in this, as becomes him in all things, he is willing to rest on your Excellency's decision. Should your Excellency be induced to favor his wishes in this respect, he hopes to be faithful and assiduous in the discharge of his duty. And your petitioner shall ever pray, etc.[1]

WILLIAM C. BRYANT.

MANUSCRIPT: Unrecovered TEXT: Bigelow, *Bryant*, pp. 32–33, note.

1. John Bigelow reported in 1890 the discovery of this letter in the "Massachusetts State Archives," but its present location is undetermined. It seems to have been written during Cullen's visit to his family between November 11 and December 5, and reflects the successful outcome of the argument offered his father in 15.5. Ironically, the commission was not awarded him until nearly two years later, when his circumstances and those of his "country" (Massachusetts) had changed so radically that he resigned the commission within six weeks after being sworn in at Worthington. "Youth," p. 183. See also the certificate of appointment dated July 25, 1816, and that accepting Bryant's resignation on February 8, 1817, both in NYPL–GR.

21. [*To* Elisha Hubbard][1]

[Cummington, cDecember 1, 1814]

To a Discontented Friend

The hills are white with new fall'n snow,
Beneath its weight the forests bow,
The ice-clad streams can scarcely flow,
    Constrained by hoary winter.
Haste, to the cheerful parlour fly,
And heap the generous fuel high,—
And then—whenever thou art dry,
    Why, broach the bright decanter.

To Providence resign the rein,
Nor vex with idle care thy brain,
To know if thou shalt go to Maine,
    Ohio, or Kentucky.
Nor give to moping dread thy mind;—
The man to gloomy dreams inclin'd,
The ills he fears will always find,
    And always be unlucky.

Submit, if troubles cross thy way—
Smooth up thy brow—enjoy the day—
For age steals on without delay—
    Repress thy wish for roving.
The man who thinks—(whate'er his case)

To cure life's ills by changing place,
Will find it but a *'wild goose chase,'*
>   And ever be removing.

Fortune may frown and friends desert,
Domestick sorrows wring the heart—
Yet surely 'tis the wisest part
>   To yield without repining.
Enjoy the good, kind heav'n bestows—
Leave sullen discontent to those,
Who fear a *thorn* in every rose,
>   To God thy all resigning.

MANUSCRIPT: Unrecovered TEXT: *NAR*, 5 (September 1817), 336.

1. Published in the *NAR* for September 1817 on the pages just preceding "Thana-topsis," as an imitation of Horace I.ix, this poem and another entitled "Horace, Ode II. B. I. Translated" have been all but overlooked by Bryant scholars. The present editors owe a debt to the late Tremaine McDowell for his identification of both author and addressee. "Youth," pp. 173–174. George Downes had written Bryant on July 6, "You know how unhappy our friend Hubbard made himself when he was with us and yet he has made a stand in Williamsburg and is doing all the business of the town. . . . Thus you see how miserable we may make ourselves by anticipating evils which never will happen." Hubbard had complained to Bryant on September 13 of his uncertainty "where to turn or to go or to rest." (Both letters are in NYPL–BG.) The date assigned this verse letter is conjectural. The snowy hills and forests, and the icy streams, suggest Cummington, and Bryant's comment to Baylies after his visit at home in November–December that, while there was no snow at Bridgewater, there was excellent sleighing at Cummington (Letter 22), confirms this supposition.

22. *To* William Baylies

>   Bridgewater   Dec. [*c*15]   1814
Dear Sir

   I have got back to Bridgewater safe and sound and in much better trim than I went from it. All the people in this quarter are well and kicking except old Mrs. [Lake?] who was in the ground before I returned. But here is no snow. All the indication of winter here is very cold weather. But from Boston to Albany there is excellent sleighing, and on the *hills* of Hampshire, the best I ever saw.

   —I paid a visit to my old instructor Mr. Howe. I found him amongst his sheep in deshabille—[1] Business he tells me is languishing—only 70 actions were entered at the November term of C[ourt of] C[ommon] P[leas] for that county, whereas there are generally from 200 to 250. He entered himself but one—and had but one continuing from the last term notwithstanding his isolated situation with some half dozen towns round him of which he enjoys the almost exclusive practice.—

   I met at Mr. Howe's with "Lara a Tale"—which is advertised on the cover of the Analectic Magazine as being written by Lord Byron. It seems intended as a sequel to the Corsair— It possesses some merit but I think it cannot be written by Lord Byron— The flow of this poet's versification is admirably copied—but it seems to me to want his energy of expression, his exuberance of thought, the peculiar vein of melancholy which imparts its tinge to everything he writes—in short all the stronger features of his genius— Conrad, whose character you used to admire and who makes his appearance in this tale as a Spanish peer under the name of Lara, —is degenerated into a lurking assassin—a midnight murderer— But perhaps you have seen the poem— For my part I never heard of it till I met with it at Mr. Howe's. May it not be the effort of some American Genius? Perhaps— A notion has got into my head that it is of Cisatlantic origin.[2]

[unsigned]

MANUSCRIPT: NYPL–GR (draft) PUBLISHED (in part): Life, I, 132–133.

1. With his law practice declining because of the war, Samuel Howe had begun breeding Merino sheep, recently introduced from Spain. Some months after this letter was written George Downes, still studying with Howe, wrote Bryant, "Mr. Howe I suspect has given up all Idea of being a judge, he has given up study entirely has bought him a lot of land and has become a great farmer—these damn'd Merinos have been the ruin of him. He actually has not studied in the office more than one week since he first became connected with them. I am clearly of an opinion that a man in our profession ought not to engage in any active employment it entirely unfits him for study. Mr. Howe occasionally of an afternoon comes into the office and takes his book and attempts to read but in vain for not five minutes elapse before he is in the arms of Morpheus." July 6, 1815, NYPL–BG.

2. Lara (1814) was, nevertheless, Byron's. But Bryant's judgment was sound; Lara was one of Byron's poorest works. The Corsair had been published earlier that year.

23. To Peter Bryant

Bridgewater— Dec. 20 1814

Dear Father—

I got to this place last Thursday week—and upon putting myself into Eaton's scales found myself ten pounds heavier than when I started from Bridgewater.— For the use of my horse I paid $7.20—at the rate of 6 cents per mile—the usual price here—it being the verdict of a jury of horse-jockeys that the horse returned in no better trim than he went— My shoes cost me $2.25— When I came here I found not a particle on the ground—although the sleighing was tolerably good at Worcester— Now there is considerable snow here not enough however to make very good sleighing—but there is said to be more as you go farther north. If any body was to come down after your sleigh between now and February (in January they tell me the sleighing is the best here) I have no doubt but he might return in it without any difficulty— I have written to Dr.

Richards.[1] There is a dancing school about to be kept in this neighborhood— It is to be kept two evenings in a week— The terms are seven dollars pr quarter. You will decide for me whether it would be proper to take advantage of this opportunity or not—

It has been whispered to me that I should do well to attend— You will decide for me— I should like to know your opinion soon as it is to commence in a few days— I have not heard from *my country* to know whether it is her pleasure to accept of my services or not. I begin to suspect that the jade is determined to take no notice of me.[2]

[unsigned]

MANUSCRIPT: NYPL–GR (draft).

1. Presumably a Dr. Richards of Abington owed Peter Bryant money for medical consultation. See Letter 31.
2. See Letter 20.

24. *To* William Baylies

Bridgewater   Dec   27, 1814

Dear Sir

I have not been able to find the bar-rules of the Old Colony—a circumstance which I fear will occasion me some inconvenience—as I have had the satisfaction of adding since my last about half a dozen more names to your *docket*—

A Bridgewater winter is more intolerable than a Bridgewater summer—the wind perpetually shifting from out to in—now rain, next snow —now a frozen collection of rough points for one to hobble over—then a swimming ocean of mud for one to wade through—one day carrying off the snow that fell the day before—and while you are disappointed of your sleighing you may console yourself with the philosophical reflection that you enjoy in return the grateful vicissitudes of white and brown—

I have been much engaged in reading Saunders. It is a feast compared with the chaotic miscellany of Comyns—[1]

We hear that you Legislators have got through with the conscription bill, and it is presented to the president to receive his sanction— God forgive the poor perjured wretch if he dares sign it— If the people of New England acquiesce in this law I will forswear federalism forever—[2]

I remain Sir
With the utmost respect
W. C BRYANT

MANUSCRIPT: NYPL–GR (draft) PUBLISHED (*in part*): *Life*, I, 130.

1. See Letter 19.
2. Daniel Webster had warned Congress that Massachusetts would nullify a conscription law. But this proved unnecessary; peace had been signed three days before the date of this letter. Morison, *History of the American People*, pp. 398, 401.

25. *To* Austin Bryant

Bridgewater   Feb. 5, 1815

Dear Sir—

Yours of the 25 ult I received yesterday— I am much afflicted at the news of my father's sickness— I trust you are doing every thing in your power to make his situation as comfortable as possible—[1]

—The Governor's message, at the beginning of the present session of our Legislature, will be a sufficient answer to those people, who ascribe the failure of my application for a commission, to the want of a recommendation from some military character.—[2]

You inform me that your federalists are much disappointed at the proceedings of our Convention— This is not much to be wondered at— considering the general character and feelings of the citizens of Hampshire— They are impatient of oppression and prepared to resist the least encroachment upon their rights— But what do they want done? Shall we attempt by force what we may perhaps obtain peaceably? The plan proposed by the Convention, if it should meet with success, certainly appears competent to secure the interest of the Eastern States at the same time that it preserves the Union: —if it should fail, it will not be our fault nor that of our Convention.— In that event we might resort to the first principles of things—the rights of mankind—the original, uncombined elements of liberty— But in the mean time it appears to my judgement proper to make use of all the means for our relief which the constitution allows. For this purpose our delegates were chosen—this was the tenour of their instructions—all that the constitution would permit they have done—and they could not have done more without transgressing the commands of the people in whose service they were employed— They have publickly proclaimed the terms on which depends the continuance of the union—they have solemnly demanded of the national government that the rights taken from them should be restored, and barriers erected against future abuses of authority— Now if these things could be effected by a peaceable compromise would it not be better than to resort to sudden violence? —We should then be in possession of all the advantages which could be derived from a separation without hazarding any of its dangers— Even if it were certain that this plan will fail—yet perhaps it would be necessary that we should adopt it, to hold up our justification to the world as we go along—to show that we act not from factious motives —or from a temporary burst of popular turbulence—to unite the wishes of all honest men in favour of our cause and take from the mouths of our enemies all occasion of contumely. And this effect is in a great measure produced. Our southern friends (and Mr. Baylies gives me a very good opportunity of inspecting the southern papers) can scarcely find terms to express their approbation of the proceedings of our convention, while the ingenuity of Democracy is vainly exercised to find some plausible occasion to revile them— I calculate that the plan of conduct which they have recommended will make more proselytes and acquire more respect to the federal party than any thing that has been done for these ten years— It will strongly impress our adversaries with the idea of that dignified and temperate firmness which steadily advances to its object—and it is not altogether impossible that it may alarm them into compliance. —If not;—next June will be the season for further deliberations—then may be the time to tell the world that the original compact between the States is dissolved—[3] But, in my opinion, you people of Hampshire expected too much— You thought that the Eastern States were in a moment and by a single effort to be restored to peace liberty and independence—how, you did not know but the Convention were to devise the means— But the delegates were no necromancers;—they were men like ourselves. They could not draw rain from the clouds nor call ghosts from the ground. Evils of the magnitude which we suffer they knew were not easily removed nor were they to be approached by rash hands— They have conducted themselves like men aware of the high responsibility which rests upon them.—

The reasons in favour of the conduct of our convention may therefore be reduced to the following heads:

1st. Because their instructions limited their deliberations to constitutional measures.

2d Because even if their authority had been unlimited, yet it were better to exhaust the catalogue of peaceable and constitutional expedients before we proceed to violence, especially as the plan now recommended has never been tried—and as it is calculated to bring the parties to a certain and speedy issue upon the great points in dispute—

3d. Because the plan now recommended bids fair to be a popular one and to overcome by its moderation that strenuous opposition to our wishes which a more violent one would be likely to encounter.

4th Because it is necessary to make one [bold?] and distinct expression of the general will of the Eastern States to give them an opportunity of granting our demands in preference to risquing a separation before we appeal to those immutable principles of right and liberty given by God with his own divine image to man.

—Such are my ideas upon the subject though I confess they are changed from what they were when I first saw the report of our delegates— I am however far from censuring, or even wishing to diminish the high spirit and quick sensibility to oppression that prevails in your county— It is necessary to counterbalance the sluggishness of our towns on the shore—

—There is now on the ground a much greater quantity of snow than is often seen in Bridgewater, and the sleighing is very good— The season is pretty healthy—

[unsigned]

MANUSCRIPT: NYPL–GR (draft) PUBLISHED (in part): Life, I, 134–136.

1. On January 25 Austin wrote Cullen reporting their father had been ill for a month with liver trouble. Life, I, 133. By the time Cullen wrote this letter, however, Dr. Bryant had begun to recover. See Lydia Richards to Charity Bryant, February 6, 1815, Sheldon Museum.

2. Austin had remarked on January 25, "I have heard nothing of your commission. People here tell me that you ought to have applied to some military character for a recommendation." Governor Strong's message on January 18 endorsed the Hartford Convention's pacific recommendations.

3. On January 5 the Hartford Convention had proposed that the four states represented—Connecticut, Massachusetts, New Hampshire, and Vermont—assert their right to unite for defense, and retain for this purpose a portion of their federal tax revenues. The delegates refrained from urging withdrawal from either the war or the Union, which extremists had urged, and their proposals were quickly ratified. But lest the national government should not meet their terms, they called for another convention, at Boston on June 15, "with such powers and instructions as the exigency of a crisis so momentous may require." Henry Adams, History of the United States During the Administrations of Jefferson and Madison. II. Madison. Abr. with Introduction by George Dangerfield and Otey M. Scruggs (Englewood Cliffs: Prentice–Hall, 1963), pp. 139–142.

26. *To* Peter Bryant

Bridgewater   Feb. 28, 1815

Dear Father

Mr. Starkweather has just called on me & handed me yours of the 23. I am very happy to hear that you are in a state of recovery.[1] The money which was sent in Austin's letter I received. As it was mentioned in the letter, I should most certainly have let you know it had the case been otherwise.[2] —The news of peace has been received here with the most extravagant demonstration of joy. —I have been very curious to know what the democrats say about it—and the following seems to be a favourite method with them of getting rid of the unlucky stumbling block that we have obtained none of those objects for which the war was declared— It is true, say they, that there is no express stipulation in the treaty about sailors rights and impressment and the principle of search, but the British have received such a drubbing that they never will dare again to impress a seaman nor search an American ship—[3]

—I wrote to Dr. Richards myself in compliance with your directions immediately after I returned to Bridgewater—

—I thank you for cautioning me about my morals and habits— I hope to profit by it—but I believe that the Bridgewater people give me the character of being pretty steady.[4] There is now a great deal of snow on the ground.

I am sir—in haste
Your affectionate son
W C BRYANT

MANUSCRIPT: NYPL–GR ADDRESS: Dr. Peter Bryant / Cummington / By the Politeness of / Mr. Starkweather.

1. Dr. Bryant's letter to Cullen is unrecovered, but in an accompanying one to Dr. Philip Bryant he wrote, "I am considerable better . . . and am daily but slowly gaining strength." February 24, 1815, BCHS. Rodman Starkweather was one of Peter Bryant's medical students.

2. The excerpts from Austin's letter of January 25 in *Life*, I, 133, do not mention money, but Cullen probably refers to the cost of his rented horse and his new shoes; see Letter 23.

3. News reached this country in mid-February of the Treaty of Ghent, in which there was no reference to earlier American demands that Great Britain cease the impressment of American seamen. Bailey, *Diplomatic History*, pp. 154–157.

4. We may suppose word had reached Dr. Bryant of Cullen's boasts to such friends as George Downes of his amorous conquests at Bridgewater. See Letter 11.

27.   *To* Samuel Howe

[Bridgewater] March 19, 1815

Yours of the 1st of this month by one of those vexatious blunders which frequently take place in conveying the mail from Boston to this place did not reach me till the 15th when the time of service for the writ you sent me had expired. If you think proper I will alter it to the next term—or do any thing you please with it—[1]

I thank you for the information you give me of the state of my father. I am very happy to hear that he is in so good a way of recovery—[2] Mr. Baylies yesterday returned from Washington after an absence of more than six months— He has had a horrid time of it.

I reciprocate most cordially your congratulations on the return of peace. This event, so much desired, and so little expected, seems to have excited in every part of the Union a delirium of transport which has not even yet subsided. Yet whatever may be our feelings on this occasion I trust that we shall not *feel* much gratitude to the man who has so long and so successfully been employed in wasting the strength and debasing the character of the nation, merely because he has not suffered its very life-blood to flow from the arteries of the Union—still less when it is recollected that he was compelled to the present treaty only by the necessity of affairs— In that hour of danger and dismay from the terrors of which we have but just now escaped we were told by the democratic party, and, for the truth must not be dissembled, by some of our own, that *then* was no time for the bickerings of party dispute, that we ought to unite to repel the invader from our soil and to secure an honourable peace—and then would be the time to call our rulers to an account— We are now told by the same party that we have been conducted through many dangers and troubles to an honourable peace—that Commerce is restored uninjured to our arms and now when federalism has gained all we have been clamouring for her mouth ought to be shut forever—what are you quarreling about?—unite.

But God forbid that the federalists should relax their exertions to drag back into that obscurity from which they ought never to have emerged the men who have brought upon the country so much distress and disgrace— I much fear however that this accommodation will incline the federal party to indolence and that in the convalescent prosperity of the country they will forget to chain that mighty influence which has brought us so near to our ruin, and now wearied with its efforts, perhaps only pauses for some more favourable opportunity to destroy us.

If the peace has blown my military projects to the moon—it perhaps may be a question whether it has not a little shattered your Merino speculations. I say a question because I do not think it yet ascertained whether we might compete successfully with other nations in the exportation of wool—but our prospects in the law are I think rather brightened— However this may be I am certain that you would not have wished your country in its late state of hazards for all the Merinos in the world—

[unsigned]

MANUSCRIPT: NYPL–GR (draft) PUBLISHED (in part): Life, I, 136–137.

1. With his letter of March 1 Howe had forwarded a writ against a man in Plymouth County, asking Bryant to hand it to a sheriff for immediate service. NYPL–GR.

2. Howe reported that Peter Bryant had so far recovered as to attend a meeting, the day before, of "our society" to celebrate the peace. This was probably the Washington Benevolent Society, a popular Federalist group for whom Cullen had written an "Ode for the 4th of July, 1814," which was published in the Hampshire Gazette for July 6, 1814, and reprinted in In Memory of William Cullen Bryant, Born, 1794— Died, 1878 ([New York: Evening Post Steam Presses, 1878]), pp. 18–19.

28. To Peter Bryant

Bridgewater   April 27, 1815

Dear Father

When Mr. Starkweather was here Captain Ames[1] was from home— which was the reason that I could not let you know his terms of board at that time—though I omitted to mention that circumstance in my letter. I have since inquired of him and he tells me that he intends to charge at the rate of $2.25 a week— I began to board with him on the tenth of June 1814— From Nov. 8 to Dec. 8 I was absent—[2] Deducting that time therefore, there will be according to my calculation 48 weeks from the tenth of last June to the ninth of next. And $48 \times 2.25 = 108.00 =$ Capt. Ames's demand at that time— As I shall probably be admitted next August[3] and return to Cummington—I make it in the whole from the tenth of June 1814 to the second Monday in August 1815 57 weeks & 3 days and Capt. Ames's bill at that time $129.25— If there are any mistakes in this calculation you can correct them from the premises.

I believe the federalists may thank their own laziness for letting Strong's majority sink so much this year—[4] Much has been said concerning the great number of voters who have gone from the state since the peace—for purposes of commerce or other business—but it is impossible I think that it should amount to four thousand—

It would be convenient for me to have an additional pair of thin pantaloons this summer— If my mother should think proper to send down a pair by you next June I should like to have them middling large —and made upon the tight-knee and bell-muzzle plan—[5]

After my return to Bridgewater I did considerable business for Mr. Baylies—and had a good many tedious clients to talk to but never brought any thing to the grand consummation—a trial— So that I have done no arguing since I came to Bridgewater.

Speaking of hats—they are now made in this neighbourhood— Some are manufactured in town I believe but they are good for nothing—

I was at my Grandfather's a day or two ago and found him with his family in good health—

Since I left Cummington last I have been so tormented with boils on my face that I pity poor Job if he had worse ones or more of them than I have had— There is now a great fellow of this breed over my left eye—and I can scarcely see to write—as you have perhaps already suspected—

People in Bridgewater call this a late spring because they have not planted their corn yet— The snow has been off the ground for more than a month—

There is no news here—nothing stirring—and I cannot think of another single item to add to my letter—

Believe me Sir
Your dutiful Son
WILLIAM C BRYANT

My regards to my friends—

MANUSCRIPT: NYPL–GR ADDRESS: Dr. Peter Bryant / Cummington / To go to the Worthington Post office POSTMARK (in script): W. Bridgewater / May 1st POSTAL ANNOTATION: 18¾.

1. Cullen's landlord at West Bridgewater; see 13.3.
2. Visiting his family at Cummington.

3. I.e., to practice law.

4. Caleb Strong had just been re-elected governor of Massachusetts.

5. Sarah Bryant customarily made her sons' clothes as well as her husband's. Peter Bryant wore to the legislature in Boston a broadcloth suit she had cut and stitched; her diary records her making an overcoat for Cullen just before he left home in December 1811 to study law. "Youth," pp. 34, 137.

29. *To* George Downes

[Bridgewater, *c*May 1, 1815][1]

[Dear Si]r

I am a little at a loss to comprehend why in the course of nearly six months I have not received a single line from you—when certainly it was your turn to write— But perhaps your time is so totally engrossed by law-affairs and love-affairs—by the constant devotions which you pay to *Themis* and *Venus*—that you have no leisure for any thing else— If so I believe I must try to muster good nature enough to pass over the offence —upon promise of better behaviour in future— Bridgewater—my friend —grows rather dull to me—but [the next 3?] months will carry me away from it— I got sick of an eternal obsequiousness to the petticoated gentry. I neglected them—and now I am at sword's-points with above half of them— Once in a while, however, we contrive to get up a bobbery of some sort—a ball or so—and *election day* we are to have what we call a *tea party*—[2] I wish you had been at Bridgewater when the news of peace arrived— We had fine sport—and celebrated the event in repeated festivities— But I soon grew weary of them and now there is not a greater drone in Massachusetts than I am— The nearer I approach to the conclusion of my studies the more I am convinced of the necessity of industry.

You, my friend were born under [a more fortunate?][3] star than I— You have every [advantage in?][3] entering upon the practice of law of accommodating your conversation to ev[ery sort of?][3] people and rendering yourself agreeable to all— The maturity of your manners will add much to the respect you will receive upon entering into life and the natural placidity of your temper will enable you to contemn the little rubs which will of course attend the young practitioner—

But I lay claim to nothing of all these—and the day when I shall set up my gingerbread board[4] is to me a day of fearful expectation— The nearer I approach to it the more I dread it— I feel much anxiety about our friend Hubbard— I am afraid he will never practice in his profession at all— I should lament that his talents should lie unemployed and his acquisitions become useless to him— From his unbending independence and integrity I had conceived a hope that he would have increased the respectability of the profession by adding one more to the list of *honest lawyers*.[5]

Write me something to put me in good humour. Your gallantries have generally something *unique* in them—and I should like to hear what you are doing in that way—[6]

Adieu— God bless you—
WILLIAM C. BRYANT

MANUSCRIPT: NYPL–GR (draft) PUBLISHED (*in part*): *Life*, I, 138.

1. Since this letter was apparently written before election day, May 3, it is dated conjecturally about May 1.

2. In colonial New England elections were held the Wednesday before Easter, which was then also "Inauguration Day," when governor and council were seated ceremoniously in a holiday atmosphere, with "Election Cake" and more convivial refreshments. This custom was continued into the ninteenth century, though the celebration came at a later date after votes had been counted. Inauguration Day, still also called "Election Day," was held on the first Wednesday in May, which in 1815 fell on the third. Samuel Eliot Morison, *Builders of the Bay Colony* (Boston: Houghton Mifflin, 1964), p. 86; *A Dictionary of Americanisms on Historical Principles*, ed. Mitford M. Mathews (Chicago: University of Chicago Press, 1951), p. 548.

3. Manuscript torn here.

4. The use of this picturesque term for the professional man's signboard, or "shingle," derives perhaps from an early slang characterization of money as "gingerbread."

5. Bryant was obviously out of touch with Elisha Hubbard, who, according to Downes, was now settled in a comfortable law practice at Williamsburg. See 21.1. Cullen was probably ascribing to Hubbard the uncertainty he was beginning to feel of his own readiness to enter the courtroom.

6. Downes obliged him, writing on July 6, "I think you do injustice to your talents and your application. If I were conscious of possessing those qualities in the degree you do I should have no fear for the future." NYPL–BG.

30. *To* Peter Bryant

Bridgewater   May 24, 1815

Dear Father

I have found a good opportunity to send to Cummington—but unluckily have nothing to write. I am however alive, as this scrawl will abundantly testify—and well—as to which point you must be satisfied with my own affirmation.

—I presume that you in Cummington as well as we in Bridgewater were a little surprised that Bonaparte should so suddenly resume the sceptre of France.[1] The exile of Elba has outwitted all Europe. We, I think, may dread, in common with other nations, the consequences of this event. They, by due concert and proper measures, may perhaps ensure their own safety, even if they should not have the power or inclination to pull him again from the throne—we have no security against his artifices and emissaries but in the virtue of the people, which I fear is not wonderfully great.—

I am told that you have half a score of pupils—that you have bought another farm,[2] and that matters are going on at Cummington, in high stile. At Bridgewater, on the contrary, nothing is taking place to diversify the dull uniformity of existence—except that a neighbouring house caught fire yesterday—which I helped to extinguish—and brought away water enough in my clothes to have put out the conflagration of a city—

We have had a late and very disagreeable season— The earth has been

> A naked subject to the weeping clouds,[3]

with short intermissions, for more than six weeks. But the weather now begins to be mild and pleasant.

In July next there will be a Term of the Supreme Court at Plymouth, for the decision of law questions only—where, I am informed, some of the great luminaries of the law from Boston will be present.

Bridgewater has been remarkably healthy since I have resided in it— I marvel greatly that there should be so little sickness here—amongst so many filthy bogs, lazy streams, and stagnant puddles.

My regards to all my friends

I am Sir
Your affectionate Son
WILLIAM C. BRYANT

MANUSCRIPT: NYPL–GR ADDRESS: Dr. Peter Bryant / Cummington / Favd by Mr. Otis PUBLISHED (in part): Life, I, 138.

1. Escaping from exile on Elba, Napoleon I entered Paris on March 20 to re-occupy the throne of France.
2. This farm, acquired from a neighbor named Dwelly Cotterell, was occupied by Austin Bryant for several years after his marriage in 1819. Sarah to Charity Bryant, March 1, 1821, NYPL–Berg; Bryant Record, p. 45; Only One Cummington, p. 350.
3. 2 Henry IV I.iii.61.

31. *To* Peter Bryant

Bridgewater   11 July 1815

Dear Father

I intend to set out for Cummington on Monday the 21st of next month, and barring all extraordinary occurrences, shall of course get to Northampton on Tuesday night, or if the stage does not arrive there on Tuesdays—Wednesday night. I have seen Richards; he promises to let me have part of the money due on the note you sent me towards the close of the month.[1] If you can contrive to see Mr. Howe soon I wish you would desire him to let me know what he wishes to have done with his writ against Litchfield. The sooner you speak to him the better, otherwise I may not get word from him before suing time for August Term expires. If I do not hear from him I shall conclude that he does not mean to have the writ altered to that Court.[2]

There is no news stirring in these parts— The weather for some time past has been extremely dry—and not more than two thirds of the usual quantity of hay will be cut this year—as the farmers tell me—.

Your affectionate son

WM   C. BRYANT

MANUSCRIPT: NYPL–GR ADDRESS: Dr. Peter Bryant / Cummington / To be left at the Worthington post office POSTMARK (*in script*): W. Bridgewater / July / [12?] POSTAL ANNOTATION: 18¾.

1. Richards is unidentified, except as described in Letter 32. The occasion for his debt to Dr. Bryant is not known.

2. See 27.1. On July 19 Samuel Howe wrote Cullen, "I wish you would alter the writ I sent you for the third Monday in August & get it served in season." NYPL–BG.

32.   *To* Peter Bryant

Bridgewater   31 July 1815

Dear Father

I was mistaken in writing to you that I should take the stage from the North Parish to Boston on Monday. I have since seen Marshall who informs me that it passes by his tavern on Tuesday— I shall therefore set out from Bridgewater on Tuesday, the twenty second of next[1] month and arrive at Northampton on Wednesday or Thursday evening—you will be able to satisfy yourself which.

Nothing new or strange has occurred since you left us.[2] As for our people some of them are sick with the measles—as for our weather it is very warm and very dry—as for our Indian Corn—it never looked better. This is the summary.—

I was at meeting at the North Parish yesterday—and saw my Grandfather and his wife there—[3] They were well.

I have not seen Richards yet— The Abington people are engaged in settling a minister; he is one of the active characters in the business; his attention may be totally absorbed by this affair, and I may be under the necessity of recalling him again by a gentle hint to his recollection.

My regards to my friends

I remain

Your affectionate Son

WM C. BRYANT

MANUSCRIPT: NYPL–GR ADDRESS: Dr. Peter Bryant / Cummington / To be left at the Worthington Post Office POSTMARK (*in script*): W. Bridgewater / Aug. 1st POSTAL ANNOTATION: 18¾.

1. Bryant mistakenly wrote "this month."

2. Peter Bryant and his son Austin had apparently visited Bridgewater earlier that month. See Peter to Philip Bryant, February 24, 1815, BCHS; Samuel Howe to Cullen Bryant, July 17, 1815, NYPL–BG.

3. Cullen's grandmother, Silence Howard Bryant, had died when his father was nine years old. Peter Bryant's stepmother, Hannah Richards Bryant (d. December 18, 1816) was by all accounts a stern taskmaster who inspired little affection among her stepchildren and step-grandchildren. See *Life*, I, 53; Abigail Snell to Charity Bryant, January 17, 1817, Sheldon Museum.

33. *To* Samuel Howe

Bridgewater   8 August 1815

My dear Sir

I enclose you the writ you sent me last spring. I put it into the hands of an officer as soon as I received your last, but the creature neglected to make service of it till yesterday—the last moment of grace.

Your remarks upon publick speaking I read with the more interest as they come from one who has practised that art with such distinguished success. Yet I must acknowledge that their effect upon me was considerably lessened by the reflection that mere industry could never have supplied that eloquence—you must be content sir not to claim the whole merit of producing it, to yourself—you must ascribe much of it to the bounty of Nature, assisted I have no doubt, by art but still entitled to the credit of furnishing the raw material which was afterwards to be worked up into such polish and elegance.[1]

I never could believe that the maxim *Orator fit* holds good in its full extent. It may be true that any man of common sense and common utterance may by practice and diligent endeavour be brought to talk decently well upon some occasions—but, what we currently term *Eloquence* according to my weak judgement depends as *much* upon the original constitution of the mind as any other faculty whatever. This however is not the place for a disquisition of this kind.

Next week by the leave of Providence and the Plymouth bar I become a limb of the law.[2] You inquire in what part of the world I intend to take up my abode. This is a hard question. I have formed a thousand projects; I have even dreamed of the West Indies—after all it may be left to mere chance to determine— I hope soon to see you and have the benefit of your advice upon this subject— My best remembrances to all who have not forgot me—and tell Mr. Downes that I should write to him did I not expect to see him so soon.

believe me sir
with the highest esteem & respect
Yours etc
W C BRYANT

MANUSCRIPT: NYPL–GR (draft) PUBLISHED (*in part*): *Life*, I, 139.

1. Howe had written Cullen on July 17 a long letter of advice and reassurance, addressing himself to the problem which he realized was most unsettling to his former pupil: "You are soon I suppose to become one of the brotherhood & from your habits

& progress in your professional studies while with me I hesitate not to predict you will become a distinguished member of that fraternity. I hope you have availed yourself of every opportunity to accustom yourself to speaking in publick. The manner of speaking which you know Demosthenes is reputed to have said was one of the three first requisites for an Orator is wholly a matter of habit. Some persons acquire this habit more readily than others yet no person was ever able to speak gracefully & powerfully upon a first attempt. I hope also that a want of success in the first instance will not be suffered to discourage you." NYPL–BG.

2. On August 15 Bryant left the Court of Common Pleas at Plymouth with a certificate entitling him to practice as an attorney in any circuit of that court in the State of Massachusetts.

II

Following Two Professions
1816–1821
(LETTERS 34 TO 80)

HAVING BEEN ADMITTED TO THE BAR on August 15, 1815, Byrant—as he put it to a former fellow-student—"lounged away" three months at his home in Cummington. His phrase was surely imprecise, for during this time he wrote the first draft of "Thanatopsis" and an incomplete version, or "Fragment," of the poem later entitled "Inscription for the Entrance to a Wood." And he busily hunted a community in which to locate his legal practice.

Bryant's problem was troublesome. To settle in a large town or a city, such as New Bedford or Boston, which he saw as the most attractive prospect, would require capital his father could not provide. William Baylies urged on him, as offering a young lawyer the best opportunities, certain rural towns such as Truro on Cape Cod, or Freetown, between Bridgewater and New Bedford, but to Cullen these seemed to promise only more of the isolation in which he had once been unhappy at Worthington. Northampton, where his father's friends Samuel Howe and Judge Joseph Lyman might have helped, was the Hampshire County seat and already well served by attorneys. Having explored possible openings in towns nearer home, such as Williamsburg and Ashfield, Bryant finally accepted, in December 1815, what seemed the least attractive choice, the little farming village of Plainfield just north of Cummington where he had prepared for college under Moses Hallock.

Six unhappy months at Plainfield, which Bryant describes rather bitterly in the first letter written thereafter which is now recovered, ended with his receiving through Samuel Howe an invitation to enter into partnership with an established lawyer, George Ives, at Great Barrington in the Housatonic Valley, forty miles from Cummington. Here, after eight months with his more experienced partner, Bryant bought Ives out and began practice by himself.

The young poet who had now "mixed with the world" and been "stained" by its "follies" could still look only "coldly on the severe beauties of Themis," as he told Baylies a few days after parting from Ives in May 1817. Meanwhile, Peter Bryant furthered his son's literary interests. In a desk drawer in his office he happened on some of Cullen's verses. Taking them to Boston when he attended the legislature in June, he left them with his friend Willard Phillips, then an editor of the *North American Review*. The anonymous appearance in that journal in September 1817 of "Thanatopsis" and "A Fragment" ("Inscription for the Entrance to a Wood"), incomplete as they then were, encouraged Cullen four months later to submit two finished poems to the *North American Review*, one of which was "To a Waterfowl."

Soon afterward, at Phillips' invitation to contribute a prose article to his journal, Bryant produced a critical essay on American poetry which showed him to be a perceptive student of his own craft. Several more of his articles were accepted by the *North American Review* in 1819 and 1820. But its conductors had decided, soon after the publication of "To a Waterfowl," that because they could not hope for equally good verse from other writers they must discontinue their poetry department, so Bryant was left once more to solitary composition.

Despite distaste for his profession, Bryant persevered at the law, and earned recognition in Berkshire County in other ways. During his first two years as an attorney he was limited by his license to appearances in justice courts and in the Court of Common Pleas, but in September 1819 he was admitted to full practice in the Supreme Judicial Court of Massachusetts. In the same month he was surprised to receive an honorary Master of Arts degree from Williams College. Between 1819 and 1821 he was elected or appointed to a series of village offices in Great Barrington: tithing man, town clerk, justice of the peace, and clerk of the center school district. He wrote odes for agricultural celebrations, a speech for the Bible Society, and in 1820 an oration which he delivered at Stockbridge on the Fourth of July.

The years 1820 and 1821 were eventful for him in more personal ways. In March 1820 Dr. Peter Bryant died of the chronic lung trouble from which he had suffered increasingly for five years. In January 1821 Cullen married Frances Fairchild, a Great Barrington girl he had met during his first few months in the village. In April he was invited to compose a longer poem than he had heretofore attempted, and to read it before the Phi Beta Kappa Society in Cambridge the following August, learning—belatedly—that he had been elected to the Harvard chapter of that society four years earlier.

The circumstances of this invitation make it evident that the Cambridge friends Bryant had made during his writing for the *North American Review*—Willard Phillips, Edward Channing, and Richard Dana—had been so impressed with his poetic talent that they were eager to encourage it further. They made his visit to Cambridge for the Harvard commencement in August the occasion for the realization of a project which Channing had urged on him more than two years before, the publication of a collection of his poetry. They offered suggestions and frank criticism toward its preparation, and guided the slim volume of eight poems through the press in September. And by securing favorable notices of Bryant's *Poems* at Boston and New York, they encouraged him to make a resolution four years later of the dilemma which was becoming ever more frustrating—whether to lodge his career finally in literature or the law.

34. *To* an Unidentified Friend[1]

[Great Barrington, December? 1816?][2]

I am told you complain that I have not kept my word in writing to you whenever I should establish myself in business. I had indeed forgotten that I ever made such a promise; but a late repentance will sometimes wipe out an error if made as soon as that error is discovered. I too have great cause to complain of my Bridgewater friends many of whom promised to write to me & who seem to have forgotten both me & their promises. After leaving Bridgewater and lounging away three months at my father's I went to practice in Plainfield a town adjoining Cummington— I remained there eight months but not being satisfied with my situation & prospects in that place I left it for Great Barrington—a pleasant little village in Berkshire County on the banks of the Housatonick, where I am now doing business in partnership with a young man of the name of Ives.[3] This town was originally settled by the Dutch about the year 1730—& many of their descendants compose about one tenth of the present inhabitants.— Its politics are highly federal. I live about 5 miles from the line of the state of New York & 10 from that of Connecticut— In Plainfield I found the people rather bigoted in their notions, and almost wholly governed by the influence of a few individuals who looked upon my coming among them, with a good deal of jealousy— Yet I could have made a living out of them in spite of their teeth had I chosen to stay, but Plainfield was an obscure place & I had little prospect of ever greatly enlarging the sphere of my business— My present situation I am better pleased with—[4]

Such is my history. I have been very solicitous to hear from my friends in Bridgewater since I left it;—but without much success— I should be extremely glad to receive a line from you or any of my friends who may condescend to write. I shall always be glad to hear of their welfare & always interested in their history. Of all the places in which I ever resided there is none in which I passed my time more pleasantly, & none in which I would rather wait for the close of my life than in Bridgewater— I hope you continue as cheerful, as good-humoured & as hospitable as ever— I hope that the young ladies of your parish are getting well-married and that those who are not will preserve their bloom till they do— I came into this place about the first of last October— Since I have been here I have been wasted to a shadow by a complaint of the lungs but am now recovered—

I am very desirous to hear from friends in Bridgewater.

[unsigned]

MANUSCRIPT: NYPL–GR (draft) PUBLISHED (*in part*): *Life*, I, 145–146.

1. The recipient of this letter is identifiable only as a friend, and probably a former fellow-student, of Bryant's at Bridgewater.

2. The date is conjectural. This letter must have been written between Bryant's

removal to Great Barrington in October 1816 and the dissolution of his partnership with George Ives in May 1817.

3. Soon after beginning law practice in Plainfield, Bryant had apparently heard through Samuel Howe that George Ives (1789–1825), son of Gen. Thomas Ives of Great Barrington, Massachusetts, was looking for a partner. After an exchange of letters, Ives wrote Bryant on June 24, 1816, inviting him to join in a busy practice which might produce as much as $2,000 a year with a partner in his office. NYPL–BG. Having looked into other possibilities, perhaps at Dalton and Northampton, Bryant accepted Ives's invitation about September 1. Sarah Snell Bryant, "Diary," August 6, 10, 19, 22, 1816; "Youth," pp. 183–185.

4. Although these brief comments are apparently Bryant's only surviving reaction to his eight months' law practice at Plainfield, we know from William Baylies' reply to an unrecovered letter he wrote after only a month's residence there that his situation was uncongenial. Writing Cullen on January 24, 1816 (NYPL–BG), Baylies remarked, "I suppose from your description that Plainfield does not furnish a very *polished society*," but "If the people are honest & industrious it is sufficient— Indulge not in an *over-refined* taste— It is the enemy of our peace—a destroyer of our comfort." It seems likely that Cullen's return, as a fledgling lawyer, to the village he had left only six years earlier as a schoolboy of fifteen did not win him easy acceptance among the opinionated farmers who were his neighbors there. That his unhappy experience was not unique is made evident by his friend Jacob Porter, who wrote later of Plainfield, "Several attornies have practiced here, each for a short time; but no one has met with sufficient encouragement to make it his permanent residence." *Topographical Description and Historical Sketch of Plainfield* (Greenfield, 1834), p. 26.

35. *To* William Baylies

Great Barrington   25 Jan'y 1817

My dear Sir

It is a long time since I have heard from you and perhaps I have only to reproach my own remissness in writing to you with being the cause. If my conduct in this respect should seem to you of sufficient consequence to need an apology I beg that you will impute it to any thing else, rather than a forgetfulness of my obligations to one whom I shall ever remember with esteem and gratitude. I am naturally indolent & negligent enough but I thank God that whatever faults have been permitted to grow up in my disposition he has kept my heart warm towards my friends.

I have removed my residence to the place from which I date this letter. I am in partnership with a young man of the name of Ives and have the honour of occupying the office where your colleague Mr. Hubbard received his professional education.[1] This is a pretty little village in a very pleasant part of the world and if it has not every advantage I could wish I ought perhaps to remember that since the Garden of Eden was drifted by the deluge to take root in the main ocean

an Island salt and bare
The haunt of Orcs and seals and sea-mews' clang[2]

Paradise is no longer to be found on earth.

The act reducing the pay of members of Congress gave me some surprise. I thought perhaps that they might agree to receive a daily instead of annual compensation but I little dreamed, after reading the report of the committee appointed upon the question, that they would consent to return to their old allowance of six dollars a day. I did not look to see so easy a triumph of what seemed the publick will over the settled opinions of a very large majority of their legislators—[3]

—I see that you are not a candidate in the next election of Representatives in Congress. I expected that you would leave the theatre of publick life not only because you intimated to me a disposition to do it but because I knew you loved retirement better than distinction.[4] I should be much gratified to receive a line from you.

[unsigned]

MANUSCRIPT: NYPL–GR (draft) ADDRESS: Hon   William Baylies / Representative in Congress / Washington.

1. Possibly Henry Hubbard (1783–1863, Williams 1803), a Lanesboro lawyer and member of the Massachusetts legislature during Baylies' tenure there. Bryant and Ives occupied an office on Main Street near a lane later called Bryant Court. This had once been used by Gen. Thomas Ives, George's father, and earlier Judge Theodore Sedgwick (1746–1813) had begun his law practice there. [Beers] *Berkshire County*, I, 308; Taylor, *Great Barrington*, p. 421; Sedgwick, *Life and Letters*, p. 24.

2. Cf. *Paradise Lost* XI.834–835.

3. Replying on February 7, Baylies pointed out that repeal of the Compensation Law, of which he did not approve, at least left the next Congress free to fix its own pay. NYPL–BG.

4. After two terms in Congress, from 1813 to 1817, Baylies returned to full-time law practice. Between 1820 and 1831 he served several one-year terms in the state legislature, of which he had been a member from 1808 to 1813, and in 1833 returned to Congress for another term. *BDAC*.

36. [*To* George Downes][1]

Great Barrington   17 March 1817

I have now on my hands about half-a dozen correspondents to whom it is my duty to write. That duty I have delayed to perform till I am ashamed of my neglect, and I have now deliberately addressed myself to the task. Your claims are superiour to those of any other and I begin by writing to you. I have heard that you are married— Alas! Sir, I little thought when I saw you last October that the chain was then forging which was to fetter your freedom so soon. I did not dream that with all that unconsciousness of air and innocence of countenance you were meditating any special enormity. You in the mean time, I suppose, look without envy on the restless and unsatisfied liberty of us who are yet without the pale of matrimony—you hug your irons and love the blissful slavery to which you have transferred yourself—in like manner as it is said that a people are happier under the soft and easy sway of a wise & virtuous monarch than the turbulent and anxious administration of a republick— But my dear Sir— You say with Milton

Hail wedded love mysterious law true Source
Of human offspring sole propriety.[2]

Marriage is a lottery—and little does one know when he chuses the number of his ticket whether it draw a blank or a prize. He may have some particular partiality for the number—he may have dreamed about it. I will not disturb your felicity on this occasion with many unlucky reflections of my own upon the subject of marriage. Though I have always felt a secret horrour at the idea of connecting my future fortunes with those of any woman on earth yet I reverence the institution which had its origin in paradise, and without which Eden was not happy.[3]

You, I suppose, with your accustomed judgement, have made choice of the future companion of your life rather for solid than showy qualities, you have wisely reflected that woman was formed for domestic life that her husband's fireside is the only place where she should be ambitious to shine—that home is her province—and that, in proportion to her usefulness, there is the real value of her character— May God bless your union & crown it with an offspring who shall be a blessing to the world.—

[unsigned]

MANUSCRIPT: NYPL–GR (draft).

1. It is evident that this letter and the one dated April 17, 1818, are intended for the same recipient. He is identified conjecturally as George Downes, because of Bryant's comment, "Your claims are superiour to those of any other," and because they had in all probability met at Cummington or Worthington the previous October.

2. *Paradise Lost* IV.750–751.

3. Bryant's first letter to his future wife, Frances Fairchild, two weeks later (Letter 38) suggests he may himself have been contemplating marriage just then.

37.   *To* John E. Howard[1]

Great Barrington   25 March 1817

My dear Sir

Yours of the 27 of Dec. I received and read with great pleasure. It was the the first letter that has reached me from Bridgewater since I left it—a period of nearly two years. Yet there was one part of it which, while it equally excited and disappointed my curiosity, gave me some alarm. You inform me that you are————. How shall I understand this————? What meaning shall I give this blank? It made my blood run cold in every vein and my hair rise "like quills upon the fretful porcupine"[2] when I reflected that the word "married" might complete the sentence, and possibly give the meaning so mysteriously withheld— Dii omen avertant![3] Yet, if there was no special enormity behind the curtain, it seems to me that you might have spoken out—and you would do me great injustice to suppose that I should not be very much gratified to know any circumstance relating to your present situation. In your next I shall expect to learn all. You will tell me whether you are employed as when we parted in the labours of agriculture, or the contemplative pursuits of study—single, or in the yoke— Miss x x x x x x x x x you say is more blooming than ever. Long may she bloom—late may her eye lose its brilliance, and the roses of her cheek their freshness. Such are my wishes for her and for all the fair-ones of Bridgewater.[4]

Poor Allen. I am sorry for him. He had good traits in his character, but I was always afraid whither certain propensities of his would lead him. I knew his want of settled principles.[5]

Present my affectionate remembrances to Mr. Baylies, and to your family, and to all my friends in Bridgewater,—and tell Mr. Baylies that I am on the eve of writing him a longer letter than he will have patience to read.

I remain Sir
with the highest esteem
WM C BRYANT

MANUSCRIPTS: Middlebury College Library (final copy); NYPL–GR (draft) ADDRESS (from draft): Mr. John E. Howard / Bridgewater / Massachusetts.

1. John Edward Howard (d. 1854, Brown 1815) was Bryant's second or third cousin and one of his companions in the balls and outings described in letters written during his law study at West Bridgewater. *The Historical Catalogue of Brown University 1764–1934* (Providence: Brown University, 1936), p. 121; Howard to Bryant, April 7, 1815, and December 27, 1816, NYPL–BG.

2. Cf. *Hamlet* I.v.19–20.

3. "Heaven forbid!"

4. Howard wrote on December 27, "You don't know how much we want your company to enliven our parties. . . . Miss ———— continues to be the rage."

5. Allen is unidentified (but see Letter 12).

38. *To* Frances Fairchild[1]

Great Barrington   31 March 1817

Dear Frances

It is so long since we have heard from you that some of us begin seriously to doubt whether there ever was such a young lady as Frances Fairchild. Others pretend to say that the reason why we hear nothing of Frances Fairchild is that she has changed her name to Frances Wells— but I am pretty certain that if you were either dead or married or run away you would let us know it. I have been disappointed of the high gratification I anticipated in hearing that you had become the bride of some illustrious western sachem—Walk-in-the-Water, or Split-log, for instance. I expected much pleasure in learning how you appeared in your new dignity, wearing the wolf-skin, bedizened with wampum, and brightened up with bears-grease;—but since your hand was not solicited on your first arrival among them, I have abandoned all hope of your being elevated to that splendid station. Upon the whole, I believe that you may as well give up all expectations from the Indians, and return to Great Barrington.[2]

There are some very disagreeable reports current here concerning the state of your health. It has been said that you are confined by indisposition to your room. If this is not true, and I hope it is not,—you would relieve your friends here from many unpleasant apprehensions by writing to them on the subject. With all due respect for your western country, I doubt whether the lake-air, and bad water, and quack doctors of that territory are the safest hands to which a young lady of your delicate constitution might be trusted.[3]

Your favorite—little Hannah, grows handsome and good tempered, runs all over the house, chatters like a swallow, and has become as plump as a bean.—[4]

One of our neighbours as you have probably heard has got married, and some others seem to contemplate following his example. Who they are you will probably hear when that event takes place.— You promised to return to us in the *Spring*. We shall expect you along as soon as the roads become settled. Maj. Hopkins desires me to present his affectionate remembrances to you,[5] and so would forty more if they knew that I was writing.

I remain
with high esteem
Yours &c
W. C. BRYANT

MANUSCRIPTS: NYPL–GR (draft and final) ADDRESS: Miss Frances Fairchild / East Bloomfield / New York.

1. This is the first known letter from Bryant to his future wife. See "Bryant's Correspondents." In December 1816 Frances Fairchild had gone with her sister Eugenie, Mrs. P. G. Tobey, to visit in East Bloomfield, New York, near the head of Canandaigua Lake, where her brother Moses had settled earlier. She did not return to Great Barrington until July 1818. No letters from her to Cullen at this time seem to have survived. Frances Bryant, "Autobiographical Sketch," and "Mrs. F. F. Bryant's Genealogy," NYPL–GR.

2. A treaty had been signed in 1794 between the American government and the Iroquois Confederacy at Canandaigua, near East Bloomfield. But Cullen's fanciful image of Frances among savages was probably suggested by groups of Stockbridge Indians, then domiciled with the Oneidas in central New York, whom he had seen on their periodic pilgrimages to their ancestral homesite in the Housatonic valley, near Great Barrington. See his note to "Monument Mountain," *Poems* (1876), p. 490.

3. Cullen was apparently already aware of the poor health from which Frances would suffer during most of her married life.

4. Probably a child of Frances' older sister Esther, Mrs. Allen Henderson, with whom she lived after her return to Great Barrington.

5. (Militia) Major Charles W. Hopkins of Great Barrington, husband of Frances' sister Mina.

39. *To* Peter Bryant

Great Barrington   29 April 1817—

Dear Sir

I have been several times on the eve of writing to you since I visited Hampshire[1] and am a little ashamed that I have no better excuse than that of indolence for neglecting it. I enclose you a ten dollar bill which I wish you would take the trouble to forward to Dr. Porter and get endorsed on the note he holds against me.[2] I have an agricultural question to submit to you. Whether Plaister of Paris would not be a good manure for your Cummington soil. I have been induced to think on this subject by observing the immense advantages which attend its use here where there is a plaister-mill, and where the farmers scatter it on their grounds as regularly as the manure of their barn-yards. In cold wet lands it is said to be of little or no benefit but dry sterile hungry soils overgrown with five-finger and other rigid worthless plants have been rendered fertile by its use and now produce fine crops of clover and other grasses. It is spread on the surface of the soil in ploughed lands immediately after the seeds are committed to the earth;—on pastures at any time of the year. It is usual to allow a bushel to the acre, but many are of opinion that a much smaller quantity a peck for instance—if evenly distributed over the ground would be of equal advantage.[3]

My business goes on at the old rate. I have been well since I saw Hampshire except another little touch of the pleurisy—which went off with a little blood from the arm— I write with a lame hand which must be my apology for not writing more and for writing so illegibly— Remember me to the family and all my friends— I should be happy to hear from you—

Your affectionate Son
W   C   BRYANT

MANUSCRIPTS: NYPL–GR (draft and final) ADDRESS: Dr. Peter Bryant / Cummington.

1. Sarah Snell Bryant's diary, cited in "Youth," p. 199, reports two visits by Cullen to Cummington in 1817, but indicates no dates.

2. Jacob Porter; see 6.1. No details of this debt have been recovered, but it was probably incurred during Bryant's removal from Plainfield to Great Barrington the preceding fall.

3. This is the earliest indication of a studious interest in agricultural problems which Bryant took during his later life, after he had acquired large country properties. In October 1817 he composed an ode for the annual celebration of the Berkshire Agricultural Society, as he did in several subsequent years. These were widely printed in the newspapers of neighboring villages and towns. See *Poetical Works*, I, 71–72, 336–338, for three of these odes.

40. *To* William Baylies

Great Barrington [*c*May 27] 1817[1]

My dear Sir

I have at length summoned up industry enough to answer yours of the 7th of February last. I am obliged to you for the kind inquiries you make concerning my situation. —You ask whether I am pleased with my profession— Alas, Sir, the Muse was my first love and the *remains* of that passion which not *rooted out* yet chilled into extinction will always I fear cause me to look coldly on the severe beauties of Themis. Yet I tame myself to its labours as well as I can, and have endeavoured to discharge with punctuality and attention such of the duties of my profession as I was capable of performing— When I wrote you last[2] I had a partner in business. —He has relinquished it to me. *I bought him out* a few days ago for a mere trifle. —The business of the Office has hitherto been worth about 10 or 12. hundred dollars a year. —It will probably be less hereafter yet I cannot think it will decrease very materially, as I am well patronized here and have been considered with more kindness than I could have expected— There is another Office in town kept by Genl. Whiting— one of the Senators from this district,[3] who has a partner—Mr. Hyde—[4] In "arguing" cases I have not been very frequently employed. I never spouted in a courthouse. While in Hampshire County I did something in that way and began to make long speeches at references and Justice courts, but since I came here my partner—who was respectable as an advocate & has the advantage of ⟨superior⟩ longer experience took that trouble off my hands—since our separation however I have [been] trying my hand at it again—[5]

Upon the whole I have every cause to be satisfied with my situation, for place a man where you will it is an easy thing for him to dream out a more eligible mode of life than the one which falls to his lot. —While I have too much of the mauvaise honte[6] to seek opportunities of this nature I have whipped myself up to a desperate determination not to avoid them.[7]

I should be much delighted to visit Bridgewater again, and mean to do so at no very distant period. I believe however that the circumstances of my business and the hard times will keep me at home the present season—

[unsigned]

MANUSCRIPT: NYPL–GR (draft) ADDRESS: To the Hon   William Baylies PUBLISHED (*in part*): *Life*, I, 147–148.

1. The date of May 27 is a likely one, for this letter accompanied that of the following day to Peter Bryant.
2. January 25, 1817, Letter 35.
3. See 41.2.

4. James A. Hyde (d. 1836, Williams 1807) was admitted to the bar in 1811, served as Great Barrington town clerk from 1813 until Bryant's election to that office in 1820, and was re-elected when Bryant left for New York City in 1825. Thereafter, for several years, Hyde handled Bryant's unfinished legal business. Taylor, *Great Barrington*, p. 371; Hyde to Bryant, December 14, 1829, NYPL–GR.

5. During his brief practice in Plainfield in 1816, Bryant appeared at least four times in the Court of Common Pleas at Northampton, and argued other cases before justices of the peace in Cummington as well as in Plainfield. "Youth," pp. 181–182.

6. "Bashfulness."

7. This sentence seems to belong with the preceding paragraph, where it probably appeared in the final draft.

41. *To* Peter Bryant

Great Barrington   28 May 1817

Dear Father

I have at length effected a change of the *"Stile royal," we*, into the less ostentatious but full as important pronoun *I*. My partner has relinquished the business of the office to me. I made a very good bargain with him, and got it for a mere trifle. When I see you I will tell you more about this affair.[1] Genl. Whiting, with whom, I hope, you will become acquainted, will deliver you, together with this, a letter for Mr. Baylies which I wish you would try to forward to him, as the General is not probably acquainted with the Bridgewater representatives.[2]

Your affectionate Son
Wm C. Bryant

Manuscript: NYPL–GR address: Dr. Peter Bryant / Boston / By the politeness of Genl. Whiting.

1. The exact date on which Bryant and Ives dissolved their partnership is uncertain. They last appeared in court together as counsel on April 26, 1817; Bryant handled his first case alone on May 24. Without doubt they parted amicably, for they remained personal friends, and Bryant and his bride shared a house and kitchen for a year with George Ives and his mother in 1821–1822. Taylor, *Great Barrington*, pp. 417–420.

2. (Militia) General John Whiting (1770?–1846) had practiced law at Great Barrington since his admission to the bar in 1792. From 1816 to 1817 he was a state senator. Taylor, *Great Barrington*, p. 370.

42. *To* Miss Sarah S. Bryant[1]

Great Barrington   8 Sept. 1817

Dear Sister

I believe that this is the first letter I ever wrote you, and I design it, if you will consent, as the beginning of a regular correspondence between us. You are now at the most interesting period of your life—[2] a period when a thousand circumstances are busy in forming and settling the character and when impressions are easily taken and perhaps more deeply made and longer retained than at any other age; because the understanding, then arrived at a degree of maturity, begins to join its more vigorous operations to those of the fancy and feelings. Could I assist in rendering those impressions what they ought to be, I would do and sacrifice much. Next to her parents, a young lady ought to consider her brother as her best friend—a friend whose affections even misconduct can hardly alienate and with whose admonitions and kind offices selfish considerations cannot well mingle. There is a degree of unreserve too, and confidence, in the communications between brother and sister, which can hardly have place between them and their parents—a kind of freedom arising from equality of years and the absence of authority, and in most instances from their having passed part at least of their juvenile days together, in the same domestick circle and under the same discipline.

These are some of the reasons which led me to solicit this correspondence—you I am persuaded will look at it in the same light that I do—nor will you let any timidity or delicacy deter you from it—for you were brought up in a family the members of which were never taught to prefer what is expedient to what is right. In desiring you to write to me regularly, I do not seek a detail of the passing events of Cummington, nor a meteorological journal of the weather, nor notices of how the corn looks and the pigs thrive; though these I confess are convenient topicks to swell a letter to the desired size— I want a transcript of your sentiments and feelings. Neither my letters nor yours, unless you chuse it, need be exhibited—and whatever information you may require on any subject with which I am acquainted will be cheerfully afforded, and whatever advice you may need will be sought as well from me as from the friendships of the world, many of which I know to be frivolous (for though I am yet young something has made me grey) and many hypocritical.

I wish you to request my father to procure for me *Pickering's Vocabulary* which I suppose will be found at Butler's Bookstore—that I may have it when I visit Cummington this fall.[3]

I am obliged to break off here— I remain

Your affectionate Brother, and friend

W. C. BRYANT

MANUSCRIPTS: Weston Family Papers (final); NYPL–GR (draft) ADDRESS: Miss Sarah S. Bryant / Cummington.

1. See "Bryant's Correspondents."
2. "Sally," then fifteen and hoping to attend a boarding school at Middlebury, Vermont, entered instead, the following spring, Miss Bancroft's school for girls at Northampton. *Bryant Record*, p. 91; Sally to Charity Bryant, February 15, 1819, Sheldon Museum.
3. Probably John Pickering, *A Vocabulary; or, Collection of Words and Phrases . . . Peculiar to the United States of America* (Boston, 1816). Butler's bookstore was in Northampton.

43.   *To* Frances Fairchild

Great Barrington   30 Sept. 1817

Dear Frances

To punish you for not having returned long since to Great Barrington, I have at length determined to put you to the penance of reading another of my letters. I have heard with much pleasure, the favourable accounts which have been received amongst us, concerning your health,[1] and the restoration of your tranquility—and though at first I was half inclined to be angry with you for being contented in a place so far to the west, yet the warm interest which I take in your welfare soon reconciled me to the idea. It is whispered that you have lost much of that interesting pensiveness of countenance which you used to exhibit here so often in the morning, and that you have acquired a plumpness of figure which would not disgrace a Turkish beauty who had gone through a course of camel's milk. I have been long in doubt to what cause to impute this alteration, for I am sure it cannot be owing to any particular influence of your western air and climate. The fat old Falstaff ascribed his corpulence to sighing and grief, which he said had blown him up like a bladder;—but if they could have had any such effect upon you, you would have exceeded all reasonable dimensions before you left us.[2] It must therefore be attributed to some other cause. Is there no young *Adonis* of the West, who is permitted to sun himself in the brilliance of your eyes, and to whisper soft things in your ear, and who, in your case, has successfully taken upon himself the office of restoring your serenity of mind, and of *"ministering to a mind diseased"*?[3]

You will receive this letter by the hand of Capt. Hopkins, with whom I hope you will conclude to return to Great Barrington.[4] As an inducement, I must acquaint you that matrimonial business has taken a sudden spring here—young ladies are in great demand—the continual cry is, *"going, gentlemen, going—gone!"*—and the list of those who have been married this fall, or are about to be married, is too long to insert in this letter.[5] I must tell you however that Parson Griswold has attended the auction—outbid the unfortunate Mr. Brooks—and had struck off to him the fair Maria R.————[6]

If, however, you should not find a sudden market amongst us, you will at least see many faces wearing their warmest smiles to welcome your return—smiles which are not those of the countenance merely, but which come from the heart. The general regret which attended your departure, and to which I then called your notice, I can assure you has not diminished. You too, if I have rightly interpreted a disposition so open as yours, must sometimes think with strong emotion on the friends you have left, and often indulge the wish of returning to the place where your earliest years were past, and to which belong your tenderest and most delightful recollections.

If these last sentences are a little dull you need not read them over again.

> I remain
> with the highest esteem and regard,
> Your friend
> WILLIAM C. BRYANT.

MANUSCRIPTS: NYPL–GR (final; also draft dated 13 September) ADDRESS: Miss Frances Fairchild / [E]ast Bloomfield / New York.

1. See Letter 38.
2. See *1 Henry IV* II.iv.362–366.
3. Cf. *Macbeth* V.iii.40.
4. Probably Frances' brother-in-law Charles W. Hopkins, to whom Bryant referred earlier as "Major." See 38.5.
5. This "spring" must have been recent indeed, for in the draft of this letter written only two weeks earlier Bryant had warned, "I cannot however promise you a very quick market amongst us. Matrimonial business is become very dull here—very dull indeed. None of the young people have been coupled together in the yoke of wedlock since you left us nor do they seem much nearer marrying than they did at that time."
6. Rev. Samuel Griswold was rector of Saint James's Episcopal Church in Great Barrington from 1805 to 1820. Taylor, *Great Barrington*, p. 345. Brooks is unidentified.

44. *To* Willard Phillips[1]

Great Barrington   26 Oct   1817

Sir

An association of young men amongst us having *agreed* to take a few of the best literary journals—the North American Review was of course one of the first for which we determined to subscribe—[2] I have one of the numbers of that work in my possession but do not learn from it the terms nor the mode of its publication— You will have the goodness to place my name in the list of subscribers and inform me by mail concerning the terms. I will enclose the money to whomever you shall direct—. If three numbers or more compose a volume you may begin at the number for last May—if but two—from the Number for September—[3]

I am much gratified at the high reputation which your journal has attained—and that it continues to increase— I have been accustomed to consider as an absurdity the idea that the first city in this large empire in point of literature and science could not support one respectable literary Journal— Powerfully sustained as that work is it cannot, I think, fail of the ample success I wish it.—[4]

> I am Sir
> with much respect
> Your obt. Servt—
> WILLIAM C. BRYANT

MANUSCRIPT: NYPL–GR (draft) PUBLISHED (*in part*): *Life*, I, 152.

1. See "Bryant's Correspondents."

2. Phillips then edited the *NAR*, founded two years earlier. The nature of the "association" to which Bryant refers is obscure, but that it was short-lived is evident in his remark to Phillips' successor Edward Channing in a letter dated March 25, 1819, "It is true that I subscribed for the work at first, in behalf of a Literary association— but that association came to nothing before I received my first Number." See Letter 56.

3. Whether the number in Bryant's possession was that for September, or whether he knew this contained five of his own poems which his father had submitted unsigned to Phillips in May or June, is uncertain. These poems were a translation from Horace, an imitation of the same author (see Letter 21), a blank verse fragment later called "Inscription for the Entrance to a Wood," four stanzas on death he had written three years earlier, and another incomplete blank-verse poem of forty-nine lines for which the editor coined the title "Thanatopsis." *NAR*, 5 (September 1817), 336–341.

4. Probably Bryant's characterization of the *NAR* as "powerfully sustained" indicates he was aware that, although at its inception in 1815 it had been simply the successor of the *Monthly Anthology*, a feeble if hopeful review edited by William Emerson, the *NAR* had been taken over the following year by a "Club" formed by such Harvard stalwarts as Edward Tyrell Channing, Richard Henry Dana, Willard Phillips, and Jared Sparks. Rusk, *Emerson*, p. 18; H. B. Adams, *The Life and Writings of Jared Sparks* (Boston, 1893), I, 225–234.

45. [*To* John E. Howard][1]

[Great Barrington, cOctober 1817][2]

I am happy to learn that you have quietly set yourself down to the study of law in Mr. Baylies's office. It is at least something to have made choice of a profession, and you have commenced your studies in a place which I should prefer, all things considered, to any I know of. It may be said with more truth of our profession than of any other that industry is the road to success—and you I hope will be more diligent in the pursuit of knowledge than I was or even seemed to be for while I appeared to study I was half the time only dreaming with my eyes open. As essential to these habits of diligence you are doubtless as well aware as I am that one should make himself satisfied with the profession he has chosen— and our profession may be a hard task-master but its rewards are proportioned to its labours which is as much as any way of life has to say for itself— I was much gratified at receiving your favour of the 14th of July[3] not only because it seemed a proof that I was not quite forgotten amongst my Bridgewater friends but because of the interest with which I always hear of their welfare.

It is now more than two years since I left Bridgewater—since I *tore myself away* from the fair ones of Bridgewater—since I caught the last beams of their bright eyes and gazed for the last time on forms which seemed to have been moulded by nature to realize the ideal beauty of the painter and statuary. —Is it possible that all these lovely rosebuds yet remain ungathered on the stalk *"wasting their sweetness on the desert air"?*[4] Can it be true that all these fair ones are still the votresses of the coy and sullen Diana *"chaunting cold hymns to the pale fruitless moon"?*[5] and have none deserted to the seducing rites of Hymen? —If two years have gone by without an instance of this sort—build a cloister in your parish and whisper in the ears of these obdurate nymphs—*"Get thee to a nunnery, Ophelia, go."*[6]

[unsigned]

MANUSCRIPT: NYPL–GR (draft) PUBLISHED (*in part*): *Life*, I, 148.

1. This unaddressed draft letter seems related in tone and content to that of March 25, 1817, to John Howard (Letter 37). It is clearly not, as suggested in *Life*, I, 148, intended for a former fellow law student.
2. The date is assigned conjecturally on the basis of Bryant's remark that he had been away from Bridgewater for more than two years.
3. Letter unrecovered.
4. Cf. Thomas Gray, "Elegy," stanza 14.
5. Cf. *A Midsummer-Night's Dream* I.i.73.
6. Cf. *Hamlet* III.i.142.

46. *To* Peter Bryant

G[reat] Barrington   10 Jan. 1818

Dear Father

I suppose that probably I am not honoured with a place in your list of *very punctual* correspondents if you have any such—but when one has nothing to write that he thinks his friends will care to read it seems to me that he has a pretty tolerable reason for letting his pen lie idle in the inkstand. I have now however so fair and convenient an opportunity for writing you, that I should deem it no very trivial sin of omission to let it pass without making use of it.

I have nothing to tell you about myself except that since my return from Cummington I have by no means enjoyed the perfection of *high rude health*—but the lancet has relieved me[1] —and that business is dull enough with me.—

We have subscribed for the North American Review here. I wrote to Mr. Phillips for it and received an answer from him in which he gives you the *credit*—if it can be called by that name—of the writing [of] Thanatopsis.[2] I have sent you inclosed a correct copy of my version of the fragment of Simonides together with a little poem which I wrote while at Bridgewater which you may get inserted if you please in that work.[3] I would contribute something in prose if I knew on what subject to write. I must likewise request of you the favour to pay Mr. Phillips for me $2.50, for the Review.

You may perhaps ascribe it to a discontented and uneasy disposition —but for my part I regret that I was not able to go to Boston in the first instance, and commence the practice of Law there.[4] I do not relish this business of skulking about *in holes and corners of the earth*.[5]

If you will obtain the January number of the N. A. Review for me, if it is not already sent by mail—and send it me by Gen. Whiting, you will oblige me much.—

I am, as ever,
Your affectionate Son
WM. C. BRYANT

MANUSCRIPTS: NYPL–GR (final, and draft dated 9 January) ADDRESS: Hon. Peter Bryant / Boston / favd. by Hon. Jno. Whiting PUBLISHED (*in part*): *Life*, I, 152.

1. Cullen's lung trouble, reported earlier (Letters 34 and 39), seems to have ceased soon after this time. In 1821 he wrote his sister Sally, then within three years of her death from consumption, "I myself, at your age, and all along since till within two or three years was occasionally affected with symptoms similar to those you describe." Letter 269.

2. See Letter 44. Phillips had written on December 2, "Your 'Fragment' was exceedingly liked here; among others Mr. Channing the clergyman spoke very highly of it. All the judges here say that your fragment and your Father's Thanatopsis are among the very best poetry that has been published in this country." NYPL–BG. Phillips' supposition that Dr. Bryant had written "Thanatopsis" was shared by Edward Channing and Richard Dana. Their misunderstanding is accounted for in Peter Bryant's reply to this letter: "With respect to 'Thanatopsis,' I know not what led Phillips to imagine I wrote it, unless it was because it was transcribed by me; I left it at his house when he was absent, and did not see him afterward. I have, however, set him right on that subject!" *Life*, I, 152–153. The original fair copy of "Thanatopsis," in HEHL, is in Dr. Bryant's handwriting, while the accompanying manuscript "Fragment" ("Inscription for the Entrance to a Wood") is in Cullen's hand. The resulting confusion, perhaps the most notable of its kind in American letters, has provoked much discussion and embellishment. For the clearest account of the facts, see "Youth," pp. 205–209.

3. These were "Version of a Fragment of Simonides" and "To a Waterfowl," published in *NAR*, 6 (March 1818), 382–384. Bryant's failure here to name the second poem caused much subsequent confusion in his biographers, and gave rise to the fanciful tale of its composition told in *Life*, I, 143–144. See William Cullen Bryant II, "The Waterfowl in Retrospect," *New England Quarterly*, 30 (June 1957), 181–189.

4. See Letters 9 and 11.

5. Cf. *The Winter's Tale* I.ii.289.

47. *To* Miss Sarah S. Bryant

Great Barrington   17 Feb. 1818

Dear Sister

It gave me the more pleasure to receive a line from you as, from your delaying to write for so long, I had almost abandoned the hope of drawing you into correspondence.[1] You plead indolence—if you knew as well as I do the pernicious influence of this palsy of the faculties you would not call it by the soft name of an *"apology"* for any thing. When you have drunk as deeply of the cup of this enchanter as I have done you will find that he comes not alone but quarters on his wretched votary a numerous brood of unavailing regrets—*seven devils* or more, worse than himself, enter and dwell with him in the *empty* mansion.[2] The inert strength of this habit must be wrestled with and subdued and when once you have your foot on his neck you will find a pleasure in this kind of victory and will prefer the habit of exertion to the habit of idleness. Want of talent and talent unemployed amount to pretty much the same thing. I am sure it requires no great mental exertion to write a letter. If it does—write frequently—and from a task it will soon become an amusement. You think of attending an academy—if you do I hope you will learn as much there in as short a time as possible.[3] You expect to gain there some knowledge of the *manners and customs of the world* as you call them. The fact is that too many of the *manners* and *customs* of the *world* are acquired in places where numerous young persons of either sex are collected together—some schools are however more eligible than others both on these and other accounts—you I hope will select one of the best and I shall have great confidence in your good sense and firmness of principle to escape the dangers attendant on such a situation.

Works of amusement you tell me are apt to interfere with your severer studies. Thousands split upon that rock. You are now at the season of life when a foundation should be laid of just and solid thinking, and the mind stored with the materials of future reflection. The immoderate perusal of works of mere amusement weakens the mind and unfits it for any other employment.[4]

I looked for a visit from you and Austin this winter—but winter is almost over. Next week I shall be at Lenox.[5] I hope you will write soon and a longer letter than your last.

> I remain
> with much affection
> Yours
> W. C. Bryant

MANUSCRIPTS: Weston Family Papers (final); NYPL–GR (draft dated February 7) ADDRESS: Miss Sarah S. Bryant / Cummington.

1. Sally's letter is unrecovered.
2. Cf. Luke 11:26.
3. See 42.2.
4. Cullen was less complacent in the earlier draft of this letter, where he added, "You may perhaps say that all this is fine—but that a certain brother of yours appears to preach better than he practices— The repartee will be fair enough but what I have said will not be the less true.—"
5. The Court of Common Pleas convened on the fourth Monday of February, June, and October at Lenox, the Berkshire County seat a dozen miles north of Great Barrington. During sessions, lasting about two weeks, visiting lawyers formed a congenial club at the boardinghouse of Bradford Whiting, opposite the courthouse. "Youth," 191–193.

48. *To* Peter Bryant

Great Barrington   20 Feb. 1818.

Dear Father

Yours of the 15th and 16th by Gen. Whiting have been received.[1] I feel obliged to you for the trouble you have taken on my account. I suppose I am to review the book mentioned by Phillips.[2] If I can procure it I will undertake the task. My situation here is not such as to afford me much opportunity of adding to the information which I already possess respecting this subject. This is like most other villages—there are not many who suffer an excessive passion for books to interfere with other employments or amusements—they incumber their houses with no overgrown libraries. This scarcity of books I find extremely inconvenient.[3] As you observe, I believe I have read most of the American poets of any note—Dwight—Trumbull—Barlow—Humphreys—Paine—Clif[f]-ton—Honeywood. The writings of Hopkins I have never met with. I have seen Philip Freneau's poems and some things by Francis Hopkinson. I have read most of Mrs. Morton's productions and turned over a volume of stale and senseless rhymes by Mrs. Warren. There was a Dr. Ladd (I believe I am right in the name) of Rhode Island, who it seems was considerably celebrated for his poetical talent, of whom I have seen hardly any thing—and another Dr. Church a Tory at the commencement of the revolution who was compelled to leave the country, and some of whose satirical verses which I have heard recited possess considerable merit as specimens of forcible and glowing invective. Before the time of the writers whom I have enumerated,[4] some of whom are still living and the rest belong to the generation which has just passed away, I imagine that we could hardly be said to have any poetry of our own—and indeed it seems to me that American poetry may justly enough be said to have had its rise with that knot of Connecticut poets Trumbull and others, most of whose works appeared about the time of the revolution or soon after.

Any facts relating to the subject which may occur to you, of which I may be ignorant or not aware, I should be obliged to you to suggest to me. Perhaps I may visit Cummington before next June in which case opportunities will be greater. I remember in the American Review and Monthly Magazine published some eighteen or twenty years ago considerable information on this subject and some biographies of our poets.[5]

It is not in my power to send you the address you mention as it was printed in the Berkshire Star and I have not the paper in which it appeared.[6] It was hasty and very imperfect and I was reluctant to suffer it to be published and should not have consented but for the solicitation of Mr. Wheeler, our parson. The good man was so importunate and so confident that it would be good on account of the quarter from which it came it not being usual for young lawyers in this part of the country to harrangue upon such subjects that I could not well refuse him—but stipulated that it should appear without my name. It was notwithstanding by some mistake or misunderstanding printed as the production of Wm C. Bryant to which was carefully subjoined, *Attorney at Law*.[7]

I remain your affectionate Son
WILLIAM C. BRYANT

MANUSCRIPTS: NYPL–GR (final and draft) ADDRESS: Hon. Peter Bryant / Cummington PUBLISHED (*in part*): *Life*, I, 153–154.

1. Though Dr. Bryant's letters are unrecovered, undated quotations in *Life*, I, 152–153 seem to be portions of one or both of these.
2. Peter Bryant had passed on to Cullen Willard Phillips' request that he interest his son in noticing for the *NAR* a recently published versified survey of ancient and modern poetry. "I think it is a very good subject for Cullen," Phillips remarked; "Let him if he has the means give a short history of and criticism on our poetry." Letter dated February 14, 1818, in NYPL–BG. The book was Solyman Brown, *An Essay on American Poetry* . . . (New Haven, 1818).
3. In the first draft of this letter Cullen added here, "after having been accustomed all my life to have access to very respectable libraries."
4. These poets were, in the order listed: Timothy Dwight (1752–1817), John Trumbull (1750–1831), Joel Barlow (1754–1812), David Humphreys (1752–1818), Robert Treat Paine (1773–1811), William Clifton (1772–1799), Saint John Honeywood (1763–1798), Lemuel Hopkins (1750–1801), Philip Freneau (1752–1832), Francis Hopkinson (1737–1791), Sarah Wentworth Morton (1759–1846), Mercy Otis Warren (1728–1814), Joseph Brown Ladd (1764–1786), and Benjamin Church (1734–1776).
5. The *Monthly Magazine and American Review* (1799–1800).
6. ["Address on the Bible"] *Berkshire Star*, Stockbridge, January 29, 1818.
7. Rev. Elijah Wheeler (1774–1827) was pastor of the Congregational Church at Great Barrington from 1806 to 1823. Taylor, *History of Great Barrington*, p. 343. Bryant's evaluation of this speech, given before the Auxiliary Bible Society of Great Barrington on January 1, 1818, was probably just; it was a perfunctory performance aimed at an orthodox audience, notable only for its early hint of the religious toleration which would later characterize his writing and speaking. For its full text, see "Youth," pp. 276–284.

49.   *To* Willard Phillips

Great Barrington   13 Apl. [1818]

Yours of the 2d. I received on the 11th instant—[1] I had undertaken to write the article you speak of but it will not be possible on account of some arrangements which I have made to have it ready by the middle of May— I can get it to you probably by the first of June—if that should not be soon enough to insert it in the number for July it can perhaps be deferred.[2] In that case it will not be necessary to have it so early as June—and if you will be good enough to inform me I will keep it longer on my hands and make it more fit to be read—[3] I think if your work sustains its present character it will soon acquire a reputation not easily to be shaken— A good review has been a desideratum in our literature—

The publick taste requires to be guided and informed— Our countrymen are assisted in forming their opinion concerning the numerous modern publications imported into this country from Great Britain by the judgement of the criticks of that island—but with respect to our native works we have hitherto had no such guide on which we could safely rely— Your work with its present promise I think will supply this want—and constituting a kind of censorship which assigning to merit its just applause and exposing unsupported pretensions shall give a proper direction to our national taste—

[unsigned]

MANUSCRIPT: NYPL–GR (draft) ADDRESS: Willard Phillips Esq. / Boston. PUBLISHED (*in part*): *Life*, I, 152.

1. Phillips wrote on April 2 asking Cullen to supply the article on American poetry by the middle of May, in time for the July number of the *NAR*. NYPL–BG.

2. These arrangements were apparently for a visit to Cummington to consult books and magazines in his father's extensive library which were unavailable at Great Barrington. According to Mrs. Bryant's diary, Cullen was at home from April 27 to May 1.

3. Phillips replied on April 30 that June 6 or 7 would be time enough for a July printing. NYPL–BG.

50.   *To* William Baylies

Great Barrington   14 Apl. 1818

Dear Sir

I have neglected writing to you so long that I am almost ashamed to write at all—[1] I could however bring a host of formidable advocates for my fault who if they could not convince you would at least terrify you into a pardon— *Ill health, Blue Devils* and a demon of softer look but more deadly purpose than these, *Laziness*—will attest how often they have pinioned my arms and withheld my fingers from the pen— Can you refuse any thing to these powerful pleaders?—

I believe that we shall send to Boston a brace of democratick senators from this county this year. —There has been some dissatisfaction amongst the federal party with the nomination excited I suppose by men who wish to be candidates themselves— Much mischief has been done by this course and I apprehend that it will lose us the election.—[2]

The great folks at Washington I see make themselves pretty busy with the difficulties between this country and Spain— If we should have a war with that country and one could get a commission in the army he might perhaps before it was ended have an opportunity of garnishing his private history with a few South American adventures—[3]

Do you read the North American Review? —In the number for September (I believe) 1817—perhaps in the preceding number—there are some lines entitled "*Thanatopsis*"—and "*a fragment*" by an old friend of yours, and in the No. for March 1818—three more *pair of varses* from the same hand—[4]

[unsigned]

MANUSCRIPT: NYPL–GR (draft) PUBLISHED (*in part*): *Life*, I, 155–156.

1. Bryant had last written his former law tutor nearly a year earlier (Letter 40), and Baylies had replied on November 18, 1817. NYPL–BG.

2. Though still identifying himself as a Federalist, Bryant reflects here the growing doubts about his party's merits which would within a few years lead to his support of Jacksonian Democracy.

3. Sympathy in this country for Spain's rebelling South American colonies led to the introduction in Congress of a resolution recognizing their *de facto* governments. This was defeated in the House of Representatives on March 30, 1818, by a vote of 115 to 45. Bailey, *Diplomatic History*, p. 168. Bryant's earlier hope for military "adventures" had earned him a belated commission in the Massachusetts militia in July 1816, which he resigned within six weeks, after deciding to enter law practice at Great Barrington. "Youth," pp. 183–184.

4. There is a note of casual pride in this report of poetic recognition, for Bryant had written Baylies, two years after composing these poems, "You ask whether I am pleased with my profession— Alas, Sir, the Muse was my first love and the *remains* of that passion which not *rooted out* yet chilled into extinction will always I fear cause me to look coldly on the severe beauties of Themis." See Letter 40. His pose of nonchalance seems evident, too, in his professed uncertainty over when the first two poems were published, in view of his remarks about them to his father in Letter 46. Bryant's phrase, *"pair of varses,"* suggests the anecdote he is said to have enjoyed repeating about a village rhymester who once exclaimed, "Well, Squire Bryant, they say you are a poet like me; is that so? I've never heerd any of your varses; would you like one of mine?" *Life*, I, 204.

51. [*To* George Downes]

Great Barrington   17 April 1818

Dear Sir

I hardly know what apology to make for so long delaying to answer your very agreeable favour of July last.[1] I might plead indolence but you would not admit it— [I] might offer the excuse, business, but it has the misfortune of not being true—yet, perhaps, it might avail something to tell you that for some months past my hours of leisure have been poisoned by ill-health and depression of Spirits—

I did not expect that you would make the use you have done of my remarks upon the subject of matrimony.[2] My object was to offer you comfort in your misfortunes— I was influenced solely by the charitable motive of persuading [you] to be as contented as possible and I wished to make your fetters sit light on you by telling you that they were bright and tinkled delightfully— Was it generous to turn the consolations with which I was humanely endeavouring to save you from despair into weapons against me? Would you make your physician swallow the contents of his own saddle-bags?

—To be serious. All cannot receive the same [saying?]— With respect to marriage it seems to me that we must [collect?] our duty from the circumstances of our lives— Expedience, convenience, inclination, opinion may be permitted to guide our conduct in this respect— The Apostle of the Gentiles discoursing on this subject, and holding the balance between a single and a married life could derive no casting weight from revelation to determine the dispute but he threw into the scale of celibacy the opinion of one who knew much of human life and human nature—[3] Others, perhaps with equal opportunities of judging correctly have thought differently— Who shall decide when doctors disagree? And soundest casuists doubt like you and me?[4]

You desire me to give my opinion on the present pacifick condition of the European powers—of the vast and increasing efforts made for the purpose [of] Christ'izing the world and the part which it is the duty of you and me to take in regard to these exertions— You have imposed on me a task beyond my abilities— I cannot however believe that the peace of Europe will be materially disturbed for some years at least still less for centuries to come and I pray God never that the destructive and wasting contest. . . .

[unsigned]

MANUSCRIPT: NYPL–GR (incomplete draft).

1. Letter unrecovered.
2. See Letter 36.
3. Saint Paul wrote, "Those who marry will have pain and grief in this bodily life, and my aim is to spare you." 1 Corinthians 7:28.
4. Pope, *Moral Essays*, Ep. III.1–2.

52. *To* Peter Bryant

[Great Barrington] 20 June 1818

Dear Father:

Yours of the 11th instant I received on the 13th[1] by my uncle,[2] whom I had little time to see, as I was then just setting off to attend a court in Sheffield. I am obliged to you for the concern you express respecting my health. It has been considerably improved by my journey to New York. I was absent a fortnight; we were three days coming up the river, beating up one day and night against a furious head-wind, during most of which time I was obliged to lie flat on my back in my birth[3] to prevent sea-sickness, of which I felt some qualms. While in New York I kept running about continually, and this constant exercise, together with being rocked and tumbled about in the vessel, operated on me as a restorative, and since my return my pain in the side and night-sweats have left me.[4] I believe my affairs will not permit my visiting Cummington at present. My several absences of late render it proper that I should now give a little attention to my office, and, as I have taken off the tether from Major Ives and let him loose into the field of practice again, it has become necessary that I should use some diligence to prevent any part of that share of practice which I have obtained from falling into his hands.[5] Perhaps however, I may see Cummington some time in the course of the summer or autumn. I have written a review of Mr. Brown's book, and forwarded it to the publishers of 'The North American Review.'[6] Luckily, I found the volume in this neighborhood, and escaped throwing away my money on it. It is poor stuff.

[unsigned]

MANUSCRIPT: NYPL–GR (draft) TEXT: *Life*, I, 156.

1. Unrecovered.
2. Peter Bryant's only surviving brother, Bezaliel (1765–*ante* 1833), was then returning from a visit with the Cummington family to Bedford, New York, where he kept an apothecary shop. Bezaliel to Charity Bryant, June 24, 1818, Sheldon Museum; Sarah to Cullen Bryant, June 12, 1833, NYPL–GR.
3. Bryant's customary spelling of "berth" as "birth" will be silently corrected hereafter.
4. On this, his first visit to New York City, Bryant had represented in a court action one Abraham Meyer, for whom William Coleman, editor of the New York *Evening Post*, appeared as a witness. MS receipted bill, "William Coleman Esq. to Abm. Meyer Dr. 1818 June," in HEHL. Thus Bryant met his future employer eight years before joining the *EP* in 1826. Another memento of this visit is a memorandum in NYPL–GR in which he recorded peculiar pronunciations he heard in the city. See [William] Cullen Bryant [II] " 'Dictionary of the New York Dialect of the English Tongue,' " *American Speech*, 16 (April 1941), 157–158.
5. When the partnership of Bryant and Ives was dissolved in May 1817 (see 41.1), it was apparently with a stipulation that Ives should not practice law in the same court district until at least a year had passed.
6. Notice of Solyman Brown, *An Essay on American Poetry* (New Haven, 1818), in *NAR*, 7 (July 1818), 198–211. This was the first of five prose articles Bryant wrote for the *NAR* before moving to New York City in 1825. He appraised most of the poets listed in Letter 48, and called for a higher standard of American literary taste: "The poetical adventurer should be taught that it is only the production of genius, taste, and diligence that can find favour at the bar of criticism—that his writings are not to be applauded merely because they are written by an American, and are not decidedly bad; and that he must produce some satisfactory evidence of his claim to celebrity than an extract from the parish register" (p. 198). Turning to the author whose verse essay he was discussing, Bryant added, "Mr. Brown has fallen into a great mistake in thinking himself qualified to write a book. In the present instance, with talents of a very humble order, he has assumed a very pompous tone, and made a great parade of small acquisitions" (p. 211).

53. *To* Peter Bryant

Great Barrington 1 Sept 1818

Yours of the 22d I received on the Friday evening following.[1] On Saturday I was engaged so that it was out of my power to visit Cummington that week independent of other reasons. —As the Supreme Court is in session next week at Lenox you will see the propriety of my staying at home the present week—[2] besides—though I should be happy to see my friends—I do not much relish Williamstown Commencements—nor indeed any thing that belongs to that place or that ⟨beggarly⟩ institution— You will therefore have the goodness to excuse me from attending —especially as I hope before long—at some time when there is no prospect of having any thing else to do, to have the pleasure of seeing my friends in Hampshire.—[3]

I have been in tolerable health this summer— I think I can [perceive] a gradual augmentation of my business. The gentlemen of our profession on the frontiers of Massachusetts are often employed to collect demands for creditors living [in] adjoining states which is not only a profitable but pleasant branch of our business. I have formed some acquaintances in the State of New York who already begin to be of use to me.—

Excuse the brevity of my letters.

[unsigned]

MANUSCRIPT: NYPL–GR (draft) ADDRESS: Dr. Peter B[ryant].

1. Letter unrecovered.
2. At the September 1817 term of the Supreme Judicial Court of Massachusetts Bryant had been admitted to practice as an "Attorney" before that court, which meant that he might manage, but not argue, cases. At the September 1819 term he was admitted to full status as a "Counselor." *Berkshire Eagle*, June 20, 1878, quoted in Bigelow, *Bryant*, pp. 37–38.
3. That Cullen's youthful antipathy toward the college where he had spent only eight months as a sophomore should have persisted so long is surprising, particularly in view of the fact that only a year later Williams College awarded him an honorary Master of Arts degree (diploma, dated September 1, 1819, in Homestead Collection).

54. *To* Edward T. Channing[1]

Great Barrington   6 Sept. 1818

Dear Sir

I am much gratified with the favourable reception that my contribution to the North American Review has met with from the proprietors of that work, as well as with the obliging manner in which it has been communicated to me, and feel myself happy if I may be esteemed to have done any thing for the literature of my country.[2] In the mean time I may occasionally attempt something for your journal, and lend such assistance as might be expected from one situated as I am,

—Musis procul et Permesside lymphâ,[3]

distant from books and literary opportunities, and occupied with a profession which ought to engage most of my attention. I have tried to write an essay for your next number, but could not satisfy myself. There is hardly any spot in the department of Essays unoccupied. With respect to writing a review, I will be contented with such a work as you may think proper to mention—provided you do not set me too difficult a task.[4] I enclose you a small poem which I found by me, and which you may give a place in your journal, if you think it will do.[5]

I am Sir

very respectfully

Yours

Wм. C. Bryant

MANUSCRIPTS: HCL (final); NYPL–GR (two drafts, one mistakenly dated October 6) ADDRESS: Edward T. Channing Esq / Boston POSTMARK (*in script*): Great Barrington / October 7th—1818 POSTAL ANNOTATION: 12½ ENDORSEMENT: Wm C Bryant / G. Barrington / Sept. 6, 1818 / *The Yellow Violet—* / This poem was not / published in the North / American. I suppose we / had just determined to pub- / lish only prose. PUBLISHED: *Life,* I, 157–158.

1. Edward Tyrell Channing (1790–1856, M.A. Harvard 1819), brother of the Unitarian minister William Ellery Channing and cousin of Richard Henry Dana, had succeeded Willard Phillips the preceding April as editor of the *NAR.* The following year he became Boylston Professor of Rhetoric and Oratory at Harvard. Here, for a third of a century, he was an outstanding teacher, counting among his students Emerson, Holmes, Thoreau, and Lowell. See Rusk, *Emerson,* pp. 77–78.

2. Channing had written on September 3 thanking Bryant for his article on American poetry, and adding, "I doubt not you have heard in many ways of the great pleasure which our readers have received from that & your earlier communications to the work. You know how important it is that those, who have helped to give a character to a work of this sort, should continue their exertions. . . . Excuse me then, when I ask you to spare a little time from your profession, & give it to us." NYPL–BG.

3. The source of this quotation, which Bryant himself so ably translated, has not been identified.

4. Channing asked for a book review, and perhaps also an essay, for the November number.

5. "The Yellow Violet." Despite Channing's complaint that it was "next to impossible" to maintain a "uniformly respectable" poetry department, he asked for more poetry from "you and your father"—apparently still thinking Peter Bryant had composed "Thanatopsis." Channing's endorsement on Cullen's letter indicates the immediate fate of "The Yellow Violet," written in 1814, but unpublished until its inclusion in Bryant's 1821 volume. See *Poems* (1876) pp. 24–26.

55. *To* Miss Sarah S. Bryant

Great Barrington   22 Feb. 1819

Dear Sister

I plead guilty to the charge of negligence and acknowledge the justice of your reproof.[1] I might urge however in extenuation of my offense, that it was not a premeditated one; it was a sin of omission merely. This, after all, is a species of transgressions to which our race would still be subject, were the bad passions entirely removed from our hearts and the blameless intentions of the *age of Paradise* restored. The zealous pursuit of one duty might lead us to overlook another. A thousand seductions would still lie in wait to make us relax the activity required of us. The persuasions of ease, the more powerful suggestions of weariness might induce us to defer doing our duty to some other moment when it might be done as well, and the opportunity of performance might thus imperceptibly go by and escape us forever. So powerful is the influence of the feelings over the reason.

Excuse this effusion of philosophy.— I hope you study to make the situation of our father during his illness as comfortable as possible. I had long been anxious without much success to hear of his health before I received your letter, and had hoped to hear that it was better.[2]

I was much pleased with the specimen of your drawing which you sent me. It was well done, and I think you have made unusual proficiency.

I would write you a longer letter if I had time. I think you will see in this the marks of haste.— But you may write me in answer as long a letter as you please— My love to the family—

Your affectionate brother and friend
WM. C. BRYANT

MANUSCRIPTS: Weston Family Papers (final); NYPL–GR (draft, mistakenly headed "Cummington").

1. Sally's letter is unrecovered. She was obviously impatient with her brother for his neglect, for she had written her mother several months earlier from Northampton, "I do not take it very kind of Cullen that he did not either come and see me or write to me." Undated letter [cNovember 10, 1818], BCHS.
2. Peter Bryant had been ill again with lung trouble since October. Though he had been able to "ride out" in an emergency to "set a couple of broken arms" suffered by two neighboring ladies who were thrown from a wagon, his practice was now borne largely by his former pupil Samuel Shaw, whom he had taken as a partner. Sarah to Sally Bryant, November 2, 1818, and Peter to Sally, November 13, 1818, Weston Family Papers; *Bryant Record*, pp. 92, 94. Sally had left school in Northampton about the middle of January and come home to Cummington. Sally to Charity Bryant, February 15, 1819, Sheldon Museum.

56.   *To* Edward T. Channing

Great Barrington   25 March 1819

Dear Sir

Your favour of the 8th. inst. has been received. To commendations so flattering as you are pleased to bestow on me, coming from such a quarter, I hardly know what to say.[1] Had you seen more of those attempts of mine concerning which you express yourself so favourably, your opinion would perhaps have been different— [I]f in some instances I have been successful, I may have been so by accident. The lines I sent you you are at liberty to dispose of as you think proper; but do not, by any means, take any trouble to make a place for them in your Journal, and above all, do not let them appear if they are not worthy of it.[2]

I have not the Backwoodsman but I have seen some extracts from it —enough to give me some opinion of the work and I agree with you in thinking that it is bad enough. If I can procure it at any of the neighbouring bookstores I will review it for your June No. If I do not get it I will send some article for the Miscellaneous department.[3] I return you one of the Numbers for December. I supposed, when I received it, that it was sent me by some mistake, and I ought to have returned it before. It is true that I subscribed for the work at first, in behalf of a Literary association—but that association came to nothing before I received my first Number—and I was left to take it on my own account.[4]

I may perhaps, some time or other, venture a little collection of poetry in print,—for I do not write much—and should it be favourably received, it may give me courage to do something more.[5] In the mean time I cannot be too grateful for th[e] distant voice of kindness, that cheers me in the pursuit of those studies which I have nobody here to share with me.

I remain Sir
Yours truly
Wm. C. Bryant

MANUSCRIPT: HCL ADDRESS: Edward T. Channing Esqr. / Counsellor at Law / Boston POSTAL ANNOTATION: 12½ DOCKETED: Wm C Bryant / G Barrington March 25, 1819 PUBLISHED (in part): *Life*, I, 158–159.

1. Acknowledging receipt on March 8 of Bryant's poem "The Yellow Violet," and an essay "On the Happy Temperament" (*NAR*, 9 [June 1819], 206–210), Channing remarked, "Everybody here is asking after you, & I believe blaming me a little for not doing more to secure something from you. . . . The Author of the 'Waterfowl' & 'a fragment' is under higher obligation than any American bard to do more. If I had any right or wish to commend you—in your hearing—I should have urged your obligation to write by comparing you with greater men than we can boast of." March 8, 1819, NYPL–BG.

2. Channing had regretted that, in the absence of other verses, "The Yellow Violet" would not fill space enough to form a "poetical department." He asked Bryant's permission to insert the lines in an appropriate review, and to "give a copy to one or two who will make no use of them but to love them as they should be loved" (March 8).

3. Asking if Bryant cared to review James Kirke Paulding's *The Backwoodsman* (Philadelphia, 1818), an appeal in verse for novelty in American writing, Channing added, "We think it not worth reviewing unless it is severely handled both for its bad politics & bad poetry" (March 8). Bryant did not review this book.

4. Channing had offered Bryant on March 8 two free subscriptions to the *NAR*— one for himself, and one for the now defunct "association." See Letter 44.

5. Channing had inquired, "May I not ask you, if we may not expect a volume from you in spite of your profession?" (March 8).

57. *To* Austin Bryant

Newport [Rhode Island]   Aug 3   1819

Dear Brother.

As my father wrote home from New-Bedford and probably informed the family concerning his health I have delayed to write till this time—[1]

Immediately after writing my last he became very much worse—and found himself obliged to send for medical assistance.[2] Dr. Warren[3] came —bled him and put a seton into his side— On Monday we set out from Boston and arrived at Milton—[4] Tuesday the rain prevented us from travelling and my father still continued very ill— Wednesday we set out again—on Friday we arrived at New-Bedford—[5] Yesterday we set out from that place—and this morning came to Newport— Our father has been gradually getting better since leaving Milton and is now as far as I can judge as comfortable as when he left Cummington if not more so.

Your affectionate brother
WILLIAM C. BRYANT

Excuse my brevity & haste. We cannot write long letters while travelling— We shall probably get home some time about the middle of *Next Week.*

MANUSCRIPT: BCHS.

1. During the spring of 1819 Peter Bryant's health steadily worsened. A premonition of his early death was suggested in Cullen's essay "On the Happy Temperament" in the *NAR* for June, where he wrote, "Hard and bitter is the trial when we see those whom we love drawn toward the grave by the irresistible progress of disease and decay." By early summer the doctor became convinced that his only hope for recovery lay in a journey to the seashore, and on July 19, accompanied by Cullen, he left Cummington by buggy for Newport, Rhode Island, by way of Boston. Peter to Sarah Bryant, July 30, 1819, BCHS.

2. Cullen's letter of July 23 from Boston is unrecovered.

3. Dr. John Collins Warren (1778–1856, Harvard 1797), dean of the Harvard Medical School and Peter Bryant's warm friend. Hemorrhaging profusely the day he reached Boston, Dr. Bryant was treated by Warren and his Harvard colleague Dr. James Jackson (1777–1867). Their advice, Peter wrote his wife on July 30, was that "nothing short of a long voyage—either to Italy, E. Indies, or New Orleans, would benefit me."

4. Cullen and his father spent two nights at "Brush Hill," the Milton home of Mrs. Samuel Howe's father, Judge Edward Hutchinson Robbins (1757–1829, Harvard 1775), a former lieutenant governor of Massachusetts. Here, Dr. Bryant reported to his wife, he was "nursed very tenderly" by Mrs. Robbins. See also Lesley, *Recollections of My Mother*, pp. 20–21, 101.

5. At New Bedford the travelers spent three nights with Dr. Bryant's cousin (Gamaliel Bryant, Jr.?), a sea captain.

58. *To* Charity Bryant[1]

Cummington   March 21st. 1820.

Dear Aunt

I sit down to give you the melancholy news of the death of my father. He expired on Sunday last between the hours of seven and eight in the evening. It was not his fate to wait the gradual extinction of life which is the usual termination of that disorder under which he laboured and which in its natural course would probably have carried him off soon. His death was occasioned by an effusion of blood into the lungs brought on by a violent fit of coughing. When the blood first began to flow he expressed his opinion that it would prove fatal, and the event too fully verified his prediction—he did not survive more than fifteen minutes. The blood in spite of the violent efforts he made to throw it off, filled his lungs—all that we could do for him was in vain, and he expired by a kind of suffocation. I was present when this melancholy event took place having arrived here on a visit the evening before. I never saw any body die before, but judging as well as I am able I should think his death on the whole, more easy than is generally the case. He died sitting in his chair with his hands in his lap holding his handkerchief and his feet crossing each other—but there was no convulsion, no discomposure of attitude— no appearance of distress or agony except what was occasioned by the violent exertion he made at first to throw off the blood from his lungs.[2] Today we attended his funeral.[3] Let us hope that our departed friend after all his sufferings is gone to a better and happier world. Let us trust that a man so upright and just in his conduct, so gentle in his temper, so forgiving of injuries, so full of good will to all mankind, and of offices of kindness and humanity to which he certainly sacrificed his health and probably his life, is one of those whom God has rewarded with felicity. Indeed, if this be not the case I think there is little hope for any of the human race.

My mother and the family desire their affectionate remembrances.—

I am, dear aunt,

Your affectionate nephew

WILLIAM C. BRYANT.

MANUSCRIPTS: University of Texas (final); NYPL–GR (draft dated March 22) ADDRESS: Miss Charity Bryant / Weybridge / Vermont / To go to Middlebury post office POSTMARK (*in script*): Cummington Ms / March 23 1820 POSTAL ANNOTATION: Wm C Bryant / 12½ PUBLISHED (from draft): *Life*, I, 162.

1. Charity (1777–1851), younger of Peter Bryant's two surviving sisters, had lived since 1806 in Weybridge, Vermont. With a girlhood friend, Sylvia Drake (1784–1868), another spinster, she ran a busy tailor shop. See unpublished address by Mrs. H. B. Hagar, dated January 21, 1935, in the Sheldon Museum. Charity had once taught school in Plainfield, living with her brother's family at Cummington, and had since visited them occasionally.

2. By the preceding October Dr. Bryant had begun to recover from his long illness, but, soon after, the rigors of winter calls on his patients brought on a severe cold and hemorrhages. By early January he was confined to the house, and soon afterward to his bed. He had bled himself, he wrote Charity, "near 30 times in the course of the year past," thinking this his only means of survival. During the week before his death on March 19 his wife checked two hemorrhages by feeding him salt, but on the evening he died "the blood flowed so fast he could not swallow." Peter to Charity Bryant, January 5, 1820, Sheldon Museum; Sarah to Charity Bryant, March 1, 1821, NYPL–Berg.

3. Dr. Bryant's funeral showed the high regard in which he was held by his community, drawing the largest crowd of mourners ever assembled in Cummington. The

open coffin stood on the snow under tall poplars in front of the house for all to see; burial was in a hilltop cemetery above the homestead, the grave marked by a simple slate for which Cullen later composed the epitaph:

PETER BRYANT
A studious and skillful
Physician and Surgeon,
And for some time a member
of the State Senate,
Born in North Bridgewater,
August 12, 1767
Died March 19, 1820.

See Jacob Porter, "Some Account of Cummington, in Hampshire County, Massachusetts," *Collections of the Massachusetts Historical Society*, Second Series, 10 (1823), 44; Lydia Richards to Charity Bryant, April 2, 1820, Sheldon Museum.

59. *To* Miss Sarah S. Bryant

Great Barrington   Apl. 22nd. 1820.

Dear Sister

Though I cannot say much in praise of the length of your last letter,[1] yet I am very glad that you thought of writing to me at all. Let me beg of you, the next time you write to send me a good long letter—it can do you no hurt—the exercise will tend to give you greater ease in composition, and perhaps more steadiness in pursuing a train of thought—not to mention that, being a female, your Laconism is what the criticks might call a fault in *costume*.[2] I have thought much of the subject concerning which you desire my opinion. Upon the whole, I think your plan a good one, and I am pleased with the spirit in which it originated. Your good sense has probably taught you long since that no kind of honest employment is disreputable. The occupation of keeping school may not be the most pleasant in the world—or it may—for I have had no experience to enable me to decide this question—but habit has rendered it agreeable to many who have followed it;—and though I judge differently of your qualifications for that employment from what you appear to do, yet even if you are not perfectly well prepared to teach certain branches of learning you can easily make yourself so, in the leisure hours before and after school. I do not exactly know how well instructed you are in arithmetick grammar &c., but I feel very certain that if you undertake to teach these branches, you can, by a little attention, easily keep ahead of your scholars. Indeed I think that the opportunity of acquiring knowledge, and of fixing in the memory what is already acquired is the principle advantage to be reaped from the employment you propose to yourself. Yet I should not wish to have you always a school mistress. The habits of continually dwelling on those minor branches of learning which are merely the stepping stones to higher knowledge, is apt at length to lead the mind to consider these petty studies as the sum of all human science—a fact of which we see daily examples. If the mind cannot always enlarge itself, it will generally contract itself to the limits in which it is employed. A short time spent in keeping school will not however be apt to produce this effect, but would probably be to your advantage.[3] I have no news to tell you. The world rolls about in the old way.

My love to the family and my affectionate remembrances to all my friends. God bless you—

Your affectionate brother
WM. C. BRYANT

The first copy of this letter was written a week ago—but by some mistake I missed the mail.

MANUSCRIPTS: Weston Family Papers (final); NYPL–GR (draft dated April 17) ADDRESS: Miss Sarah S. Bryant / Cummington / To go to the Worthington Post Office.

1. Unrecovered.
2. I.e., her Lacedaemonian, or Spartan, brevity is not the female fashion.
3. Sally taught school at Plainfield the following summer. Lydia Richards to Charity Bryant, September 24, 1820, Sheldon Museum.

60. *To* Charles Sedgwick[1]

Great Barrington   July 30   1820—

Dear Sir

I have altered the second stanza of Paine's Ode[2] in the following manner—

> In a clime, whose rich vales feed the marts of the earth,
>   Whose shores are unshaken by Europe's commotion,
> The fleets of the world to the land of your birth
>   Shall come—as the billows come in from the ocean.[3]
>   But should pirates invade, &c.

The other exceptionable passage I have altered in two ways [neit]her of which exactly pleases me— You may chuse, or think of something better—

> Then unite, heart and hand,
> Like Leonidas' band,
> In a vow to the God of the ocean and land
> That ne'er shall the sons of Columbia &c

—which however does not mend the matter much. —More devoutly and more tamely thus—

> And ask of the God of the ocean and land
> That ne'er *may* the sons of Columbia &c.—[4]

I am Sir
Yours sincerely
WILLIAM C. BRYANT

MANUSCRIPT: Pierpont Morgan Library ADDRESS: Charles Sedgwick Esq. / Stockbridge PUBLISHED: Charles I. Glicksberg, "Bryant and the Sedgwick Family," *Americana*, 31 (October 1937), 627–628.

1. Bryant apparently met Charles Sedgwick (1791–1856) at the county court in Lenox soon after starting law practice in Berkshire County. Admitted to the bar in 1814, Sedgwick became clerk of courts in 1821, and served in this position until his death in 1856. In 1874 the town of Lenox established in his name the Charles Sedgwick Library, in the handsome former courthouse, built in 1816, in which he served so long, and which is still occupied by the Lenox Library Association. Sedgwick, *Life and Letters*, p. 121; [Beers] *Berkshire County*, I, 303, 329; II, 209. Charles Sedgwick's *Letters to His Family and Friends* was privately printed at Boston in 1870.

2. Robert Treat Paine, Jr. (1773–1811), "Adams and Liberty: The Boston Patriotic Song" (1798). It is not clear for what purpose Bryant and Sedgwick wished to improve this popular ode. It may have been recited or sung at the Fourth of July celebration in Stockbridge, where Bryant, discussing the recently adopted Missouri Compromise, made his first public attack on the institution of slavery. *An Oration, Delivered at Stockbridge, July 4th, 1820* (Stockbridge, 1820).

3. Cf. Paine: "The trident of commerce should never be hurl'd, / To incense the legitimate powers of the ocean."

4. Cf. Paine, stanza 9: "And swear to the God of the ocean and land, / That ne'er shall the sons of Columbia be slaves."

61.   *To* Willard Phillips

Great Barrington   Aug. 19, 1820

Dear Sir—

I have just been able to procure Percy's Masque—and now that I have got it, will set about reviewing it as fast as I can. I will send the article as early at least as the middle of September—perhaps earlier. I am told the author of Percy's Masque is a countryman of ours.— I think it a very creditable specimen of our genius in the way of tragedy.[1] —My regards to my Boston acquaintances—

Yours sincerely
WILLIAM C. BRYANT

MANUSCRIPT: MHS ADDRESS: Willard Phillips Esq—.

1. Phillips wrote on August 4 (NYPL–BG) asking Bryant to review for the October *NAR* James A. Hillhouse's verse drama, *Percy's Masque* (London, 1819). Its publication in England accounted for Bryant's initial uncertainty of its author's nationality. In his notice Bryant stressed the special understanding of character and feeling for natural speech demanded of the tragic dramatist who would succeed in this, the most difficult of poetic tasks. He thought the author had succeeded only in making a "respectable production." *NAR*, 11 (October, 1820), 364–393.

62.   *To* Miss Sarah S. Bryant

Lenox, Oct. 20, 1820

Dear Sister—

I expected to have heard from you before this time when I saw you last, as I believe you owe me a letter or two; but my communications with the shades are almost as frequent as with my friends at Cummington unless I go purposely to visit them. I wrote a letter to my mother in September enclosing a bill of what was due to the publisher of the Evening Post and an account against the Estate in favour of Colt of Pittsfield; this letter Mr. Howe tells me he has mislaid—[1] I can perhaps get Colt's account again before I come to Cummington which will probably be in two or three weeks.

I should have been glad—indeed I hoped to have received a line from you by Mr. Howe, from which I might have learned how you all did and how you were getting along. I shall know soon probably—but you should not forget to write— The time may perhaps come when we shall not see each other so frequently as now, and should we not keep up an occasional correspondence of one letter at least in half a dozen years we might go near to forget each other.

For myself I am in the old way pretty much, as to business and health excepting a touch of influenza with which every body is attacked— I have written an article for the last North American Review—on Percy's Masque, a tragedy lately published by an American writer.

I am told you are going to lose your neighbours—for such they have always seemed to our family—Mr. and Mrs Howe.—[2] I think you will regret Mrs. Howe's departure very much and with good reason—for though I once was a little prejudiced respecting her, it was impossible to retain my prejudices long—and I must do her what is no more than justice—I must say that I think her an excellent woman, of a sound understanding and good heart.—

I believe I have nothing more to write that would look well on paper.— I shall see you soon, and if I have forgotten any thing I suppose I may have the privilege of communicating it verbally.— Excuse this rambling letter—one of the most so I ever wrote. I write in the common sitting room of my boarding house with half a dozen people about me.—[3]

Your affectionate brother
WILLIAM C. BRYANT

MANUSCRIPT: Weston Family Papers ADDRESS: Miss Sarah S. Bryant / Cummington / (By the politeness of S. Howe Esq.)

1. Bryant's letter is unrecovered, and nothing further is known about these accounts against Peter Bryant's estate.

2. See "Bryant's Correspondents." In 1820 Samuel Howe entered a law partnership in Northampton with Elijah Hunt Mills.

3. See 47.5.

63. *To* Henry D. Sewall

Great Barrington   Nov. 1, 1820

Dear Sir

I intended when I received yours of the 29th of August to have given it an earlier answer and to have accompanied my answer with further contributions to your new work.[1] —But I did not get your communication till the 12 of September and since that time we have had a Term of the Supreme Court which lasted a fortnight—one of the Court of Sessions and another of the Court of Common Pleas and these together with my other engagements and some ill health have obliged me to delay it till it was too late for any thing but apologies.—

I felt obliged to you for pointing out those topicks which have not been often touched upon by writers of devotional poetry.[2] Your conjecture was right that the choice of a subject was more difficult than the composition of the hymn. I made some attempts to write but could not satisfy myself, and I would not send you impromptus nor the stale efforts of languor and lassitude—nothing which was not written in moments of enthusiasm and excitement and carefully corrected at my leisure—

I ought to thank you for the good opinion you are pleased to express concerning my hymns. "Praise" says a poet, is "the poets best reward,"[3] and I should forfeit my pretensions to be considered one of the fraternity were I to deny that I am pleased with the commendations of literary [. . . whose applause confers?] reputation—

[unsigned]

MANUSCRIPT: NYPL–GR (draft).

1. *A Collection of Psalms and Hymns for Social and Private Worship*, ed. Henry D. Sewall (New York, 1820). In July Catharine M. Sedgwick (see "Bryant's Correspondents") had reminded Bryant of his earlier promise to compose hymns for this collection, designed to honor William Ware at his ordination in 1821 as pastor of the new Unitarian church in New York City. Catharine M. Sedgwick to Robert Sedgwick, May 17, 1820, *Life*, I, 163; Miss Sedgwick to Bryant, [July] 17 [1820], NYPL–BG. She forwarded to Sewall five hymns which Bryant sent her, and Sewall wrote Bryant on August 29 thanking him and soliciting further contributions. NYPL–BG.

2. Sewall proposed additional hymns on neglected subjects, such as the paternal character of God and the duties of parents and children, because, he wrote, "A minister discussing on these obvious topicks will find it difficult to select a hymn at all adapted to them." He went on to list changes he had made in Bryant's verses, concluding abruptly, "I have no room to enter into a critical defense of these alterations —nor am I disposed." Bryant ignored these changes when in 1864 he printed these and others of his hymns privately.

3. The source of this quotation is uncertain.

64. *To* Mrs. Sarah S. Bryant

Great Barrington, Jan. 16th, 1821

Dear Mother:

I hasten to communicate to you the melancholy intelligence of what has lately happened to me.[1]

Early in the evening of the eleventh day of the present month, I was at a neighbouring house in this village. Several people of both sexes assembled in one of the apartments—three or four others, together with myself were in another. At last came a little elderly gentleman, pale, thin, with a solemn countenance, a pleuritic voice, hooked nose, and hollow eyes.[2] Presently we were summoned to attend in the room where he and the rest of the company were assembled. We went in, and took our seats; the little elderly gentleman with the hooked nose then prayed, and we all stood up. When he had finished, most of us sat down. The little elderly gentleman with the hooked nose then asked those who remained standing for something which he called a *certificate*—which seems to be of as much importance in the solemnization of these mysteries as one of St. Peter's tickets to a dead Russian.[3] A paper was accordingly produced, inscribed with certain significant characters,[4] upon which having mused a little while, he turned to us and pronounced several cabalistical expressions, which I was too much frightened to remember—but I recollect very well, that, at the conclusion, I was given to understand that I was married to a young lady of the name of Frances Fairchild, whom I perceived standing by my side, and whom I hope, in the course of the next few months, to have the pleasure of introducing to you as your daughter-in-law; which is a matter of some interest to the poor girl who has neither father nor mother in the world.

I have not played the fool, and married an Ethiop for the jewel in her ear.[5] I looked only for goodness of heart, an ingenuous and affectionate disposition, a good understanding &c. &c., and the character of my wife is too frank and single-hearted to suffer me to suppose the possibility of my being disappointed. —I misstate the matter—I did not look for these, nor any qualities—but they trapped me before I was aware, and now I am married in spite of myself. When we shall begin to keep house will depend, as everything else does, *altogether upon* circumstances.[6]

Thus the current of destiny carries us all along. None but a madman would swim against the stream, and none but a fool would exert himself to swim with it. The best way is to float idly with the tide.

So much for philosophy—now for business. I wrote again to Mr. [William] Coleman the Publisher of the [New York] Evening Post, and received their account, which I will forward to you by some convenient opportunity. The amount due is $34. They constituted me their agent to see to the collection of the money, with a commission of 12½ per cent.

If, therefore, you will send me $30 I will get you a Rect. for the whole a/c and let the $4. go towards paying for the books I have taken.[7]

I doubt much whether Dr. Rogers will conclude to take the surgical instruments and books.[8] —Remember me to the family—I should be glad to hear from you—

Your affectionate son
W. C. BRYANT

MANUSCRIPTS: Weston Family Papers (final); NYPL–GR (draft) ADDRESS: Mrs. Sarah Snell Bryant / Cummington PUBLISHED (in part): Life, I, 169–170, from draft, and mistakenly dated June 1821.

1. Bryant's earliest surviving letter to his mother, this has been variously interpreted as evidence of his real bewilderment at finding himself married ("Youth," p. 231), a "humiliating surrender" for which his pride seemed to be "awkwardly seeking excuses" (Life, I, 170), or simply wry Yankee humor. Its quite different origin is intimated in Letter 65.

2. Rev. Elijah Wheeler. See 48.7.

3. Bryant's allusion may be to the Eastern Orthodox belief which does not recognize the papacy, of which Saint Peter was by tradition the first representative.

4. As town clerk, Bryant had issued his own marriage license. "Youth," p. 234.

5. Cf. Romeo and Juliet I.v.47–48.

6. The couple were married in the home of Frances' sister Esther, Mrs. Allen Henderson. This house, still standing, was even then notable for having sheltered British General John Burgoyne briefly after his surrender at Saratoga in 1777, as well as for having been entered by a mob during Daniel Shays' Rebellion in 1786. Frances Bryant, "Autobiographical Sketch"; [Beers] Berkshire County, II, 10.

7. Neither letter to Coleman has been found.

8. Bryant evidently hoped that Dr. Benjamin Rogers, in whose home he then had his law office, would buy his father's medical books and instruments.

65.   To Miss Sarah S. Bryant[1]

Great Barrington, Feb. 4th, 1821

Dear Sister,

I received yours of the 7th of January but this morning.[2] You must prepare yourself for a long letter.

You have heard you tell me that I am about to be married to a poor young lady and so ignorant that she does not know poetry from prose.[3] Again you tell me that you have heard that I am married. You then hint something about the truth of the reports you have heard. If you mean that you give credit to every scandalous story that may be circulated, about me, or about the young lady who has done me the honour to bestow her hand upon me is to say the least of it, an unkind insinuation, and might lead me to think that I did not stand very high in your good opinion or your affection.

But I acquit you of any such meaning, though I cannot believe that you would have mentioned any such idle reports had they not made some impression upon your mind. At all events I will give them a short examination and see what stuff they are made of. —That I am married, you have probably learnt long since, from my letter to my mother.

That my wife is not rich I acknowledge and it was the solemn vow of my heart made and registered in heaven years ago never to marry a rich wife—never to humble myself by obligations of that kind to any woman on earth—never to reverse the natural order of things and instead of earning a subsistence for my family to marry a woman who should provide for me. Destined as I am to be poor, the fate of a poet, I would not unite myself to one who could reproach me even by her tears with having squandered her fortune. There is another reason for my resolution—rich girls are hardly ever worth marrying. They may sometimes be tolerably accomplished—but the vulgar pride of wealth from which they are rarely free taints the whole moral constitution. If riches are a necessary qualification in a wife who, my dear sister will ever think of marrying you?—

The question of riches you see is easily disposed of and the slander of ignorance might be dispatched in three or four expressive monosyllables—but I have something to say on that head too.

Nothing offends young ladies in general so much as that any young lady in particular should have the good fortune to get married. Every young man of tolerable promise and respectable expectations taken up in this way is so much deducted from the number of their chances to get married, and their disappointment is generally in proportion to the consideration in which he is held in society. Accordingly, for some time before and after the event takes place, the most malicious scrutiny is at work upon the character of the unfortunate fair one with a determination to make faults where they are not found. A dialogue similar to the following may be imagined to take place:

"Is Mr. A. going to be married?"

"So it is said—to Miss B, but I can hardly believe it—I do not believe that he would have such a creature. I shall be perfectly astonished if he does."

"She is handsome I suppose."

"Handsome!—no indeed—some people pretend to call her well-looking, but for my part I always thought her very plain."

"Rich then."

"Not worth the linen on her back and yet she holds her head as high and gives herself as many airs as if she were mistress of a fortune."

"Good tempered perhaps."

"Her friends would be glad to have people think so, but I know that she was always extremely disagreeable to me."

"He is thought to be something of a scholar—undoubtedly he has made choice of a young lady of good education."

"Not if he marries her— She pretends to read indeed and to study this thing and that but I do not believe that she understands any thing that she reads."

"I wonder if she is as fond of poetry as he is?"

"Pooh— My dear Madam, what a question! Poetry! Why she is perfectly ignorant—she does not know anything—she can't tell poetry from prose."

This is an old tune—it is repeated on every such occasion—I myself have heard it a hundred times. It is as silly as the disputes between children about the biggest piece of cake and yet the scandals you have heard came from this very respectable source.

About three years since when Highland Mary, Forever Fortune, When Bidden to the Wake or Fair, &c. were worn out by being sung over and over at the parties in our village a bran new song was imported from Albany, the most perfect nonsense in the world, beginning thus—

> "Come here thou blue-eyed stranger,
> Ah, Whither dost thou roam!
> Through this wide world a ranger,
> Hast thou no friends—no home?" [4]

And this stanza was followed by three others each surpassing the others in silliness. Now there are a vast many people in the world who are mightily in love with what is beautiful and elegant &c. and a very few who are disgusted with nonsense. Accordingly our new song being sung by a pretty girl with a good voice became all the rage, was admired and encored and the young ladies were all dissolved in ecstacy. "Beautiful! Charming! Affecting! Exquisite!" &c. &c. "I must have a copy—I must have the notes. I must learn the tune— How does the first line run? 'Come here thou blue-eyed ranger'?" All was rapture and pathos and elegance. It would have been a pity to disturb this delightful trance and accordingly they who knew how ridiculous it was said nothing. Encouraged by this seeming acquiescence the amateurs proceeded a step farther. Four additional stanzas to the same ballad were picked up some where, still more silly if possible than the others. The raptures of the young ladies were redoubled. "How much the song is improved!" Parties were made for the purpose of singing *Blue-Eyed Mary*. Young ladies were on a visit here from neighboring towns— *They* must hear Blue-Eyed Mary too— They heard, joined in the applause. "How beautiful! What a pathetic sentiment in the concluding stanzas,

> 'Come here thou blue-eyed stranger
> I'll find thee friends and home.' "

At last the secret came out that some people were laughing in their sleeves, at their raptures and their beautiful new song. The celebrity of Blue-Eyed Mary sunk immediately and the beautiful song has never been

heard of since. Such are they who talk of *ignorance* and *poetry* and *prose*
—such are their qualifications to decide—from such people came the
effusion of spite which reached you in the form of a rumour—I despise
the calumny—I despise its authors whom I believe I know and I would
not condescend to notice it but on your account.[5]

As for the education of the young lady who is now my wife, I will
only say that she has diligently improved her opportunities of information—that she is fond of reading—that she has both too much good taste
and good sense to praise nonsense because it is fashionable and too much
goodness of heart to say of others, though she might justly do it, what it
seems they are so ready to say unjustly of her—

I am now boarding out and shall not begin keeping house till next
spring or summer— You talk of going to keeping school—if you will
come and stay with Frances and myself next summer, I shall be glad to
have you with us. I shall probably come to Cummington next spring
when the roads are settled.

Your affectionate brother
WM. C. BRYANT.

MANUSCRIPT: Weston Family Papers ADDRESS: Miss Sarah S. Bryant / Cummington.

1. This letter, unknown to any of Bryant's biographers, lifts much of the obscurity
heretofore surrounding his courtship and marriage.

2. Sally's letter is unrecovered.

3. A month earlier Sally had written her cousin Eben Snell at Williams College,
"William C. has been at home a few weeks since; he was in high health and spirits.
We have frequently heard that he was going to take an helpmate. Since he went back
we heard that he was going to marry a young lady very poor and so ignorant that she
could not distinguish poetry from prose." But that she was mainly teasing the older
brother who had offered her earlier homilies is evident from her added remark, "However I do not feel at all troubled about his marrying a fool." January 1, 1821, Weston
Family Papers.

4. The version of this popular song to which Bryant refers was probably that published in New York in 1817 by William Dubois. Richard J. Wolfe, *Secular Music in
America: 1801–1825* (New York: New York Public Library, 1964), pp. 92–93. There
was irony—although perhaps unintentional—in Cullen's scornful account of this song's
sudden oblivion, for, according to her younger brother John, it was one of Sally's fa-
vorites. *Bryant Record*, p. 94.

5. This "effusion of spite" may be explained in Cullen's case by pique at his reported attitude toward some of his fair neighbors: "The young women liked his bright
eyes and clustering light-brown hair, and 'set their caps for him,' but he once gave
them great offense by saying that 'farmers' daughters always walked as if they were
carrying swill-pails!' " *Life*, I, 203. Such a feeling toward Frances Fairchild is more
difficult to account for, unless it was because her long absence from Great Barrington
(see 38.1) in the supposedly primitive West had disposed her fellow-townswomen to
think her illiterate.

66.   *To* Henry D. Sewall

                                    Great Barrington   March 29th   1821.
Dear Sir

A few weeks since I received from you a letter mentioning that you had sent me a copy of your collection of hymns[1] and a pamphlet which I suppose is the answer to Dr. Spring's attack on the Unitarians.[2]

I have not received either of them, owing probably to some accident as the letter was mailed at New York. You politely offer to send me any number of copies which I may want for my friends if I should find the work so well done as to induce me [to] make use of the proffer. I have not seen the work yet but I have no fear that I shall not like it. For what little of my own there is in it I shall of course feel a parent's particularity and report speaks highly of the general merit and good taste of the compilation. I will avail myself of your politeness so far as to request you to send me by Mr. Pynchon the bearer two copies of your work.[3]

I congratulate you on the prosperity of the religious society for whose particular use your compilation was undertaken. Judging from the circumstances in which it is placed, I should wonder if it did not number among its members many of the most enlightened liberal candid and intelligent of the inhabitants of yr city animated with much of that fearless and commanding virtue which pursues its duty in spite of consequences. It is from such men that the cause of liberal Christianity must look for prompt spirited vindication against the attacks of bigotry and insolence.[4] —I have seen Mr. Everett's dedication sermon—and admired it—[5]

                                                        [unsigned]

MANUSCRIPT: NYPL–GR (draft).

1. See 63.1. Sewall's letter, dated January 2, 1821, is in NYPL–BG.
2. Rev. Gardiner Spring (1785–1873) was pastor of the Brick Presbyterian Church in New York City. His criticism of Unitarianism, and the reply to which Bryant refers, were contained in Spring's *A Tribute to New-England: A Sermon Delivered Before the New-England Society . . . on the 22d of December, 1820* (New York, 1821), pp. 39–43; and [Henry D. Sedgwick?] *Remarks on the Charges Made Against the Religion and Morals of the People of Boston and its Vicinity by the Rev. Gardiner Spring D. D. . . .* (New York, 1820).
3. Probably George Pynchon, a Great Barrington storekeeper whom Bryant had represented in several court actions.
4. Though Bryant attended the Great Barrington Congregational Church, the established church to which his duties as town clerk and tithing man led him, he was not a member. This is his first recorded expression of interest in Unitarianism, of which he became an adherent upon moving to New York City in 1825. "Youth," pp. 195–196, 242, 246.
5. See Edward Everett, *Sermon Preached at the Dedication of the Congregational Church in New York*, Jan. 20, 1821, 2nd ed. (Boston, 1821).

67. *To* Miss Sarah S. Bryant

Great Barrington   Apl. 10, 1821.

Dear Sister

I wrote to you some time since with an invitation to pass the summer in Great Barrington. In your reply I did not understand you to give me a direct answer.[1] I hope that on reflection you will conclude to come. Frances joins me in this request and will do every thing in her power to render your stay here pleasant to you. I do not think that the occupation of keeping school is the best for your health that you could pursue—it would be much better for you to come and work a little and study a little with Frances—and try a new air, in this charming village. As for your earnings—I think you ought not to sacrifice your constitution to such considerations. I hope that some of us will always be able to give you a home—we shall certainly be willing to do it as long as we have homes of our own—so that you will probably be provided for somewhere, although you should not keep school this summer.[2] Will you have the goodness to write me immediately and inform me whether you will accept my proposal that I may make the necessary arrangements for bringing you down with me when I visit Cummington.

Yours affectionately
WM. C. BRYANT

MANUSCRIPT: NYPL–GR ADDRESS: Miss Sarah S. Bryant.

1. Sally's reply is unrecovered.
2. The reassurance that she would "probably be provided for somewhere" must have struck Sally as somewhat patronizing, and even ironical, for it is said that her brothers as well as her parents had for some time opposed her wish to marry her father's young partner, Dr. Samuel Shaw. *Bryant Record*, pp. 92–93. See 69.3.

68. *To* William J. Spooner

Great Barrington   Apl   2[6?] 1821

Sir

I have just received yours of the 17th instant communicating a vote of the Phi Beta Kappa Society. The honour thus conferred upon me is as unlooked for as it is flattering. I did not even know that I was a member of your society till I was informed of it by your letter.[1]

I have concluded to accept the appointment and discharge myself of it as well as I can.

I have never attended an anniversary of the Φ. B. K. Society and must profess myself entirely unacquainted with the order of proceedings on that occasion. Of the general character of the performances I know only so much as might be gathered from reading a few of them, which have occasionally fallen in my way. As you have kindly offered to give me any information I may desire on those subjects I shall be obliged to you if you will mark out for me such a brief general outline as may prevent me from doing any thing outré, or getting foul of an interdicted subject.[2]

[unsigned]

MANUSCRIPT: NYPL–GR (draft) ADDRESS: Wm. J. Spooner Esq. PUBLISHED (*in part*): *Life*, I, 170–171.

1. William Jones Spooner (1782?–1824, M.A. Harvard 1813) wrote Bryant on April 17 that he had been unanimously chosen by the anniversary committee of the Harvard Phi Beta Kappa Society to read a poem on the day after commencement that summer, adding casually, "I believe you have not attended any meeting of the society since you were elected a member." Writing again on May 29, Spooner expressed surprise that the secretary had forgotten to notify the poet of his election, but "if he forgot the fact, the rest of the society have not." Bryant had apparently been proposed for membership—probably by Willard Phillips—soon after the publication of his first poetry in the *NAR* in 1817. See *Phi Beta Kappa Directory: 1776–1941* (New York, 1941), p. 200. Spooner's two letters are in NYPL–BG.

2. In his second letter Spooner discussed at some length past performers and their subjects, audience reaction, and critical reception, concluding with the suggestion that Bryant do "just what pleases yourself—I will warrant its pleasing the audience."

69.   *To* Miss Sarah S. Bryant

Great Barrington, May 5, 1821

Dear Sister

I have this day received yours of the 28th of April.[1] I am much concerned at the account you give of your health. I hope however that you have not all the cause for apprehension you suppose. I myself, at your age, and all along since till within two or three years was occasionally affected with symptoms similar to those you describe, and I have known others to be so, who yet escaped the consumption. I think, therefore, that though there is every reason for prudence and caution in every thing that concerns your health, yet you ought not to give way to despondency.

I am glad you have concluded to come and stay awhile with me. You shall not be troubled with too much company—at least you will not if you choose—there is no compulsion here about paying visits. If you will invest me with authority for that purpose which I think you ought to do, and which I must claim (for persons who have your complaint, although they acknowledge the necessity of prudence in regard to their health as a general rule, are often perversely imprudent in particular instances) I will order the matter so, that you will not visit too much; and people, you know, are visited in proportion as they visit.

I like your plan of studying Botany this season. I think it will be apt to improve your health and strengthen your constitution. I know not where health abides, if it be not in the fields; and when the capricious nymph deserts me, as she often does, in my office, I am driven to seek her in the open air, and dig for her in my garden, or go after [her] to the groves and mountain tops. I think you can pursue the study of that science to great advantage with me. I have several books on that branch of natural history. The plants of this region will, many of them, interest you by being new to you, and my wife who has paid considerable attention to the subject, shall be your companion in your rambles, and your instructress.[2]

I think I cannot well visit Cummington till about the middle of June. I have made arrangements to come about that time, but if any thing should happen to prevent it, you must not be surprised, but expect me about the beginning of July. When I come, I shall expect to bring you back with me if you are well enough, which I pray you may be.—[3]

Your affectionate brother
WM. C. BRYANT

MANUSCRIPTS: Weston Family Papers (final); NYPL–GR (draft) ADDRESS: Miss Sarah S. Bryant / Cummington PUBLISHED: *Bryant Record*, p. 98.

1. Unrecovered.

2. In 1820 the distinguished naturalist Amos Eaton (1776–1842, Williams 1799) gave a series of popular lectures on botany in Great Barrington and nearby towns. An early friend of Peter Bryant's, he took a particular interest in Cullen and Frances, who became his avid pupils. Eaton to Bryant, June 21, 1833, NYPL–BG. By 1821 Cullen was a "passionate botanist" whose accurate knowledge of the flora of Berkshire and Hampshire Counties has been remarked by several historians. See *Life*, I, 165, 203; D. D. Field, *History of the County of Berkshire* (Pittsfield, 1829), pp. 61–67; McDowell, *Representative Selections*, p. xxxiv. Cullen's assurance that many local plants would be new to Sally is explained by the difference in altitude of nearly one thousand feet between Cummington and the valley of the Housatonic at Great Barrington.

3. It is unlikely that Sally visited Great Barrington that summer, for from May 1 until her marriage to Dr. Samuel Shaw on September 13 she was constantly under his medical care. "Samuel Shaw Day-Book No. 3 Began April 1st 1821," Homestead Collection.

70. *To* Edward T. Channing

Great Barrington   June 2nd. 1821.

My Dear Sir.

If I pursued my *grave legal studies*, as you call them, so diligently that a letter from you could be said to interrupt them—I can assure you that the interruption would be a very agreeable one. But you certainly need use no apology to one who does not follow the study of law very eagerly, because he likes other studies better; and yet devotes little of his time to them, for fear that they should give him a dislike to law.[1]

I wish Mr. Dana all success in his new literary project; and as you tell me he intends to give his exclusive attention to the work, I cannot doubt of its being well received.[2] I shall be happy if any assistance I can render will be of any use to him. I write some trifles occasionally, which I might look over, make better, and send to be printed; —though in requesting my aid I fear you do me more honour than I shall do the work good. The little poem I sent you some time since, you may dispose of according to your pleasure;[3] and I will trouble you with another for Mr. Dana's work, —which you will find on the other side of this leaf.[4] I shall send you a copy of my 4th of July Oration, though, as it is nearly a year old, I doubt you will find the topicks there treated of a little stale.[5] I intend being in Cambridge next August, when I promise myself the pleasure of seeing you and my other friends there.[6] In the mean time believe me

Yours truly

WM. C. BRYANT

MANUSCRIPTS: HCL (final); NYPL–GR (draft) ADDRESS: Edward T. Channing Esq / Cambridge / Mass. POSTMARK (*in script*): Great Barrington   June 9th POSTAL AN- NOTATION: 12½ ENDORSED: Wm C. Bryant / Gt. Bar. June 2, 1821 / The "Green River" PUBLISHED (*in part*): *Life*, I, 165–166.

     1. Channing wrote on May 15 that, though he had not bothered Bryant by "solic- iting literary favours" since he had ceased editing the *NAR* in 1819, he now hoped the poet would contribute to a periodical Richard Dana planned to publish. NYPL–BG.

     2. *The Idle Man*, Part 1, Number 1, was published in New York by Wiley and Halsted in June 1821. With the exception of five poems contributed by Bryant to as many numbers of this short-lived periodical in 1821–1822, its contents, consisting mainly of essays and fictional articles, were written by Dana.

     3. Channing repeated his earlier request to be allowed a free hand in disposing of "The Yellow Violet." See 56.2.

     4. "Green River," printed in *The Idle Man*, 1, No. 2 (1821), 61–63. See *Poems* (1876), pp. 31–35.

     5. Learning that Bryant's oration at Stockbridge on July 4, 1820, had since been published, Channing had asked for a copy of it. See 60.2.

     6. Although Channing had hinted that he might have had a part in securing the Phi Beta Kappa invitation to Bryant for the coming Harvard commencement—"Have you any thing to draw you this way next summer?"—Bryant's guarded reply gives no indication he suspected this.

71.   *To* Richard H. Dana[1]

Great Barrington   July 30   1821.—

Dear Sir.—

     Yours of the 18th of June together with the first No. of the Idle Man I received some time since, for both which accept my thanks.[2] I would have answered your letter earlier, but I was pestered with several engagements, and among the rest with the composition of my poem, which I find a harder task than I expected, —owing partly to my having written but little in that way lately, and partly to the difficulty of the stanza I have chosen;—the labour has gone near to make me sick.[3] —I am delighted with the Idle Man and I shall think better of the world if it likes it too. It is an attempt to bring them back to the power and better feelings of our nature. When I saw one of the articles headed "Mr. Kean" —(this was immediately after I heard the news of his unlucky manoeuvre at Boston) I wished you had chosen a subject for your first number more likely to be *popular*[4]—but before I had finished reading

it you had engaged me in it so much that I would not have exchanged it
for any other.[5] It is not possible for me, in this retirement, to judge of
the progress it is making in the literary world; —all however that have
read it, whom I have seen, speak favourably of it. —You should not wish,
however, that it might start into popularity all at once—that would be a
bad omen. You must suffer the world to get in love with it gradually, if
you mean they shall remain attached to it long. —I feel, on the whole, a
strong confidence that it will succeed.—

> Please to give my regards to all my friends in Cambridge—
>
>   I am Sir
>   Yours truly
>   WILLIAM C. BRYANT

MANUSCRIPT: NYPL–GR ADDRESS: Richard H. Dana Esq DOCKETED: W. C. Bryant / July
    30—21 PUBLISHED (in part): Life, I, 166, 171.

1. This is the first of more than one hundred letters Bryant wrote Richard Henry
Dana (1787–1879) over a period of fifty-seven years. See "Bryant's Correspondents."
    2. Dana gave high praise to "Green River," Bryant's first contribution to The
Idle Man: "I do not say that it is better than the Water Fowl, but with that exception it is beyond any thing that I have read of American poetry." June 18, 1821, MHS.
    3. Bryant was writing his Phi Beta Kappa poem, "The Ages," in Spenserian
stanzas, difficult because of their tight rhyme scheme and end-stopped thought units.
He used this form only once again, in "After a Tempest" (1824). Another troublesome
problem was oral delivery, which Willard Phillips had anticipated in a letter dated
July 13. Remembering Bryant's early fear of public speaking, and anxious that his
protégé should perform well before a Cambridge audience, Phillips gave him a thorough lesson in elocution, passing from practice, breathing, voice placement, diet, and
rest, to phrasing, rhetorical embellishments, and gesture. NYPL–BG.
    4. After triumphs in Boston, New York, and Philadelphia during his first visit to
this country, the British tragedian Edmund Kean (1787–1833) returned to Boston in
May 1821 just as the theater season was waning. After playing two nights to poor
houses, he left the theater abruptly during his third performance and refused to return. "Boston was vastly incensed, regarding the tragedian's action as an insult; other
cities took up the quarrel, recrimination followed, a newspaper war began, Kean apologized in the public prints, but to no avail; his season was wrecked, and he hastily returned to England." George C. Odell, Annals of the New York Stage (New York:
Columbia University Press, 1927), II, 591–592.
    5. Having seen Kean play Hamlet, Richard II, Lear, Othello, and Sir Giles Over-
reach, Dana wrote in The Idle Man, "How can I describe one who is nearly as versatile and almost as full of beauties as nature itself? . . . Kean, in truth, stands very
much in that relation to other players whom we have seen, that Shakespeare does to
other dramatists." "Kean's Acting," reprinted in Dana's Poems and Prose Writings
(Philadelphia and Boston, 1833), pp. 421–422.

72. *To* Frances F. Bryant

                                  Boston   Aug. 25   1821

My dear Frances—

    You observed in what an elegant style I went from Great Barrington
to Sheffield. Seated on a rough board, laid on top of a crazy waggon whose

loose sides kept swinging from right to left and back again, with a coloured fellow at my right hand, and a dirty old rascal before me who kept spitting on me all the way, I was jolted over a road that filled my mouth and ears and clothes with dust, and which the mulatto observed was "very much like de desert of Arabey." At Sheffield I was put into Ensign's pleasure [w]aggon, with a decent looking man on the same seat—the negro was put into the back seat, and the dirty fellow with him, —upon whom I had the pleasure of spitting in my turn. At Norfolk [Connecticut] we found no dinner ready for us, and were obliged to wait for it till about four o'clock. Then I got into the stage, and about half past eleven in the evening arrived at Hartford. —At half past six the next morning I was on my way to Boston and about twelve o'clock at night I saw the rows of lamps along the great western avenue and beyond them those of the Cambridge and Charlesto[w]n bridges. We entered Boston over the great western avenue which is not yet finished. It is an immense causey of a mile and a half in length over a kind of bay made by [the] Charles River part of which is sometimes left bare at the ebbing of the tide. It is built by driving piles into the mud and erecting on them a causey of solid stone with openings beneath for the tide to pass and return. At half past twelve I got into Boston. —I am now at Mrs. Vose's.[1] Yesterday in the afternoon Mr. [Willard] Phillips called on me in a chaise and carried me to Waltham. —We passed by the seat of Mr. Otis a fine large building on a smooth round eminence at a little distance from the road with a wood on the west. The approach to it was through a gravelled road of about an eighth of a mile in length with a thick dark row of trees and shrubbery on either side.[2] —He took me to the seat of Mr. Lyman a Boston merchant who has acquired great wealth in the India trade—[3] the father of that Mr. Lyman who wrote the book about Italy.[4] It is a perfect paradise— Phillips tells me that there is not a country seat in the United States on which so much expense has been laid out. The owner is continually engaged in making improvements and alterations the annual cost of which is estimated at not less than twenty thousand dollars. The house is a handsome building shaded with exotick trees—the mountain ash of Europe— with its large numerous cymes of red berries—the English beech with its smooth coleus-coloured stem and purple foliage— Here I saw the Chinese Sumach—a sort of apple tree which Phillips called the crab apple—a pretty tree load[ed] with fruit of a delicate light yellowish red colour, about twice the size of a thorn berry—& various other shrubs whose names I did not learn. In front of the house, to the south was an artificial piece of water winding about and widening into a lake, with a little island of pines in it, an elegant bridge crossing it, and swans swimming on the surface. —A hard rolled walk, by the side of a brick wall, about ten feet in height and covered with peach and apricot espaliers which seemed to grow to it, like the creeping sumach to the bark of an elm—

led us to a grove of young forest trees on the top of [an] eminence in the midst of which was a Chinese temple— North of the house was a park, with a few American deer in it and a large herd of spotted deer—a beautiful animal imported from Bengal. —We visited the green-house. Here were pine apples gro[wing. T]he rafters were covered with the grape vine of Europe whose clusters were nearly ripe. —Here was an American aloe whose ensiform leaves are as thick and as large as I am—a species of datura with large white flowers of the size of a half pint tumbler—and a thousand other curious matters—

More than a hundred acres lie about this seat without any enclosure most of which is fine smooth turf with occasional cornfields— We took tea at Mr. Lyman's, with several agreeable ladies. —They said there was some elegant poetry in the last Idle Man—[5]

Phillips has seen my thing—and tells me it will go well.[6]

Your affectionate husband

W. C. BRYANT

MANUSCRIPT: NYPL–GR ADDRESS: Mrs. Frances Bryant / Great Barrington / Mass / Via Hartford POSTAL ANNOTATION: 12½ DOCKETED: W. C. B. from Boston PUBLISHED (*in part*): *Life*, I, 171–173.

1. Peter Bryant had often stayed, with fellow-members of the legislature, at Mrs. Vose's boardinghouse, which was first on School Street and later on Franklin Street. He and Cullen were there in July 1819 when the doctor was treated for hemorrhages by his friends, Drs. Warren and Jackson. See 57.3.

2. "Oakley," at Watertown, the country home of Harrison Gray Otis (1765–1848, Harvard 1783), then United States senator from Massachusetts and later mayor of Boston.

3. "Waltham House," the estate of Theodore Lyman (1753–1832), was described by the landscape architect Andrew Jackson Downing as one of the earliest and most celebrated country residences in the United States, remarkable for "extent, elegance of arrangement, and the highest order and keeping, . . . bear[ing] witness to a refined and elegant taste in rural improvement." *A Treatise on the Theory and Practice of Landscape Gardening Adapted to North America . . .* , 4th ed. (New York and London, 1850), pp. 41, 44.

4. Theodore Lyman, Jr. (1792–1849, Harvard 1810), later (1833–1835) mayor of Boston, had spent some years in Europe and written two travel books. Bryant no doubt refers to *The Political State of Italy* (Boston, 1820).

5. Bryant's own "Green River."

6. Though Bryant spent nearly two weeks at Boston and Cambridge, in all likelihood reporting further experiences to his wife, this is his only surviving account of his visit. At the home of Richard Dana's brother Edmund Trowbridge Dana (1779–1859, Harvard 1800) in Cambridge he met Edward Channing and the Danas' brother-in-law, Washington Allston (1779–1843, Harvard 1800). See Richard Dana to Bryant, May 10, 1859, in *Life*, II, 126. There the poet was coached by Phillips and his new friends, who were eager that he distinguish himself on August 30. His audience that noon in the First Congregational Church of Cambridge included Secretary of State John Quincy Adams, Dr. William Ellery Channing, President John Thornton Kirkland of Harvard, Professor Edward Everett, Gen. Timothy Pickering, Justice Lemuel Shaw, and perhaps Ralph Waldo Emerson, a Harvard senior. Although Bryant read "The

Ages" in what one listener recalled later as a quiet, monotonous delivery demanding close attention, he was warmly applauded. Another auditor reported that the poem was "generally considered the finest that had ever been spoken before the Phi Beta Kappa Society." On the other hand, periodical notices were either perfunctory or ill-informed. *The Galaxy* for August 31 called Bryant's carefully wrought Spenserians "blank verse"; the *Columbian Centinel* found them, surprisingly, "replete . . . with patriotic sentiments." *Life,* I, 174–175; Rusk, *Emerson,* p. 87; "Youth," pp. 262–263. Richard Dana's reassuring letter of November 4, 1821, struck a balance: "You must not think that there are but two or three to relish your longest poem. I've heard a good many out of those I know express themselves in quite warm praise, for Americans, about it." MHS.

73. *To* Messrs. Hilliard and Metcalf[1]

Boston—Sept 4th 1821.—

Gentlemen—

I have made Willard Phillips Esq. of Boston my agent to superintend the publication and sale of my poems which are now in your press.[2] —You will therefore observe his directions, concerning the work, and deliver to him or to such persons as he shall order the whole impression or any number of copies.

Yours &c

William C. Bryant.

MANUSCRIPT: MHS ADDRESS: Messrs. Hilliard & Metcalf / Boston / Massachusetts.

1. Publishers of the *NAR,* as well as of Bryant's *Poems* (1821).
2. Bryant makes it clear that his slim volume of eight poems was submitted to a publisher only five days after his Harvard recitation, and before he left for home. This suggests that he had brought with him from Great Barrington revised versions of "Thanatopsis" (with introduction and conclusion added) and "Inscription for the Entrance to a Wood," had made minor changes in "To a Waterfowl" and "Translation of a Fragment of Simonides"—all first published in the *NAR*—and, adding "Green River" from *The Idle Man* and "The Yellow Violet," which Channing still held unpublished, had rounded out his little collection with "The Ages" and a "Song," later entitled "The Hunter of the West," also previously unpublished.

74. *To* Richard H. Dana

Great Barrington   Sept. 15th. 1821.

My dear Sir

Yours of the 8th. I received day before yesterday, and today the copy of my poems. I am definitely obliged to you for the trouble you have taken with them—and submit as quickly as you could wish to your restoration of the altered passages. As to *the pale realms of shade,* I have not a word to say in its defense. I dislike it as much as you can, and I had a secret misgiving of heart when I wrote it.[1] I am now engaged with all my might in reviewing your book [*The Idle Man*] and will send on the fruit of my labours soon. I sent a communication concerning the Idle Man to the Editors of the N. Y. Spectator, a paper which has a wider circulation in the country than any other, printed at New York.[2] One of my friends told me some time since that he had seen it very favourably noticed in one of the Albany papers. I am glad you do not mean to be discouraged by any symptoms of coldness with which the public have received it at New York. —If it goes off well in Boston, and at the South, there is no fear that it will not soon do well enough in New York. The fires kindled at both ends of the pile will meet at last and be hottest in the middle.

Mrs. Bryant and myself will be very glad to see you and your lady here, whenever the pursuit of health, or of pleasure, shall draw you into the country. When you come, we shall expect that the scenery of our region will give birth to something for the Idle Man.[3]

In the mean time, I send you something of my own for your next No. It is a poem which I found unfinished among my papers on my return from Boston, and added the latter half of it on purpose for your work. —You see my head runs upon the Indians— The very mention of them once used to make me sick—perhaps because those who undertook to make a poetical use of them have made a terrible butchery of the subject. —I think however, at present, a great deal might be done with them.—[4]

My compliments to Mrs. Dana & your Brother and Mr. Channing and Mr. Phillips and all my friends at Cambridge.—

Your friend
WILLIAM C. BRYANT.

You may give what name you please to the poem.—

MANUSCRIPT: NYPL–GR PUBLISHED (in part): Life, I, 177.

1. Seeing Bryant's poems through the press, Dana and his friends restored many earlier readings which they thought better than Bryant's hasty revisions. On September 8 Dana wrote him (MHS), "I believe that a poet should not be allowed to alter in cold blood—he grows finical. . . . Forgive me for the liberty I took part in, & I will forgive you your bad alterations, and we will shake hands." The phrase, "The pale realms of shade," in "Thanatopsis," appeared in the 1821 Poems as "the pale realms of death," and in subsequent editions as "that mysterious realm." See Poems (1876), p. 23.

2. Letter 75.

3. Dana wrote in his September 8 letter, "I long to be clambering some of your grand rocks with you; &, the lord willing, I will before the leaves turn red & yellow once more."

4. The untitled verses enclosed in this letter were given by Dana the title, "A Walk at Sunset," and published in The Idle Man, 1, No. 3 (1821), 74–76. This was the first of five poems concerned with Indians and their legends published by Bryant between 1821 and 1824. One may only ponder which earlier poets had, in Bryant's opinion, made "terrible butchery" of Indian subjects, for the noble (or the brutal) savage had figured often in English poetry since he had appeared in Spenser's The Faerie Queene and Milton's Paradise Lost, and he had been a favorite subject of Bryant's American predecessors, such as Joel Barlow, Timothy Dwight, Philip Freneau,

Francis Hopkinson, and Sarah Morton. See Benjamin Bissell, *The American Indian in English Literature of the Eighteenth Century* (New Haven: Yale University Press, 1925), pp. 163–211, *passim*.

75. *To* Messrs. Lewis and Stone, for the COMMERCIAL ADVERTISER[1]

[Great Barrington, cSeptember 15, 1821]

I lately met with the second number of the Idle Man, published in New-York. I was not prepared to expect much from it, as most of the attempts of our countrymen in that way of writing, have been decided failures. Although my curiosity induced me to look into it, I had made up my mind, resolutely, that I would not like it. —I therefore dipped into it—read a page or two—liked it—read farther to find something wrong—and at length became so delighted with it, that I could not lay it down until I had finished the perusal. I immediately bought the first number, which I found equally interesting with the other. I owe this public testimony to the merits of a writer from whom I have received at once so much pleasure and improvement. If choice and elegant diction, and a quick and deep sensibility to all that is beautiful in nature, or high and holy in feeling, are any recommendation to a work, I am sure the public will give the Idle Man their warmest patronage. The tender and delicate tone of sentiment, that runs through the article entitled *Domestic Life*, the deep pathos of *The Son*, the wit of *The Hypocondriack*, the contemplative and gentle beauty of the lines *Written in Spring*, are enough to fix the character of the author, as one who must do honor to our literature. It is upon works like these—the fruits of original, but mature and cultivated talent, that our country must rely to disprove the scandals circulated among foreigners, concerning the state of letters in this country. I have seldom met with any writer who employs a style so unaffected and unambitious, and at the same time so strikingly elegant, as the author of the Idle Man. There is no confusion of Metaphor, no vague and indeterminate phraseology, no false brilliancy; but every word adds to the meaning; his conceptions are brought out in all their force and freshness, nothing is chilled, nothing is obscured, all lies before the mind with the distinctness and vividness of a landscape in a clear pure atmosphere, and under a bright morning sun.

Since I read the Idle Man, I have seen favorable notices of it in the newspapers in different parts of the Union, but not one in those of the city of New-York. I am surprised that the inhabitants of this polished metropolis should be so insensible to the merit of native genius among themselves, and that they alone should withhold their patronage from a work which does them so much honor. For my part, I hope that the writer will meet with such encouragement, that he will long continue to entertain me and my friends with his beautiful speculations on life and manners.

Y.[2]

MANUSCRIPT: NYPL–GR (incomplete draft) TEXT: New York *Spectator*, September 21, 1821.

1. The daily New York *Commercial Advertiser* had as its semi-weekly edition the New York *Spectator*, in which this letter was printed.

2. Bryant occasionally used the initial *Y* in later anonymous writings. See, for example, Letter 86.

76. *To* Willard Phillips

Great Barrington   Oct   1st   1821.

Dear Sir—

I send you my *critique* on the Idle Man.[1] I hope it is not too late. —Since I returned there has been a Term of the Supreme Court in this County whic[h] lasted a fortnight and at which by good luck I had a little business—and another of the Court of Sessions—and the second No. of the Idle Man got carried off by somebody and it was some time before I could get it again &c. &c.—all which must be my apology for the delay. —The review I submit to your revision. —Draw your pen through any part you please, without mercy, and interline where you please. —Will you be so good as to see that about a dozen copies or more of my poems are reserved for me to give my friends.—

Yours sincerely—

WM. C. BRYANT

MANUSCRIPT: MHS ADDRESS: Willard Phillips Esq—.

1. This critical notice, written for the *NAR* at Dana's request, was not published therein because, in Dana's words, his "enemies" among the members of the "Club" (Edward Everett in particular) asked Phillips to "qualify or omit the praise, & retain the censure." Dana to Phillips, December 2, 1821, MHS; 78.1.

77. *To* Gulian C. Verplanck[1]

Great Barrington   Oct. 10, 1821.

Sir—

Yours of the 4th inst together with the N. Y. American of the same date and a copy of your Anniversary Discourse[2] have just reached me.

I had before seen the greater part of your Discourse in the shape of extracts, in various publications, but I am happy in an opportunity to read, in its original connection, the whole of a work the free and liberal spirit of which, to say nothing of its other merits too generally acknowledged to need any testimony of mine, had already so much interested me.

Whether you think highly of my poems or otherwise I hope at least that you think more of them than I was able to find in the paper you sent me. On unfolding it I found the two inside pages entirely blank—through some blunder, I suppose, of the press. I conclude however from the intimation in your letter that the notice was a favourable one, and I am grateful for the assistance afforded me at a time when it may do me much service.[3]

> I am Sir
> With much respect
> Yours &c
> WM. C. BRYANT

MANUSCRIPTS: NYPL–Berg (final); NYPL–GR (draft) ADDRESS: Gulian C. Verplanck Esq / New York POSTMARK (*in script*): Great Barrington / October 11th—1821 POSTAL ANNOTATION: 12½ PUBLISHED: *Life*, I, 179.

1. This is the first of more than fifty letters Bryant wrote to Gulian Crommelin Verplanck (1786–1870, Columbia 1801) during their intermittent friendship of half a century. See "Bryant's Correspondents."

2. *An Anniversary Discourse, Delivered Before the New-York Historical Society, December 7, 1818* (New York, 1818). Fifty years later Bryant characterized this early declaration of cultural independence as "one of the happiest examples in our language of the class of compositions to which it belongs." "Verplanck," p. 217.

3. Dana had sent a copy of Bryant's *Poems* to Verplanck, who wrote for the New York *American* of October 4 the notice to which Bryant refers. Here Verplanck was the first critic to suggest a similarity between Bryant's poetry and that of Wordsworth. See Verplanck to Bryant, October 4, 1821, NYPL–BG.

78. *To* Richard H. Dana

Great Barrington   Oct   30   1821

My dear Sir.

I had made up my mind to defer writing to you till I had received the 3d. No. of the *Idle Man*. But it does not come, and as I am bound to answer your letter and the grave inquiry in it, I may as well do it now I am in the humour. I am sorry that my review was so late, but if you knew how many rascally accidents laid their heads together to [thw]art and delay me, and the anxiety I felt about it, you would forgive me even more freely perhaps than you do now. Your question about the Letter from Town I am glad you have put to me as you did for I should not certainly deserve many of your thanks, if in reviewing your work I had not been contented with stating such objections to it as might occur to me, but had set the invention of others to work to look them up for me.[1] Truly and frankly then—the objection did occur to me on reading the article. I promised myself at the beginning more than I found at the conclusion, and the whole affected me like a sort of disappointment. I am far from denying that there is merit in the article—spirit & sense and fine touches—but the plan as it seemed to me was faulty. It is possible however that I have expressed myself on this point in the review, more strongly than I ought or meant to do. Indeed I did not think any of the criticisms I passed upon the book when I pretended to find fault with it, of much importance. But I would not speak of its merits with less enthusiasm than

I felt, and when I had done so, I bethought myself of looking up something to find fault with, in order to secure to my review the reputation of impartiality, and induce reade[rs] to give more credit to those parts in which I had praised the book. Besides I knew your work did not need to have any defects which might happen to be in it kept out of sight through tenderness to its character, and that any appearance of a disposition to do such a thing would be very silly and ill-judged. Thus, though my objections were such as I honestly believed in, I thought them of very trifling consequence, and if they are stated in the review in such a manner as to make a different impression, for heaven's sake let them be qualified and softened down into what I meant they should be—or, if thought best, struck out altogether. I will leave this task to the practical genius of Mr. Phillips, if he will undertake it—and I know him to be too friendly to the success of your work to suffer any thing to go to the press which shall tend to its disadvantage.[2]

The notice of the *Idle Man* in the N. Y. Spectator was mine.[3] The Commercial Advertiser and the N. Y. S. are printed at the same office— the one a daily and the other a semi weekly paper. Since that was published I have seen another very favourable and extremely sensible and well-written notice of your work in the N. Y. Daily Advertiser. I had written before the receipt of your last, an article on the Idle Man for the Northern Whig printed at Hudson,[4] and another for one of the Albany papers[5]—but I have kept them by me that I might say something about the 3rd No. You need not return the manuscript of my article for the N. A. R. I believe that I shall be able with the help of the original notes of it to get in a notice of the 3d No. of the Idle Man.—

In the mean time I will trouble you with a little commission— I want about 20 copies of my poems. Will you be so kind as to see them packed up, and directed to *George Whitney Esq*. Stockbridge, to be left at Hicks's Tavern—and sent by the driver of the *Springfield stage*. I do not like to have them sent me immediately by the way of Hartford because there is a delay of a day there, and they might get mislaid—

Will you also have the goodness to give a copy for me to Prof. Norton who has had the politeness to send me some of his publications.[6] I should be glad also to get a copy to my friend the Hon. William Baylies of Bridgewater—

I have just taken yr. 3d No. from the Post office.—

Yours truly, W   C   BRYANT

MANUSCRIPT: NYPL–GR ADDRESS: Richard H. Dana Esq. / Cambridge / *Mass*. POSTMARK (*in script*): Great Barrington / November 1st— POSTAL ANNOTATION: 12½ DOCKETED: W. C. Bryant / *Oct   20   1821*.

1. On October 8 Dana had written Bryant indignantly of those members of the *NAR* "Club" who wished Phillips to modify Bryant's praise for *The Idle Man*. Worried lest his favorable criticism be toned down and his adverse comments let stand,

Dana asked if hostile reaction elsewhere had influenced Bryant's opinion of the article called "Letter from Town." MHS. See 76.1.

2. Subsequently Dana demanded that Bryant's review be printed in the *NAR* as written, or not at all. On these terms Edward Everett, then the editor, rejected his article. Dana to Phillips, December 2, 1821, and Dana to Bryant, December 9, 1821, MHS.

3. Letter 75.

4. Since no copy of the *Northern Whig* for this period has been recovered, it is uncertain whether Bryant completed and submitted this article. A short fragment of such a letter is in NYPL–GR.

5. See Letter 79.

6. Andrews Norton (1786–1853, Harvard 1804), Dexter Professor of Biblical Criticism and Sacred Literature at Harvard, was a leading Unitarian and a poet of modest pretensions. It is not known which publications he sent to Bryant.

79. *To* the Editor of the Albany EVENING GAZETTE[1]

[Great Barrington, cNovember 15, 1821]

In the Evening Gazette of Saturday last I observed a notice of the 2nd No. of the Idle Man, which the Editor says is written on the plan of the Sketch-Book,[2] and that the author has copied the style of Leigh Hunt[3] Hazlitt[4] and other aimers at simplicity.

I went home in some pain for the poor gentleman whose intellectual poverty had forced him to adopt the plan of one author and the manner of another and being curious to know what sort of patchwork would come of all this I took up the Idle Man which I had lately purchased but had only hastily looked over. —I must confess that I was unable, even with the assistance of the light I had received from the editor of the Gazette, to see in what way the plan of the Sketch book had been followed or the style of Hunt and Hazlitt imitated. —If the Editor is speaking after the manner of printers, the plan of the Sketch book has indeed been followed in a considerable degree—the work appears in a cover of exactly the same colour—the paper is of much the same whiteness and fineness and the type is large brilliant and beautiful. But here ends the identity of plan in these two works. The Sketch book is composed of the recollections narratives and reflections of a travelled man, wrought up into elaborate and highly-finished essays. The Idle Man is the vehicle of the speculations of a gentleman of literature and observation upon all subjects connected with manners, and letters—the communications of his friends and occasional articles in poetry— It is no more upon the plan of the Sketch book than the Edinburgh review upon the plan of Blackwood's Magazine. —Then, with respect to the style, I could see no traces of an imitation of Hunt and it is actually ungenerous to charge him with having copied Hazlitt, to which his manner is as unlike as the ancient Grecian costume is to the dress of a Merry Andrew. The truth is that his sentences are not made in a mill, nor has he trimmed or stretched them as Procrustes did his captives without regard to [the] vital spirit that was in them. If this is a kind of style with which the Editor of the Gazette is not familiar let him at least be careful how he classes it with others, and remember that there is a sort of writing equally distinct from the tame and the extravagant.—

The Editor says that the Idle Man contains many acute observations but often carelessly expressed—I should think them very carefully expressed. —The author is careful to body them forth in all the vividness and beauty of nature, and to give them the same freshness of feeling with which they first presented themselves to his mind. —He has not it is true studied to be uninteresting—he has not thrown cold water on his own conceptions and chilled them down to the standard of those who criticize mechanically and by a few coarse rules without a single spark of sensibility to what is grand beautiful or touching.

I cannot speak with the same confidence of the poetry in the Idle Man, part of which the Editor extracts as a confirmation of the position that the author belongs to the school of Hunt, as I have no pretensions to the character [of] a critick in that sort of composition. Whether it bears out the Editor in such a charge the readers of the Idle Man will judge.—[5]

[unsigned]

MANUSCRIPT: NYPL–GR (draft).

1. No printed version of this letter has been located in the Albany *Evening Gazette*; the text is taken from the manuscript draft.

2. Washington Irving's collection of loosely related essays and tales, *The Sketch Book of Geoffrey Crayon, Gent.*, appeared in New York in seven parts during 1819 and 1820. Wright, *American Fiction 1774–1850*, p. 151.

3. James Henry Leigh Hunt (1784–1859), whose essays in the *Indicator*, 1819–1821, fixed him in conservative American minds as the leader of a "Cockney School" of writing.

4. William Hazlitt (1778–1830) was then best known for his several courses of lectures on English literature and drama, published between 1818 and 1821.

5. The poetry alluded to was mostly Bryant's own. The complaint that it followed the "school of Hunt" was a common reaction of readers conditioned by eighteenth-century neo-classical verse to contemporary romantic poetry, particularly that of Wordsworth, Keats, and Shelley.

80. *To* Richard H. Dana

Great Barrington   Nov   21, 1821.

My dear sir.

I have two of your letters by me unanswered.[1]

I send you herewith some remarks on the 3d No. Idle Man, and have given directions as nearly right as I could for their insertion in the main article.[2] I think your Edward & Mary will take well. You have addressed the sympathies of a large class of readers. Your pages will be turned by fair hands, and gentle eyes that have seen thirteen summers, and mayhap some that have seen thirty will dissolve over the sentimental narrative. You have now nothing to do but [write on?]. Somebody has come out in the N. Y. Spectator in raptures with this No. From his style and his verbal criticisms, I take him to be Stone, the principal Editor.[3] The other day I saw an extract from the Article on domestic life in the N. Y. Daily Advertiser.

I thought of adding something to my remarks on the Letter from Town intimating that my objections related only to the plan, and commending its other qualities; and I prepared a paragraph for that purpose. But on reading your last, and reflection that it was important to give no handle to any body to say that the review was a partial one, I concluded not to send it. As the Letter is the least important article you have written, you will I hope be content to let it be sacrificed to appease the literary enemies you mention, as magicians are said, on certain occasions, to make a burnt offering of a dog to his imperial majesty.

Coleman[4] was always a mere verbal critic. His blunder about *fugitive* was a good one, and I hope will make him more careful. The phrase "life takes of," I confess I do not like. I believe that I have seen a precedent for it in some old writer; but when I met with it in the Idle Man, I looked at the passage again to see if I had read it right. You will see that I have animadverted a little upon these things in the second additional paragraph of my review.

You will please to see that the heading of my Article is altered so as to include the 3d No. —Give my thanks to Mr. Phillips for his elegant but partial review of my book.[5] Walsh[6] says the review is in bad taste;—meaning thereby I suppose that it is not in his own taste. Your partiality for my book makes you too severe upon the public because of its unpopularity. There is nothing about the principal poem[7] that would be likely to catch the public favour. A didactic subject, an unusual stanza, a deliberate avoidance of that balanced monotony and jingle that many ears are tickled with,—all these are sadly in its way,—and for aught I know a hundred other things. So I have made up my mind not to be disappointed if it should not be generally much thought of; the approbation of a few whose judgment I value most, as it was much beyond what I expected, so it is enough in all reason to content me.[8] I am sorry you have had so much trouble with the copies I requested you to send. I supposed they might be entered on the way-bill in the same manner as a passenger and sent to the place to which they were directed without difficulty. It is practised so in this part of the country, and packages trunks &c. are often received by us in the stages. If you have not sent them on take no more trouble with them. I will get our representative to call for them in the winter.

I send you another poem, which I made up for you as I have the others, drawing it from among my old papers and putting it into shape.[9] When you write me again will you tell me who is the author of the review of Sewall's collection of hymns in the Christian Disciple? Perhaps you know that I wrote a few for that compilation. They are enumerated in that review, but are said to be too fine for the sanctuary. I am half inclined, myself, to suspect that some of them are not written in the properest style for devotional poetry.[10]

I hope that you will have the pleasure of enjoying a triumph at last over those friends of yours who say your book ought not to go, by convincing them that it *must* go. It will be unfortunate, however, if the literary men of this country are to be divided into parties; for, when a good book comes out it is a pity that it should not obtain all the patronage that would naturally be given to such things. Yet one good grows out of this evil, the zeal of its friends is quickened, and a little party feeling is better than indifference.

My regards to all my friends in your quarter.

[signature missing]

MANUSCRIPT: NYPL–GR ADDRESS: Richard H. Dana Esq / Cambridge / Mass. POSTMARK *(in script)*: Gt   Barrington, Nov. 23— POSTAL ANNOTATION: *50* DOCKETED: W. C. Bryant, Nov 2[1]   1821.

1. November 4, and 9, 1821. MHS.

2. For the *NAR*. Willard Phillips reported to Bryant on February 17, 1822, the final disposition of his review of Dana's *The Idle Man*: "For various and weighty reasons your piece upon the Idle Man was suppressed. It was gravely settled that you praised the Idle Man *plus quam satis* [more than enough], and more than would go down." NYPL–BG; see 76.1, and Letter 78.

3. William Leete Stone (1792–1844) was also editor of the weekly *Spectator*'s parent daily, the New York *Commercial Advertiser*.

4. William Coleman (1766–1829), editor since 1801 of the New York *Evening Post*, one of whose stated aims was to "cultivate a taste for sound literature." Nevins, *Evening Post*, p. 99.

5. Phillips' notice of Bryant's *Poems* in the *NAR* (13 [October 1821], 380–384) was so enthusiastic as to draw the charge of partiality from those who knew him as both critic and manager of the book's sales.

6. Robert M. Walsh (1784–1859), founder in 1811 of the first American quarterly, *The American Review of History and Politics*, became in 1820 editor and publisher of Philadelphia's leading political newspaper, the *National Gazette*, and in 1827 of the *American Quarterly Review*. A facile and often quoted political writer, Walsh was nevertheless a heavy-handed literary critic of no lasting reputation. See Letters 159, 194, 195.

7. "The Ages."

8. Dana's vain efforts to get Verplanck's notice of Bryant's *Poems* reprinted in Boston newspapers led to his comment, in a letter to Bryant on November 4, 1821: "The truth is, you know, that real first-rate American poetry is as cheap & of great & easy growth amongst us as pumpkins. We can talk about the Western country, the Ontario & Mississippi, our canals & steam-boats, but are as cold as oysters about all the higher movements of the soul;—there is nothing here within sight of a man, but what God shows him in nature, to satisfy the reaches of his mind or longings of his heart." MHS.

9. "The West Wind," *The Idle Man*, 2, No. 1 (1822), 155. See *Poems* (1876), pp. 41–42. The manuscript is unrecovered.

10. Though Dana did not identify this reviewer, the notice in *The Christian Disciple and Theological Review* (N.S. 3 [July–August 1821], 364) was so similar to Henry D. Sewall's earlier reactions to Bryant's hymns as to suggest that he might have inspired the reviewer's critical judgments.

III

The Roads Diverge
1822–1825
(LETTERS 81 TO 127)

WITH THE PUBLICATION OF HIS BOOK of verse in September 1821 Bryant had, within four years of his first appearance in the *North American Review*, earned some fame as both poet and critic, and found friends at Cambridge, Boston, and New York who watched his progress sympathetically. Meanwhile, he made his living at the law and followed a course which, among his Berkshire County contemporaries, not seldom led to the legislature and to the national Congress. As tithing man, town clerk, Supreme Judicial Court Councilor, justice of the peace, clerk of the center school district, secretary of the Berkshire Federal–Republican party convention, and occasional public orator, he was often in the public eye.

During his bachelor years in Great Barrington, Bryant had suppressed his distaste for what he termed to his father "skulking about *in holes and corners of the earth.*" For a time he thought he had broken the "spell" of his early enchantment with the "dear, dear witchery of song." As a justice of the peace, he settled his neighbors' disputes; as an attorney, he pressed their claims in the county courthouse at Lenox. He tilted with legal opponents in the courtroom and quarreled with them outside, and he caricatured their craggy faces on drafts of his letters and poems. In the guise of a sophisticated social critic, he ridiculed in newspaper essays his neighbors' oddities and affectations in home, office, pulpit, and barnyard. He attended agricultural fairs and Fourth of July festivities, danced at parties and balls, played whist, and poked fun at popular songs and common gossip. And he sang to the Barrington girls he courted, as he once had to those of Worthington and Bridgewater.

But Cullen's marriage in 1821, the birth a year later of a daughter, and his gradual assumption after his father's death of the responsibility for the well-being of his younger brothers and sisters, on the one hand, and the insistence of his literary friends, on the other, that he increase his poetic output, sharpened his dilemma. He had defined this earlier for Edward Channing: "You certainly need use no apology to one who does not follow the study of the law very eagerly, because he likes other studies better; and yet devotes little of his time to them, for fear that they should give him a dislike to law."

Between 1822 and 1824 Bryant busied himself with several diverse activities which, though they broadened his preparation for a later career, must at the time have seemed, even to him, to be at variance with his natural genius.

The liberalizing influences of Peter Bryant and Samuel Howe on Cullen's religious thought, and of William Baylies on his sense of social responsibility, were enhanced by his friendships with the Sedgwicks, especially Henry and Theodore II. Bryant's long report to Andrews Norton at Cambridge on the condition of religion in Berkshire County in 1822 defined the beliefs which underlay his expression thereafter. His public appeal, at the close of 1823, for aid to the Greek revolutionaries in their struggle against Turkish rule led to the composition of several poems hailing their cause, and showed his growing concern with world affairs. His study of French with a sometime Napoleonic officer, L[ouis?] Boutin, joined in by his wife and child, initiated his acquisition of half a dozen modern languages during the following decade. And occasional letters to village and city newspapers reflected an impulse to propose opinions on social, political, and literary matters to a wider audience than that of the *North American Review*.

The apparent paucity of his verse composition during this period is evidenced by his accepting a dare from several lawyer friends to write a political farce for the stage, only to lay it forever aside, and his quitting midway the composition of a long narrative poem on a mythic theme from Cotton Mather's *Magnalia Christi Americana* of the early-eighteenth century. Not until he was asked at the end of 1823 to furnish verses on a continuing basis to the *United States Literary Gazette* at Boston, and offered payment for them, did Bryant recover his best mode of composition.

In the meantime, his friendly critics had not forgotten him. Dana and Phillips, worried at his distraction with politics and other matters, wrote of their concern to the Sedgwick brothers. Accounting to Bryant in October 1823 on the slender sales of his 1821 *Poems*, Phillips remarked, "I wish you to write something more by and by that with these shall make a volume that can be bound." And he confided the following spring to Henry Sedgwick at New York City, "I am apprehensive that he grows careless of poetry, and will let his talent sleep." Their encouragement brought Bryant to visit the Sedgwicks in New York in April 1824. At Robert's home he met Cooper, Halleck, Sands, Sparks, and other busy writers. Here he began to think he might make a living at the literary career he had followed only fitfully for a decade.

His visit to New York that spring did not, by itself, impel Bryant to abandon the law. His final frustration with "legal chicanery," as he later called it, came in the fall, when a verdict for slander he had twice won for a client, before first judge and then jury, was overturned on appeal by a hair-splitting decision. But his resolution to quit his profession coincided closely with published praise of his poems in the *Literary Gazette* and of those which were reprinted in Great Britain. When the Sedgwick brothers invited him to revisit them in the spring of 1825, while they completed arrangements for him to edit a new literary monthly, the *New-York Review*, Bryant went eagerly.

Returning to Berkshire after successful negotiations in the metropolis, Bryant exulted over his imminent escape from the "disagreeable drudgery" of the law. Charles Sedgwick wrote to his brother Henry, "Every time I saw him, every muscle of his face teemed with happiness. He kissed the children, talked much and smiled at every thing. He said more about your kindness to him than I have ever heard him express before, in regard to any body." On May 1, 1825, Bryant left Great Barrington and the law for an editorial career in New York City which would occupy him for the rest of his life, extending over more than half a century.

81. [*To* Nathaniel Preston?][1]

Great Barrington   March 12   1822.

Dear Sir,—

As you seem determined not to stand midwife at the bringing forth of *John Calvin* & the *Saybrook platform*[2] in Sheffield,—I have sent you some prescriptions for retarding the parturition.— I think however that they will come into the world too late to do much harm and that the wonderful birth will prove to be nothing more than a super foetation, or stillborn perhaps—or at most that the only signs of life attending it will be the few feeble wailings it may utter before it is silent forever—

To be serious however as you are in want of books on the Unitarian controversy I will recommend some and others I will send you.— In the first place then—I recommend the Old and New Testaments as the best Unitarian books I am acquainted with— Read the 17th chapter of St. John's Gospel, the perusal of which eight years since convinced me of the inferiority and subordination of the Son to the Father.[3]

I send you Dr. Ware's Letters a good summary and defence of those points of Doctrine on which rational Christians differ from the orthodox, with the exception of the Doctrine of the Trinity which is not treated of in that publication.[4]

On the subject of the Trinity particularly, I se[nd yo]u a pamphlet written by Jacob Norton who belongs to the *Arian* division of Unitarians —those who hold to the preexistence of Christ his superangelic nature &c—points which are denied by us plain humanitarians. I wish I could send you a better book on this subject—but as he attacks the Trinitarian hypothesis with considerable spirit, and gives a sort of review of the text commonly cited to support it—and moreover as it is the only connected treatise I have on the subject I have concluded to send it to you—[5] There is a book entitled *Yates's Reply to Wardlaw*, which contains a most admirable argument on this subject and which I hope to own before long.—[6]

I have several Numbers of the *Unitarian Miscellany* which carry on a sort of skirmishing warfare on the fra[il]ties of orthodoxy.[7] —If what I have sent you sh[ould] agree with your digestion better than the knotty and ligneous points of Calvinism—I will send them also. —With those sentiments of esteem which I trust ever [entitles] those whose independence of intellect leaves them to examine for themselves the subjects which interest them most

I am sir—

Yr friend

W. C. Bryant

MANUSCRIPT: NYPL–GR (draft).

1. This letter was probably intended for Dr. Nathaniel Preston, postmaster at Sheffield, Massachusetts. See Letter 90.

2. New England's "peculiar church polity" was codified at the Massachusetts synod of 1648 in the Cambridge Platform, formalizing Puritan theocratic rule. In 1708 its tenets were subscribed to by the Connecticut Congregationalists in the adoption of the Saybrook Platform. See *The American Puritans: Their Prose and Poetry*, ed. Perry Miller (Garden City: Doubleday [1956]), pp. 37, 121.

3. At the Last Supper, Jesus raised his eyes toward Heaven and said, "Father, . . . This is eternal life: to know thee who alone art truly God." John 17:1–3.

4. Henry Ware, Sr., *Letters Addressed to Trinitarians and Calvinists, Occasioned by Dr. Woods' Letters to Unitarians* . . . (Cambridge, 1820).

5. Jacob Norton, *Things as They Are; or, Trinitarianism Developed* . . . (Boston, 1815).

6. James Yates, *A Vindication of Unitarianism, In Reply to Mr. Wardlaw's Discourses on the Socinian Controversy* (Glasgow, 1815; Boston, 1816). Bryant's remark that he had gained Unitarian beliefs eight years earlier suggests that he may have first met with Yates's *Reply* while studying law with Samuel Howe at Worthington. Mrs. Howe wrote later that, though her husband strongly opposed her liberal views when they were married in 1813, soon afterward Henry D. Sedgwick, a zealous Unitarian, lent him " 'Yates's Answer to Wardlaw.' This book and the New Testament he read with care, . . . comparing it with Scripture; and was entirely convinced of the truth and reasonableness of the Unitarian faith, which he afterwards held through life." Quoted in Lesley, *Recollections of My Mother*, p. 237.

7. *The Unitarian Miscellany and Christian Monitor*, published at Baltimore by the Unitarian Book Society, was edited at that time by Jared Sparks.

82.   To Richard H. Dana

Great Barrington   March 28th, 1822.

My Dear Sir

I have just received yours of the 15th inst. together with the 5th No. of the Idle Man. I ought certainly to apologize for not having written to you earlier and you would have heard from me immediately after I received your 4th No.—but you are to know that a trifling enlargement of my family took place about that time and though I can hardly tell why it should be so yet the fact is that this circumstance has kept my affairs particularly of a literary kind in a sort of hassle ever since.—[1]

I will own to you that of late I have been deterred from writing by the cause to which you allude.[2] The sorrow that I felt must attend such a loss had to me a kind of sacredness about it which I feared to violate, and I knew that I could bring no consolation.

I must not suffer you to speak so slightingly of your 4th No. The second letter from town has more than made amends for any faults of its elder brother.[3] But the story of *Thomas Thornton*[4] which I have just read has in my opinion merit of a higher, and more decided kind than any thing you have written for the Idle Man except *The Son*.[5] It has one species of merit which does more to render an author immediately popular than any other— I mean that of exciting a deep interest in the event of the story. I have great hopes from it.

You are right in believing that my principal feeling when I was made acquainted with the rejection of my review was that of regret at being disappointed in the hope I had formed that I might be of some service to you. I did not indeed feel altogether certain that it would be admitted, from what I knew of the opposition made to you by some of those concerned in the North American Review, but when I thought of the praises sometimes lavished by that work on productions which your most strenuous opposers could not think for a moment of putting in comparison with yours I must confess I hardly expected it would be refused admission. If however the reason for rejecting it was that it was badly written, it was a good one, if true, and ought to have prevailed.[6] If the article can be made to answer any purpose I hope you will not hesitate to make use of it— though I do not know of any periodical work in which it could be inserted with the hope of its doing you much good— I do not know any thing about the Literary Repository.[7] Has not the *Analectic Magazine*[8] more reputation? But of this subject you have better means of judging than I. I do not regret the labour of composing the article. I only regret that that labour has been of so little service to you.—

I hope the unpleasant sensations in the head of which you complain will make you look carefully to your health. My experience has taught me that the state of the head depends very much on that of the stomach and the condition of the stomach is again dependent on the due regulation of diet and exercise. But exercise ought to be taken at proper times. A few minutes violent exercise or half-an-hour's intense study immediately after a meal have put my head in confusion and kept it buzzing for a whole day.—

You greatly overrate the help your work receives from my verses. If the readers of your work have the same sort of feeling about the poetical part of your work that I have about that of most periodical publications, they care very little whether they read it or not. However, that you may not be out of poetry for your next number I send you what follows.[9] In the mean time you may depend on my doing every thing I can for you in the Newspapers. My regards to all my friends.

Yours truly
William C. Bryant

MANUSCRIPTS: LH (final); NYPL–GR (draft).

1. The Bryants' first child, Frances (Fanny), later Mrs. Parke Godwin, was born at Great Barrington on January 2, 1822. Dana's letter of March 15 is unrecovered.

2. Dana had apparently reported the death on February 10, at the age of thirty-four, of his wife, Ruth Charlotte (Smith) Dana, mother of four young children. *Richard H. Dana, Jr.: An Autobiographical Sketch*, ed. Robert F. Metzdorf (Hamden, Connecticut, 1953), p. 99.

3. "A [Second] Letter from Town" and "A [First] Letter from Town," reprinted in Dana, *Poems and Prose Writings* (Philadelphia and Boston, 1833), pp. 411–419, 390–401.

4. See "Tom Thornton," *ibid.*, pp. 151–220.

5. *Ibid.*, pp. 378–389.

6. See 80.2.

7. The *Literary Repository and Scientific and Critical Review* (1820–1827?), published in New York, which, in January 1821, had printed Fitz-Greene Halleck's notable elegy on his friend Joseph Rodman Drake. Adkins, *Halleck*, pp. 118–119.

8. The *Analectic Magazine*, of Philadelphia, edited during its first two years (1813–1815) by Washington Irving. Williams, *Spanish Background*, II, 5.

9. Bryant enclosed with this letter "The West Wind" (see *Poems* [1876], pp. 41–42), and "Her Last Adieu," three stanzas first composed at Bridgewater in 1814. This is the only one of his early love poems he ever offered for publication. Dana printed "The West Wind" in *The Idle Man*, 2, No. 1 (1822), 155, but seems never to have commented on "Her Last Adieu," which remains unpublished. The 1814 manuscript is in NYPL–GR. See *Life*, I, 107–118; Bryant II, "Thanatopsis," pp. 174–177.

83. *To* Richard H. Dana

Great Barrington   July 20, 1822.

Dear Sir—

I cannot tell how it is, but when I have a letter to write and at last set myself seriously about it I am always surprised at seeing how long I have delayed it. But I have infinitely less patience [when] I expect one from a friend.

I know in some measure how to feel for you under the dreadful misfortune you mention.[1] I have myself a little daughter playing under my roof and when I make your case my own I can judge of the sharpness of your sufferings. Yet you know how to apply to these sorrows the best consolations in store for them. It is true that nature must have its way, and the first burst of grief cannot be restrained, but the memory of those whom we loved so much at last becomes a sacred and cherished companion to us, that comes in aid of our virtue and comforts us under the falsehood and unkindness of the world. We find that desolate as our situation at first seemed to be, our friends are not altogether lost us; we commune with their images in our own hearts.

And then we reflect that we ought [not] to grieve, for they have past through all the sufferings that God has provided to educate and chasten those he loves, and now they can suffer no longer;—and with regard to ourselves, life has something more and better for us to do than to brood forever over the loneliness and darkness of our own lot.

I hope you will get the better of your *invisible enemies* as Dennie once called them the nerves.[2] Let me be your physician. I rec[om]mend then the air of the fields, and exercise in the garden. To talk of early rising I suppose would do no good—you and your doctor have settled that point.

The review of the Idle Man in the North American is certainly a very cautiously written production.[3] I have, as well as you, no doubt that the author was instructed where he ought to find fault, and how small a measure of reluctant praise it would do to bestow. Why should he couple the Club Room[4] with the Idle Man in that article? I cannot tell, unless it was to insinuate the notion that they were works of nearly equal merit. They seem to me oddly yoked, and I cannot see in the extracts he gives from the Club Room quite merit enough to justify his encomiums. But the thing is done, and may good come of it.

I have received the paper you forwarded to me, and about the same time somebody else sent me another like it. —The paragraph relating to me has been copied in the Newspapers in this vicinity, and people here are just beginning to enquire about my book.[5]

Miss Sedgwick's New England Tale is quite popular.[6] A second edition is in the press. I hope you like it. —You see that American productions are coming into fashion a little.

If Verplanck's plan for you should take effect I wish you a good salary, an agreeable situation and a pleasant duty.[7] —Should you visit New York this season you will not only *try* to take me in your way but will actually *do* it. Take the steam boat or a packet to Albany, —from that place the stage runs to Hartford through this town. From this place you can go home by the way of Hartford, or I will carry you [to] Stockbridge and you can go by way of Springfield.—

Remember me to all my friends in your part of the world.

Your friend
W. C. Bryant

Manuscript: NYPL–GR address: Richard H. Dana Esq. / Cambridge / Mass postmark (*in script*): Great Barrington   July 30th postal annotation: 12½.

1. Dana's letter of *c*July 1 is unrecovered. A brief quotation, apparently from this letter, in *Life*, I, 196, concerns only his comment on a notice in *Blackwood's Edinburgh Magazine* of William Roscoe's *Specimens of the American Poets* (see Note 5). Dana had evidently written of his depression over his wife's death, recorded later by his son: "To those of us who saw our father's grief, which no description we have read of agony short of madness has equalled, . . . it might well be a peculiar lasting & sacred thing." *Richard H. Dana, Jr.: An Autobiographical Sketch*, ed. Robert F. Metzdorf (Hamden, Connecticut, 1953), p. 34.

2. Joseph Dennie (1768–1812), essayist and editor of the weekly *Port Folio* at Philadelphia.

3. William H. Prescott, later the distinguished historian, had written for the *NAR*, 14 (April 1822), 319–350, a long article titled "Essay Writing" in which, having discussed in detail the form initiated in England by Addison and Steele and brought to America by Irving, he tackled the deficiencies of both the short-lived *The Club-Room* (Boston, February–July, 1820) and the principal author of *The Idle Man*. He found Dana guilty of "hopeless perversity of taste" and "mystical, vague and unintelligible phraseology," and suggested that his uniformly "amiable" and "beautiful character" could interest only the few, rather than the many (pp. 340–347). But his praise for Bryant's poetry was unrestrained: "We cannot quit the Idle Man, without expressing our obligation to the Muse, who has enriched these pages with such eloquent pictures of American scenery, as must add new and valuable treasures to descriptive poetry" (p. 349).

4. *The Club-Room* was founded in 1820 by Joseph T. Buckingham, later more successful as editor of the *New-England Magazine* (1831–1835) and the *Boston Courier* (1824–1848). Mott, *American Journalism*, pp. 187, 208, 262.

5. Early in 1822 a volume entitled *Specimens of the American Poets; with Critical Notices and a Preface,* containing the eight poems in Bryant's collection, was published at London. The editor, William Roscoe, introduced these in a laudatory notice which was copied in Berkshire County papers. On July 18 the Stockbridge *Berkshire Star* printed a letter (probably written by Bryant's friend Charles Sedgwick) from "An American," who complained, "It is not much to the credit of American discernment . . . that we do not value our diamonds till the rays of their brilliance come to us reflected back from across the Atlantic. . . . This distinguished individual is not only an American but an inhabitant of Massachusetts, and not only an inhabitant of Massachusetts, but of the County of Berkshire." The writer then quoted Roscoe's notice, including the remarks, "The publication of this small volume of poems by Mr. Bryant, will induce a belief that America is destined very speedily to become the mother of poets. . . . If the approving judgement of the English public can add any weight to Mr. Bryant's claims to the admiration of his countrymen, his Poems only require to be known to entitle him to it" (pp. 189–191). Having read a similar comment, in a notice of Roscoe's *Specimens* in *Blackwood's* for June 1822, Dana wrote Bryant, "They seem to be fully aware that you are another sort of man from those bound up with you." *Life,* I, 196.

6. [Catharine M. Sedgwick] *A New England Tale; or, Sketches of New England Character and Manners,* . . . (New York, 1822).

7. Gulian Verplanck had helped Dana arrange the publication of *The Idle Man* by Charles Wiley of New York. Subsequently Verplanck had apparently urged Dana to come to New York and take an editorial position, a suggestion he repeated four years later. See Letters 149 and 159; July, *Essential New Yorker,* p. 117.

84. *For* the BERKSHIRE STAR. *To* the Electors of the Berkshire District.[1]

[Great Barrington, *ante* October 31, 1822]

GENTLEMEN.—

I cannot resist the desire I have of saying a few words to you on the subject of the approaching election of a Member of Congress for this District.

I am no proficient in the Art of Rhetoric, and shall not be able to give you such an eloquent and florid address as I read in the Pittsfield Sun of last week, on the same subject, some parts of which exceeded my poor capacity and learning to comprehend.[2] I am only a plain man, speaking to plain men like myself, and shall be satisfied if I can state a few simple facts in such a way as to meet the approbation of those among my fellow citizens, who, like myself, make no pretensions to the character of scholars and critics. Indeed, if I were able to amuse you with a flourish of fine sentences on this occasion, it would answer no purpose for me to try; for my design is not to pervert the truth, or to deceive any man, but only to state to you my ideas on this subject in the clearest manner I am able.[3]

In the first place, then, I hope you are all aware of the importance of being represented in Congress by a man of ability and integrity. I do not know that this consideration is more important at the present time than at any other. But I know that the nation has interests, which ought always to be watched over, and should never be entrusted to the care of those whom we do not know to be perfectly capable of managing them. None of us would trust himself in a public coach, on a dangerous road, with a postillion, who, we suspected, did not know how to drive; or embark on board a vessel, even for a short voyage, with a pilot who never saw salt water before. We are guilty of a similar folly when we put the interests and welfare of our country into the hands of those with the correctness of whose political principles, or with whose capacity in a political situation, we are not acquainted.

But this is not all. The candidate for whom we give our votes ought not only to be *a fit man,* but *the fittest man.* When we find it necessary to entrust any body with the management of our private concerns, we apply to the best man for that purpose whom we know. When we would employ an artist, or a mechanic, or a laborer on our farms, we engage the man who will do our work best and most profitably. We ought not to do worse [f]or our country than we do for ourselves. It is our duty to give her the best servants we can get.

Now it is extremely fortunate for us, that at the present time we can sit calmly down and weigh the merits of the different candidates who are held up for the next election, without having our minds influenced or agitated by any of the prejudices and passions that have prevailed in party times. It is my earnest wish that all considerations of this sort may be entirely laid aside on the present occasion. There are now two candidates in this district, of whom I am told that one receives his principal support from the Democratic party, and the other from the Federal. But this surely is no reason why we should vote for one or the other. Let us look to their real and substantial qualifications, for the office of Member of Congress. I will just ask you to go along with me in a brief review of these; and hope that our minds will be made up on this subject, exactly as we find the one to have an advantage in this respect over the other.

With regard to Col. DWIGHT—[4]

He is a man whose abilities and integrity are not questioned even by his opposers.

He has been tried and found faithful, having already served us ably and uprightly in the same office for which he is now a candidate.

His political principles are well known to be sound, enlarged and liberal.

His political conduct has been remarkable for dignity, moderation, and freedom from party bias.

He is no less qualified to serve us by his personal influence and interest with those among whom he will find himself at the seat of government, than by his acquaintance with the principles of sound legislation.

He is a native of Berkshire, and attached to us and our interest by the strongest ties.

He is a farmer, and thus intimately connected with the most numerous, useful, and responsible class of men in the District.

I can say all this of Col. DWIGHT. I could say no more of any man.

If a candidate is able and upright; if he is well acquainted with the duties of the office for which he is supported; if habit has given him skill in the practice of those duties; if he has peculiar advantages and opportunities for performing them; and if circumstances of a peculiar kind dispose him to perform them with greater readiness, I see not what more can be required or had.

Examine this list of qualifications, my friends, and see whether it is not singularly fortunate that they are all found in one individual! I cannot think that you will at present leave out a man thus rarely gifted, from an office which he has discharged so creditably to himself and to his constituents. You would not be apt, in your private concerns, to decline availing yourself of the services of one who had been faithful, diligent, and useful in your employment, merely for the sake of employing another with whose merits you were not so well acquainted.

With respect to Mr. Jarvis, the other candidate,[5] I admit with pleasure that his integrity is not to be doubted. He has also shown great talents in the exercise of his profession. In the course of my business, I have been sometimes led to attend the courts at Lenox, and have been entertained by his ingenious manner of managing causes, and the flashes of wit with which his arguments are usually enlivened.

I am told also that he has written a book entitled the Republican, containing many excellent observations on the science of government, taken from a variety of authors; and that copies of this work have been sent to Mr. Adams and Mr. Jefferson, each of which gentlemen has had the civility to write the author a very polite letter on the subject.[6]

I am told likewise that he has gained great popularity in the town of Pittsfield, by supporting certain measures very offensive to the town of Boston, lately proposed in the Legislature of this State.[7]

But after all it seems to me that the balance of fitness and qualifications for the place of Member of Congress is in favor of Col. DWIGHT. I cannot help saying also, that I regret very much that Mr. Jarvis should have consented to become a candidate against him. I should have been glad to see all opposition to the re-election of Col. DWIGHT laid aside. He has entered upon his parliamentary career with great promise of success and usefulness;—I should be glad to have him continue in it, till he gains that rank and influence on the floor of Congress that he soon must; —till he has had time to do for the reputation and interests of the North, all that his talents enable him to do. These are my feelings. I claim no credit for them—but in his opposers they would have been magnanimous. They have, however, chosen to take a different course,—but in this, I am inclined to think, that the great body of our citizens will have too much prudence and good sense to follow them. The electors of the Berkshire District will, I hope, bear in mind a certain passage of Scripture, which I take the liberty to quote, not irreverently, but as a maxim of practical wisdom— *No man having drank old wine straightway desireth new for he saith the old is better.*[8]

DRAPER.[9]

MANUSCRIPT: NYPL–GR (draft) TEXT: *Berkshire Star*, Stockbridge, Thursday, October 31, 1822.

1. This letter concerns the imminent election in the congressional district which included Berkshire County and several towns in western Hampshire County, including Cummington.

2. An anonymous article in the *Pittsfield Sun* of October 24, 1822, urged the election to Congress of William C. Jarvis of Pittsfield.

3. Bryant adopts here the guise of the untutored rural commentator on public affairs popularized earlier by John Dickinson (1732–1808) in his *Letters from a Farmer in Pennsylvania to the Inhabitants of the British Colonies* (1767–1768), and by Samuel Seabury (1729–1796), who published a series of Loyalist pamphlets in 1774–1775 under the pseudonym "The Westchester Farmer."

4. Henry Williams Dwight (1788–1845), the incumbent, was a Stockbridge lawyer and a breeder of sheep and cattle who was at one time president of the Berkshire Agricultural Society. First elected to Congress in 1820, he represented his district there until 1830, when he declined renomination. *BDAC.*

5. William Charles Jarvis (c1786–1836), a native of Boston, was a lawyer who then represented his adopted town of Pittsfield in the state legislature. Joseph Ward Lewis, "Berkshire Men of Worth," *Berkshire County Eagle*, August 14, 1935, p. 12.

6. *The Republican; or, A Series of Essays on the Principles and Policy of Free States* (Pittsfield, 1820). Jarvis' "respect for the bench and indeed for the whole judicial process which amounted almost to reverence," drew from Thomas Jefferson the caustic "civility," "You seem . . . to consider the judges as the ultimate arbiters of all constitutional questions; a very dangerous doctrine indeed, and one which would place us under the despotism of an oligarchy." Quoted in Birdsall, *Berkshire County*, pp. 248, 250, from a letter from Jefferson to Jarvis dated September 28, 1820.

7. Jarvis' proponent in the *Pittsfield Sun* had demanded, "On questions when the gigantic powers of eastern talents and eastern wealth were reared against the country interest, was he not the bold and fearless advocate of your rights?" Had he not urged a tax on "the immense sums of money invested in Insurance Companies, and which heretofore have escaped unnoticed and untaxed?"

8. Luke 5:39.

9. In adopting this pseudonym, which suggests the humble weaver, Bryant probably had in mind Jonathan Swift's Dublin draper in *The Drapier's Letters* (1724).

85.   *To* Richard H. Dana

Great Barrington   Nov. 17   1822.

Dear Sir

I have been some disappointed at not having seen you in Great Barrington this fall—though I hardly expected you would tempt the Yellow Fever, in New York.[1]

There is some justice in your reproofs. I acknowledge myself to be a bad correspondent—but I am not without apology. I write very little— there is a sort of sterility, I believe, in my genius,—but why, my dear sir, must you always wait for an answer from me before you write again— I hold that in a correspondence it is the duty of each party to contribute according to his ability. Now, as you are a practised and experienced author, fertile in intellectual resources, with a host of fine ideas at your command, and a rich wardrobe of fine dresses for them, if you were to write two letters to my one, you would hardly do your share.—

Yesterday I received the Centinel of Wednesday the 13th. It contains a furious attack on your last Number of the Idle Man. I send you an answer to it, which I would have directed immediately to the Editor of the Centinel without troubling you with it—but I recollected the squeamishness of the Boston Editors, and fearing that if I sent it to Russell I should hear no more of it, I concluded to inclose it to you.[2] If you should think it worth while, you will hand it to Mr. Phillips or some other friend with my request that he would get it inserted in one of the Newspapers. —It is amusing to think that any body should take alarm at your books, but at all events it is a fortunate circumstance. There is no class of works that excite so much curiosity and get so much notoriety and so great a *run*, as those of which the ability is undisputed but the morality a little doubtful. —Therefore, though the fears of your *well wisher*, as he styles himself, appear to me supremely ridiculous and groundless—and though I am half inclined to believe them affected yet I am not sorry that he has come out with them. —It will draw more attention to the work,—besides giving me the pleasure of telling the public what I think of it— But if, as may perhaps be the case—and I do not know that this is not the most probable event—the attack on your work should be only laughed at by those who may meet with it, and then forgotten—why then it will do you no harm you know.—

I rejoice at what you tell me, that you have in some measure regained your composure and serenity of mind.[3] It must be so;—life must have its cheerful as well as its gloomy moments, or it would be insupportable. It is a common and rather trite topic with moralists to compare the life of man to the natural year, and to run a parallel through their various stages of youth maturity and decline, but they resemble each other quite as much in the alternations of storm and sunshine with which they are diversified.—

> Non semper imbres nubibus hispidos
> Manant in agros; aut mare Caspium
> Vexant inaequales procellae
> Usque; nec Armeniis in oris
>
> Amice Valgi, stat glacies iners
> Menses per omnes; aut Aquilonibus
> Querceta Gargani laborant
> Et foliis viduantur orni.[4]

Is your work sold at any of the bookstores in Albany? I have heard several persons complain that they have sent there for it without being able to get it.

Now it is healthy again in New York I suppose you will go there. I shall expect to see you here either on your way thither or your return. —Remember me to all my friends in your quarter & believe me

Truly yours
WM. C. BRYANT

MANUSCRIPT: NYPL–GR ADDRESS: Richard H. Dana Esq. / Cambridge / Mass POSTMARK *(in script)*: Great Barrington November. 18th— POSTAL ANNOTATION: 25 ENDORSED: Wm. C. Bryant / Nov. 17, 1822 / in this he sent an / answer to remarks in / Columbian Centinel on my / story of "Paul Felton," The / remarks were published in / the Centinel soon after I recd. / them, which newspaper I have.

1. See *A Statement of Facts Relative to the Late Fever Which Appeared in Bancker-Street and its Vicinity* (New York, 1821).
2. The conservative *Columbian Centinel* of Boston had been edited continuously since 1784 by its founder, Benjamin Russell. Mott, *American Journalism*, pp. 131–133. For Bryant's reply, see Letter 86.
3. See 83.1.
4. Horace, *Odes* II.ix.1–8: "Rough storms do not always beat from the clouds onto already sodden fields; nor do rain squalls continually stir up the Caspian Sea. The snows eventually melt from the Armenian countryside, dear Valgius; mountain oak groves cease to bend under the north wind's blasts; and ash trees recover their leaves."

86. *To* the COLUMBIAN CENTINEL, Boston

[Great Barrington, cNovember 17, 1822]

THE IDLE MAN. Vol. II.—No. 1.

It is a common amusement with a certain class of ingenious gentlemen, when there are no convenient objects at hand on which to exert their spirit of adventure, to conjure up scare-crows of their own invention, equip them in the most frightful manner their imagination can suggest, and when they have made them sufficiently hideous, to fall foul of them tooth and nail, batter them terribly, and scatter about without remorse the horrible paraphernalia in which they had just drest them up. Somebody, who calls himself a well wisher to the Author of the Idle Man, has given the public an entertainment of this kind in the *Centinel* of Nov. 13th. I must confess I was a little startled at the zeal and fury with which he assaulted his chimera; I began to think him in blood earnest, and to have some apprehensions that what he flew at so fiercely was in reality the dangerous and detestable thing he seemed to think it.

But as it is not my way to make up my opinion hastily on such subjects, I thought it might be well just to look at the book which had the odd fortune to call forth so much clamour from the well wisher of its Author. I took up the 1st No. of Vol. 2d. of the Idle Man, to see if I could find in it those pernicious tendencies which the writer in the *Centinel* considers as so apparent. At first the narrative seemed to me rather heavy, but, as I proceeded, my attention became strongly fixed, and I was soon so absorbed in the perusal that I wholly forgot my original purpose.[1]

I was carried along by a sort of fearful interest which I had not the power to resist. I was made to watch, from its very birth, the progress of the latent distemper of the imagination, the secret predisposition to insanity that sometimes lurks in minds otherwise finely constituted, to see its gathering strength from a variety of circumstances, and at length breaking out in the commission of acts of horror, and finally destroying its wretched victim.[2]

When I had done reading the work, I set myself to reflect on its moral tendency, and I have the pleasure of assuring those who have not seen this Number of the Idle Man, that it is as harmless as it is profoundly interesting. I cannot see that the Author's aim is to show, as the writer in the *Centinel* would seem to insinuate, that society exerts an unfriendly influence on great minds, and that to such, the soft and gentle ties of society are a curse and a spell of evil. It seems to me that he only attempts what is innocent enough, namely, to describe the workings of a disease of the imagination, from the first morbid speck, to the time when it has wholly mastered the reason; to show by what strange and unthought of means it is fostered and how perversely it makes its food of what would produce in other minds only a healthful and cheerful excitement. Such is the plan, nor is it executed in such a manner as to give any just occasion for censure. We acknowledge the power of genius, but it is not employed to make us in love with the deeds or the fate of the hero of this story. The very strength and pathos with which his reasonings, his fancies, and his feelings are given, only serve to make us see more clearly the error that pervades them. The path he has trod is shown to us in dark and fearful colours. I am sure that it is not drawn so as to excite in anyone the wish to tread it after him. Let us rather say that it is marked out that it may be dreaded and avoided.

The writer in the *Centinel* has some very pretty sentiments about the beneficial influences of society—the misfortune is that they are nothing to the purpose. There is no attempt in the narrative of PAUL FELTON to disgust men with society—its effect upon the mind of PAUL is not represented as more unfortunate than that of solitude, each is made to do its work. It was in solitude that his mind was cultivated and impressed with its peculiar bias; it was there too that the malady grew upon him and was nourished, which finally destroyed both him and the innocent creature connected with him.

But though the writer in the *Centinel* has succeeded very well in the province of sentiment, he seems to have failed in that of reasoning. "Unable," says he, "to display the workings of a mighty mind engaged in a mighty cause, with all its vast faculties intensely bent to the accomplishment of an adequate object, he [the author of the Idle Man][3] has represented his hero as yielding to the morbid influence of a diseased imagination," &c. The influence of a *diseased* imagination must be *morbid* of course, and so far the writer's logic is good, though at the expense of a little tautology; but when he says, that because the author of the Idle Man has done one thing, it is therefore certain that he is unable to do another, it seems to me that he strains hard for an inference. If the author of that work has chosen to represent his hero under the dominion of a distempered fancy, (a subject by the way which Shakespeare has not disdained, and which has called forth some of the proudest efforts of his genius) are we therefore to conclude that he was not capable of showing him in his sober senses? I might as well conclude that because Shakespeare wrote Hamlet, it is impossible that he could have written Julius Cesar; or that because I have seen the writer in the *Centinel* fighting with his own shadow, he is incapable of doing any thing else.

But the writer says that the developements of the mysteries of the human soul exhibited in this No. of the Idle Man are unnecessary, and asks why they were made. Alas! many things have been written both in the olden time and in these days of degeneracy quite as unnecessary as the story of Paul Felton.— Beautiful revelations of love and pity, powerful representations of stronger and fiercer emotions have been given us and continue to be given, by gifted spirits, without the least necessity in the world. For my part, I rejoice that my countryman has contributed his share to these; and am far from dreading any pernicious consequence from what he has done. I dwell with interest on the disclosures he has made of what is in man, and am conscious of no evil influence. To the sound mind they can do no harm, and he who is predisposed to insane wanderings, would extract melancholy, I suppose, from a description of Adam and Eve in Paradise.

Y.[4]

MANUSCRIPT: Unrecovered TEXT: *Columbian Centinel*, Boston, November 27, 1822, p. 1.

1. "Paul Felton," the last of three short novels Dana wrote for *The Idle Man*, was reprinted in his *Poems and Prose Writings* (Philadelphia and Boston, 1833), pp. 271–377.

2. This story reflects the deep impression Edmund Kean's acting of Shakespearean roles had made on Dana the preceding year, when he had written, "It has been said that Lear was a study for any one who would make himself acquainted with the workings of an insane mind. There is no doubt of it. Nor is it less true, that the acting of Kean was a complete embodying of these working." See 71.5. Paul Felton's derangement on the desolate heath, and his companionship with the mad boy Abel, strongly suggest Lear and Edgar. Felton's suspicion of his innocent wife, Esther, his jealousy of her rejected suitor Ridgley, and his eventual murder of Esther, unmistakably echo *Othello*.

3. Brackets as in printed text.

4. This is the second known instance of Bryant's use of the initial "Y" in anonymous letters to the press. See Letter 75.

87.   *To* Charles Sedgwick and Others

Lenox   Jan   29th. 1823.

I, William C. Bryant of Great Barrington in the County of Berkshire & Commth of Massachusetts for a valuable consideration do hereby transfer and convey to Charles Sedgwick, Robert F. Barnard, Thomas Twining Benjamin Sheldon & Henry W. Dwight Esquires the Copy Right of the annexed production, written by me entitled—The Heroes—a Farce, in three Acts.[1]

WILLIAM C. BRYANT

MANUSCRIPT: HEHL.

1. On February 2, 1823, Peter Rush Bryant, then in Great Barrington being tutored by his brother for entrance to college, wrote his mother, "Cullen has written a farce upon the late duel and sent it somewhere by the mail. He is very secret when writing anything." Weston Family Papers. This *jeu d'esprit* was evidently the product of a dare by Bryant's fellow-lawyers during a county court term. An agreement signed at Lenox on October 31, 1822, by those named in his conveyance states, "We the subscribers hereby engage & promise to pay to Wm. C. Bryant Esqr. the sum of Two hundred [fifty] Dollars within three months from date, provided the s⁴ W. C. Bryant shall within that time write a farce founded on the story of Col. Cumming & George McDuffie [see 88.3] & transfer the copy right thereof to the subscribers." NYPL–BG. Barnard was the father of Frederick A. P. Barnard, president of Columbia University from 1864 to 1889. Twining and Sheldon are otherwise unidentified. In the margin of the above-mentioned agreement Bryant wrote, "This paper was ret⁴ to me in Apl 1823 cancelled without a farthing being paid upon it."

88.   *To* Charles Sedgwick

Great Barrington   Feb. 12, 1823.

Dear Sir.—

The line you sent me last week I did not receive till Wednesday afternoon, when it was handed me by Mr. Griswold;[1] and since that time I have found no opportunity to get a letter to Lenox.

You request me to give you my opinion on the best method of disposing of the farce. I may come too late with what I have to say on that subject—if so let this be a letter of apology.

In the first place then I say— That the decision of this question must depend very much on the merits of the production. If it is not likely to succeed on the stage my advice is to do nothing with it. I am really so doubtful of my abilities in the department I have attempted, that were you to be of opinion that it would not take with the public, I should be neither disappointed nor mortified in the least, and should cancel a certain paper that I have,[2] as readily as I would blot a bad line out of a poem. Therefore I entreat you to lay aside all respect for the vanity of authorship, in making your decision—and all apprehensions of offending a sensitiveness in regard to their own works which afflicts most writers, and which I myself have my full share of in other instances but which in the present, I can assure you has no place. Then again, if the public have already got enough of Cumming and McDuffie and are glutted with the witticisms and squibs and moralizing on that subject, as may well be the case (you can judge better than I) then I would give the same advice and should myself take the same course as if the play were good for nothing. But if, not merely from the intrinsic merit of the production but from other circumstances there is a good prospect—not a probable one merely but a pretty certain one that it will succeed on the stage—then I would offer it to the managers of some theatre and get it printed at the same time. If not likely to succeed on the stage it is not likely to succeed at all—for who ever heard of such a thing as a closet farce!—In case you do any thing with it I cannot tell which would be the better place for bringing it out. The subject, I think would be less stale at Boston than at New York—but then the Boston folks are so full of notions. If they get a maggot in their heads they will cry up a thing at a furious rate—if not it falls like lead. At New York the gale of patronage blows more steadily; and the rain of public favour drops upon what is mediocre and tolerable as well as upon what is taking and fashionable— Albany I know nothing of. —The mail bag is come—Goodbye—[3]

Yrs truly
W   C   BRYANT

I leave the whole matter with you to decide—

MANUSCRIPT: MHS ADDRESS: Charles Sedgwick Esq / Lenox POSTAL ANNOTATION: PAID 6.

1. Sedgwick's letter is unrecovered. For Griswold, see 43.6.
2. The agreement of Sedgwick and others to pay $250 for the finished play. See 87.1.
3. "The Heroes" ridiculed an extraordinary series of duels, then much in the news, between the sharp-tongued South Carolina congressman George McDuffie and an obscure, vindictive political opponent, Col. William Cumming. See Edwin L. Green, *George McDuffie* (Columbia, South Carolina: The State Company, 1936), pp. 33–36. Sedgwick tried, through his brothers Henry and Robert in New York, to find a producer for the farce, writing Bryant on February 14, "In regard to the satire of the play we both know that it is excellent— As to its success neither you nor I nor any body else can tell before hand. . . . One word abt. the contract—the *bond*—the money is fairly earned & fairly due" (but was not paid; see 87.1). NYPL–BG. Six weeks later Charles reported to Bryant his brothers' lack of enthusiasm: "Happily for me you are too well acquainted with the opinions of the Sedgwick tribe to take in dudgeon Mr. Harry's free sayings abt. the farce." March 28, 1823, NYPL–BG. So Bryant filed his play with other discarded manuscripts, and seems never to have mentioned it again. See *Life*, I, 187–188; Birdsall, *Berkshire County*, pp. 278–279.

89.   *To* Charles Webster, Editor, BERKSHIRE STAR

[Great Barrington, *c*April 15, 1823][1]

Mr. W.

It is no uncommon thing either with individuals or bodies of men when galled by the utterance of unwelcome truths against which they cannot well defend themselves to give vent to the violence of their feelings and endeavour to divert the attention of the publick by making a great clamour about something else. A few harmless remarks in the Star of the 27th of March last on the course it was expected the federalists of Pittsfield would take in relation to the late Senatorial election drew forth from a writer in the last Star a most bitter tirade against a *certain town in the South part of the County*. —I expected to have seen some justification of the conduct of our Pittsfield friends or some extenuation at least, if not an absolute denial of the charge brought against them.[2] No such thing. The writer has done like a man who because ⟨his windows had been pelted by mischievous boys⟩ he had heard some unfavourable report about himself, should start out into the highway to horsewhip the first man he meets. In answer to the accusation against Pittsfield he has presented us with a long list of political sins committed by the inhabitants [of] a certain other place of which he deigns to give us no other information than that it lies in the south part of Berkshire—[3] I applaud the ingenuity of the stratagem. I must own that it was the wisest course that an inhabitant of Pittsfield could take on this delicate occasion. It was natural too that one trained to legal investigations should betray some traces of his profession in his mode of thinking on political subjects, and following in some sort the analogy of that rule by which counsel select the proper evidence to support the causes they undertake, should endeavour to get rid of an unwelcome accusation against his townsmen by the best expedient the nature of the case will admit of. —On the subject which called forth the remarks of this writer, I have nothing to say. The charge has not been denied or extenuated; the mischief has already been done and cannot be repaired by talking about it. But it may not perhaps be altogether unamusing or uninstructive to see in what manner the writer, who signs himself No Town Sticker has made and supported the charges which he intended to divert the publick odium from the town of which he himself is an inhabitant. —If I can form any judgment of that place meant by this writer I feel no more partiality for it than I do for Pittsfield, and whenever it shall so far forget itself as to assume an impunity that does not belong to it let the publick [. . .].

There was says the writer a gross and palpable compromise made in the Nomination of Senators for 1819 for the purpose of aiding the Congressional Ticket. I was not better pleased with this [picked?] Nomination than the writer himself— It was too much like the Pittsfield nomination of 1822. But I never thought of ascribing it to interested motives. It was the opinion of many worthy and judicious men all over the state at that time that a union of the Parties was both desirable and practicable when there was no storm and stress. But the attempt to effect that union I think in this County failed. The break was too green to heal over, the two parties retained too much personal feeling and too much recollection of past animosity to coalesce. The experiment was an unfortunate one indeed, but who has authorized the writer to say that it was got up to serve a local ambition?

There is no action that can be performed,—the most virtuous the most disinterested & praiseworthy, to which a malignant ingenuity cannot assign some sinister purpose.—

The next political crime laid to the charge of a certain town in the south part of the County is that its delegates in the convention of 1820 were desirous of furnishing a candidate from their own town. Granting this to be true, and I do not know or care whether it is so or not, was this an offence of unusual enormity? —Have not the delegates from other towns committed the same crime with impunity—and is it not natural that gentlemen should give their suffrages on such occasions for those with whose deserts they are best acquainted? —But it would seem not so when the town to which the writer alludes acquiesced in the decision of the convention.—

But there was no nomination in 1821 except one made by an individual and an inhabitant of the nameless town [who] went to a gentleman of Pittsfield and proposed to him to stand candidate at the approaching election of Senators. —I have no means of knowing whether this story be true or not, but suppose for a moment that it is— Will it be said that the individual who made this proposal had not as much right to meddle with the nomination as the individual who finally published it? Or if the people do not choose to send their delegates and make a nomination themselves is it the pleasure of this writer that nobody shall be permitted to propose a candidate to the suffrage of the people through the medium of the newspapers? Or when a gentleman is to be nominated by his friends would he forbid that they should first consult him respecting it?

The writer then goes on to say that in 1822 Mr. Jarvis[4] was put in nomination to the exclusion of a candidate from the southern part of the county, that this nomination originated in a local feeling wholly foreign to the interests of Pittsfield or the honour of the candidate, and that the object was entirely different from the one indicated by the measure. That this measure had the effect of preventing the nomination of a candidate from the south, I admit—that it was intended to produce that effect I deny. Equally unfounded is the assertion that the nomination was made without regard to the merits of the candidate, or that its object was different from what would naturally be inferred from the measure itself.

—These bold assertions are as gratuitous as they are bold. —They have been made in the face of the county— In the face of the county I challenge the writer to produce a shadow of proof in their favour. Let him make his words good if he can.—

The writer conceives that the nomination of Mr. Leavenworth was not correctly made.[5] I hardly know how it should have been made to suit the fastidious humour of this writer. He is dissatisfied with nominations made in conventions and with nominations made out of them. But a nomination of a gentleman who had only one vote less in the caucus than one of the persons who was at length agreed on as candidate, made at a time when it was too late to call a convention seems to me liable to as few objections as are usually brought against any nomination whatever. —The writer thinks on the whole that he shall vote for Mr. Leavenworth. If he kept this resolution he deserves credit for it. Let him share the praise of fidelity and constancy with the Seraph Abdiel.

> ---------------- faithful found
> Among the faithless - - - - - - - - - - - - -[6]

Of the various charges of *artifice, treachery, impudence stupidity dishonour faithless ingratitude and pertinacious selfishness* I do not think it necessary to take any notice. They are cheap terms of vituperation and may be applied with as much ease where they are not deserved as where they are. —But when the writer of the article I have been considering looks over it in his cooler moments and sees into what intemperance of language his passions have betrayed him, when he sees how indifferent and inconsequential in themselves are the facts on which he has founded his charges, and how destitute of all proof is the assertion that they originated in bad motives, if he is a person of that fair and candid mind that I am still willing to believe him notwithstanding his heat on this subject I am sure that his natural ingenuousness will summon the blood into his cheeks.—

[unsigned]

MANUSCRIPT: NYPL–GR (draft).

1. Its context suggests that this undated draft was written soon after local and state elections on April 7, 1823. The printed version has not been found.

2. Neither article referred to has been located. On March 5 Bryant had served as "Secretary of the Federal Republican Convention for the District of Berkshire," held at Lenox, which nominated for state senators George Conant of Becket and Douglas Sloane of Williamstown. They were defeated by their Democratic–Republican opponents, Jonathan Allen of Pittsfield and George Hull of Sandisfield, gaining only about forty-two percent of the vote. *Berkshire Star*, March 13 and April 24, 1823.

3. Pittsfield, then as now the most populous town in Berkshire County, lies north of its center. Great Barrington, the "certain town" referred to, is about twenty miles southward.

4. William C. Jarvis of Pittsfield. See 84.5.

5. David Leavenworth (1769–1831), a Great Barrington storekeeper, was long a justice of the peace. Bryant represented many legal clients in his court. Taylor, *Great Barrington*, pp. 318, 358, 420.

6. Cf. *Paradise Lost* V.896–897.

90. *To* Andrews Norton[1]

[Great Barrington, cAugust 1, 1823]

There are three religious societies in Great Barrington —the Congregational—the Episcopal—& the Baptist Societies. —The two former are nearly equal to each other in point of Numbers and include about two thirds of our population. The Baptist Society comprises about three fourths of the remaining third, and the rest are with hardly an exception Methodists.

The Congregationalists are mostly Calvinists, the Episcopalians Arminians— The members of these two societies living every where intermixed with each other and having churches in the same neighbourhood and settled ministers of a very respectable character there prevails a good deal of jealousy among them— The Congregationalists cannot see in the Episcopalians the proper mystical evidences of Richard Sullivan's regeneration[2] and the Episcopalians accuse the Congregationalists with neglecting those positive ordinances which are presented as the conditions of salvation or what is the same thing suffering them to be administered by unauthorized & unconsecrated hands. —The C are continually labouring to get up a high state of religious excitement—the Ep discourage & retard it. The Baptists living in a separate quarter of the town and including in their number many who have no other care about religion than to get rid of being taxed for its support seem pretty indifferent about other sects. The more conscientious among them however prefer the Congregationalists & sometimes attend their worship— The Methodists are rather inclined to the Ep form of worship—though they are apt to consider its followers as too cold & doubt the vitality of their religion—

In almost every Town in this vicinity there is a society of Congregationalists of the Calvinistic persuasion with a settled minister. There are however several Baptist congregations one or two Methodist Societies and a sprinkling of Universalists and Episcopalians.—

2. Of the inhabitants of Great Barrington a very few only are professed Unitarians— The Unitarians of this Town are generally men of correct morals and upright dealings—but from having taken a disgust to religion in the status in which it is taught in the Calvinistic pulpits are not I fear the most devotional or pious. They would however I have no doubt be willing to promote any project which has for its design the diffusion of correct views of Christianity—

3rd. Our Representative Dr. B Rogers[3] might perhaps communicate some information on the subject.—

4th & 5th The measures used to oppose the spread of Unitarianism are violent denunciations of its doctrines from the orthodox pulpits and exhortations to read no publications written for the purpose of insinuating into the mind the dangerous and seducing doctrines of that sect. Unitarianism is put on the same footing with Mahometanism & Deism, and its followers are denied the name of Christians and its doctrines represented as bringing eternal perdition on those who embrace them.[4] The Unitarian clergy are represented as artful & subtle reasoners who have refined away all the essentials of religion, and though they may be in the main tolerably moral are attached to the pleasures of the world & destitute of real piety— Harvard University comes in for its share of vituperation, and is in fact the great dread of most of our orthodox clergy.[5] —Sometimes the opinions of the Unitarians are [much misre]presented—

6th. The effects of these representations are what might naturally be expected— Those who place implicit confidence in the opinions of the clergy have imbibed a sort of horror at the mysterious heresy whose doctrines they are forbidden to look too narrowly into, and some of this feeling is naturally extended to the persons of its professors. Upon others, and their number is increasing, the only effect of so much noise about Unitarianism has been to excite their curiosity to know what it is—and having been acquainted with its tenets they are grown more charitable [. . .].

7th Unitarianism is not by any means declining— Six years since when I came to the County of Berkshire there was not to my knowledge a Unitarian in it— Now there is scarcely a town in which there are not a few—professedly so—in some numbers who enter into its views of Christianity— It was about three years since that the Orthodox clergy of this county were apprised that the heresy of Unitarianism had passed the barriers of our mountains, and general agreement was entered into by the association of this district to preach it down. —They preached accordingly till they had wearied both themselves and their hearers—till the spirit of enquiry had gathered strength from the means used to suppress it, and they whose tenets were denounced had been stimulated to make some exertions in their turn— At present the clergy seem to have varied their mode of warfare. They appear to consider the heresy of Unitarianism as an evil whose growth cannot be checked by Human means, and are employing the usual means to produce in all those possible that preternatural state of religious feeling called an awakening by which they hope to effect at last [its] extermination.

8th. In addition to the distribution of tracts I should think that a few discourses from a preacher of rational Christianity in some of our best towns would be attended with great advantage and tend very much to remove the erroneous notions entertained concerning these doctrines, and prove what many profess to doubt the connection between them and piety— Many from motives of curiosity would go to hear an Unitarian preacher who could not be persuaded to read a tract.—

9th. The Christian Disciple is taken in this Town and some other parts of the County— The Unitarian Miscellany has an agent here and several subscribers. The Christian Register is taken in one of the Towns of this vicinity— Some Episcopalians take the Churchman's Magazine. But the great vehicle of religious intelligence—the great conduit of spiritual nourishment to the good people of this place is the Religious Intelligencer, to which its importunate agents have secured a wide circulation, and of which at least 300 copies come weekly to the inhabitants of the County of Berkshire— Orthodox tracts are almost the only ones circulated and read, and these are distributed with great assiduity.[6]

10— I think that well chosen Unitarian tracts would be read with some interest and with a good effect in this vicinity—

11th. 12 & 13— Among the Orthodox strictly so called there is but little charity toward Unitarians. They are lost without exception. But in many of those societies which support orthodox clergymen there are numbers favourably disposed toward Unitarianism. —The Towns of Stockbridge & Pittsfield contain many Unitarians—gentlemen of great respectability. —I would mention the following as gentlemen from whom information might be obtained upon the questions addressed in your circular & with whom the committee might correspond. —Dr Nathaniel Preston, Postmaster, Sheffield[7]—Geo. Whitney Esq. Stockbridge[8]—Chas. Sedgwick Esq., Lenox—Saml. McKay Esq. Pittsfield[9]—Hon George Hull Sandisfield—[10]

14. The Universalists have many followers in the neighbouring towns of Sheffield Egremont & Washington & some very respectable ones— One Pickering from Andover—a man of considerable talent at extemporaneous speaking has been the great apostle of that sect, and done much to diffuse its doctrines— Many Universalist tracts written by him have been distributed in the vicinity— It is difficult to say what description of Universalism is most prevalent— Pickering discarded the doctrine of future punishment altogether—but other teachers introduced by him favour the notion of a limited punishment—[11] The former doctrine as it appears to me however is caught up eagerly by the profligate and desperate—though

it is embraced by many virtuous people— The Universalists in this neighbourhood seem sometimes a little inclined to identify themselves with
Unitarians, & some preachers among them (they have no pastorates) have
argued agst. the Error of the Trinity— I have given Unitarian tracts to
some of them & had the satisfaction to see that they were read with interest & effect. I have never found Unitarian books in their homes.

[unsigned]

MANUSCRIPT: NYPL–GR (draft).

1. On July 15 Professor Norton (see 78.6) had sent Bryant a questionnaire beginning, "What is the state of Religion in Barrington and its vicinity?" with the explanation, "The preceding . . . has been sent round by a committee of a society composed
of gentlemen in Boston and its neighborhood—several of the Boston clergy, of the officers of the college, and some laymen such as Mr. Quincy, Mr. R. Sullivan &c. No gentleman of the committee having the pleasure of your acquaintance, I was requested to
forward it to you; and you can if you please return an answer directed to me."
NYPL–BG. Bryant replies here to a series of categorical questions. See Letter 117 to
Rev. Henry Ware, chairman of what was perhaps the same committee.

2. Probably Richard B. Sullivan (1779–1861), an overseer of Harvard College
from 1821 to 1852. See Note 1.

3. Dr. Benjamin Rogers, then a member of the legislature for Great Barrington.
See 64.8.

4. The previous year Catharine Sedgwick had written a friend, "I quite long to
look upon a Christian minister who does not regard me as a heathen and a publican.
. . . Some of my friends here have, as I learn, been a little troubled [at her becoming
an author], but, after the crime of confessed Unitarianism, nothing can surprise them."
Her devoted aunt remarked to Miss Sedgwick about that time, "Come and see me as
often as you can, dear, for you know, after this world, we shall never meet again."
Sedgwick, Life and Letters, pp. 156–157.

5. Under the influence of such Unitarian pioneers as Henry Ware, Sr. (1764–
1845) and William Ellery Channing (1780–1842), Harvard had become the center of
liberal religious views. The citadel of Calvinistic orthodoxy was now Andover Theological Seminary. Rusk, Emerson, p. 99.

6. The Christian Disciple and Theological Review (1813–1823), then edited at
Boston by Henry Ware, Jr., was succeeded by the Christian Examiner. The Unitarian
Miscellany and Christian Monitor (1821–1824), begun at Baltimore by Jared Sparks,
was conducted at this time by Francis W. P. Greenwood, later pastor of King's Chapel
at Boston. The Christian Register: An Evangelical Magazine (1822–1823), edited by
James Blythe of Lexington, Kentucky, lasted only one year. The Churchman's Magazine of New Haven appeared intermittently between 1804 and 1827, when it gave way
to the Episcopal Watchman. By the Religious Intelligencer, Bryant probably meant
the Religious Informer (1819–1825), edited at Enfield, New Hampshire, by E. Chase.

7. See Letter 81.

8. George Whitney, a state representative for Stockbridge in 1822, and registrar
of probate for Berkshire County from 1823 to 1825. [Beers] Berkshire County, I, 313,
345.

9. Samuel M. McKay (1793–1839, M.A. Williams 1823), a founding trustee in 1823
of the Berkshire Medical College at Pittsfield, and president of the Berkshire Agricultural Society in 1824, long represented Pittsfield in the legislature. [Beers] Berkshire
County, I, 311, 392, 409.

10. George Hull (1788–1866), postmaster at Sandisfield and state senator, served

from 1836 to 1843 as Whig lieutenant governor of Massachusetts. Joseph Ward Lewis, "Berkshire Men of Worth," *Berkshire County Eagle*, March 25, 1936, p. 12.

11. In 1822 David Pickering published at Hudson, New York, *Psalms and Hymns, for Social and Private Worship*. This included a summary of Universalist beliefs.

91. *To* Mrs. Sarah S. Bryant

Great Barrington—Sept. 15, 1823.

Dear Mother—

Peter has concluded to apply for admission at the Academy at West Point. But as it is uncertain whether he will be received, and as he will not enter the institution until June, if at all, he has concluded in the mean time to apply himself to his college studies so that if he should be rejected at West Point he might not miss the opportunity of entering some one of the colleges without losing a year.[1]

I am not certain that West Point would not be a good place for him. The learned professions a[re] getting to be a poor way of making a livelihood, and he will at least have the advantage of being able to choose the military profession if he should happen to like it.—

Peter says that he wishes you to send for him about the [. . .][2] see that it will be convenient [. . .][2] Frances has been this summer in a state of health far from being firm, and she finds herself uniformly ill on any unusual fatigue. —I think therefore that I must get my household into such a state as to give her as little hard work to do as I can.—

Peter seems to think that he must have a cloak but wishes that the plaid may not be bought till he comes home, as he would like to have a voice in the choosing of it. It took nine yards for my cloak but it is made very full. —He likewise wishes me to say that he will need another pair of pantaloons this winter. —

If he should apply himself to his studies this winter—you will not of course think of getting a school for him.[3] —It is possible however that he may not study so well at home as at some other place; and if he should find that to be the case with him I would advise him to leave home instantly.

We are all tolerably well—Frances desires her love—

Your affectionate son
[signature missing]

MANUSCRIPT: BCHS.

1. Since the middle of January Peter Rush Bryant, then nineteen, had been living with Cullen and Frances in Great Barrington, where Cullen helped him prepare for college. Peter to Sarah S. Shaw, February 2, 1823, BCHS. In the spring Cullen failed to get him a scholarship at Harvard College. Willard Phillips to Cullen Bryant, May 5, 1823, NYPL–GR. Later that year Cullen asked William Baylies to enlist the help of his brother, Congressman Francis Baylies of Taunton, in securing for Peter an appointment to West Point. William Baylies to Bryant, December 26, 1823, NYPL–BG. He also appealed to Congressman Henry Dwight (see 84.4) and Senator Elijah Mills (see

10.3) toward the same end. In March 1824 Mills reported he and Dwight had arranged Peter's admission to the United States Military Academy in June. Mills to Bryant, March 19, 1824, NYPL–BG.

2. Manuscript torn.

3. I.e., a position as district schoolmaster.

92.   To Isaac Parker[1]

Great Barrington   Oct 5   1823

Sir—

In the action Grotius Bloss vs Augustus Tobey on which a verdict was rendered at the last Term of the S[upreme] J[udicial] C[ourt] in Berkshire & a motion made in arrest of judgment, I have just been told that a written argument was expected of me as counsel for the pl[aintif]f immediately.[2] I have not [had] time since I learnt this to prepare one, and as the cause is an important one to my client on account of the magnitude of the Bill of Cost, and several questions of some nicety are involved in it I hope that a little time will be indulged us, and as soon as may be, Mr. Jarvis & myself will transmit written arguments.

At the time the motion in arrest of judgment was made which was immediately before the close of the session I was absent and the associate counsel in the haste of the moment & without time for deliberation moved to take judgment on the first & seventh counts. I am at present rather inclined to think that these are not the best in the declaration, particularly the former.— The reason why an earlier election was not made will be understood from the following circumstances. Mr. Jarvis at the time the verdict was rendered recommended to me to look over the declaration and select such counts as I thought most proper to receive the verdict on— The Judge informed us that we had a right to receive the verdict on any of the counts as it was a general one—but went on to say that he did not see why we were not safe enough in taking a general verdict—adding however that we must "judge for ourselves." —In consequence of this intimation, I did not request that opportunity of examining the several counts which without doubt would have been allowed us and a general verdict was entered.—

Under these circumstances I am not without hopes that the court will suffer us to amend our motion,—particularly as the other party cannot in any manner be prejudiced by it.

As soon as I can consult Mr. Jarvis I will forward the amended motion for the consideration of the Court.—

I remain Sir

very respectfully yrs.

WM C. BRYANT—

MANUSCRIPT: NYPL–GR (draft) ADDRESS: Hon Isaac Parker.

1. Isaac Parker (1768–1830, Harvard 1786), Chief Justice since 1814 of the Massachusetts Supreme Judicial Court, was also Royall Professor at the Harvard Law

School, of which he had been the principal founder. Bryant knew Parker would hold court terms at Lenox in March and September 1824.

2. At the June 1823 term of the Court of Common Pleas Bryant won for storekeeper Grotius Bloss of nearby Alford a judicial assessment of damages and costs against a neighbor, Augustus Tobey, who had accused Bloss publicly of burning his own store to collect the insurance on its goods. This judgment was confirmed by a jury in September at the Supreme Judicial Court term. But Tobey's lawyers, led by veteran John Whiting (see 41.2), moved successfully in arrest of judgment. As Bryant explains, during his absence his associate counsel William C. Jarvis was hurried into a decision which put the victorious plaintiff on the defensive. Bryant's later "plain, common-sense argument" failed to convince the appellate justices, who overturned the jury verdict in September 1824 and levied court costs against Bryant's client. *Supreme Judicial Court Records, May Term, 1823–May Term, 1827*, pp. 164–169, Berkshire County Court, Pittsfield, Massachusetts. See also Bigelow, *Bryant*, pp. 38–39; *Life*, I, 201–202; *Berkshire Eagle*, June 20, 1878. This reversal of judgment was crucial in Bryant's decision soon afterward to quit the law for journalism. Half a century later he wrote of the verdict, "By a piece of pure chicane, in a case the merits of which were with my client and were perfectly understood by the parties, the court, the jury and every body who heard the trial or heard of it, my client was turned out of court after the jury had awarded him damages and deprived of what they intended he should receive. This did not much heighten my respect for the law." Letter to unidentified correspondent, May 7, 1878, Lafayette College Library.

93. *To* Messrs. Robert B. Southwick & Co.[1]

Great Barrington   Dec   27, 1823.

Gentlemen.

Sometime since I wrote you that I had seen Jno. C. Deming and that he promised to call on you and make some arrangement of the demand against him and [Cyrenus] Stevens. Since that time I have not heard from you.

At present I have some news to communicate concerning him and Stevens of no very agreeable nature.

A man in West Stockbridge, a creditor of Deming to a considerable amount, and who had given him money to discharge a certain debt, which he neglected to pay over & appropriated to his own use, was sued on that debt and called on Deming for security. Deming made to him an assignment of all his effects, and in the assignment stipulated that if the property assigned upon being sold should bring more than enough to pay this debt the surplus should be applied towards the payment of other claims which were mentioned in the assignment, and among which I cannot learn that yours was named. The property however, it is said, will not more than pay the debt it was first intended to secure. In the mean time Deming went off to the State of New York, and is now in Albany on the limits. —One of the creditors, whose name was mentioned in the assignment, has attached the property assigned—and the consequence, it is expected, will be a law suit.

While these things were transacting, Stevens was buying goods in the City of New York. He purchased, it is said, a considerable assortment, but he has not sent them to this state, nor is it expected that he will. Both they and he are somewhere in your state, and it is likely will not soon be seen here. Stevens it seems owed debts to a considerable amount, and both he and Deming have mutually been security for each other.

Such are the particulars as far as I have been able to learn them. It was impossible to secure any thing on your demand; the first news of Deming's failure being after the assignment of his property.—

I hope you may be able to get something of them in your State— though they will probably attempt to keep their property as much under cover as they can—

I am Gentlemen

Yrs. Respectfully

WM C   BRYANT

MANUSCRIPT: NYPL–GR ADDRESS: Messrs. Robt Southwick & Co / Merchants / Poughkeepsie / N. Y. POSTMARK (*in script*): Great Barrington December 31st POSTAL ANNOTATION: 12½ ENDORSED: W. C. Bryant / 12 Mo. 27th 1823 / answered 2 Mo.—12th 1824.

1. This and Letters 96 and 98 concerning the same case are together representative of the kind of litigation in which Bryant was mostly involved during nearly nine years of law practice at Great Barrington. Robert B. Southwick and his brothers, Edward C. and Willet H. Southwick, operated a tannery on the Hudson River shore at Poughkeepsie, New York. James H. Smith, *History of Dutchess County, New York* (Syracuse, 1882), p. 392. No other record of this case has been found.

94.   *To* Theophilus Parsons[1]

Great Barrington   Dec   29   1823.

Dear Sir.

I have just received yours of the 19th. —The proposal contained in it is of too flattering a nature not to be accepted, at the same time that my circumstances do not permit me to decline the pecuniary compensation you offer.[2]

As to the amount of this compensation, I am not sufficiently acquainted with the price which literary wares bear in market to form any judgment. If I were to say that I leave [it] wholly to your generosity, I should show *myself* destitute of that quality—for you might then be induced to give *too much* through fear of giving *too little*. I will not therefore leave it to be settled exactly in that way. You say that you are offered terms which put it in your power to pay for what assistance you want, and that you have engaged the support of some of the best writers in Boston and its vicinity.[3] Let the compensation you allow me be proportioned to what you allow others, and such as the terms offered you by your publishers enable you easily to make, and whatever it may be, I

shall be entirely satisfied. I hope, at least, that you will think my assistance of sufficient value to entitle me to receive the "Gazette," as it comes
out.

On such conditions I will send to the publishers of your [work in th]e
course of the year, the number of poems you men[tion. In][4] the mean
time you will permit me to express the hope that your undertaking may
be successful. I have no doubt that it will be so; the demand for such
things is increasing, and what is of more consequence they are getting
into better hands.

I am Sir
Yr. obt. humble Servt.
WM. C. BRYANT.

MANUSCRIPT: BPL ADDRESS: Theophilus Parsons Esq. / ⟨Boston⟩ / Taunton / Bristol
County POSTMARK ⟨(*in script*): Great Barrington   December 29th / 12½⟩: BOS-
TON / MS / JAN / 1 POSTAL ANNOTATION: 10.

1. Theophilus Parsons (1797–1882, Harvard 1815), lawyer and editor of the Taunton, Massachusetts, *Free Press*, later edited the *New England Galaxy*, a Sunday newspaper, at Boston. From 1848 to *c*1869 he was Dane Professor of Law at Harvard.
2. Parsons wrote Bryant on December 19 that he would edit a new periodical, the
United States Literary Gazette, and was "very anxious" to have Bryant's contributions: "If you can confer upon me this great favour, will you have the goodness to
inform me, how much money I may have the pleasure of sending you for ten or
twenty pieces of poetry to be sent to Cummings, Hilliard & Co., in the course of the
ensuing year." NYPL–GR.
3. Parsons did not identify these writers. Among them, the following year, was a
Bowdoin College junior, Henry Wadsworth Longfellow.
4. Manuscript damaged here.

95. *To* Theophilus Parsons

Great Barrington   Jan   19, 1824.—

Dear Sir—

Yours of the 6th I received on the 16th.[1] —Below I give you a list of
persons who are as likely to take the Gazette as any I can think of in these
parts;—and on the other side of the leaf I send you a little poem for your
first No., if you receive it in season.—[2]

With great respect & esteem
Your obt Servt.
WM C. BRYANT.—

Lester Filley[3] } Otis		Daniel Noble	
Robt. F. Barnard ⎤		Douglass W. Sloane	⎤ Williams-
William B. Saxton ⎱Sheffield		Chas. A. Dewey	⎰ town
Edward F. Ensign ⎦		Chester Dewey	
Henry W. Bishop } Richmond		Eben. Kellogg	⎦

Ralph Taylor ⎤
Allen Henderson ⎬ Great Barrington
Thomas Hopkins ⎦
William Porter jr. } Lee
Edward Stevens } New Marlborough
Theodore Sedgwick ⎤
Theodore S. Pomeroy ⎥
Robert E. Galpin ⎬ Stockbridge
George Whitney ⎦

Charles Sedgwick } Lenox
Thomas Gold ⎤
Henry Hubbard ⎬ Pittsfield
Saml. M. McKay ⎦
Asa Burbank } Lanesborough
William Ward ⎤
Elisha Mack ⎬ Worthington
Jacob Porter } Plainfield

MANUSCRIPT: HEHL ADDRESS: Theophilus Parsons Esq. / Taunton / Mass. POSTMARK
(*in script*): Great Barrington. Jany   19. POSTAL ANNOTATION: 12½.

1. Parsons wrote Bryant on January 6 asking for "a few lines" for the first number of the *Gazette*, and "two or three dozen names in the west of the State, to whom
the Gazette might be sent with any chance of its being retained." He could not yet
define the terms of payment for the poet's contributions, but he had "no reason whatever, to fear their inadequacy." NYPL–BG.
   2. "Rizpah," *USLG*, 1 (April 1, 1824), 12. See *Poems* (1876), pp. 64–67.
   3. The men listed are identified as follows, though it is not known how many of
them subscribed to the *USLG*. Except when indicated otherwise, references are to
[Beers] *Berkshire County*.
   Lester Filley (d. 1859) was the leading lawyer in Otis, where he tutored many
Berkshire County law students. II, 262, 514.
   Col. Robert F. Barnard. See 87.1.
   William B. Saxton was later president of the Housatonic Agricultural Society, and
town clerk of Sheffield. I, 412; II, 553.
   Edward F. Ensign (d. 1853?, Yale 1815), lawyer and state legislator, later became
Berkshire County High Sheriff. I, 303, 312.
   Henry Walker Bishop (1796–1871, Williams 1817), then a practicing lawyer, was
later Registrar of Probate for Berkshire County, and a judge of the Court of Com-
mon Pleas. I, 329–330, 347.
   Col. Ralph Taylor, a Great Barrington storekeeper, was Bryant's roommate from
1818 to 1821, and often his walking companion. II, 2, 30; Taylor, *Great Barrington*,
p. 419.
   Deacon Allen Henderson was the husband of Frances Bryant's sister Esther.
   Thomas Hopkins is unidentified.
   William Porter, Jr., a lawyer, was later a state representative and senator. I, 304,
309; II, 181.
   Edward A. Stevens was for many years a member of the legislature. I, 304, 309.
   Theodore Sedgwick II (see "Bryant's Correspondents") was then president of the
Berkshire Agricultural Society.
   Theodore S. Pomeroy, a lawyer, later represented Stockbridge in the legislature.
I, 313, 347.
   Robert E. Galpin was afterward a state legislator and president of the Housatonic
Agricultural Society. I, 313, 412.
   George Whitney. See 90.8.
   Daniel Noble (1776–1830, Williams 1796) was a founder of the Berkshire Medical
Institute at Pittsfield. I, 304, 314, 392.
   Douglas W. Sloane (1784–1839, Williams 1807), then a practicing attorney, was
later principal of a boys' school at Williamstown. I, 340; II, 679.
   Charles A. Dewey (1793–1866, Williams 1811, Harvard LL.D. 1840), son of Justice

Daniel Dewey (see 17.1), was an attorney and for nearly thirty years a justice of the Massachusetts Supreme Judicial Court. I, 338, 344.

Rev. Chester Dewey (1784–1867, Williams 1806) was from 1810 to 1827 professor of Mathematics and Natural Philosophy at his alma mater, and the founder of its museum. Thereafter he had a long and distinguished career as principal of the Berkshire Gymnasium at Pittsfield (1827–1836), principal of the Collegiate Institute at Rochester, New York (1836–1850), professor at the medical school in Woodstock, Vermont (1842–1849), and first professor of Chemistry and Natural Sciences at the University of Rochester (1850–1861).

Ebenezer Kellogg, a professor at Williams College, gave his name to a building on the campus. II, 685.

Charles Sedgwick. See 60.1.

Thomas A. Gold (1788–1854, Williams 1806) was a lawyer and principal organizer of the Hudson and Berkshire Railroad in 1828. I, 341, 418.

Henry Hubbard (1783–1863, Williams 1803), lawyer and organizer in 1827 of the Berkshire County School Society, edited the *Berkshire County Whig* at Pittsfield from 1840 to 1849. I, 340; Birdsall, *Berkshire County*, pp. 109–110.

Samuel M. McKay. See 90.9.

Dr. Asa Burbank was first Professor of Obstetrics at the Berkshire Medical Institute. Smith, *Pittsfield*, I, 360.

Col. William Ward (1781–1849?) had been postmaster at Worthington since 1805. He was the son of William Ward (1743–1820), a first Selectman of Cummington and, in 1790, principal founder of Cummington Academy (often called "Ward's Folly"), which was attended by Bryant's mother as well as by his brother John. *Only One Cummington*, pp. 348, 376; Brown, *John Howard Bryant*, p. 13; *Town of Worthington, Massachusetts Bicentennial 1768–1968* (Worthington?, 1968?), p. 151.

Elisha Mack was later a Middlefield lawyer. *Gazatteer of Hampshire County, Massachusetts, 1654–1887*, ed. W. B. Gay (Syracuse, 1887?), p. 329.

Jacob Porter. See Letters 6 and 7.

96. *To* Messrs. Robert B. Southwick & Co.

Great Barrington Feb 23 1824.

Gent.

Yrs. of the 12th inst was duly received—[1] You wish to know where Stevens is. A few days after I wrote you last[2] he called on me, and said that he came to see about your demands against him. I told him what I had written to you, and in answer he said that he did not mean to leave the country—that he intended to remain in West Stockbridge—that he could not pay your debt at present—but would pay it if you would give him time—and finally that he intended before long to call on you and make some arrangement of the affair with you. I believe that one item of his information is true—namely that he does not mean to pay the debt at present. I do not know of any way to secure it. Stevens is now in West Stockbridge. What is become of his goods I cannot tell. Some hides purchased by him in New York were brought from Poughkeepsie by one Brown of Pittsfield who I am told claims them.—[3]

Yours respectfully
WM. C. BRYANT

MANUSCRIPT: NYPL–GR ADDRESS (address leaf torn): [Messrs.] R. B. Southwick & Co. / Merchants / Poughkeepsie /N. Y. POSTMARK *(in script)*: [Great Barrington, February 23? 182]4 POSTAL ANNOTATION: 12½ DOCKETED: Wm C Bryant / 2 Mo 23d—1824.

1. Letter unrecovered.
2. Letter 93.
3. The brothers James and Simeon Brown had operated a tannery on Water Street, Pittsfield, since 1800. Smith, *Pittsfield*, I, 41.

97. *To* Theophilus Parsons

Great Barrington   March 10, 1824

My dear Sir.

Yours of the 2nd. I received yesterday,[1] and some time previous I had received your letter stating the terms upon which C[ummings] H[illiard] & Co. would engage me.[2] I regret that any misapprehension should have occasioned you any trouble;—it did not occur to me that, although I had told you that I should be satisfied with any compensation the publishers should think fit to offer,—they might notwithstanding like to know to what extent I should be willing to contribute to their work. It was from this mistake that I neglected to write.

I think the terms offered perfectly reasonable, and accept them with pleasure.[3]

In answer to one of your letters I enclosed you a little poem for your first No. and a list of persons in this County who I thought might take the Gazette.[4] You have not acknowledged the receipt of that letter, in any of those which you have written to me—but I expect to see by your first No. whether you have received it or not.—

In the mean time, with all good wishes for the success of your undertaking, I am Sir

Your obedt. & much obliged Servt.

WM C. BRYANT

MANUSCRIPT: BPL ADDRESS: Theophilus Parsons Esq. / Taunton / *Mass.* POSTMARK *(in script)*: Great Barrington   Ma[rch 1]0th POSTAL ANNOTATION: 12½.

1. Letter unrecovered.
2. Parsons replied on February 14 to Bryant's suggestion, "Let the compensation you allow me be proportioned to what you allow others" (Letter 94): "You speak of the terms we offer other gentlemen, but the plain truth is, there are almost none whose aid we should value so much, and therefore think compensation greater in proportion to the amount received than they have, less than that you should have. —The result to which we come, is, that we ask you to furnish us, an average of about 100 lines a month, and receive for it, $200 a year—Less than this we could not offer, and more we cannot afford." NYPL–BG.
3. Bryant's acceptance of Parsons' terms corrects Godwin's statement, "When Mr. Bryant was asked to name the compensation he expected for these writings, he fixed upon two dollars for each piece." *Life*, I, 192. Godwin had accepted Parsons' mistaken recollection in old age, "I asked him, for the proprietors of the paper, to

name his own price. And he named two dollars a poem! And this, I think was all that he was paid." Parsons to Godwin, October 27, 1879, NYPL–GR. In fact, between April 1, 1824, and May 15, 1825, Bryant's contribution of twenty-three poems totaling 1,187 lines was almost precisely that asked by Parsons. His compensation was thus nearly nine dollars a poem, rather than two.

4. Letter 95.

98.   *To* Messrs. Robert B. Southwick & Co.

Great Barrington   Apl   10   1824.

Gentlemen.

On last Monday all the hides in the vats of Cyrenus Stevens in West Stockbridge were attached and taken out on a writ in favour of Spencer & Crocker of West Stockbridge[1] against Stevens. As soon as I learnt this fact which was yesterday I went to W. Stockbridge to learn more particularly what had been done. On my arrival I found that 500 hides had been attached, of which 400 were afterwards replevied as the property of Simeon Brown of Pittsfield who had taken them away with him to Pittsfield. The remaining 100 were slaughter hides. I have thought it my duty to give you this information that you might take such steps as you may think expedient.—

Yrs. respectfully
WILLIAM C. BRYANT

MANUSCRIPT: NYPL–GR ADDRESS: Messrs. R. B. Southwick & Co   Docketed: Wm C. Bryant / Apl 10th   1824.

1. Unidentified.

99.   *To* Theophilus Parsons

Great Barrington   Apl   12   1824.

My Dear Sir—

Yours of the 31st ult. I received two or three days since;[1] and I have inclosed you a few contributions for your paper as soon as I could find time to copy them.—[2]

Every letter I have received from you has been something more than a week on the road. If you will take the pains to direct them *via Hartford* they will get to me in two days. Will you be so obliging as to give orders that my copy of the Gazette and other copies which may be taken in *Gt Barrington* be directed in that manner.—

As for the payment of the $200.00—it is an old maxim that a good paymaster pays when his work is done:—that, I suppose will be at the end of the year. —It might however be convenient for me to receive $100.00 at the end of 6 mouths— It may be sent by mail, unless I should previously direct otherwise.

I am sir
Truly yours
WILLIAM C. BRYANT

MANUSCRIPT: BPL ADDRESS: Theophilus Parsons Esq / Tauton.— / Mass. POSTMARK (*in script*): Gt Barrington Apl. 12. POSTAL ANNOTATION: 25.

1. Parsons wrote on March 31 that the first number of the *USLG*, though delayed, was in type, and "you will shortly see Rizpah in print." He asked contributions for the second number by return mail, inquiring how Bryant would like to receive his compensation. NYPL–BG.

    2. These were "The Old Man's Funeral," *USLG*, 1 (April 15, 1824), 31; "The Rivulet," *ibid.* (May 15), 69–72; and "March," *ibid.* (June 1), 64. See *Poems* (1876), pp. 67–73. The manuscripts of these poems are in HEHL.

100.   *To* Frances F. Bryant

New York, Apl. 29, 1824.

My dear Frances—

    I have on the whole made up my mind not to come home this week[1] —the weather has been so bad that I have seen little of the city as yet— and as there is no knowing when I shall be here again, I think I had better take time to look about me before I leave the place.—Miss [Catharine] Sedgwick has undertaken the charge of getting a bonnet for you, but as the weather has been rainy for two or three days past she has not been out, *and I do not intend to come away till the bonnet is bought.*

    I dined yeste[rda]y at Mr. Robert Sedgwick's in a company of *authors.* Mr. [James Fenimore] Cooper the novelist—Mr. [Fitz-Greene] Halleck author of Fanny—Mr. [Robert Charles] Sands author of Yamoyden —Mr. Johnson the Reporter[2]—& some other literary gentlemen— Mr. Cooper engaged the whole conversation to himself—he seems a little giddy with [the] great success his works have met with.[3]—Hier, au soir, nous allâmes Mons. Ives[4] et moi, chez une famille Française, ou nous jouâmes au whist, et parlâmes Français tout le temps.[5] Thomas has insisted upon my accompanying him two or three times to Mr Robt Sedgwick's whose lady[6] has a very pretty sister with whom he seems (but that is between ourselves) *épris* [smitten], and the ladies say there is something in it;— and that is scandal enough for *one* letter.—

    I got in on Sunday Morning at 5 o'clock & heard two sermons from *Parson Ware*[7] & very good ones too— Tuesday we had [Jared] Sparks Editor of the N. American Review to dine with us—a man of very agreeable manners—he was on his way to Boston from Baltimore.—

    Please to tell Dr. Leavenworth, if I do not get home Monday—to make my apology to the world—& get somebody to take down the votes for me, and make the proper memorandums.[8] —Good bye— Baisez la petite Fanchette pour moi [kiss little Fanny for me]—and give my regards to the family—

Your affectionate husband
WM C. BRYANT.

P. S. I have not told you when to expect me. —If I do not come home this week you may expect me next Wednesday—

W[illiam?] has been very busy with Ama[nd]a—he tells me this morning that she has comp[leted] her purchases of furniture & will probably have a house more magnificently furnished than any other in G. B. which information you may give to all whom it may concern.—[9]

WCB

MANUSCRIPT: NYPL–GR ADDRESS: Mrs. Frances Bryant / Great Barrington / Mass.—
DOCKETED: W. C. B. NY. PUBLISHED (*in part*): *Life*, I, 189–190.

1. Henry Sedgwick, aware of Bryant's growing distaste for legal practice and for Great Barrington, had invited him to visit New York City in the Spring. Sedgwick to Bryant, March 20, 1824, NYPL–BG.

2. William Johnson (1769–1848, Yale 1788), a legal scholar, was Reporter for the Supreme Court of New York and for the Court of Chancery.

3. In his memorial discourse on Cooper in 1852 Bryant recalled having been "somewhat startled, coming as I did from the seclusion of a country life, with a certain emphatic frankness in his manner, which, however, I came at last to like and to admire." See Bryant, "Cooper," p. 60.

4. Thomas Earl Ives (1802–1843, Yale 1822), third son of the late Gen. Thomas Ives of Great Barrington and brother of Bryant's former law partner, George Ives, was later a practicing lawyer at New Orleans. Dexter, *Graduates of Yale*, Supplement, pp. 93–94.

5. "Last evening Mr. Ives and I went to the home of a French family, where we played whist and spoke French the whole time."

6. Mrs. Elizabeth Ellery Sedgwick, of Newport, Rhode Island, was herself a woman of notable beauty who had been Washington Allston's model for his painting of a prophetess. Sedgwick, *Life and Letters*, pp. 148–150.

7. Rev. William Ware (1797–1852, Harvard 1816), pastor since 1821 of the Second Congregational (Unitarian) Church in New York City. See 63.1.

8. As town clerk of Great Barrington, Bryant was responsible for recording votes in the imminent election for local and state officers. David Leavenworth, a justice of the peace, was then his landlord. See 89.5.

9. Probably William Sherwood of Great Barrington and his bride. See Sherwood to Bryant, February 22, 1823, NYPL–BG. Sherwood later owned the boardinghouse at 385 [West] Fourth Street in Greenwich Village where the Bryants lived after their return from Europe in 1836.

101. *To* Theophilus Parsons

Great Barrington   May 26, 1824.
My dear Sir.

Yours of the 5th. reached Great Barrington during my absence in attending the Sup. Court at Lenox, where I was detained about a fortnight, and I received yours of the 18th. a day or two after my return. I see that you have found out my foible—a propensity to procrastinate, but I am ashamed to think that it has given you any trouble, and I do not mean that for the future you shall have any cause to reproach me for any want of punctuality.—[1]

In the little poem entitled—*The Oldman's Funeral*—at the end of the first line of the third Stanza *run* is printed for *won* in the Gazette.—

You can correct this in an erratum if you please—but it is not of much consequence.[2]

For prose—I have several little matters of that sort by me, but they are all unfinished— I will by and by put the last hand to some of them, and send them down for insertion in the Gazette—[3] In the mean time, I send you a supply of verse,[4] and will take care that you have more before you are out.

Yours truly

WILLIAM C. BRYANT

MANUSCRIPT: BPL ADDRESSS Theophilus Parsons Esq / Taunton / *Mass.* POSTMARK (in *script*): Great Barrington   May 28th POSTAL ANNOTATION: 18¼.

1. Parsons wrote on May 5 that he would "economize" Bryant's "three delightful pieces" (see Letter 99) by stretching them over three numbers of the *USLG*, hoping meanwhile to receive more. NYPL–BG. Parsons' letter of May 18 is unrecovered.

2. See *Poems* (1876), p. 68: "Why weep ye then for him, who, having won / The bound of man's appointed years, at last, / . . . / Serenely to his final rest has passed."

3. On May 5 Parsons asked whether Bryant had any prose pieces on hand which might help fill the department of Miscellany, offering to pay one dollar a column. There is no evidence that Bryant sent any "little matters" of prose to Parsons, unless —as seems unlikely—the brief notice of Catharine Sedgwick's novel *Redwood* (1824) which appeared in the *USLG*, 1 (July 15, 1824), 101–102, was his.

4. This included a sonnet, later entitled "Consumption," *USLG*, 1 (June 15, 1824), 75; "An Indian Story," *ibid.* (July 1), 92; and "Summer Wind," *ibid.* (July 15), 107. See *Poems* (1876), pp. 75–81. The manuscripts of these are in HEHL. The sonnet reflected Bryant's concern over his sister Sally's worsening health, which resulted in her death six months later.

102. *To* Theophilus Parsons

Great Barrington   June 22, 1824.

Dear Sir.—

I send you another cargo of verse. The lines entitled *Autumn Woods* I would print the 1st. of October. I hope you will receive the enclosed before you have disposed of what you have on hand—[1]

yrs truly

W. C. BRYANT

MANUSCRIPT: HEHL ADDRESS: Theophilus Parsons Esq / Taunton / Mass. POSTMARK (*in script*): Gt   Barrington. June 23 POSTAL ANNOTATION: 25.

1. In addition to "Autumn Woods," *USLG*, 1 (October 15, 1824), 203, the manuscript of which accompanied this letter, the other poems in this "cargo of verse" were a "Song," later entitled "Love's Seasons," *ibid.* (August 15), 141; "An Indian at the Burying Place of His Fathers," *ibid.* (August 1), 125; and "Hymn of the Waldenses," *ibid.* (September 1), 156–157. See *Poems* (1876), pp. 81–88, 96–98. The manuscripts are in HEHL.

103. *To* Richard H. Dana

Great Barrington   July 8th. 1824

My dear Sir

It made me very happy to receive a letter from you again, even though it brings me a reproach for my negligence. I believe you are a little mistaken when you say you have writ[ten] to me twice before without receiving an answer. I think it was only *once*. Be this as it may, I should have more reason than I ever yet had, to be angry with myself for that indolence which is my besetting infirmity, were it to deprive me of the pleasure of your correspondence.[1]

You say nothing of what you are bound to know must interest me exceedingly, your present employment and prospects now that you have given up the trade of authorship.[2] I have [made] many enquiries about you to little effect. [Fenimore] Cooper, whom I met in New York last May, could only say that he had seen you, and Mr. Dexter of Boston,[3] whom I saw at Lenox last week, only knew that you were yet in Cambridge. He said moreover that there was a story which has obtained considerable currency that you were the author of the new novel *Saratoga*; but added that he thought it impossible you should be. If in fact you are the author, I shall take it in high dudgeon that you are all along holding yourself out to me as a man who has thrown by his pen. At all events I shall read Saratoga since it has the honour of being attributed to you.—[4]

You inquire whether I have written any thing except what I furnished to Parsons— Nothing at all. I made an engagement with him with a view, in the first place, to earn something in addition to the emoluments of my profession which as you may suppose are not very ample, and in the second place *to keep my hand in*, for I was very near discontinuing entirely the writing of verses. As for setting myself about the great work you mention, I know you make the suggestion in great personal kindness towards myself, and I cannot sufficiently express my sense of that unwearied good-will which has more than once called my attention to this subject.[5] But I feel reluctant to undertake such a thing for several reasons. In the first place a project of that sort on my hands would be apt to make me abstracted, impatient of business, and forgetful of my professional engagements—and my literary experience has taught me that it is to my profession alone that I can look for the steady means of supplying the wants of the day. In the second place I am lazy. In the third place I am deterred by the difficulty of finding a proper subject. I began last winter to write a narrative poem which I meant should be a little longer than any I had already composed; but finding that would turn out at last a poor story about a spectre ship and that the tradition on which I had founded it had already been made use of by Irving, I gave it up.[6] I fancy that it is of some importance to the success of a work that the subject should be happily chosen. The only poems that have any currency at present are of a narrative kind—light stories in which love is a principal ingredient.

Nobody writes epic and nobody reads didactic poems; and as for dramatic poems they are out of the question. In this uncertainty what is to be done? It is a great misfortune to write what every body calls frivolous, and a still greater to write what nobody can read.

I am glad to hear that Miss Sedgwick's new novel finds so much favour with your friends, and I think that when you have read it you will call it a good book.[7] What you told me of the success of our countryman Cooper in England is an omen of good things.[8] I hope it is the breaking of a bright day for American literature, the glory and gladness of which shall call you again from your retirement.—

And now, as I have opened my heart to you and told you all that is in it, I shall expect a similar confidence from you to be manifested soon in a similar manner.

Remember me to all the friends who compose your Attic circle & believe me

Truly yours

W. C. BRYANT

MANUSCRIPTS: NYPL–GR (draft and final) ADDRESS: Richard H. Dana Esq. / Cambridge / Mass. POSTMARK (in script): Gt Barrington, July 9. POSTAL ANNOTATION: 12½ ENDORSED: From / Wm C. Bryant / July 8th 1824 / Ans Nov 16, 1824 PUBLISHED (in part): Life, I, 195–196.

1. No letter from either correspondent has been located, between Bryant's to Dana of November 17, 1822 (Letter 85) and Dana's to Bryant dated July 4, 1824, quoted in part in Life, I, 194.

2. See 83.7.

3. Probably Franklin Dexter (1793–1857), a lawyer.

4. Saratoga: A Tale of the Revolution was written by Mrs. Eliza Lanesford (Foster) Cushing and published anonymously at Boston in 1824. Wright, American Fiction 1774–1850, p. 84.

5. Dana had urged Bryant to tackle a long poem: "A man does not feel himself completely till he grapples with something that will hold him a tug." Quoted in Life, I, 194.

6. The theme of this poem, which survives in a manuscript fragment in NYPL–GR, was drawn from an incident recounted in Cotton Mather's Magnalia Christi Americana (1702), I, vi. Irving had used this legend in the tale "Dolph Heyliger" in Bracebridge Hall (1822). In 1850 Longfellow incorporated it in his ballad, "The Phantom Ship." See Longfellow, Letters, II, 350–351; Life, I, 197; 162.5.

7. Redwood (1824).

8. Dana wrote on July 4, "Two gentlemen, lately from England, report that Cooper is in high snuff there. They say he ranks at least with Irving, and that no works meet with a quicker sale."

104. *To* Charles Sedgwick

Great Barrington   July 10   1824.

My dear Sir.

I send you the April No. of the N. A. Review which Mrs. S. & your-self expressed a desire to read. For Greenwood's article I must bespeak a favourable perusal beforehand; for I once heard it censured by one who was yet Wordsworthian enough as I found afterwards, to speak of the tie that associates natural and moral beauty, and of the voice of divinity issuing from the eloquent places of nature.[1]

I did not want a writ of partition in the School District case—partition having already been made in due form of law by three disinterested and discreet freeholders, resident in the County of Berkshire. But the statute provides that the return of the partitioning Com^{te} upon being accepted shall be recorded in the Clerk's office & also in the Office of Register of Deeds. If you ever do such a thing as to let such a paper go from your hands I should like to have it sent to me that I may get it recorded here—[2]

I believe your sister, Miss Sedgwick, sometimes interests herself in what is going on in the literary world. Will you tell her as [a] piece of literary news, that my latest advices from Cambridge inform me that a certain work entitled Redwood, the production of an anonymous writer, whose name was so well concealed that it did not come to the knowledge of the public much sooner than the name of the work itself, is in such high esteem there that it is absolutely dangerous and unsafe not to admire it—that the unfortunate critic who is sufficiently hardy & unreasonable to find fault with it suffers an immediate forfeiture of reputation in matters of taste; and what is better still that those who from some reason or other (probably religious prejudices) did not like the New England Tale[3] have come out its decided and redoubtable champions.[4]

In the midst of these acclamations of praise which I hear from all quarters, it is a matter of no small pride to me that the unexpected and flattering honour which the author has done me in dedicating the work to me has permitted me to "Pursue the triumph & partake the gale," as Pope says.[5]

I have scribbled you a slovenly letter here; but we do not always dress to see our friends.—

Yrs. truly

W. C. Bryant

Manuscript: Pierpont Morgan Library address: Charles Sedgwick Esq. / Lenox endorsed: W. C. Bryant / July 1824 / In Re C. M. S's "Redwood" published: Charles I. Glicksberg, "Bryant and the Sedgwick Family," *Americana*, 31 (October 1937), 629.

1. This notice by Francis W. P. Greenwood in *NAR*, 18 (April 1824), 356–371 was entitled "Miscellaneous Poems of Wordsworth, London, 1820," but concerned itself

largely with Wordsworth's *Poetical Works* (Boston, 1824), the first American printing of his poetry since the republication at Philadelphia in 1802 of the *Lyrical Ballads*. See William Charvat, *The Origins of American Critical Thought 1810–1835* (Philadelphia: University of Pennsylvania Press, 1936), pp. 89, 91.

2. Bryant was appointed clerk of the center school district of Great Barrington on April 4, 1821, at about the same time that Sedgwick became clerk of the Court of Common Pleas at Lenox. "Youth," p. 235.

3. [Catharine M. Sedgwick] *A New England Tale; or, Sketches of New England Character and Manners* (New York, 1822). Miss Sedgwick had planned this, her first book, as a Unitarian tract, but her brother Henry persuaded her to write a full-length novel instead. Anti-Calvinistic in plot and characterization, the tale was either censured or slighted by reviewers. However, it soon went into a second edition (New York, 1822), despite—or perhaps because of—the fact, Henry wrote Catharine, "The Orthodox do all they can to put it down." Letter dated May 25, 1822, Sedgwick, *Life and Letters*, pp. 152–153.

4. See 103.7. Bryant apparently summarizes here comments omitted from that part of Dana's letter of July 4 printed in *Life*, I, 194.

5. *Essay on Man*, Ep. IV.385–386.

105. *To* Willard Phillips

Great Barrington   July 14, 1824.

My dear Sir.—

You have probably long before this seen the new novel Redwood. It is written by a friend of mine and I am extremely anxious that it should be noticed in the N. A. Review. My acquaintance with Mr. Sparks is very slight or I would have written to him on the subject.[1] I therefore take the liberty to add to the many requests with which I have already troubled you by desiring you to inquire whether the article is already engaged or not. I should be very glad to hear that it has got into hands willing to do it justice. —But if it is not already taken up, or if nobody who is like to treat the work as it ought to be, will think of doing it, I propose to review it myself; though I confess I should prefer to have it done by somebody else.[2]

It gives me great pleasure and some pride to hear of the reputation of your book on Insurance. I am told that the profession call it the best book on the subject.[3] (You have however never told me anything about its success.) It is something that ones book has a good reputation but it is also a very pleasant thing to have it sell well— A work in our profession is not however like the popular works of the day sought after with eagerness hastily read and then forgotten—it takes some time for it to get a reputation, and then men buy it as they find they want it—and the market for it if not so quick at first is more steady—it is like those articles of necessity & use which are bought daily while articles of ornament, after which there is a great rush while they are in fashion, are a mere drug as soon as the mode changes.—

[unsigned]

MANUSCRIPT: NYPL–GR (draft) ADDRESS: To Willard Phillips Esq.—.

1. See Letter 100. Bryant's critical writing for the *NAR*, interrupted more than two years earlier with the rejection of his notice of Dana's *The Idle Man* by editor Edward Everett, had just been resumed, under the more sympathetic editorship of Jared Sparks (1789–1866, Harvard 1815), with the publication of his review of Henry Pickering's *The Ruins of Paestum; and Other Compositions in Verse* (Salem, 1822), and *Athens, and Other Poems* (Salem, 1824), written at Phillips' request. Phillips to Bryant, November 11, 1823, NYPL–BG. This review appeared in *NAR*, 19 (July 1824), 42–49.

2. Because Miss Sedgwick had dedicated *Redwood* to Bryant; see Letter 104.

3. *A Treatise on the Law of Insurance* (Boston, 1823). A year earlier Phillips had sent Bryant a copy of this work. Phillips to Bryant, September 10, 1823, NYPL–BG.

106. *To* Mrs. Sarah S. Bryant

Great Barrington   July 30   1824.—

Dear Mother.—

I have just received a letter from Peter.[1] He tells me that Sarah was worse when he left Cummington; that he had written home to know what was the state of her health, but had received no answer; and that he wished me, if I had heard any thing lately respecting it to let him know it. —I am however so unfortunate as to know less about it than he does. —Frances and myself feel a great deal of solicitude upon this subject; and entreat you to write immediately and let us know how Sarah does.—[2]

I suppose that Peter also would be glad of a letter from home instead of getting his news at second hand from me. —According to his own account he is subjected to a pretty rigid discipline; and which along with some hardship, obliges him to a good deal of activity—enough one would imagine to root out all remains of laziness in his disposition, after being continued for four years. This mode of combining athletic exercises with a course of literary instruction is in my opinion the only true mode of education—and I should think its effect would be found equally favourable on the health, the intellects, and the morals of the pupils.—[3]

I thought of visiting Cummington this month. But Frances's health is at present extremely infirm; and I must defer it till she is better. —She sends her love to you and all the family.

Your affectionate Son
WM. C BRYANT

MANUSCRIPT: BCHS.

1. Letter unrecovered. Peter Rush Bryant had been admitted to the United States Military Academy at West Point on July 1, 1824, as a member of the class of 1828. Cadet records, Archives and History Section, USMA Library, West Point, New York.

2. Failing rapidly that summer and the ensuing autumn from tuberculosis, Sarah Bryant Shaw (Sally) died on December 12, 1824, leaving a two-year-old daughter, Ellen Theresa, later Mrs. Clark Ward Mitchell.

3. Peter was soon ill and unhappy at West Point. On February 25, 1825, having

gained his mother's leave to withdraw, he was discharged from the military service after having been "absent sick" from two mid-year examinations. USMA records; Peter to Sarah Bryant, October 29, 1824, BCHS.

107. *To* Theophilus Parsons

Great Barrington   Aug. 20   1824

My dear Sir

Just as I had copied the enclosed, I received yours of the 16th.[1] I send it on with all possible expedition.—[2]

Yrs. truly

W. C. BRYANT

MANUSCRIPT: BPL ADDRESS: Theophilus Parsons Esq / Taunton / *Mass* POSTMARK (*in script*): Great Barrington August 21st— / POSTAL ANNOTATION: 25.

1. Letter unrecovered.
2. Bryant apparently sent with this letter the poem "Monument Mountain," *USLG*, 1 (September 15, 1824), 173–174. See *Poems* (1876), pp. 89–93. Manuscript in HEHL.

108. *To* Theophilus Parsons

Great Barrington   Oct. 16, 1824.

Dear Sir

I send you three little poems.[1] What is a very unusual occurrence with me, my professional business for a few weeks past has left me little leisure to write poetry:[2]—In the winter I expect to have nothing else to do.—

Yrs. truly—

W. C. BRYANT.

MANUSCRIPT: HEHL ADDRESS: Theophilus Parsons Esq. / Taunton / Massachusetts.— POSTMARK (*in script*): Sheffield / Oct   23 POSTAL ANNOTATION: Way 18½.

1. These were a sonnet later entitled "Mutation," *USLG*, 1 (November 15, 1824), 237; another sonnet, later called "November," *ibid.*; and "Song of the Grecian Amazon," *ibid.* (December 1), 253. See *Poems* (1876), pp. 98–101. Manuscript in HEHL.
2. At the October 1824 court term at Lenox Bryant entered at least twenty-four writs for court action, as compared with six during his first term before the Court of Common Pleas seven years earlier. "Youth," pp. 191–192; MS "Docket of Cases, 1823 to 1825," NYPL–Miscellaneous Bryant Papers. In addition, the *Bloss vs. Tobey* case, to which he had given much time during the past year, was finally decided against his client in the Supreme Judicial Court during its September–October term. See 92.2.

109. *To* Henry D. Sedgwick

Great Barrington   Oct. 18. 1824.

My Dear Sir.

If I thought the conductor of the N. A. guilty of a wilful neglect of the work you mention, it would be a sin of omission for which I should feel little disposition to offer any apology.[1] But that department of the review which includes the notice of works of this kind, is one with which Sparks has never to my knowledge, meddled:—if it had depended on him I am sure the work would have been noticed as early as in the October number, which is as soon as it could possibly have been done.[2]

He intends however that Redwood shall be noticed in his review, and noticed as it ought to be. Last summer I wrote to a friend of mine in Boston on the subject,[3] and after some delay on account of Mr. Sparks's absence received an answer, from which the following is an extract:

"Mr. Sparks has made an unsuccessful attempt for a review of Redwood, has another importunity pending, and, in case of its failure, another party in reserve. It cannot appear until January, as the press is to be delivered of the next in a few days. There is no danger of rough usage of your said god-child, which Mr. Sparks has determined shall fall only into good hands. If all these resources fail, Mr. Sparks has agreed to advertise me and I will let you know of it. He thinks, with me, that the thing were better to be done by some other hand if practicable."[4]

If I rightly remember, the former Editor of the N. A., in a note to an article on the Spy, gave a sort of pledge to review the New England Tale, which was never redeemed. The religious tendency of the work might have been the reason for this.[5] But if we are not to have the pleasure of seeing a work so eminently honourable to our Literature as Redwood, noticed in our principal journal of criticism, with the eulogium which is its due, why, I think we may as well give up the reading of reviews altogether—

You call the last No. of the N. A. dull. I am certain the article on Counsellor Sampson's Discourse was not a dull one.—[6]

Yours truly,
W. C. BRYANT

MANUSCRIPT: MHS ADDRESS: Henry D. Sedgwick Esq / Counsellor at Law / New York POSTMARK (*in script*): Great Barrington, Oct. 18. POSTAL ANNOTATION: 12½.

1. *Redwood.* See Henry Sedgwick to Bryant, October 13, 1824, NYPL–BG; Letter 104.

2. Editor Jared Sparks of the *NAR* usually left the criticism of fiction and poetry to the charge of Willard Phillips. See Phillips to Bryant, November 10, 1823, and April 6, 1824, NYPL–BG.

3. Willard Phillips; see Letter 105.

4. Phillips to Bryant, September 13, 1824, NYPL–BG.

5. In noticing Fenimore Cooper's *The Spy: A Tale of the Neutral Ground* (New York, 1821), Edward Everett had commented in a footnote: "When [these] remarks were prepared for the press, we had not read the New England Tale, a beautiful little picture of native scenery and manners, composed with exquisite delicacy of taste, and great strength of talent. . . . If rumor has rightly attributed this excellent production to a female pen, we may with far greater confidence boast of a *religious* Edgeworth in our land, than of a wonder-working Scott." *NAR*, 15 (July 1822), 279. See 104.3.

6. Notice of "An Anniversary Discourse delivered before the Historical Society, on Saturday, December 6, 1823, showing the Origin, Progress, Antiquities, Curiosities, and Nature of the Common Law, By William Sampson, Esq.," *NAR*, 19 (October 1824), 411–439.

110. *To* Jared Sparks[1]

Great Barrington Oct 23 1824.

My dear Sir.

The article on Redwood for your next number, the writing of which you so obligingly offer me,[2] I should hardly venture upon, were it not that the omitting to notice a native work which has had so considerable a circulation, in a journal of the high reputation of the N. A. Review, might be looked upon by the public as equivalent to something like disapprobation. This neglect would have a still more decided squinting that way, after the elaborate articles on several American works of the same class that have lately appeared in your journal.

I had hoped that the work of reviewing Redwood would have been undertaken by somebody more competent than I am to do it justice. I have also some apprehensions that those who may know who is the writer of the article may be apt to suspect that his eyes were a little dazzled by the dedication. This is a predicament of some delicacy—not to say an awkward and embarrassing one; and on this account it were certainly better that the article should be done by some other hand. I undertake it however rather than that the work should fail of being noticed in your review.[3] But if after receiving this you should find any body willing to write the article to whom you would be willing to dispose of it, let me beg of you to press him into the service, and inform me of it,—and should I have made some progress in writing the article no harm will be done, you know. I am Sir

yours sincerely

WM. C. BRYANT

MANUSCRIPTS: HCL (final); NYPL–GR (draft).

1. Briefly editor of the *NAR* in 1817–1818, Jared Sparks had held a Unitarian pastorate for four years at Baltimore before returning to Boston in 1823 as owner–editor of the review. Soon after, through Willard Phillips, he asked from Bryant prose contributions for which he offered payment. Phillips to Bryant, October 2, 1823, NYPL–BG. But no record has been found of what if any compensation Bryant received for the two articles he wrote for the *NAR* in 1824–1825.

2. After failing to enlist a satisfactory reviewer of *Redwood*, Sparks asked Bryant to take this "good opportunity for speaking of the resources of this country for successful novel writing." Sparks to Bryant, October 16, 1824, NYPL–BG. See also Phillips to Bryant, September 13, 1824, NYPL–GR.

3. Bryant's anxiety that *Redwood* be fully and fairly treated in the *NAR*, even at the cost of embarrassing himself, reflected his warm friendship for the author and her brothers, of whose concern he was made fully aware. Henry Sedgwick wrote him

on October 13, "I will say frankly to you—what I would not to any one else—that I feel somewhat disappointed that there is no review of Redwood. . . . The total & repeated neglect of a native work . . . in a periodical devoted to domestic literature & native concerns—is by many deemed equivalent to disapprobation." NYPL–BG. When Charles Sedgwick learned that his friend would review the book, he wrote Bryant, "I made H[enry] D. S[edgwick] very happy by communicating the information you gave me at Court. He has more interest in my Sisters favor than his own." December 15, 1824, NYPL–BG.

111. *To* Jared Sparks

Great Barrington   Nov   5, 1824.

My Dear Sir.—

I have just recd yrs. of the 30th.[1] I regret that you should have been put to the trouble of writing to me a second time about the Review of Redwood—but I can assure you that the delay did not arise from any fault of mine. I got your letter of the 16th Oct. on the 23d. and on Monday the 25th I addressed an answer to you, agreeing to undertake the article, and handed it to the post master in Lenox where I was attending the Court of Common Pleas.[2] Letters sent from Boston to Great Barrington are generally a long time on the road unless directed *via Hartford.* —I hope you have received my answer before this time—if not this will serve the same purpose. I repeat my thanks for the obliging manner in which you have offered me the article— In haste—

Yours sincerely
W. C. BRYANT

MANUSCRIPT: HCL ADDRESS: To / Mr. Jared Sparks / Boston POSTMARK *(in script)*: Great Barrington November 6 POSTAL ANNOTATION: *Paid 12½* Docketed: Mr. Bryant / Nov. 11. / 1824.

1. Letter unrecovered.
2. Letter 110 (dated October 23, however).

112. *To* Theophilus Parsons

Great Barrington   Nov. 26   1824

My Dear Sir.—

Lest you should be out of poetry I send you a small supply subjoined.[1] The *money* due me from the Publishers of the Lit. Gazette may be remitted by mail; a circumstance which, although of some consequence I forgot to mention in my last.

Yrs truly
WM C   BRYANT

MANUSCRIPT: HEHL ADDRESS: Theophilus Parsons Esq. / Taunton / *Mass.* POSTMARK *(in script)*: [Great Barri]ngton, November 26th POSTAL ANNOTATION: 12½.

1. The poems enclosed were "To a Cloud," *USLG*, 1 (December 15, 1824), 267; and "The Murdered Traveller," *ibid.* (January 1, 1825), 286. See *Poems* (1876), pp. 101–103. Manuscript in HEHL.

113. *To* Jared Sparks

Great Barrington   Nov. 29, 1824.

My Dear Sir;

I send the Review of Redwood which I hope will come to your hands in season.—[1]

Your Obt. Servt.

WM. C   BRYANT

MANUSCRIPT: HCL ADDRESS: Mr. Jared Sparks.

1. Sparks replied on December 20 that, though he was much pleased with the review, it was too late for the January *NAR*, and would have to wait for the April number. NYPL–BG. The manuscript of Bryant's article is unrecovered.

114. *To* Charles Sedgwick

Great Barrington   Dec. 21, 1824.

My dear Sir,—

I finished the work I told you I had undertaken, a day or two before the first of December, and forwarded it immediately. I would have been glad to have had more time for it—but to have delayed it till another number of the N. A. would have been quite too bad—for the Article will be late enough in all conscience—that is if Sparks concludes to print it—and if he does not he will I hope furnish a better.—[1]

Since writing the article I have been twice to New Haven as a witness in an action against one of my neighbours.[2] This must be my apology for not earlier attending to your second call for the Report of partitiong. Comttee. in the case of the Cent. School Dist. in this Town. I have found it in the Register's Office but owing to some mistake of the Agent who left it, it is not recorded— I will send it as soon as it is recorded.—[3]

As for my plans for the future which you are so kind as to inquire about—they are much in statu quo.—I am fixed in my determination to leave this beggarly profession. —I am obliged to you for your counsel to see what I can do in New York and I think I shall *reconnoître* the ground in the Spring.[4] —Mr. Hillhouse who called on me about three weeks since told me that he thought there would be no obstacles in the way of my success, &c, &c—[5]

I am quite obliged to Mrs. Sedgwick for the honour she is doing me, and am proud of the opportunity of supplying the deficiency in her collection by the Copy of M[onument] M[ountain] which I enclose.—[6]

You have seen I suppose the extract which the last L. Gazette contains from a notice of Redwood in the New Monthly Magazine.[7] —Indeed I think it cannot fail to take with the English public: —A faithful picture of our domestic manners drawn by a writer of genius in addition to that celebrity which is created by qualities which must delight at all times and in all countries, must have, with English readers, the more *piquant* and popular attraction of novelty and of the promise it holds forth of gratifying a curiosity in relation to our Country that is every moment more & more stimulated. —In the mean time, I am gratified at seeing so many handsome things said of it on both sides of the water—and must confess that the other day it gave me no little pleasure to see in a letter from a certain literary gentleman at the eastward an apprehension expressed that Miss Sedgwick was in some danger of remaining stationary in her literary progress from the *indiscriminate* commendation as he called it, bestowed upon her last work— It was a remark that showed at least that the book was in great favour with the public.[8]

Yrs. truly

W C BRYANT

MANUSCRIPT: Pierpont Morgan Library ADDRESS: Charles Sedgwick Esq / Lenox PUBLISHED: Charles I. Glicksberg, "Bryant and the Sedgwick Family," *Americana*, 31 (October 1937), 630–631.

1. See 113.1. Bryant was then obviously unaware that publication of his *Redwood* notice would be delayed until April 1825.
2. Details of this case are unrecovered.
3. See Letter 104.
4. Charles Sedgwick had written Bryant soon after reversal of the Bloss–Tobey verdict (see 92.2) that though the Law was a "hag" with the "wrinkled visage of antiquity," full of "tricks in practice which perpetually provoke disgust," he would regret to see his friend quit the profession; yet he would respect Bryant's decision to seek a literary career, and suggested he ask help from Henry and Robert Sedgwick in New York. November 5, 1824, NYPL–BG. On December 15 he simply asked if Bryant had yet formed a plan. NYPL–BG.
5. James A. Hillhouse (1789–1841, Yale 1808, M.A. 1811) of New Haven had recently spent three years as a hardware merchant in New York City, where he had been an intimate of Cooper, Halleck, and other writers, as well as a friend of the Sedgwick brothers. He had recently brought Bryant at Great Barrington the manuscript of his verse drama, "Hadad," asking for it a critical reading. Hillhouse to Bryant, October 1, 1824, NYPL–BG.
6. Elizabeth Sedgwick had been clipping Bryant's poems as they appeared in the *USLG*, and her husband had mislaid "Monument Mountain." Charles Sedgwick to Bryant, December 15, 1824, NYPL–BG.
7. A British periodical (1814–1884) then edited by the poet Thomas Campbell.
8. The "literary gentleman" was Richard Dana, who had written, "The danger is . . . that Miss S——— will be injured by indiscriminate praise, rather than by too much censure." Dana to Bryant, November 16, 1824, MHS.

115. *To* Theophilus Parsons

Great Barrington   Dec   30, 1824.

My dear Sir—

I have received a letter from you enclosing a check on the U. S. Bank for $200.—, for sending which I am much obliged to you.[1] In the mean time here is something for your next.[2] I hope to send you soon a more ample supply.

Yrs truly
W   C   BRYANT

MANUSCRIPT: HEHL ADDRESS: Theophilus Parsons Esq. / Taunton / *Mass.* POSTMARK (*in script*): Sheffield Jan   1 POSTAL ANNOTATION: 18.

1. Parsons had written on December 18 enclosing the check and thanking Bryant for the "promptitude and regularity" with which he had submitted his "beautiful poems," for which he hoped the *USLG*'s success would soon bring the poet "compensation more adequate to the value of your aid." NYPL–BG.

2. Bryant enclosed "Hymm to the North Star," *USLG*, 1 (January 15, 1825), 298. See *Poems* (1876), pp. 105–107. Manuscript in HEHL.

116. *To* Sarah L. Howe[1]

Great Barrington   Jan. 10   1825.

Madam.—

I received your obliging note by Mr. Ives,[2] and avail myself of this opportunity to express my thanks for the kindness that dictates the suggestion it contains.

I think, with you that the subject you mention would afford a happy opportunity for a writer of talents, and that few public occasions of the kind would admit of allusions to the history of the past that might be introduced with such striking effect.

I have however always hitherto wholly abstained from coming upon the arena with those who write poetical Addresses for prizes. Along with perhaps a respectable competitor or two, one approaches the tribunal who are to decide upon his production, to have his merits weighed against those of a swarm of rhymsters and poetasters, the most miserable of the tuneful tribe. In such a contest a defeat would be intolerably shameful, and a victory inglorious. Besides, although the poem may be the best that is offered, there is no certainty that it will be pronounced such by those who are appointed to settle its merits—and then it will figure in a volume of Rejected Addresses. Such is the diversity of tastes, that a poem offered to the public in the usual manner, if it has any excellences will be sure of finding somebody to acknowledge and admire them. The very same work submitted at first to the judgment of two or three literary men might be decidedly condemned or at least placed below one of inferior value. Whether these considerations have kept first rate poets from writing for prizes, or whether the anxiety of competition neutralizes their enthusiasm when they write, is more than I know—but all the prize poems I have ever read are second rate—very elaborate and very frigid.[3]

My respect for your opinion has however led me to suspect that there is not quite so much in all this as I am apt to think. I had even almost

made up my mind to follow your suggestion and was about sitting down
to write an address in good earnest. I have been prevented however by
finding that it would be difficult to spare, from my other engagements, the
time necessary for such a composition.—

Present my compliments to Judge Howe— Mrs. Bryant desires her
best regards—

I am Madam
Your obt. & much obliged Servt.
WILLIAM C. BRYANT

MANUSCRIPTS: UVa (final); NYPL–GR (draft) ADDRESS: Mrs. Sarah L. Howe / Northampton.

1. Wife of Bryant's first law tutor, Judge Samuel Howe, who was now conducting
the Northampton Law School with his partners Elijah Hunt Mills and John H. Ash-
mun. See Letter 62.
2. Probably Thomas Ives; see 100.4. Mrs. Howe's letter is unrecovered, and the
subject and occasion for a poem which she apparently suggested to Bryant is unknown.
3. Bryant's youthful composition of odes for Independence Day and Agricultural
celebrations seems to have left him with a reluctance to write occasional poetry which
was evident throughout the rest of his life.

117. *To* Henry Ware [Sr.][1]

Great Barrington   Jan. 15, 1825.

Sir.

I have this day received a circular from a committee of whom you
are the chairman requesting my attendance in Boston on the 27th at a
meeting of the friends of religion from various parts of New England.[2]

I regret that it will not be in my power to attend the meeting. My
heart however will be with them in the important object they propose to
themselves, and any judicious & moderate measures calculated to promote it will have I am persuaded the hearty concurrence and assistance
of many friends of rational Christianity in this part of the country. Indeed it seems to me that it is high time that some sort of concert *should
be entered* some systematic combination—some degree of mutual understanding & united exertion should take place among those who profess
to hold liberal principles on the subject of religion were it for no other
purpose but to confirm & encourage those who like us in the County of
Berkshire dwell in the very shadow—and under the very frown of orthodoxy. —It is true that many of us while we do not wish to make our faith
a subject of wrangling & contention, yet make no secret of their opinions
on religious subjects; but is probably no less true that many who have
in their hearts embraced the same opinions are restrained from avowing
them by the dread of unpopularity. We do not suffer ourselves to doubt
that religious truth will ultimately prevail, but the distance at which we
live from the places where it is taught and our comparatively small com-

munication with them makes its progress among us so slow that we are sometimes ready to fear that i[t]s general diffusion here is a blessing reserved for the next generation. If the doings of your meeting are published in the news papers or in any of the periodical religious publications we shall see them of course—if not we hope that some way will be taken to communicate the results to the Unitarians of Berkshire.

[unsigned]

MANUSCRIPT: NYPL–GR (draft) ADDRESS: Revd Henry Ware—D. D.

    1. Henry Ware (1764–1845, Harvard 1785), professor of theology at the Harvard Divinity School, was one of the principal founders of Unitarianism in this country.
    2. On December 29, 1824, Ware, Alden Bradford, and Richard Sullivan invited Bryant, as one "known to take a deep interest in religion," to confer at Boston "on the expediency of appointing an annual meeting for the purpose of union, sympathy, & cooperation in the cause of Christian truth & Christian charity." NYPL–BG. In all likelihood the invitation resulted from Bryant's careful analysis for Andrews Norton, in Letter 90, of the state of religion in Berkshire County.

118. *To* Messrs. H. C. Carey & I. Lea[1]

Great Barrington   Jan. 15 1825

Gentlemen,

    I am very sensible of the compliment you pay me in applying to me as a contributor to your new work along with authors so celebrated as those whom you mention in a letter ⟨of the 5 inst.⟩ which I have just received from you.[2]

    You may consider me as a contributor, in my way, that of verse I mean, to the work.

    As to the matter of compensation I am too poor to work for nothing and we have a great modern authority for the maxim, that a man ought to be paid as well for the sweat of his brains as that of his brow.

    I do not however wish to fix upon any definite compensa[tion] myself. —I am willing to leave it to you to judge of the value of the articles I shall send you & shall be content with whatever amount you shall think I ought to receive.—[3]

Your obt servt
WM C BRYANT

P. S. I shall expect to receive a copy of the work.

W C BRY'T.

MANUSCRIPT: NYPL–GR (draft).

    1. Henry C. Carey (1793–1879) and his brother-in-law Isaac Lea (1792–1886) were partners in a highly successful Philadelphia publishing firm (1821–1851).
    2. This work was the first American gift annual, *The Atlantic Souvenir: A Christmas and New Year's Offering. 1826* (Philadelphia, 1826). Other writers in the first volume were James Kirke Paulding and Catharine Sedgwick. Carey and Lea's letter is unrecovered.

3. After hesitating because of his coming move to New York City, Bryant sent three poems to *The Atlantic Souvenir* for 1826: "June," pp. 64–66; "O Fairest of the Rural Maids," p. 135; and "Nature" (later titled "I Broke the Spell That Held Me Long"), p. 184. See *Poems* (1876), pp. 116–121. Pleading they made "little or nothing by the book," its publishers paid him only ten dollars for three of his most notable poems! Carey & Lea to Bryant, February 20, 1826, NYPL–BG.

119. *To* Theophilus Parsons

[Great Barrington, *c*February 1, 1825]

Dear Sir.

Above you have 2 poems. In haste. Yrs truly.

W. C. BRYANT.[1]

MANUSCRIPT: HEHL ADDRESS: Theophilus Parsons Esq / Taunton / Mass. POSTMARK *(in script)*: Sheffield.

1. This note was appended to the manuscript of "The Lapse of Time," *USLG*, 1 (February 15, 1825), 330, and "Song of the Stars," *ibid.* (March 1), 349. See *Poems* (1876), pp. 107–110.

120. *To* Henry D. Sedgwick

Great Barrington   Feb. 7. 1825.

My dear Sir

Since writing my letter of the 15th of January[1] I have received two from you, for which I thank you very much. I am exceedingly obliged to you for the readiness with which my enquiries have been answered, and still more so for the benevolence which has anticipated them, and which has proved, that, in applying to you, I was not mistaken in the opinion I had formed of your willingness to be of service to me, or at least was only mistaken in estimating it too low.[2]

I intend to set out for New York, next Tuesday, with a view of seeing what arrangements can be made for getting employment there, agreeable to your obliging suggestion. —I saw your brother, Charles, last week; he partly agreed to go down with me, and promised to let me know his final determination on the subject by last Friday's post—but I have not heard from him since. I hope however to have the pleasure of his company on the journey.—

My compliments to Mrs. & Miss Sedgwick and believe me—

Your sincere & much obligd
Friend & Servt.
WM. C. BRYANT

MANUSCRIPT: MHS ADDRESS: Henry D. Sedgwick Esq. / Counsellor at Law / New York POSTMARK *(in script)*: Great Barrington February 7th POSTAL ANNOTATION: 12½.

1. Unrecovered.
2. Charles Sedgwick had reported to Henry Bryant's decision to quit the law and

to look for literary employment in New York. In a letter which crossed Bryant's of January 15, Henry invited him to be his guest for a week or ten days while looking about the city. January 16, 1825, NYPL–BG. On January 23, having received Bryant's direct appeal for help, Henry wrote again urging him to come down at once and to explore the possibility of editing a literary review then being planned by the New York Athenaeum, for which, he said, "there is just now a rage." NYPL–BG.

121. *To* Charles Sedgwick

Great Barrington   Feb. 9   1825

My dear Sir.

I did not hear from you last Friday as I expected— I took it for granted, therefore, that you had not made up your mind not to go with me to New York next week, and wrote to your brother in such terms, that he will probably expect to see us both. You will not I hope disappoint either his expectations or mine. As it depends upon you whether I shall have a very solitary uncomfortable journey, or a very pleasant one I hope that, all other circumstances being equal, you will take the *humane* side of the question.[1]

I have made some inquiries about the Stages between Hudson and New York. They run every day and set out from Hudson at eleven o'clock in the forenoon. On Wednesday and one other day in the week (I forget which) comes along another Stage which travels all night for the dispatch of the mails. If you go, I hope you will come down Monday night, and if we can get to Hudson the next morning by eleven o'clock, *à la bonne heure*, well and good—if not we have the next day before us—but we will talk of these things when you come.[2]

Believe me
Ever truly
Yours &c
WM C   BRYANT

MANUSCRIPT: Pierpont Morgan Library ADDRESS: Charles Sedgwick Esq. / Lenox / Judge Walker DOCKETED: Wm C Bryant / Gt—Barrington / Feb— 1825 PUBLISHED: Charles I. Glicksberg, "Bryant and the Sedgwick Family," *Americana*, 31 (October 1937), 633–634.

1. Bryant made the trip alone, for Charles wrote him the next day that his wife was "reluctant to be left alone, & besides she '*knows* that I shall not take her to N. Y. in the spring if I go with you, for she has never heard of my makg two journies in one year.'" February 10, 1825, NYPL–BG.

2. Lying twenty-five miles west of Great Barrington and 110 miles north of New York, on both the Hudson River and the New York–Albany post road, Hudson was the usual point of departure for travelers from southern Berkshire County to New York City.

122. *To* Frances F. Bryant

New York   Friday   18 Feb   1825

My dear Frances

I have got here at last after being three days and one night on the road. —The first day brought me to Hartford—the next carried me to New Haven, and finding no packet nor steam-boat there which would set for New York till Friday, I kept on in the stage, and the next morning at sunrise found that I had travelled the immense distance of twenty six miles during the night. Yesterday at 7 o'clock in the evening I came into New York in the midst of a smart shower of rain—and this morning, after a good long nights sleep at the City Hotel, am as well as when I set out last Monday.[1]

On m'a fait beaucoup de questions au sujet de vous et de votre petite fille—[2] I find that the Influenza has been quite as prevalent here as with us and they say it is travelling through the city— Mrs. S[edgwick] s[ai]d this morning that the physicians computed that about four thousand people were sick with it in the city.—

Je n'ai pas eu le loisir de rien dire ni faire au sujet de mon projet— mais je prétends de faire le meilleur usage de mon tem[p]s pendant que je reste ici, et de décider au plutôt possible ou de m'établir ici ou non. Mons. S[edgwick] est bien occupé ce matin comme il l'est tous les matins —je lui parlerai ce soir.[3] I mean at present to set out for Hudson next Wednesday morning—and I should be very glad if H. Seley could be there so as to bring me out on Saturday morning—and if you can contrive [to] give him the information so that he may make it in the way of his business to be there at that time I should be glad.—[4]

Adieu—baisez pour moi la petite Fanchette.[5]

Your affectionate husband

W   C. BRYANT

I hope you are recovering as rapidly from your late indisposition as when I left you— Be careful of yourself—and if it [is] necessary to have any thing done for you do not be backward about asking it.—

W. C. B.

MANUSCRIPT: NYPL–GR ADDRESS: Mrs. Frances Bryant / Great Barrington / Mass. POST-MARK: NEW-YORK / FEB / 18 POSTAL ANNOTATION: 12½ DOCKETED: W. C. Bryant / N. Y—.

1. It is uncertain why Bryant took this slower route to New York City, rather than by way of Hudson.

2. "Many questions have been put to me on the subject of you and your little daughter."

3. "I have not had leisure to say or do anything about my project—but I intend to make the best possible use of my time while I remain here, and to decide as far as possible whether to establish myself here or not. Mr. S[edgwick] is very busy this morning as he is every morning—I shall talk with him about it this evening."

4. Probably a son of John Seley, a Great Barrington storekeeper whom Bryant had represented in several court actions.

5. "Goodbye—kiss little Fanny for me."

123. To Frances F. Bryant

New York   Monday—Feb. 21, 1825.

My dear Frances,

It will not be possible for me to set out from here till Thursday next, which will bring me to Hudson on Friday afternoon. I have a little Justice action before Dr. Leavenworth on Saturday morning—if I can get home early enough to attend to it I shall be glad, if not I must let it go by the board & pay the cost myself unless it can be adjourned—at all events I cannot leave town on Wednesday, for I have just got affairs into a promising train and it will not do to run away from them till I have brought them to some conclusion—unless I would return immediately. Will you speak to Elias and request him to enter any actions that may be returnable before his father on Sat. morning if I do not get home in season.[1] I do not recollect that there are any but there may be.

My friends here are making some interest to obtain the approbation & patronage of the Athenaeum for a literary paper to be established here under my direction, and I think there is a pretty good prospect that they will succeed. The Athenaeum at present is all the rage here[2] and I think there is great probability *q'un journal établi sous ses auspices aurait une circulation fort étendue.*[3] At all events I shall make the experiment. Mons. Hillhouse, Dr. Wainwright, prêtre de l'église Anglicane,[4] Mons. Verplanck, et beaucoup d'autres savan[t]s de N. Y. se sont intéressés pour moi, dans ce projet, et j'ai, à ce que je pense, sujet d'espérer que, mon attentat n'échouera pas. —Baisez la petite Fanchette pour moi— Ayez je vous prie un soin particulier de votre santé—et croyez moi

pour la vie
avec la dernière passion
votre ami[5] &c.
W. C. BRYANT

MANUSCRIPT: NYPL–GR ADDRESS: Mrs. Frances Bryant / Great Barrington / *Mass.* POSTMARK: NEW-YORK / FEB / 21 POSTAL ANNOTATION: 12½ PUBLISHED (*in part*): *Life*, I, 210.

1. David Leavenworth's son Elias (1803–1887, Yale 1824) was then a law clerk in Bryant's office. "Youth," p. 197. Admitted to the bar in 1827, he moved to Syracuse, New York, where he was successively mayor, state assemblyman, Secretary of State for New York, and member of Congress. *BDAC*, p. 1203.

2. The New York Athenaeum, a popular lyceum founded in 1824, before which Bryant would deliver four lectures on poetry the following spring. See Bryant II, "The Middle Years," pp. 24–26; *Prose*, I, [3]–44.

3. "that a journal established under its auspices would have a wide circulation." Italics Bryant's.

4. Rev. Jonathan Mayhew Wainwright (1792–1854, Harvard 1812), then Rector of Grace Episcopal Church, was an officer of the Athenaeum, as were James Hillhouse, Gulian Verplanck, and Henry and Robert Sedgwick. See MS volume, "Recording Secretary of New York Athenaeum," New-York Historical Society.

5. "Mr. Hillhouse, Dr. Wainwright, priest of the Anglican church, Mr. Verplanck, and many other New York scholars have interested themselves on my behalf in this project, and I think I have cause to hope that my venture will not run aground. Kiss little Fanny for me— Take particular care, I pray you, of your health—and believe me / for life / with the utmost devotion / your friend."

124. To Theophilus Parsons

Great Barrington   Feb. 28, 1825.
Dear Sir.—

I have received yours of the 18th.[1] As I was absent at the time it came and have just returned, I hope you will excuse my not answering you earlier. I have also received a letter from Mr. Carter[2]—and although he offers me an easier engagement with the Gazette than that of the present year (inasmuch as I am requested to furnish half the matter for half the money) yet I have found myself obliged to decline it, having made arrangements for leaving Great Barrington, and not expecting much leisure for the next year. For the matter of prose, [about which I believe I said something in one of my former letters, why, I have not found time to write any. —I send you one piece more, with which I take my leave of the Literary Gazette, for which my connexion with it, independently of its own merits, has given me a sort of affection, wishing it all manner of success with the public—][3]

I am Sir
very respectfully & truly
Yours &c &c—
WM C. BRYANT

MANUSCRIPT: HEHL ADDRESS: Th. Parsons Esq.

1. Acknowledging Bryant's "A Forest Hymn," USLG, 2 (April 1, 1825), 28–30—see Poems (1876), pp. 111–116—Parsons wrote on February 18 that he would be succeeded as editor of the USLG on April 1 by James Gordon Carter (1795–1849), an educational writer. NYPL–BG.

2. Dated February 15, 1825. NYPL–BG.

3. Matter between supplied brackets is so heavily lined through as to be nearly illegible. The enclosed poem was "The Grecian Partizan," USLG, 2 (May 15, 1825), 142–143. This is titled "The Greek Partisan," in Poems (1876), pp. 153–154. Manuscript in HEHL.

125. To Frances F. Bryant

New York   March 23, 1825.
My dear Frances

I suppose you would like to know whether I broke my neck in going out to Hudson last Thursday. I can assure you that it is as sound at this moment as your own, notwithstanding your prediction. However, I met with what was almost an equivalent. I got wet by riding half a mile in that tremendous thunder shower, and afterwards drove to Hudson, a distance of ten miles in a damp great coat and pantaloons. I waked the next morning giddy and almost blind with a cold.

I thought to go to New York in the steam boat on Friday—but none went down that day. Then I engaged a passage in a sloop, and had my baggage carried on board of her, and after waiting there from three o'clock till six in the afternoon, during which time I was briefly employed in pulling at a rope to help get her away from the dock, against a strong northwest wind, the vessel ran upon the bottom of an old dock in the river, and stuck. I went back to my quarters in the city. The next day (Saturday) the Olive Branch came along, about noon; I got on board of her and the next morning at 5 o'clock, found myself in this city.[1]

Here I am, trying to starve myself well, going hungry amidst a profusion of good cheer, and refusing to drink good wine amidst an ocean of it. But all will not do; I am continually in the steam-boat. Sitting or standing I feel the roll and swell of the water under me; the streets and floors of houses swing from side to side as if they were floating in a sea. However I am not much alarmed as long as my lungs are free from the distemper, which they seem to be hitherto.

My negociations with the Atl[antic] mag[azine] are going on, but I do not exactly know what will come of them.[2] I shall probably be able to tell you all about it when I get home. When that will be I know just about as well as when I left Barrington. I should think however that I might return in the course of next week.—

Mr. Hillhouse's Hadad is out.[3] He has presented me with a copy, which I shall bring up with me.

Monday evening I was at one of the soirées of Dr. Hosack.[4] There was a crowd of literary men—citizens & strangers—in fine apartments splendidly furnished—hung with pictures &c. &c. Here I saw Capt. Franklin, who is just arrived from Europe, and is going on another Polar Expedition, by land— Two other gentlemen of the expedition were with him. —He does not look lik[e a] man who had suffered the hardships of which his narrative gives an account—[5] He is square built rather short, inclining to corpulence, with the complexion of a shoemaker. Kiss F[anny] for me—

yr affectionate husband
W. C. BRYANT

MANUSCRIPT: NYPL–GR ADDRESS: Mrs. Frances Bryant / Great Barrington / *Mass.* POSTMARK: NEW-YORK / MAR / 23 POSTAL ANNOTATION: 12½ PUBLISHED (*in part*): *Life,* I, 211–212.

1. The "Olive Branch," a small steamboat, was the same one Peter Rush Bryant had taken from Albany to West Point the previous June. Peter to Sarah Bryant, July 1, 1824, BCHS.

2. The *Atlantic Magazine*, a literary monthly conducted by Robert Charles Sands (1799–1832, Columbia 1815), was absorbed in May in the *New-York Review*, Sands assisting editors Bryant and Henry Anderson in conducting the new journal. See Letter 126.

3. The dramatic poem Bryant had read and criticized in manuscript in December at James Hillhouse's request. See 114.5. He later reviewed it in the *NYR*, 1 (June 1825), 1–13.

4. Dr. David Hosack (1769–1835, Princeton 1789) was then a professor at Columbia College and the College of Physicians and Surgeons, and president of the New-York Historical Society.

5. Sir John Franklin (1786–1847), British explorer, had published in 1823 *Narrative of a Journey to the Shores of the Polar Sea in 1819–1822.*

126. *To* Richard H. Dana

New York, March 30, 1825.

My dear sir.—

I enclose you a prospectus of a work of which I have just engaged to become one [of] the Editors.[1] I beg that you will take the trouble to show it to such persons in your neighbourhood who will be likely to subscribe, and return the paper by Mr. Payne the bearer. He will leave Boston on Wednesday next.[2]

I have given up my profession which was a shabby business—and I am not altogether certain that I have got into a better— Bliss & White, however, the publishers of the N. Y. Review, allow me a compensation, which at present will be a livelihood for me, and a livelihood is as much as I got from my profession.—[3] Being one of the Editors of the work, though not a proprietor, I feel some anxiety that it should have a respectable circulation. —I rely upon its having your good word as far as may be consciencious to give it.—In great haste and hoping soon to find time to write you a longer letter—I am

Ever sincerely
yrs &c
W. C. Bryant

MANUSCRIPT: NYPL–GR PUBLISHED (*in part,* as of April): *Life,* I, 213.

1. The enclosed printed prospectus follows:

"E. Bliss & E. White,
No. 128, *Broadway, New-York,*
WILL RECEIVE SUBSCRIPTIONS TO THE
NEW-YORK REVIEW
AND
Monthly Magazine.

———

"This work is, with some modification, a continuation of the Atlantic Magazine. The first number will be issued on the first day of May, 1825.

"The price to subscribers will be *Six Dollars per annum,* payable at the end of six months by city subscribers. Country subscribers are expected to pay in advance.

———

"The recent development and rapid progress of native literature and science have created a corresponding necessity and demand for such periodical publications, as aim at exhibiting comprehensive views of the increase of knowledge, the progress of opinion, and the vicissitudes of taste in the political world. For this reason, the Conductors of the Atlantic Magazine, encouraged by a steadily increasing approbation and support, have determined to devote a greater portion of their journal to the purposes of criticism. It is hoped, that their associates will be thus enabled to analyse the plan and investigate the merits of almost every new publication, which in their opinion has a well-founded claim upon the notice, or a serious influence upon the interests of the people of this country.

"The Magazine department of the journal will still consist of such articles in the lighter and more attractive kinds of literature, as may serve to relieve the attention of the reader, and diversify the character of the work. For this purpose the Conductors have secured the co-operation of several gentlemen amply qualified to furnish the departments of Intelligence, Poetry, and Fiction.

"In consequence of the intended alteration, the present title of the journal will cease to be appropriate. The Atlantic Magazine will therefore be conducted, after the termination of the second volume, under the name of the *New-York Review and Monthly Magazine*.

"The journal will be issued monthly. In a country circumstanced like ours, the propriety of publishing a work on the plan herein proposed, every month instead of every quarter, is too obvious to insist upon. While the necessity of limiting the length of contributions will increase their number and variety, and prevent at the same time all unnecessary prolixity of argument or style; the contents of a critical journal are thus brought promptly and repeatedly before the notice of the public, while they still retain the opportunity of application, and the interest of novelty.

"☞ All letters, communications, contributions, and books intended for review, are to be addressed (post paid) to the Editors of the *New-York Review and Monthly Magazine*, care of the Publishers, E. Bliss, and E. White, No. 128, Broadway, New-York.

"New-York, January 1, 1825."

[appended in Bryant's handwriting] "Since the publication of this Prospectus, the subscribers have associated themselves for the purpose of conducting the 'New York Review and Monthly Magazine'; and have made such arrangements as, in their opinion, will enable them fully to accomplish all the objects which have led to the establishment of the Review.

"New York, March 30, 1825.

[signed] WILLIAM C. BRYANT
[signed] HENRY JAMES ANDERSON."

Henry James Anderson (1799–1875, Columbia 1814), professor of mathematics and astronomy at Columbia College, and Bryant's co-editor of the *NYR*, was described by Henry Sedgwick as "a young man of great attainments, industry & merit, who indulges the pride (or whim) of supporting himself altho' his father is a man of wealth." Sedgwick to Bryant, January 23, 1825, NYPL–BG. According to Sedgwick, Anderson, who had been conducting the *Atlantic Magazine* since January, had conceived the plan for a new review such as is outlined in the prospectus just quoted. The text of this, with Bryant's added comment, is taken from a copy in the Williams College Library.

2. Thatcher Taylor Payne (1796–1863), younger brother of the actor–playwright John Howard Payne, was a lawyer and occasional critic who had become one of Bryant's new friends in New York. See Taft, *Minor Knickerbockers*, p. lxxxi. Bryant mistakenly wrote "Paine."

3. An undated draft "Agreement" between editors and publisher, in Bryant's hand, specifies that he would receive $250 in salary each quarter, and in addition twenty-five cents on each pay day for each subscriber in excess of five hundred. Bryant's sober comments to Dana contrast sharply with his delight on returning home, as reported by Charles Sedgwick in a letter to his brother Henry: "Every muscle of his face teemed with happiness. He kissed the children, talked much and smiled at every thing. He said more about your kindness to him than I have ever heard him express before in regard to any body." April 1, 1825, MHS.

127. *To* Frances F. Bryant

New York   May 24   1825.

My dear Frances

Mr. James Hayward[1] being about to go to Plainfield in his way through this place I avail myself of his politeness to make him the bearer of a letter to you. Miss Sedgwick also hearing last evening that he was going near you handed me a book of Geography in French with showy prints, which she desired me to "send to Fanny." I hope *you* will be able to read it if our little girl is not.

I am now boarding at Mons. Evrard's.[2] The family speak only French and what is better very good French, and what is better yet are very kind and amiable people. Mons. E. is a bigoted Catholic and is taking great pains to convert me to the true and ancient faith. I have been so far wrought upon by his arguments that I went yesterday to Vespers in Saint Peter's Church; but my convictions were not sufficiently strong to induce me to kneel at the elevation of the host.[3] As I have a great respect for family prayer among all denominations of Christians, I intend asking of Mons. Evrard the favour of being permitted to attend his. On these occasions, it is said he utters with inconceivable rapidity a long list of such petitions as the following—

> Sainte Marie, priez pour nous.
> Chaste Vierge, priez pour nous.
> Mère adorable, priez pour nous.
> *Mère de Dieu,* priez pour nous.
> Maison dorée, priez pour nous.[4]

This is as good, at all events, as a Calvinistic or a Trinitarian prayer and as I have been able to swallow those I do not see why I should stick at this.—

I have had one or two turns of being a little homesick since I have been here, but I think that if you and Frances were with me I should pass my time, quite as pleasantly, to say the least, as I did in Great Barrington.[5] In the mean time I have become a great church-goer; I went three times yesterday including the Roman Catholic service, which is more I believe than I have done before these ten years.—

Tell my mother, that I have looked a little for the calico that I was to get,—I found a very pretty piece of 2½ yards, a yard in width, at 35 cents; but I have not taken it. Will you inquire & when you write will you let me know if this will be enough—if not how much more I shall want—

I might procure for you, at this moment, a very pleasant residence in Bloomingdale, at a house which Miss Eliza Robbins[6] has taken for the season—about 6 miles from the city and very beautifully situated—but the ladies tell me *"it will not do"—particularly, on your account—* So I must look again.—[7]

Embrassez pour moi la petite Fanchette—& give my love to all the family.—

Your affectionate husband
W. C. BRYANT

MANUSCRIPT: NYPL–GR ADDRESS: Mrs. Frances Bryant / Cummington / Mass. / Mr. Hayward PUBLISHED *(in part)*: *Life*, I, 214–215.

1. Probably the James Hayward who, with Stephen Hayward, had earlier operated a woolen mill and store at Cummington. *Only One Cummington*, pp. 256–257.

2. Francis A. Evrard, a former plantation-owner in Santo Domingo, had escaped the slave insurrections there of 1802–1804 and come to New York. Bryant wrote here "Everhard's."

3. Saint Peter's Roman Catholic Church, on Barclay Street west of Broadway, was a short walk from Evrard's house on Chambers Street.

4. "Holy Mary, pray for us, / Chaste Virgin, pray for us. / Adorable Mother, pray for us. / Mother of God, pray for us. / House of Gold, pray for us."

5. On May 1, after taking his wife and daughter to Cummington to spend the summer with his family, Bryant went to take up his new editorial position at New York. Frances Bryant, "Autobiographical Sketch"; Taylor, *Great Barrington*, p. 420.

6. Miss Eliza Robbins (1786–1853), elder sister of Mrs. Samuel Howe, and author of a number of elementary school textbooks, was a family friend of the Bryants'. Lesley, *Recollections of My Mother*, pp. 308–309, 369–370.

7. Bloomingdale was a rural village overlooking the Hudson River at what is now Broadway and 106th Street, a few blocks south of the present Columbia University campus.

IV

Sitting in Judgment
1825–1827
(LETTERS 128 TO 194)

SOON AFTER SETTLING DOWN in May 1825 as co-editor with Columbia professor Henry Anderson of the *New-York Review and Atheneum Magazine*, Bryant wrote Richard Dana, "The business of sitting in judgment upon books as they come out is not the literary employment the most to my taste nor that for which I am best fitted." But, he added, "It affords me for the present a *certain* compensation—which is a matter of some consequence to a poor devil like myself."

Bryant's later characterization of himself in 1825 as an "unknown literary adventurer" is hardly accurate. Though he had published fewer than fifty poems between the appearance of "Thanatopsis" in 1817 and his removal to New York eight years later, this modest production had steadily enhanced his reputation. His poetry had been received enthusiastically in England as well as at home, and even to some extent in France. During the same period he had written half a dozen prose articles which proved his to be one of the ablest pens in American literary criticism.

The many book reviews and notices Bryant wrote during thirty months as an editor of the *New-York Review* and its successor, the *United States Review*, though often produced simply to fill space the harried editor would have preferred to allot to others, constitute a considerable portion of the writing now recognized as the "beginning of a more discriminating criticism in America." But the most influential of his critical judgments were contained in four Lectures on Poetry he read to the New York Athenaeum in March and April of 1826. Here he urged members of this popular lyceum to turn their attention from neo-classicists such as Dryden and Pope to the romanticism of Southey, Wordsworth, Coleridge, Byron, and Shelley, whom he placed more directly in the great English tradition of Spenser, Shakespeare, and Milton.

Bryant's lectures were paired with those given by Samuel F. B. Morse on the history of painting. His poems had drawn praise from William H. Prescott in the *North American Review* for their "eloquent pictures of American scenery." A student since boyhood of drawing and sketching, Bryant quite naturally emphasized in his lectures the close affinity between the poet and the painter.

Bryant had been elected the preceding November to Fenimore Cooper's Bread and Cheese Lunch Club, an informal grouping of writers, artists, and business and professional men interested in the arts. Here he formed friendships with writers Fitz-Greene Halleck, Gulian Verplanck, and Robert Sands, and with artists Morse, Asher Durand, Henry Inman, Robert Weir, and Thomas Cole. His warm sympathy with the artists led him to support their attempt to improve the training and increase the patronage of young painters and sculptors which resulted in their formation in May 1826 of the National Academy of Design, under the aggressive leadership of Morse. He printed notices of the Academy's exhibitions in his *Review*, and, after he joined its staff in the summer of 1826, in the *Evening Post*. He opened the *Post*'s columns to Morse and his associates to reply to attacks on their growing institution by friends of the moribund American Academy of the Fine Arts, which it was replacing in public esteem. Early in 1828, Bryant addressed to the National Academy, as its "professor," a series of five lectures on Mythology which he repeated annually for some years thereafter.

Bryant's first venture as editor of a literary journal ended in June 1826, when publication of the *New-York Review* was suspended. The next month he made what he thought at first would be only a temporary connection with the New York *Evening Post*, when its editor William Coleman, the paper's founder, suffered a serious accident. But by the end of 1827 Bryant was its responsible editor, guiding the policies of a journal which he soon made the leading organ of radical Democracy, and which would be identified with his name for more than half a century.

Like its predecessor the *New-York Review*, the *United States Review*, launched in October 1862, lasted for only one year. Issued simultaneously at New York and Boston, with Bryant and Charles Folsom joint editors, it was an interesting experiment, undertaking as it did to overcome the critical hegemony of Boston and Cambridge, exerted through the *North American Review*, by offering readers a national monthly literary journal. Bryant took responsibility for all poetry, and for reviewing books published at New York and cities farther south, while Folsom and his reviewers cared for works appearing "to the Eastward." But Bryant became increasingly uncomfortable with his associate's tendency to introduce conservative political views into what he insisted must remain a literary journal. Thus he was almost relieved at the failure of the *United States Review* to survive beyond its first anniversary, for this freed him for consideration of the political and social questions now absorbing much of his time. To Dana's accusation that he was wasting his talents on a "vile blackguard squabble," he replied, "Politics and a bellyfull are better than poetry and starvation."

Just as his review failed, Bryant found a more congenial outlet for his literary energies. In August 1827 Robert Sands won the backing of bookseller Elam Bliss for a project which would join Bryant, Gulian Verplanck, and himself with Cole, Durand, and other artists in preparing for Christmas publication an illustrated gift-book of fiction, poetry, humor, legend, and criticism in the manner of the then popular German literary almanacs. Bryant happily seized this opportunity for literary fellowship as an antidote to the serious and solitary business of political journalism. The publication of the first *Talisman* in December 1827 began a collaboration which subsequently exerted, through the Sketch Club, the American Art Union, and the Century Association, a profound influence on the artistic growth of America's metropolis.

128. *To* Richard H. Dana

New York   May 25, 1825.

My dear Sir.

On coming to New York about a week since I found two letters from you which seemed from their dates to have been waiting for me some time. In one of them I was very glad to find a contribution in verse for my magazine.[1] I am surprized after reading it to hear you say that you never wrote thirty lines before in any measure. You have come into your poetical existence in full strength, like the first man. Not that I was surprized to find the conceptions beautiful—that I was prepared for, as a matter of course—but you write quite like a practised poet. The printer has got it and you shall see your first born in print next week— It will be admired without doubt. The only fault I find with it is that you give rather too many magnificent titles to a bird the popular associations connected with which, are not generally of the dignified kind you mention. I can speak also of his character from my own experience, having once kept a tame crow and found him little better than a knave a thief and a coward. As for the trochees &c. &c. never *fash yourself* about them. They are well enough—I would not alter them even if it could be done without injuring the beauty of the expression. I hope to receive more favours of the same kind from you. Choose a subject worthy of your genius, and you will do well enough. In the mean time if you have any prose that you can spare I should be very glad to publish it in my journal. We pay $1.00 a page, and I am sorry that we cannot give any thing that can be called a compensation for poetry. You mention an *Essay* which you enclosed me in a note. I have not received it though I have enquired at all the places where I thought it could be left for me. If it is a good one as I have no doubt it is from your recommendation I am sorry that it has not come to my hands—more especially as I suspect that in the course of the work we shall be sorely perplexed to get matter for our magazine or miscellaneous department. A talent for such articles is quite rare in this country and particularly in this city. There are many who can give grave sensible discussions on subjects of general utility—but few who can write an interesting or diverting article for a miscellany. If your friend does these things well I should be glad to have him write for us—though I hope he will not be too sensitive upon the subject of altering his contributions. When an Editor is responsible for the several articles inserted in his journal, and pays for them, it is hard that he should not be permitted to make them what he thinks they ought to be—

I believe you are right about the $6.00 but it is the fault of the publishers.[2] Wells & Lilly will not be the agents for the journal—though I do not know whom the publishers will appoint.

I do not know how long my connection with this work will continue— My $1,000.00 is no great sum to be sure but it is twice what I got by my practice in the country. —Besides my dislike for my profession was augmenting daily, and my residence in Great Barrington in consequence of innumerable local quarrels and factions which were springing up every day among an extremely exciteable, and not very enlightened population, had become quite disagreeable to me. It cost me more pains and perplexity than it was worth to live on friendly terms with my neighbours—and not having as I flatter myself any great taste for contention I made up my mind to get out of it as soon as I could and come to this great city where if it was my lot to starve I might starve peaceably and quietly. The business of sitting in judgment upon books as they come out is not the literary employment the most to my taste nor that for which I am best fitted—but it affords me for the present a *certain* compensation—which is a matter of some consequence to a poor devil like myself.

In the mean time I am greatly obliged to you for the pains you have taken in looking up subscribers—tho to say the truth I expected no less from your friendship.—Please to remember me to Prof. Channing if he is still with you—& believe me

Ever sincerely
Yrs &c
W. C. Bryant

Manuscripts: LH (final); NYPL–GR (draft) Address: Richard H. Dana Esq / Cambridge / Mass. Postmark: BOSTON / MS / MAY / 31 Endorsed: Wᵐ C. Bryant / May 25—1825— / Answered Published (*in part*, from draft): *Life*, I, 215–216.

1. "The Dying Raven," *NYR*, 1 (June 1825), 76–78.
2. Dana had evidently complained of the high price of a subscription to the *NYR*. That portion of his letter dated April 15 (manuscript unrecovered) was omitted from the selections published in *Life*, I, 213–214.

129. *To* Richard H. Dana

New York, May 28. 1825.

My dear Sir.

You will see in the copy of my Magazine which I send you that I have changed your crow to a raven. I do not know how you will like the metamorphosis—but it is a change only of the title of your poem, and I have not ventured to take any such liberty with the verses.[1] My reason for doing this was that the *title* was not a taking one—Anderson[2] was of the same opinion and urged me strongly to make the alteration—and Mr. [Fitz-Greene] Halleck (author of Fanny &c) to whom it was shown, while he admired the beauty of the poetry, thought the title an unfortunate one.— The raven is a North American bird, common in the interior of the U. S. and naturalists say that his habits are similar to those of the crow. I hope you will forgive the liberty I have taken—as it was only with a view to draw to your poem the attention it deserves.—

You will appear in our magazine in company with Mr. Halleck. The poem entitled Marco Bozzaris was written by him—and I think it a very beautiful thing.[3] Anderson was so delighted with it—he got it from the author after much solicitation—that he could not forbear adding the expression of his admiration at the end of the poem.— For my part, tho' I entirely agree with him in his opinion of the beauty of the poem, I have my doubts whether it is not better to let the poetry of magazines commend itself to the reader by its own excellence.—

The lines, which follow yours, were written by your humble servant.—[4]

There is an article on Verplanck's Evidences of Christianity in our review as you will see.— It was written by Bruen—[5] I do not think it does justice to the work—but it was furnished at the particular solicitation of Anderson—and was written by a gentleman of considerable ability who might have made something of the subject if he had pleased— I am sorry that so good a book was not better handled— But this is *entre nous.*

Now I am at New York whither you sometimes come it seems—I hope I shall see you again one of these days— In the mean time I hope you will not forget me but send often one of your good long letters and occasionally a poem—for he who has begun to woo the muses at your age is not soon cured of his passion, I trow. And remember me to Prof. Channing if he is still in your neighbourhood, and tell him, that if he has more things on hand than he wants for the North American Review that he will do well to send them for insertion in mine.—

I am dear sir
Yours truly
WM. C. BRYANT

MANUSCRIPT: NYPL–GR ADDRESS: Richard H. Dana Esq / Cambridge / *Mass.* POST-MARK: NEW-YORK / JUN / 9 POSTAL ANNOTATION: 18¾ PUBLISHED (*in part*): *Life,* I, 216–217.

1. See 128.1.
2. See 126.1.
3. *NYR,* 1 (June 1825), 72–74.
4. "A Song of Pitcairn's Island," *ibid.,* 78–79.
5. [Matthias? Bruen] Notice of Gulian C. Verplanck, *Essays on the Nature and Uses of the Various Evidences of Revealed Religion* (New York, 1824), *ibid.,* 26–33.

130. *To* Henry C. Carey[1]

[New York   *c*May 1825]

Dear Sir

I have just received your polite note of the 18th.[2] I should be willing to make some sacrifice of my own ease and convenience for the sake of complying with a request expressed in such handsome terms. I fear however that it will not be in my power. My present pursuits leave me little time; and poetry you know is not to be written in a hurry—at least mine is never written so, and the habit has continued too long with me to be broken now.

If however I should find leisure to write any thing for your work I will send it as early as the middle of June.[3] I should prefer taking a subject of my own choice [to] illustrating any of the plates you mention.

                              I am Sir
                                   very respectfully
                                        Yr obt humble Servt.
                                             W. C. BRYANT.

MANUSCRIPT: Haverford College Library ADDRESS: Henry C. Carey.

   1. See 118.1.
   2. Unrecovered.
   3. Soon after writing this letter Bryant seems to have sent Carey three poems for *The Atlantic Souvenir* for 1826. See 118.3.

131.   *To* Frances F. Bryant

                                   New York[1]   June 3, 1825.
My dear Frances—

   I send you by Mr. Ch. Sedgwick who is about setting out for Lenox the first No of the New-York Review—which he has kindly undertaken [to] put into the post office there along with this letter. —I think it is a pretty good number—I speak with reference to the articles which I did not write myself— The articles are by the following authors— Art. I by myself[2] II by Mr. Dix—[3] III by Revd. Mr. Bruen—IV by myself—[4] the review of Lionel Lincoln by a *Mr. Payne I think*—[5] and the three other articles in the Review department by Dr. Anderson.[6] —In the Magazine department—the poem entitled Marco Bozzaris is the work of Mr. Halleck —the account of the proposed publication of Mrs. Barbauld's works by myself—[7] the Dying Raven by Dana, the Song of Pitcairn's Island by myself and the Spirit of Spring by Professor Doane of Washington College, Connecticut.[8]

   Our subscription list is going on pretty well—we have already about 500 in the city—and 100 in the Country, besides the Boston subscribers, of whom no return has yet been made.—

   I have written you two letters previous to this—one by mail, and the other by Mr. James Hayward, who also undertook the conveyance of a little Book of Geography in French, with plates, for Frances. —Since writing my last I have received yours of the 21st of May. —I am glad that you pass your time so pleasantly as you seem to do from your letter. —Frances will probably be more contented as she recovers her health—

I hope you will take good care of your own— As a medicine I recommend plenty of walking; provided always, that you do not go so far as to fatigue yourself. I am obliged to walk a good deal every day as I lodge at some distance from the Bookstore of my publishers—and I find my health much improved by it.—

This week has been a chapter of terrible accidents in N. Y. Last Friday a Swiss who had just arrived in this country was murdered by two of his fellow passengers. Yesterday morning at 6 o'clock the boiler of one of the Steam boats plying between this city and Brunswick, exploded at the wharf, as she was just setting out with about 100 passengers on board,—and four of [her] hands were scalded to death, and others badly injured—and this morning about 2 o'clock a Mr. Lambert returning from a party a little out of the city with some of his friends was assaulted by a party of drunken apprentices, and a fray ensued in which he was killed.—

I like my boarding house better and better— It is almost impossible to conceive of a man of more goodness of heart and rectitude of principle than Mons. Evrard. He is very religious—very charitable—and very honest—a proof of the utter folly and presumption of all those who arrogate to their own sect the exclusive title Christians. Here is a bigoted Catholic—a man who believes that miracles are wrought by good men at this day—who kneels to the consecrated wafer as to the body of God himself—and who invokes saints and angels to pray for him—and yet his religion, mistaken as it is in these points, is as full of piety towards God and kindness to his neighbour, as that of any man I ever knew, while it is much more amiable and cheerful than that of many sects. —On the whole I think that a *good Catholic* is quite as good, and much more amiable than a *good Calvinist*. Kiss little Frances for me and give my love to all—

Your affectionate husband
W C Bryant

Saturday June 4th I open my letter to tell you that I have just received your letter of the 28th— I am sorry to hear that Frances is no better— I hope that you will not forget the calomel and if one dose will not do try another—

W[9]

MANUSCRIPT: NYPL–GR ADDRESS: To / Mrs. Frances F. Bryant / Cummington. / Massachusetts POSTMARK (*in script*): June 8 POSTAL ANNOTATION: 10 PUBLISHED (*in part*): *Life*, I, 217.

1. Bryant mistakenly wrote "Great Barrington."

2. "*Hadad, a Dramatic Poem, By James A. Hillhouse,*" NYR, 1 (June 1825), 1–13.

3. [John A.? Dix] "Report of the Secretary of War," *ibid.*, 13–26.

4. "*The Travellers: A Tale, Designed for Young People.* By the Author of '*Redwood*' [Catharine M. Sedgwick]," *ibid.*, 34–38.

5. [Thatcher Taylor Payne] "*Lionel Lincoln* [by James Fenimore Cooper]," *ibid.*, 39–50.

6. [Henry J. Anderson] "The Journal of Madame Knight," *ibid.*, 50–55; "The New York Medical and Physical Journal No. XIII," *ibid.*, 55–56; "*John Bull in America; or, The New Munchausen* [by James Kirke Paulding]," *ibid.*, 57–71.

7. "Mrs. Barbauld," *ibid.*, 74–76.

8. A poem by George Washington Doane (1799–1859, Union 1818), who was later the Episcopal bishop of New Jersey.

9. Before his marriage, Bryant had always been called "Cullen" by family and friends. Frances referred to him as "William," and after their marriage some of his brothers followed her custom.

132.   *To* Theodore Sedgwick[1]

New York, June 11th, 1825.

My dear Sir—

Your polite attention to a letter that I wrote you at the last session of the legislature, encourages me to apply to you on an occasion which I hope will not be quite so unpleasant,—since it regards the conferring of an obligation, instead of the taking away of a good office from a reluctant incumbent.[2]

Capt. Pope of Great Barrington,[3] about a year since, presented to the Governor & Council an application from some of the most respectable inhabitants of Egremont of different political parties, desiring that Mr. Charles Leavenworth,[4] a member of the bar living in that town might be appointed Justice of the Peace. This petition has never been attended to, although as it seemed to me it contained some very good reasons for the appointment.

Mr. Leavenworth has been for some years in the profession—long enough to have been made a Counsellor of the Supreme Court had he applied for it.— The reason he has never done so is I think a very good one considering the present state of the profession. Before being admitted as Counsellor one must be admitted as Attorney of that Court, and previous to being admitted as attorney a handsome sum must be paid which it well becomes any young lawyer to consider whether he is likely to get back again.—

Soon after being admitted as Counsellor, it is common for gentlemen of the profession to receive a commission of the peace.[5] Now I can see no reason why those young men who have [been] long enough in the profession to be made counsellors should not be equally entitled to a commission provided their respectability in their profession is as well ascertained.—

On this point Mr. Leavenworth need not fear inquiry. I know him very well, and can bear witness that [he] is well versed in his profession, industrious, and possessed of more than common acuteness of mind. His practice has always been honourable— I have known frequent instances of his having discouraged suits for trivial causes, and put an end to petty controversies between his neighbours which some others whom I know would have suffered to ripen into great ones—in short, his example in this respect is such as some who are his seniors might well take for a pattern.— The town of Egremont is also indebted to him in other respects—and he has done a good deal for objects of public utility & if the character of the inhabitants has been considerably improved and elevated within a few years past (as I believe it has, and there certainly has been great room for it,) it is in some measure owing to his exertions.—

I do not know what Mr Hollenbeck[6] the representative from Egremont, may be disposed to do in this matter. There is a local feud in Egremont,—as where is there not?—and he and Leavenworth are on different sides of the question. Hollenbeck whom I know very well, is not of a very milky dove-like disposition towards those who are not of his side. I presume therefore he would not care to have Leavenworth appointed.

I presume, that by this time you have perceived the object of my letter. It is to request that you see to this thing a little, unless you should find that there exists some objection to it—and, what I believe may be done without difficulty, procure for Mr Leavenworth an appointment which he deserves, and which would be quite convenient to him in the way of his profession, as well as to his neighbours.—

I am to be sure no longer a citizen of Massachusetts, but I am certain that I need not apologize to you for meddling a little with the matters of some of my friends whom I have left there. I have written to Col. McKay[7] on this subject and also to Capt. Pope.— I am Sir

with great respect and esteem
your friend
WM. C BRYANT[8]

MANUSCRIPT: MHS ADDRESS: Theodore Sedgwick Esq. / Member of the Legislature / ⟨Boston⟩ Stockbridge POSTMARK: BOSTON / MS / JUN / 15 POSTAL ANNOTATION: 12½ DOCKETED: Wm Bryant / 11 June / 1825.

1. Theodore Sedgwick II (1781–1839). See "Bryant's Correspondents."
2. In an unrecovered letter dated January 20, Bryant had apparently urged Sedgwick to recommend the removal from office as justice of the peace in Berkshire County of Gen. John Whiting, Bryant's legal opponent in the *Bloss vs. Tobey* action. See Sedgwick to Bryant, February 11, 1825, NYPL–GR; 92.2.
3. Ebenezer Pope (1782?–1841) was Frances Bryant's maternal uncle. "Mrs. F. F. Bryant's Genealogy," NYPL–GR; Pittsfield *Sun*, March 18, 1841.
4. Charles Leavenworth (1796–1829, Yale 1815), eldest child of Bryant's former landlord David Leavenworth, of Great Barrington, had prepared for the law under Col. Robert Barnard at Sheffield (see 87.1). After practicing briefly in Great Barrington, he had opened an office at nearby Egremont in 1819. Dexter, *Graduates of Yale*, VI, 771–772.
5. Bryant had followed this course, having been admitted to the Supreme Judicial

Court in September 1817 as an Attorney and two years later as a Counselor, then receiving an appointment as justice of the peace in May 1820. "Youth," pp. 234–236.

6. Probably the father of Elias R. Hollenbeck, medical student of Bryant's former office-mate Dr. Benjamin Rogers, and briefly custodian of Bryant's legal accounts after his removal to New York. See Elias Hollenbeck to Bryant, June 9, 1826, NYPL–BG; Taylor, *Great Barrington*, p. 323.

7. Samuel McKay (see 90.9) represented Pittsfield in the legislature.

8. A postscript to this letter by Catharine Sedgwick explains that she took it from New York to Boston, then forwarded it to her brother at Stockbridge. No reply has been located.

133.   *To* Frances F. Bryant

New York, June 12, 1825.

My dear Frances

I envy you very much the pure air, the breezes, the shade and the coolness which you must enjoy in the country, while I am sweltering under a degree of heat which I never experienced in my whole life time for so long a period. For six days the thermometer has hardly been below 80 degrees—day or night. I cannot write, except in the morning when the air is a little cooler—but in the middle of the day when the thermometer is at 85 or 87 it is almost impossible to collect resolution enough even to read. Yesterday in the afternoon I rode out a few miles into the country— I found it worse if possible than the city. The roads were full of carts, barouches, chaises, hacks and people on horseback, passing each other; and a thick cloud of dust lay above the road as far as the eye could follow it; it was almost impossible to breathe the stifling element.

Along with these inconveniences however there is one advantage which to me is of considerable importance. The nights are very dry. I do not perceive that the night-air is at all more damp than that of the day. There is a window at the head of my bed, and I have slept with it wide open for six nights past, without experiencing the least inconvenience— without perceiving any thing like that current of moist air which in the country you always feel coming from an open window in the stillest nights. A cough, which I have had hanging upon my lungs ever since last March, has left me entirely. Upon the whole I think that the change of climate is likely to prove rather beneficial to my health than otherwise.

I lodge in Chambers Street—near the Unitarian Church which, of course, I attend pretty regularly.[1] Mr Evrard, my host, has lived here twenty years—and during that time no epidemic fever has prevailed in this quarter— His house is at some distance from that part of the city in which the yellow fever made so many victims a few years since. The north river is at a short distance from us—I see it whenever I put my head out of the window—and whenever the wind is westerly it comes to us from over a body of water several miles in width.[2]

Monday June 13th.— I have not received a letter from you as I expected, this morning— I should think that it would be well to write your letters on Saturday and let Austin or Peter hand them to the Post Master on Sunday.— But if you have been unmindful of me, I have not been careless of you for I have been making enquiries, of every body who I thought could tell me, concerning a boarding house for our little family this summer.— I shall go to Brooklyn this afternoon to look at a boarding house which has been recommended to me.—

Tuesday morning June 14— Yesterday afternoon was somewhat cooler—quite agreeable weather—and I went over to Brooklyn. I found most of the houses where board could be procured quite full.— I found one however, a public house kept by a Swiss family, about half a mile from the ferry, bearing a very unpromising name—The *Military Garden* —where I was told that we might be accommodated. A gentleman, an acquaintance of Mr. Evrard who had taken the trouble to make some enquiries about it, for me, assured me that notwithstanding it was a public house, I could be as much by myself there as I could wish.— I could not however do any thing with the old Swiss, his wife not being at home, and she as far as I could understand him has the management of these matters.— I shall go over again in a day or two.—

There will be no difficulty in getting received at Mr. Duflon's, for that is the name of the Swiss,[3] unless it should be respecting the price— Mr. Evrard's friend however s[ai]d he had conversed with the Lady and she sd that she [wou]ld board me on the most reasonable terms.— But old Duflon said that his price for a single gentleman was $6.00 pr week— I cannot pay twice that sum— Besides board ought to be cheaper there—than in New York.— Good bye— Give my love to the family

Yours affectionately

W. C. Bryant

P. S. If you see Deac. Briggs[4] tell him that I called more than once at the office of the N. Y. Observer but could not find Abel Packard[5] nor hear any thing of him—

I sent you a letter last week together with a copy of my journal No 1 by Ch[arles] Sedgwick Esq. who promised to take them to Lenox and there put them into the mail— Our subscription list goes on very well in the city—and the first number has met with a most flattering reception. We have at present more than 500 subscribers in the city besides 150 in the country. These are exclusive of the Boston and Northampton subscribers— If we do not get the number up to a thousand before the end of the year, I am deceived by present appearances—several notices which have been given of the work in the Newspapers are favourable in the highest degree.— W. C. B—

MANUSCRIPT: NYPL–GR ADDRESS: Mrs. Frances F. Bryant / Cummington / Massachusetts. POSTMARK: NEW-YORK / JUN / 14 PUBLISHED (*in part*): Life, I, 218.

1. The Second Congregational (Unitarian) Church, of which William Ware was then pastor.

2. Although the Hudson River at that point is a scant mile wide, Bryant probably referred to the prevailing southwest wind across New York harbor.

3. No doubt this was the John Duflon, builder of a large "military Garden," whom Walt Whitman remembered in *Specimen Days*, and in articles in the Brooklyn *Standard*. See *The Uncollected Poetry and Prose of Walt Whitman*, ed. Emory Halloway (Garden City and Toronto: Doubleday, Page & Co., 1921), II, 298.

4. Deacon James W. Briggs (1782–1837?) was a son of Rev. James Briggs (1745–1825), first pastor of the Cummington Church, 1779–1825. Deacon Briggs had been Cullen's primary school teacher. "Youth," pp. 25, 27; *Only One Cummington*, p. 253.

5. *The New York Observer and Religious Chronicle* was soon afterward edited by Gerard Hallock of Plainfield, son of Bryant's early tutor Moses Hallock. Dr. Abel Packard practiced medicine at Cummington from 1824 to 1828. *Only One Cummington*, p. 398.

134. *To* Frances F. Bryant

New York   June 20   1825.

My dear Frances.

I hope that this letter which I shall send by Col. Ward of Worthington,[1] who is now in this city will have the good fortune to reach you earlier than most of my letters that you have received by mail. I got yours of the 11th last Friday. You mention the letter brought by Mr. Hayward as the last that had come to your hands—though I had sent off two since that, before receiving yours. I hope this will incline you to qualify your accusation of my being a negligent correspondent.

I intended to have gone over to Brooklyn, and to have finished my arrangements for our lodgings during the warm weather, before I wrote you again. I have not however been able to do it,—partly owing to the heat, which on some days has been quite oppressive—and partly because I am pretty busy in getting together matter for our next number. I shall probably be in Cummington in about 3 weeks from this time. I shall think of remaining there about a fortnight, and intend to stay about 5 days, or a week, in Great Barrington, on my return. In short I mean to make my arrangements so as to get back to New York somewhere about the first of August.—

I have not seen, nor heard any thing from your brother Egbert.—[2] Wm. Leavenworth[3] is now in town. Miss Sedgwick went about a fortnight since to Boston, to be present at the great occasion at Bunker Hill.[4]

I send you along with this, by Col Ward, a little roll containing 4 lithographic prints, which I thought you might perhaps amuse yourself by copying, and then bestow them as you pleased.

Notwithstanding the heat, the noise, and the unpleasant odours of the city, I think that if you and Frances were with me, I should pass my time here much more pleasantly than at Great Barrington. I am obliged to be pretty industrious, it is true, but that is well enough.— In the mean time I am not plagued with the disagreeable disgusting drudgery of the law—and what is still better am aloof from those miserable feuds and wranglings that make Great Barrington an unpleasant residence, even to him who tries every method in his power to avoid them.

If you have any time to spare I think you would do well to set about putting your name on every article of clothing that you are likely to have washed here. Last Saturday my laundress came with my linen and brought one cravat two pairs of stockings and a flannel wrapper that did not belong to me and I found that two cravats of my own and two pairs of stockings were missing. I sent her away with the things that did not belong to me, and have not seen her since, though it has been her usual practice to call Monday morning to take my dirty linen—and it is now five o'clock in the afternoon. I do not expect however to lose them, for she seems to be a very honest old lady, washes at the reasonable rate of 50 cents the dozen, and was sent to me by Miss Sedgwick who was kind enough to look her out for me.—

I am very glad that Frances makes such progress in learning to read, [and you must tell her that when I see her again I shall expect that she will be able to read any where in Cobwebs].[5] Mr Ward has called for the letter.—

> Good bye
> yrs affectionately
> W   C   BRYANT

MANUSCRIPT: NYPL–GR ADDRESS: Mrs. Frances F. Bryant / Cummington / Mass / W   Ward Esq. PUBLISHED (in part): Life, I, 219.

1. See 95.3.
2. Egbert Nelson Fairchild (1802?–1864) was the youngest of Frances Bryant's nine brothers and sisters.
3. After Bryant left Great Barrington William, son of David Leavenworth, built a dam and mill near the grove of which the poet had written in "Green River," "And the plane-tree's speckled arms o'ershoot / The swifter current that mines its root." Taylor, Great Barrington, p. 358. See Poems (1876), p. 33.
4. Daniel Webster's speech at the dedication of the Bunker Hill Monument on June 17, 1825, was the subject of an article by Bryant in NYR, 1 (August 1825), 214–219.
5. The lines between supplied brackets are in block print, presumably for little Fanny's eye. "Cobwebs" is unidentified.

135. To George Bancroft[1]

New York   28 June 1825.

My dear Sir

I yesterday received your beautiful translation of Goethe's ballad. We shall venture to print it—there is nothing in it with which true delicacy can be offended. I have however ventured to take the liberty you

grant me, of slightly varying the phraseology in one or two instances,—
not with a view of improving, but of softening the expression.[2]

I expected to have seen you on your return from West Point, and
to have talked with you about the review of Everett's Orations. We
should be very glad of it for the August number—the article will be
rather late for September. If you will do me the favour to write it, I
should like to receive it by the 15th of July.[3]

Allow me to express my gratitude for the friendly interest you take
in our journal. We shall be exceedingly glad of all the help you may be
disposed to give us, and I hope that you will not be impatient if I show
you the value I set upon your promise of assistance, by occasionally re-
minding you of it.

I am sir
yours sincerely &c &c
WILLIAM C. BRYANT

MANUSCRIPT: MHS ADDRESS: Mr. Geo. Bancroft.

1. George Bancroft (1800–1891, Harvard 1817), then joint conductor with Joseph
Green Cogswell of the experimental Round Hill School at Northampton, had published several articles on German literature in the NAR since his return from Europe
in 1823. This is Bryant's first letter to the historian and diplomat who would become
his intimate friend.

2. "The Indian God and the Bayadeer," NYR, 1 (July 1825), 165–168.

3. Bancroft did not send this article until September. It was published in the October number of the NYR.

136. To George Bancroft

New York   Aug   10, 1825.

My dear Sir

I am afraid you may not altogether be pleased with the form in
which your translation of Schiller's Division of the Earth appears in our
last number.[1] I have been absent from the city for about four weeks past
and your translation was received and printed in my absence.[2] I am just
returned and Dr. Anderson has told me that not being pleased with the
measure he took the liberty to alter the last line in every stanza in such
a manner as to make it two syllables longer.—

I regret that it has been done—but the blame is principally if not
wholly my own. I should have mentioned to Anderson, before I left the
city, your protest against the alteration of any of your contributions without first consulting you.[3] It did not occur to me however that any poetical
articles might be received from you during my absence.

Dr. Anderson states to me that he has hitherto in all cases taken the
liberty to make alterations in the poetical contributions sent him, without the least scruple, wherever his taste or fancy dictated, and that in
most instances his correspondents had given him an unqualified license

of doing it.— That the measure of your translation, although the same
with that of the original, seemed harsh and unpleasant to his ear, and
that without intending any disrespect to the author, or disparagement
of the merit of the translation, he had followed his old habit of making
such alterations as pleased him. On learning from Anderson what he had
done I determined to give you this explanation immediately that you
might be satisfied that the fault was an accidental one, and would not be
committed a second time.

The translation is a beautiful one and we are greatly obliged to you
for it.— I have heard nothing of your article on Everett's Orations yet.—

I am dear Sir
yrs truly &c &c
W. C. BRYANT

MANUSCRIPT: MHS.

1. *NYR*, 1 (August 1825), 242–243.
2. Bryant had passed most of July at Cummington and Great Barrington, bringing his family back with him to Evrard's boardinghouse for the month of August.
Frances Bryant, "Autobiographical Sketch," NYPL–GR.
3. This was evidently a sensitive point with Bancroft. When editor Jared Sparks
of the *NAR* cautioned him against "certain effulgences of style," Bancroft warned him
to "make no omissions nor alterations. . . . I have written with great care, and will
be personally responsible for every word of the article." Russell B. Nye, *George Bancroft: Brahmin Rebel* (New York: Knopf, 1945), pp. 78–79.

137. *To* Richard H. Dana

New York   Sept. 1, 1825.

My dear Sir

I intended to have answered your letter before this but I have been
exceedingly lazy, and somewhat hurried, during the hot weather that
has continued almost ever since I received it. I have found time however
to look over the lines you sent me, and as you seemed to give me leave,
to make some alterations.[1] I have in particular taken the liberty, whenever I found you out of the pale which the lawgivers of versification have
put up to confine poets in,—to catch you and bring you back and put on
your fetters again. There are two lines which I am confident you left on
purpose to try me

O'er hills, through leafy woods, and leafless;—
To me—who love the stream to trace, &c

I tried, by reading these lines over and over, to make them agree in
rhyme and measure—but finding that impossible, I altered them, and in
doing this was obliged to alter several of the neighbouring lines. I must
confess that you had one good reason—I have written *good reason* but
that is wrong—you had one apology for leaving the lines as they were,
namely, the difficulty of making them otherwise,

I have also ventured to make some changes where the sentences were continued from one couplet to the beginning of another, or where they began near the end of one couplet and were continued to the middle of the next—a practice sometimes exceedingly graceful in the heroic measure, but which if frequently introduced in octosyllabic verse produces a harshness. In other cases where I thought the idea not sufficiently brought out I have taken the liberty to amplify it a little. But you will see all the mutilations I have made when you receive the journal which I shall send on the heels of this letter.—

One thing I have done—I have respected the thoughts in all the alterations I have made—and it is a great excellence of your verses that they are full of thought. You are however more at home in blank verse than in rhyme—at least you are so in the specimens you have sent me.

I saw Cooper yesterday. He is printing a novel entitled *The Last of the Mohicans*: the first volume is nearly finished.[2] —You tell me that I must review him, next time, myself. Ah, sir, he is too sensitive a creature for me to touch.[3] He seems to think his own works his own property instead of being the property of the public, to whom he has given them— and it is almost as difficult to praise or blame them in the right place as it was to praise or blame Goldsmith properly in the presence of Johnson.—

The language held by a certain gentleman in this city,[4] whom you do not name, concerning Cooper's novels, may have other causes besides the one you mention, that a certain other person has written a very clever novel.[5]— There was once I am told a very warm friendship between them —this was broken by some misunderstandings and supposed causes of complaint—and now matters are so ripe that there is a law suit pending.[6] I should be very sorry to suppose that mere jealousy of Cooper's literary reputation should make such excellent people his enemies, and I beg you will set what you heard to some other ac[count.]

My encomiums on the *"beautiful style"* of which you speak, were attended with some qualifying animadversions, which were not printed.[7]

I hope to continue to receive contributions from you. Any thing you have on hand, poetry, or prose, I shall be grateful for.— Remind [Edward] Channing of his promise to write for me—and tell him that it was time he was in print again.— My regards to all my friends in Cambridge.

[signature missing]

Manuscript: NYPL–GR Address: Richard H. Dana Esq. / Cambridge / Massachusetts. Postmark: NEW-YORK / SEP / 1 postal annotation: 18¾ published (*in part*): *Life*, I, 220–221.

1. "Fragment of a Poetical Epistle," *NYR*, 1 (September 1825), 319–322. Dana's letter is unrecovered.

2. *The Last of the Mohicans: A Narrative of 1757.* 2 vols. (Philadelphia, 1826).

3. Thatcher Payne had written the article on Cooper's *Lionel Lincoln* for the first number of the *NYR*. When *The Last of the Mohicans* came up for review Bryant gave

the task to Robert Sands, whose notice appeared in *NYR*, 2 (March 1826), 285–292.

4. Robert Sedgwick. See Note 6.

5. Catharine Sedgwick's *Redwood*. See 103.7.

6. In 1818–1819 Robert Sedgwick repeatedly lent Cooper money, not pressing him for repayment. But in 1824–1825, after differences between them, Sedgwick sued for payment. The next year he dropped the suits, with Cooper liable for the costs. *The Letters and Journals of James Fenimore Cooper*, ed. James Franklin Beard (Cambridge: The Belknap Press of Harvard University Press, 1960), I, 124–125.

7. In his review of Hillhouse's *Hadad* in the *NYR* for June, Bryant had remarked on the "great beauty" to be found in the dialogue between Hadad and Tamar. It is perhaps this passage to which Dana had referred.

138. *To* Frances F. Bryant

New York Sept. 17, 1825.

My dear Frances

I remembered after I sent off my last[1] that I had not given you the number of our new lodgings in order that you may tell the coachman where to set you down. It is 88 Canal St.[2] Do not forget to take the stage that goes to N. Y. by the Williamsburg ferry instead of that to Brooklyn. It costs but 6 pence more.

I am just returned from a call on Miss W————. I went to the intersection of Essex and Rivington Streets, and knocked at the door of a house at one of the corners, in which I judged it most likely that she lived. It was a two story brick house standing quite by itself with jars of flowers on the outside of the upper windows. The lower story had been evidently built for a shop of some sort, but the front door was shut and I went to a side door. A woman between thirty and forty years of age put her head out of a window above the door and asked what I wanted, and at the same time a pretty little girl about twelve years of age opened the door. I inquired if a Mr. Simpson lived there? The woman said that he did not—but a Mr. Sinclair did. "An Englishman?" demanded I. "No, no such person lives here." The little girl said there was a Mr. Brown who lived there. "And what business does he follow?" "He is a blacksmith." "Then I have come to the wrong place," and turning away I went to the opposite corner where there was a grocery. I enquired for a tall Englishman who drove a cart with two horses. The grocer said that there was such a man who lived in the house which I had just quitted but he did not know his name. "There he is now, going in." I returned to the house but Simpson had got in and shut the door. I knocked again; it was opened by the woman whom I had seen at the window. I told her, that the man who had just entered was the person whom I wanted to see. "Oh, it is Mr. Sinclair!" "Aye, aye, Mr. Sinclair." Mr *Sinclair* who was going up stairs now looked down: I accosted him; he returned my salute good naturedly, and asked me to walk up. I went up; and stood on the landing-place, while he opened the door of a chamber, announced my name, and then said that the lady would be ready to see me in a moment. A[t] length I was permitted to enter, Mrs. W. rose from her chair and gave me her hand. She was in a dark dress open in front with a white under dress—and her cheeks had the same unnatural colour that we used to remark when she lived in Great Barrington—*rouge* probably. But she was exceedingly emaciated, her figure thin, and her cheeks hollow. I was astonished at the change in her appearance. My astonishment however did not last long; hearing an odd sort of noise in the room I turned my eyes to the quarter from which it proceeded and saw a fine plump infant, four or five weeks old as I should judge, in the arms of the woman whom I saw at the window. There was a cradle too in the room, and some squares drying at the fire. Mrs. W. looked quite sober and Mr. S. a little silly. I began to suspect that my intrusion could not be very welcome; and as the child began to grow uneasy I staid but little time. On taking my leave I gave the lady the name of Mrs. W. and to make amends for this blunder I called Mr. Simpson, Mr. Sinclair.[3]

Kiss little Frances for me—

Yr affectionate husband & friend

W C BRYANT

Let nothing be said nor written about this— It is evident that the gentleman and lady do not mean to have their history made public, from the circumstances of their taking feigned names. You recollect that Bellamy[4] hesitated about letting me know their place of residence—and I have no doubt that they mean to conceal it from those who would be likely to talk about it. People have enough to talk about already—there is no necessity that we should provide them with any new topics. W. C. B.

MANUSCRIPT: NYPL–GR ADDRESS: Mrs. Frances F. Bryant / at Mr. Lord's / Jamaica / Long Island POSTMARK: NEW-YORK / SEP / 18 POSTAL ANNOTATION: 6.

1. Letter unrecovered.

2. About September 1 Frances and Fanny had gone to board with a Mr. Lord at Jamaica, Long Island. Soon after, Bryant found winter lodgings for his family with a Mrs. Meigs at 88 Canal Street, Manhattan. Frances Bryant, "Autobiographical Sketch," NYPL–GR.

3. Nothing further has been learned about the persons described here.

4. Unidentified.

139. *To* Frances F. Bryant

New York[1] Sept. 19, 1825.

My dear wife

I wrote you last Friday, enclosing a ten dollar bill, and informing you that I had made arrangements for being boarded at Mrs. Meigs's this winter. I requested you also to acknowledge the receipt of my letter without loss of time. Yesterday I put another letter into the post office informing you what I had forgotten to say in my first, that our lodgings were at 88 Canal Street. And to day, not having received any answer to my first letter which I fear may have miscarried, I write to say that I think you may as well come in without any delay. The weather is become quite cool—and you will find things very convenient here—and I am impatient to have you and Frances with me.—[2]

Yours affectionately
WM. C. BRY[ANT]

MANUSCRIPT: NYPL–GR ADDRESS: Mrs. Frances F. Bryant / Jamaica / (L. I.) POSTMARK: NEW-YORK / SEP / 19 POSTAL ANNOTATION: PAID.

1. Bryant mistakenly wrote "Great Barrington."
2. Although Frances implied that she and Fanny stayed at Jamaica until the end of November, it seems more probable that they returned to New York soon after this appeal, for no further letters to her from her husband that autumn have been recovered. See her "Autobiographical Sketch," NYPL–GR.

140. *To* George Bancroft

New York   Sept 19 1825.

My dear Sir

I have received your article on Everett's Orations, read it and handed it to the printer.[1] Dr. Anderson has seen it, and agrees with me in thinking the style as spirited and eloquent as the thoughts are ingenious and just. I found the word *transitory* twice in one sentence, used in such a manner that I was convinced that there must have been a slip of the pen, and therefore took the liberty to substitute another word. I have also omitted the clause where, speaking of the poet who should write what would be the best of its kind, you say, "the maritime cities will vie with each other to secure his presence." As I sometimes write poetry myself, and am lately removed to the principal maritime town in the United States, a reader who was not very charitably disposed, and who was ignorant that you were the author of the article might make these words the subject of a mischievous construction. Except these alterations which I am convinced you would have made had you been here I have changed nothing; indeed there was nothing which could be changed for the better.

As for the Polyglott Grammar[2]—do as you judge proper about reviewing it. The only reason that I can see for doing it is the pretensions which the author makes to learning &c.—and it is proper enough to put down such pretensions when they are empty ones. A short notice of the work, briefly exposing its worthlessness, would answer every purpose, should you think proper to write at all.

I am sir
yrs. truly
WM. C. BRYANT.

MANUSCRIPT: MHS DOCKETED: Recd   Oct. 1825.

1. See *NYR*, 1 (October 1825), 333–341.

2. Listed among new books in *NYR*, 1 (August 1825), 248, was "A Polyglot of the Hebrew, Chaldee, Syriac, Greek, Latin, English, French, Italian, Spanish and German Languages, reduced to one common rule of Syntax, &c. with an extensive Index, intended to simplify the study of Languages," by Samuel Barnard, New York, Wilder and Campbell. This was not reviewed in the *NYR*.

141.   *To* Maria Lovell Edgeworth[1]

New York, October[2] 1st. 1825.

Madam,

I am indebted to the politeness of Mrs. Griffith[3] for an opportunity of forwarding to your hands the little volume which accompanies this note. I take the liberty to request that you will accept it as a testimony of respect from one [of the] citizens of a country which, no less than the kingdom that has the honour of your birth, has been delighted and instructed by your writings.[4]

> I have the honour to be,
> Madam,
> > your most obedient and
> > most humble Servt.
> > WM. C. BRYANT.

MANUSCRIPT: NYPL–GR ADDRESS: To / Miss Maria Lovel[l] Edgeworth.

1. The Irish novelist Maria Edgeworth (1767–1849), then widely read in Great Britain and the United States, was best known for such stories of Irish life as *Castle Rackrent* (1800) and *The Absentee* (1812).

2. Bryant mistakenly wrote "Sept."

3. Mrs. Mary Griffith was the American author of several novels, including *Camperdown* (Philadelphia, 1836), for which Bryant helped her find a publisher.

4. James Hillhouse reported to Bryant that Miss Edgeworth had expressed interest in him in a letter to Mrs. Griffith, and asked Bryant to send her an inscribed copy of his poems. Hillhouse to Bryant, September 15, 1825, NYPL–BG; M[ary] G[riffith] to Bryant, September 23, 1825, NYPL–GR.

142.   *To* Richard H. Dana

New York   Jan   11th   1826.—

My dear Sir

I have been making some enquiries concerning the business about which you wrote me the other day.[1] I find by the books of Wiley that a balance is due to him of 25 cents—but Mr. Cooper tells me that Wiley's books were so negligently kept that there is not the least probability that they exhibit the true state of the account.[2] However it is not worth while to pursue the enquiry any farther—for every body tells me that there is not the least prospect of getting a sou,[3] even if the balance were a million in your favour.

I was informed that there were a considerable number of copies of the Idle man in the Bookstore and that they would be delivered to your order.— If you will send me an order directed to Samuel S. Gardiner Esq. assignee of the effects of the late Chas. Wiley or any persons having charge of the same—I will attend to the business and see that they are housed where you can be sure of getting at them when you want them. A man in the shop told me that he wished I would get the order immediately for he wanted to get all the books out of the shop.—

I like your poem very much[4]—by the bye I have not yet been able to discover the popular name of your bird—but I wish you would take the trouble to make a little change in the metrical construction of it and send me the alterations in your next. I refer to the following lines.

> "With the motion and roar
> Of waves driving to shore"

and also

> "To thy spirit no more
> Come with me quit the shore—
> For the joy and the light
> When the summer birds sing"

These lines do not correspond in measure with the lines which occupy the same place in the other stanzas. All the other lines in the poem are such as the ear will acknowledge for Iambics but these are in a kind of tripping measure, which is not in harmony with the rest of the poem and is disagreeable from its unexpectedness. Besides they do not as it seems to me suit with the general solemn and plaintive effect of the whole.— Cannot you substitute Iambics for these?[5] The abbreviation 'long I should be glad to see altered—for it is certainly an innovation—but if you insist upon it I will retain it.

It is true as you say that there is a want of *literary entertainment* in our Journal. But as to the multitude of clever men here who might furnish it vous n'y êtes pas [you are wrong].— We have some clever men to be sure, but they are mightily given to instructing the world—to elucidating the mysteries of political economy and the principles of jurisprudence &c &c—they seem to think it a sort of disgrace to be entertaining— Since the time of Salmagundi[6] the city has grown exceedingly grave and addicted to solid speculations. Paulding sometimes writes for our Magazine[7] and we pick up the rest of it as well as we can.—

I have written this letter very hastily and carelessly as you see, at a bookstore—for I wish to send it off this morning—and my lodgings are [a] good way out of the busy part of the town.— I would write you a longer letter to convince you of your mistake in supposing that there was any matter of offence between you and me, but I have not time. When I write again I mean to tell you all about myself and my prospects —and in the mean time I beseech you to tell me if the public good does not require that it should be kept secret,—what is the mighty task to which you are devoting your time and of the success of which you speak so despairingly.— Be it what it may—may it meet with the success which I am sure it will deserve— I am reading Cooper's novel and have been exceedingly delighted and interested as far as the middle of the first volume and expect to be so to the end.[8]

Since my residence here my wife has been very sick—she was at one time at death's door—but by the blessing of God she is now recovered—[9]

Yrs truly &c

W. C. BRYANT

MANUSCRIPT: NYPL–GR ADDRESS: Richard H. Dana Esq / Cambridge / Massachusetts POSTMARK: NEW-YORK / FEB / 11 POSTAL ANNOTATION: 18¾ ENDORSED: W. C. Bryant, Feb 11th / 1826. Ans Feb. 18th 26 PUBLISHED (in part): Life, I, 222.

1. Dana's letter is unrecovered.

2. Charles Wiley (1782?–1825?), New York bookseller since 1807, had published Cooper's first three novels and Halleck's Fanny, as well as Dana's The Idle Man. In a back room of his bookstore at Wall Street and Broadway Cooper had presided over meetings of The Den, literary forerunner of the Bread and Cheese Lunch Club. Adkins, Halleck, p. 152; Wright, American Fiction 1774–1850, pp. 69, 71–72, 75.

3. Bryant mistakenly wrote "sous."

4. "The Little Beach Bird," NYR, 2 (April 1826), 397.

5. Dana revised these lines to read: "With the motion and the roar / Of waves that drive to shore," and "Thy spirit never more. / Come quit with me the shore, / For gladness and the light / Where birds of summer sing." See Poems and Prose Writings (Philadelphia and Boston, 1833), pp. 129–130.

6. [Washington Irving, William Irving, James Kirke Paulding] Salmagundi; or, the Whim-Whams and Opinions of Launcelot Langstaff, Esq. and Others (New York, 1807–1808).

7. James Kirke Paulding's contributions to the NYR were a "Letter of Adrian Lubberson" in 1 (November 1825), 461–471, and another letter in 2 (December 1825), 66–70; and "The Beau's Tale," 2 (January 1826), 133–146.

8. The Last of the Mohicans: A Narrative of 1757. 2 vols. (Philadelphia, 1826).

9. No other record remains of Frances Bryant's serious illness at this time.

143.   To Messrs. H. C. Carey & I. Lea

New York   Feb   21, 1826—

Gentlemen—

I think of publishing before long a small volume of poems, and write to enquire whether you have any objection to the republication by me of the three little pieces which I contributed to the Atlantic Souvenir for 1826, entitled "June," "Nature," and "Oh, fairest of the rural maids." You will oblige me by giving as early an answer as may be consistent with your convenience.[1]

I am Gentlemen

your obt   humble Servt.

W. C. BRYANT

MANUSCRIPT: The Historical Society of Pennsylvania ADDRESS: Messrs H. C. Carey & I. Lea ENDORSED: Rc Feb 24 / Ansd same day.

1. See 118.3. Perhaps Carey & Lea's letter of February 20 (NYPL–GR) sending only $10.00 for the poems named, which crossed this letter, discouraged Bryant from publishing a book of verses at this time, for he seems not to have mentioned the prospect again. A year later he wrote to Dana, "I have no idea that were I to publish a volume of poems I could get any thing like *handsome wages* for the time I might spend in putting them in order and superintending their publication—that is, I should not be as well paid as a merchants clerk commonly is." See Letter 165. When he made this comment, he had just received from Willard Phillips a five-year accounting of the sale of his 1821 *Poems*, showing net proceeds of $15.07! February 21, 1827, NYPL–BG.

144. *To* Harrison Gray[1]

New York   July 21, 1826.

Dear Sir

I received your letter on the 18th. A short but somewhat troublesome indisposition has prevented me from answering it till now. I am sorry that you could make no better arrangement with Mr. Folsom,[2] as I cannot by any means consent to the condition he requires, namely that he shall be the sole judge of what articles are to be inserted in the journal and what rejected. I explained to you fully my views on that subject in our last conversation and supposed that I had made myself understood. Had such an arrangement been insisted on in the first place as necessary to the union of the two works I would never have taken a single step in the affair.

In all my conversations with yourself and Mr. Carter on this subject, and in all the letters I have written about it, I have ever kept in view the necessity of the new work being both really and apparently as much under the control and direction of the New York as of the Boston Editor.[3] Mr Carter for whose opinion I have great respect will I believe consider this matter in the same light that I do.[4] He will readily agree with me that we of New York are exceedingly jealous of the reputation of what literature we have, and that a work is not likely to be patronized and fostered with any unusual zeal of which the sole direction and responsibility is to remain with the literary men of another city. The New York Review has been cherished because the people of New York have considered it as a creature of theirs and I am confident that when they learn that it is to become a Boston work as it will be when conducted solely by a Boston Editor the favour with which it is regarded will be materially diminished. Indeed I have no doubt that a rival journal would be immediately set up.

To show what are the feelings of the booksellers on this subject, (and I believe they may be considered as pretty fairly representing the sense of the public on such subjects) I will mention that I inquired of the Carvills[5] what would be the consequence if it were to happen that the direction of the work should be entrusted solely to a Boston Editor.

They answered that in that case they should not consider themselves as bound by the contract they had made for it was made with the understanding that the work should be as they expressed it a *New York thing* and as much under the control of the New York as of the Boston Editor, without which they could not expect its success.

Besides, this subject is a matter of feeling with me as well as intimately connected with the prosperity of the work here. I was the proprietor of the N. Y. Review and had it not been united with the Literary Gazette I should have gone on with it as the sole Editor. I do not like to give up its management entirely, nor can I submit to wear the name and bear the responsibility of an Editor when I have none of the privileges of one. I have [all] along assured my friends here that in uniting the two journals the New York character of the work would be preserved—that the N. Y. Review would not be merged in the Lit Gazette, but that the two would be blended and that I should stand before the public as one of the responsible conductors of the journal. They will be disappointed if any other arrangement is made, nor can I suppose that they will consider themselves as under any further obligation to patronize the journal.

In agreeing that Mr. Folsom should have the sole power of judging respecting the admission of the Boston contributions, I consent to a great deal, but to no more than what the circumstances of the case make necessary. I should like to have a voice in the decision also were it not that no convenient arrangement could be made for that purpose. In the mean time however he has an advantage which I have not. He will see all my communications before they go to press, and [if] there is any thing in them which he may think objectionable he will have the opportunity of writing to me on the subject before they are inserted. It is not necessary therefore that he should have the same degree of confidence in me that I must have in him in consenting to what I do. If he has not this degree of confidence it is not fit that we should conduct the work together.

You say you think that I should be persuaded by Mr. F's reasoning on the subject were I to see him. I have great respect for Mr. F's reasoning powers but I doubt whether he will be able to advance any thing new on this subject. I know that a great deal may be said about the character of a work for consistency and all that—but I have heard a great many discussions *pro* and *con* on this subject. I am weary of them and my mind was long ago made up. If Mr. F. wishes as you say he does to please the New York public it must be done by letting them have a New York Editor.

As to my coming to Boston immediately it will be out of my power for two reasons. In the first place it will be inconvenient for me to leave New York to which I returned some time since, until after the first of

August.[6] In the next place I do not exactly see what I am to go to Boston for unless to disagree to the condition insisted upon by Mr. Folsom, which I can as well do on paper, without the expense and fatigue of a journey to give a verbal assurance of my determination. It will not be expected of me I suppose that I should undertake the journey for the sole purpose of being persuaded out of my firmest resolutions and convictions both of duty and interest. In the mean time [if] it be absolutely necessary that the work should be under the sole management of the editor in Boston I can think of only two methods by which I am willing it should be done: Either to dissolve the union of the two works, or to suffer me to divest myself entirely of the name and character of Editor of the work and become a contributor merely—in which case I should immediately retire from New York.—

I have written you a long letter. If I have in any part of it expressed myself with warmth it is not with an intention to give offence—but because the point for which I am contesting is a vital one with me, and one in which I consider my reputation as in some measure concerned. I believe I have shown myself pretty easy and accommodating in all the other particulars of the bargain—but this is a point which on looking over what I have said I am sure you will not wish me to yield.—

I remain—

Yours truly

Wm C. Bryant

I hope to hear from you soon and to learn that you have made some less objectionable arrangement with respect to the Editorship— The Lit. Gaz. has not yet arrived.—[7]

MANUSCRIPT: Haverford College Library ADDRESS: Mr. Harrison Gray / Bookseller / Boston POSTMARK: NEW-YORK / JUL / 22 POSTAL ANNOTATION: single / 18¾.

1. Early in 1825 the Boston bookseller Harrison Gray had bought control of the *USLG*, to which Bryant had contributed twenty-three poems during the past year. At that time James Gordon Carter succeeded Theophilus Parsons as editor. In April 1826 Bryant proposed to Carter a union of his magazine with the *NYR*, the joint work to be published simultaneously at Boston and New York. But after they had worked out an amicable merger and prepared its first number (July 1, 1826), Gray notified Bryant that Charles Folsom would replace Carter, and suggested a revised plan of procedure which Bryant here rejects. Parsons to Bryant, February 18, 1825; Carter to Bryant, February 15, 1825, and April 11 and June 22, 1826, NYPL–BG.

2. Charles Folsom (1794–1872, Harvard 1813), until recently Harvard College Librarian, was then an editor for his alma mater.

3. Though Bryant's letters have apparently been lost, Carter's replies make evident their agreement that each would be responsible for prose matter contributed in his area, with Bryant in charge of all poetry, and that Bryant would be an equal owner with Gray, Carter, and one other, of the new review. See Carter to Bryant, May 3 and May 17, 1826, NYPL–BG.

4. Having read Bryant's letter, Carter wrote him on July 30, "I should have been

exceedingly sorry to have had you answer the proposition in any other manner. It was contrary to the spirit of the agreement by which the works were united, . . . and if I had been here when the proposition was about to be made I should have protested against [it] most vehemently, as alike impudent in its nature, and hostile to the interest of all parties." NYPL–BG.

5. G. and C. Carvill had agreed to be the New York publishers and distributors of the *United States Review and Literary Gazette*, as the new journal would be called.

6. Bryant had recently taken his wife and daughter from Orange Springs, New Jersey, where they had boarded for a month, to Cummington. Frances Bryant, "Autobiographical Sketch," NYPL–GR.

7. In his July 30 letter, Carter assured Bryant, "I believe I have convinced Mr. G. that the condition proposed by Mr. Folsom would be prejudicial to his interest and to the interest of all concerned. And I do not think any more such propositions will be made." The matter seems to have rested here, for in spite of their growing differences of opinion during the ensuing year, Bryant and Folsom ran the *USR* on the terms agreed to earlier.

145. *To* Frances F. Bryant

New York   July 29   1826.

My dear Frances.

I am obliged to you for your letter notwithstanding there was some obscurity in certain passages. On the evening of your arrival at Great Barrington, you say that you walked up to Hopkins and back again. Now the greatness of this exploit you will please to observe depends entirely on the place where Hopkins was when you walked up to him—if for instance he was only the other side of the room it was a very little matter —if he was at his house it was fetching a considerable walk.[1]

But leaving the solution of this knotty point until we have an opportunity to discuss it verbally I proceed to mention that I have been a little unwell since I wrote you last.[2] I was then somewhat out of order with what I thought a pretty hard cold—but the next day I had a head ache and fever and a strong desire to take medicine which I indulged, and in a day or two began to get better and am now nearly as well as usual. You may believe this when I tell you that yesterday I went to Communipaw and in the evening to the opera. Communipaw as you may perhaps know is the oldest settlement in these parts except New York. It lies southwest of Paulus Hook and consists of about half a dozen low stone Dutch houses ranged along the shore, the inmates of which talk Dutch yet. We went into one of the houses, a girl had just finished churning. She gave the party some buttermilk—a delicacy of which you know I am not particularly fond. We saw nothing else except a young negro about two years old in "*mudder's nakedness*," as the Irish say. As to the Opera I was pleased—more so than I expected to be. The piece was Don Giovanni, a well known plot borrowed from the Spanish I think by Molière, and since reproduced in a great many dramatic forms.[3] The hero, Don Giovanni Don Juan or Don John, marries all the wives he can persuade to have him commits murders and all sorts of iniquities, and fears neither God nor man. He invites the statue of a man whom he has murdered to supper with him—the statue accepts his invitation, comes at the hour appointed—takes Don Giovanni by the hand—who expires in the most cruel torments—whereupon hell opens and the devils drag him in among the fireworks.— Don Garcia is a good actor as well as a celebrated singer, but his lower notes are a little husky—his voice is somewhat worn.— His daughter the Signorigna as she is affectedly called, is little and pretty, with a liquid voice and skinny arms which she does not [know] how to use—a good actress however. Angrisani with a fine deep bass voice is also an excellent performer. The three other performers were poor. Madame Barbieri, a French woman, just tolerable—with a great deal of mannerism. Signora Garcia, not so good, and Mons. Milon intolerable. There was another, however, young Garcia who *enacted* the servant of Don Juan who was passable. —So much for the Italian Opera.—[4]

I have had a melancholy time however till now since you have been absent. Sick, just able to crawl down town, and obliged to work—passing the rest of the day alone in my room with nobody to talk to, nor to talk to me, you will not wonder if at times I have been a little out of spirits. —I hope you will succeed in making Fanny contented—as for yourself I do not suppose that among so many friends and old acquaintances you can be low spirited.

PETITE FANCHETTE!

IL FAUT QUE TU SOIS TOUJOURS DE BONNE HUMEUR QUE TU N'INCOMMODES-PERSONNE, QUE TU RÉPONDES PROMPTEMENT ET CIVILEMENT À TOUTES LES QUESTIONS QU'ON TE FAIT, QUE TU OBÉISSES TOUJOURS À TA MÈRE, QUE TU LISES ET DU FRANÇAIS ET DE L'ANGLAIS TOUS LES JOURS; ET ÉPELES DE MÊME, QUE TU TE SOUVIENNES DE TON PÈRE, MAIS QUE TU NE CRIES POINT EN VOULANT LE VOIR, ET ALORS VOUS SEREZ BONNE, ET TON PAPA SERA BIEN-AISÉ D'AVOIR DES NOUVELLES DE VOUS ET ENFIN DE VOUS REVOIR.[5]

Monday   July 31

I think I shall go to Boston in a week or ten days from this time.[6] Therefore if you write to me again at New York I wish you to write as soon as may be convenient after you receive this. If you get the money from Comstock you need not trouble Hollenbeck— But if you cannot get it before next Friday you may as well not send it at all. I have a little money and will make a shift to get along without it. Tomorrow is Commencement day here. I shall attend— The literary exercises of the day will be held at St. John's Church—and the other exercises which consist in eating and drinking will take place at the College Hall. I have an invitation, and think I shall go.[7]

There is an ordination to take place at Northampton a fortnight from next Wednesday. I think I shall so arrange my journey as to be there. Could not you and one of my brothers meet me there? If you should think of doing this, please when you get to Cummington write me at Boston. They have had a most furious awakening in Northampton— the orthodox have been praying preaching and exhorting at the poor heretics for several months—but they mean to have an ordination not-withstanding.[8]—Most of the ladies of your acquaintance are gone out of town. Mrs. Schuyler & Miss Morton are gone notwithstanding the dread the latter has of the country—the one to Massachusetts & the other to Rhinebeck. Mrs. Russell has gone to Boston, Mrs. Sedgwick to New-port— Mr. Balestier and his family have set out today for Catskill & per-haps for Niagara. Mrs. Ware whose children are sick thinks she shall go soon. Whether Mrs. Sewall & Mrs. Wheaton are at home I do not know. Mrs. Ledyard I believe is.[9] Pray take good care of your health— Do not fatigue yourself with too much walking— Kiss little Frances for me—& be-lieve me—with great affection &c

your friend & husband

W. C. BRYANT

MANUSCRIPT: NYPL–GR ADDRESS: Mrs. Frances Bryant / Great Barrington / Massachu-setts. / pr. Mr. Sherwood.

1. Frances was probably visiting her sister Mrs. Allen Henderson, and had walked to the home of her sister Mrs. Charles W. Hopkins.

2. Letter unrecovered.

3. The libretto for Mozart's *Don Giovanni* (1787) had been written at Vienna by his collaborator Lorenzo Da Ponte (1749–1838), who now lived in New York, where he was the first professor of Italian at Columbia College. In 1825 he wrote "A Critique on Certain Passages in Dante," published in *NYR*, 1 (September 1825), 325–327. Like Molière in *Le Festin de Pierre* (1665), Da Ponte had drawn for his plot in *Don Gio-vanni* from an early Spanish play, *El Burlador de Sevilla y Combidado de Pietra*, 1630, by Tirso de Molina. See Fitzlyon, *Libertine Librettist*, pp. 139, 246–258.

4. Manuel Garcia (1775–1832) and his Spanish opera company had opened in New York on November 29, 1825, the first season of Italian opera ever heard in America, and on May 23, 1826, given the first performance of *Don Giovanni*, with Da Ponte in the audience. Garcia's daughter, eighteen-year-old Maria Felicita (1808–1836), the "Sig-norigna," was later the celebrated Mme Malibran. His son Manuel (1805–1906) was, from 1830 to 1895, a distinguished teacher of music, first at the Paris Conservatory, and later at the Royal Academy of Music in London. For further information about this remarkable company, see Fitzlyon, *Libertine Librettist*, pp. 260–264; George C. Odell, *Annals of the New York Stage* (New York: Columbia University Press, 1927–1949), III, 182–187, 222, 268, 399.

5. (in block letters) "Little Fanny! You must always keep your temper so that you do not trouble anyone; answer promptly and politely all questions asked you; always obey your mother; read both French and English every day, and likewise spell; remem-ber your father, but do not cry because you wish to see him; and in that case you will be good, and your papa will be very glad to have news about you, and, at length, to see you again."

6. At the beginning of July, after an inquiry to editor William Coleman, Bryant had taken a temporary position with the New York *Evening Post*. Early the next month, at Gulian Verplanck's suggestion, he went to Boston to offer Richard Dana a permanent position with the paper. Nevins, *Evening Post*, p. 123; Letter 159.

7. Bryant reported the Columbia College commencement in the *EP* for August 2.

8. The Second Congregational (Unitarian) Church at Northampton was dedicated on December 7, 1825, with a sermon by Henry Ware, Jr. See his *A Sermon Preached at the Dedication* . . . (Northampton, 1825).

9. The persons named were probably acquaintances Frances had made at the Unitarian church and at the Bryants' boardinghouse. The only ones certain of identification are Mrs. Robert Sedgwick and Mrs. William Ware, wife of the Unitarian pastor. Two others were perhaps Mrs. Henry Sewall (see Letters 63 and 66) and Mrs. Henry Wheaton, wife of the jurist and diplomat whose life of William Pinckney Bryant had reviewed in the *NYR* (2 [May 1826], 435–444).

146. *To* Frances F. Bryant

New York   Aug. 2, 1826.

My dearest Frances

I have just got your letter by Mr Van Deusen[1] for which I am much obliged to you,—meaning to include in the expression of my gratitude the forty dollars it contains. I could have made a shift to get along without it, for Coleman[2] pays me enough to go to Boston with; but now I shall have enough to settle with Mrs. Meigs,[3] and something to get us all to New York again.

While you were writing me your *short* letter I was writing you a very long one which I suppose you have received before this time by Mr. Sherwood.[4] As soon as you get to Cummington I wish you would write to me at Boston for I shall probably be at the latter place almost as soon as you will have arrived at the former and if you do not write immediately I may not get the letter.

I shall send you a number of the Evening Post either by Mr. Van Deusen or by the Mail containing an account of the Commencement of Columbia College and will also mark with a pencil such paragraphs as are written by me. I have got to be quite famous as the editor of a newspaper since you were here and some of my friends—Mr. Verplanck in particular are quite anxious that I should continue so. Some compliments have been made to me about the improvement in the Evening Post &c. The establishment of the Evening Post is an extremely lucrative one. It is owned by two individuals—Mr Coleman and Mr. Burnham.[5] The profits are estimated at about thirty thousand dollars a year—fifteen to each proprietor.[6] This is better than poetry and magazines.

Mrs. Meigs's family is much reduced. Last week Nott and Lovejoy went away, this week Mr. Stoddard.[7] *He* however expects I believe to return next month. No new boarders come, though Mrs. Meigs has what she calls applications quite frequently. I do not hear of her refusing any body; but nobody goes so far as to engage board. Tommorrow Aunt Sally[8] goes to Connecticut, I believe in good earnest.

Thursday Aug. 3.

Aujourd'hui je vais diner chez Madame Ledyard.[9] Vous n'avez pas, je sais, beaucoup de goût pour elle, mais il faut qu'elle soit une très aimable et très excellente personne, puisqu'elle m'a invité à dîner. Je vous dirai pour votre satisfaction que si vous jouissez des plaisirs de la campagne, d'un air pur, de la fraîcheur, et de la verdure, au moins n'avez vous pas de si bons dîners qu'on a à la ville. Mais à présent nous avons un bon temps aussi. Les dix jours qui viennent de passer, il a fait assez frais. Les chaleurs de la canicule ont été si agréablement temperées, que tout le monde en est en joie. Je ne me souviens d'avoir jamais eprouvé un temps qui soit plus à mon goût.[10]

Votre mari
GUILLAUME C. BRYANT

MANUSCRIPT: NYPL–GR ADDRESS: Mrs. Frances Bryant / Great Barrington / Mass. / pr. I. L. Van Deusen Esq. PUBLISHED (*in part*): *Life*, I, 229.

1. Isaac L. Van Deusen represented Great Barrington for several terms in the Massachusetts legislature. Taylor, *Great Barrington*, p. 365.

2. See 145.6. Bryant mistakenly wrote "Colman."

3. The Bryants had moved in May 1826, with their landlady, Mrs. Meigs, from Canal Street to Laight Street, nearer the Hudson River. Frances Bryant, "Autobiographical Sketch," NYPL–GR.

4. Probably William Sherwood. See 100.9.

5. Michael Burnham (d. 1836), business manager of the New York *Evening Post* since 1806. Nevins, *Evening Post*, p. 93.

6. Nevins suggests (pp. 135–136) that these were gross rather than net profits. In the first year of Bryant's participation in *EP* ownership, its net profits were about $13,500; his one-eighth share in 1827–1828 yielding just under $1,700. See "*Evening Post* Accounts," NYPL–GR.

7. Perhaps Nott was Josiah Clark Nott (1804–1873), then studying at the College of Physicians and Surgeons, and later a distinguished ethnologist as well as physician. Lovejoy is unidentified. Solomon Stoddard (Yale 1820, M.A. 1828, M.A. Middlebury 1838), later wrote a book notice for the *USR*. See *Historical Register of Yale University* (New Haven: Yale University, 1939), p. 496.

8. It seems likely that "Aunt Sally," apparently Mrs. Meigs's cook, was the "Aunt Sallie" to whom Lorenzo Da Ponte taught the "mysteries of the Italian *cuisine*" so that members of the Garcia opera troupe would feel at home in their New York boardinghouse. Fitzlyon, *Libertine Librettist*, p. 263. Godwin wrote that for a time the Bryants occupied the same lodgings as the Garcias, "where they learned to admire the wild fawn of the herd, the Signorita Felicite." *Life*, I, 227.

9. Unidentified.

10. "Today I shall dine at the home of Mme Ledyard. I know you care little for her, but she must be a very kind and excellent person, since she has invited me to dinner. I will say, for your benefit, that while you enjoy the pleasures of the country, pure air, freshness, and greenery, at least you haven't such good dinners as we have in the city. But at present we have good weather, too. For the ten days just past it

has been cool enough. The heat of the dog-days has been so pleasantly moderated that everyone is happy. I do not remember ever having experienced weather more to my liking."

147.   To Fanny Bryant

à la Nouvelle York
le 2 jour d'Août, 1826

Ma chère fille.

Je suis sûr que vous savez assez de Français et d'écriture, pour lire couramment ce que je vais vous écrire. Je suis bien-aisé d'entendre de si bonnes nouvelles de vous. Votre mère m'a averti que vous vous conduisez comme une bonne fille, et que vous êtes presque toujours de bonne humeur. Eh bien, si vous continuerez d'être sage et obéissante, et que tu lises et épèles comme il faut, tous les jours, je vous apporterai, quand je viendrai de Boston, quelque chose que vous donnera bien du plaisir.

J'ai vu, l'autre jour, tante et Donnie.[1] Ils m'ont fait bien des questions au sujet de vous, et de votre mère, mais je ne pouvais pas leur répondre, parce que vous étiez bien loin.

Au reste, j'espère de vous voir dans quinze jours, au plutôt. Mais n'oubliez pas d'être une bonne fille.

votre très affectioné père[2]
WILLIAM C. BRYANT

MANUSCRIPT: NYPL–GR ADDRESS: Madamoiselle Fanchette Bryant.

1. Aunt and Donnie are unidentified.
2. "My dear daughter. I am sure you know enough French and handwriting to read readily what I am going to write you. I am very glad to hear such good accounts of you. Your mother has informed me that you behave yourself like a good girl, and that you are almost always good-tempered. Well, if you continue to be good and obedient, and read and spell properly, every day, I shall bring you, when I come from Boston, something that will please you very much. The other day I saw aunt and Donnie. They asked me many questions about you and your mother, but I could not answer them, because you were very far off. Moreover, I hope to see you in a fortnight, or sooner. But don't forget to be a good girl. Your very affectionate father."

148.   To John W. Francis[1]

[New York, cAugust 5, 1826]

Dear Sir.

You were kind enough to promise me an article on the IIId. Vol. of Smith's History of New York which is about to appear.[2] I am now going out of town and shall remain out of town till the first of October next. I should be exceedingly glad to have the article for the October number of the U. S. Review—and for that purpose it would be well that it should be ready before the middle of September. If it cannot be ready for the Oct. No. I hope to have it for the next. Whenever it is finished if you will be so obliging as to send it to the store of Messrs. G & C Carvill it will be immediately forwarded for publication.[3]

I am sir

With great respect &c—

Yrs &c—

W. C. BRYANT.

MANUSCRIPT: Columbia University Libraries ADDRESS: Dr. J. W. Francis.

1. Dr. John Wakefield Francis (1789–1861, Columbia 1809), professor of obstetrics at the College of Physicians and Surgeons and a frequent writer on medical subjects, was an early member of Cooper's Bread and Cheese Club. His literary intimacies are recounted in his *Old New York; or, Reminiscences of the Past Sixty Years*, ed. Henry T. Tuckerman (New York, 1865).

2. William Smith, *History of the Province of New York* (London, 1757). Volume IV was reprinted in 1826 in *Collections of the New-York Historical Society.*

3. This article did not appear in the *USR.*

149. *To* Gulian C. Verplanck

Cummington   Aug. 26   1826

My dear Sir

I have been at Boston and seen Mr. Dana and spoken with him about the Evening Post.[1] He seemed to think favourably of the plan, but mentioned that he had some thoughts of making an arrangement of the same nature with Russell, the Editor of the Boston Centinel,[2] which would be more convenient to him on a variety of accounts, particularly as it would not oblige him to leave his home in Cambridge and the Centinel being a semi-weekly paper, would not require a greater degree of attention than his health would permit. He seemed however desirous to have the place in the office of the Post kept in reserve until he had tried what could be done nearer home.

I told him that I should write to you on the subject, and that from what I had heard Coleman say, I had no doubt that any suggestion of yours respecting the choice of an Editor would be followed by him. In the mean time I do not exactly see what can be done. Dana does not wish any thing to be done that will commit him, and any thing short of that would do little good. I have thought however that it would be well to let you know these circumstances, satisfied that if you could think of any thing which would be of service to Mr. [Dana in this?][3] affair you would be glad to do it.

I saw Mr. [Washington] Allston at Cambridge. He spoke of his intimacy with you in Europe, and desired me to give you his particular regards.

Yrs truly

W. C. BRYANT

MANUSCRIPT: NYPL–Berg PUBLISHED (*in part*): *Life*, I, 229.

1. See 145.6.

2. The *Columbian Centinel,* for which Bryant had written a notice of Dana's *The Idle Man* in 1822 (Letter 86).

3. Manuscript torn.

150. *To* Charles Folsom[1]

Cummington Sept 11 1826.

My dear Sir

I send you an article for the Miscellany and a piece of poetry.[2] I had another poetical article sent to me on which I had bestowed a good deal of labour but I cannot find it to send with this. Perhaps I may send you another of my own in season for the Oct No.

I wish that whatever is sent to me during my residence in Cummington by mail, may be directed *to be left at the Post Office in Worthington.* I shall then get it earlier.

I shall be glad to hear from you and from the Review.

Yrs truly
W C BRYANT

MANUSCRIPT: HEHL ADDRESS: Mr. Charles Folsom / Editor of the U. S. Review / Care of Harrison Gray / Boston POSTMARK (*in script*): [Worthing?]ton Ms POSTAL ANNOTATION: [½?] oz 75.

1. See Letter 144. The *NYR* having ceased publication with the May number, Bryant had served as a nominal editor, first with James G. Carter and later with Charles Folsom, of the *USLG* while its fourth volume was being completed with the July, August, and September numbers. The new joint publication, the *United States Review and Literary Gazette,* began publication on October 1.

2. Bryant's prose tale, "A Border Tradition," *USR,* 1 (October 1826), 40–53, and his verse translation, "Mary Magdalen" (see 151.1).

151. *To* Charles Folsom

Cummington Sept. 14 1826

My dear Sir.

I did not get your letter of the eighth until last evening. I had previously sent on an article for the Miscellany and some lines from the Spanish. I wish you to make a correction in the title of the latter. Instead of *To Mary Magdalen*—let it be *Mary Magdalen*—otherwise I am afraid that those who are not well versed in Scripture History on reading the title may expect a copy of amatory verses addressed to some Mary or other.[1]

I send you a *critical notice* and some more poetry for the Oct. No.[2] I supposed that I had already contributed my proportion to the Sept. No and that the account of the N Y Lyceum would go into the Oct. No.[3] As it seems this has not been convenient I fear my contributions for this No will not amount to my 20 pages. If I could get at new books I could soon dish up Critical Notices enough to make out the quantity but in my situation it is not easy to get at these. I told Mr. Carvill to send me the new publications that appeared in N. Y. or at least such as could be conveniently sent, but I have as yet received nothing. I hope therefore that if there should be any deficiency in furnishing my quota while here in the country you will let me make it up as soon as I am returned to town, where I shall probably be in 3 weeks. I shall let you know when I go.—

I have not yet received the Sept. No. which I suppose is published before this time. The August No was I am told very well received in New York, and if we do nothing to lose the public favour in that quarter I think it stands on at least as good ground there as the N. Y. Review did.

As for Gaston de Blondeville I intended to have made an article about that novel and the other pieces published with it—but I cannot lay my hands on them. You may as well take it before it is stale.[4] Vivian Grey and the Highlands you are welcome to.[5]

I think we spoke of the alteration you mention in the mode of printing the work—viz to put running titles in Italics over the several articles—and I agreed to it. We also spoke of putting the Miscellany and Critical Notices into the same type with the Reviews. What do you think of this alteration? These articles are not more easy to write than the Reviews and are perhaps of as much consequence. Putting them into smaller type seems, however to imply that one of these two things is the case. Besides ought not he who furnishes a Critical notice to be paid as liberally as he who furnishes a Review? I mention these things for the consideration of yourself and Mr. Wigglesworth.[6]—if you make the changes I shall think it well—if not I do not regard it as very important.

I believe there was some understanding between us, or at least between myself and the gentleman who conducted the Lit Gaz. respecting the books to be reviewed similar to what you mention.—[7] I am obliged to you for the further light you give me on the Ode of Villegas. I mistook the sense entirely and mean sometime or other to correct the translation. In the mean time the original has exercised the critical ingenuity of others besides yourself. You recollect we vainly tried to find the word *hicella* in the dictionaries. A friend of mine in New York writes me that he is told by Cubi that it is an obsolete word, signifying "favour, complexion" &c.[8]

I have just received a letter from Mrs. Simmons in which she solicits the immediate remittance of the money for the two letters of Mr. Simmons. I wish she had it. I have no doubt that she is in distress. Cannot the type be set up the number of pages ascertained and the money sent without delay? I left with Mr. Carter the letter from her to me containing her address. If you should not find it—her address is *Mrs. Eliza Simmons, care of John Vaughan corner of Front & Walnut Streets.*[9] My compliments to Mrs. Folsom & believe me

Yrs truly
W. C. BRYANT.

I hope to be informed of the names of the writers of the articles in the Journal as they appear, and shall make a point of letting you know by whom the articles that I send are written.—

MANUSCRIPT: BPL ADDRESS: Mr. Charles Folsom / Editor of the U. S. Review / Care of Harrison Gray / Boston POSTMARK (*in script*): Worthington Ms / Sept—15 POSTAL ANNOTATION: 25 DOCKETED: Bryt.

1. "Mary Magdalen, from the Spanish of Bartolome Leonardo de Argensola," *USR*, 1 (October 1826), 59–60. See *Poems* (1876), p. 199.

2. "The New York Lyceum of Natural History," *USR*, 1 (October 1826), 53–58; "Sonnet" (later titled "October"), *ibid.*, 59. See *Poems* (1876), p. 142. The article was also Bryant's.

3. Folsom had complained on September 8 that nothing had yet come from Bryant for the October number, since his "Celestial poetry & 'Lyceum' " would appear in September. NYPL–BG. The poem referred to, "The Conjunction of Jupiter and Venus," appeared in *USLG*, 4 (September 1826), 451–453. See *Poems* (1876), pp. 156–159.

4. Richard Dana reviewed Ann Radcliffe's posthumous novel *Gaston de Blondeville* (Philadelphia, 1826) in *USR*, 2 (April 1827), 1–8.

5. Benjamin Disraeli's *Vivian Grey* (Philadelphia, 1826) was noticed briefly in *USR*, 1 (December 1826), 231–232, by Edward Wigglesworth (see Note 6). Bryant probably refers to [Ambrose Walker] *The Highlands: A Tale of the Hudson* (Philadelphia, 1826), which, though not noticed in the *USR*, drew Bryant's censure for its inflated style, in the *EP* for July 22, 1826.

6. Edward Wigglesworth (1804–1876, Harvard 1822), a recent law school graduate, had been assisting Carter on the *USLG*, and continued to do the same for Folsom on the *USR*. *Appleton's Cyclopaedia of American Biography*, edd. James Grant Wilson and John Fiske (New York, 1887–1900), VI, 501.

7. Folsom's understanding of their agreement, outlined on September 8, was that his writers would review books published in the Boston "quarter," and Bryant's the New York State publications, while "all books printed south of New York shall become our prey, *of course*, except such as you shall expressly retain for the New York critics."

8. "From the Spanish of Villegas," Bryant's first verse translation from that language, *USLG*, 4 (July 1826), 294. See *Poems* (1876), p. 198. Bryant's New York friend was Robert Sands, who reviewed, in *USLG*, 4 (September 1826), 460, *A New Spanish Grammar*, 3d ed. (New York, 1826), by Mariano Cubi y Soler, a Spanish teacher with whom both Bryant and Sands were acquainted. Sands to Bryant, August 27, 1826, NYPL–BG.

9. The letters to which Bryant refers were apparently [R. J. Simmons?] "Letter from an Adventurer in England," *USLG*, 4 (September 1826), 443–448, and "Letter from an American in Europe," *ibid.* (July 1826), 290–293. See Folsom to Bryant, September 8, 1826, NYPL–BG.

152. *To* Messrs H. C. Carey & I. Lea

New York   Sept. 22d. 1826

Gentlemen.

I have received your letter enclosing Mr. Tone's poem. I think highly of parts of it which are truly poetical and full of spirit, but other portions, particularly those which contain the political disquisitions, are somewhat prosaic. There are also some verbal changes which might be made to great advantage. I am exceedingly desirous to publish the poem but I think that it should first be revised, and that those parts which are evidently inferior to the rest should be abridged and compressed. The poem should be given to the public divested of every thing that could weaken the effect of the better portions. Mr. Tone should do this as an act of justice to his own powers.[1]

I showed your order for a copy of the Atlantic Souvenir to young Mr. Wiley.[2] He would not understand it as an order for the absolute delivery of the volume, and would suffer me to take it only on condition of returning it. I took it—made a notice of it for the next No. of the U. S. Review—and handed it back to him. —It is certainly got up better than the last year's, and cannot fail of success.[3] I am Gentlemen

with great respect
yr Obt humble Svt.
W. C. BRYANT

MANUSCRIPT: The Historical Society of Pennsylvania ADDRESS: Messrs H. C. Carey & I Lea. ENDORSED: Recd & Ansd Oct 27.

1. See 153.7.
2. John Wiley, son of the late New York bookseller Charles Wiley, was apparently handling local sales of *The Atlantic Souvenir.*
3. Notice of *The Atlantic Souvenir* for 1827, *USR*, 1 (November 1826), 144–150.

153. *To* Edward Wigglesworth

New York   October[1] 6   1826.

Dear Sir

I have just arrived at New York.[2] I received your letter while in the country nearly a week since, but have hardly had time to reflect on its contents until now.[3]

If Mr. Gray and Mr. Folsom are agreed I have no objection to increasing the fund for the payment of contributions another hundred dollars. The amount of matter which [you would] be obliged to furnish by the present arrangement appears from your estimate to be considerably greater than I had supposed it would be.

I shall very shortly send on the matter I may collect for the Nov No. I shall send a notice of Mr. Brooks Phi Beta Kappa poem[4]—another of the Atlantic Souvenir [for] 1827—and one of Count Segur's Four Ages of Life. I have also hopes of getting an article from Mr. Wm. Ware on Alexander's Canon of the Old and *New Testaments.*—
Monday   October[5] 9th—

I got yours of the 5th. as postmarked while writing this—and I have delayed finishing it until I could enclose the poetry for the next No. I have altered Mellen's poem a little.— The *Night Scenes* I have made as you will see sad havoc with— It has yet too many words and the verse has no modulation, but if you have not an abundance of poetry on hand besides I believe it may do.—[6]

I have in my hands a poem by W. T. W. Tone of Alexandria which has been sent me for publication in the U. S. Review. Parts of it have great merit—, & parts are somewhat prosaic— It is long—it would take up 10 pages at least in the journal—but as it is in several canto's it might be divided. I must however look at it again before I venture to send it on.[7]

I shall in a day or two send you the prose.

I will be very much obliged to you to mention to Mr. H. Gray that Mr. Sedgwick has paid my note to Bliss and White—I not being in funds.—[8]

We have not recd. the Oct　No. yet but suppose that it is on its way. I do not mean that after this month there shall be any delay in getting to you my proportion of the matter for the journal. It may as easily be sent you by the tenth of the month preceding the publication as at any time.—

Mr. Carvill has taken pains to ascertain whether the subscribers in this city will continue to take the journal and finds that they are generally willing to do so.—

I am sir

Yrs [respectfully?]

W. C. Bryant

MANUSCRIPT: HCL.

1. Bryant mistakenly wrote "Sept."
2. On October 2 Cullen had taken Frances and Fanny from Cummington to Great Barrington, leaving them there for a visit while he returned to New York. Louisa to Cyrus Bryant, October 1, 1826, BCHS.
3. Wigglesworth had written Bryant on September 21, with Folsom's endorsement, asking that his excessive share of criticism be lightened by the provision of extra fees for other contributors. NYPL–BG.
4. See 154.4.
5. Here, as above, Bryant mistakenly wrote "Sept."
6. With his letter of October 5 (NYPL–BG) Wigglesworth sent Bryant Frederick Mellen's "The Seaman's Burial," *USR*, 1 (November 1826), 142–143, and William P. Lunt's "Night Scenes," *USR*, 2 (April 1827), 56–58.
7. This poem was not published in the *USR*.
8. This debt to Bliss and White was probably incurred to obtain for the *USR* the former subscription list of the *NYR*. See James G. Carter to Bryant, May 17, 1826, NYPL–BG.

154. *To* Charles Folsom

New York　Oct. 13, 1826.

Dear Sir

I enclose you a Review of Carey & Lea's Atlantic Souvenir[1] a notice of Segur's Four Ages[2] a letter from Dupin a French Jurist handed me by

Mr. Sampson,[3] and an article on Brooks's poem by a Mr. Lawson who wishes to remain anonymous.[4]

With the latter article you may perceive I have taken some liberties —but I am not certain that it is yet exactly what it ought to be. Mr. Brooks has really written a good poem and deserves to be praised for it, but I do not know what you may think [of] the degree of approbation bestowed upon it. The article may also need some further corrections in the diction.— Will you look over it and make such further amendments and omissions as my haste has not permitted me to make.—

For the next number I shall probably have an article on Smith's History of New York[5] another on Alexander's Canon of the Scriptures,[6] another on Torrey's Compendium of the Flora of the Northern & Middle States,[7] and I do not know what else.

There was no copy of the last No. sent to me with those directed to the Carvills—so I got one of his. Should there not be a few numbers sent on to me every month in order that I might make such a use of them as I may judge best for the interest of the work? Do you distribute no numbers gratuitously from Boston?[8]

The Revd. R. R. Gurley Secretary of the Colonization Society, and Editor of the *African Repository* has sent his work to me desiring to exchange with the U. S. Review—and I am desirous that it *should* be done.[9] I believe that the owners of the Literary Gazette exchanged with the several periodical works—but I do not remember that any arrangement was made for doing the same thing with the U. S. Review. Will you be good enough to mention this subject to the other proprietors & write me about it? It is not a pleasant situation to be the editor & one of the proprietors of a public journal and yet not to have a copy of it to dispose of.—

Some time since I received a letter from Mr. Abel Patten who writes by order of the *Society of Social Friends* Dartmouth College sending six dollars and requesting me to send them the New York Review. I wrote to him explaining the change that had taken place in the journal, adding that if his Society were already subscribers for the U. S. Lit. Gaz. or did not choose to take the new work I would return the money provided they gave me notice within a reasonable time. I have heard nothing from them since. It will be most convenient for them to receive the work from Boston, & for me to keep the money as a fund for the payment of postage— Will you request the agents to put them down as subscribers—credit them with the money and charge it to my account?[10]

What is become of the *"Wallet"*?[11]

The 1st No of the United States Review[12] arrived to-day. It seems to take very well. The mechanical execution delights every body.—

My compliments to Mrs. Folsom & believe me

Yrs. truly

W. C. BRYANT

MANUSCRIPT: BPL ADDRESS: Mr. Charles Folsom / Editor of the U. S. Review / Boston / Care of Bowles & Dearborn   Booksellers[13] POSTMARK: NEW-YORK / OCT / 14 POSTAL ANNOTATION: 2 Oz / 150.

1. [Bryant] "The Atlantic Souvenir, A Christmas and New Year's Offering, 1827," *USR*, 1 (November 1826), 144–150.
2. [Bryant] "The Four Ages of Life: a Gift for Every Age. From the French of Count de Segur. N. Y., Carvill, 1825," *USR*, 1 (December 1826), 223–225.
3. "Letter on the Napoleon Code. By Dupin," *USR*, 1 (November 1826), 125–128. William Sampson (1764–1836), a lawyer and Irish patriot living in New York, had been invited by Bryant to contribute to the *USR*. Sampson to Bryant, August 16, 1826, NYPL–BG.
4. The critic was probably James Lawson (1799–1880), a Scotsman, then an editor of the New York *Mercantile Advertiser*. James Gordon Brooks (1801–1841, Union 1819) had read his *Anniversary Poem* before the Phi Beta Kappa chapter at Yale before its publication in New York. Lawson's review appeared in *USR*, 1 (January 1827), 303–305.
5. This review, which Bryant had requested of Dr. John W. Francis, was apparently not written. See Letter 148.
6. By William Ware, in *USR*, 1 (February 1827), 327–336.
7. By an unidentified reviewer, *USR*, 1 (January 1827), 290–291.
8. Marginal note by Folsom: "Send him 4 [numbers of each?] for his file."
9. Marginal note by Folsom: "let Mr   B   exchange with Mr   Gurley."
10. The society named was a student organization founded in 1783 which had as one of its aims the enlargement of library holdings. Ralph Nading Hill, *The College on the Hill: A Dartmouth Chronicle* (Hanover: Dartmouth Publications [1964?]), p. 208.
11. Harrison Gray had arranged with steamboat and stagecoach companies to carry a special weekly mail pouch between Boston and New York. James G. Carter to Bryant, July 15, 1826, NYPL–BG.
12. Bryant mistakenly wrote "New York Review."
13. On October 1, 1826, Bowles and Dearborn replaced Harrison Gray as publishers of the journal. There is no indication of a change in ownership at that time.

155. *To* Frances F. Bryant

New York   Oct   21, 1826.

My dear Frances

I take this opportunity of sending a letter as far as Great Barrington by B. F. Rogers who is now in this city with his sister and Mr. Saxton,[1] although I have little to write.

The controversy about the Greek vessels occasions some noise here. I shall send on some newspapers directed to Austin which will give you an account of the matter. In the Albany Daily Advertiser you will see Mr. Sedgwick's narrative of the affair and in the Evening Post a little sparring between a foolish young Mr. Platt, and Mr. S. Mr. Sedgwick has done himself great credit by the fearless manner in which he has come forward to expose the frauds of these people, and the Greek agent has written a pamphlet which is printed but not yet published, and which shows the infamy of these proceedings in the strongest light.[2]

I have not seen Mr. Payne lately and can tell you nothing about our boarding house.[3]

I expected to get a letter from you before this time. I grow anxious to learn how you do, and what you do, and whether you continue to pass your time agreeably. We have had some delightful weather since I have been here—but it is now getting to be rainy. I am not quite so pleasantly situated at Mrs. Meigs's as I could wish. They have put me as [I] think I mentioned to you before into the same room with Mr. Stoddard[4]—and he is so terribly dyspeptic and whimsical that my comfort and quiet are not a little abridged.

The new Unitarian Church is to be finished by the first of December.[5] Mr. [William Ellery] Channing is invited to preach at the dedication. You will then be in town I hope, and have an opportunity of hearing him.

It is possible that G. & C. Carvill may have sent to Austin the first No of the U. S. Review as they have taken the list of subscribers from Bliss & White. It would probably be more convenient for him to receive it from Boston—I am certain that it would arrive earlier in that way. If he and Dr. Dawes[6] & others conclude to take it, I think he had better return the No he has received immediately to G. & C. Carvill according to their card enclosed in the No. and send to subscribe to the agent in Boston, or write to me about it and I will have the work sent to him from thence.—

I write this in haste at the office of the Evening Post and therefore you must excuse its brevity and its dulness.

Pour la petite, j'ose croire qu'elle continue à être bonne, et qu'elle joue, travaille, tricote, épèle, lit du Français, et fait du bruit, comme autrefois! Son papa lui envoit un baiser.[7]

I hope you will take good care of yourself and Frances in order that by and by you may report yourselves to me safe and sound. My love to the family. Your affectionate husband

Wm C. Bryant

P. S. The persons indicted for a conspiracy to defraud the Fulton Bank, to wit Jacob Barker Henry Eckford & others do not yet know their fate. Their crime is a state prison offence— The jury came in this morning & stated that they could not agree—the court sent them out again. It is said that ten of the jury were for convicting & two for acquitting them. The jury will not probably agree at all.—[8]

Manuscript: NYPL–GR address: Mrs. Frances F. Bryant / Cummington / Massachusetts / pr. Mr. Rogers postmark (in script): Great Barrington. Oct 25 postal annotation: 10.

1. The first-named was probably a son of Bryant's former office-mate, Dr. Benjamin F. Rogers of Great Barrington; the second, William B. Saxton of Sheffield. See 95.3.

2. Henry Sedgwick had worked, to the detriment of his health and sanity, to free from legal attachment two frigates loaded with supplies for the Greek revolutionaries. He managed to clear one so that it could sail for Greece; the other was detained. [Henry D. Sedgwick] *Vindication of the Conduct and Character of H. D. Sedgwick Against Certain Charges Made by Jonas Platt . . . in the Case of the Greek Frigate* (New York, 1826); John Duer and Robert Sedgwick, . . . *Examination of the Controversy Between the Greek Deputies and Two Mercantile Houses . . .* (New York, 1826); *EP*, October 17–19, 1826; Sedgwick, *Life and Letters*, pp. 182–185; Alexander Contostavlos, *A Narrative of the Material Facts in Relation to the Building of the Two Greek Frigates.* 2nd ed. [with a postscript by Henry D. Sedgwick], New York: Elam Bliss, 1826.

3. Since Bryant was then lodging with Mrs. Meigs, this comment is obscure.

4. See 146.7.

5. At the corner of Mercer and Prince Streets.

6. Dr. Howland Dawes, a practicing physician at Cummington from 1795 to 1845. *Only One Cummington*, p. 398.

7. (In block letters) "As for the little one, I dare say she continues to be good, and that she plays, works, knits, spells, reads French, and makes noise, as of old. Her papa sends her a kiss."

8. Jacob Barker (1779–1871), a banker, was then the employer of Fitz-Greene Halleck. Henry Eckford (1775–1832), a wealthy Scottish shipbuilder resident in New York since 1796, had been the father-in-law of Halleck's close friend and fellow-poet, the late Joseph Rodman Drake (1795–1820). Bryant's guess that the jury would disagree at this, the first of several trials, was borne out; the case was in the courts for several years longer. Adkins, *Halleck*, pp. 47, 167–177.

156. *To* Charles Folsom

New York   Oct   29   1826.

My dear Sir.

I write to you at this time principally to say that I have put Mr. *Strickland's Reports* into the hands of Mr. [James] Renwick who will prepare an article for the Dec   No.[1] and that I shall also have a notice of the *Rifleman* and another of a Spanish Tale by Dr. Sanuza of this city— I forget the name of the Tale.

The Review has been well received here, and the subscription list is going on well in the city although some of the country subscribers are taking advantage of the gap in the work to have an apology for returning their numbers. I am very much delighted with the typographical arrangement and execution and hear it spoken of in terms of admiration by every body.[2]

I shall send on the matter shortly for the Dec. No. and hope it will reach you by the tenth.

The poem of B. L. de Argensola from which I made my translation I found in Bouterwick's History of Spanish and Portuguese Literature a work which contains a great deal of poetry in these languages, placed in the notes and serving as a series of illustrations to the text. The publication in which I found it is a translation from the German published at

London in two volumes a few years since. If I could come at it I would send you the original of the lines.[3]

Our contributor Cushing it seems is in some difficulty—I suppose it is he. I do not however think the evidence arising from comparison of hands conclusive, and I should be satisfied with his denial. Mr. Verplanck once handed me an article for the New York Review written by one of his friends the hand writing of which so nearly resembled his own that I could almost have sworn to it.—[4]

I fear that three pages of political intelligence every month might be deemed a pretty large proportion— I do not know however that I should be for excluding a contribution of that sort provided it seemed likely to be interesting to the public.[5]

In haste
yrs truly
W. C. BRYANT

MANUSCRIPT: BPL ADDRESS: Mr. Charles Folsom / Editor of the U. S. Review / Boston / Care of Bowles & Dearborn   Booksellers— POSTMARK: NEW-YORK/ OCT / 31 POSTAL ANNOTATION: 18¾.

1. James Renwick (1792–1863, Columbia 1807, M.A. 1810), professor of Natural Philosophy and Experimental Chemistry at Columbia from 1820 to 1853, and a member of the Bread and Cheese Lunch Club, was father of architect James Renwick (1818–1895, Columbia 1836). See Adkins, *Halleck*, p. 153.

2. Folsom had written on October 10 that Bryant's suggestions for typographical changes (Letter 151) had been incorporated in the first number of the *USR*, though this had delayed its publication. NYPL–BG.

3. In his October 10 letter Folsom commented, "I have made a keen search after the original of your beautiful translation of 'Mary Magdalen,' but in vain. . . . Will you do me the favour to direct me to it?" From Friedrich Bouterwek's *Geschichte der Poesie und Beredsamkeit*, 12 vols. (Göttingen, 1801–1819), James Ross had published a translation of Volumes III and IV as *A History of Spanish and Portuguese Literature* (London, 1823). Williams, *Spanish Background*, I, 375–376; II, 333.

4. Caleb Cushing (1800–1879, Harvard 1817) had contributed to the *USLG*, and had written for the *USR* (1 [October 1826] 1–9) an article, "The Diplomacy of the United States." As a candidate for election to Congress from Massachusetts, he had been accused, on the basis of his supposed handwriting, of an unfair attack on his opponent in a Boston newspaper. Claude M. Fuess, *The Life of Caleb Cushing* (New York: Harcourt Brace, 1923), I, 56, 73–74.

5. Folsom had written Bryant on October 10, "Cushing . . . has proposed to furnish a monthly political summary of three pages. I spoke of allowing one page, if we liked the matter & the plan. . . . He has replied that he cannot do with less than three pages. So the thing rests. What do you think?" NYPL–BG.

157. *To* Edward Wigglesworth

New York   Nov   5   1826

Dear Sir

I return the poetry you sent me altered for the press, except the "fragment" which will not do. Do you want it again? I am not for receiving the poetry of Mr. Mellen on the terms he expects—we cannot afford it—and I think this was understood by us all when I saw you last. He can probably make a better bargain elsewhere. —Nor should I think the piece itself worthy of insertion unless altered.[1]

I send you also a review of the "Young Rifleman."[2] I shall have Mr. Renwick's Review of Strickland this week, on Friday at latest—a notice of Alexanders Canon by Mr. [William] Ware and a Review of some work on Banking by Wm. Coleman jr. who is a great Political Economist with us.

> I am Sir
> yrs in haste—
> W C BRYANT

If you have not the Young Rifleman let me know it & I will send you the book or the leaves from it, containing the extracts—

MANUSCRIPT: BPL ADDRESS: Edward Wigglesworth Esq / Boston— / Care of Bowles & Dearborn.

1. Grenville Mellen (1799–1841, Harvard 1818) had contributed verse to the *USLG*, and in noticing his prize poem, *The Rest of the Nations* (Portland, 1826), Bryant had commented, "It may be very old fashioned in us to recommend the free use of the *file* to this writer, but it is only recommending the example of the greatest poets, both ancient and modern." *USLG*, 4 (September 1826), 461–462. Mellen wrote an indignant protest to Bryant (n.d., NYPL–BG), and asked more money of Folsom for his verses. Reporting his request to Bryant, Folsom remarked, "I think he is not a valuable contributor, & is likely to be a troublesome one." October 30, 1826, NYPL–BG.

2. Bryant's notice of *The Adventures of a Young Rifleman* (Philadelphia, 1826), appeared in *USR*, 1 (December 1826), 178–190.

158.   *To* Charles Folsom

New York   Nov. 9, 1826.

My dear Sir

I received at nearly the same moment your last letter and Prof. Renwick's Review of Strickland's Reports. I saw with some alarm that you had on hand a critical notice of Strickland's Reports—as the article furnished by Renwick is a very good one and contains matter which we cannot well spare. I have sent it on however and hope that it will be printed in some form or other. Could not the critical notice of Mr. Treadwell be incorporated into it? The work of Strickland is one of no small importance, and is got up at an expense quite unusual in this country. It seems to me deserving of more notice than could be taken of it in a page or two. Or if this plan will not answer could not Mr. R's article be provided with a new title and placed in the miscellaneous department? One of these things, I should imagine, might easily be done.[1]

I send you also an article on Alexanders "Canon of the Scriptures" by Mr. William Ware[2] and another on "Thoughts on Banking" by Mr. W. H. Coleman.[3] The latter has been examined by some of our most erudite political economists here, and as they approve of it I think it entirely safe to publish it—more especially as Mr. Coleman has studied very carefully and for a considerable time the subjects on which he has touched and has the reputation of understanding them very well. He desires however to be kept anonymous, as there are some brokers of his acquaintance of a different opinion from himself and being ill, does not want to have any controversies.—

You have shortened somewhat the time allowed me to get my articles to Boston but as you have only given me information of it since the month came in you must excuse me for not obeying you this time. I will endeavour to do it hereafter.—

Mr. Renwick Mr. Ware & Mr. Coleman are men who write for pay. The first and last of these articles, I hope you will contrive to put at all events into the next number as I promised the writers it should be done; and my promise was made before you informed me that the first of the month was not soon enough.

In respect to Mr. G. Mellen's poetry we are quite agreed.[4] Our *concern* is too poor to buy much poetry; and I dare say that Mr. Mellen will make more by writing prize poems than he could do by writing poetry for us at the rate we can afford to pay. I have handed to Mr. Halleck the author of *Fanny* & of *Croaker*[5] a copy of the first and second numbers; and unless he disappoints me much I shall have from him something for the next No. He is exceedingly popular here—more so than you can well imagine—and a little assistance from him would help the work exceedingly.

Sandoval,[6] *Boyne Water*,[7] & the *other novel*[8] you are welcome to. I have not read them, and do not intend to do it, nor am I certain that I can get any body to notice them. For your next I shall have an article on Jicotencal a Mexican Tale by a Spaniard of this city[9]—another on a translation of *Las Partidas* or the code of Spanish Law lately published in Louisiana[10] with such other matters as it may please fortune to send in my way.

As for Mrs. Hemans have you forgotten my telling you that Mr. [George] Bancroft of Northampton requested of me some time since while I was editor of the N. Y. Review the privilege of reviewing that work when it appeared, and that I promised it to him? And do you not recollect that I desired, that if you had no objection, he might be the person to do it—and that you agreed to it? I cannot, to be sure, recollect quite so well as Mrs Quickly in another case, whether you were at that time sitting by a sea-coal fire or not, nor what dish you were eating, nor whether it was Wednesday, nor who came into the room nor what the person who came into the room said;[11]—but I recollect the *substance of the conversation* very well which is as much as is necessary, and I have no doubt that you do also on being reminded of it. I spoke to Mr. Bancroft about it afterwards and I suppose he expects to do it. Whatever may be thought of Mr. Bancroft's poetical talent, of which there are some specimens in Carey & Lea's Souvenir of this year, he shows no want of ability in prose.[12]

Make what you please of the article on Brooks's poem.[13] I will give you in my next what you desire, an abstraction of *my opinions* on the U S. Review & Literary Gazette and its several articles.—[14]

My compliments to Mrs. Folsom & Believe me

Yrs truly

W. C. BRYANT

I observe that copies of the U S Review are sent hither to several editors of Newspapers who publish the contents of the numbers as a kind of equivalent. These are the *Statesman* the *National Advocate* and the *Daily Advertiser*. Of these the two former have a small circulation, and neither of the three ever have noticed or ever would notice the work in any other way than by performing their bargain that is by publishing a list of the contents. There are other papers whose opinions on subjects of literature are somewhat more likely to be right, who have a larger circulation & whose Editors are either my personal friends or acquainted with me & well disposed towards me. These, such as the Editor of the N. Y. *American*, the *Commercial Advertiser*, the *Enquirer* as it is now conducted, the *Times* &c do not receive the work—yet they are friendly to it—and all noticed the union of the two journals in the kindest terms.—[15]

MANUSCRIPT: BPL ADDRESS: Mr. Charles Folsom / Editor of the U. S. Review / Boston / Care of Bowles & Dearborn / Booksellers.

1. James Renwick's review of William Strickland, *Reports on Canals, Railways, Roads, and Other Subjects* (Philadelphia, 1826), appeared in *USR*, 1 (December 1826), 198–204. Daniel Treadwell (1791–1872), an inventor and popular lecturer on the steam engine, as well as Rumford Professor at Harvard, had recently patented a very successful printing press. His article was not printed in the *USR*.

2. William Ware, notice of Archibald Alexander, *The Canon of Old and New Testaments* (Princeton, New Jersey, 1826), in *USR*, 1 (February 1827), 327–336. In an undated note to Folsom, in BPL, Bryant wrote, "I have marked a passage at the end of Mr. Ware's article which I think should be struck out—as it may not be palatable to the orthodox."

3. *USR*, 1 (December 1826), 190–197.

4. See 157.1.

5. Fitz-Greene Halleck, *Fanny* (New York, 1819); Halleck and Joseph Rodman Drake, *Poems, By Croaker, Croaker & Co. and Croaker, Jun. As Published in the Evening Post* (New York, 1819).

6. Not reviewed in the *USR*.

7. Edward Wigglesworth noticed *The Boyne Water*, "By the O'Hara Family" (New York, 1826?), in *USR*, 1 (January 1827), 300–301.

8. Jane and A[nna] M[aria] Porter, *Tales Round a Winter Hearth* (New York, 1826?), was noticed by Theophilus Parsons in *USR*, 1 (January 1827), 296–297. The three novels named were American reprints of earlier British publications.

9. In reviewing the anonymous Spanish language novel *Jicotencal* (Philadelphia, 1826), based on Cortés' conquest of Mexico, Bryant rendered more than two pages of the text into English—his first known prose translation from the Spanish. *USR*, 1 (February 1827), 336–346.

10. Not published.

11. Cf. *2 Henry IV* II.i.92–112.

12. Bancroft's review of Felicia Hemans, *Poems* (Boston, 1827), in *USR*, 1 (March 1827), 401–406, preceded a longer notice he wrote of the work for the *NAR*, 24 (April 1827), 443–463.

13. See 154.4. Folsom thought this article should be "considerably shortened," which it was. Folsom to Bryant, October 30, 1826, NYPL–BG.

14. In his October 30 letter, Folsom asked Bryant to give his candid opinion of the review, "so far as it is made up in this quarter, with all the freedom of a friend & the unsparingness of an enemy."

15. These friendly New York editors were Charles King of the *American*, William L. Stone of the *Commercial Advertiser*, Mordecai M. Noah of the *Enquirer*, and Nathaniel P. Tallmadge of the *Times*.

159.   *To* Richard H. Dana

New York   Nov   11   1826.

My dear Sir.

I do not write with your last letter[1] before me and may perhaps fail of answering some things that are in it. If so I shall try to make up the deficiency in my next.

I am quite sorry that you did not write the article on Mrs. Radcliffe. I think you would have done justice to the subject and I am pretty certain that there are few who can.[2] In the mean time do not forget us, and if [a] subject occurs to you on which you can write *con amore*, put your thoughts immediately into black and white for the U. S. Review. I shall think a great deal better of the journal for your contributions.

By the way [Robert] *Walsh*[3] is to be the Editor of a new literary journal to be published by Carey & Lea at Philadelphia under the name of the American Quarterly Review. I have seen the prospectus which has just been received here and is one of the most clumsily written things that can be imagined. It says that "Philadelphia contains a large fund of talent science and erudition—larger perhaps than any other American city" —and observes that as very little of this vast fund is expended in any of our journals, it might be laid out to great advantage in one of their own.—

By the way how is my *godson* should I call it? the poem I looked over with you when I saw you last. He was a likely bantling I remember, and did honour to his parent.[4]

You will recollect I spoke to you about having something to do with a daily paper here— You say nothing about it in your letter. Have you thought of the plan any further and what do you think of it?—[5]

If you do not like our *reviews* you must give us something better.— You have friends who can write *well* and I wish you to tell them that I say they *must* write.— I am as sick of addresses and eulogies &c &c as you are— I have not read any of them—some I have looked into—but I feel a sensation of nausea a rising of the gorge at the very sight of their covers.

Mr. Verplanck has just called on me— He says I must tell you that he will write you soon and send you *something* what it is I do not know. Mr. Verplanck has been successful in the late election—he goes in by 1800 majority.[6]

I write this in haste as Mr [Henry] Sedgwick is just setting out— By and by I shall write to you at my leisure and perhaps at more length.— My regards to your brother and sisters— I remember with great pleasure my visit to Cambridge.

Yrs truly
W. C. BRYANT

P. S. There has been a very villainous transaction here in which the poor Greeks have been fleeced horribly. Mr. [Henry] Sedgwick has gained infinite credit for the courage and zeal he has shown in the cause. The story of the transaction in the pamphlets of Contostavlos & Mr S. is worth reading.[7]

MANUSCRIPT: NYPL–GR DOCKETED: W C Bryant / Nov 11–26.

1. Unrecovered.
2. But Dana subsequently did write the review. See 151.4.
3. See 80.6.
4. This was Dana's first long poem, "The Buccaneer," published with other poems in 1827, and reviewed by Bryant in *NAR*, 26 (January 1828), 239–247.
5. See Letter 149. Dana seems by this time to have given up the idea of editing a newspaper, and no more was said on the subject.
6. This was Gulian Verplanck's second election to the United States House of Representatives, in which he served from 1825 to 1833.
7. See 155.2.

160. *To* Charles Folsom

New York   Dec   8, 1826.

My dear Sir.

I send you two Critical Notices with Dr. Lindsley's pamphlet.[1] I have also enclosed a *good deal* of poetry—more perhaps than can be printed in the next No. The articles sent me by Mr. Wigglesworth I do not return because I have not had time to examine and correct them.

The poem on Burns is by Halleck the author of Fanny and is altogether [the] noblest monument that has been erected to the memory of him whom it celebrates.[2] It is the tribute of one great poet to the genius of another. You will oblige me by giving it the first place among the poetry of the January number. It will have a great run here, as every thing written by Halleck is sought and read with the greatest eagerness. Halleck of all the literary men of the age except the author of the Waverly novels[3] is the most universal favorite with the New York public. The poem entitled My Native Village is by a brother of mine—[4] That entitled a *Changeful Picture* is anonymous.[5] The translation from Heredia is not *wholly* made by myself and therefore I have not felt justified in putting my signature to it. It seems to me that the poetry of Heredia is the best which has been written about the Great American Cataract.—[6]

Mr. Halleck is fond of having his poetry handsomely and correctly printed, and as he was not to see the proof sheet he showed some anxiety on the subject. I tranquillized him by referring to your well known care and accuracy, and promised him in your name that his poem should have all the advantages which typographical arrangement correct orthography and careful punctuation could give it. I hope you will not disclaim my authority to make such a promise.

I am in hopes of getting up a kind of association of literary gentlemen here each of whom will contribute yearly a certain proportion—a small one—to the contents of our journal— Mr. Verplanck suggested it the other day and offered to be one of them provided 7 or 8 others could be induced to engage in it.

I would write about some further matters as I promised to do in my last—but the boat would be off before I could finish my letter.[7]

Yrs truly
W   C   BRYANT

P. S. I see nothing of the Review of *Brooks's* poem— I fear his friends will grow impatient.—[8]

MANUSCRIPT: BPL ADDRESS: Mr. Charles Folsom / Editor of the U   S. Review / Boston / Care of Bowles & Dearborn.

1. [Eliza Robbins] Notice of Philip Lindsley, *The Cause of Education in Tennessee, USR*, 1 (January 1827), 293–296. The critical notices mentioned were probably those of John Torrey, *A Compendium of the Flora of the Northern and Middle States* (New York, 1826?), *ibid.*, 290–291; and Count Xavier de Maistre, *Russian Tales* (New York? 1826?), *ibid.*, 291–293. Reviewers unidentified.

2. "Burns," *ibid.*, 277–282.

3. Sir Walter Scott.

4. "My Native Village," by "J[ohn] H[oward] B[ryant]," *USR*, 1 (January 1827), 286–287.

5. "A Changeful Picture," by W. G. C.," *ibid.*, 287–289. This was sent to Bryant by Willis Gaylord Clark (1808–1841), later an editor of the *Knickerbocker*, with the plea, "I know it has many imperfections—alter it wherever you may please." Undated letter, with manuscript poem showing Bryant's radical revisions, HEHL.

6. "Niagara. From the Spanish of José Maria Heredia," *USR*, 1 (January 1827), 283–286. This letter and the original manuscript poem in HEHL resolve often expressed doubts whether the translation was Bryant's. See Williams, *Spanish Background*, II, 145–146, 333.

7. See 158.14.

8. See 154.4.

161. *To* Charles Folsom

New York   Jan   8   1827.[1]

Dear Sir

I send you notices of Mitchill's Discourse[2] & the Essay on Boring for water[3]—and some poetical contributions. I intended to have sent a poem of my own but I delayed it till an Influenza or something of the kind stupified me and I could not *concoct* any thing poetical. As a substitute which you will be glad to see I send you another poem of Mr Halleck's entitled *Wyoming*.[4] If you have time enough, he would like to see the proofsheet as before.— By the bye there was an error in the poem called Niagara in the last No.—*feelingly* for *feebly*.

Tor Hill I wish to notice myself as I am going to read it.

Yrs truly

W. C. Bryant

P. S. Dont print what I have *marked out* with red ink.

MANUSCRIPT: BPL ADDRESS: Mr. Charles Folsom / Editor of the U   S. Review / Care of Bowles & Dearborn / Boston.

1. Bryant mistakenly wrote "1826."
2. [Bryant] Notice of Samuel L. Mitchill, *A Discourse on the Character and Services of Thomas Jefferson* . . . (New York, 1826), *USR*, 1 (February 1827), 384–387.
3. [Bryant] Notice of *An Essay on the Art of Boring the Earth for . . . Water* [anon.] (New Brunswick, 1826), *USR*, 1 (March 1827), 461–462.
4. "Wyoming," by "F. G. H., June, 1821," *USR*, 1 (February 1827), 376–379. Despite its early date, this was the first appearance of this poem in print. Adkins, *Halleck*, pp. 180–181.

162. *To* Charles Folsom

[New York, *c*February 10, 1827]

Dr   Sir

I send   Notes on Colombia—Review[1]
Hillhouse's Oration   Crit. Notice[2]
The Stars—Mr. Sands—please to put this first.[3]
Sonnet &c. Miss Manley[4]
The Parting—*Myself*.[5]

A Stroll to Sweet Auburn—This was enclosed to me by Mr. [William] Emerson who wrote that Mr. Wigglesworth sd   he must send it to me.[6]

I send by *mail* as the steam boats do not go to New London.

W. C. B.

MANUSCRIPT: HEHL.

1. [Bryant] *Notes on Columbia, Taken in the Years 1822–3 . . . By an Officer of the United States Army* (Philadelphia, 1827), *USR*, 1 (March 1827), 418–432.

2. [Bryant] James A. Hillhouse, *An Oration Pronounced at New Haven, Before the Society of Phi Beta Kappa, September 12, 1826, "On Some of the Considerations Which Should Influence the Epic or Tragic Writer in the Choice of an Era"* (New Haven, 1826), *ibid.*, 462–463.

3. [Robert C. Sands] " 'The Stars,' . . . From de La Martine," *ibid.*, 445–449.

4. [Emma C. (Manley) Embury] "The Bride," and "Sonnet," *ibid.*, 452–454.

5. [Bryant] " 'The Parting,' from an Unfinished Poem," *ibid.*, 449–452. This was a portion of Bryant's discarded narrative poem, "The Spectre Ship." See 103.6.

6. Probably " 'Song': I have a sprig of myrtle," signed "E," *USR*, 2 (April 1827), 61. William Emerson (1801–1868), several of whose letters from Europe were published in *USLG* and *USR*, was the elder brother of Ralph Waldo Emerson. He had recently entered law practice in New York. Mount Auburn Cemetery at Cambridge, Massachusetts, was often referred to there as "Sweet Auburn," in tribute to Oliver Goldsmith's "The Deserted Village." Here Waldo Emerson walked "almost every day when he was in Cambridge." Rusk, *Emerson*, pp. 71, 188.

163. *To* Charles Folsom

New York   March 1   1827.[1]

Dear Sir

I enclose you an article on Halleck's poems for your next[2]—and a Review of the Life of Lindley Murray written by Miss E[liza] Robbins[3] together with two pieces of poetry sent me by Mr. Wigglesworth. Miss Robbins will expect to be paid for what she writes. There is also an article for the Miscellaneous department about the Fine Arts in the age of Charles 5th. The writer brought it to me with some pieces of poetry. I was obliged to reject the poetry, and to alleviate the matter as well as I could I told him I would send on to you the prose article for insertion in case you thought it worthy. Do as you think proper with it. The author did not give me his name but spoke of *Morse the painter* as his particular friend &c. which is something in any man's favour; and he requested that if you thought the article worthy of insertion *6 copies* of the No. containing it might be sent to New Haven directed to the signature, n——C. and the money should be remitted. I hope you will see this part of the request attended to, if the article is admitted.[4] As to the books Honor O'Hara, Last of the Lairds, Hosack's Address, The Young Rifleman & Bull on Fuel which Mr. Wigglesworth wrote me about I give them up to your writers with pleasure. But do not forget that Bull is said to have slandered the Rhode Island Coal and Dr. Hosack the Western Medical College, and that a prosecution is actually pending against the latter gentleman. Bull is Secretary of the Lehigh Company.[5] —As for Rome in the 19 Cent. & Almacks I have articles promised on those subjects— I shall send next week some verses of my own and several Critical Notices, and a long letter to yourself about many things.

Yrs truly
W   C   BRYANT

MANUSCRIPT: BPL ADDRESS: Mr. Charles Folsom / Editor of the U S. Review / ⟨Care of Bowles & Dearborn / Boston⟩ Cambridge.

1. Bryant mistakenly wrote "1826."
2. [Bryant] Review of [Fitz-Greene Halleck] *Alnwick Castle, with Other Poems* (New York, 1827), *USR*, 2 (April 1827), 8–13.
3. Not published.
4. Not published.
5. Neither Bull's nor Hosack's publication was noticed in the *USR*.

164. *To* Charles Folsom

[New York] March¹ 9, 1827

Dear Sir

I send notices of Letters from the Bahama Islands & Simms's *poems*,² and of *Almacks* and Paul Jones.³ The two latter are written by R. C. Sands Esq who wrote the translation of the *Stars* from De La Martine in the last No. and who will expect to be paid for them and also, as I should have mentioned before, for the Stars, the poetry to be paid for of course at the same rate as the prose.

I send also some verses of my own⁴ and the poem by Digamma, who as you may perhaps know is Professor G. W. Doane of the new College at Hartford (Conn.).⁵ He has published a volume of poems, and although *somewhat* inferior to Lord Byron and a few others in the poetic line, is said to be a good scholar and a man of considerable talent. I do not think the verses enclosed particularly fine, but the[y] will do, and the author has written and may write better—

Yrs truly

W. C. BRYANT

MANUSCRIPT: BPL ADDRESS: Mr. Charles Folsom / Editor of the U S. Review / Care of Bowles & Dearborn / Boston.

1. Bryant mistakenly wrote "Feb."
2. [Bryant] Notice of *Letters from the Bahama Islands, Written in 1823–4* (Philadelphia, 1827?), *USR*, 2 (April 1827), 62–64; [Bryant] notice of William G. Simms, Jr., *Lyrical and Other Poems* (Charleston, 1827), *ibid.*, 70–71.
3. "*Almack's: a Novel*," *ibid.*, 64–66; "*Paul Jones: a Romance*, by Allan Cunningham," *ibid.*, 66–68.
4. "Spring in Town," *ibid.*, 54–55. See *Poems* (1876), pp. 146–148.
5. [George Washington Doane] "Another Vision in Verse," *USR*, 2 (May 1827), 141–143. The new college was Washington (later Trinity) College, founded in 1823.

165. *To* Richard H. Dana

New York March 10 1827.¹

My dear Sir.

I am quite sorry not to be able to send back by Mr. Reed² your manuscript poem, as you requested. I have not yet completely fulfilled my function of critic upon it. It is as you know a manuscript of considerable length and of course offers considerable occasion for remark.[3]

There are three classes of things to be done; or at least I divide them so. In the first place there are things that must be done immediately. These I contrive to do. In the second place there are things which must be done soon. These I put off as long as I can, and in some instances I believe I have missed doing them at all. In this class I put writing answers to letters, writing articles for my journal, &c &c. The third class consists of those things which may be done at any time. These for the most part I never do at all; and that I believe has been the reason I did not write the long poem of which you speak.[4] My reason at present is that I have no leisure to do such things.

No[w,] I had placed the revision of your manuscript in the second class; and the serious truth is that since I received it I have had so many things of the first class on my hands, that I have had no leisure to give it that attention which I could wish before I send it back to you. I read it over immediately on receiving it, and solely with a view to its general effect as you requested. I was pleased with it. I have read it twice since and have made some progress in my observations and annotations but have not yet completed them. I shall now have an interval of some leisure and will finish the work in a few days; and if I have no other opportunity I can send it to Bowles & Dearborn, as there is an opportunity of doing this twice a week by an arrangement with the steam boats. I will then write you more particularly about your poem.

The folks who said I was out of my wits were guilty of some exaggeration. Dr. Channing is an eloquent preacher, he has a manner quite different from any body else I ever heard, and it is difficult to listen to him without excitement.[5]

You handled Miss Yorktown I thought quite tenderly. I found the book unreadable, and gave you great credit for your perseverance in getting through with it, and felt much obliged to you, as a philanthropist, for speaking of it with so much forbearance. I was surprised therefore to see by a very very angry article in the Galaxy that your criticism was not taken in good part, by the lady's friends.[6]

The article on "Nature" has been very highly spoken of here. I thought parts of it somewhat obscure but nobody agreed with me.[7]

I sincerely regret that any thing should happen to prevent your writing for the work. As to the gravity of it—I have heard that complained of by others—but what can one do? Fine writing is rare in this country—wit and humour are scarce—if we can get tolerable good sense I suppose we must be content with it although not delivered in a very sprightly manner. I have never been more strongly impressed with the extreme heaviness of American compositions than in reading the first No. [of] Walsh's Quarterly just out. The articles are furnished in most instances by men of considerable reputation for ability, but the book is much duller than ours has ever been.[8]

As for the circulation of the U. S. Review I believe it is increasing. If I keep to it I may possibly find it a source of some profit in time, but these things you know are built up slowly, and no man must expect in this country to grow rich by literature. I have no idea that were I to publish a volume of poems I could get any thing like *handsome wages* for the time I might spend in putting them in order and superintending their publication—that is, I should not be as well paid as a merchants clerk commonly is.[9] What reputation I have depends in a good measure, I have no doubt upon my having written so little. I began to write a great while since, and I have no doubt that if I had written voluminously at first I should have given the public a surfeit at once. I hold therefore that my best way of keeping in favour with the public is to appear before them rarely. —But I have talked enough about myself.

I like Mr. Reed very much and regret that I could not see more of him. Present my regards to your sisters and your brother and the rest of my friends about you and believe me

very truly yrs
W. C. BRYANT

MANUSCRIPT: NYPL–GR ADDRESS: Richard H. Dana Esq. / Cambridge / Mass / pr. Mr. Reed ENDORSED: W. C. Bryant / 10 March 1827 / Ans—Mar. 26.

1. Bryant mistakenly wrote "1826."
2. Possibly Sampson Reed (1800–1880), a Boston druggist whose *Observations on the Growth of the Mind* (Boston, 1826) had been reviewed by Jonathan Porter in *USR*, 1 (November 1826), 109–118.
3. "The Buccaneer." See 159.4.
4. For several years Dana had been urging Bryant to write a long poem. See, for example, 103.5.
5. On December 7, 1826 William Ellery Channing had preached the sermon at the dedication of the new Unitarian church in New York. See 155.5. Although Bryant's comment is somewhat obscure, he maintained the highest regard for Channing's eloquence. In an obituary article in the *EP* for October 5, 1842, he wrote of Channing, "So admirable is his use of language, that phraseology, which, when analyzed, seems to have no character but that of simple propriety, has in his hands a poetic effect, and an irresistible power of kindling emotion in the reader."
6. [Dana] Review of [Mrs. Eliza Lanesford (Foster) Cushing] *Yorktown: An Historical Romance* . . . (Boston, 1826), *USR*, 1 (January 1827), 241–245. The *New England Galaxy* was a weekly newspaper published in Boston.
7. [Walter Channing] "What is Nature," *ibid.*, 263–269.
8. The *American Quarterly Review*.
9. See 143.1.

166.   *To* Charles Folsom

New York   March 20   1827.

My dear Sir.

I ought to have answered some things in your letters earlier—but some how it has happened that whenever I have written to you lately it has been in haste so that I was obliged to defer or at least forgot many things which I had to say.

In answer to a question you put me some time since concerning the nature of the articles furnished from your quarter and the manner in which the work has been conducted there,[1] I answer that I have been well pleased with the former, and particularly gratified with the latter. I believe that the later numbers are, if any thing, superior to the others and as far as I can judge the work is gaining in the good will of the public. I have however something to say on two or three articles. In the first place, although I doubt not that the utmost care is taken to prevent it, one or two articles of intelligence have found their way into our pages which are not quite new. For example the *Chinese Advertisement* in the first No. was published in *all* the newspapers five or six years ago. The *Turkish Anecdote* is more modern but I had seen it before—I cannot tell where— some time since. I do not know from what sources this part of the Journal is gleaned but I should think the Revue Encyclopedique, might furnish a good many valuable items.[2] It seemed to me that the article on Williston's Tacitus was too caustic and contemptuous in its tone.[3] Had you no doubt about the insertion of *Micromegas*?[4] It was well-translated I allow—exceedingly so—but it is not new to many of our subscribers in N. Y. who have read Voltaire in the original. Besides, Micromegas had been translated into English already—the translation was published in London in 1753 along with that of the Universal History. It has been intimated to me that the extracts from the eulogies on Adams and Jefferson were a little too liberal for the taste of readers in this quarter—but this remark might have its origin in a feeling of local jealousy—the authors of those eulogies being all except Mr. Sergeant New Englanders.[5]

As to Jones's Indian Tales of which you ask my opinion[6] I confess that I did not like his Nantucket at all—the attempt at humour was too violent and outrageous if I may so speak. But the *Indian Tradition* I thought a great deal better—indeed it was quite good in its way—with the exception of the interview between the Great Spirit and the Evil Spirit which is altogther too extravagant for my taste. This tale if divested of the blemish to which I allude I should think a desirable contribution—but of the nature of the rest in Mr. Jones's collection I can of course form no judgment.

Prof. Renwick's article of which you speak occasioned no complaint here. I believe it is thought a fair exposition of the imperfections of the plan of execution of the Grand Canal.[7]

And as to the article entitled "Nature" before I give my opinion of it I would say that it is in high favour with readers here.[8] Several persons for whose literary opinions I have great respect voluntarily expressed to me the pleasure they had experienced in reading it—among these was Miss Sedgwick the author of Redwood. I said that I thought parts of it a little obscure—but I could not find any body to agree with me. This obscurity is in fact my principal objection to it—but even with this defect, which does not after all exist in it to a very great degree, I like the article. I like it, partly because it is an instance of that moral and intellectual speculation which is rare in our country, and which therefore I think may very agreeably diversify the pages of our journal. I do not understand the author as you seem to do, to bring a general condemnation against learning, and if he does, I do not agree with him. I understand him to say that too close and exclusive attention to particulars is apt to disqualify the mind for broad and comprehensive views of things. This I believe is as true as that a man who gives his sole attention to watchmaking will not be likely to be a good architect. This however is, or should be, no objection to the trade of watchmaking, for we must have watchmakers and we must have architects. I am myself an admirer of *learning* though not one of her most favoured admirers—but I would not exclude speculations on the moral and intellectual capacities of our nature when they were ingenious and intelligible, particularly from the Miscellaneous part of our Journal. With respect to the style of "Nature" I must confess I do not see any great objection that can be made to it,—except the mistiness in one or two places.

Of Swedenborg I only know that I cannot understand or read his works— Concerning Mr. Reed I agree with you.[9] And as to Wordsworth, although he is a sort of poetical master of mine I do not believe that we should much disagree in opinion.[10] I like his Peter Bell tho'. To my shame be it spoken I had never read it when I received your letter, but I have read it since with great pleasure, and think that Wordsworth has written worse things. Wordsworth has his faults I know and among them is I think a want of terseness, an occasional fine drawing and extenuation of meaning which I do not like and should be loth to imitate. But his spirituality and his vein of lofty and profound meditation I admire and am awed by it whenever I take up his works. I think that in the literature of our own country as compared with that of England there is apparent something of a worldly material spirit such as might be expected in the literature of a people devoted to trade and gain. I could wish that some remedy might be applied with a view of correcting our character through our literature—but I do not know that it is possible. You see sir that this is a subject upon which much may be said. I shall leave it with observing that I am not more a friend to childishness or obscurity than you are. I do not feel any strong sympathy for the former and the latter I labour to avoid.—

I do not know who W. G. C. is—but he has lately written me from Onandaga in the western part of this State enclosing a poem which I fear I cannot publish.[11] The Reviewer of Mr. Brooks was at first a little ill-natured about the alterations in his article but I apologized for you as well as I could. He wishes that the article might be sent to him. If you have it by you I wish you would let it be sent to me with some of the parcels that come to N. Y.—but I would not make a very *painful* search after it—for really I hope you have lost it.[12] Mrs. Simmons also wants the manuscript of her husbands letters entitled Letters from an Adventurer in London or England I forget which. I hope they are preserved, for the poor woman has dunned me several times for them. Will you be so good as to send them yet to me if they are to be found. I suppose that Mr. Wigglesworth will know something about them.[13]

Mr Grenville Mellen wrote me a very long and strange letter about three months ago and since that he has written me a very short one.[14] He wants to get back some poetry of his which he thinks I have got, and also speaks of a prose contribution to the Journal. For my own part I am innocent of having in my possession any thing of Mr. Mellen's writing but his letters. He says that he has written to you on the subject but has received no answer. I have seen I believe two of his poems and sent them to Boston again— His prose I never heard of before.—

Mr. Renwick told me the other day that if I pleased he would prepare an article on Sganzi's Civil Engineering a work published I believe at Boston. As it had been published some time, and you had done nothing about it I told him I thought he might venture to do it. If you have disposed of the art. or have any objection to Mr. Renwick's making an article on it will you inform me immediately.[15] Mr. Halleck has been quite pleased with the manner in which his poems were printed in the Review —but I suppose the newspaper Editors in Boston do not know that there is such a work as ours for I saw the poem on Burns in the Evening Gazette,[16] credited to the Montreal Herald. Carey & Lea manage differently. I do not suppose there is an Editor of a Newspaper in America to whom they have not sent their new *Quarterly*[17] with a written request that it might be noticed.

Yrs truly.
W   C   BRYANT

I have received no list of the names of the contributors to the two last Numbers of the Journal. It places me in rather an awkward situation not to know the names of the authors of the articles in a work of which I am one of the Editors. I ought to be able to answer the first inquiries on the subject—as a knowledge of the writers adds much to the interest of such a work. Could not the names be sent me along with the 6 copies forwarded me? I should think that the best way, and it would certainly be the best way as respects myself.

I have no great objection to reviewing Milton's Prose works but I cannot do it for the next No. Such a book you know must be read with great care—and reflected upon a good deal.[18]

MANUSCRIPT: BPL ADDRESS: Mr. Charles Folsom / Editor of the U. S. Review / Care of Bowles & Dearborn / Boston / POSTMARK: NEW-YORK / MAR / 22 POSTAL ANNOTATION: 18 [¾?].

1. See 158.14.

2. Published at Paris from 1819 to 1835. While Bryant was at Cummington in the summer of 1826, an article from the *Revue* praising his poetry appeared in the *EP* for September 5, apparently translated from the French by Robert Sands.

3. [James L. Kingsley] Review of *The Histories of Tacitus*, ed. E. B. Williston, *USR*, 1 (December 1826), 171–177.

4. [Edward Wigglesworth] "Micromegas," *USR*, 1 (February 1827), 369–375; *ibid.* (March 1827), 438–444.

5. [Edward Wigglesworth] Review, "Eulogies on Adams and Jefferson," *USR*, 1 (October 1826), 30–40. Bryant evidently meant liberal in length, not political opinion.

6. James Athearn Jones had contributed two tales to the *USR* and its predecessor: "Indian Traditions. The Creation of the Island of Nantucket," *USLG*, 4 (August 1826), 357–361; and "An Indian Tradition," *USR*, 1 (December 1826), 204–218. This and subsequent comments are Bryant's responses to questions raised by Folsom in a letter dated January 11, 1827, NYPL–BG.

7. See 158.1. The term "Grand Canal" was then often applied to the Erie Canal, opened in 1825.

8. See 165.7. In commenting on this article, Bryant was necessarily discreet. Folsom had printed it with "great misgivings," and only because it had been offered him by Bryant's close friend Dana as a "choice morsel." Folsom was certain the unnamed writer was Dana's cousin Walter Channing, dean of the Harvard Medical School, whose writings, he informed Bryant, had been previously rejected by the *USLG* as "affected and mystical, &, where intelligible, overstrained." Folsom to Bryant, January 11, 1827, NYPL–BG.

9. Folsom had praised "the poetry, the spirituality," in the "Swedenborgian" style of such writers as Sampson Reed. See 165.2.

10. Folsom professed himself a "great admirer of Wordsworth, Peter Bell, &c excepted."

11. See 160.5.

12. See 158.13.

13. See 151.9.

14. See 157.1. Mellen's second letter is unrecovered.

15. This article did not appear in the *USR*.

16. See 160.2.

17. The *American Quarterly Review*.

18. Folsom had remarked on January 11, "Mr. Jenks, the Editor of Milton's Prose Works, is very desirous that you should review it." No notice of this publication appeared in the *USR*.

167. *To* Charles Folsom

[New York, cApril 1, 1827]

Dear Sir

I meant to have sent you by Mr. Gray[1] a Review [of] the life of E. D. Clarke the traveller—but I am unable to f[ind] it in season. I shall send it by Friday's boat. It will [make][2] 10 or twelve pages—so that you may calculate upon me for tha[t] amount for the Review part.—

yrs truly

W. C. BRYANT

MANUSCRIPT: BPL.

    1. Probably Harrison Gray.
    2. Manuscript torn.

168. *To* Charles Folsom

N. Y.   Apl   5   1827—

Dear Sir

I send you an article on Dr. Clarke.[1] —I suppose you have the book at Boston. If there are any inaccuracies in the language I beg you will correct them. I send you also some poetry I have received from Jones. He wishes that the three sonnets should not all appear in the same No. I wish you therefore to print the first and second in the next No. and reserve the other for the June No.[2]

Yrs truly

W   C   BRYANT

P. S. Next week I shall send you some verses of my own & some critical notices.—

MANUSCRIPT: BPL ADDRESS: Chas. Folsom Esq / Editor of the U   S. Review / Care of Bowles & Dearborn / Boston / Wm. C. Goff.

    1. [Bryant] Review of William Otter, *The Life and Remains of Edward Daniel Clarke* . . . (New York, 1827), *USR*, 2 (May 1827), 109–123.
    2. [James Athearn] Jones. See 166.6. The poems were "To a Western Mound," and "On the Same," *USR*, 2 (June 1827), 220; and "To the Mississippi," *ibid.* (July 1827), 304.

169. *To* Charles Folsom

New York   Apl 11   1827

Dear Sir

I send you a batch of poetry which I have been trying to patch up for the U. S. Review.[1] Some critical notices which I intended to send are not finished. They will make 2 or 3 pages & will go by the next boat.—

I am obliged to your attention in regard to the names of writers of the articles.[2]

I have just read an article in the Statesman of yr city on the March No. The writer of it complains that we review books that have been published a good while. I cannot believe however that he very sincerely disapproves this practice—since his own article on the *March* No is published on the 9th of *April* several days after the April No. was out.[3]

Yrs truly.
W. C. BRYANT

I send also a sentence or two about Mr Cubi's proposed work which I suppose may go in at the end of the list of New publications.[4]

MANUSCRIPT: BPL ADDRESS: Mr. Charles Folsom / Editor of the U. S. Review / Care of Bowles & Dearborn / Boston / Goff.

1. These poems apparently included Bryant's own "The Life of the Blessed," from the Spanish of Luis Ponce de León, *USR*, 2 (May 1827), 136–137. See *Poems* (1876), pp. 200–201.

2. Reacting to Bryant's rebuke in Letter 166, Folsom sent him early in April lists of contributors to the *USR* for February, March, and April. Manuscript in NYPL–BG.

3. The *Statesman* (1825–1829), conducted by Nathaniel Greene, was then Boston's leading Democratic newspaper. Mott, *American Journalism*, p. 218.

4. This was probably to be a reissue of Mariano Cubi y Soler, *A New Spanish Grammar*, which reached a sixth edition by 1847. Williams, *Spanish Background*, I, 373. See 151.8.

170. *To* Charles Folsom

New York   Apl. 12, 1827.

Dear Sir

I send you Notices of Tor Hill & another book.[1] If the article about the Fine Arts in the reign of Charles V is not printed I think it would not be best to do it—for I have just seen it in a Weekly newspaper—[2]

yrs truly
W C BRYANT

MANUSCRIPT: BPL ADDRESS: Charles Folsom Esq / Editor of the U. S. Review / Care of Bowles & Dearborn / Boston / Drop this in Post Office.

1. "*The Tor Hill.* By the author of *Brambletyre House* [Horace Smith]," *USR*, 2 (June 1827), 232. The second article is unidentified.

2. See Letter 163.

171. *To* Charles Folsom

[New York, *ante* May 1, 1827]

Dear Sir

I send you a review of Mercer's discourse &c by Miss Robbins.[1] I shall pay for this article myself and it will therefore be included in my 20 pages. I also send a piece of poetry by Ianthe—(Miss Manley).[2]

I shall shortly send something more. I mean to do something with Everett's America—but it is difficult to know how to treat it. I think it contains some capital errors—and what perplexes me more, it has a political tendency, more properly speaking a leaning upon some of the questions that divide the two principal parties in the country. I spoke to a distinguished literary gentleman about making a review of it but he, after having read it, said that he could not make such a review as I would be willing to publish.—[3]

yrs truly
W. C. BRYANT

MANUSCRIPT: BPL ADDRESS: Mr. Charles Folsom / Editor of the U. S. Review / Care of Bowles & Dearborn / Boston.

1. [Eliza Robbins] Review of Charles F. Mercer, *Discourse on Popular Education: Delivered in . . . Princeton . . . Sept. 26, 1826* (Princeton?, 1826), and *Plans for the Government . . . of Boys* [no further identification], *USR*, 2 (July 1827), 264–272.

2. "Spring Breezes," *USR*, 2 (June 1827), 220–221.

3. Bryant refers to Alexander H. Everett, *America, or a General Survey of the Political Situation of the Western Continent* (Philadelphia, 1827), reviewed by Theron Metcalf in *USR*, 2 (August 1827), 348–368.

172.   *To* Charles Folsom

[New York, cMay 7, 1827]

Dear Sir

I send you a notice of Del Mar's Sp[anish] Grammar by Mr. Stoddard formerly a tutor at Yale College,[1] & one of the Biblical Repository,[2] & two pieces of poetry.[3]

I shall have by & by something about Sismondi's History of the Literature of the South, & Dr. Miller's Clerical Manners & Habits.

Yrs truly
W   C   BRYANT

MANUSCRIPT: BPL ADDRESS: Mr. Charles Folsom / Editor of the U S. Review / Care of Bowles, & Dearborn / Boston.

1. Notice of Emanuel Del Mar, *Grammar of . . . Spanish*, *USR*, 2 (June 1827), 231–232. For Stoddard, see 146.7.

2. Notice of *Biblical Repertory: A Collection of Tracts in Biblical Literature*, III, No. 2, ed. Charles Hodge, *USR*, 2 (June 1827), 225–226.

3. [Bryant] "Is This a Time to be Cloudy and Sad," *USR*, 2 (June 1827), 217–218. See *Poems* (1876), pp. 149–150, where it is entitled "The Gladness of Nature." [George B. Cheever] "Passage of the Red Sea," *USR*, 2 (June 1827), 218–219.

173. *To* Richard H. Dana

New York   June 1. 1827.

My dear Sir

There was no occasion for so much spirit in your last letter—the one previous had moved my bowels, and I would have done what you desired immediately if I could. I am now quite well and the first moment I was able I finished the examination of your work.[1] I should however apologize. I have a good deal of work to do. I drudge for the Evening Post, and labour for the *Review,* and thus have a pretty busy life of it. I would give up one of these if I could earn my bread by the other, but that I cannot do. I have delayed attending to your manuscript, from time to time just as I often delay writing poetry, until I should feel able to do it better justice. I have delayed it too long, but it was not from mere laziness.

You are mistaken in supposing the poem did not take well with me. I think very highly of it. It has passages of great power and great beauty, and the general effect to my apprehension is very fine. Did you tell me not to show it? I cannot find the letter which accompanied the manuscript and I may have sinned, for I *have* shown it to Verplanck who thinks highly of it, and we have agreed that it should be printed.

As for the mode of publication, I would get the booksellers interested if possible in the sale. But these gentry pay nothing for manuscript works, at least they do not in New York unless the previous reputation of the author makes the sale *sure.* Generally booksellers here are not willing to undertake any risk. The old race of booksellers who did these things, such as Wiley & Eastburn[2] have passed away and their successors are careful men who do what is called *safe* business. There is now a great deal more bookselling enterprize in either Boston or Philadelphia than here. If you could get a bookseller to publish at his own risk and allow you a certain portion of the profits I should think it the best way. But you must not *expect* to make a great deal of money by a first poetical publication, and then if you should you will be agreeably disappointed.

It is difficult to judge in what manner the public will receive your work. I believe the reception will be respectful. I hope it will be cordial, but fashion has a great deal to do with these things, and though there is a better taste for poetry in this country than there was ten years ago, there are yet a great many who count the syllables on their fingers e. g. Mr. [Robert] Walsh and all that class of men. But we will try what we can do for it.

I have not marked quite all the passages which I thought required amendment, because I was not certain where the fault lay. There is occasionally a startling abruptness in the style, and Matt is treated by the poet who relates the story with a sort of fierce familiarity which is sometimes carried too far. If I have thus, both here and in the notes I have made, dwelt upon the blemishes it is not because they are more numerous than the beauties, but because I wish the work to be entirely free of them. They are blemishes of execution merely, and I who have been an apprentice in the trade of verse from nine years old, can only wonder how with so little practice you have acquired so much dexterity. [There] are passages of strong pathos, indeed the whole work is instinct with this quality, the descriptions are also striking and as many powerful lines might be picked out of the poem as out of any other of the size that I know.

I am obliged to conclude in haste

yrs truly
W. C. BRYANT

MANUSCRIPT: NYPL–GR ADDRESS: Richard H. Dana Esq. / Cambridge / Mass. DOCKETED: W C. Bryant / June 1   1827 PUBLISHED (in part): Life, I, 233–234.

1. Dana's long poem, "The Buccaneer." See 159.4. Neither letter has been recovered.

2. James Eastburn, friend of Drake, Halleck, Sands, and other New York writers, was an "intelligent publisher and learned bibliophile." Adkins, Halleck, pp. 126, 132. For Charles Wiley, see 142.2.

174.   *To* Charles Folsom

New York   June 1, 1827.

Dear Sir

I send you a Review of the Catalogue of the Exhibition of the National Academy of Design. I send at present part of it only but you will receive the rest in 3 or 4 days at farthest, as the gentleman who is writing it only retains the last sheets in his hands to make a few additions & alterations. It may make 16 or 17 pages. I wish you would give it as conspicuous a place in the Review as possible as it is a subject quite interesting to us in New York and somewhat so to other cities.[1]

I have been so ill lately as to be unable to write myself but you shall have a notice of the Prairie next week.[2] I am out of poetry. If you have any I want it.

Cooper's pamphlet on the Constitution relates to a question that divides the two parties of the U. S. I should think it had better not be meddled with at least as respects that question.[3] If Mr Everett reviews Clay's speeches I hope he will also steer clear of that question—since it is made a party question—and that he will not get in any of his *new fashioned* notions on political economy.[4]

I think Verplanck will be persuaded to review Cooper's Political Economy but I will let you know next week. If he will not I think Porter will do it well.[5]

Yrs truly—
W. C. BRYANT

MANUSCRIPT: BPL ADDRESS: Mr. Charles Folsom /Editor of the U S. Review / Care of Bowles, & Dearborn / Boston.

1. See 175.4.
2. See 175.1.
3. Thomas Cooper (1759–1839), president of South Carolina College, was an ardent anti-tariff man, as is evident in his pamphlet, *On the Constitution* (Columbia, South Carolina, 1826), to which Bryant refers. This was not reviewed in the *USR*.
4. Edward Everett reviewed *The Speeches of Henry Clay* (Boston, 1826) in *USR*, 2 (July 1827), 278–285.
5. Thomas Cooper's *Lectures on the Elements of Political Economy* (Columbia, South Carolina, 1826), was not treated in the *USR*.

175. *To* Charles Folsom

[New York, *c*June 5, 1827]

Dear Sir

I shall send a notice of the Prairie,[1] & by and by something about Keppel's Travels. The rest of the books mentioned in Mr. Wigglesworth's letters I am willing to leave to you.

There are several works published your way which you do not "seize upon," some of them American works: Johnston's Narrative, Porter's Analysis of Delivery—Miss Bowdlen, Rambles in Germany &c. &c. &c.— What do you mean to do with all these?

I sent 3 months ago a review of Lindley Murray's Life. I have not heard of it since.[2] I sent also in some of the last days of last April a review of Mercer's Discourse on Education as a part of my contributions for the *June No*. Will you inform me whether you have received it?[3]

The enclosed is the rest of *Mr. Morse's* article on the Exhibition— Mr. S. F. B Morse the painter & president of the National Academy. —He is to be kept anonymous. It is of the utmost importance that the article should appear in the July No. If the whole cannot be got in it may be partial.[4] I shall write again this week.—

yrs truly—
W C Bryant

MANUSCRIPT: BPL.

1. It is likely that a notice of Fenimore Cooper's *The Prairie, A Tale* (Philadelphia, 1827) in *USR*, 2 (July 1827), 306–308, was written by Bryant—despite his earlier remark to Dana, "Ah, sir, he is too sensitive a creature for me to touch" (Letter 137). The comment that Leatherstocking is the character on whom Cooper "must mainly depend for his future fame" is echoed a quarter century later in Bryant's memorial discourse, and in each instance he is called the "philosopher of the woods." See Bryant, "Cooper," pp. 56–57.
2. See Letter 163.
3. See 171.1.
4. [Samuel F. B. Morse] Review of *The Exhibition of the National Academy of Design* (New York, 1827), in *USR*, 2 (July 1827), 241–263. Bryant's concern that this

should appear in July is accounted for by a notice in the same number, pp. 308–310, of Morse's *Academies of Art: A Discourse . . . May 3, 1827 . . . on the First Anniversary of the National Academy of Design* (New York, 1827), which Bryant himself probably wrote.

176. *To* Charles Folsom

[New York, June 10, 1827]

Dear Sir

The above lines are by Sands.[1] I sent you the beginning of this week an article by Mr. Morse who is to be kept anonymous. I wish that that article should be considered as a part of my contribution for the July No. so far as is necessary but if what I have sent exceeds my 20 pages I wish that for the surplus he may be paid by the proprietors. The rest I shall advance myself. I have been somewhat out of health and unable to write till lately. I have for that reason sent no verses of my own. —Ianthe is Miss Manley—an old correspondent of the U. S. Lit. Gaz.

yrs truly,
W. C. Bryant

I shall review Miller's Letters, on Clerical Habits—

MANUSCRIPT: BPL ADDRESS: Charles Folsom Esq / Editor of the [U. S. Review] / Care of B[owles & Dearborn / Boston][2] POSTMARK: NEW-YORK / JUN /10 ENDORSED: Ianthe: I asked Bry who she was / E. W.

1. Poem, "The Butterfly," from the French of de Lamartine, *USR*, 2 (July 1827), 302.
2. Manuscript torn.

177. *To* Charles Folsom

[New York, June 15, 1827]

Dear Sir

I believe that you may as well get a review of the life of Napoleon in your quarter. Dr. Anderson has called to tell me that he could not make an article on Everett's America that would not lose us 150 subscribers in Boston. The work is excessively unpopular here.[1] It is a political work as it seems to me, and if it were laid on the same shelf with Cooper's pamphlet on the constitution no harm would be done I think.[2] Verplanck has talked about an article on Cooper's Political Economy, but he is lazy and I believe will never do it. Suppose you give the book to Porter.[3]

Mr. Blunt wants to exchange his American Annual Register for the U. S. Review.[4] I have no objection if the other proprietors agree to it. I am making a notice of Elliott's Address.

I have heard nothing from you about the review of Lindley Murray's life and Mercer's discourse—[5]

Yrs truly
W. C. Bryant.

The review of Fowle's Grammar is much liked here[6] & also that of Brown's philosophy—[7] I inclose the poetry you sent me the other day—a little altered.

MANUSCRIPT: BPL ADDRESS: Charles Folsom Esq. / Editor of the U. S. Review / Care of Bowles & Dearborn / Boston POSTMARK: NEW-YORK / JUN / 15 POSTAL ANNOTATION: 18¾.

1. See Letter 171.
2. See 174.3.
3. See 174.5. Jonathan Porter, a Boston lawyer, wrote several articles for the *USR*.
4. Joseph Blunt (1792–1860), lawyer and politician, edited the eight volumes of this annual chronicle of news events published from 1827 to 1835 by G. & C. Carvill, New York publishers of the *USR*. Drake, *Dictionary of American Biography*, p. 99.
5. See Letter 175.
6. Review of William B. Fowle, *The True English Grammar*, USR, 2 (June 1827), 201–208.
7. Review of Thomas Brown, *A Treatise on the Philosophy of the Human Mind*, *ibid.*, 161–184.

178. *To* Frances F. Bryant

New York   June 30   1827.

My dear Frances

I arrived at New York about half past two the morning after I left you and passed a tolerably comfortable time in my berth until about 5 o'clock when I turned out and went to my boarding house. But my misery was yet to come; the cherries I had swallowed at Fishkill[1] were discontented with their imprisonment in the stomach of a New Yorker and in the afternoon I became terribly sick. I was in great misery until late in the evening when with the help of some soda I was relieved, and the next morning found me only a little weaker than ordinary.

I have got home our matters from Mrs. Meigs's.[2] I saw Mrs. & Miss Johnson who enquired very affectionately about you and hoped for Fanny's sake that you would come to New York soon.[3] I shall certainly expect you on Thursday. It will be the day after the 4th of July you know and all the tumult will be over.

Austin [Bryant] is in the city. He came down yesterday. He left all our Friends in Cummington well. I suppose he will return Monday or Tuesday. I have given him the cloak. He stays with me at Mrs. Tripler's one of whose boarders went away by good luck the very day he came.

I have been looking quite anxiously for a letter from you and hoped at least that I should receive one this morning but I have not seen it yet.

À FANCHETTE

PETITE J'ESPÈRE BIEN DE VOUS VOIR JEUDI PROCHAIN EN MEILLEURE SANTÉ QUE VOUS N'ÉTIEZ LORSQUE JE VOUS AI QUITTÉ À NEWBURGH.[4] EN ATTENDANT JE VOUS PRIE DE VOUS MONTRER PATIENTE ET SAGE D'AIMER VOTRE MAMAN ET LUI OBÉIR, ET DE PENSER QUELQUEFOIS À VOTRE PÈRE.[5]

Mr. Field[6] has just told me that Mr. H D Sedgwick's friends have heard from him within a day or two and that he is no better.[7] Mr. Field & Mr. Griffith[8] desire their respects. I write this in Mr. S[edgwick]'s office.

yr affectionate husband
W. C. BRYANT

MANUSCRIPT: NYPL–GR ADDRESS: Mrs. Frances F. Bryant / Care of Mr. Wm Teller / Fishkill Landing / N. Y. POSTMARK: NEW-YORK / JUN / 30 POSTAL ANNNOTATION: 10.

1. Frances and Fanny were summer boarders at Fishkill Landing (now Beacon) on the east bank of the Hudson sixty miles north of New York. Frances Bryant, "Autobiographical Sketch," NYPL–GR.

2. Two months earlier the Bryants had moved with their landlady Mrs. Meigs from Laight Street to Thompson Street. Soon afterward Bryant took new rooms with a Mrs. Tripler, at Walker Street and Broadway, where his family joined him in September. *Ibid.*

3. The Johnsons, apparently boarders with Mrs. Meigs, are otherwise unidentified. But see Letter 313, and Cullen to Frances Bryant, April 14, 1836, NYPL–GR.

4. Little Fanny had the whooping cough that summer.

5. (in block letters) "To Fanny / Little one, I hope very much to see you next Thursday in better health than you were when I left you at Newburgh. Meanwhile, I beg you to show yourself patient and well-behaved, to love your mama and obey her, and think sometimes of your father."

6. David Dudley Field, Jr. (1805–1894), of Stockbridge, was then a law student in the Sedgwick brothers' office. He was later distinguished for reforming the New York State civil and criminal codes.

7. Henry Sedgwick, whose unremitting work for the Greek revolutionary cause (see Letter 155) had seriously impaired his eyesight, suffered this summer the first attack of an intermittent insanity which continued until his death four years later. Sedgwick, *Life and Letters*, pp. 184–185.

8. Unidentified.

179. *To* the Editor of the U. S. REVIEW[1]

[New York, cJuly 10, 1827]

Dear Sir

Hope Leslie has been placed by Miss Sedgwick's brother in the hands of a person who has undertaken to give a review of it. Indisposition has prevented its being ready for this number.[2] The other books you mention you may take if you please.[3]

The address of Mr. Elliot[t], which I send you to print from, I wish you would return, as it belongs to Mr. Verplanck.[4] Along with this I send you some poetry of my own,[5] a piece signed W. G. C. by Willis G. Clark of Onondaga,[6] another signed J. H. B. by my brother,[7] with several from your quarter, and two reviews.—[8]

You put a heavy load on my shoulders in printing the article on Clay's speeches,[9] and I have had occasion for some dexterity in parrying the attacks made upon me for it. Clay is a political man and the article is written by one of Clay's political admirers and of course, cannot be expected to suit those who are not of that class. Besides, I have some doubts whether a literary journal is the place for discussing the question concerning the propriety of Mr. Clay's appointment as Secretary of State. For my part I always thought the appointment a very bad one—never having much respect for Mr. Clay's principles nor a high estimate of his political knowledge. But the article has [been] inserted and though I cannot say much for it I put the best face on the matter I can.[10]

I like Metcalf's article and not only consent but even wish that it may be published with the exception of one or two sentences through which I have drawn a pencil. These passages contain sentiments in which I cannot quite agree with the writer.[11]

yrs truly.—

[unsigned]

MANUSCRIPT: BPL ADDRESS: Editor of the U. S. Review.

1. Bryant's addressing the "Editor of the U. S. Review" suggests uncertainty over the identity of his current Boston counterpart. Though he had continued writing to Folsom, replies had been coming since April from Wigglesworth. On June 23 Willard Phillips had written him that he had been offered the direction of the *USR*, and asked Bryant's confidential advice on its financial shape and prospect of continued New York support. NYPL–BG. Apparently Bryant was not consulted by his partners on this matter of direct concern to himself.

2. [Catharine M. Sedgwick] *Hope Leslie; or, Early Times in the Massachusetts . . .* (New York, 1827).

3. Bryant refers to titles named in Wigglesworth's letters of June 28 and July 2, 1827. NYPL–BG.

4. [Bryant] Review of Stephen Elliott, *Address Delivered at the Opening of the Medical College in Charleston . . . November, 1826* (Charleston, 1827), *USR*, 2 (August 1827), 368–376.

5. "The Disinterred Warrior," *ibid.*, 386–387. See *Poems* (1876), pp. 150–151.

6. Not published.

7. [John Howard Bryant] "The Traveller's Return," *USR*, 2 (August 1827), 387–388.

8. One of these was Bryant's, of Samuel Miller, *Letters on Clerical Manners and Habits . . .* (New York, 1827), *ibid.*, 377–386. The other was probably Richard Dana's review of *The Novels of Charles Brockden Brown*, 7 vols. (Boston, 1827), *ibid.*, 321–333.

9. See 174.4.

10. Only six months before Bryant would assume editorial responsibility for the *EP*, a strong Jackson paper, he could hardly justify to Democratic friends and associates his review's praise of President Adams' Secretary of State.

11. See 171.3.

180. *To* Frances F. Bryant

[New York, cAugust 1, 1827]

My dear Frances,

Mr Verplanck being [about] to go to Fishkill tomorrow[1] I write this rather than lose the opportunity, although I have very little to tell you.

I am yet hard at work writing my tale for the next number of the review. It is a story of a man killed by an explosion of fire and water from the ground like that which happened at Alford a few years since on old Patterson's farm. I hope I shall get it finished in season but I find it slow work.[2] The August number of the work has appeared and I shall send it to you with *Cubi*[3] and some other books if Mr. Verplanck will carry them.

Col. Loomis is gone to the Springs.[4] Mrs. Tripler would have visited Fishkill this week but her friend's house there, she hears, is so full of boarders that there is no room for her. She will not take either of the new houses now building in Walker Street. I undertook to see the proprietor for her, and having learned of him that he intended to ask $900 rent, I dropped the conversation.

The heat here has been excessive for three or four days. I do not recollect that I have known it greater. One poor fellow, a mason dropped down dead yesterday while at his work at about half past six in the afternoon. I have heard of nobody dying from drinking cold water. To day it is cooler and I am able to write, which I was not yesterday. The Commencement of Columbia College took place today. I looked in a few minutes, there was a well dressed audience but I could hear nothing and the heat was suffocating—so I came out again. An invitation to the dinner was sent me but I did not go.

Kiss Fanny for me and believe me

with the greatest affection
your husband & friend
W. C. BRYANT.

MANUSCRIPT: NYPL–GR ADDRESS: Mrs. Frances F. Bryant / at Mr. Wm. Teller's / Fishkill Landing / N. Y. / Mr. Verplanck.

1. Gulian Verplanck's ancestral home, "Mount Gulian," stands one mile north of Fishkill Landing, now Beacon, where it has recently been reconstructed after a disastrous fire.

2. [Bryant] "A Narrative of Some Extraordinary Circumstances That Happened More Than Twenty Years Since," *USR*, 2 (September 1827), 447–459. This was the fourth of thirteen prose tales Bryant wrote for publication during his first seven years in New York. Its melodramatic plot is lightened by poetic descriptions of nature, and his portrayal of villagers and their customs, reflecting the observation of his years in Berkshire County. Alford, about five miles from Great Barrington, was Frances Bryant's birthplace.

3. Mariano Cubi y Soler, *A New Spanish Grammar*. See 151.8. Frances and five-year-old Fanny seem to have joined Cullen about this time in studying Spanish.

4. Col. Loomis may have been Arphaxed Loomis (1798–1885), a New York lawyer and legislator who was later associated with David Dudley Field on the New York commission for legal reform. Frances Bryant had visited Orange Springs, New Jersey, the previous summer. See 144.6.

Dr. Peter Bryant (modern portrait, from an early pen-and-ink sketch).

Mrs. Sarah Snell Bryant

Frances Fairchild Bryant, *ca.* 1820.

Dr. Bryant's office, built in 1801 and restored a century later by Mrs. William Vaughan Moody as a writers' retreat (see Letter 30 and p. 62).

Dr. Bryant's gravestone in the Bryant Cemetery, Cummington, with the inscription composed by his son (see Letter 58).

The home of Judge Samuel Howe at Worthington, where Bryant studied law
1811–1814 (see Letter 8).

The building in Plainfield believed to have been Bryant's law office
1815–1816 (see Letter 34).

St. James's Episcopal Church, Great Barrington

The Cottage Seminary at Great Barrington, attended by Fanny Bryant; the central building had been Bryant's law office in the early 1820s. Letters 92, 93, 96, and 98 were probably written here.

Charles Sedgwick Library, Lenox

Whiting's boardinghouse in Lenox, where Bryant lived during court sessions (see Letter 47).

"Scene on the Hudson" from *The Talisman* for 1828.

Weir's "Fort Putnam" etched by Durand for *The American Landscape* in 1830
(see Letter 215).

A pencil sketch characteristic of Bryant's artwork in the 1830s.

A French diligence, *ca*. 1830 (see Letters 295 and 312).

Trustees of Reservations

Bryant's 1832 pencil sketch of a cabin on the Illinois prairie: probably Whiswall's, described in Letter 245.

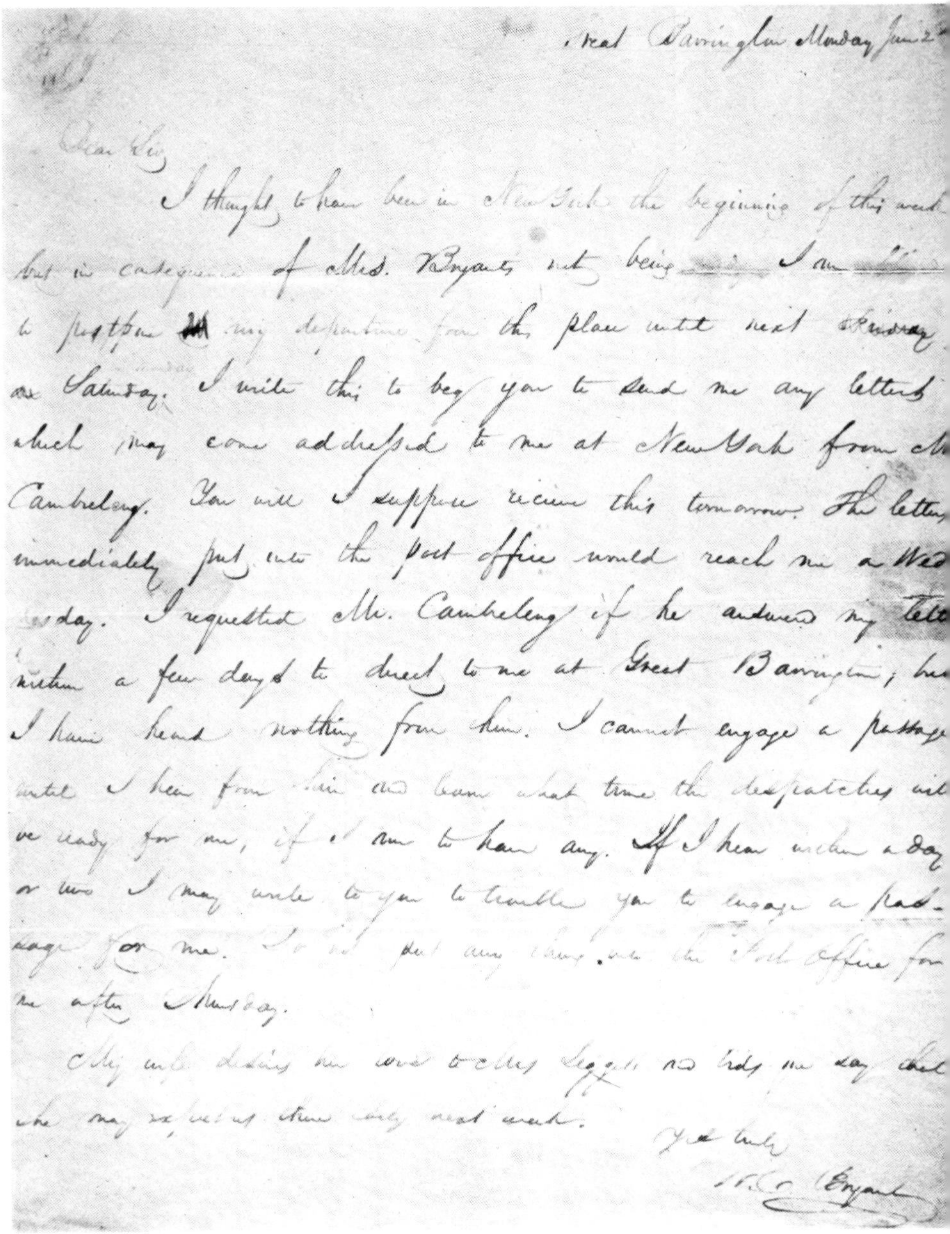
Great Barrington Monday June 2nd

Dear Sir,

I thought to have been in New York the beginning of this week but in consequence of Mrs. Bryant's not being well I am obliged to postpone my departure from this place until next Thursday or Saturday. I write this to beg you to send me any letters which may come addressed to me at New York from Mr Cambreleng. You will I suppose receive this tomorrow. The letters immediately put into the post office would reach me on Wednesday. I requested Mr. Cambreleng if he answered my letter within a few days to direct to me at Great Barrington; but I have heard nothing from him. I cannot engage a passage until I hear from him and learn what time the despatches will be ready for me, if I am to have any. If I hear within a day or two I may write to you to trouble you to engage a passage for me. Do not put any thing into the Post Office for me after Thursday.

My wife desires her love to Mrs Leggett and bids me say that she may expect us there early next week.

Yrs truly

W. C. Bryant

The original holograph of Letter 283.

181. *To* Charles Folsom[1]

N Y Aug 10 1827.

Dear Sir

I send you a Tale which has given me some trouble to write— A page or two more will be sent on, next Monday which will finish it—[2] I shall send some poetry and perhaps a critical notice or two. I expected a Review of Miss S[edgwick]'s Book Hope Leslie—but it does not come—

yrs truly
W. C. BRYANT

MANUSCRIPT: BPL ADDRESS: Charles Folsom Esq. / Editor of the U S. Review / Care of Bowles & Dearborn / Boston / Mr. James M. Russell.

1. During the final month of his association with the *USR*, which ceased publication after the September 1827 issue, Bryant continued to address Folsom on editorial matters, but no replies from Folsom have been found.
2. "A Narrative of Some Extraordinary Circumstances." See 180.2.

182. *To* Frances F. Bryant

New York Aug 13. 1827.[1]

My dear Frances

I received your letter yesterday (Monday). I am very sorry to see you give such an account of yourself. If you find your situation not what you desire I do not wish you to remain a moment in it on my account. When Mr. Van Polanen[2] comes down I shall send you some money and request you to do just as you please. I should send it now did I know who is to carry this letter.

Mrs. Tripler will go to Fishkill on Tuesday next. If I do not have an earlier opportunity I shall send by her. I wish you to consult your own comfort and that of Frances entirely. As to my being in the country a week or two it is not of much consequence.[3]

In haste
with great affection
Yours—
W. C. BRYANT.

MANUSCRIPT: NYPL–GR ADDRESS: Mrs. Frances F. Bryant / Fishkill Landing / N. Y.

1. Bryant mistakenly wrote "1826."
2. Roger Van Polanen, a Dutch diplomat long resident in this country, with whom Bryant had recently become acquainted. *Life,* I, 320.
3. Although Frances' letter is unrecovered, it is evident from Letters 185 and 186 that she was unhappy in her summer boardinghouse.

183. *To* Richard H. Dana

New York   Aug   13, 1827.

Dear Sir.

I have heard nothing from you since I sent you your poem.[1] I write now to mention a mode of publishing it if you should not have thought of a better.

A book is to be published in this city by Bliss the bookseller[2] a kind of Miscellany beautifully printed and embellished in the way of the London Souvenirs &c.[3] The contributors will be Mr. Verplanck Mr. Sands and myself, and perhaps one or two more. The profits of the publication, if there are any are to be divided between the bookseller and the authors. That *something* will be made by it there is little doubt considering the great run that Carey's *Souvenir* had last year bad as it was,[4] and considering also the great demand there is for the London works of that kind.

Now if you will trust us with your poem it shall be published, in the finest style, with or without your name, just as you please and shall lie in the parlour windows of the rich and fashionable—not the best judges of literary merit to be sure, but the best purchasers of showy books. Your interests in the matter we will make the same provision for as for our own.

There is one recommendation to this plan—it will cost you nothing and you may even get something by it. By publishing in the common way you run some risk of losing and the probability of getting any thing as times go is I can assure you from experience very small. Whether this mode of publication however is as likely to advance your literary reputation as the other is for yourself to consider. It is better generally to write a book of one's own, and to be responsible only for one's own productions, but I should think that a *poet* might as well make a beginning in this way as the other.[5]

My regards to your sisters & brother. Let me hear from you soon,—& believe me,

Ever faithfully yours,

W. C. BRYANT.

MANUSCRIPT: LH.

1. "The Buccaneer."

2. Elam Bliss (d. 1855), publisher of the *NYR*, brought out Poe's 1831 *Poems* and Bryant's first collection in 1832 (see 229.1). According to Verplanck, Bliss, "desirous to try his fortune in [gift annuals], pressed Mr. Sands to undertake the editorship of an annual volume." [Gulian C. Verplanck] "Memoir of Robert C. Sands," *The Writings of Robert C. Sands, In Prose and Verse* (New York, 1834), I, 20.

3. *The Forget-Me-Not* (London, 1823) was the first illustrated annual gift-book in English. Modeled on earlier German *Taschenbücher*, or "pocketbooks," it began a vogue for "Christmas and New Year's Offerings" which saw sixty-three such works published in a single year, 1832. In the United States their popularity increased steadily until an average of sixty appeared annually between 1846 and 1852. See Frederick W.

Faxon, *Literary Annuals and Gift-Books* (Boston: Boston Book Company, 1912), pp. xi–xii.

4. *The Atlantic Souvenir* for 1826 was the first American gift-annual. *The Talisman for MDCCCXXVIII*, described by Bryant in this letter, was the second—followed closely by the Boston *Token*. Thompson, *American Literary Annuals*, pp. 1, 49, 56.

5. Dana had found a publisher elsewhere, and on October 18 Jared Sparks wrote asking Bryant to review *The Buccaneer, and Other Poems* (Boston, 1827). NYPL–BG. Bryant's article appeared in *NAR*, 26 (January 1828), 239–247.

184. *To* Charles Folsom

N Y   Aug. 13   1827.

Dear Sir

I send you a critical notice of Sismondi[1]—a sonnet[2] & the rest of the story[3]— There are several books lately published here of which I think I shall have some notices for yr. next—The Baroness of Reidesdel—[Mde?] Haufert &c.[4]

yrs truly
[unsigned]

Hope Leslie I suppose I shall have a review of by & by—

MANUSCRIPT: BPL ADDRESS: Charles Folsom Esq / Editor of the U. S. Review / Care of Bowles & Dearborn / Boston / Politeness of / Mr. I. H. Buckingham.

1. [Bryant] Notice of J. C. L. Sismonde de Sismondi, *Historical View of the Literature of the South of Europe*, trans. Thomas Roscoe (New York, 1827), *USR*, 2 (September 1827), 467–468.

2. [Bryant] "A Power is on the Earth and in the Air," *ibid.*, 460. See *Poems* (1876), p. 152, where the poem is entitled "Midsummer."

3. Bryant's "Narrative of Some Extraordinary Circumstances." See 180.2.

4. Neither of these was noticed in the *USR*.

185. *To* Frances F. Bryant

[New York, August 21, 1827]

My dear Frances.

I enclose you $25.00 that you may be able to make such arrangements as you please about your boarding house. It is possible, though not certain, that I may come up the latter part of the week and if you go to another place I wish you to let me know where without delay. The reason for my not coming at present is that I am busy correcting the translation of Mignet which is printing,[1] and besides, young Coleman[2] is absent on a journey. If you should leave the place where you are let me beg you to remember that you are in a village, and to say not a syllable to any living soul about the place you have left.[3]

I have found 3 Bedticks which I took to Mrs. Van Polanen's last evening. If they are not the right ones let me know without delay. As to the length of the sofa do as you please. I should like however to have it proportioned to its *width* so that it may not look like a great chair. Kiss Frances for me.

> your affectionate husband
> W. C. BRYANT

MANUSCRIPT: NYPL–GR ADDRESS: Mrs. Frances F. Bryant / Fishkill Landing / N. Y.

1. A. F. Mignet, *History of the French Revolution, from 1789 to 1814. Revised and Corrected from the London Edition* (New York: G. & C. Carvill, 1827). The "Advertisement" states that this translation, published at London in 1826, was "disfigured with mistakes of the meaning of the original, with numerous Gallicisms and frequent obscurities of expression," and that "the present corrections and revision have been made by a gentleman thoroughly conversant with the French Language and History." This publication has been overlooked by Bryant's biographers.

2. Bryant mistakenly wrote "Burnham." W. H. Coleman, son of the ailing publisher of the *EP*, had been Bryant's editorial associate since William Coleman's injury in June 1826. Nevins, *Evening Post*, p. 123.

3. At about this time Frances Bryant moved from William Teller's boardinghouse at Fishkill Landing to one operated by a Mr. Wyatt. Francis Bryant, "Autobiographical Sketch," NYPL–GR.

186. *To* Frances F. Bryant

[New York] Aug. 21   1827.

Dear Frances

I wrote a letter this morning by Mrs. Tripler enclosing you twenty five dollars. I do not learn by your last whether you received a letter written by me about a week ago in answer to your last letter but one. In that I mentioned that I should soon send you some money and begged you not to stay any longer in a situation that was not pleasant to you, but either to come to New York or find another place in that neighbourhood, just as might be most agreeable to you. At present I hope you will be able to find a place in your neighbourhood because I believe there is some prospect of my coming up this week to pass a week or fortnight with you. Young Coleman has returned, and thinks himself able to attend to the paper a little while. But Mignet is not yet done though I am finishing it as fast as I can. Whatever change you may make let me know it immediately.—

> Yrs affectionately
> W. C. BRYANT

MANUSCRIPT: NYPL–GR ADDRESS: Mrs. Frances F. Bryant / Fishkill Landing / N   Y.

187. *To* Charles Folsom[1]

[New York, cSeptember 10, 1827]

Dear Sir.

I send you an article for the next No.—a review of Hope Leslie. It was written by Miss E. Robbins by whom Mr. H. D. Sedgwick was desirous that the work should be reviewed.[2] I also enclose a piece of poetry which I have looked over.[3] If there is any thing in the review that does not suit you we have a *carte blanche* to expunge or alter any excep[tion]-able passages.

Yrs. truly

W. C. BRYANT

MANUSCRIPT: BPL ADDRESS: Charles Folsom Esq. / ⟨Editor of the U. S. Review / Care of Bowles & Dearborn / Boston⟩ / Cambridge.

1. This is the last letter in Bryant's editorial correspondence with Folsom, who had apparently ended his association with the *USR* without Bryant's having been made aware of it.

2. See 179.2. Since the *USR* ceased publication after the September number, Miss Robbins' review went unpublished.

3. Poem unidentified.

188.   *To* Jared Sparks

New York   Oct. 23   1827.

Dear Sir.

I have just received yours of the 18th. I am pestered with several things which I am doing about this time, but rather than that any body else should review Mr. Dana's book I will undertake it. You shall have the article by the time you mention. In the mean time I hope that the publishers will forward me the sheets or book as early as possible, that I may be able to speak more understandably of the work—and perhaps I may have occasion to make some extracts.[1]

I remain sir

with great respect & esteem

yr friend & Servt

WM. C. BRYANT

MANUSCRIPT: HCL ADDRESS: Mr. Jared Sparks / Editor of the N. A. Review / Boston DOCKETED: From Wm. C. Bryant / Oct. 29 / 1827.

1. See 183.5.

189.   *To* Jared Sparks

New York   Nov. 8   1827.

Dear Sir.

Mr. Verplanck Mr. Sands and myself are engaged in getting up a little work in this city, on the plan of the German Literary Almanacks, with embellishments &c. which will soon be published by E[lam] Bliss. A friend of ours and an accomplished scholar, Mr. [Thatcher Taylor] Payne, a brother of John Howard Payne—has engaged to prepare a notice of it for some of the reviews and I have been commissioned to inquire of you whether you would oblige us by permitting it to be inserted in your January number provided you should like the article. Will you be good enough to inform me soon?

I have received the entire sheets of Dana's poems—and will have the article ready in season. It will not however be possible for me to make a very long one owing to my other engagements.—

Yrs. truly
WM. C. BRYANT

P. S. If you think you can insert the article on the *Talisman* for so our work is to be called—it will be sent on as early or earlier than mine.—

MANUSCRIPT: HCL ADDRESS: Mr. Jared Sparks / Editor of the N A Review / Boston DOCKETED: From / Wm. C. Bryant / Nov. 12 / 1827.

190.   *To* Jared Sparks

[New York, November 16, 1827]

My dear Sir

I have just received your letter. I believe I did not explain to you fully the plan of the Talisman, and in what respect it is unlike the other works you mention.[1] The *Talisman* then, is written wholly, with the exception of three small poetical pieces, by the three persons mentioned in my last. We look upon it as a very different thing from those pretty miscellanies which are made up of contributions, solicited from a thousand sources, and which, being regarded as a kind of New years toy, are scarce ever made the subjects of very serious criticism. It resembles them in its accidents, being an 18mo and bound up with engraving, but intrinsically it is quite another matter. It is meant to be such a thing as the Sketch Book would be if published in that shape,[2] or rather like the Salmagundi, for that was written by three,[3] or like the Scriblerus papers put into a neat little volume and embellished with plates.[4] We should therefore feel the same reluctance to being reviewed in the same article with the *Atlantic Souvenir* which is no great matter in a literary point of view, or with the other works got up in the same miscellaneous way, as you would at seeing your Life of Washington[5]—from which I wish you a great increase of reputation and great emolument—reviewed in the same article with the *Beauties of History*.

But if the difficulty cannot be got over in any other way we should prefer that the Talisman should not be spoken of at all in the January number, but that the notice if it appears at all should be delayed to the next—though it is of some consequence that the work should be noticed early.

If you think that the objections to admitting a notice of the work separately are removed by any thing I have said I should be glad if you would let me know. If I hear nothing from you I shall take it for granted that you do not see the propriety of putting them into distinct articles, and in that case I should prefer that the work might not be noticed at present.

Yrs sincerely
WM. C. BRYANT

MANUSCRIPT: HCL.

1. Sparks' letter is unrecovered.
2. Washington Irving's *The Sketch Book of Geoffrey Crayon, Gent.* appeared in installments in the United States during 1819 and 1820, before its publication in England as a single work in 1820.
3. *Salmagundi*, a semi-monthly periodical written by Washington Irving, his brother William, and James Kirke Paulding, ran for twenty numbers in 1807–1808.
4. *The Memoirs of Martinus Scriblerus*, written principally by John Arbuthnot, with the collaboration of Alexander Pope, Jonathan Swift, and other members of the Scriblerus Club, was first published with Pope's *Works* in 1741.
5. Sparks was then gathering material for his chief historical work, *The Life and Writings of George Washington*, published in twelve volumes in 1834–1837.

191.   *To* Jared Sparks

New York   Nov   30   1827.

Dear Sir,

   Mr. Payne has been so ill with the rheumatism that he could not sit to do the mechanical part of writing which is the reason that the article of the Talisman has not been sent on to you. He is now better, and the article was nearly finished to send off by this morning's mail. It shall certainly be sent by tomorrow's, and I hope that still it will not be too late. If it should be you have only to leave it out.—

Yrs. truly
W. C. BRYANT

MANUSCRIPT: HCL ADDRESS: Mr. Jared Sparks / Editor of the N. A. Review / Boston POSTMARK: NEW-YORK / NOV / 30 POSTAL ANNOTATION: 18 / PAID / [¾?] DOCKETED: From / Wm. C. Bryant / Dec. 3. / 1827.

192.   *To* Jared Sparks

New York   Dec   1. 1827.

My dear Sir

   I send you herewith by today's mail Mr. Payne's article respecting the Talisman.[1] It would have been finished earlier as I mentioned in my last had it not been for an ill-timed and somewhat severe fit of indisposition which quite disabled him from writing till within a day or two. If it should not arrive in season for insertion we must submit as well as we can to what we cannot help.

   A part of the article—that relating to the history of a popular branch of German literature I think you will like—both as it is entertaining, and as it contains information not accessible to general readers.[2] I see that you pay great attention to this latter point in the management of your review —and Mr. Payne's studies and opportunities enable him to "speak scholarly and wisely" [3] on the subject he has undertaken.

The writer of the article whose rheumatism seems to have disgusted him with the things of this world, and more particularly, and the authors of the Talisman think unreasonably, with the article itself, commits it into your hands with a desire that you should take such liberties with it as may suit your notions of propriety or your convenience. If the article be too long omit such passages as may most conveniently be spared—if it contains any thing you do not like expunge it.

I send you in another envelope the printed sheets containing the extracts noted in the manuscript.

Yrs truly

W. C. BRYANT

MANUSCRIPT: HCL ADDRESS: Mr. Jared Sparks / Editor of the N. A. Review / Boston DOCKETED: From / Wm. C. Bryant / Dec. 3. / 1827.

1. "The Talisman for MDCCCXXVIII," NAR, 26 (January 1828), 258–274.
2. Payne discussed the influence of the popular German Taschenbücher (pocket books) and Taschenkalender (pocket almanacs) on the vogue for gift-books and literary annuals begun in England with the publication in 1823 of The Forget-Me-Not.
3. Cf. The Merry Wives of Windsor I.iii.1–3.

193. To Jared Sparks

New York   Dec   7th. 1827.

Dear Sir.

I got your letter this morning and enclose the extracts from the Talisman as you request by return of mail.[1] I believe I have sent them all, though from being obliged, with the assistance of Mr. Payne to make them up from memory it is possible that some may be omitted. If so you can vary the phraseology of the manuscript so as not to show the *lacuna*. You will have no difficulty I think in referring them to their proper places in [the] article—with the exception perhaps of The Butterfly[2] which is not paged— I believe however that the initial and final words of the poem are given in the manuscript.—

Yrs truly

W. C. BRYANT

MANUSCRIPT: HCL ADDRESS: Mr. Jared Sparks / Editor of the N. A. Review / Boston / Mass.tts POSTMARK: NEW-YORK / DEC / 8 POSTAL ANNOTATION: PAID 75 DOCKETED: From / Wm. C. Bryant / Dec. 10. / 1827.

1. On December 5 Sparks had acknowledged receipt of Payne's notice of The Talisman and Bryant's review of Dana's poems (see 183.5). Columbia University Li-

braries. The printed sheets Bryant had sent separately on December 1 had gone astray, so Sparks suggested cutting out the extracts and sealing them in a letter.

2. [John Nielson, Jr.] "The Butterfly [from the French]," *The Talisman for MDCCCXXVIII* (New York, 1827), p. [119].

194. *To* Gulian C. Verplanck

New York   Dec. 28. 1827.

Dear Sir,

The review of the Talisman was despatched so says Mr. Sands on Monday—you must therefore I suppose have received it before this time. It is pretty well done, but owes I suspect all the touches of liveliness that are to be found in it to the active fancy of our friend who forwarded it.[1]

We are very much interested for the fate of the Talisman. So far things go on auspiciously. Sparks was here the other day—he says that the article is inserted and professes himself exceedingly pleased with it as being a sprightly amusing article which he was very glad to have for his review. The work was quite cordially noticed in the Courier.[2] I did what I could for it in the Post[3]—Stone puffed it in the Commercial,[4] Maxwell in the Journal of Commerce,[5] Morris in the Mirror[6]—and besides Dwight spoke of it as favourably as could be expected from *him*[7]—and the Statesman said something about it in the same article in which it noticed the Token.[8] The Albion gave a notice of it which I did not see,[9] and the New York Observer devoted nearly two columns to remarks on the work [and] extracts from it.[10] This latter paper however was a little too free in its mention of names and gave you the credit to which I believe you are not entitled of having principally written the "Thoughts on Handwriting" from which it gave a long extract.[11] You think that Noah did not blow the horn loud enough[12]—two gentlemen of your acquaintance thought so too, and therefore furnished him with another article on the subject which appeared last Monday.[13] On the whole if the Talisman should not succeed it must be because puffing does not help a book on.

And as to the actual sale of the work [Elam] Bliss says what I believe is true, that it is *fair*. The other booksellers however have set their faces against the book not having been able to obtain of Bliss such terms as suited them, so that its sale such as it is is altogether in spite of them. From appearances I should think Bliss might be able to get off a thousand, (half the impressions) by Newyears day.

As to what the critics say of the work I believe the general opinion to be quite favorable. Bliss has a "legend" of the whole set of American and English Souvenirs lent to Dr. [Jonathan M.] Wainwright to take home with him in order that he might make a choice of the best and how the Dr. returned all but the Talisman giving that the preference. The book has also found favour with the trustees of the high school who have bought a dozen of them—for premiums, on the recommendation, as I heard one of the same trustees say to Dr. Bliss, of certain young Misses who had compared it with the Atlantic Souvenir. I am also told that the work is on the whole a favorite with the ladies. To the tale of our friend Viellecour, the Jackson man, two objections have been made—one that it is too short, the other that it is too long. The first class of objectors say that it is very witty but that it is spun out to such an immoderate length that the wit palls upon the reader—the second class complain that the story ends abruptly and say that if the author had made it about a third longer and *given himself* room to tell why Mr. Viellecour came back and some other particulars about which the reader is now left in the dark the story would have been a capital one.[14] So you see that it is talked of, and that is the great point.

Walsh has done a scurvy thing[15] and the Editor of the Aurora[16] has done another in a critique on the several works of this kind which he says are for sale by Carey & Lea. He echoes Walsh's words. It is high time that Mr. Walsh was attended to a little— His critical sufficiency might be lowered a peg or two greatly to his own advantage an[d] that of the public. It is a service that must be done him one of these days.

I do not know why I did not republish your notice of Dana.[17] It is always easier to tell why we have done a thing than why we have not done a thing.

Sparks says that Dana's poems sell well in Boston, that he is in high spirits about it, and that he has never seen him more cheerful in his life. He intends to write something else.

The Post gets along as usual—I am an owner of one eighth of the establishment,[18] but otherwise the paper I believe is just what it used to be.

Bliss tells me he has sent on some copies of the Talisman for you by water not having been able, after a great deal of looking, to find any other conveyance. There is a copy for Buckingham[19] and one for Bradford.—[20]

My wife desires her respects and tells me to say that Mrs. Ledyard[21] is a great admirer of the Talisman—

Yrs truly
W   C. BRY.

MANUSCRIPT: NYPL–Berg ADDRESS: Hon. Gulian C. Verplanck / Member of Congress / Washington / (D. C.) POSTMARK: NEW-YORK / DEC / 30 POSTAL ANNOTATION: FREE DOCKETED: W. C. Bryant.

1. This notice appeared in the first number of the *Southern Review*, published at Charleston (1 [February 1828] 262–271). See 196.5.

2. The New York *Morning Courier*, edited by James Watson Webb (1802–1884).

3. *EP*, December 18, 1827.

4. William Leete Stone (1792–1844) edited the New York *Commercial Advertiser*.

5. William Maxwell (1784–1857, Yale 1802) was briefly editor of the New York *Journal of Commerce* after its founding in 1827.

6. George Pope Morris (1803–1864), founder and principal editor of the weekly *New-York Mirror*, to which Bryant later contributed many poems.

7. Theodore Dwight (1764–1846), editor of the New York *Daily Advertiser*, was a younger brother of President Timothy Dwight of Yale, and a grandson of Jonathan Edwards.

8. The New York *Statesman* was a short-lived paper of small circulation. See Letter 158. *The Token* (Boston, 1828) very nearly shared with *The Talisman* the distinction of being the second American gift-book.

9. The weekly New York *Albion*, edited by John Sherren Bartlett (1790–1863), British-born physician and journalist.

10. The *New York Observer and Religious Chronicle*, a weekly founded by Samuel F. B. Morse's younger brothers, Sidney Edwards and Richard Cary Morse, was then edited by Gerard Hallock (1800–1866), son of Bryant's early tutor Moses Hallock.

11. "Thoughts on Hand-Writing," *The Talisman for MDCCCXXVIII*, pp. 28–44, was written by Robert Sands.

12. Mordecai M. Noah (1785–1851), playwright and early Zionist, edited the New York *Enquirer*.

13. The two gentlemen were probably Bryant and Sands.

14. [Sands and Verplanck] "Mr. De Viellecour and His Neighbours. A Tale, Moral and Chronological," *The Talisman for MDCCCXXVIII*, pp. [45]–113.

15. Robert M. Walsh. See 80.6.

16. The Philadelphia *Aurora*, edited from 1822 to 1827 by the playwright Richard Penn Smith (1799–1854).

17. This notice has not been identified. It is not included in the bibliography of Verplanck's writings in July, *Essential New Yorker*, pp. 291–294.

18. Bryant's one-eighth share in the *EP*, acquired in December 1827, yielded him about $1,700 a year at that time. "*Evening Post* Accounts," NYPL–GR.

19. Possibly Joseph T. Buckingham. See 196.6.

20. Possibly Samuel Bradford. See 210.5.

21. Unidentified.

V

Fellow in the Arts
1828–1831
(LETTERS 195 TO 222)

THE YEARS FROM 1828 TO 1831 were as happy as any Bryant had ever enjoyed and, despite growing responsibility for his newspaper, as carefree. Through his active part in the programs of the New York Athenaeum and the National Academy of Design, and his collaboration with writers and artists in preparing the successive *Talisman* volumes, he assumed a central role in the city's cultural life. And his fondness for satire, indulged as a youth in "The Embargo," and as a village lawyer in newspaper essays and in his farce "The Heroes," found targets among the city's fashionables in "The Legend of the Devil's Pulpit," published in *The Talisman*, and in *jeux d'esprit* in the *Evening Post*, such as a verse lampoon of Fanny Wright and repeated spoofs of editorial opponents.

As the second *Talisman* appeared at the close of 1828, its creators formalized their association in a "Sketch Club," or "Twenty-One," which provided convivial gatherings at the homes of its members in rotation, at which they exercised their artistic skills and put together another edition of their annual. The club's intimacy as well as its secrecy were fostered by its limitation to twenty-one members and its obscure announcements of weekly meetings published among the obituaries in the *Evening Post*. Its gatherings were for the most part frolicsome, with serio-comic themes proposed by the host for varied expression in sketches, verses, or prose articles. But its members also collaborated in more serious projects. Among these were a third *Talisman* early in 1830, and at the end of that year *The American Landscape*, a volume of landscape paintings by Cole, Durand, Weir, and others, engraved by Durand and accompanied by letterpress written by Bryant, and in 1832 two volumes of stories by Bryant, Leggett, Paulding, Sands, and Catharine Sedgwick, called *Tales of Glauber-Spa*.

Bryant's appreciation of other arts was likewise quickened by friendships with their practitioners. Lorenzo Da Ponte and Manuel Garcia drew him to the Italian opera and the oratorio, which led him to review their performances in the *Post*. He found a warm friend in the young tragedian Edwin Forrest; when Forrest offered a prize in 1829 for the best play on an American aboriginal theme, Bryant headed the committee which chose John Stone's *Metamora*, providing Forrest with his most popular starring vehicle. The following year Bryant chaired a similar group which selected James Kirke Paulding's *The Lion of the West* for the comedian James Hackett, who found, in Nimrod Wildfire, his most enduring role.

When the *Evening Post*'s veteran conductor William Coleman died in July 1829 Bryant became at once the editor-in-chief, soon engaging as his assistant William Leggett, magazine editor and writer of tales, poems, and theatrical reviews. Reluctant at first to discuss politics, Leggett quickly became, in Bryant's words, a "zealous democrat, and an ardent friend of free trade." Within two years Leggett had become a partner in the establishment. His help freed the senior editor from much daily tedium, allowing him more time to discuss in his leaders the central issues facing the new Democracy of Andrew Jackson. Soon after he joined the *Post* in 1826, Bryant had made it the "only journal north of the Potomac" to develop a rational argument against the protective tariff then in force. Now he joined his friends Verplanck and Churchill Cambreleng, Jackson leaders in Congress, in their opposition to federally financed public works and the private Bank of the United States. As Bryant's editorials drew increasingly acrimonious replies from anti-administration editors, the saucy ribbing which had marked his earlier thrusts at his foes took on a sharper tone. The resulting exchange of insults in April 1831 reached its climax on the 20th, when editor Stone of the *Commercial Advertiser* printed the charge that Bryant was a liar, whereupon Stone's furious adversary horse-whipped him the next morning on Broadway opposite City Hall.

The explosion of a temper he had kept in close check since boyhood—except in one rare instance at the Berkshire courthouse when he had threatened to thrash an opposing lawyer "within an inch of his life"—was a chastening experience for Bryant. The account he gave his readers the next day, over his signature, of the quarrel and its causes, was both apology and justification. A few days later he urged his fellow-editors to heed Hamlet's advice to his players that "in the very torrent and tempest of passion, one should acquire and beget a temperance that may give it smoothness," and Samuel Johnson's admonition to his friend Boswell to "oppose, without exasperating." Bryant's remorse over his rage against Stone underlay his last—and probably best—short story, "Medfield," published the following year. In his poem "The Future Life," composed a few years afterward, he wrote, "Wrath has left its scar—that fire of hell / has left its frightful scar upon my soul." A later editorial associate remarked of Bryant, "He impressed me as a man of strong feelings, who had at some time been led by a too explosive expression of them to dread his own passions, and who had therefore cultivated a repression which became the habit of his life."

195. *To* Richard H. Dana

New York   Feb. 16, 1828.

My dear Sir.

I am glad you are so well pleased with my review of your poems. It is pretty well received I believe by the reading world and thought a fair criticism. Mr. Walsh to be sure says that your poems are "too broadly and strongly eulogized," but Mr. Walsh's opinion on poetry you know is not worth any thing, and although it yet passes for more than it is worth, its real value is beginning to be better understood than formerly. Mr. Walsh is the greatest literary quack of our country and deserves to be taken down a peg or two. It would do him good for the creature really has some talent; and if he would be content to drudge in a plain way might be useful.

I saw Mr. Greenough and am obliged to you for introducing me to so agreeable a man and one of such genuine tastes and right opinions.[1] You must excuse me for not filling the sheet—

In haste yrs. truly

W C. BRYANT

P. S. I ought to answer your question about the New York Evening Post. I am a small proprietor in the establishment, and am a gainer by the arrangement. It will afford me a comfortable livelihood after I have paid for the *8th. part* which is the amount of my *share*.[2] I do not like politics any better than you do—but they get only my mornings—and you know politics and a bellyfull are better than poetry and starvation.

I should also express my pleasure at learning of the success of your poems in Boston. To confess to you the truth, I had strong misgivings as to their reception—very strong—but I knew that there had been a change in the tastes of the people there, and that the popularity of Wordsworth's poems whether real or factitious had prepared the way for you. As to their reception here, you know we are a prosaic money making community and nothing takes unless it be a new novel, or some work on a subject of immediate interest—but they have been read with pleasure by the [few] who know how to value such things. We did what [we] could in the papers both before and after the work appeared.

W C B.

MANUSCRIPT: NYPL–GR DOCKETED: W C. Bryant Feb / 16–28 PUBLISHED (*in part*): *Life*, I, 235–236.

1. Horatio Greenough (1805–1852, Harvard 1825), a young Boston sculptor home after brief study in Italy, was then on his way to Washington, where he would execute busts of John Quincy Adams and John Marshall, among others. Elected that year to honorary membership in the National Academy of Design, Greenough probably attended one or more of the lectures Bryant gave before the academicians that month as their newly elected Professor of Mythology and Antiquities. Their meeting began a

warm friendship unbroken until Greenough's death. See *Letters of Horatio Greenough to His Brother, Henry Greenough, with Biographical Sketches and Some Contemporary Correspondence*, ed. Frances Boott Greenough (Boston, 1887), pp. 25, 28, 153; *Morse Exhibition of Arts and Science Presented by National Academy of Design in Commemoration of the 125th Anniversary of its Founding* . . . (New York: National Academy of Design, 1950), p. 97; T. Addison Richards to Parke Godwin, January 1, 1880, NYPL–GR. Bryant referred to his friend here as "Greenhow," probably associating his name with that of Robert Greenhow (1800–1854), a New York physician of his acquaintance.

2. See 194.18. John Bigelow recorded that Henry Sedgwick lent Bryant $2,000 to buy this share. *Bryant*, p. 69n.

196. *To* Gulian C. Verplanck

New York   Feb 16 1828.

My dear Sir,

I have not written I believe since Mr. Herbert got his letter containing an account of the reception of his ode at the dinner at Washington. He was wonderfully delighted with it and so also were his friends.[1] The artist who made Plutarch Peck's coat with his usual interest in every thing that relates to American letters called to obtain a sight of it[2] and a copy was despatched to Mr. Viellecour who returned a note expressive of the gratification with which he had perused it. Mr. Herbert was observed to look wonderfully complacently for a day or two—but his face grew longer when Mr. Walsh said that the ode had been praised too highly and the critical Charles King[3] declared it prosaic. However a couple of articles which lately appeared in the Enquirer in which justice is done both to Mr. Walsh and his Jack Rugby[4] have restored their usual serenity to the features of our excellent friend.

I have not got the Southern Review yet nor can I learn that a single copy of it has been received in the city. When it comes I shall trumpet it as loudly as it will bear. Noah had an article about it yesterday morning which smells of Washington.—[5]

The Talisman continues to sell a little. Have you heard that Mr. [James Kirke] Paulding has declared it to be the best work of its kind that has appeared in England or America? He said he had read them all.

The Tariff does not seem likely to be popular to the eastward. It was amusing to observe by the papers how it was received. The Jackson papers in that quarter seized upon it as a proof that the Jackson party was friendly to manufactures—or at least willing to give their friends fair play. The Adams papers presented a dead silence for a while—and then the storm broke forth. The Boston Courier attacks the whole bill tooth and nail as you probably have seen by this time.[6] The dissatisfaction with the tax on Molasses seems to be pretty general—it reaches from Albany to Portland. An article from the National Journal in which it is said that the bill does not meet the views of the real friends of the American System is copied into almost every administration paper that I take up, and they are all taking their cue from it.[7] —I think the New England members will be forced—as you predict—to vote against it.[8]

Yrs truly

W. C. BRYANT

MANUSCRIPT: NYPL–Berg ADDRESS: Hon. Gulian C. Verplanck / Representative in Congress / Washington POSTMARK: NEW-YORK / FEB / 16 POSTAL ANNOTATION: FREE DOCKETED: W. C. Bryant PUBLISHED (*in part*): *Life*, I, 244–245.

1. "Francis Herbert" was the fictive author of *The Talisman*. Bryant, who served as its editorial co-ordinator and contributed the largest share of original copy, was often called "Francis" by his two associates. Verplanck so addressed him on January 9 in reporting the reception given his reading of Bryant's ode, "Drink to Those Who Won," at the Jackson Day celebration the previous evening: "V. P. Calhoun nodded approbation. Van Buren was in extacies. . . . The company . . . shouted and clapped, the music brayed, the cannons fired, & Col. Hayne swore that the Jackson cause had all the poetry as well as all the virtue of the land." NYPL–GR. The text of this ode, which was sung at New York's Masonic Hall the same evening, has eluded Bryant's biographers; see, for instance, *Life*, I, 244. It has lately been found in a scrapbook in NYPL–GR, and is here reproduced:

> "Ode for the Eighth of January
> From the New York Committee
>
> Not for a realm o'erthrown,
>   Bowed to receive the chain;
> We raise the song of victory—
>   A loud exulting strain:
>
> But for a City saved,—
>   Its streets from slaughter free:
> And those who rushed to smite its sons,
>   Driven back into the sea:
>
> Backward, with blood and death,
>   Driven from the rescued strand:
> On the proud day whose memory gilds
>   The records of our land.
>
> Pure drops from woman's eye,
>   And grateful tears of age,
> And those of childhood's tender lids,
>   Shall consecrate the page.
>
> Then drink to those who won
>   That meed of deathless fame,
> And let our festive halls this day
>   Re-echo Jackson's name."

2. Plutarch Peck was a comic character in the tale, "Mr. De Viellecour and His Neighbours." See 194.14. The "artist" was probably Robert Sands, one of its authors.

3. Charles King (1789–1867), earlier a banker and state assemblyman, and now editor of the New York *American*, was afterward president of Columbia College.

4. Servant and foil to the comic Doctor Caius, in *The Merry Wives of Windsor*. A writer in the New York *Enquirer* of February 13 (Bryant?) remarked, "Charles King, who is Walsh's Jack Rugby, is degraded by living as he does, on the offals of the twice cooked and originally stale game falling from Walsh's table." That Bryant may have written this article is suggested by Verplanck's reply, to this letter, that he was happy

to learn that "our friend Herbert" had not "lost his taste for anonymous authorship, having observed the best late number of the N. Y. Enquirer was wholly from his pen." February 17, 1828, NYPL–BG.

5. The first number of the *Southern Review* (1828–1832), published at Charleston, appeared in February 1828. Mott, *American Journalism*, p. 208.

6. Joseph T. Buckingham's Boston *Courier* (1824–1864) strongly advocated a protective tariff. *Ibid.*, p. 187.

7. The Washington *National Journal* (1822–1842) had been the administration's organ briefly during President Monroe's second term. *Ibid.*, p. 178*n.*

8. The "Tariff of Abominations," adopted in May 1828, was politically motivated. "Pro-Jackson congressmen wished to present their candidate to the South as a free trader, and to the North as a protectionist; they therefore introduced a bill with higher duties on raw materials than on manufactures, hoping that New England votes would help defeat it, and Adams be blamed." Morison, *History of the American People*, p. 431. Despite the expectations of Bryant and Verplanck, nearly half the New England congressional delegation favored the bill, which was passed with their aid.

197. *To* Richard H. Dana

New York March 5 1828

My dear Sir

I enclose you the little poem which you were so good as to send me some time since for the United States Review.[1] I am sorry that the premature decease of my work did not permit me to grace its pages with so agreeable a composition, but the fates would have it so.

I have just looked at Walsh's fourth No.[2] I was glad to see that it contained a favorable notice of your poems notwithstanding the churlish manner in which he spoke of the praise I gave them and which I thought they deserved. I suppose however that what he said on that occasion was only to show his critical acumen. Walsh is a poor made up creature—a thing of shreds and patches[3] that has no more real enjoyment of literature than a sophomore's common place book has. He has taken it into his head, however, to set up for a judge in these matters, and half the readers in America are ready to believe him so.

Yrs truly
WM C. BRYANT

MANUSCRIPT: NYPL–GR DOCKETED: W C Bryant / Mar. 5—28.

1. Dana's poem is unidentified.
2. Of the *American Quarterly Review*.
3. *Hamlet* III.iv.102. Hamlet, seeing his father's ghost: "A king of shreds and patches!"

198. *To* Gulian C. Verplanck

[New York, March 7, 1828]

Dear Sir.

I have made inquiry respecting the French order of 1826 relaxing the regulations of foreign commerce to Martinique and Guadaloupe and

I am convinced that there is not the least doubt in the world that it was never made public in this city until the printing of the order itself a short time since by the Senate.[1] Our merchants at least never heard of it before and there is no probability that so shrewd and sharp-sighted a class of men would have failed to take notice of a fact of this kind or having noticed it would have forgotten it. I have not looked over the files of the Evening Post to see if it ever appeared in them—that would be a long job you know, but I will do it if necessary.

I suppose you got the *tuneful nine;*[2] if you did not let me know. I directed a copy to be sent you.

Dana I observe has been *very* well treated in the American Quarterly. The notice was undoubtedly written by some personal friend of his—perhaps Ticknor might have done it.[3] Walsh I perceive is uncomfortable about the Southern Review, and is indiscreet enough to make a parade of his jealousy in his paper. It will do the Southern Review no harm and himself some hurt.

The Talisman seems coming into vogue again. Bliss is in high spirits about it. He has got an order for a new supply from Boston, and sells them almost daily in the city.

Your *literary intelligence,* Burnham, the "literal" Burnham was afraid of. "Wait [till] they come out and contradict it," said he— So to humour him I made a sort of introduction to it and told the public that "I did not come here as a lion."[4]

Somebody told me that you were negotiating with Da Ponte for rooms &c. Da Ponte moves this spring.[5]—I am now situated with a Spanish family very respectable deserving people, protégés of our friend Thatcher T. Payne, the author of the celebrated critique on the Talisman. They intend to take a house somewhere in the neighbourhood of St. John's Square next May, and would be glad to furnish you with lodgings &c in the manner to which you are accustomed, and on satisfactory terms. If you should think of them you will please to let me know.[6]

In haste
yrs truly
W. C. BRYANT

MANUSCRIPT: NYPL–Berg ADDRESS: Hon. G. C Verplanck / Member of Congress / Washington / D. C. POSTMARK: NEW-YORK / MAR / 7 POSTAL ANNOTATION: FREE DOCKETED: W. C. Bryant.

1. Bryant refers to a translation published in United States Senate Document No. 89, Twentieth Congress, First Session, February 8, 1828, of an order dated at Paris, February 5, 1826, titled "Ordinance of the King Authorizing the Importation, by National and Foreign Vessels, into the Islands of Martinique and Guadaloupe, of the Several Articles Designated by the Annexed Tariff."

2. An engraving in the *NYM,* 5 (January 26, 1828), 225, of nine "Eminent Living American Poets, copied from Original portraits, . . . and Engraved by James Eddy, Boston, 1827." In this picture, grouped clockwise around a bust of James Gates Perci-

val, are similar likenesses of Fitz-Greene Halleck, Edward Coote Pinkney, James Brooks, Samuel Woodworth, Washington Irving, John Pierpont, Charles Sprague, and Bryant. Halleck wrote Bryant on January 16: "Mr. Morris, the Editor of the Mirror, has asked me to say to you that his engraving of the Seven, or Nine, I forget which, 'Illustrious Obscure' is completed. He has made me what I dare say I ought to have been and very possibly shall be, a Methodist Parson. . . . The Barber-Shop sort of immortality with which this engraving honors us, is most particularly annoying, but how could we help ourselves?" NYPL–BG. The drawing of Bryant's head followed that of his earliest known portrait, an 1827 watercolor by Henry Inman now in the New-York Historical Society, and reproduced as the frontispiece to this volume.

3. George Ticknor (1791–1871, Dartmouth 1807), Smith Professor of French and Spanish at Harvard.

4. Michael Burnham, the business manager who shared with William Coleman financial control of the *EP*, seems to have spoken out occasionally on editorial policy. The "literary intelligence" he questioned was probably a compliment to Bryant, in an unrecovered letter on political affairs, like that in the *NYM*, 5 (December 22, 1827), 191. Noting with the "greatest satisfaction that this gifted individual" had been made joint editor of the *EP*, the article enlarged on Bryant's "rich and vivid fancy," and his "keen perception of whatever is beautiful in creation."

5. See 145.3, 146.8.

6. On March 1, 1828 the Bryants moved from Mrs. Tripler's boardinghouse on Broadway to one on Hubert Street run by Adelaida de Salazar, wife of a Spanish immigrant doing business in New York. Here they made warm friends of the Salazars, and began regular study of the Spanish language. In May the Bryants moved with the Salazars to 92 Hudson Street, near Saint John's Park. Frances Bryant, "Autobiographical Sketch," NYPL–GR; Williams, *Spanish Background*, II, 128.

199. *To* Gulian C. Verplanck

New York   March 24   1828.

Dear Sir,

You are acquainted I believe with Dr. Revere of this city. He has a son a promising lad of fifteen whom he desires to make a midshipman in the U. S. Navy. The young man is I am told of excellent moral habits, and uncommonly good education, and a great passion for the navy. If you have any influence by which you could aid him in procuring the place, you would oblige a very worthy and intelligent man, the father.[1] Mr. Coleman has promised to write to Cambreleng on the subject.[2] Dr. Revere has a brother-in-law in the House, Mr. Gurley of Louisiana, with whom he has corresponded on this subject.[3]

Yrs truly

W   C. Bryant

P. S. Mr. De Viellecour is much delighted at the success of his old acquaintance Plutarch Peck—such is his benevolent nature—although he acknowledges that "the dog" as he calls him "dont deserve it."[4]

Bliss is very desirous to go on with the Talisman another year. He thinks he has sold enough to indemnify him for the expenses of the last. An order for ten copies from Philadelphia, where you know they did not sell at first, has put him in good spirits.

I have put a paragraph in the Post about the letter in the American.

Noah has behaved shabbily in the affair and I did not know what to do with it at first but a letter from Washington in his paper of this morning with the signature of A. L. has given me an opportunity to say what I wished.[5]

Your report on the state of the finances is well received.[6] Mr. Coleman has made an article about it for the Post which lauds it to the skies, and which I have *"fixed over"* as Sands says—but I believe it is not very elegant after all.

W. C. B.

MANUSCRIPT: NYPL–Berg ADDRESS: Hon. Gulian C. Verplanck / Member of Congress / Washington / (D. C.) POSTMARK: NEW-YORK / MAR / [25?] POSTAL ANNOTATION: FREE DOCKETED: W. C. Bryant.

1. John M. Revere (1787?–1847, M.D. Edinburgh 1811, M.A. Harvard 1812) was a professor at the medical college of New York University after its founding in 1832.

2. Churchill Caldom Cambreleng (1786–1862), born in North Carolina, became a properous merchant in New York City, which he represented in Congress from 1821 to 1839. House majority leader during the administrations of Jackson and Van Buren, he was a friend and confidant of Bryant's. In 1832 Cambreleng advanced $7,000 to enable Bryant and William Leggett to gain control of the EP. BDAC, p. 651; "Evening Post Accounts," NYPL–GR.

3. Henry Hosford Gurley (1788–1833, Williams 1805–1808, class of 1809) was a congressman from Louisiana from 1823 to 1831. BDAC, p. 983. Bryant wrote "Gourlay."

4. See 196.2. This reference is probably to the success of Peck as a character, and to that of the story in which he appeared, since he was decidedly unsuccessful as a defeated candidate for the New York State legislature who had to run from his creditors.

5. A letter in the New York American of March 18 attacked Verplanck for sending letters to a "Jackson paper." Sands's letter to Verplanck dated March 25 explains this editorial tiff. "I gave my authority to Col. Stone," he wrote, "that you were not a regular correspondent of Noah or the Post, and not the writer of a letter ascribed to you in the American. It was so stated in the Commercial [Advertiser]; but from the foolish notices in which Noah replied, people inferred the contrary. He has since inserted a stupid and misprinted note from some scrub correspondent, which is equivocal. Bryant however timed it properly yesterday." NYHS. Mordecai Noah edited the New York Enquirer. See 194.12.

6. Twentieth Congress, First Session, House of Representatives Report Number 185 of the State of the Finances. Verplanck was a member of the House Committee on Ways and Means, of which he was later (1831–1833) the chairman.

200. *To* Gulian C. Verplanck

New York. May 9. 1828.

Dear Sir.

I publish to day yours of the 5th or at least a part of it—but so altered that the authorship need not be claimed by you unless you please. It has also been thought best to publish Mr. McDuffie's letter. I made an apology for you on the day after the article appeared in the Commercial; but the merchants said it was *sly* and did not think it quite satisfactory.

It however had the effect of disgusting them with Blunt if they were not disgusted before. The letters published to day, particularly Mr. McDuffie's will set the matter right. The anti-auction party are making a great noise here but I am not certain that they are very strong; although a good many of them are valuable subscribers to newspapers. They are however the only party that show any activity or make any clamour. When you get here you will be able to judge better than I can. For my part I think that both they and Mr. McDuffie are clearly in the wrong—but we of the Post have thought it prudent to take no part in the controversy.[1]

The demand for the Talisman continues—and you must do your share for another year. Inman has a design illustrating Moore's poem of the Dismal swamp which I hear spoken highly of, and which he wishes engraved for the Talisman. Will you pick up from the Virginians some particulars of the Dismal Swamp while you are at Washington which some of us may weave into a narrative or make a florid description out of?[2]

yrs truly

W   C   BRYANT

MANUSCRIPT: NYPL–Berg ADDRESS: Hon   Gulian C. Verplanck / Member of Congress / Washington / D. C. POSTMARK: NEW-YORK / MAY / 10 POSTAL ANNOTATION: FREE DOCKETED: W. C. Bryant.

1. George McDuffie (1790–1851) of South Carolina (see 88.3) was the leading Southern proponent of free trade in the House of Representatives; Joseph Blunt (see 177.4) was a high-tariff man. The letters and articles referred to concerned the national debate preceding the passage by Congress that month of the "Tariff of Abominations." See 196.8. The auction of cheap foreign goods imported at a low rate of duty, a state-licensed monopoly, had by 1828 become so obnoxious to conventional New York merchants that an anti-auction movement of prominent New York City businessmen entered a slate of congressional candidates against Democratic Congressmen Cambreleng and Verplanck. See Walter Hugins, *Jacksonian Democracy and the Working Class: A Study of the New York Workingmen's Movement 1829–1837* (Stanford: Stanford University Press, 1960), pp. 150–151.

2. Henry Inman (1801–1846), popular portrait and figure painter, was from its inception in 1826 until 1830 vice president of the National Academy of Design. He did six illustrations for the three *Talisman* volumes. His "The Dismal Swamp," engraved by Peter Maverick, accompanied Verplanck's article of the same title in *The Talisman for MDCCCXXIX*, facing p. 255.

201.   *To* Cyrus Bryant[1]

[New York, June 12, 1828]

Dear Brother

I sent on your boxes to Hartford day before yesterday. The freight to [N. Y. was] $1.00 the cartage to Thorburn's $.25 and the cartage to the steamboat $.25. I went to Thorburn's on that morning and found them just arrived. I directed them as you requested.

I do not find that I have any particular intelligence [to] communicate to you. Matters are much in the same state as when you left us. We are all well.

yr. affectionate brother
W. C. BRYANT

MANUSCRIPT: BCHS ADDRESS: Cyrus Bryant / Cummington / Mass. DOCKETED: Wm C. Bryant / June 12, 1828.

1. Cyrus, Cullen's next younger brother, returned to Cummington in June, after working four years in South Carolina, to begin studying the natural sciences under Amos Eaton, at the Rensselaer Polytechnic Institute. He stopped on the way north to see Cullen and Frances. Dr. A. Fitch to Cyrus Bryant, July 22, 1828, BCHS. See "Bryant's Correspondents."

202.   To John Pierpont[1]

New York   Oct. 30th. 1828.

My Dear Sir

At your request I enclose a copy of the little poem which I am flattered to hear has made so favorable an impression upon any body that it could be copied from memory.

Yrs truly
WILLIAM C. BRYANT

MANUSCRIPT: Pierpont Morgan Library ADDRESS: Revd. John Pierpont / Boston / [fwd?] by Mr. Goodwin DOCKETED: Wm C. Bryant / 30 Oct. 1828.

1. Rev. John Pierpont (1785–1866, Yale 1804), pastor of the Hollis Street Unitarian Church in Boston, was best known for his long religious poem, "The Airs of Palestine" (1816). Though his letter is unrecovered, he had apparently asked for a copy of Bryant's "The Death of the Flowers," published in NYR, 1 (November 1825), 485–486. See Poems (1876), pp. 132–134.

203.   To Gulian C. Verplanck

New York, Dec. 29, 1828.

My dear Sir

If I have not written to you earlier it was because I had nothing to say. Now that I am furnished with a subject I write with the greatest punctuality and alacrity. You know I suppose that the Talisman was published the day before Christmas.[1] It seems to be favorably received— puffed stoutly in the Mirror, Critic,[2] and Commercial, and faintly in the Albion and Journal of Commerce—but how it will sell I cannot say. There seems to be a law of primogeniture in relation to these books—the eldest born has the market.[3] Bliss however says he does not complain. I suppose you will have seen a communication on the subject of the work which appeared in this morning's Enquirer, praising it highly—particularly the Reminiscences, and attesting to the authenticity of the anecdotes of Billy the Fiddler and Hewlett the dancing master.[4] It was written I doubt not by Paulding. When he took a copy of Bliss a few days since he said that if it was as good as the last years he should notice it in some way. Sands declared himself vanquished by this magnanimity of Paulding's.[5]

Mr. Sands wrote you a fortnight since concerning a proposition of Dr. Bliss to publish another volume of the Talisman as a matter of business—the matter to be ready at an assigned day, say the first of July—the embellishments to be more splendid than hitherto—the size of the book larger to distinguish it from other *Annuals* of this country, and the writers to be liberally compensated. He has received no answer and fears the letter may have miscarried. How does the plan strike you? Bliss wants an answer, either negatively or affirmatively—early in order that he may immediately engage his artists.[6]

I have got the Kentucky Message. It is in pickle and will have a "benefit" in the Post tomorrow.

A Mr. E. H. Cummings of Baltimore has written to the proprietors of the Post offering to furnish us upon our own terms with reports of what is doing in Washington between the 1st of Jan. and the inauguration. Do you know this Cummings? Would it be worth while to employ him? Will you answer these questions in your next.[7]

I suppose you have heard that it is intended to displace Maxwell. At least such is the talk and that Ogden Hoffman is spoken of to fill his place.[8] General Morton[9] they say is to be removed from the office of Clerk to the [Municipal] Corporation to make way for [Mordecai] Noah, an arrangement for which I am a little sorry.

Miss Sands does not mean to forgive you for not coming to Hoboken to bid the family good-bye before you went to Washington. So there is something for you to settle when you get back.[10] The weather is quite vernal and they say Hoboken is quite verdant and spring-like in its appearance. I shall go there this afternoon—and also as I think on the 2nd of Jan. when the 8th is to be celebrated by anticipation and Sam. Swartwout is to preside over the patriotic festivities of the occasion.[11] The city dinner on the 8th, I do not intend to countenance with my presence.

The American Academy of [Fine] Arts have filled their gallery with copies of Italian and Flemish paintings which an Italian has brought over for originals. Some good copies say Morse and the other artists but for the most part daubs. By the bye—do not let Col. Trumbull paint the other 4 national pictures. They will [be] taken down again in 20 years, and the Col. has got 32,000 dollars already for his copies. Give one to Allston while he is not only alive but in the vigor of his genius. Give one to Morse who is going abroad next spring to Rome, who will study it there, and give 5 years of his life to it. Give one to Sully and if the Col. cannot do without the remaining one, let him have it as a matter of grace.—[12]

I suppose you have got the copy for Elliot.[13] Palfrey could do nothing for us—the N. A. being taken up with other matters.[14] We have told Bliss to send a copy to Mr. Gouge of the Phil. Gaz.[15]

Yrs truly
W. C. BRYANT

MANUSCRIPT: NYPL–Berg PUBLISHED (in part): Life, I, 246.

1. The Talisman for MDCCCXXIX.
2. William Leggett's weekly literary magazine, The Critic, which first appeared on November 1, 1828, failed the following June shortly before its editor–publisher became Bryant's associate on the EP. Proctor, "Leggett," p. 242.
3. Bryant alludes to The Atlantic Souvenir, of which 7,000 copies were sold in 1828. Thompson, American Literary Annuals, p. 50. An impression of two thousand copies of The Talisman for MDCCCXXVIII had not been disposed of by May 1829.
4. In "Reminiscences of New York," written jointly by Bryant and Verplanck, "Francis Herbert" guided the reader through old New York, "a sort of thoroughfare of the world; a spot where almost every remarkable character is seen once in the course of his life, and almost every extraordinary thing once in the course of its existence." Billy the Fiddler was a dwarf who played beautifully at dancing parties, and claimed to have composed one of Mozart's "six sonatas." David Hewlett was the last representative of four generations of American dancing-masters who were succeeded by emigrés from the French Revolution. The Talisman for MDCCCXXIX, pp. 311, 317–318.
5. James Kirke Paulding had called the 1828 Talisman the best gift-annual in England or America. Whatever his difference with Sands, it had been resolved when Verplanck wrote Bryant on January 1, 1829, "I rejoice that Sands is mollified towards Paulding to whom he has never done justice." NYPL–BG.
6. Sands wrote Verplanck on December 18, "Dr. Bliss wishes to publish another Talisman. He proposes to print an edition of 5,000, to pay an artist for superintending the engravers etc. and to take all the trouble from the writers and to pay Mr. Herbert $1,200 or $1,500 if he can have the manuscript by the first of July or August. . . . Bryant assents to it, and I am disposed to." NYHS.
7. Replying on January 1, Verplanck said he knew nothing of Cummings, and advised against hiring a special Washington correspondent, since his own confidential reports were more accurate. He thought, however, that during the "gala days of Jackson's entry" Bryant might wish to pay some "agreeable writer" visiting Washington to report the inaugural for "your fashionable readers." NYPL–BG.
8. Hugh Maxwell (1787–1873), an early political collaborator of Verplanck's, had been New York County district attorney since 1821. He was succeeded in 1829 by Ogden Hoffman (1793–1856, Columbia 1812), who served until 1835.
9. Gen. Jacob Morton (1761–1836).
10. Julia M. Sands (1805?–1888) and her brother Robert lived with their widowed mother in Hoboken, New Jersey, directly across the Hudson River from New York City. At their home The Talisman's authors did much of their collaborative writing.
11. The annual celebration of Andrew Jackson's victory over the British at New Orleans on January 8, 1815. Samuel Swartwout (1783–1856), Collector of the Port of New York (1829–1838), was a prominent Democrat who had captained a company of stay-at-home militia, composed of "men from the best families of New York," at the time of that battle. Schlesinger, Age of Jackson, p. 233; Adkins, Halleck, p. 38.
12. Morse and Trumbull were the rival presidents, respectively, of the new and energetic National Academy of Design and the soon-to-be-defunct American Academy of the Fine Arts. Earlier in 1828 Bryant had printed in the EP half a dozen letters

written by these two men and others in what was then known as the "War of the Academies." In 1824, heroic copies of four historical paintings by John Trumbull (1756–1843) had been installed by commission from Congress on huge panels in the Rotunda of the National Capitol. The four remaining panels went unfilled until many years later, when they were allotted to John G. Chapman (1808–1889), William H. Powell (1823–1879), John Vanderlyn (1775–1852), and Robert W. Weir (1803–1889). As chairman of the Committee on Public Buildings of the House of Representatives, Verplanck was soon in a position to help his friends among the artists of the National Academy to secure commissions to execute works for the government, and in a number of cases was successful. For a detailed account of his efforts, see Callow, *Kindred Spirits*, pp. 45–50.

13. Stephen Elliott (1771–1830) was editor of the *Southern Review*.

14. John Gorham Palfrey (1796–1881, Harvard 1815), later distinguished as an historian of New England, wrote often for the *NAR*, and from 1835 to 1843 was its owner and editor.

15. William M. Gouge (1796–1863), editor of the Philadelphia *Gazette and Daily Advertiser*, would soon become the leading Jacksonian writer on finance.

204. *To* Gulian C. Verplanck

New York   Jan   27   1829.

My dear Sir

I have not written to you since the *contract* with Bliss was agreed to by you. I believe we shall have a splendid book so far as respects the embellishments. Neilson takes hold of the thing with zeal and is assisted by the opinions of the artists.[1]

As to the degree of favour with which the Talisman has been received—I can only say that the *impartial* opinions seem to place it even higher than last years. I suppose you have seen Buckingham's opinion of it—placing it in point of literary merit above all other works of the kind.[2] The Middletown Gazette—a paper in which I showed you a criticism on Ch[arles] King's style—expressed the same opinion, but committed a great blunder as to the authors—ascribing the book to Paulding Halleck and myself.[3] The Norfolk Herald paid a high compliment to Maverick's engraving of the Dismal Swamp, which it said gave a pleasing view of the Great Feeder with a lady crossing the lake by the fire-fly lamp in a canoe rowed by an Indian.[4] As I told you before hand Coleman cannot abide the Scenes at Washington—not liking the ridicule of fat women[5]—and Lewis Tappan is outrageous against the Simple Tale which he looks upon as an impious sneer at the charitable and religious societies of many of which he is a principal pillar.[6]

I suppose you saw an Ode to Miss Wright in the Post not long since. It has passed for Halleck's among most of the knowing ones—and Carter was so cock-sure of it that he republished it in the Statesman and laid a wager with Col. Stone that Halleck was the author. Mr. Walsh I suppose fell into the same mistake for he republished it with praise.[7]

You have doubtless seen the learned epistle of a Mr. John Smith to the editors of the Evening Post. The prose was concocted—as well as the major part of the translations by Sands and myself. The other translations were furnished by Dr. Anderson, Payne, and Da Ponte. Anderson was excessively interested in the thing and superintended the revision of the translations made by him. We look upon it here as a very learned jeu d'esprit.[8]

The Senate will not receive a great accession of strength in Mr. Dudley, as I take it[9] —But he is better than the Lieut. Gov. the "Earthen Pitcher of the State."[10] —You have seen Halleck's epistle to the Recorder?—[11]

yrs truly
W. C. BRYANT

I have spoken to Inman. He knows Berrien and has I suppose written to him.[12]

MANUSCRIPT: NYPL–Berg PUBLISHED (in part): Life, I, 239, 246–247.

1. Dr. John Neilson, Jr. (1798?–1851), lecturer on anatomy at the National Academy of Design, contributed drawings to each of the three Talisman volumes, and coordinated literary material and illustrations for that of 1830. He also wrote articles for the NYR and the Knickerbocker. EP obituary, September 22, 1851; Callow, Kindred Spirits, pp. 15, 25. Bryant mistakenly wrote "Nelson."

2. Joseph Buckingham was a highly respected journalist, and his Boston Courier has been termed "perhaps the most lively and literary of the city's dailies." Mott, American Journalism, pp. 187, 262.

3. The weekly Middlesex Gazette, published at Middletown, Connecticut. See Clarence Saunders Brigham, History and Bibliography of American Newspapers 1690–1820 (Worcester, Massachusetts: American Antiquarian Society, 1947), I, 35.

4. The Norfolk (Virginia) Herald, edited by Thomas G. Broughton. Ibid., II, 1126–1127. See 200.2.

5. [Sands and Verplanck] "Scenes at Washington," The Talisman for MDCCCXXIX, pp. 77–152. William Coleman, ill at home since his 1826 accident, was still nominal editor of the EP. Nevins, Evening Post, p. 134.

6. [Sands] "A Simple Tale," The Talisman for MDCCCXXIX, pp. 224–252. The Tappan brothers, Lewis (1788–1873) and Arthur (1786–1865), prosperous merchants and pietistic reformers, founded the New York Journal of Commerce in 1827.

7. Frances Wright (1795–1852), wealthy and attractive young Scottish crusader, had just begun in New York a series of lectures advocating radical social reforms. The avowed admiration of editor William L. Stone of the Commercial Advertiser for Miss Wright led Bryant to link their names in this "ode," one of several satires he aimed at Stone early in 1829:

> "O, 'tis a glorious sight for us,
> The gaping throng, to see thee thus
> The light of dawning truth dispense,
> In that rich stream of eloquence,
> While Colonel Stone, the learn'd and brave,
> The Press's Atlas, mild but grave,
> Hangs on the words that leave thy mouth,
> Slaking his intellectual drouth. . . ."

See "Ode to Miss Frances Wright," EP, January 17, 1829. Halleck is said to have denied authorship with the comment, "There is but one man in New York who could have written it, and that is Bryant." *Life*, I, 239*n*. Nathaniel H. Carter (1787–1830, Dartmouth 1811) edited the New York *Statesman*. Drake, *Dictionary of American Biography*, p. 166.

8. The authors of this "letter," published on January 24, went to absurd lengths to prove that Col. Stone's supposed English version, in the *Commercial Advertiser*, of some French verses showed him to be a clumsy translator. The letter was reprinted in *The Writings of Robert C. Sands, in Prose and Verse* (New York, 1834), II, 309.

9. Charles Edward Dudley (1780–1841), British-born mayor of Albany, was chosen in 1829 to fill the unexpired United States Senate term of the newly elected governor of New York, Martin Van Buren.

10. Lieutenant Governor Enos Thompson Throop (1784–1874) became acting governor a few weeks later, when Van Buren went to Washington as Secretary of State.

11. Halleck's "The Recorder, A Poetical Epistle by Thomas Castaly," published in *EP*, December 20, 1828, satirized Richard Riker, the Recorder of New York City, whom Halleck's employer, Jacob Barker, believed responsible for the prosecution described in Letter 155. This poem contained verses highly complimentary to Bryant. Adkins, *Halleck*, p. 172; *Prose*, I, 376–377*n*.

12. On January 9 Verplanck wrote Bryant that he hoped to join the Capitol Art Committee in the next Congress, and would then try to "serve my friends as well as the arts." Meanwhile, he thought he might get for Henry Inman "a minor job"—a portrait of Washington "for our hall"—to go with one of Lafayette already hung. NYPL–BG. But this commission went to John Vanderlyn. John M. Berrien (1781–1856), senator from Georgia, would soon become President Jackson's attorney general. Inman had probably met Berrien during his seven years as an itinerant portrait-painter in the West and South.

205. *To* Gulian C. Verplanck

New York Feb 9 1829.

Dear Sir.

You are to be accommodated in the matter of a view near Albany. Mr. Morse has a sketch. I have not seen it but Neilson who is the regularly employed connoisseur of the work says it is the thing.[1] We had a chase after *Rebecca*, Allston's picture, but could not find it. Neilson seems to think there may be some difficulty in getting the picture from Winthrop and getting it properly engraved.[2]

As to what you call the test of the favour of the Talisman with the public—the sale—I am sorry that I cannot speak very encouragingly. It is so slow that poor Bliss is very much disappointed. He has golden hopes however of the next year's volume. Somebody has promised to take 50 copies of him to send out to England—Wardell of Philadelphia I believe.[3] And then the work is to be in the market in season to stand a fair competition with the earliest of the annuals. The necessity of putting the designs immediately into the hands of the engravers will oblige us rather to illustrate their designs than to have designs illustrating what we write. We shall have enough to do, I fancy, after your return to finish the literary part of the work by the 1st of July.

Did you see a learned article in the Post the other day about Pope Alex. VI and Cesar Borgia? Mat. Patterson undertook to be saucy in the

Commercial about a Latin quotation in the Evening Post—so we—that is Sands and myself sent him on a fool's errand. He has not been able as yet I believe to find the *Virorum Illustrium Reliquiae*—though he says he believes Da Ponte has a great many queer old Latin books, and he has some indistinct reminiscences of a book that had something about *Virorum Clarorum* in the title page.[4]

People have done talking about Miss Wright here—and now the common topic is Gen. Jackson's health. As often as about once a week somebody sets on foot a report that he is dead. This morning there is a good deal of anxiety because he has not got to Washington yet, although he has been allowed eight whole days to travel thither from Pittsburgh. As we have all set our hearts upon his being president, I solemnly believe that if he were to take it into his head to die before he is declared to be elected it would occasion tenfold more vexation and disappointment than if Mr. Adams had received a majority over him. We should all think it very unkind of him after all the trouble we have been at on his account. Besides you know that every body is in an agony of curiosity to know who he will put into his cabinet. If he should slip off to the other world without solving this pickle we should never forgive him.[5]

Do you not intend to make some great speech this session that we can publish in the Post with *remarks* "earnestly inviting the attention of our readers"? Or will it be soon enough to take that trouble another session?

[signature missing]

MANUSCRIPT: NYPL–Berg PUBLISHED (*in part*): *Life*, I, 238–239, 247.

1. Verplanck's "Gelyna, a Tale of Albany and Ticonderoga Seventy Years Ago" was prefaced by an engraving by F[rancis] Kearney of Thomas Cole's 1826 painting, "View Near Ticonderoga." *The Talisman for MDCCCXXX*, pp. 302–335. Morse's sketch was not used.

2. Possibly Francis Bayard Winthrop, of New Haven, who owned another Washington Allston painting titled "The Angel Releasing St. Peter from Prison." Edgar P. Richardson, *Washington Allston: A Study of the Romantic Artist in America* (Chicago: University of Chicago Press, 1948), p. 126n. Allston's "Rebecca at the Well," which had been shown at the National Academy in 1826, was then owned by M. Van Schaick of New York. Mary Bartlett Cowdrey, *The National Academy of Design: Exhibition Record 1826–1860* (New York: New-York Historical Society, 1943), I, 8. No illustration by Allston appeared in *The Talisman*.

3. Probably Thomas Wardle, an importer of English books. See H. Glenn Brown and Maude O. Brown, "Philadelphia Book Trade to 1820, Part XI," *Bulletin of the New York Public Library*, 54 (March 1950), 138.

4. In their "learned article," quoted in Nevins, *Evening Post*, p. 128, the authors countered a charge of having used incorrect Latin with the comment, "If any of the Popes spoke bad Latin, two or three hundred years before we were born, it should be recollected that it was not in our power to help it." Mat. Patterson, otherwise unidentified, was apparently an assistant editor of the *Commercial Advertiser*.

5. Repeated rumors of Andrew Jackson's death were finally refuted by his arrival

at Washington two days after Bryant wrote this letter. Schlesinger, *Age of Jackson*, pp. 5–6.

206. *To* Gulian C. Verplanck

New York Feb 27 1829.

Dear Sir.

Having a spare moment I think I cannot employ it better than in taking you to task for letting Gen. Jackson make so bad a cabinet.[1] Van Buren is very well—but how comes Ingham to be the Secretary of the Treasury? It does not signify to say that he is not exactly in favour of the Tariff as it now stands—he is a tariff-man, infected with the leaven of the American System.[2] Then as for capacity I should judge from what I have seen of him in letters and speeches that he is no great matter. We are very much inclined to grumble here at the appointment of Ingham. Eaton I have no doubt would have stood quite as high in the general estimation,—as to talent I mean—if he had never written the Life of Jackson.[3] Branch too is a man of whom we know little in this quarter, and that little does not give us a high opinion of him. Berrien's appointment will be highly satisfactory.[4] I allow the cabinet is as good as the last—the Treasury department is a little better filled—but where are the great men whom the General was to assemble around him—the powerful minds that were to make up for his deficiencies? Where are the Tazewells, the Livingstons the Woodburys, the McLanes &c?[5]

How happens it that the [Adams] administration papers are the first to announce this Cabinet and correctly too or nearly so? while our mouths are shut? Here we have a letter from Cambreleng[6] giving the arrangements—private as death—of which we are not to suffer a word to escape us—and on the very same day the American and Commercial both get letters from Washington which they publish, announcing the very same arrangement without the least variation.[7] I wonder who keeps the Jackson secrets so well at Washington? Who continues the admirable system by which the enemies of the President elect are informed of every thing that is going on while his friends are kept in the dark?

Your friend Mr. Baylies I saw when going on to Washington. I do not expect any thing for him from the new administration. Talents so resplendent as those of Genl. Eaton must throw those of the author of "Catullus," as Coleman named him into the shade.[8] Is Mr. Noah to be provided for?[9]

I shall see you I suppose after the ceremonies and festivities of the coronation are over and then I shall hear your frank opinion of the new cabinet as I have given you mine. There is nothing new here of any importance. Barker swears that Riker must leave his office and confidently expects that he will be removed by an unanimous vote of the Senate.—[10]

We have had slippery weather here. Sands has been obliged to pass an hour or two every morning in agreeable meditations in the cabins of the Hoboken ferry boats. It took them as long as that to get through the ice. For two days [pa]st he has not been over at all and I have just learned that on Tuesday he slipped up and broke his head to use a good old phrase.— My little daughter has been quite sick for several days. She has been thought in some danger—but I believe her case looks a little better now.

Yrs truly—

W C BRYANT

P. S. Why do you never write?

MANUSCRIPT: NYPL–Berg ADDRESS: Hon. G. C. Verplanck / Member of Congress / Washington / D. C. POSTMARK: NEW-YORK / FEB / 28 POSTAL ANNOTATION: FREE DOCKETED: Wm C. Bryant PUBLISHED (in part): Life, I, 247–248.

1. President-elect Jackson had named Martin Van Buren of New York as his Secretary of State, and Samuel D. Ingham to the Treasury, John Branch of North Carolina to the Navy, and John H. Eaton to the War Department. John M. Berrien of Georgia would become Attorney General, and William T. Barry of Kentucky Postmaster General.

2. The "American System," with which Ingham's name had been associated since its inception in 1815, combined the subsidy of manufactures through a protective tariff, government subsidy of roads and canals, and the regulation of currency by a national bank. Charles M. Wiltse, The New Nation 1800–1845 (New York: Hill and Wang, 1961), p. 55.

3. John Eaton's The Letters of Wyoming, to the People of the United States on the Presidential Election and in Favor of Andrew Jackson (Philadelphia, 1824), was influential in creating an image of Jackson as noble statesman–farmer. John William Ward, Andrew Jackson: Symbol for an Age (New York: Oxford University Press, 1962), pp. 44, 68–69.

4. Except for his over-estimate of Berrien, Bryant's appraisal of these choices accords with that of most modern historians, one of whom concludes that the cabinet, "save for Van Buren, . . . was composed of mediocrities, or worse, and was destined to be of little use to its chief." Van Deusen, Jacksonian Era, p. 32.

5. Of those named, all but Littleton Tazewell of Kentucky would enter Jackson's reorganized cabinet two years later—Edward Livingston of Louisiana as Secretary of State, Louis McLane of Delaware as Secretary of the Treasury, and Levi Woodbury of New Hampshire as Secretary of the Navy.

6. Bryant found a continuing source of confidential political intelligence in Churchill Cambreleng. See 199.2.

7. The American and the Commercial were unfriendly toward Jackson. Schlesinger, Age of Jackson, p. 276.

8. Francis Baylies (1783–1852) of Taunton, Massachusetts, was the younger brother of Bryant's law tutor. The only New England congressman to vote against John Quincy Adams in the run-off election of 1824, he was defeated for re-election in 1826. Verplanck and other friends failed to get him a cabinet appointment in 1829, but in 1832 Jackson sent him to Buenos Aires as acting American minister during crucial negotiations over fishing rights at the Falkland Islands. Since Baylies had published some historical writings as well as a significant report on western exploration, perhaps Bryant was suggesting that William Coleman had confused the Latin poet Gaius Valerius Catullus with the Roman consul Quintus Lutatius Catulus, a bitter opponent of Julius

Caesar—as Baylies was of John Quincy Adams. July, *Essential New Yorker*, pp. 137–138; *BDAC*. See also *NYR*, 2 (March 1826), 274–285.

9. Mordecai Noah had edited a Tammany Hall organ, *The National Advocate*, before founding the Democratic New York *Enquirer* in 1826. In 1829 he was appointed Surveyor of the Port of New York.

10. See 155.8; 204.11. Richard Riker remained in office.

207. *To* Fanny Bryant

Nueva York   8 de Julio 1829

Querida hija mia

Te mando un libro que quizas te divertirá. Tu lees sin duda Español y Frances todos los dias, para que no olvides esas lenguas. En il mismo tiempo creo que no negliges la aritmética. Espero que todo el tiempo que pasarás en el campo non solamente *estes* buen[o], mas que *seas* buena, lo cual es mucho mas importante. Deseo mucho ver te y á tu madre.

Dios guarde tu vida los muchos años que te desea tu cariñoso padre.[1]

WILLIAM C. BRYANT

MANUSCRIPT: NYPL–GR ADDRESS: Senorita Francisca Bryant / Great Barrington / Massachusetts.

1. "My dear daughter / I send you a book which will perhaps amuse you. Without doubt, you study Spanish and French every day, so as not to forget those languages. At the same time I am sure you do not neglect arithmetic. I hope that not only will the entire *time* you spend in the country *be* agreeable, but that *you will be* agreeable, which is more important. I would like very much to see you and your mother. / May God watch over your life for many years is the wish of your loving father."

208. *To* the Trustees of Columbia College

[New York] July 31 [1829].

Mr. Bryant will do himself the honor of accepting the invitation to the Commencement dinner on the 4th.

MANUSCRIPT: Columbia University Libraries.

209. *To* Frances F. Bryant

New York   Wednesday   Aug. 5   1829.

My dear wife

This morning Mr. Burnham set out for Connecticut. How long he will be absent I cannot say—he said he should return in a fortnight at least. Whenever he returns I shall set out for Cummington. As that may be any time from ten days to three weeks from this time I think you would do well to set out for Cummington the latter part of next week or the beginning of the week following at furthest. I should be very much disappointed not to find you there when I arrive.

In the mean time, if you want me to bring you any thing from New

York or to do any thing before I leave it write me immediately and I will attend to it.

I wrote, as you perhaps know by this time, to Mr. Hyde to pay Maj. Hopkins. Hopkins took up some notes for me of Col. Thomas Hopkins and his father which he has handed over to Mr. Hyde, I suppose, in the settlement. I wrote to Hyde to give them to you.[1]

Peter left here on Sunday morning— He might as well have waited till Monday, for the boat in which he took passage met with an accident and was obliged to return. He got here about night, and putting his baggage on board the Constellation started again the next morning. So you see nothing is gained by travelling Sundays—at least nothing was gained in that instance.[2]

Mr. Oya has been in the city. He called on me at the office and afterwards at the house. He inquired after you and Fanny very particularly and charged me to give you both his regards. He has been living in Germantown in New Jersey[3] and was here to see his brother, who is one of the old Spaniards expelled from Mexico. He speaks English tolerably, considering that he began to learn it so late. He told me he had seen Mrs. Tripler.[4]

You will see in today's Evening Post an extract from a letter concerning a new picture by Washington Allston of a Mother and child. I copied it from a letter which Verplanck had just received from Dana.[5] D. says that "The Past" suited him exactly, and spoke of its "naked strength" in which he thought it exceeded any thing I had written.[6] He added that if Bryant must write in a newspaper to get his bread he prayed God he might get a bellyfull. Dana speaks in the same letter of a poem he has been writing and says he thinks he shall deliver it at Andover. What has he to do with Andover I wonder! I hope he is not studying divinity to make himself a Calvinistic parson. He is inclined to Calvinism you know, but I hope he will not Andoverize himself.[7]

Yesterday was the Commencement of Columbia College. It rained violently and therefore I neither attended the exercises nor went to the dinner. Theodore Sedgwick the younger had the valedictory and acquitted himself with great credit. Mr. Verplanck spoke highly in praise of his performance. His father and Chas. Sedgwick were here by the latter of whom I send this letter.[8]

I like Leggett, so far, very much. He seems to be an honest man, of good principles, industrous, and a fluent though by no means a polished writer.[9]

Mr. Field returned to day.[10] We are all well here except Christoval who has been sick and cross ever since you went away, notwithstanding the great superiority of the Spanish mode of dieting children.[11] The Coleman family are all gone into the country; they are travelling I believe towards the western part of the state. Mrs. R[obert] Sedgwick has gone to Newport.—

I believe I have no more news to tell you at present. *Adios—un besito para Frazquita* [Goodbye—a kiss for Fanny].

Your affectionate husband
W. C. BRYANT

I shall not write you again until I get an answer to this, having written I believe two or three letters to your one.[12]

MANUSCRIPT: NYPL–GR ADDRESS: Mrs. Frances F. Bryant / Great Barrington / Mass PUBLISHED (*in part*): *Life*, I, 248.

1. James A. Hyde (d. 1836, Williams 1807) had assumed Bryant's Great Barrington law practice in 1825. A balance sheet dated December 14, 1829, with which Hyde sent Bryant a credit of $72, seems to have been in final settlement of their accounts. NYPL–GR. The relationship of Charles Hopkins, Frances Bryant's brother-in-law, to the others named is uncertain.

2. Peter Rush Bryant had been teaching in the New York high school since May. Failing to get employment in the customs house, he then returned to Cummington. Eliza Robbins to Frances Bryant, July 24, 1829, NYPL–BG; John Bryant to Cyrus Bryant, September 27, 1829, BCHS.

3. Bryant must have meant Germantown, Pennsylvania, a suburban town near Philadelphia.

4. Señor Oya and the Bryants had apparently been fellow-boarders at Mrs. Tripler's the preceding year.

5. Allston's painting "Mother and Child" had just been acquired from the artist by the Boston Athenaeum. Edgar P. Richardson, *Washington Allston: A Study of the Romantic Artist in America* (Chicago: University of Chicago Press, 1948), p. 209.

6. Bryant's "To the Past" (retitled "The Past" in his *Poems* [1847], and thereafter) appeared in *The Talisman for MDCCCXXIX*, pp. 73–75. See *Poems* (1876), pp. 171–173. Dana's praise for this poem, and Verplanck's reported exclamation, "Gray's 'Elegy' is nothing to it," accounted in part for Bryant's later opinion that it was his "best thing."

7. Dana, then a strong adherent of the Trinitarian faction within the Congregational Church, in opposition to Unitarianism, later became an Episcopalian. See 216.1.

8. Theodore Sedgwick III (1811–1859), son of Bryant's old friend Theodore II (1780–1839), later became a distinguished lawyer and frequent contributor to the *EP*.

9. On July 13 William Coleman had died of a stroke, and Bryant was at once made editor-in-chief. He engaged immediately as his assistant William Leggett (1801–1839), until lately conductor of *The Critic*. Leggett had spent three years on the Illinois prairie and three more in the navy before returning to his birthplace, New York City. Here he published a book of verse, *Leisure Hours at Sea* (1825), and won praise for a frontier tale, "The Rifle," in *The Atlantic Souvenir* for 1828. He wrote poems, essays, tales, and theatrical criticisms for periodicals, and served briefly as assistant editor of the daily *Merchants' Telegraph*, before founding the short-lived *Critic* in 1828. Though he stipulated to Bryant, on joining the *EP*, that he should not be asked to discuss politics, "on which he had no settled opinions, and for which he had no taste," he had gained from his unhappy experience under a despotic naval commander, Bryant thought, a hatred for tyranny in all forms—and soon found himself in the heat of the *EP*'s opposition to the American System. Bryant, *Reminiscences of EP*, p. 12, and "William Leggett," *Democratic Review*, 6 (July 1839), 17–28; Proctor, "Leggett," pp. 241–242.

10. Ferdinand E. Field, an English horticulturalist, was then Bryant's fellow-boarder and frequent walking companion. During a correspondence of more than forty years, Bryant visited Field several times in England, and they saw each other

again in this country. In 1869 Bryant secured publication in New York of Field's *The Green-house as a Winter Garden: A Manual for the Amateur*, for which he wrote the preface.

11. Christoval was the small daughter of the Bryants' current landlady, Adelaida de Salazar.

12. Bryant's other letters are unrecovered.

210.   *To* Gulian C. Verplanck

New York, Dec   [*c*15], 1829.

Dear Sir.

We are greatly obliged to you for such oracular hints, for so they are received, as you have occasionally given us since you went on to the capitol. They are copied every where, even into the *American*. The President's Message has been very favorably received here. Almost every body speaks well of it as a whole. Those who are concerned in the United States bank did not like that part relating to that institution—but even on that subject there is not much excitement notwithstanding the opposition journals have tried hard to kindle one.[1] How came Eaton to suffer his report to appear so overcharged with verbal inaccuracies? Partly I suppose by having an ignorant copyist for the press and partly by his own ambition to be fine, but in either case he is inexcusable. It has given the small critics of the opposition something to talk about.[2]

We see but one side of the parties at Washington. The Telegraph has not been sent us for ten days past. A line was put into the Post mentioning the fact, but it has not brought us the paper. If you should see the Editor will you mention it to him.[3]

The Talisman I have little to tell you about. If you see the Courier you must have seen Paulding's article about it, and Brooks's certificate to its merits.[4] Sands's negotiation with Bradford has come to no fruit yet.[5] Bliss does not talk of making much money by the concern.—

Yrs truly

W. C. BRYANT

MANUSCRIPT: NYPL–Berg ADDRESS: G. C. Verplanck Esq. / Washington / D. C. DOCKETED: W. C. Bryant PUBLISHED (*in part*): *Life*, I, 248–249.

1. President Jackson's first message to Congress, on December 8, 1829, was cautious on the question of tariff reduction, but expressed real concern over the power and constitutionality of the private Bank of the United States, the renewal of whose charter he later vetoed. Schlesinger, *Age of Jackson*, pp. 80–81, 89–90; Van Deusen, *Jacksonian Era*, pp. 38–39, 66.

2. Secretary of War John H. Eaton.

3. Duff Green (1791–1875) edited the Washington *United States Telegraph*, the administration organ during Jackson's first two years in office. Mott, *American Journalism*, p. 179; Van Deusen, *Jacksonian Era*, p. 45.

4. James Gordon Brooks (1801–1841) was then an editor of the New York *Morning Courier*.

5. Robert Sands negotiated with several booksellers hoping to find continuing

sponsorship for *The Talisman*; among them, apparently, was Samuel Bradford of New York, grandson of the "patriot printer" of Philadelphia, William Bradford. See Mott, *American Journalism*, pp. 25–26. Another was Henry C. Carey, publisher of *The Atlantic Souvenir*.

211. *To* Gulian C. Verplanck

New York   Dec. 24th   1829.

Dear Sir

I shall communicate to Mr. Coleman the fate of his packet which was committed to the post office in perfect forgetfulness of the spirit of reform now infused into all public departments, and which I hope will produce as much accommodation in some respects as it deprives us of in others. I believe the packet consisted of Coleman's article on the subject of Banking which appeared in the United States Review either in the original pamphlet or transcribed, with perhaps some additional manuscript.[1]

You have accounted satisfactorily enough for Eaton's failure, but has he no friends who write English and who can look over his official communications for him?

The other day Mr. Sands showed me the third volume of [a] work called Tales of an Indian Camp published in England by Colburn and which Carey & Lea are to republish here. You may perhaps have seen some preliminary puff of the book in which the author is said to be a Mr. Jones—J. A. Jones I believe—the same who wrote the sonnet on Webster, and then edited a Jackson paper in Philadelphia. And what do you think I found Mr. Jones had been doing in his third volume? Only transplanting my story of the Cascade of Melsingah bodily into his work leaving out my introduction, and fitting it with a short one of his own, altering slightly the beginning and end of several of the paragraphs, and putting a new sentence at the close of the whole, but otherwise copying verbatim about twenty pages of Mr. Herbert's composition.[2] It is the same old coat with a new cuff and collar. Not the slightest acknowledgment of the obligation is made in any part of the book. What adds to the man's impudence he relates in the course of the work with the utmost gravity as Mr. Sands tells me that in his childhood he was attended by an Indian servant from whom he learned the superstitions and traditions he has made use of in compiling the book. This theft from me is not however the only one the work contains. The Notes to Yamoyden are stolen in the same wholesale manner.[3] It will be necessary that the critics should be prepared to vindicate Mr. Herbert's literary rights when the book comes out. For my own part I intend to expose the robbery, and if the book comes in your way you will not forget what is due to our old friend.[4]

Sands has seen Carey. He seemed to entertain the proposition favorably and promised to write with an offer of terms.[5]

Yrs truly

W. C. Bryant.

MANUSCRIPT: NYPL–Berg ADDRESS: Hon. G. C. Verplanck / Member of Congress / Washington /D. C. POSTMARK: NEW-YORK / DEC / 24 DOCKETED: W. C. Bryant PUBLISHED (in part): Life, I, 249–250.

1. "Thoughts on Banking," by W. H. Coleman, son of the late publisher of the EP, had been printed in USR, 1 (December 1826), 190–197. Verplanck's letter presumably reporting the packet's loss is unrecovered.

2. Bryant's tale, "The Cascade of Melsingah," appeared in The Talisman for MDCCCXXVIII, pp. 198–227.

3. Sands's and James Wallis Eastburn's dramatic poem "Yamoyden" (1820) was accompanied by extensive notes reflecting its authors' research into the tragic history of King Philip of the Wampanoags.

4. James Athearn Jones had published a Revolutionary War tale, The Refugee: A Romance, in New York in 1825. In 1829, according to Sands, he was London correspondent for the New York Commercial Advertiser, and had sold his Tales of an Indian Camp to the publisher Colburn for 1,000 guineas. Sands to Verplanck, December 27, 1829, NYHS. When Henry Carey learned of the plagiarisms in this book, he refused to publish it. On December 30 Verplanck wrote Bryant, "I will have the piratical depredation on Mr. Herbert's property punished in a way he little dreams of— By a singular but agreeable coincidence I received the other day a long & interesting letter from Washington Irving. . . . I shall in my next make a reclamation upon him both in his literary & diplomatic character to have this literary pirate broken up & pilloried by his friend [Thomas] Campbell or some other officer of the London critical police." NYPL–BG.

5. Sands's attempt to sell the copyright of The Talisman to Carey & Lea for $2,000 soon failed. Sands to Verplanck, May 11, 1830, NYHS. See Letter 212.

212. To Gulian C. Verplanck

New York   Jan   11th   1830

Dear Sir

I suppose you may have seen before this something in the city papers or in the Albany Argus[1] on the subject of Mr. Webb's plans to get a law passed giving the printing of all legal notices in the city to the Courier and Enquirer.[2] We published a protest against it on Saturday.[3] We had early notice of what Mr. Webb was going to do and had written to our friends in Albany and had been answered that there was no probability that the legislature would do any thing affecting the interests of the Evening Post. But as the devil would have it, Col. Stone took it into his head to go to Albany for the purpose of "defeating Webb." Before he had been there two days Stilwell[4] wrote to us in great alarm urging us to lose no time in making every exertion in our power for that Stone's arrival had made the question a Jackson and Adams question, and there was every reason to fear that Webb would succeed. These letters were received Saturday but since that time we have been informed that Mr. Webb's prospects did not look quite so well. If you have any confidential friend in the Legislature to whom you could write on the subject and who could be made to see the impropriety and injustice of the measure to say nothing of its inexpediency and impolicy, you might do us a service. I have just heard that there was a meeting on Saturday night at Tammany Hall called by the creature Sibell for the purpose of denouncing the Evening Post. You may recollect that Sibell a year or two since had a battle with Stevens. He now thinks that in the contest between the friends of Walter Bowne and the other party headed by Stevens the Evening Post was lukewarm and did not sufficiently revenge on Alderman Stevens the ancient drubbing he gave Sibell. The friends of our paper were however too strong for him and it was not denounced as he intended. The meeting was called privately.[5]

Bliss made a better sale of the Talisman on the last days of the year 1829 than he expected, and he now informs me that he shall probably lose but little. His forehead has grown considerably smoother and he is evidently less nervous and in better spirits. Sands as he has perhaps written to you had an interview with Carey on the subject of the "Miscellanies." Carey professed to receive the suggestion with great gladness of heart and promised to write the next week making an offer. He went home and more than a fortnight elapsed without hearing from him when a letter arrived in which he said he had forgotten the subject altogether, and that he had on "mature deliberation" made up his mind to make no offer at all, having already as many irons in the fire as he well knew how to manage, and being determined to give up the publication of American light literature.[6]

Carey has discovered Jones's plagiarisms from the Talisman and refuses to publish the book. Leggett I believe informed him.

Yrs truly
W. C. BRYANT

P. S. I have seen [Francis] Baylies who visited the city about a fortnight or three weeks since. What a queer affair that was at Boston.[7]

MANUSCRIPT: NYPL–Berg ADDRESS: G C Verplanck / Washington / D. C. DOCKETED: W. C. Bryant.

1. The Albany *Argus*, edited by Edwin Croswell (1797–1871), state printer and conservative member of the Albany Regency, was for a time the most influential Democratic newspaper in the North. See Benson, *Jacksonian Democracy*, pp. 67–68; Mott, *American Journalism*, p. 257; Schlesinger, *Age of Jackson*, p. 179.

2. Col. James Watson Webb (1802–1884), precocious soldier in the War of 1812, left the army in 1827 to buy the New York *Morning Courier*. In 1829 he acquired the *Enquirer*, and with it editor Mordecai Noah and Washington correspondent James Gordon Bennett. This merger produced the enterprising and aggressive *Courier and Enquirer*, most widely read of New York papers. Mott, *American Journalism*, pp. 182–183, 260–261.

3. In an open letter to the legislature in the *EP* for January 9 Bryant called Webb's proposal a "direct attack on our interests." He pointed to Webb's "vehement opposition," a year earlier, to the regular Democratic ticket. Webb would, in fact, desert the Jackson cause two years later, under the suspicion that he had been bought off by Nicholas Biddle's Bank of the United States. Mott, *American Journalism*, pp. 182–183, 232; Van Deusen, *Jacksonian Era*, pp. 63–64.

4. Silas Morse Stilwell (1800–1881) was then a Democratic state assemblyman from New York City. Four years later he switched parties and ran for lieutenant governor on the Whig ticket. Benson, *Jacksonian Democracy*, p. 45n.

5. Walter Bowne, Tammany Democrat and opponent of Governor DeWitt Clinton on the powerful state Council of Appointments until its dissolution in 1821, naturally opposed the rise of the Workingmen's faction in his party. Samuel Stevens, a mechanic and an Antimason, was nominated for the lieutenant governorship in 1832. Willis Fletcher Johnson, *History of the State of New York Political and Governmental*. I. *1776–1822* (Syracuse: The Syracuse Press, 1922), pp. 394–395; Walter Hugins, *Jacksonian Democracy and the Working Class: A Study of the New York Workingmen's Movement 1829–1837* (Stanford: Stanford University Press, 1960), p. 21. The "creature Sibell" is otherwise unidentified.

6. Three years later Elam Bliss reprinted the three volumes of *The Talisman* (1828–1830) with the title, *Miscellanies. First Published under the Name of The Talisman* (New York, 1833).

7. Bryant's reference here is obscure.

213.   *To* Gulian C. Verplanck

New York   Feby 1   1830

Dear Sir

I send you Irving's letter having already forwarded the other several days since. The part that relates to the Talisman I copied and sent to Sands. I am much obliged to you for permitting me to avail myself of the information they contain. The articles I made from them are, I observe, republished in most other papers out of the city except perhaps in the violent opposition papers.[1]

Mr. Burnham told me he had written you two letters on the subject of city and state politics. He has I fancy given you a view of things *peint en laid* [i.e., an ugly picture]. There has been a good deal of noise here about various matters within a few weeks. Throop's appointments of Masters in Chancery, Commissioners &c. have not been very popular. Many of them are Adams men, some are minors it is said and some aliens. Dean[2] said he had refused to administer the oath to two or three of the commissioners on the ground of being aliens— Thomas Bolton a good Jackson man and an old federalist has been turned out of an office which he filled to great acceptance, and this has displeased many.[3] I heard Dean —a regular Tammany man you know—[prating?] most vehemently the other day about the whole list of appointments, declaring them the shabbiest he had ever known made.

Then there is Mr. Webb's attempt to get the printing of the legal notices—but we are assured from Albany it will go no further. I cannot learn that his project received any strong support from the party here— the strongest and most respectable of them I believe were against it.

I have begun my letter on the wrong side—no matter—I proceed to the next subject—the New University.[4] You have read all about it and know the different projects and the nature of the controversy. The New

University has many active friends—Wainwright[5]—Matthews[6]—Maxwell[7] and others—Loundy the former sheriff is much interested in the project[8] —Delafield, he of the Bank,[9] Mercein,[10] &c. &c. These men are writing in the newspapers and stirring up everybody in whom they find any disposition to encourage the project. Wainwright says there is a wonderful excitement among the Working Men on the subject, that is, the plainer part of the Community, respectable mechanics and trades people, and that they are all for a University. On the other side *the Bishop*[11] carries on the war almost alone—writing for the papers, calling upon editors, and upon others likely to be influenced one way or the other, either for the sake of counteracting the representations of the other party or for the sake of securing them before hand in favor of Columbia College. The activity of these clergymen has been incessant and somewhat amusing to the laity. Dr. Spring[12] who was expected to favor the project bolted because there was *no religion in it* and came out in a most vehement attack upon it in the Commercial under the signature of Theophilus declaring the attempt to disjoin learning and religion a piece of flagrant impiety and one which would draw after it the most terrible moral consequences and the curse of heaven besides. I asked one of the champions of the new institution what he would do now—he replied *"we will fix that"* and I have since been told that it is expected to make the thing palatable to the ultra-religionists by a theological professorship or something of that nature. Dr. Augustine Smith[13] was at first very warmly in favor of the New University, but I have heard nothing of him lately, nor do I know what has cooled his zeal. Dr. McNeven[14] is tooth and nail against Columbia College, and the other gentlemen of Rutgers College are I am told by no means disposed to stand by it. The first project of a new system of instruction for Columbia College included as you might perhaps have seen, medicine and jurisprudence —but when it came to be adopted the provision for instruction in these branches of knowledge was struck out. McNeven said it was done at the instigation of Dr. Watts[15] who was afraid of raising up an institution to rival his own, and attacked the Trustees in the Post, charging them with being under the control of men who consulted other interests besides those of the institution. In the mean time Bishop Hobart has called on the Very Revd Mr. Power who has assured him that the Catholics will take no interest in the New University as they are going to have a University of their own in New York and have at present an agent in Europe collecting funds for the purpose.[16]

Now as to the Working Men. It is likely I believe to turn out a very harmless concern—somewhat troublesome to party men perhaps, but morally and politically harmless. The party has abjured the Agrarian doctrine. The Evening Journal their paper the other day had an account of one of their meetings at which the "Agrarians aided by the Tammanyites and the aristocrats" attempted to appoint a chairman and secretary but were defeated and put down by a triumphant majority. The Evening Journal has a subscription of about 2000. Dr. Wainwright says they are decent people and he has enlisted the paper in favor of the New University. There is no doubt I believe that the better sort of the mechanics and trades people by uniting themselves to the knot of Agrarians have smothered and overpowered them. The party is now very strong—so much so that some very shrewd Tammany men begin to think that if they hold together they will prevail at the next election.[17] A   Hamilton has become a great friend of the Working Men. He says they will get up a good ticket and will prevail.[18]

Yrs truly,
WILLIAM C. BRYANT

MANUSCRIPT: NYPL–Berg.

1. On January 11 Verplanck wrote Bryant, "I send you [Washington] Irving's first letter . . . the substance of which you may throw into scattered paragraphs—but it must not be printed as a whole, or a letter from London." NYPL–BG. On January 22 he forwarded another Irving letter, "to the first paragraph of which you & Sands are parties. The remainder must not be for the profane, but must be used with the same discretion as the former, which I see you have husbanded with marvellous mystery & advantage." NYPL–BG. Verplanck refers to *EP* editorials of January 14 and 16, in which Bryant praised the skill of the American minister to London, Louis McLane, in his efforts to re-open American trade with the British West Indies, at a standstill since the Revolution. Bryant thought McLane's negotiations hampered by British resentment at John Quincy Adams' denunciation of England in a July 4 oration while Secretary of State, and by the Tariff of Abominations, passed in 1828 during his presidency. Echoing Irving's words, Bryant commented on January 14, "We learn that [McLane] has already made a highly favorable impression in [England]," and on January 16 that he was an "excellent negotiator." McLane's success enabled President Jackson to announce, the following October, the re-opening of direct trade with the West Indies. Bailey, *Diplomatic History*, pp. 193–195; Van Deusen, *Jacksonian Era*, p. 57. Irving's comments on *The Talisman* apparently reported his exposure of the literary thefts discussed in Letter 211.

2. Probably Amos Dean (1803–1868, Union College 1822), lawyer and city judge.

3. Bolton had been a member of the Common Council of New York City who served on the testimonial committee during the Erie Canal celebration in 1825. Martha J. Lamb, *History of the City of New York: Its Origin, Rise, and Progress* (New York and Chicago [1877]), II, 700–702.

4. The private, non-sectarian University of the City of New York was opened in 1832, and renamed New York University in 1896. Bryant discussed its plan of operation and controversy with Columbia College in *EP* editorials on January 12, 13, 15, 16, and 26, 1830.

5. Rev. J. Mayhew Wainwright. See 123.4.

6. Rev. James McFarland Mathews (1785–1870), first chancellor of the new university, describes its genesis in his *Recollections of Persons and Events* . . . (New York, 1865), pp. 189–258, *passim*.

7. Hugh Maxwell. See 203.8.

8. Otherwise unidentified.

9. John Delafield, Sr. (1786–1853, Columbia 1802?), a shipowner and banker who was then treasurer of the New-York Historical Society. See Vail, *Knickerbocker Birthday*, pp. 70–78, *passim*.

10. Thomas F. R. Mercein (d. 1856), an early member of the New-York Historical Society, was later pastor of the Methodist church at Sheffield, Massachusetts. *Ibid.*, p. 56.

11. Rev. John Henry Hobart (1775–1830, Princeton 1793), rector of Trinity Church and bishop of the Episcopal diocese of New York since 1816.

12. Rev. Gardiner Spring. See 66.2.

13. Virginia-born John Augustine Smith (1782–1865, William and Mary 1800), trained in medicine at London, was a professor at the College of Physicians and Surgeons in New York. In 1831 he became its fifth president.

14. William James McNeven (1763–1841, M.D. Vienna 1784) had been a fellow-prisoner in Ireland with the revolutionary Thomas Addis Emmet, whom he followed to New York in 1805. Professor of obstetrics at the College of Physicians and Surgeons from 1808 to 1826, he resigned to help found the short-lived Rutgers Medical School. Bryant wrote "McNevin."

15. John Watts, a graduate of Edinburgh University, was the fourth president (1826–1831) of the College of Physicians and Surgeons, then an independent institution, but after 1891 a part of Columbia University. See *A History of Columbia University 1754–1904* . . . (New York: Columbia University Press, 1904), pp. 316–317. Watts's article in the *EP* has not been located.

16. John Power (1792–1849), vicar general of the Roman Catholic diocese of New York, and since 1819 pastor of Saint Peter's Church. In 1841 Saint John's College, later Fordham University, was founded by John Joseph Hughes (1797–1864), then bishop and later archbishop of New York.

17. The Workingmen's Party, formed in 1829 by dissident Tammany Hall Democrats who were merchants and professional men as well as mechanics and clerks, opposed the Albany Regency and the Jackson administration. That November they won nearly as many votes for their legislative slate as did the party regulars. A year later, however, their party had fractured, and Jackson supporters won city as well as state elections. The New York *Evening Journal*, edited by Noah Cook, and the *Working Man's Advocate*, by George Henry Evans, spoke for the two factions of the Workingmen's Party. See Benson, *Jacksonian Democracy*, pp. 33–40, *passim*; Walter Hugins, *Jacksonian Democracy and the Working Class: A Study of the New York Workingmen's Movement 1829–1837* (Stanford: Stanford University Press, 1960), pp. 12–23, *passim*; *EP* for November 18, 1829.

18. James Alexander Hamilton (1788–1878, Columbia 1805), son of the first Secretary of the Treasury, was an influential adviser of Presidents Jackson and Van Buren, serving from 1830 to 1833 as United States Attorney for the Southern District of New York. See Benson, *Jacksonian Democracy*, p. 6.

214. *To* Gulian C. Verplanck

New York   Feb   23   1830.

Dear Sir

Mr. Wade—Durand's Wade, desired yesterday to know whether Francis Herbert would give a hundred pages of letter press for a Landscape Annual. He said that he had learned from Dr. Bliss that the publication of the Talisman would not be continued, that Durand and he, and I believe Hatch, also, had projected the publication of a series of engravings of American artists ten or twelve which they had intended to publish in a portfolio form with very brief descriptions, but that he did not like the idea of Francis Herbert going into retirement, and that he and Hatch were determined to alter their plan and engage Mr. Herbert if possible to write descriptions stories and other articles for the work after his own manner. Durand is yet to be consulted and he is at St. Augustine in Florida with his wife. I have seen Sands and he has no objection to do the thing. What do you say?— The pictures can be sent to you at Washington and you can do your part which will amount to between 30 and 40 pages before you return—if you please— The compensation can be fixed upon after Durand's consent is obtained—[1]

Yrs in haste,
W. C. BRYANT.

The book is to be as large or [a] little larger than the English Landscape Annual.[2]

MANUSCRIPT: NYPL–Berg.

1. Asher Brown Durand (1796–1886) was then a leading engraver, having executed plates from such notable paintings as Trumbull's "Declaration of Independence" and Vanderlyn's "Ariadne," as well as designs for American banknotes, on which his symbolic figures may still be seen. He engraved paintings by Inman, Morse, and Weir for *The Talisman*, and he rendered scenes by Cole, Weir, and William J. Bennett, in addition to two of his own, as illustrations for *The American Landscape*, published by Elam Bliss (New York, 1830). Bryant wrote the preface and letterpress; there is no evidence that either Sands or Verplanck contributed to this, nor was the name of the fictive "Francis Herbert" mentioned in the volume. George W. Hatch (1805–1867), one of Durand's pupils, had engraved illustrations by Inman, Weir, and John Neilson, Jr., for *The Talisman*, but apparently had no part in *The American Landscape*, of which printer Edward Wade, Jr., was the co-proprietor with Durand. See *DAA*, pp. 196–197, 300.

2. *The Landscape Annual*, London, 1830–1839.

215. *To* Gulian C. Verplanck

New York   March 5   1830.

Dear Sir

I send you back Mr. Sarchet's letter. You will see that I have made a report of your speech. I presume that it was what you did say, if I understand your letter.[1]

I have just seen Mr. Wade. He showed me a beautiful drawing of a Weehawken scene by Bennett intended for the Landscape Annual. It is taken from the big rocks near the end of the wood just before you come upon Swartwout's dike.[2] You remember them—two or three cedars grow up by their side. —There is a view of the Delaware Water Gap, of which he showed me a proof,[3] a[nd] a proof of an etching of Fort Putnam.[4] The plates are about this size.[5]

Yrs
W. C. BRYANT.

MANUSCRIPT: NYPL–Berg ADDRESS: Hon. G. C. Verplanck / Member of Congress / Washington D. C. POSTMARK: NEW-YORK / MAR / 6 DOCKETED: W. C. Bryant.

1. Verplanck's letter is unrecovered. Neither Mr. Sarchet nor Bryant's report of Verplanck's speech has been identified.

2. The English-born artist William James Bennett (1787–1844), an early member of the National Academy, furnished two pictures for *The American Landscape*. These were "Weehawken," facing p. [7], and "Falls of the Sawkill," facing p. [14]. Both were engraved by Durand.

3. "Delaware Water-Gap. Drawn and engraved by A. B. Durand," *ibid.*, facing p. [13].

4. "Fort Putnam. Painted by Robt. W. Weir. Etched by J. Smillie, finished by A. B. Durand," *ibid.*, facing p. [11].

5. Here Bryant drew a box about 5½″ by 6½″, with the comment, "Some of the Plates—perhaps they are a little longer."

216. *To* Richard H. Dana

New York   April 17   1830.

My dear Sir.

I am writing this to send by Prof. Channing of whom I have un-luckily seen less during his visit to the city than I could desire. From him and Mrs. Channing I learn that you are still a sufferer occasionally from the disorder your old enemy particularly during damp weather. If we had you here in New York I think one of our long hot summers might sweat a little of the rheumatism out of you. To the climate I believe it is owing that I have got rid of some unpleasant symptoms of a tendency to pul-monary complaints, that I once had.

I should have written to you on the receipt of your poem delivered at Andover, but having said what I thought of it in the newspaper it did not occur to me that I ought in some manner to let you know that I had received it.[1] I did not think it equal to the second long poem in your previous volume,[2] but I liked it, it was characteristic, original in diction and thought, and contained matter enough to have furnished a common writer with his poetical stock for life. You talk of laying by your pen. Why should you do so? You have gained nothing yet but praise—you answer— But this is as much as could be expected to be gained by a first attempt. I do not take your last publication into account, for that was a pamphlet and nobody ever makes any thing by pamphlets. A work in-tended to have a steady sale and to interest beyond the present moment should be printed in such a shape that it can stand upon a shelf with other good books. What acknowledged standard in classical work is printed in the pamphlet form? If you ever print again make a volume. You have gained a reputation, the tide of taste has taken a surprising turn in your favour, and now you must take advantage of it to obtain some-thing more solid. —Not that I believe that poetry can be to any great ex-tent a money-making business here under any circumstances—though if I had nothing else to do I believe I should print in the expectation of realizing some profit—small indeed—but better than nothing.

I shall not apply for the commission you talk of.[3] Half if not two thirds of the old General's cabinet are *old federalists*, and they have concluded not to hang the Hartford Convention men this year. Besides some of the principal diplomatic and other appointments have been made from the federal party, and I am afraid they are all likely to escape the reward of their political sins. The other job you mention, that of writing a long poem, I have not undertaken yet, and though I sometimes think of it I doubt whether I ever shall. The great difficulty is to know what it shall be about. Hillhouse disclaims having any thing to do with a great poem.

I do not know that there is any thing doing here at present the history of which would interest you, except that an exhibition of fine old pictures has been opened of which Mr. Channing will tell you. The great city keeps on growing a little every year, and filling up with adventurers from all lands. Here is no literary circle to give the law of taste as in your neighborhood. This is a comfortable thing, but then on the other hand nobody cares any thing for literature here; and the man of genius is the man who has made himself rich.

My regards to your brother and sisters and to Mr. Allston and to Mr. Phillips if you should ever get beyond the nod you give him now and then. He is as bad a correspondent as I and there is an old debt of a letter from him of four years standing or more.

Yrs truly
W. C. Bryant

MANUSCRIPT: NYPL–GR ADDRESS: Richard H. Dana Esq. / Cambridge / Mass. / fav. of Prof. Channing DOCKETED: From / Wm. C. Bryant / Ap. 17, 1830.

1. Bryant's notice of Dana's "Thoughts on the Soul" has not been recovered.
2. Probably "The Changes of Home," in *The Buccaneer, and Other Poems* (1827).
3. In an unrecovered letter of uncertain date, Dana had apparently urged Bryant to seek an appointment from the Jackson administration.

217. *To* Gulian C. Verplanck

New York   April 22   1830

Dear Sir

I find the following in Walsh's paper of yesterday.[1]

This was taken from the New York American of *Tuesday* where it appeared with the same heading which it has in the above. In copying it however Mr. Walsh omitted the following part which immediately follows in the same paragraph— "We have also been amused with some of the references such as 'Acts of Faith, see Inquisition' 'Actors see Actresses' &c. The volume extends from the letter A. to the word 'battle,' and is altogether a well-executed design and replete with information judiciously compressed. Such biographical sketches as it contains (Joel Barlow for example) are well done and add much to the value of the work for English readers."

The American very honestly took the whole but Mr. Walsh was so modest that he could not bear to republish the particular eulogium bestowed upon *his article* on the life of Joel Barlow among the "original articles furnished by the accomplished Robert Walsh jr." I have looked at the preface by Lieber.[2] It is positive as to the articles of American biography being all signed and written by Mr. W. I think that I cannot do less than reprint the article from the Literary Gazette, accompanied with a statement of the facts respecting the Barlow article! I will send the paper containing what I shall say to Lieber.[3]

> Yrs truly
> W C BRYANT

MANUSCRIPT: NYPL–Berg ADDRESS: Hon. G. C. Verplanck / Member of Congress / Washington / D. C. POSTMARK: NEW YORK / APR / 22 POSTAL ANNOTATION: FREE DOCKETED: W. C. Bryant.

1. Here Bryant attached a clipping, reading as follows:

"*The Encyclopedia Americana*, now in the course of publication by Messrs. Carey, Lea & Carey, of Philadelphia, is thus spoken of in the London Literary Gazette:

" 'This is the beginning of an important and laudable undertaking; and such as, if skilfully and industriously conducted to an end, of which the volume before us gives fair promise, is likely to redound to the credit of American literature. A popular dictionary founded on the German Conversations-Lexicon, and consequently embracing all the latest knowledge of Europe, and containing also a copious collection of original articles in American biography, and other American topics, must recommend itself to notice and favour. It is a curious circumstance, that in order to make room for more valuable matter the editor has altogether omitted heraldry, as a subject of no consequence in the eyes of so new a nation as the United States; this is rather characteristic.' "

Robert Walsh edited the Philadelphia *National Gazette*.

2. Francis Lieber (1800–1872), a German liberal who came to the United States in 1827 after political imprisonment in his own country, edited the *Encyclopedia Americana* in thirteen volumes (Philadelphia, 1829–1833). Thereafter he taught history and political philosophy at South Carolina College (1835–1856) and at Columbia College (1857–1872).

3. See Letter 218. Bryant's article has not been located in the *EP*

218. *To* Gulian C. Verplanck

New York   May 21   1830.

Dear Sir

I wrote you a day or two since an awkward letter about Mr. Dodge, which I did at the urgent request of Mr. White the younger who was anxious that something should be said to you on the subject of his father-in-law's application. Of course I know nothing about him except what his recommendations say, and you will know more about him when you see them than I do, since you are better acquainted with the persons who signed them.[1]

Mr. Walsh as you have doubtless seen, gives a very lame explanation of his conduct in stealing your life of Joel Barlow.[2] He did not notice what I said until more than a week after it appeared notwithstanding the Philadelphia Inquirer endeavored to call him out by hoping that I did not mean to accuse Mr. Walsh of plagiarism. I sent the Evening Post containing my article, immediately to Wigglesworth one of the editors of the *Encyclopedia Americana* whom I know. It is possible that some communication between him and Walsh occasioned the article in the National Gazette. It appears after all that the life of Barlow was imposed upon the editors of the Encyclop Am   as original and that Mr. Walsh's conduct was nothing better than downright theft. The most amusing part of his apology is the passage where he intimates that when he sent the article to Boston he had forgotten that he did not write it himself. Scarcely less curious however is the part where he infers that as the biographer cannot make lives he has a right to steal lives written by other men.

Of Mr. Herbert whom you still speak with so much affection I have nothing good to tell you. I am I must confess a little inclined to think that the old gentleman had better give up publishing any more for the present. To write three thick volumes, and get little cash and less circulation, is not certainly very encouraging.

There is talk of establishing an evening paper here to support the cause of the Tammany Society. The editor is to be Mr. Hagedorn of the Newark Intelligencer. You may have seen his prospectus or advertisement.—

Yrs truly

W. C. BRYANT

MANUSCRIPT: NYPL–Berg ADDRESS: Hon. G. C. Verplanck / Member of Congress / Washington / D. C. POSTMARK: NEW-YORK / MAY / 21 POSTAL ANNOTATION: FREE DOCKETED: W. C. Bryant.

1. Bryant's earlier letter is unrecovered. Perhaps Mr. Dodge was David Low Dodge (1774–1852), a New York dry-goods merchant and founder, in 1815, of the New York Peace Society. White is unidentified.

2. Verplanck had published a "Sketch of the Life and Writings of Joel Barlow" in the *Analectic Magazine*, 4 (August 1814), 130–158. See July, *Essential New Yorker*, p. 291.

219. *To* Thomas Cole[1]

New York   June 15   1830.

My dear Sir,

I take the liberty, I hope it is no improper one, of introducing to your acquaintance Mr. William Cox of this city, the bearer of this letter, a gentleman of talent and merits. He has been for some time past connected with the New York Mirror in which his articles under the signature of C. have attracted much attention. An arrangement has been made by which he is henceforth to devote his whole time to that publication, and during his absence in Europe will write for it in the character of a foreign correspondent. He is desirous of the acquaintance of some American painter in England, and it has struck me that you might enable him to make his communications to the Mirror serviceable to the cause of the Fine Arts in this country.[2]

I am Sir
With the greatest respect and esteem
Your obt. Servt
WILLIAM C. BRYANT

MANUSCRIPT: New York State Library ADDRESS: Thomas Cole Esq.

1. This is Bryant's earliest known letter to Thomas Cole (1801–1848), with whom he became acquainted soon after moving to New York. Cole had left his native England at eighteen, and after study at the Pennsylvania Academy of the Fine Arts and several years as a wood-engraver and itinerant portrait-painter in Ohio, had come to New York in 1825. A founder of the National Academy in 1826 and a contributor to *The Talisman*, Cole had become an intimate of Bryant's by the time he left in June 1829 for three years of study in England and Italy. Bryant marked his departure with a sonnet, "To Cole the Painter on his Departure for Europe," published in *The Talisman* for 1830. See *Poems* (1876), p. 181. By then Cole was the leading landscape-painter in what would later become known as the Hudson River School. See Gardner and Feld, *American Paintings* I, pp. 223–224; Bryant II, "Poetry and Painting," pp. 860–861, 874–882; Merritt, *Thomas Cole*, pp. 12–14.

2. William Cox (1805?–1847), like Cole, was an Englishman who had seen much of America before coming to New York in 1825. In 1827, a printer in Jonathan Seymour's shop on John Street, he set type for the first *Talisman* volume, meanwhile composing a notice of the gift-book which, when published in the *New-York Mirror*, greatly pleased the authors. For several years thereafter Cox's literary and dramatic criticisms and familiar essays in the *Mirror* were widely admired. After his return to England he continued to write for that magazine, as well as for several British periodicals and the American *Atlantic Club-Book*. His *Mirror* articles were collected in two volumes as *Crayon Sketches* (New York, 1833), and reprinted in London and Edinburgh. From 1840 until his death Cox edited the *Bristol Mercury* in England. See *Prose*, I, 413; Taft, *Minor Knickerbockers*, pp. 266–267; John Paul Pritchard, *Literary Wise Men of Gotham: Criticism in New York, 1815–1860* ([Baton Rouge] Louisiana State University Press [1963]), pp. 124, 174–175.

220. *To* Cyrus Bryant

New York   Dec   3, 1830.

Dear Brother.

Not long since I received a letter from you by some unknown hand. It purported to have been sent to Hartford by Mr. Ford, but who brought it to the office I was not able to learn, nor where he was to be found. I presume however it was Mr. Ford, and that he either was going immediately out of town, or did not care to be incommoded by taking back any parcel.[1] I had Dr. Meade's books[2] by me for the Cummington Lyceum,[3] which I should have asked him to carry if I had seen him. I spoke to Verplanck about his books the other day—he said he had no copies—such of them as were not out of print being the property of the booksellers. As to Dr. Ackerly,[4] of whom you ask, it is possible that you may get something of him by writing—some of the works he has republished are good things *per se* though he is but a poor creature himself.

I have no letters for Peter from old Munn yet— He is a queer sort of being. He made the offer of furnishing the letters, and professed himself exceedingly desirous to do it—but though Peter's name and place of residence in Illinois were sent to him some time since, he has done nothing about the matter. I will write him a note.[5]

Miss Robbins called yesterday, to enquire whether I had heard any thing from Cummington and to express her anxiety on Edward Harte's account, having heard nothing from him or from the family, though she had written two or three times desiring that he might be sent to New York, and requesting that her letters might be answered. The place at Lockwood's for which he is destined has been kept vacant for him for two or three months and unless he comes down within a fortnight he will probably lose it, as she says. I hope therefore that you and the rest of the family will set your wits to work and contrive a plan for getting him down without delay. You have no idea how much good you will do by it.[6]

We are going to keep house. I have hired a House in Broome Street No. 571, and tomorrow we move into it.[7]

My wife desires her love to yourself and the family— We are all well—

Yrs affectionately
W. C. BRYANT

MANUSCRIPT: BCHS.

1. Probably Andrew Ford, Jr., or Elijah Ford, of Cummington.

2. Dr. Meade is unidentified.

3. In 1829–1830 Cyrus Bryant organized and acted as corresponding secretary of the Cummington Lyceum. See Cyrus Bryant to Timothy Pitkin, June 8, 1830, HEHL; "Letters addressed to the Cummington Lyceum Commenced A. D. 1829," MS notebook, NYPL–BFP.

4. Probably Samuel Akerly (1785–1845, Columbia 1804), brother-in-law of Dr. Samuel Latham Mitchill, and author of many articles and books on medical and scientific subjects. Drake, *Dictionary of American Biography*, p. 11.

5. Failing of employment in New York, Peter Rush Bryant emigrated to Illinois that autumn, reaching Jacksonville the day after this letter was written. Peter to Austin Bryant, December 30, 1830, BCHS. Munn is unidentified.

6. Earlier that year Eliza Robbins had put her nephew Edward Harte in the care of Austin Bryant, to learn farm work while attending the Cummington Academy. Eliza Robbins to Cyrus Bryant, May, n. d., 1830, NYPL–BFP. Edward had perhaps been promised a clerkship in the office of Ralph Ingersoll Lockwood (1798–1858?), a New York equity lawyer who also published novels. See Wright, *American Fiction 1774–1850*, p. 182.

7. This was between Hudson and Varick Streets, in an area now largely displaced by the approaches to the Holland Tunnel.

221. *To* Mrs. Sarah S. Bryant

New York   March 14, 1831.

Dear Mother,

I should have written earlier, but that I expected from one day to another to be able to give you news of the river's being open. It is several days since a steamboat went to Newburgh, and last evening one was advertised to start for Albany. Whether the river is open the whole distance to Albany or not, I cannot tell, but I doubt not that it will be, before you receive this letter. I hope therefore that as soon as you get it you will make immediate arrangements for coming down. If one of your boys has a fancy for visiting New York I will pay his expenses down. I think it will be almost as cheap as for me to go to Albany for you, and you being unused to the North River will want somebody to escort you. If either of them is willing to come you need not be at the trouble to write me fixing a day; but I think you should nevertheless set out without delay. Whoever comes should bring a trunk big enough to carry back the bundle of cloth left here by Miss Robbins, together with Faraday's book on Chemical Manipulations,[1] and some publications left by Dr. Akerly for the Cummington Lyceum. If however nobody will come down with you let me know immediately what day you will be at Albany and how you will come out. If you are brought out in a waggon, I will take up Miss Robbins's bundle, and will also deliver to the person who brings you out the money from her for Austin, but if you come out alone I will mail it at Albany. Tell Cyrus that I have written to Lieut. Waite on his account and on the 11th received the following answer   "In answer to your letter of the 7th I have to say that I am at this moment entirely uninformed of the contractors views in relation to future operations and consequently I cannot say whether it will be in my power to give your brother a situation. Should the business go on as I presume it will 15 or 20 persons will be wanted. If however your brother is in good business at present, I would not advise him to leave it, as it is a matter of some uncertainty whether I shall be able to grant his request."[2] I enclose you twenty dollars. It is now my wifes turn—perhaps I shall add a postscript—

Your affectionate son.

W. C. BRYANT.

[by Frances Bryant]
Dear Mother

By the time you receive this, probably the river will be open, and I hope you are ready to come. The traveling *to Albany* will be much better now, than when it gets to be muddy and the Boat you will find very comfortable. There will be no racing now, which might give you anxiety, neither will the boat be crowded with passengers. I would recommend it to you, to put into your Basket a night-gown, Cap, Needle, Thread, Thimble, Pins, and a little luncheon; for in none of the boats are trunks allowed in the cabin, and in most of them they refuse to let a Band-box be carried in. If you come in a Night-boat, ask the Chambermaid soon after you get on board, which berth you shall take, and there put your cloak, shawl, Basket, or any thing else—you must keep a little watch of them. At one end of the cabin you will see two doors, one opens into a place where you will find a wash-bowl, Towel, Looking-glass &c. The other into a *privy*. If you want drink or any thing else, ask the Chambermaid for it. I should not be so particular in giving you information, did I not know how awkward one feels in a strange place. If you are in a day-boat, choose a berth for yourself, and lay down your things. Lie down yourself when you please. When the meals are ready, go with the rest; and take care of yourself, ask for any thing you see on the Table that you may like. You need not give yourself any uneasiness about your Trunks if you see them put into the Baggage-room at Albany, they will be safe until you get to New York, but when you arrive you must begin to look out for them, for the baggage is then taken out, and every body is then to keep watch of the trunks &c. When you get here, have the baggage put into a Coach, get in yourselves and tell the coachman to drive to 571 Broome Street. I think you will want your Hood and blue silk shawl. If perfectly convenient and agreeable to you, I should like to have you bring me an old flannel Sheet, for an ironing sheet, also a few old rags for dishcloths.

We have thought it would save you a good deal of anxiety to have some one start to come down with you. I know how uneasy one feels in such a situation, on account of the weather, accidents misunderstandings &c. And as William offers to pay the expense of some one of your boys to accompany you, I hope you will take your choice and make them come with you. I dont think of any thing more—so I will leave the rest of the sheet for W^m to write to John— Tell Adeline and Louisa I want to see them very much; I have a great deal to say to them.—[3]

Yours affectionately
F. B.—

[by Cullen Bryant]

P. S. With respect to the expense of the two different routes to Illinois I am doubtful whether there is much difference. Mr. Leggett says that one might go from here to Shawneetown very comfortably for forty dollars;[4] the conveyance from here to Baltimore is rapid and cheap—the expenses on the road would not be more than nine dollars—thence by the way of Pittsburg to Wheeling say $12—thence down the river in a Steamboat to Shawneetown say $9. —But probably he would not go quite down to Shawneetown—stopping at Cincinnati and striking overland to the westward. How this is I do not know and am not able to learn. As to John's going on with a party from Massachusetts I question very much whether he would gain any thing by it. If he is going to settle there he had better not trammel himself with any connections of the sort but settle where he can find the best situation. If he should come this way with you he might take the money of Miss Robbins as he went along.[5] He will find the waters all open, and the roads will be settled by the time he gets down. But if he waits for the [Erie] canal to open he must delay his journey for several weeks yet. I do not say this because I would have you wait for John in case he should conclude on going this way. On the contrary I hope you will not, for if you are late it will spoil your visit and Frances by what I can learn intends to leave the city early.[6]

W. C. B.

A steam-boat went up to Poughkeepsie on Saturday and returned yesterday. The ice is cracking and the water rising every where in the neighborhood of Hudson, Albany and Troy.

MANUSCRIPT: BCHS ADDRESS: Mrs. Sarah S. Bryant / Cummington / Mass. POSTMARK: NEW-YORK / MAR / [14] POSTAL ANNOTATION: PAID 37½ / double-paid.

1. Michael Faraday, *Chemical Manipulations* (London, 1827).

2. Probably Carlos A. Waite (1800–1866), then a first lieutenant in the United States Army, who later distinguished himself in the war with Mexico, retiring in 1865 as a brigadier general. William H. Powell, *List of Officers of the Army of the United States from 1779 to 1900* (New York: Hamersley, 1900), p. 650. Since neither Bryant's letter of inquiry nor Waite's reply has been recovered, it is uncertain what employment Cullen was trying to secure for his brother—perhaps on War Department construction in the West.

3. Adeline Plummer Bryant, Austin's wife, and Charity Louisa, Cullen's sister.

4. William Leggett had lived as a youth in the village of Edwardsville, Illinois. Shawneetown was not far above that place on the Ohio River. Proctor, "Leggett," p. 241. John Howard Bryant, Cullen's youngest brother, was planning to join his next older brother Peter Rush as a homesteader on the prairie at Jacksonville, in west-central Illinois. Cullen mistakenly wrote "Legget," and "Shauneetown."

5. In late March John brought his mother to New York City, from which he left on April 18 for Illinois by way of the Hudson River, the Erie Canal, and overland, reaching Jacksonville about May 23. Brown, *John Howard Bryant*, p. 17.

6. During Sarah Bryant's visit Cullen and his family moved from Broome Street to rooms at Fourth Street and Broadway. On June 1 Frances and Fanny returned with her to the Cummington homestead, where Frances gave birth to her second daughter, Julia Sands Bryant, on June 29. Frances Bryant, "Autobiographical Sketch," NYPL–GR.

222. *To* the Readers of the EVENING POST[1]

New York, April 21, 1831.

It is with the greatest reluctance that I obtrude anything relating to my personal concerns on the public. I observe, however, in last evening's *Commercial*, a false account under the signature of William L. Stone, of an affair between myself and him, which took place yesterday. Lest my silence might be construed into an admission of its truth, I have thought it my duty to present to the public a correct statement of the transaction, beginning with the provocation out of which it arose.

A few days after the late dinner given in this city to the Hon. Tristam Burges,[2] an article appeared in the Evening Post in which that festivity was made the subject of some harmless pleasantry, founded on an allusion to the story of the quarrel between the painter Hogarth and the Freemasons.[3] The town did this paper the honour to be amused with the article, and some of the persons who were at the dinner were good humoured enough to join in the laugh. The Commercial, however, answered in an angry paragraph, in which the following toast was inserted,

"The Evening Post, and the Courier and Enquirer.
—Stupidity and Vulgarity."

This toast the Commercial commended for its propriety and justice, and affirmed that it was drunk with cheers and great applause at the Burges dinner. As William L. Stone, the conductor of the Commercial, was one of the committee of arrangements, and as the toast appeared in his paper, in an editorial article, without a name, it was natural to suppose it his own. —No notice was, however, taken of the toast until a day or two after we received a communication from a person styling himself a *Looker On*, affirming Stone to be its author.[4] It was then mentioned in the Evening Post that a correspondent had informed us that the toast was manufactured by Stone. It was natural to suppose that he would be gratified with being thought the father of a toast he commended so highly, instead of which however he, on the next day, addressed an insolent note to the proprietors of this paper, demanding the name of our correspondent. I was not in the office when it came; but one of the proprietors, rightly judging that it deserved no other answer, sent him the communication mentioned in our paper the day previous. On the same day, which was the 12th instant, there appeared in the Commercial an article, of which we publish the material part below. It contains the note from Stone to which we have alluded, and the article in the Evening Post which called forth that article.

" 'New York, April 12

To Messrs. Michael Burnham & Co.

Much to my surprise, I find the following paragraph in your paper of last evening:

"A correspondent informs us that the toast given at the Burges dinner and published in the Commercial about ten days afterward, respecting the Evening Post and the Courier and Enquirer was given by COL. WM. L. STONE. That the public may see what kind of toasts this person is in the habit of giving on such occasions we publish it. 'The Evening Post, and the Courier and Enquirer—Stupidity and Vulgarity.' "

This statement is utterly and in all respects untrue—May I therefore request the name of the correspondent who has palmed the falsehood upon you, or am I to understand that you adopt it as your own? I am, &c.

WILLIAM L. STONE.

N. B. I shall wait until 11 o'clock for a reply.'

A note, of which the foregoing was a copy, was early this morning addressed to the New York Evening Post. No answer has been received, but instead thereof, a dirty anonymous scrawl, which seems to have been the only authority for the FALSEHOOD thus editorially endorsed by the Evening Post. The Editors of that paper are understood to be William C. Bryant and a young man by the name of Leggett.

"So much for that part of the subject. It is now proper to repeat that such a toast was given at the dinner referred to, with the addition of the commentary *par nobile fratrum* [a perfect pair]. By whom it was given, or by whom written, we know not. But its truth and propriety were so manifest that it was drunk with universal applause."

The tenor of this article, as well as that of the note, were grossly insulting to the persons mentioned in it. —It was not thought, however, worthy of any other notice than an article in which the reasons for thinking the toast to be Stone's were recapitulated—namely, its appearing in an editorial of his—its being asserted to be his by a correspondent—the flimsy pretence of Stone, that he did not know who gave it or wrote it—and lastly, Stone's own denial.[5] Two or three days afterwards the following paragraph appeared in the Commercial, intended professedly as an interpretation of the article of the 12th inst., already quoted:

"After having refuted the calumny of the Evening Post in regard to the authorship of a certain toast, the truth of which seems to have cut the conductors of that paper to the quick—giving the charge a solemn denial under our own signature, and leaving the brand of a significant word spelt with four letters, which it would outrage public ears polite to repeat, to blister upon the forehead of William C. Bryant, if a blister can be raised on brass, we must confess we are not prepared to see a repetition of the base slander copied in the Albany Argus."[6]

In this paragraph it will be seen that Stone, alluding to his article of the 12th instant, boasts that in that he had bestowed upon me by name, the most insulting epithet that can be applied to a human being—an epithet never before, to my knowledge, connected with my name. I was also, in this paragraph, malignantly singled out by him from several conductors of the paper, equally responsible with myself for what appears in its columns, probably because he relied upon my known dislike of violence and of notoriety to escape punishment. The article was published in the Commercial on Saturday last. I did not see it until Monday, when the question became what course I ought to pursue on the occasion. On the one hand, it occurred to me that no glory was to be gained from personal contests between editors—and least of all from one with the individual in question—that scenes of violence were in the highest degree alien to my tastes, & that to have engaged in them, was productive of the most unpleasant kind of notoriety. On the other hand, the most outrageous possible insult had been offered me, and if I submitted to it would probably be soon repeated.

The latter consideration determined me to inflict upon him personal chastisement for a personal outrage, approaching him fairly and giving him ample opportunity to stand on his defence. This I effected as soon as I fell in with him, which was done on Wednesday morning. In what manner it was done I prefer should be related by an eyewitness. . . .[7]

In conclusion, I feel that I owe an apology to society for having, in this instance, taken the law into my own hands. The outrage was one for which the law affords no redress.

WILLIAM C. BRYANT.

MANUSCRIPT: Unrecovered TEXT: *EP*, April 21, 1831.

1. The clash with editor Stone of the *Commercial Advertiser* discussed in this letter was ignored by Godwin and most later biographers, yet it had a profoundly chastening influence on Bryant's subsequent editorial behavior. It suggested, too, the theme of his last and best short story, "Medfield," published in *Tales of Glauber-Spa* (New York, 1832), I, 243–276, but omitted by Godwin from Bryant's *Prose Writings*. See Bryant II, "The Middle Years," pp. 193–194.

2. Tristam Burges (1770–1853, Brown 1796) was an anti-Jackson, high tariff congressman from Rhode Island. *BDAC*.

3. In the *EP* of April 3 Bryant had spoofed this testimonial, which was given soon after a more elaborate one to Daniel Webster in the same room. The later affair, he remarked, being "more rhetorical, metaphorical, allegorical and ornithological, more discursive, vituperative and restrictive, . . . enabled the Clay 'Humdragons' completely to eclipse the glory of the more sober, respectable and worshipful portion of their party." The allusion to William Hogarth's demoralization of a parade of London Masons by trailing them with a swarm of chimney sweeps and other "humdragons," which Bryant was careful to explain, delighted the Democrats, but goaded Stone into hinting at his authorship of the toast quoted below.

4. The question of authorship took an ironic turn long afterward, when Stone's son attributed the offensive paragraph of April 16 (see Note 6) to Bryant's close friend Robert Sands, Stone's editorial assistant, who died the year after it was written. W. L. Stone, Jr. to Bryant, December 9, 1865, NYPL–GR. Bryant's reaction was natural: "The filial piety which induces you to exonerate your father from the share which I supposed he took in [our quarrel] does you honor but I am exceedingly pained to learn that it is to be ascribed to *Sands*, from whom, considering the friendly and intimate footing on which we stood I could not have expected it. I must, however, accept your account of the matter which although I hoped I had got rid of any rancor left on my mind by the affair, makes me think more kindly of your father." Draft letter, December 13, 1865, NYPL–GR. It is not, in fact, wholly unlikely that Sands's "excessive and unrestrained exuberance," which had once led him to insert in the *NYR* an irreverent essay for which editors Bryant and Anderson had to apologize, touched off the quarrel between the rival editors as a practical joke. If so, the remarks which brought the combatants to blows were, on each side, written by their assistants

(see Note 5). See *NYR*, 2 (March 1826), 324; Bryant, "Memoir of Robert Sands," *Knickerbocker*, 1 (January 1833), 55.

5. The article here cited, which appeared in the *EP* for April 13, suggests in its style Leggett's bluntness, rather than Bryant's deft irony. In it the *EP* rejected the "denial of Wm. L. Stone, himself, whose character is such that his denial of a fact affords the strongest presumption of its truth."

6. *Commercial Advertiser*, April 16. As the official organ of the Albany Regency, the Albany *Argus* was, like the *EP*, strongly Democratic and an arch-opponent of Stone's anti-Jackson paper.

7. Here follows Leggett's statement that Bryant met Stone on Broadway opposite the American Hotel; that Bryant carried a whip and Stone a sword cane; that the two attacked each other at about the same moment; and that Bryant appeared to get the better of his opponent. A contradictory version was recorded by Philip Hone, conservative ex-mayor, in his diary entry for April 20: "While I was shaving this morning at eight o'clock I witnessed from the front windows an encounter in the street nearly opposite between William C. Bryant, one of the editors of the *Evening Post*, and William L. Stone, editor of the *Commercial Advertiser*. The former commenced the attack by striking Stone over the head with a cow-skin; after a few blows the parties closed and the whip was wrested from Bryant and carried off by Stone. When I saw them first, two younger persons were engaged, but soon discontinued their fight. A crowd soon closed in and separated the combatants." Hone, *Diary*, I, 40. It has been suggested that the two younger persons involved were Leggett and Stone's brother-in-law. *New York Dissected, By Walt Whitman*, edd. Emory Halloway and Ralph Adimari (New York: R. R. Wilson, 1936), pp. 235–236.

VI

Journalist, Poet, Traveler
1831–1834
(LETTERS 223 TO 287)

DURING HIS EARLY YEARS IN NEW YORK, Bryant's income from editorial work barely supported his little family. But between 1829 and 1832 *Evening Post* profits increased steadily, and as Bryant's share of the paper's ownership doubled, from an eighth part to a quarter, his income was nearly trebled. The security thus provided led him to undertake several projects which promised greater satisfactions than he found in "drudging," as he termed it, for the *Post*.

First among his projects was one to gather in a single volume about ninety poems he had published during the past fourteen years, all but eight in ephemeral magazines and gift-books. He could only have been heartened, while preparing this collection at the close of 1831, by the comments of several critics, particularly a dictum in the *New-England Magazine* that Bryant stood "by common consent at the head of the list of American poets," and another in the New York *American* that "Mr. Bryant stands forth the first living poet in the language."

His *Poems* appeared in New York at the outset of 1832, in an edition of a thousand copies, half of which were sold within four months. Their early success encouraged the poet to approach Washington Irving, then living in England and at the height of his popularity, for help in securing a British publisher. Irving's sponsorship of the book, for which he wrote a generous preface, brought it cordial notices in several leading British periodicals. At home, the *North American Review* called Bryant's the "best volume of American poetry that has yet appeared." Such praise prompted Bryant, within two years, to bring out another edition to which only a handful of poems were added.

Never having seen more of his country than lower New England and the Hudson River valley, Bryant took his first trip southward in January 1832. During a ten-day visit in Washington under the guidance of Congressmen Cambreleng and Verplanck, he was entertained by cabinet members, heard remarks in the Senate by Clay, Hayne, and Webster, and in the House by John Quincy Adams and Edward Everett, and called on Andrew Jackson at the White House. In May he set out for Illinois to see his brother John, recently settled at Jacksonville. Traveling overland by stagecoach to the Ohio, and down that river and up the Mississippi and the Illinois by steamboat, he explored the prairie on horseback with John. Before turning back eastward, he bought Illinois land, in the half-formulated thought that he might one day move to the West. The following summer he and Frances traveled for the first time through northern New England, and visited Montreal and Quebec during a month's journey.

Before visiting Illinois Bryant had moved his family—enlarged the summer before by the birth of a second daughter, Julia—across the Hudson to

Hoboken, where he rented a roomy, comfortable house next door to the family of his friend Robert Sands. Here, except for the winter months of 1833–1834 when they boarded in Manhattan, the Bryants lived a quiet suburban life for two years, while Cullen commuted to the city by ferry and his family escaped the cholera epidemic which invaded New York in the summer of 1832. Intimacy with the Sands family and their friends brought the Bryants pleasant relief from the city's dirt and heat, but this was sadly interrupted in December 1832 by the sudden death of Robert Sands from apoplexy. Soon afterward Cullen prepared, with some help from its nominal editor, Verplanck, an edition of his friend's writings designed to benefit Sands's widowed mother and unmarried sister Julia.

With his newspaper's growing prosperity, Cullen could give financial help to his three younger brothers in Illinois, and could pay off for his mother some long-standing debts at Cummington. More leisure allowed him to renew a neglected correspondence with Richard Dana, and to exchange with him critical comments on their projected publications. Help for other friends, such as his successful nomination of Robert Weir to the War Department for the position of drawing instructor at West Point, occupied him frequently.

Toward the end of 1833 Bryant was becoming impatient to carry out a cherished plan to leave the *Evening Post* in the able hands of William Leggett, while he took his family for an extended visit to Europe. There, he thought, he might return to the composition of poetry and to the study of foreign languages, important as well in his children's education, while acting at the same time as the *Post*'s European correspondent. But on the eve of his planned departure in the spring of 1834 Bryant ran into unexpected obstacles. William Coleman's widow, to whom Bryant and Leggett had mortgaged the *Evening Post* property in return for her share of the paper's profits, suddenly demanded a two-thousand-dollar payment on principal before Bryant should leave the country. His spare money already shrunken by his recent purchase of an additional share from another stockholder, Bryant was further shocked at the withdrawal by Secretary of State McLane of a promised appointment as diplomatic courier which would have paid at least for his own ocean journey. He addressed an unhappy letter of protest to President Jackson, whose policies he had supported in the *Post* for five years, expressing disbelief that an administration which he had thought to be governed by a "strict sense of right" should make him the victim of such a "trivial" evasion. Hearing nothing in reply, however, Bryant adopted the expedients of serving as companion on his journey to Italy of the son of a New York merchant of his acquaintance, and of contracting with the editor of the *New-York Mirror* to send his magazine exclusive poetic contributions from Europe.

At the last moment, Bryant managed to meet Mrs. Coleman's demand by securing a bond from Michael Burnham, former business manager of the *Evening Post,* though only by pledging payment within a year of one thousand dollars on this new debt. Consequently, free at last from the "power of these people who want to hamper my movements," as he described them to his brother Cyrus, Cullen Bryant sailed with his family on June 24, 1834, on the packet boat *Poland* bound from New York to Le Havre, for an indefinite residence in Europe.

223. *To* John Howard Bryant

New York June 25 1831

Dear Brother

  I got yours of the 29th of May mailed the next day, on the 20th of this month just three weeks after it was sent.[1] I enclose you one half of a hundred dollar bill of the United States Bank in this city. You or Rush should early acknowledge receipt of it. Since you ask me what I think about the Michigan expedition I will be so frank as to tell you that although there are some arguments in its favour yet in other respects I am not greatly pleased with it.[2] In the first place you gain nothing in point of climate. You [are][3] still as far north as Cummington, and will be [pre]-vented by the latitude from raising many of the most [des]irable fruits and plants. It is possible that the winters may be somewhat milder, at least when the lakes are not full of ice—but in other seasons the effect of the proximity of the lakes must be to chill the atmosphere and to fill it with fogs. Besides the lake winds are no very comfortable things. Flint speaks often of the bleak and desolating gales from the lakes.[4] Then if timber is [plentiful] there is the labour of cutting it down and the un-healthiness consequent upon letting the sun into a new country. Is there [several words clipped] [In]diana or any other place not so [several words clipped] far north as Michigan where there is an opportunity to procure new lands? As to the want of timber where you are, is there no proba-bility that the facilities for transporting lumber will be soon greater—or may not houses be built of brick—a better material—and is there not some prospect of an improvement in the market? Almost [all] new coun-tries find a difficulty at first in sending their produce to market. I men-tion these things for your consideration. The climate I think the greatest objection to Michigan. In a description of the Huron territory the other day which I copied I saw it mentioned as a recommendation that it was removed from the influence of the air of the La[kes]. As to the young women—if they care any thing for a young man they will go with him to the world's end—[if] not they should be left at home.

  My mother and wife and daughter left here more than three weeks since for Cummington. Mother had entirely recovered from her cold and was remarkably well.

  You may of [cour]se expect to hear from me again. I shall go n[ext month?] I think into the country.

      [complimentary close and signature clipped]

MANUSCRIPT: NYPL–BFP ADDRESS: Mr. John H. Bryant / Jacksonville / Illinois POST-MARK: NEW-YORK / JUN / 25 POSTAL ANNOTATION: PAID [2]0.

  1. Letter unrecovered.

  2. John was apparently then thinking of moving on from Illinois to Michigan, to which his brother Cyrus emigrated briefly the following autumn before joining John and Peter Rush Bryant at Jacksonville, Illinois, in the summer of 1832.

3. Manuscript damaged here and elsewhere.

4. Timothy Flint, *A Condensed Geography and History of the Western States, or the Mississippi Valley* (1828).

224. *To* Frances F. Bryant

New York, Aug 21, 1831—

My dear Frances

I begin my letter today expecting to finish it tomorrow *after getting the letter you will have sent by* young Mr. Briggs.[1] I am now at Mr. Ware's where I have been ever since last Monday—that is, for these six days past.[2] When I came here I was not precisely well and wanted somebody to make my gruel which in fact has been my diet ever since. My complaint was an obscure febrile attack brought on as my physician tells me by the same causes which produce fever and ague, though differing from that in its symptoms. In the forenoon I am pretty well and go regularly to the office —but in the afternoon I am very uncomfortable, and lie on the bed [a] great part of the time. This afternoon I am considerably better and the doctor who has called on me thinks I shall be perfectly rid of the disorder in a few days. I am convinced that my complaint arose from sleeping in my house before it was properly aired. I have engaged Margaret to go to the house a day or two before you are expected, and give it a thorough airing and in particular to attend to the cellar and cellar kitchen which I mean to have properly scoured and cleaned and sprinkled with chloride of lime.

Be so good as to ask Cyrus what will take out the stain of indelible ink, or nitrate of silver from linen, and write me word in your next.

The weather here has been dreadfully hot for the week past. I did not go to church to day but Mr. Ware told me he had not had so small a congregation this year.

Monday 22 August

I have just got your letter by Mr. Briggs, together with one from Cyrus.[3] Cyrus refers me to you for the news, and your news seems to be pretty scanty. I expected a long letter considering that you had so long to write it in, but am disappointed at finding it so short. I take it for granted you think mine are too long. This shall be shorter.

Cyrus has written to me something about getting him a land agency but I think it very doubtful whether I shall be able to do any such thing.

As to your coming to New York although it is true the heat at present is great, yet September with us is rarely a hot month and I think you would be perfectly safe in coming down about the beginning of September. If you get here by a week from next Saturday—that will be the third of September;—if you wait till the beginning of week after next, you will arrive here about the sixth or seventh of the month. I would not wait longer at all events than the beginning of week after next. You will be guided somewhat by the weather. I shall be glad to see you at the earliest convenient period. —As to the money I let Austin have viz $100—when you come to settle with him you will take some kind of receipt for it— and if there is any thing yet due him I will send it up to him as soon as you arrive and let me know the amount.

Pour mon frère qui a écrit la lettre dont vous faites mention c'est une bête, et je manque d'expressions pour marque[r] mon mépris de sa conduite.[4]

Write me soon and let me know whether I am to expect you the latter part of next week or the beginning of the week following. My love to Fanny & a kiss to the infant—and regards to all.

Yr affectionate husband,
W. C. BRYANT

MANUSCRIPT: BCHS.

1. Probably James L. Briggs, a son of Deacon James W. Briggs (1782–1837?). *Only One Cummington*, p. 243.

2. Bryant passed several weeks, probably between July 19 and August 13, at Cummington after the birth of his second daughter, Julia, on June 29. On August 3 William Ware wrote asking Bryant to share his own home comforts (NYPL–GR), but Bryant went first to the house to which his family had moved on May 1, with the result described later in the letter.

3. Neither letter has been recovered.

4. "As for my brother who wrote the letter you mention, he is a fool, and I lack words to express my contempt for his behaviour." Though this letter is unrecovered, other correspondence during the ensuing year makes it clear that John Bryant felt himself badly used by his brother Peter Rush (who now called himself "Arthur") soon after reaching Illinois. See Sarah to Cyrus Bryant, September 30, 1832; John to Sarah Bryant, n. d. [October 1832?], BCHS.

225. *To* John Howard Bryant

New York, November 21, 1831

I am glad that you are so well pleased with the country, considering that you have become, as I suppose is the case, a landed proprietor; and I have no doubt, from your account, that, if you should choose to leave the place, you will be able to sell again at an advanced price.[1]

As for yourself, I hope you are not in too great a hurry to marry. When you do, I hope you will take the step with wisdom and reflection. Marry a person who has a good mother, who is of a good family that do not meddle with the concerns of their neighbors, and who, along with a proper degree of industry and economy, possesses a love of reading and a desire of knowledge. A mere pot-wrestler will not do for you. You have tastes for study and elegance, and must not link yourself to one who has no sympathies for you in your admiration for what is excellent in literature. A woman, too, whose religious notions are fanatical would be a plague to you. By the way, I suppose you have heard of the great religious excitement which prevailed last winter and spring in the western part of Massachusetts. Four-days' meetings, an expedient for the spread of fanaticism borrowed from the Methodists, were held everywhere, and when I visited Cummington, although the rage was somewhat cooled by the necessity the farmers found of attending to their business, prayer-meetings were held at four o'clock in the morning at the village, and meetings in the day-time twice a week. People would trot about after prayer-meetings for the sake of listening to unprofitable declamations about the metaphysics of the Calvinistic school, who would never stir a step to furnish their minds with any useful knowledge. . . .

I have seen several poetical things by you, some of them very well, in the Jacksonville papers.[2] I must repeat, however, the injunction to study *vigor* and *condensation* in your language and originality in your ideas. Your blank verse might also be improved by greater variety in the pauses. Affairs go on prosperously with me. The "Evening Post" has increased in subscribers within the last year, and I am in hopes by making it better to obtain still more. I shall want them to pay the new debt I have contracted.[3] I intend to visit Washington this winter to look at the old General and his Cabinet. It appears that the *unlucky*, I was going to say, but revoke the word—it appears that the late dissolution of his Cabinet has, instead of diminishing his popularity, made the old gentleman more popular than ever.[4] At the next election he will "walk over the course."

MANUSCRIPT: Unrecovered TEXT *(partial)*: *Life*, I, 280–281.

1. John's letter is unrecovered.
2. These verses are unidentified. Earlier, Cullen had published two of his brother's poems in the *USR*: "My Native Village," 1 (January 1827), 286–287; and "The Traveller's Return," 2 (August 1827), 387–388.
3. Between May 1829 and May 1830 Bryant's share in the *EP* had increased from one-eighth to one-quarter. On November 15, 1831, he incurred a further debt of $2,000, to his friend the tragedian Edwin Forrest, in order to acquire an additional one-twenty-fourth ownership. "*Evening Post* Accounts," NYPL–GR.
4. In the spring of 1831 Jackson had shaken up his initial cabinet, bringing in three of the men Bryant had thought best qualified two years earlier. See 206.5; Van Deusen, *Jacksonian Era*, pp. 45–46.

226. *To* Gulian C. Verplanck

New York, Dec. [*c*10], 1831

My dear Sir.

I have just got a letter from Miss Sedgwick agreeing to contribute to the book. Mr. Sands has seen Paulding who is much pleased with the plan and who is very desirous that the stories should be all *American*. The Harpers will want the manuscript—or a part of it at least—by the first of February.[1]

We do not like the Treasury Report here—or at least that part of it which relates to the tariff. McLane's recommendations are much of a piece with the suggestions of Mr. Clay in the Richmond Whig. McLane is just where he was when he went to England—the majority of the nation I believe is ahead of him. —The story of the American System in his report is absolutely offensive. I give him credit for honesty and frankness—but I do not believe he has thought of the subject for several years past.[2]

Yrs truly
W. C. BRYANT.

MANUSCRIPT: NYPL–Berg ADDRESS: Hon. G. C. Verplanck / Member of Congress / Washington / D. C. POSTMARK: NEW-YORK / DEC / [10?] POSTAL ANNOTATION: FREE DOCKETED: W. C. Bryant.

1. In the fall of 1831 the young and energetic firm of J. & J. Harper agreed to publish a work of fiction by *The Talisman*'s authors and others. Bryant and Sands enlisted the help of William Leggett and James Kirke Paulding, whose books the firm had issued, and of Catharine Sedgwick, who wrote Bryant on December 6 that she would gladly participate, though frightened at appearing in such "elect company." NYPL–Berg. With Verplanck, these authors were to prepare equally a volume of tales to be called "The Hexade." When Verplanck failed to make good his share, the other five produced *Tales of Glauber-Spa*, in two volumes (New York, 1832). Bryant's contributions were "The Skeleton's Cave" (I, 193–242) and "Medfield" (I, 243–276).

2. In the reorganization of Jackson's cabinet in 1831 Louis McLane was brought home from his post as minister to England to succeed Samuel D. Ingham as Secretary of the Treasury. "As Clay himself used the term, his American system was the opposite of what he was wont to refer to as the 'colonial' or 'foreign' system of free trade. It meant, basically, the use of the protective tariff to build up American industry." Van Deusen, *Jacksonian Era*, pp. 46, 51. The Richmond *Whig*, founded and edited by John H. Pleasants, was the only effective opponent in Virginia of the powerful pro-Jackson Richmond *Enquirer*, conducted by Thomas Ritchie. See Mott, *American Journalism*, p. 189.

227. *To* Gulian C. Verplanck

New York   Dec   26   1831.

My dear Sir.

I shall probably set out for Washington about the middle of the month, and shall be happy to attend to any commission you may think fit to entrust to me. Col. Wetmore will probably come on with me.[1]

Your share of the "book" will of course be between 80 and 90 pages as the volume will consist of 500. I am sorry you have not the prospect of more leisure—but you *must* write something, or the Harper's will not have the book. They bargained for it on the express condition that all the persons named should contribute. So you are pledged.[2] You say nothing about the Treasury Report. I take the liberty of imagining that it did not come up to what you expected—at all events it was much short of what I was prepared to expect from Mr. McLane. What he proposes, as concessions, as overtures of conciliation &c. amount to no more than what the manufacturers themselves with Mr. Clay at their head are willing to agree to—and will no more satisfy the south than it would satisfy them to leave things as they are at present—[3]

Yrs truly

W   C. BRYANT

MANUSCRIPT: NYPL–Berg ADDRESS: Hon   Gulian C. Verplanck / Member of Congress / Washington POSTMARK: NEW-YORK / DEC / 26 POSTAL ANNOTATION: FREE DOCK-ETED: W. C. Bryant.

1. Col., later Gen., Prosper Montgomery Wetmore (1799–1876), author of *Lexington, and Other Fugitive Poems* (New York, 1830) and a close friend of William Leggett's, was an ardent Jacksonian as well as a prosperous New York merchant. Taft, *Minor Knickerbockers*, p. 400; Vail, *Knickerbocker Birthday*, pp. 383–384.

2. Though Verplanck failed in the end to contribute to it, the Harpers published *Tales of Glauber-Spa*.

3. A year later McLane switched his position and helped draw up the Verplanck Bill, which proposed "immediate and sweeping reductions in duties." Van Deusen, *Jacksonian Era*, p. 75.

228.   *To* Gulian C. Verplanck

[New York] Dec   29   1831.

Dear Sir

I intend to send a copy of my poems to Murray of London for publication. I think of sending by the next packet and of referring him to Washington Irving, as to the character of the work. Would you be so obliging as to write a letter as soon as you receive this, to Mr. Irving informing him of the liberty I have taken, &c. Send it to me and I will forward it by the next packet which goes out after I receive it. I am desirous that if the work is printed at all in England it should be printed respectably whether I get any thing for it or not.

Yrs truly

W. C. BRYANT.

MANUSCRIPT: Carl H. Pforzheimer Library ADDRESS: Hon. Gulian C. Verplanck / Member of Congress / Washington / D. C. POSTMARK: [NEW-YORK / DEC / 29?].

229.   *To* Washington Irving

New York   Dec   29   1831.

Sir,

I have put to press in this city a duodecimo volume of 240 pages, comprising all my poems which I thought worth printing, most of which have already appeared.[1] Several of them I believe you have seen, and of some, if I am rightly informed, you have been pleased to express a favorable opinion.[2] Before publishing the work here, I have sent a copy of it to Murray the London bookseller by whom I am desirous that it should be published in England. I have taken the liberty, —which I hope you will pardon a countryman of yours who relies on the known kindness of your disposition to plead his excuse, —of referring him to you. As it is not altogether impossible that the work might be republished in England, if I did not offer it myself, I could wish that it might be published by a respectable bookseller, in a respectable manner.[3]

I have written to Mr. Verplanck, desiring him to give me a letter to you on the subject—but as the packet which takes out my book will sail before I can receive an answer, I have presumed so far on your goodness as to make the application myself.[4] May I ask of you the favor to write to Mr. Murray on the subject, as soon as you receive this.[5] In my letter to him I have said nothing of the terms—which of course, will depend upon circumstances which I may not know, or of which I cannot judge. I should be glad to receive something for the work—but if he does not think it worth his while to give any thing, I had rather that he should take it for nothing, than that it should not be published by a respectable bookseller.

I must again beg you to excuse the freedom I have taken. I have no personal acquaintance in England, whom I could ask to do what I have ventured to request of you; and I know of no person to whom I could prefer the request with greater certainty that it will be kindly entertained.

I am sir,
With sentiments of the highest respect,
Your obt humble Servt.,
WILLIAM C. BRYANT.

P. S.— I have taken the liberty to accompany this letter with a copy of the work.

MANUSCRIPT: Carl H. Pforzheimer Library ADDRESS: Washington Irving Esq. / Care of Francis B. Ogden Esq / American Consul / Liverpool DOCKETED: Wm   C   Bryant / Decr   29th   1831 PUBLISHED: *Life*, I, 264–265 (with changes).

1. *Poems by William Cullen Bryant* (New York: E[lam] Bliss, 1832). This, Bryant's first collection, included seven of the eight poems published at Cambridge in 1821 (the "Song," later entitled "The Hunter of the West," was omitted), with eighty-one others, most of which had been printed in periodicals during the preceding decade.

2. Irving's praise was probably expressed in his letters to Verplanck mentioned in 211.4 and 213.1; it is confirmed in his reply to Bryant's request (see Note 4).

3. Bryant's reiterated anxiety in this letter to find a "respectable bookseller" undoubtedly stemmed from his discovery of the plagiarism described in Letter 211. His letter to Murray accompanying the volume is unrecovered.

4. Irving replied, from Newstead Abbey, that he was "delighted" to have "a collection of your poems, which, separately I have so highly admired," and that as soon as he returned to London he would seek its advantageous publication. He regretted, however, that a copy had gone to John Murray, "who has disappointed me grievously in respect to other American works entrusted to him, and who has acted so irregularly, in recent transactions with myself, as to impede my own literary arrangements and

oblige me to look round for some other publisher." Irving to Bryant, January 26, 1832, NYPL–GR.

5. Three weeks later Irving enclosed to Bryant two notes from the Murrays regretting they could take on no new projects. He reported that he had then placed the book with a Mr. Andrews, "who has agreed to divide with you any profits that may accrue. The work is now going through the press, under my eye, and I shall do every thing in my power to launch it successfully." Irving to Bryant, February 14, 1832; J. Murray, Jr. to Irving, January 24, and February 2, 1832, NYPL–GR.

230. *To* Frances F. Bryant

Washington   Jan. 22 (Sunday)   1832.

My dear Frances

I arrived here last evening about eight o'clock after a journey of two hundred miles by land over bad roads, and thirty miles by water over rather a rough sea from New York to Amboy.[1] I have not however been at all fatigued by the journey—though I was sick a little in the boat, and for the first day sick in the stage coach. We got to Philadelphia the first night about eleven o'clock, and left it the next morning at half past two— so that I saw very little of the city. There was a bright moonlight, but riding in a close carriage I could only distinguish that the general appearance of the city before reaching the tavern at which I stopped was shabby. The country from Trenton to Philadelphia along the Delaware is not particularly beautiful—the shores are flat and have not the appearance of much fertility. Before arriving at Trenton you pass through Princeton which is rather pleasantly situated with some neat buildings. Trenton is an ugly place in a low situation on the Delaware. We breakfasted on Friday morning at Chester a rather shabby looking village in Pennsylvania sixteen miles from Philadelphia. Soon after, we entered the state of Delaware. Wilmington is rather pleasantly situated and though in a slave holding state seems to have scarcely a larger proportion of coloured population than New York. The greater number of slaves are owned in the southern part of the state. We entered Maryland a few miles before arriving at Elkton a miserable village situated on some upland meadows overlooking a dirty marsh. From Elkton we proceeded through a sterile desolate uninhabited country mostly covered with scrub oaks. The streams had no bridges and we were obliged to ford them, and the roads were bad. About four o'clock we arrived at Havre de Grace at the head of Chesapeake Bay. Here we were carried over in a ferry boat. From shore to shore the distance was about a mile and on arriving at the other side we found dinner ready. Two blacks (slaves of course) waited on the table, a man and a little girl six or seven years old, very attentive, and as silent as cats.[2] We then set out and after proceeding about twelve miles through a country mostly covered with wood arrived at a place called the Bush a little village, after which we passed through an open, but not very inviting country, as I should judge, (for it was dark) and at half past elev[en] we got to Baltimore. The next morning we took a look at the city. There is more in its public buildings to strike the eye than in those of New York. Its churches seem to be larger and built with more magnificence of architecture than ours. The private buildings, many of them at least are larger than ours, with a plainer but generally a neater exterior. Some of the best however I observed had wooden railings and steps. We went to the Washington Monument which is on a hill commanding a view of the city, and ascended to the top by a sp[ir]al stair case. The monument you know is a vast tall column with a colossal statue of Washington at the tip. The view from the summit is very extensive; the whole city and a vast extent of surrounding country lies below you like a map and the waters of the Chesapeake are seen gleaming and winding through it.[3]

Yesterday between one and two o'clock we set out in the stage coach for Washington. The country immediately after leaving Baltimore is barren and little cultivated and the whole distance from that city to this is through a region that has no attractions whatever. This morning I have been looking at the city. It is a shabby place, nearly of the size, apparently, of Hudson.[4] There are a great many wretched looking buildings some of which appear not to be tenanted. The public buildings are spacious and intended to be fine. There is nothing to mark the difference of latitude, between this and the neighborhood of New York except the greater number of negroes. I am now at Gadsby's Hotel,[5] which seems to be a very good one. Hoyt[6] is here but I have not seen him, nor have I yet called on Verplanck or any body else. I am better of my influenza—the journey has done me good. My love to Louisa[7] and Fanny and kiss the baby for me.

Yours affectionately
WM   C. BRYANT

MANUSCRIPT: NYPL–GR ADDRESS: William C. Bryant Esq / Office of the Evening Post / New York POSTMARK: WASHINGTON CITY / JAN / 22 POSTAL ANNOTATION: 18¾.

1. Perth Amboy, New Jersey, at the mouth of the Raritan River, was then the usual point of transfer from steamboat to stagecoach for travelers from New York southward.

2. Although this was Bryant's first sight of slaves, he had known Negroes since childhood; there were black laborers on his father's farm at harvest time who took their meals with the family. A Cummington census ten years before his birth showed seven blacks in town. MS "List of Inhabitants 1784," Cummington town records.

3. The monument described here was designed by the Charleston architect Robert Mills (1781–1855), who submitted the winning design in 1836 for the celebrated obelisk in Washington.

4. A Hudson River town of about 5,000 persons.

5. Gadsby's Tavern, or Hotel, had provided a refuge three years earlier for President Jackson, who escaped through the back door of the White House from his riotous inaugural reception. Van Deusen, *Jacksonian Era*, p. 31.

6. Probably Jesse Hoyt, a friend and neighbor of the Bryants', who was later appointed by President Van Buren Collector of the Port of New York. See Bryant to Van Buren, December 5, 1837, Library of Congress.

7. Cullen's sister Charity Louisa had returned from Cummington with Frances and the children in September, to remain until March. Frances Bryant, "Autobiographical Sketch," NYPL–GR.

231. *To* Frances F. Bryant

Washington   Jan   23   1832

My dear Frances

I wrote you yesterday giving an account of my arrival here. Since that time I have called on Mr. Verplanck. He took me last evening to the house of Mr. Woodbury, Secretary of War whom we found in the midst of his family and two or three friends, a fine looking man nearly as large as Col. Ward, with a prepossessing face and of agreeable conversation.[1] After a stay of about three quarters of an hour we went to Mr. McLane's Secretary of the Treasury where we found more display. Mr. McLane is a quiet cock-eyed man of small stature and unassuming manners. His wife the mother of ten children is a lady of great vivacity and as I should judge a good deal of address full of conversation and talking to all the guests with great fluency. The eldest daughter is a young lady as I should judge of sixteen. —There were several ladies, half a dozen members of Congress, and Mr. Poinsett the Minister to Mexico.[2] Among the ladies was a daughter of the Ex-Empress Iturbide, looking much as you might suppose Mrs. Salazar to have done at the age of eighteen.[3] A young lady of the name of Christie played a psalm tune or two on the piano—accompanying the music with the words. One of the hymns she sang was Watts's "Sweet fields beyond the swelling flood" &c.

This morning I went to visit the Capitol. We first entered the Representatives Hall, a splendid spacious building but not well designed for its purpose, on account of the difficulty which the speakers experience of being heard in it. Mr. Verplanck then took us to the library, a spacious and elegant room and tolerably well stocked with books. We then went to the Gallery of the Senate Chamber and waited for the Senators to assemble. The Senate Chamber is not a large nor handsome apartment compared with the Representatives Hall.[4] We saw Harry Clay who has what I should call a rather ugly face— He is a tall thin narrow-shouldered man with a light complexion, a long nose a little turned up at the end and his hair combed back from the edge of his forehead.[5] We saw also the Vice President who you know is the presiding officer of the Senate.[6] He is a man of the middle size or perhaps a little over, with a thick shock of hair dull complexion and of an anxious expression of countenance. He looks as if the fever of political ambition had dried up all the juiciness and pithiness of his constitution. —He despatched the business of the body over which he presided, with decision and rapidity. Afterwards we went to the Gallery of the other House, and saw Mr. Adams[7] Mr. Everett[8] and others, and heard two or three short speeches on trifling questions. Becoming tired we went up to the top of the great dome of the Capitol which is 185 feet from the foundation and 216 above the level of the Potomac. From this elevation we descried the whole city with all its avenues leading in various directions over a vast extent of surrounding country through which flow the waters of the Potomac. On the top of the dome is a skylight lighting a circular room of the same height with the building called the Rotunda.[9] A lady broke through the glass of this sky light about two years since and was only saved from falling through and being dashed in pieces by one of her arms catching on the sash. Since that time a railing has been placed round the sky light. This afternoon we dined with Mr. Cambreleng—Col. Drayton[10] and Mr. Poinsett two very agreeable men were of the party. We were to have gone to see Old Hickory[11] but it was too late before we were ready, as the old gentleman goes to bed at nine o'clock. We shall see him however tomorrow or the next day. I have an invitation to Mrs. McLane's on Friday evening when there is to be a party.

Wednesday   25 Jan

Yesterday I called with Mr. Wetmore on the Secretary of State Mr. Livingston.[12] Today I have dined with Mr. Verplanck. Several members of both Houses were present. Tonight I am going to see the president and afterwards to Commodore Patterson's to a party[13] —Love to all— In haste—

Yrs affectionately
W   C   BRYANT

MANUSCRIPT: NYPL–GR ADDRESS: Mrs. Frances F. Bryant / New York PUBLISHED (in part): Life, I, 267–269.

1. Levi Woodbury (1789–1851, Dartmouth 1809), former New Hampshire governor and United States senator, was Secretary of the Navy, not of War. In 1834 he became Secretary of the Treasury, and in 1846 an associate justice of the Supreme Court.

2. Joel Roberts Poinsett (1779–1851) of South Carolina, American minister to Mexico from 1825 to 1830, was later (1837–1841) President Van Buren's Secretary of War. At his plantation in South Carolina he domesticated the brilliant tropical plant subsequently named for him, the poinsettia.

3. Augustin de Iturbide reigned as Emperor of Mexico only from 1822 to 1823; he was assassinated in 1824.

4. This early Senate chamber was used by the Supreme Court after the Capitol was enlarged in the 1850s.

5. Henry Clay (1777–1852), after long service in both houses of Congress, and four years as John Quincy Adams's Secretary of State, had recently been re-elected to the Senate from Kentucky.

6. John Caldwell Calhoun (1782–1850, Yale 1804) of South Carolina was Vice President during Jackson's first term, as he had been under Adams from 1825 to 1829.

7. Having lost the presidency to Jackson in 1828, John Quincy Adams (1767–1848,

Harvard 1787) was elected to the House of Representatives in 1831, serving therein with great distinction for seventeen years.

8. Edward Everett (1794–1865, Harvard 1811, M.A. 1814; Ph.D. Göttingen 1817), earlier editor of the *NAR*, was elected in 1825 to the House of Representatives from Massachusetts, serving for ten years. He was later governor of Massachusetts, minister to England, and president of Harvard.

9. The dome Bryant describes was replaced in 1865 by the present one, more than one hundred feet higher.

10. Col. William Drayton (1776–1846), congressman from South Carolina from 1825 to 1833.

11. Jackson's nickname was the tribute of Tennessee militiamen to his toughness on a march in 1813 from Natchez, Mississippi, to Nashville, Tennessee—over eight hundred miles—most of which he made on foot with his men. John William Ward, *Andrew Jackson: Symbol for an Age* (New York: Oxford University Press, 1962), pp. 54–55.

12. Edward Livingston (1764–1836, Princeton 1781) of Louisiana, Secretary of State, 1831–1833, and from 1833 to 1835 minister to France.

13. See 232.5.

232. *To* Frances F. Bryant

Washington   Jan   29   1832.

My dear Frances,

When I wrote you on Wednesday I was about to call at the President's. We went with Mr. Cambreleng in a carriage to the palace on a bitter cold night, about 7 o'clock in the evening.[1] We were told by the servant that the President was engaged up stairs and could not be seen. C. proposed however that we should go in and see Major Lewis and Maj. Donelson—which we did.[2] Soon after I observed that C. was out of the room, and in a few minutes he entered with [the] president[3]—a tall white haired old gentleman, not *very* much like the common engravings of him. He received us very politely and after about three quarters of an hour in which he bore his part very agreeably in the conversation we took our leave. Mr. Van Buren had been rejected that day by the Senate, and when that subject was alluded to the "lion roared" a little.[4] We then went to Commodore Patterson's[5] where there was a party made up of various materials—the families of heads of departments, naval officers, members of Congress, foreign ministers and *attachés* and others. Of the ladies some were pretty but the prettiest was a Mrs. Constant from New York. On Thursday evening Mr. Verplanck took us to Gov. Cass's.[6] We saw him *en famille*, with his two daughters. He is as you may have heard a widower —a grave looking rather dark faced man of fifty years of age. On Friday evening we dined with Mr. Livingston Secretary of State. The entertainment was, I think, altogether the most sumptuous and elegant I ever witnessed. There were no guests but Major Lewis who lives with the President, Dr. Greenhow[7] and ourselves. We afterwards went to a party at Mr. McLane's. It was much like a New York party but more crowded than those generally are. Three rooms were filled with company and in two of them there was dancing. —On Saturday we dined with T. L. Smith formerly of New York now Register of the Treasury. Maj. Barry, the Post Master General was a guest—a man of slight make and apparently the wreck of a man of talents.[8] This morning we took a walk of a mile and a half to Georgetown, which is in some sort the parent of Washington.[9] It is situated close on the shore of the Potowmac and looks quite like an old town, compared with Washington. The country about it seems to be pleasant with hills vallies and woods. The shores of the Potowmac above the town are beautiful and varied. —We crossed the river on the ice to what was formerly a part of Virginia but now included in the District of Columbia,[10] and found ourselves in a wood that clothed the slope of a hill. We returned in a driving snow storm. This afternoon we are to dine at Mr. McLane's. Tuesday we shall dine with the President— Wednesday we shall set out on our return and Friday I hope will bring us to New York.

Bush from Pittsfield is here.[11] I believe he is come for an office. He has lost his wife by the influenza. Plummer of Mississippi called on me this morning. I am to dine with him tomorrow.[12]

I have heard no speeches yet from the great men, but I have heard a specimen of the manner of most of them in short debates. I have heard Hayne, Webster, Clay and others in the Senate, and Drayton Adams Cambreleng Archer[13] and Everett in the House. McDuffie I have not heard.

We have had extreme cold weather for a few days past. The thermometer has been 4 degrees below zero. I hope you continue to keep yourselves comfortable. The houses here are not built for a severe winter climate. —My love to all and a kiss to the little one.

Yr affectionate husband,
W   C   BRYANT

MANUSCRIPT: NYPL–GR ADDRESS: Mrs. Wm. C. Bryant / New York POSTMARK: CITY OF WASHINGTON / JAN / 29 POSTAL ANNOTATION: 18¾ PUBLISHED (in part): Life, I, 269–270.

1. The Executive Mansion, designated "The Palace" in architect James Hoban's original plans in 1792, was not officially called the "White House" until the end of the nineteenth century.

2. William Berkeley Lewis (1784–1866) of Tennessee was an old friend of Jackson's who became his intimate adviser and speech writer. Andrew Jackson Donelson (1799–1871, West Point 1820), Jackson's nephew, was his private secretary; his wife Emily was the widowed President's official hostess. Bryant mistakenly wrote "Donaldson."

3. This incident pointedly illustrates Cambreleng's intimacy with the President, as majority leader of the House of Representatives.

4. After Louis McLane's return from London in 1831 to become Secretary of the Treasury, Jackson appointed his former Secretary of State Martin Van Buren minister to England, but too late for congressional approval. When the nomination came be-

fore the Senate for confirmation the following January, a contrived vote allowed Vice President Calhoun, Van Buren's enemy, to cast the deciding vote, with the cry, "It will kill him, sir, kill him dead." Schlesinger, *Age of Jackson*, p. 55. But Verplanck's was the shrewder prophecy. Many years later Bryant recalled: "I was in Washington, dining with Mr. Verplanck, when the vote on this nomination was taken. As we were at the table, two of the Senators . . . entered. Verplanck, turning to them, asked eagerly: 'How has it gone?' Dickerson [of New Jersey], extending his left arm, with the fingers closed, swept the other hand over it, striking the fingers open, to signify that the nomination was rejected. 'There,' said Verplanck, 'that makes Van Buren President of the United States.' " "Verplanck," p. 224.

5. Daniel Todd Patterson (1786–1839) of New York had given Jackson vigorous naval support at the Battle of New Orleans in 1815. From 1828 to 1832 he served as one of three naval commissioners.

6. Gen. Lewis Cass (1782–1866), governor of Michigan Territory, 1813–1831, and Secretary of War, 1831–1836.

7. Robert Greenhow (1800–1854, William and Mary 1816, College of Physicians and Surgeons 1821), a fellow-lecturer of Bryant's before the New York Athenaeum, was then a state department translator.

8. William Taylor Barry (1785–1835, William and Mary 1803), former chief justice of Kentucky, dispensed Jackson's patronage. His operation of the post office, which was later the subject of congressional investigation, has been termed "wretched." See Schlesinger, *Age of Jackson*, p. 66; Van Deusen, *Jacksonian Era*, p. 35.

9. Georgetown, Maryland, settled in 1665, was not incorporated within the city of Washington until 1895.

10. Alexandria, Virginia, granted to the federal government in 1790–1791, was returned to Virginia in 1846 at the request of its residents.

11. Probably David Bush, a staunch Democrat, who ran a tavern in his Pittsfield home, later Herman Melville's "Arrowhead." Smith, *Pittsfield*, II, 7, 94, 177.

12. Franklin E. Plummer (d. 1847), member of Congress from Mississippi, was a brother-in-law of both Austin and Peter Rush Bryant. BDAC; Arthur to Sarah Bryant, March 5, 1834, BCHS. Congressman Plummer was at this time a radical Jackson-Democrat. Schlesinger, *Age of Jackson*, pp. 207–208.

13. Probably William Segar Archer (1789–1855), congressman from Virginia, 1820–1835, and, later, United States senator, 1841–1847.

233. *To* John Howard Bryant

New York, February 19, 1832.

I have received several of your poetical compositions published in the "Illinois Herald."[1] The lines on leaving the place of your nativity are very well. Those addressed to Kate are flowing and easy, but with some weak passages. The poem on winter also is unequal. The New Year's address was, I suppose, like most things of the kind, written in haste. Indeed, it is a pity to spend much time on what is so soon laid by and utterly forgotten, or what cannot possibly interest the reader afterward. As to the politics of the address, I think that, if they were not your own, I should not have put them in verse. I saw some lines by you to the skylark. Did you ever see such a bird? Let me counsel you to draw your images, in describing Nature, from what you observe around you, unless you are professedly composing a description of some foreign country, when, of course, you will learn what you can from books. The skylark is an English bird, and an American who has never visited Europe has no right to be in raptures about it. Of course, your present occupation necessarily engrosses the greater part of your time, and leaves you but little leisure for writing verses.[2] What you write, however, you should not write lazily, but compose with excitement and finish with care, suffering nothing to go out of your hands until you are satisfied with it. I have visited Washington, where I passed ten days. I saw the President, who appears to be a sensible old gentleman, of agreeable manners, and the four Secretaries who compose a very able Cabinet—the most so that we have had since the days of Washington. Of fashionable society I saw something. The only peculiarity I observed about it was the early hours that are kept—the balls beginning at eight and breaking up at eleven, and the refreshments being all light, and no supper. I heard a few words from most of the distinguished men in Congress, but no speeches of length or importance. If I come, I cannot set out until the middle of May. I shall move the 1st of May, I think, to Hoboken, and the semi-annual dividend of the profits of the "Evening Post" is made on the 15th of May.[3] My stay in Illinois will be short. The family at Cummington talk of going to Illinois next fall if the farm can be sold. . . .

I send you, by Mr. Coddington, a copy of my poems, and I have also given him one, according to your request.[4] The book sells, I believe, tolerably well—that is, for poetry, which in this country is always of slim sale. I do not expect, however, to make much by it. If it brings me two hundred or two hundred and fifty dollars, I shall think myself doing pretty well. Poetry, at present, is a mere drug, both in this country and in England. Since Byron's poetry, I am told that nothing sells. I have, however, sent my book to England to try its luck, offering it for what I can get, and if I can get nothing, consenting that it shall be republished for nothing, provided it be done respectably.

MANUSCRIPT: Unrecovered TEXT (partial): Life, I, 281–282.

1. The Illinois Herald, the state's first newspaper, was then published at Vandalia, the second capital. Mott, American Journalism, p. 191. Presumably Bryant exchanged papers with its editor, as was then the custom.

2. John was then clerking in a Jacksonville store and farming his brother Arthur's land. Brown, John Howard Bryant, p. 17.

3. On May 1 the Bryants took lodgings in Hoboken with a Mrs. Van Boskerck. For the fiscal year May 1831–May 1832 Bryant's profits were $3,485, an increase of $135 over the year before. He had, however, incurred a debt of $2,000 for an additional one-twenty-fourth over his one-quarter share. Frances Bryant, "Autobiographical Sketch"; "Evening Post Accounts," NYPL–GR.

4. Mr. Coddington is unidentified.

234. *To* Gulian C. Verplanck

New York   Feb 21 1832

My dear Sir

I got your letter today in which you mention the circumstances of the communication made to Webb about Clement and Poindexter. The matter shall be attended to—it would have been attended to [to]day but no occasion presented itself for bringing it in as if accidentally and naturally.[1]

The person I was desirous some time since of getting placed on the list of Visitors of the Institution at West Point is Col. William Swan of Cummington, Massachusetts, a man who has "done the state some service"[2] having fought under Gen. Jackson himself, —a worthy intelligent judicious man, though of little speech—much honoured and trusted by the community in which he lives—a good Jackson man of course.

I hope you have not forgot the book. We are all at work. Mr. Leggett and Mr. Sands are in the heat of composition and I have written a few pages—[3]

Yrs truly
W. C. BRYANT

MANUSCRIPT: NYPL–Berg ADDRESS: Hon   Gulian C. Verplanck / Member of Congress / Washington / D. C. POSTMARK: NEW-YORK / FEB / 24 POSTAL ANNOTATION: FREE DOCKETED: W. C. Bryant.

1. Senator George Poindexter (1779–1853) of Mississippi, a bitter opponent of Andrew Jackson who was later accused by the President of forming a plot to assassinate him, had recently supported the Senate's rejection of Van Buren's nomination as minister to England. This action drew the charge that Poindexter had tried to bribe one Samuel B. Clement to edit a newspaper hostile to Jackson. Bryant refers to an exchange of letters, lately printed in James Watson Webb's New York *Courier and Enquirer*, in which Poindexter accused several New York congressmen of instigating this charge, and tried to draw them into duels. Bryant reprinted this exchange, with caustic editorial comment, in the *EP* for Feb. 23–25, and 28. See 232.4; Van Deusen, *Jacksonian Era*, pp. 46, 99–100.

2. The USMA Archives at West Point indicate that Swan was not appointed to the Board of Visitors. The quotation is from *Othello* V.ii.339.

3. For *Tales of Glauber-Spa* (1832), then in preparation.

235. *To* Gulian C. Verplanck

New York   Feb. 28 1832.

Dear Sir,

I send you back Morse's letter, which I got this morning and for which I am much obliged to you.[1]

I hope you will find time ere long to do *something* for the book. Your name we must have, if you cannot give us a long article give us a short one, and if you cannot give us a story let us have something else.

Besides if the rest of us are not on the look out Paulding will fill the whole book.

Did you receive some papers in relation to Garcia's case? Will you let me know how it stands at present.—[2]

Yrs truly

W. C. BRYANT

MANUSCRIPT: NYPL–Berg ADDRESS: Hon. G. C. Verplanck / Member of Congress / Washington / D. C. POSTMARK: [illegible] POSTAL ANNOTATION: FREE DOCKETED: W. C. Bryant.

1. Early in 1832 Samuel F. B. Morse wrote to Verplanck, from Paris, a disconsolate letter asking whether there was still any hope that he might be commissioned to paint one or more historical pictures for the National Capitol: "I have too long lived in the hope. . . . I have studied and travelled to prepare myself, I have made sacrifices of feeling and of pecuniary interests buoyed up with this phantom of hope which is daily growing dimmer and will soon vanish." Quoted in Oliver W. Larkin, *Samuel F. B. Morse and American Democratic Art* (Boston and Toronto: Little, Brown, 1954), p. 106. See Letter 203 for Bryant's effort more than three years earlier to secure such a commission for Morse, through Verplanck's influence.

2. Garcia and his case are unidentified, but see Letter 253, which apparently concerns the same subject.

236.   *To* Gulian C. Verplanck

N   York   March 30, 1832

Dear Sir

The *Sketch Club*[1] have voted to have an Annual, —something more splendid than any which has yet appeared in this country. There are to be six copper plate engravings of larger size than is common in the American annuals—and several more cuts by Mason for head and tailpieces.[2] The book is to have a larger page than any other of our Annuals, and but half the matter. Harper is to be asked to publish it—Durand has engaged to superintend the embellishments, and you are to be asked to undertake the superintendence of the literary part.[3] The plan appears to have been got up by Ingham,[4] Durand and Weir,[5] who are full of zeal about it. The corresponding Secretary of the Club was, according to a vote, to write to you on the subject; but as I have been asked and have consented to do it in his stead, you will dispense with that formality.[6] Write me whether you will undertake the business.

Am I right in supposing your friend Barnwell to be the author of the article in the Southern Review on my poems?[7]

The authors of the "Book" are suitably vexed and disappointed that you should write nothing for it—and there are loud threats of lugging your name into the preface or some other part of the book, *en revanche.*

Dr. DeKay came into the office the other day with a Turkish salutation accompanied with an appropriate gesture. Having had an attack of the cholera he is as much a lion here—the joke is his own—as the man "qui avait vu Bolivar" was in Paris. He has now attacked the cholera in turn as you will see in the E. Post.[8]

Yrs truly

W   C   BRYANT

MANUSCRIPT: NYPL–Berg ADDRESS: Hon G. C. Verplanck / Member of Congress / Washington / D. C. POSTMARK: NEW-YORK / MAR / 30 DOCKETED: W. C. Bryant.

1. The Sketch Club, or the "Twenty-One"—often so-called because its membership was at first limited to that number—grew out of informal meetings between artists and writers for *The Talisman*. By 1829 its meetings were recorded in weekly minutes. *The American Landscape* of 1830 was the product of several of its members. During half a century the club was instrumental in founding several significant New York cultural institutions, including the New York Gallery of the Fine Arts, the American Art Union, the Century Association, Central Park, and the Metropolitan Museum. See John Durand, *Prehistoric Notes of the Century Club* (New York, 1882), pp. 9–23; Callow, *Kindred Spirits*, pp. 12–29; Bryant II, "Poetry and Painting," pp. 864–866.

2. Abraham John Mason (1794–?), an English engraver who came to New York in 1829, was then a lecturer at the National Academy and a contributor of woodcuts to the *NYM*. See *DAA*, p. 427.

3. Bryant summarizes a MS resolution dated March 15, 1832, in NYPL–GR.

4. Charles Cromwell Ingham (1796–1863), Dublin-born portrait-painter, was a founder of the National Academy and the first president of the Sketch Club. See Callow, *Kindred Spirits*, p. 13; *DAA*, p. 340.

5. Robert Walter Weir (1803–1889), for nearly half a century a close friend of Bryant's, was an historical and landscape painter who served from 1834 to 1876 as instructor in drawing and professor of painting at the United States Military Academy. In 1843 his mural, "Embarkation of the Pilgrims," was installed on one of the eight great panels in the Rotunda of the National Capitol. In this letter, and consistently thereafter, Bryant wrote "Wier."

6. The Sketch Club's corresponding secretary was then William Emerson (1801–1868, Harvard 1818), a New York lawyer, and elder brother of Ralph Waldo Emerson. Callow, *Kindred Spirits*, pp. 12–13; Rusk, *Emerson*, pp. 69, 142. This publishing venture went no further.

7. This notice was written, not by Congressman Robert Barnwell of South Carolina, but rather by Hugh Swinton Legaré (1797–1843, South Carolina College 1814), editor of the *Southern Review*, who predicted that Bryant's name would "go down to posterity as one of the first, both in time and excellence, of American Poets." *Southern Review*, 8 (February 1832), 443–462. Legaré was later a congressman, Attorney General, and briefly Secretary of State under President Tyler.

8. James Ellsworth De Kay (1792–1851, M.D. Edinburgh 1819), an early member of the Sketch Club, had just completed a study of the Asiatic cholera in Turkey. While there he had sent Bryant reports on the local political situation. See De Kay to Bryant, August 20, 1831, NYPL–BG. In later years De Kay published an exhaustive *Zoölogy of New York* in five volumes (New York, 1842–1844).

237.   *To* Richard H. Dana

New York   April 9, 1832.

My dear Sir.

It is quite a triumph for me that one who has so often rated me for a bad correspondent should himself be found guilty in a most horrible degree of the very fault he has charged upon me. You have owed me a letter for two years!— And now when you come to discharge your debt, instead of writing me a good long comfortable epistle, after your old fashion, with not an inch of blank space left that could be concealed by the folds of the letter you imitate my own brief and meagre style of correspondence.[1] Not that I am so well pleased with what you have done that I should like to have you repeat the offence—but to have a letter unanswered for two years, is I am sure a sufficient expiation for all the negligences of the kind of which I have been guilty.

You were right in expecting a copy of my poems from me. I made out a bill of persons to whom I intended to present copies, before the work was out—and I put down first the names of three old and good friends—yours and Channing's and Phillips's. That they have not been sent before is owing to circumstances that would tire you to relate even if I could recollect what they all are— Take it for granted however that the books have a very good reason for not coming to Cambridge before, and look for them as soon as I can make Dr. Bliss forward them.

The review in the American Quarterly was written it is said by Dr. McHenry, author of the *Pleasures of Friendship and other poems*, but Walsh has said in his paper that it was written at his particular request, and adopted by him as soon as he saw the manuscript.[2] It is supposed also that it received some touches and additions from his pen. Walsh has a feeling of ill nature towards me, and was doubtless glad of an occasion to gratify it; but, I believe, that as you say the article will do me no harm.

You ask about the sale of the book. Mr. Bliss tells me it is very good —for poetry. I printed a thousand copies, and more than half of them are disposed of. As to the price, it may be rather high at $1.25, but I found that with what I should give away and what the booksellers would take, little would be left for me, if a rather high price were not put upon it, and so I told the publisher to fix it at a dollar and a quarter. If the whole impression sells, it will produce me $300—perhaps a little more. I hope you do not think that too much. I have sent the volume out to England, and Washington Irving has had the kindness to undertake to introduce it to the English public. A letter I received from him two or three weeks since informs me that it is printing under his eye— It is to be published by a bookseller of the name of Andrews in Bond Street— and he is to divide with me what profits may accrue which I take it for granted will be none at all. I had an ambition, however, to have my verses published in England, in the neat manner in which they do these things—the American edition was badly enough got up in all conscience. As for the lucre of the thing on either side of the water; an experience of 24 years, for it is so long since I first became an author, has convinced me that poetry is an unprofitable trade, and I am very glad that I have something more certain to depend upon for a living.

I wish the critics of poetry in this country understood a little more of the laws of versification. The tune of

Rŭm tī rŭm tī rŭm tī &c

is easily learned, but English verse not only admits but requires some thing more. He who has got no further than *rum-ti* knows no more of versification than he knows of Greek who has merely learned the Greek alphabet. Yet people undertake to talk about the rules of English prosody who are evidently utterly unworthy of the usage, the established usage of the great mass of English poets who deserve the name. I have half a mind to write a book in order to set our people right on this matter—but I fear nobody would read it.[3]

April 10. I have this moment received the American Monthly. If you see Mr. Channing give him my best thanks for what he has so well and kindly said of my writings.[4]

As to the great poem or the long poem of which you speak I must turn it over to you to be written. One who has achieved such triumphs as you have over ill natured critics, winning a reputation in spite of them should not let his talent sleep the moment it is acknowledged.

As to the bile of which you complain why do you not shake it off by travel? Come to New York—our city is three or four times as near Boston as it used to be and a little tossing in the steam boat off Point Judith will do you good. I am going to remove to Hoboken on the first of May, where [I will give you a][5] chamber. But do not come till I get back [from the West, for] to the west I am going in the course of [three or] four weeks with no other purpose in the world but to look at it. I have a brother settled in Illinois—so I shall go down the Ohio till it mingles with the Mississippi and up the Mississippi till it meets the Illinois, and up the Illinois, to within twenty miles of Jacksonville where my brother lives.

I have written you an egotistical sort of letter but you will excuse me in consequence of having lately published a book— My regards to all my friends in Cambridge.

Yrs truly
W. C. BRYANT.

MANUSCRIPT: NYPL–GR ADDRESS: Richard H. Dana Esq / Cambridge / Massachusetts. POSTMARK: BOSTON / APR / [13?] ENDORSED: Wm C. Bryant / Ap. 9, 1832 / Ans Ap. 20. PUBLISHED (*in part*): *Life*, I, 275–276.

1. Dana's letter is unrecovered.
2. James McHenry (1785–1845) was an Irish-born author of historical novels about American life, as well as of conventional verses, such as those to which Bryant refers, published in 1822. His review, called "American Lake Poetry," appeared in the *American Quarterly Review*, 11 (March 1832), 154–174, and was extremely patronizing in tone.
3. Bryant's asperity seems to have been justified by McHenry's comment, "We cannot . . . avoid taking notice of a very awkward offence against prosody, of fre-

quent occurrence in the pages of Bryant—we mean the compressing into two syllables such words as beautiful, delicate, prodigal, merciful, innocent, horrible, &c., which no ear accustomed to pronounce English words accurately, can tolerate." A dozen years earlier Bryant had taken pains to demonstrate to such neo-classical purists as McHenry that precisely this practice had been common with great English versifiers from Spenser, Shakespeare, and Milton to Cowper. See "On the Use of Trisyllabic Feet in Iambic Verse," *NAR*, 9 (September 1819), 426–431.

4. Edward T. Channing's brief but favorable notice appeared in the *American Monthly Magazine*, 3 (March 1832), 69.

5. Manuscript torn, here and elsewhere.

238. *To* Gulian C. Verplanck

New York   April 20, 1832.

My dear Sir

Your letter seems to have been all powerful with Washington Irving.[1] I sent him a copy of my poems and another to Murray referring him to Irving. On receiving the volume Irving wrote me a letter saying that he would do what he could for me, but he was sorry that I had given the work to Murray who has occasioned him a great deal of trouble in the transactions he has had with him respecting his own works. A few weeks after receiving this letter I got another informing me that Murray declined doing any thing with the work and that it had been placed in the hands of J. Andrews of New Bond Street who was to divide with me any profits that might arise from its publication. Yesterday I received from Mr. Irving a copy of the London edition with Washington Irving's name in the title page as editor, and a dedication to Rogers prefixed to the poems, in which the kindest things are said of them. This was doing so much more than I had any reason to expect that you may imagine the agreeable surprise it gave me.[2]

Why do you never write? The Evening Post is in an eclipse since you have withdrawn the light of your countenance. The other papers are ahead of us in the revelation of state secrets and mysteries of policy.

Yrs truly

W. C. BRYANT.

MANUSCRIPT: NYPL–Berg ADDRESS: Hon. G. C. Verplanck / Member of Congress / Washington / D. C. POSTMARK: NEW-YORK / [APR] / 20 POSTAL ANNOTATION: FREE DOCKETED: W. C. Bryant PUBLISHED: *Life*, I, 273.

1. Verplanck to Irving, December 31, 1831, in Pierre M. Irving, *The Life and Letters of Washington Irving* (New York, 1864), II, 212–213. See Letter 228.

2. Irving's praise was generous; Bryant's "essentially American" poems, while "imbued with the independent spirit, and the buoyant aspirations incident to a youthful, a free, and a rising country," appeared to him to "belong to the best school of English poetry, and to be entitled to rank among the highest of their class." Preface dated London, March 1832, in *Poems by William Cullen Bryant, An American. Edited by Washington Irving* (London: J. Andrews, 1832), pp. iii–vi. Irving's dedication to

Samuel Rogers (1763–1855), wealthy patron of the arts and friend of American artists and writers, assured the book of serious attention in British literary reviews. It had cordial notices in *Blackwood's Edinburgh Magazine*, 31 (April 1832), 646–664, and in the London *Foreign Quarterly Review*, 10 (August 1832), 121–138. Irving's letter to Bryant accompanying the book, dated at London, March 6, 1832, is in NYPL–GR.

239. *To* Washington Irving

New York, April 24, 1832.

My dear Sir

I have received a copy of the London edition of my poems, forwarded by you. I find it difficult to express the sense I entertain of the obligation you have laid me under, by doing so much more for me in this matter than I could have ventured, under any circumstances, to expect. Had your kindness been limited to procuring the publication of the work, I should still have esteemed the favour worthy of my particular acknowledgments, but by giving it the sanction of your name, and presenting it to the British public with a recommendation so powerful as yours on both sides of the Atlantic, I feel that you have done me an honor in the eyes of my countrymen and of the world.

It is said that you intend shortly to visit this country. Your return to your native land will be welcomed with enthusiasm, and I shall be most happy to make my acknowledgments in person.

I am sir,
very sincerely yours,
Wm C. Bryant.

Manuscript: Yale University Library Address: Washington Irving Esqr Published: *Life,* I, 273–274.

240. *To* Washington Irving

Philadelphia May 22 1832

My Dear Sir,

I wrote to you some time since, to express my thanks for the kind interest you had taken in the publication of my book in England, but perceiving your name in the morning paper among those of the passengers in the last Havre packet, I conclude that my letter has not reached you. I take this opportunity therefore of doing what my absence from New York will not permit me to do at present in person, namely to say how exceedingly I am obliged to you for having done so much more for my book than I was entitled under any circumstances to expect.[1] I was not vain enough to hope that you would give it to the British public with the sanction of your name or take upon yourself in any degree the responsibility of its merit. To your having done so I ascribe the favorable reception, for such it is so far as I am able to judge, which it has met with in Great Britain, as well as much of the kindness with which it is regarded in this country.

I am Sir,

very gratefully & truly

yours,

W. C. BRYANT

MANUSCRIPT: Carl H. Pforzheimer Library ADDRESS: Washington Irving Esq. / New York POSTMARK: [PHILA / 22?] MAY POSTAL ANNOTATION: PAID 12½ DOCKETED: W. C. Bryant / Phila   May 22, 1832 PUBLISHED: *Life*, I, 274.

1. Leaving New York on the morning of May 22 on his way to visit his brother John in Illinois, Bryant had been unaware of Irving's arrival the previous day after seventeen years' residence in England and Europe. He missed the testimonial banquet to Irving at the City Hotel on May 30, and evidently the two men did not meet that summer during the three-week period between Bryant's return and Irving's departure on the western journey told of in *A Tour on the Prairies* (1835). See Pierre Irving, *The Life and Letters of Washington Irving* (New York, 1864), II, 258.

241.   *To* Gulian C. Verplanck

Baltimore   May 23   1832.

My dear Sir.

It may be well for me to apprise you that I am on my way to Illinois in order that if you should have any thing for the information of the public through our journal before Congress rises you may address it to Mr. Leggett.

Poor Bliss you may have heard has failed. The accident happened about three weeks since. The worthy Doctor is very much distressed, and makes though in somewhat better English, the complaint of the poor Frenchman who was pestered by Monsieur Tonson   "Oh dear I will get some sleeps—nevair!" Sleep in short has departed from his lids and the books are disappearing from his shelves—for he is paying some of his creditors in books, 10 shillings in the pound. He had sold enough of my books to be somewhat in my debt.[1]

The *Hexade* for that is the title of the new book to which you are understood to be a contributor is in the press. The first volume is printed, and the second I suppose will be finished very shortly. Sands has written a satirical story for it in which the poetical critic in the Quarterly is not spared.[2]

The Convention here have made a better job of it I believe than they expected—better certainly than I feared they would do.[3] If the Senate and House of Representatives were chosen *de novo* I fancy you would get a better set—better certainly for party purposes,—and if better organized for party purposes, there would be a better opportunity for doing business.—

I suppose you will not adjourn till July. I shall not be back until the latter part of that month. Do you know that I have taken a house at Hoboken?[4]

Yrs truly

W C BRYANT

MANUSCRIPT: NYPL–Berg ADDRESS: Hon. G. C. Verplanck / Member of Congress / Washington / Dist   of Columbia. POSTMARK: BALT / MD / MAY / 23 DOCKETED: W. C. Bryant.

1. "Dr." Elam Bliss had failed as an apothecary at Springfield, Massachusetts, before becoming a book dealer, first in Boston and later in New York. He was, in Bryant's words, "of so generous a temper as often to yield his own just rights in order to meet the expectations of authors for whom he published," yet he was at the same time "the most unenterprising and unlucky of all publishers." After this second failure, Bryant found him a position as appraiser in the New York customhouse. When, in 1844, he lost this job, Bryant appealed to Verplanck and others to help get him reinstated—with what success it is uncertain. See Bryant to Evert A. Duyckinck, May 28, 1855, Duyckinck Collection, NYPL; Bryant to Verplanck, June 10, 1844, NYPL–Berg; Arthur Ames Bliss, *Theodore Bliss, Publisher and Bookseller: A Study of Character and Life in the Middle Period of the XIX Century* (Northampton, Massachusetts: Northampton Historical Society, 1941), pp. 4–5.

2. Sands's story was "Mr. Green," in *Tales of Glauber-Spa*, II, 103–152. The "poetical critic" was evidently James McHenry; see 237.2.

3. The Democratic national convention, meeting at Baltimore on May 21 to renominate President Jackson and to give him as a running mate Martin Van Buren, had just adjourned when Bryant reached that city on May 23.

4. Frances Bryant noted that on June 15, after boarding with Mrs. Van Boskerck at Hoboken for a month and a half, she and the children "Went to Housekeeping," at an unspecified address. "Autobiographical Sketch," NYPL–GR.

242. *To* Frances F. Bryant

Hagerstown   Md.   May 24, 1832.

My dear Frances.

I am here at Hagerstown about 80 miles west of Baltimore at 6 o'clock in the afternoon, and expect to have a dull time of it until I go to bed to be waked up between three and four tomorrow morning. I left New York in the New York—there was nobody on board whom I knew and it was very cold—so I went down stairs and read Camoens.[1] A short distance from New Brunswick the passengers were landed and transferred to stage coaches. We were conveyed through a flat uninteresting country to Bordentown on the Delaware a little below Trenton. Here the sight of Joseph Bonaparte's grounds beautifully planted with trees of various kinds, with a spacious mansion and a towering observatory overlooking the Delaware made some amends for the dullness of the previous journey.[2] We embarked on board of a nice little boat with a very civil captain, and arrived at Philadelphia about five o'clock in the afternoon. Having perceived by the morning papers that Washington

Irving had arrived in New York and concluding that he could not have got my letter before he left Europe I wrote him another which I dropped in the post office. I had now a little opportunity of looking at the city by daylight. The city is better built than ours, at least more to my taste—the private dwellings being solid comfortable looking edifices without that tawdriness which you see in our New York houses—the streets were remarkably clean-looking as if just swept. At six o'clock on Wednesday morning I went on board the William Penn for New Castle where we arrived about nine o'clock and proceeded on the rail road to Frenchtown a distance of sixteen miles and a half which we travelled at the rate of 10 miles an hour. At Frenchtown the passengers were put on board the Carroll which likewise had a very civil captain an old fat rosy-faced respectable looking man. I like what I have seen of the boats on the Delaware and Chesapeake better than those on the Hudson. The commanders are as such men ought to be, *officious* smiling obliging men. We sailed down the Chesapeake a wide expanse of water with flat low shores very much indented and offering scarcely any thing to look at. We had green peas at dinner on board the Carroll—very green—pies of green currents—not larger I should think than I saw them in Mrs. Van Boskerck's garden before I left home—and to crown all a plate of very fine strawberries which I was told came from Norfolk. At five o'clock we got to Baltimore. I went to Barnum's Hotel where I found John Mumford who insisted upon introducing me to Mr. Flagg Secretary of State for New York and one of the New York delegation to the Baltimore Convention which had just finished its labors.[3] Mr. Flagg took me to a room where he made me go through the ceremony of a particular introduction to about fifteen gentlemen and their ladies. Before it was ended I began to feel and I dare say looked very foolish. I got away however—wrote to Verplanck and to Greenhow[4] and went to bed. This morning I set out again at five o'clock on the Baltimore rail road.[5] There were in the car with me three Virginia planters from the lower part of the state who had come as I judged from their conversation to attend the Baltimore Convention, and who had come out to try the rail road. They were remarkably intelligent men slovenly in their dress, —but gentlemanly in their manners, expressing themselves with uncommon propriety and good sense, and noticing very particularly as they passed every object worthy of remark offered by the journey. They did not seem to be profess[ed] politicians for they did not talk of politics at all, but well informed country gentlemen, and [one takes] them [al]together, as specimens from which I am inclined to judge well of their class. Two of them exhibited somewhat of that tendency to metaphysical speculation which I have heard mentioned as characteristic of the Virginians. Sixty miles travelling on the rail road brought us to Fredericktown.[6] The rail road is made for the greater part of the way along the Patapsco, and after it leaves that along another little stream running westerly. The work is expensive being cut through the hills and carried by high causeys through valleys with stone bridges of solid masonry over the streams. This mode of travelling is agreeable and rapid. The vegetation in this latitude is scarcely more advanced than in the neighborhood of New York. The dogwood flowers have not fallen and the azalea which I saw in flower in the southern part of New Jersey is in flower here also. Hagerstown is 25 miles west of Fredericktown; the road from the latter place is excellent being Macadamized. Hagerstown is a dirty little town built in imitation of a city. It stands in a limestone country of irregular surface rather fertile and pleasant which is more than I can say for the greater part of Maryland which I have seen.

Cumberland Md. May 25

Here I am in the midst of the ridges and spurs of the Alleganies at a little ugly town rather pleasantly situated on the banks of the Potomac near the foot of the Great Allegany or Back Bone Ridge. I have crossed today four principal ridges of the Allegany, but the greater one is to be crossed tomorrow. They are covered with forests and overlook a wide extent of wild uninhabited and sterile country. There are however among them some pleasant little sp[aces?] of rich soil. This morning when I left Hagerstown it was quite cold I took the precaution to [wear] woollen stockings which I found quite comfortable. Twelve miles beyond H I came to Clear Spring, so called from a very large spring in the village, and three or four miles beyond I passed Indian Spring which is also a large spring in an enclosure under a great tree. Near the Spring an emigrating family had halted with their waggon, and had made a fire to cook their breakfast. All along the road I observed frequently fires in the woods or enclosures by the way side where women were washing clothes at some spring or brook. I take it for granted that Friday is washing day in Maryland. At one [p]lace I saw a middleaged woman washing and a good looking young woman sitting near her on the [b]ank sewing. Just beyond Clear Spring we crossed the first ridge of the Allegany and descending on the other side came to the Potomac on the banks of which we had a pleasant ride of at least ten miles. After passing a little town called Hancock we crossed a loftier and wilder ridge, and so on ridge after ridge till we descended to the Potomac again at Cumberland having travelled 67 miles. A woman living in the mountains being in the stage with us pointed out in a lonely hollow on a stream the spot where the Cottrells[7] murdered an Englishman some years since for the sake of his money. "The Cottrells said she the father and two sons were working hare on this pike and they came on with the Englishman a little ways on pretence of chatting with him, and as if in friendship. They got him near whar yon drift wood lays and thar they killed him in a thicket." The place where this woman lives, on the wildest part of the road between two of the highest ridges I have passed, with a ragged forest on each side, is called Belgrove. The village consists of log houses—that is houses of hewn logs.

Steam Boat Transport off Marietta
Monday morning May 28.

I should have written to you on the evening of the 26th from Union in Pennsylvania at the foot of Laurel Hill the last eminence of the Alleganies but I met with an accident which took me the whole evening to repair. The baggage was badly placed and in driving furiously down a descent of near four miles in length, the *hasp* was jolted off from the lock of my trunk, my razor and box and some other little things were lost, and the trunk was considerably damaged. It rained the whole day and was very chilly. We breakfasted at Frostburg on the Alleganies, at a tavern where was a grate as large as a kitchen chimney roaring with a great fire of bituminous coal which is found in these parts in abundance. A severe frost had fallen two nights previous and the leaves of several kinds of trees had turned black as if scorched by fire. We dined at Smithfield on the Youghiogheny— We had corned beef roasted pickled eggs and boiled potatoes with gravy poured over them in the dish. Saturday night brought us to Union in Pennsylvania situated in the midst of a most beautiful and rich country of undulating surface. The buildings are mostly mean or ugly and the whole village, as are all I have seen since I left home is arranged without taste. The next day the weather was fine though cold, and I rode to Wheeling in Virginia at six o'clock in the afternoon. Here at 8 o'clock I took the steam boat for Cincinnati and having just passed Marietta 80 miles below Wheeling, I expect to arrive at Cincinnati in two days.

I have a great many things to tell you that I cannot get into a letter without writing all the time, and it is difficult to write legibly in a steam boat. I have wished a hundred times you were with me. I am sure this journey would have amused you. I have not felt the slightest fatigue since I left home. My love and a kiss to Fanny and half a dozen to the little baby.

Yrs affectionately
W   C   Bryant.

Manuscript: NYPL–GR Address: Mrs. Frances Bryant / New York Postmark (*in script*): Maysville [Kentucky] / 30 May Postal annotation: 25. Published (*in part*): *Prose*, II, 3–6.

1. Bryant was almost certainly reading Luis Vaz de Camoëns epic poem, *The Lusiads* (1572), in the original Portuguese. In 1826 he had begun to study that language. See 156.3; *Life*, I, 220. In the 1834 edition of his poems he added several to those in the 1832 collection; among these was a "Sonnet from the Portuguese of Semedo."

2. Joseph Bonaparte (1768–1844), elder brother of Napoleon, lived for most of the time between 1815 and 1841 at Bordentown, New Jersey.

3. John M. Mumford edited two short-lived New York Democratic newspapers during Jackson's first administration, the *Merchant's Telegraph* and the *Standard*. Azariah Flagg (1790–1873) was Secretary of State for New York from 1826 to 1832.

4. The letter to Greenhow is unrecovered.

5. The Baltimore and Ohio, of which an initial stretch from Baltimore to Endicott City, Maryland, was opened in 1830, was the first public railroad in the United States.

6. Now the city of Frederick, Maryland.

7. The "Cottrells" mentioned here may have been members of the same large Cummington family as Dwelly Cotterell, from whom in 1815 Dr. Bryant had bought a farm adjoining his homestead. See 30.2; *Only One Cummington*, p. 350.

243. *To* Frances F. Bryant

Cincinnati   May 31   1832.

My dear Frances

You see I loiter on my way. As I have nearly made up my mind to come home by way of the lakes, I could not pass by this flourishing and much talked of place without stopping to take a look at it. I have been detained a little longer than I intended—a boat left here for Louisville last evening but that was sooner than I wished to go—and none goes this morning. In the evening however I shall take passage in the steamboat Freedom which goes direct to St. Louis.

I wrote you on the 28th and sent the letter on shore somewhere along the river. It contained the history of my travels up to that time when I arrived off Marietta. On the 29th, Tuesday, in the morning the boat stopped at Portsmouth to land passengers and take in others. I was surprised to see come on board Dr. Jones and his family accompanied by Edward.[1] They had been fifteen days in getting to a place at which I had arrived in a week. They did not go by "the way of the lakes" properly speaking, but went to Cleveland[2] on Lake Erie, and thence passed through the middle of the state of Ohio by the canal. Contrary to their expectation, the canal was completed only to twenty miles north of Portsmouth, and the road for this distance was so bad that they were a whole day in travelling it. Edward had suffered somewhat from a toothache— he did not like the log cabins which he saw along the canal, nor the long beards of the men. We reached Cincinnati about seven on that evening. I went on shore, but Dr. Jones and his family proceeded to Louisville where they were to take a steamboat for St. Louis. —Dr. Jones expressed himself much disappointed in the appearance of the interior of Ohio both with respect to the fertility of the soil and the appearance of thrift in the inhabitants. I do not recollect whether it was that day or the day previous that the boat stopped at Maysville in Kentucky and I landed to take a look at the town which very much resembles those I saw in Maryland and is no otherwise remarkable than as being the termination of the famous proposed national road between two towns in the same state which was unfortunately strangled by what is called the Maysville veto.[3]

The shores of the Ohio have nothing to distinguish them from those of a river of the Atlantic States except the continuity of forests with which they are covered, and the richness and various forms of the foliage. The appearance of the woods is more like that of the Berkshire woods, than those of any other part of the country I have seen. They consist of oak sugar maple, hickory buckeye which is a kind of horse chestnut, the tulip tree, the button wood and sometimes the cotton wood which appears to be a gigantic poplar, and other trees common at the eastward, except evergreens of which there are none. Springing from a kindly soil they grow to a colossal size, and standing at a greater distance from each other than in our forests, and being covered with a dense foliage, the outline of each tree is perceptible to the eye, so that you may almost count them by the view you have of their summits. With us you know they appear blended into one mass. It is possible that somewhat of the effect I have mentioned may be occasioned by the atmosphere. At a little past sunset it was very striking—each treetop and each projecting branch with its load of foliage, stood forth in strong and distinct relief surrounded by deep shadows. The aspect of the shore where I have seen it did not remind me at all of the [Hudson] Highlands. The round, wooded hills which overlook it the greater part of the way, sometimes approaching close to the water and at others receding so as to leave a border of rich alluvial land, resembled to my eye the hills in Stockbridge, Lenox and some other parts of Berkshire.

I went yesterday morning to see Mr. Flint whom I found at his son's bookstore.[4] He expressed great joy at seeing me and insisted on introducing me to several of his friends. In the evening I took tea at his house where he presented me to his wife and daughter. The daughter is, I take for granted, the "great blue stocking of the west," to coin a phrase after the approved fashion. She is very intelligent—though young—and talks *remarkably* well.[5] I saw Mr. Peabody here the Unitarian minister who appears to be a sensible young man.[6] Mr. Flint talks a great deal, with much knowledge and enthusiasm, and sometimes eloquently though not always grammatically. He desired his particular remembrances to Miss Robbins,[7] from whom he had received he said several excellent letters, whose books he admired and of whom he had heard Mr. Pierpont[8] speak in terms of great respect. Will you do this errand.

This morning I climbed one of the hills overlooking the town. Cincinnati is surrounded by these and they are all covered with wood. They recede north from the river in a kind of semicircle in which lies the town, and on the southern side of the river are hills also, so that it appears to be placed in a sylvan amphitheatre, through the midst of which flows the Ohio, always quiet and placid, one of our noblest and longest streams and justifying in the placidity and evenness of its current and the beauty of its shores, the French appellation of La Belle Riviere. Opposite to Cincinnati on the Kentucky shore are the neat looking towns (so they appear at a distance) of Newport and Covington. Cincinnati contains thirty thousand inhabitants. Some of the private houses are very handsome and costly, and the public edifices equal to the average of those in New York. Many new buildings are erecting, and among others a spacious theatre. The market is well supplied—especially with strawberries of which I have seen tubsfull but have not tasted one. The inhabitants appear to be very industrious and busy. They have a sallow look in comparison with the people of the mountains of Maryland, and the hills of Fayette county in Pennsylvania, but Mr. Flint assures me that the place is healthy, and that the fever and ague does not prevail here.

Today I dine with Mr. Guilford[9] a friend of Mr. Flint, and at seven o'clock this afternoon I tear myself away from Cincinnati in spite of the attraction of a great party at which I was to have been regularly exhibited, had I consented to stay. Mr. Flint is to give me a letter to Gov. Clark at St. Louis,—the Clark who travelled with Lewis to the mouth of the Oregon.[10]

My journey has been very pleasant hitherto—but I begin to be afraid of getting homesick before it is finished. I hope you will not spare anything to make yourself comfortable. Remember that Mr. Gill / keeps the till.[11] Kisses to the babies—

Yrs affectionately
W C. BRYANT

MANUSCRIPT: NYPL–GR ADDRESS: Mrs. Frances Bryant / Care of W. C. Bryant / New York POSTMARK: CINCINNATI O / JUN / 1 POSTAL ANNOTATION: 22 PUBLISHED (*in part*): *Prose*, II, 6–7.

1. Though the Jones family were among the first settlers of Cummington, it is uncertain which of them took to Illinois young Edward Harte, Eliza Robbins' nephew. See *Only One Cummington*, pp. 199–200 and *passim*.

2. Bryant followed the early spelling "Cleaveland," after the 1796 surveyor of the Western Reserve, Moses Cleaveland (1754–1806, Yale 1777) of Canterbury, Connecticut.

3. Jackson's veto in May 1830 of a bill authorizing federal funds for this twenty-mile stretch of highway wholly within Kentucky was a calculated slap at Henry Clay's American System of making internal improvements at national expense. Van Deusen, *Jacksonian Era*, pp. 51–52. A week before the veto Bryant attacked the bill in the *EP*, writing, "It is no more a national improvement, than an ordinance to widen William St." May 19, 1830. Later he called the veto proof of the President's "resolute determination to discharge what he thinks his duty." *EP*, May 31, 1830.

4. Timothy Flint (1780–1840, Harvard 1800), of Massachusetts, spent the years 1815–1825 as a missionary, largely in the Mississippi valley. Thereafter he wrote romances and travel books, the most vivid of which was his *Biographical Memoir of Daniel Boone* (1833), which gave impetus to the Boone legend. From 1827 to 1830 he edited the *Western Monthly Review* at Cincinnati. His son, E. H. Flint, published several of his father's books. See Rusk, *Middle Western Frontier*, I, 291.

5. The derisive term "bluestocking," first applied in eighteenth-century England to women with literary pretensions, won currency in this country in the 1840s through the writings and "conversations" of such members of the Boston and Concord literary circles as Elizabeth Peabody and Margaret Fuller. Rusk, *Emerson*, pp. 232–234.

6. Ephraim Peabody (1807–1856, Bowdoin 1827), pastor of the Unitarian Church at Cincinnati from 1831 to 1838, was a founder and the first editor (1835–1836) of the literary magazine, *The Western Messenger*, published in that city. See Rusk, *Middle Western Frontier*, I, 183.

7. Eliza Robbins. See 127.6.

8. The poet–clergyman John Pierpont. See 202.1.

9. Nathan Guilford (1786–1854, Yale 1812), a lawyer and a founder of the public school system in Ohio, wrote popular frontier tales as well as school textbooks. See Rusk, *Middle Western Frontier*, I, 53, 275.

10. William Clark (1770–1838), an early Indian fighter, became federal superintendent of Indian affairs after his return in 1806 from his celebrated expedition to the Pacific Northwest with Meriwether Lewis. After serving from 1813 to 1821 as territorial governor of Missouri, he resumed charge of Indian affairs, with headquarters at Saint Louis, holding that post until his death. Bryant mistakenly wrote "Clarke."

11. Thomas Gill, bookkeeper and part owner of the *EP*.

244.   *To* Frances F. Bryant

Steamboat Water Witch on the Mississippi

Twelve miles above the mouth of the Ohio, June 3, 1832

My dear Frances,

I left Cincinnati on the 31st,—the day mentioned in my last letter. Previous to going I dined with Mr. Guilford where I met with about a dozen of what I supposed were the choice spirits of the place. Among them was Mr. King brother of Charles King—a sallow-faced man with much of his brother's manner.[1] It was a different thing from a New York dinner. The dinner hour was two—and about half past two, the lady of the house who had been sitting with the guests in the parlour withdrew and after a few minutes made her appearance again at the door, when dinner was announced and we all got up and followed her into the dining room. The lady took her seat on the *side*, not at the head of the table, and I was placed next to her. The dinner if I am not mistaken consisted of but two dishes, roast beef and roast veal—though I will not swear that there was not a piece of ham—with the usual vegetables of the season. There was a very little drinking of wine. The dessert consisted of a large dish of delicious strawberries, and as soon as these were dispatched Mrs. Guilford rose and we all followed her back to the apartment where we at first assembled. Such I suppose is the etiquette of a Cincinnati dinner. I should think we were not an hour at the table. Among the guests was a young man of the name of Thomas who I was given to understand had written poetry, who is lame, and wears his neckcloth *à la Byron*.[2] Mr. Flint at parting gave me a copy of his new edition of the Geography and furnished me with a letter to Gov. Clark of St. Louis.

On the 1st. of June between eight and nine in the morning I arrived at Louisville in Kentucky, 160 miles from Cincinnati, and the first person who fixed my eye as we approached the shore was Edward who had been detained with Dr. Jones and his family at Louisville waiting for a boat to depart for St. Louis during the whole time of my stay at Cincinnati. They had taken a passage on the Water Witch and had already been on board of her a day. As the boat on which I came would not set out for St. Louis for a day or two I transferred my baggage immediately to the Water Witch. Before she sailed I had time to look at the town. It is built almost entirely of brick, and has the appearance of a place of much business—more than Cincinnati, although it contains but twelve or thirteen thousand inhabitants. Just below the town are the falls, the only rapids by which the smooth course of the Ohio is broken from Pittsburgh to the Mississippi, a distance of nearly twelve hundred miles. They are avoided by means of a canal through [which] steam boats of the ordinary size which navigate the Ohio pass but the larger steam boats plying between Louisville and New Orleans stop below the falls. The nights are cool yet and I continue to wear my flannel. We are to set out to day June 6th to go up the Illinois as far as Naples in a boat which goes to carry supplies of corn to the troops in the Indian country.

We left Louisville at 3 o'clock P. M. and the river being quite high the captain announced his intention of going over the falls the roaring of which we could hear from where we lay. The falls are divided by a little low narrow island; on the north side of which is what is called the Illinois *shoot* and on the south the Kentucky shoot a corruption of the French word *Chute* [cataract]. We took the Illinois shoot, and when we arrived among the broken waters it was evident from the circumspection of the captain, the frequent turns we were obliged to make, and the slackening of the speed of the boat that the channel was very narrow. In one place the narrowness of the channel among the craggy rocks produced a great inequality in the surface of the stream so that the waves were almost mountainous. In passing over it the boat heeled and swung to and fro, turning up first one side of its keel and then the other, obliging the passengers to seize hold of something to keep them upright, and frightening the inmates of the ladies cabin. It was over in a moment however. A little below the falls the captain stopped the boat to let us look at the *Homer* a magnificent steam boat intended for the New Orleans trade, just built at New Albany on the Indiana side. It is as great a thing in its way as a seventy four.[3] On the lower deck is an immensely powerful engine, with, I think 11 parallel boilers. Here also is the kitchen and other offices. Below this is a spacious hold which appeared to be full of barrels of flour. On the second deck or story is the cabin, which has on each side twenty five state rooms, each as large as Fanny's bedroom in the *new house*, and each containing two berths with all the accommodations of a sleeping apartment. Each has a well-sized window of two sashes. The cabin between the state rooms is spacious and well carpeted. In one of them I saw a bedstead. The upper deck or third story is reached by a covered stair case directly from the lower deck, and is intended for what are called *deck* or *steerage passengers*. It contains berths for 220 persons.

Last night a little before sunset we stopped on the Kentucky side to take in wood. I went into a Kentuckian's garden and gathered roses. His house was a large ugly unpainted frame house with an *underpinning* like that of a New England barn, that is, consisting of here and there a log or a large stone, with wide spaces between. His peas were poled with dry young canes. About this time we passed the Wabash which is the boundary between Indiana and Illinois. Its waters are more transparent than those of the Ohio which are somewhat turbid and the difference is distinguishable for some distance below this junction. We passed the mouths of the Cumberland and of the Tennessee in the night. This morning at half past seven we came to where the Ohio empties into the Mississippi. The muddy current of the Father of Waters covered with flakes of foam, rushes rapidly by the clearer stream of the Ohio damming it up and causing it to spread into a broad expanse for a considerable distance above its mouth. Yet the Mississippi is not wider apparently than the Ohio. Its banks are low and covered with cotton wood and a peculiar species of willow, or with thick brakes of cane, the same of which fishing poles are made. Its current is so rapid that we are obliged to creep along the shore at the rate of about four miles an hour. It will probably take longer to ascend from the mouth of the Ohio to St. Louis which is but 180 miles than it did to come from Louisville to the mouth of the O. which is 500.

Mississippi river 60 miles below St. Louis. June 4th.

Yesterday the day was most beautiful—an agreeable change from the weather of the day previous which was very hot and sultry. I took occasion to go on shore in the state of Missouri while the captain was taking in wood and examined some of the plants and trees of the country. The shores for the whole distance were low and unhealthy, the banks are continually dropping into the river which is full of large wooded islands and very irregular in its course. I have seen no prairies yet, the Mississippi every where rolls through stately woods in the midst of which you see once in five or ten miles perhaps a log cabin. Yet the whole scene appeared beautiful to me; the sunshine, whether it was fancy, or reality, seemed richer and more golden than it is wont to be in our climate, and the magnificent forests, covered with huge vines of various kinds, seemed worthy to flourish under so glorious a sun. This morning we stopped to get wood at a little town called Chester, just below the mouth of the Kaskaskia on the Illinois side where we learned that all the state was in alarm about the Indians who had made an incursion to the east of the

Illinois river and murdered several families. You have probably seen that previous to this there had been an engagement between the Indians and a detachment of the whites in which the latter were defeated with the loss of 15 persons. The first story was that 52 were lost—then 27—but the truth is said to be 15. I shall be obliged to relinquish my projected route to Chicago which is said to be unsafe in consequence of the neighborhood of the savages.[4] In St. Louis where the steam boat is carrying us as fast as it can, which is slowly enough, we also learned that there had been a commotion of another nature. An inmate of a brothel, called Indian Margaret, being part Indian, stabbed a white man about a fortnight since in a quarrel, and he died of the wound. The inhabitants were so exasperated that they rose *en masse* and attacked all the houses of ill fame in the place, tore down two, set fire to a third, and burned the beds and other furniture in all of them. A black man called Abraham who was the owner of 14 houses of this description having made a fortune in this way, was seized, a barrel of tar was emptied upon him and he was then slipped into a feather bed. The people among whom were some of the most respectable inhabitants of the place began the work early in the morning and kept it up until sunset—while the magistrates stood looking on. Abraham made his escape to Canada and Indian Margaret is in prison.

Last eve. we passed Cape Girardeau a rather neat looking French settlement 50 miles from the mouth of the Ohio, on a green bluff—and a little while since we came to the old settlement of St. Genevieve where we stopped to take in freight. I went on shore and talked to the men and women who are very dark complexioned, some as dark as Indians, but with a decided French physiognomy. Most of them could speak broken English, but preferred to converse in their own tongue. The shores on the Missouri side now begin to rise into precipices some of which are highly picturesque. It is however a cold grey day and natural objects by no means have the beauty which they borrowed yesterday from the state of the atmosphere.

I am very anxious to know how you get along with the new house but I suppose I must wait until my return. I dreamed about it last night, but its situation was changed from Hoboken to the woods and rivers of the west. I think of you frequently and sometimes fear that my desire to see you will make me return before I have seen as much of the west as I intended. I shall put this letter in the post office at St. Louis as soon as I arrive there which will be early tomorrow morning—

Adieu.

W C BRYANT

St. Louis, June 5. We arrived here this morning at three o'clock. Wm. Leavenworth went away about six weeks ago for the purpose he said of raising some money to carry on a steam mill which he has been building in particular with a man named Casson. About 2 weeks since Casson went after him and the creditors seized their property. They owe eight thousand dollars and the property it is said will not fetch half the money.[5] St. Louis is beautifully situated on a hill overlooking the river. Two handsome houses a little out of town are erected on old Indian mounds on which the forest trees have been thinned out.

St. Louis   June 5. I presented this morning my letter to Gov. Clark a fine looking old gentleman but somewhat heavy though sensible. Finding him surrounded by a party of young Virginians I excused myself from his hospitalities. This afternoon I am to go to a strawberry party at the *Prairie House* between three and four miles from the city: —I have been there, and eaten strawberries gathered from the old prairie now looking like any old common field unenclosed and grazed by cows throughout the year. I have also seen a specimen of the sallow beauties of St. Louis, who however have considerable sweetness and liveliness of expression—though with us I think they would be called plain. We returned by the Rock Spring about six miles from the town. The Rock Spring is a large spring gushing out from under a cliff in a romantic little spot. There are some handsome seats near the town but the greater part of the surrounding country, though by no means sterile, is waste and wild.

There is much talk in St. Louis concerning the Indians. The true number killed in the engagement is eleven. The families murdered lived on Rock River to the west of the Illinois river. There were three families, consisting of 15 persons in all. Their bodies were left to be devoured by hogs and dogs. A man has been killed in Buffalo Grove near Galena and it is supposed that an Indian Agent has been murdered by the savages.

I set out for Jacksonville tomorrow June 6. A steam boat will take us from this place to Naples where I shall take the stage to J. a distance of 20 miles.

MANUSCRIPT: NYPL–GR ADDRESS: Mrs. Frances Bryant / Care of W. C. Bryant Esq / New York POSTMARK: ST LOUIS / JUN /5 POSTAL ANNOTATION: 25 PUBLISHED (*in part*): *Prose*, II, 7–11.

1. John Alsop King (1788–1867), founder in 1836 of the *Du Buque Visitor*, first newspaper in what was organized two years later as Iowa Territory, became in 1857 the first Republican governor of New York. See Rusk, *Middle Western Frontier*, I, 143. For Charles King, see 158.15.

2. Between 1835 and 1840 Frederick William Thomas (1806–1866), later a friend of Edgar Allan Poe's, was one of two or three leading novelists of the early Middle West. See Rusk, *Middle Western Frontier*, I, 296–300; Wright, *American Fiction 1775–1850*, p. 277.

3. A large warship carrying seventy-four guns.

4. The Black Hawk War of 1832 in Illinois marked a desperate if brief attempt by the Sac Indians and their allies, under Chief Black Hawk, to resist their forced resettlement by the federal government west of the Mississippi River.

5. William Leavenworth of Great Barrington, son of Bryant's friend and former landlord David Leavenworth, had built a dam and mill on the Green River in 1828, and owned a nearby marble quarry. It is uncertain when he went to Saint Louis or for what purpose. See Taylor, *Great Barrington*, p. 358. Casson is unidentified.

245. *To* Frances F. Bryant

Jacksonville [Illinois] June 12 1832.

My dear Frances.

I left St. Louis as I expected on the 6th inst. at eleven o'clock in the morning and proceeded up the Mississippi. I think I omitted in my last to say any thing of the scenery on the river between St. Genevieve and St. Louis. The eastern bank still continues to be low but the western is steep and rocky. The rocks sometimes rise into lofty precipices which impend over the river and are worn by some cause into fantastic figures presenting in some places the appearance of the arches, pillars and cornices of a ruined city. Near a place called Selma I saw where one of these precipices was made use of for a shot tower, for the purpose of converting the lead of the neighbouring mines into shot. A small wooden building projects over the verge of a very high perpendicular cliff and the melted lead falls from the floor of this building into a vat at the foot of the precipice, filled with water.

I saw nothing remarkable on the Mississippi until we arrived within a few miles of the junction of the Missouri with this river. I there perceived that the steam-boat had emerged from the thick muddy water in which it had been moving into a clear transparent current. We were near the eastern bank and this was the current of the Mississippi. On the other side of us we could discern the line which separated it from the turbid waters of the Missouri. We at length arrived at the meeting of these two great streams. The Missouri comes in through several channels between islands covered with lofty trees, and where the two currents encounter each other there is a violent agitation of the waters which rise into a ridge of short chopping waves as if they were contending with each other. The currents flow down side by side unmingled for the distance of twelve miles or more until at length the Missouri prevails and gives its own character and appearance to the whole body of water.

At a place called Lower Alton a few miles above the mouth of the Missouri we stopped to repair one of the boilers and I climbed a steep grassy eminence on the shore which commanded a very extensive view of the river and surrounding country. Every thing lay in deep forest. I could see the woods beyond the Missouri but the course of that stream was hidden by the gigantic trees with which it is bordered. When I awoke the next morning we were in the Illinois a gentle stream about as large as the Connecticut, with waters like the Ohio somewhat turbid. The Mississippi has generally on one side a steep bank of soft earth ten or twelve feet in height which the current is continually wearing away and which is constantly dropping in fragments into the water while on the other side it has a sandy beach. But the Illinois has most commonly a shore which presents no appearance of being eaten by the current, but which slopes as regularly to the water as if it had been smoothed by the spade. As we proceeded up the river bluffs began to make their appearances on the west side. They consisted of steep walls of rock, the tops of which were crowned with a succession of little round eminences covered with coarse grass and thinly scattered trees having quite a pastoral aspect though the country does not appear to be inhabited. We stopped to take in wood on the west shore and I proceeded a few rods through the forest to take my first look at a natural prairie. It was one of the wet or alluvial prairies. The soil was black and rather moist and soft, and as level as if the surface had been adjusted by some instrument of art. To the north and south along the river it stretched to an extent of which I cannot judge, but to the east it was bounded at the distance of about five miles by a chain of rounded eminences, their sides principally covered with grass and their summits with wood forming the commencement of the uplands on which the dry prairies are situated.[1] The prairie itself was covered with coarse rank grass four or five feet in height intermingled with a few flowers. Here and there stood a tul[ip tree?] in the midst of the wilderness of verdure.

We got to Naples a little settlement of a dozen houses on the east bank of the Illinois about three o'clock in the afternoon. This place is situated on flat rich meadows somewhat higher than the banks of the river generally are. At Naples I took leave of Mr. Maginnis a gentleman of St. Louis with whom Mr. Halleck the day before I started recommended me to become acquainted and whom I found a passenger on board the same boat. Hearing me say something of the possibility of my visiting the American camp near the rapids of the Illinois where the militia of this state drafted to repel the attacks of the Indians, are to assemble, he was so obliging as to furnish me with letters to Gen. Atkinson and other officers of the army at that station.[2] The number of passengers for Jacksonville being numerous two carriages were provided, one of them, a covered one, was instantly filled with a set of boors who obliged Mrs. Jones carrying an infant, to take the open waggon; a bad specimen of the manners of the people here. I will do them the justice to say however, that it was the only instance of incivility to ladies which I have observed in my journey. We arrived at Jacksonville about eleven o'clock. I supped at the Tavern at a long table covered with loads of meat standing in a room in which was a bed and was afterwards shown into an upper apartment where I was to pass the night in which were seven huge double beds some holding two brawny hard-breathing fellows and some only one. I had a bed to myself in which I contrived to pass the time until four o'clock in the morning when I got up and having nothing else to do took a look at Jacksonville.

It is a horribly ugly little village composed of little shops and dwellings stuck close together around a dirty square in the middle of which stands the ugliest of possible brick court houses with a spire and weathercock on its top. The surrounding country is a bare green plain, with gentle undulations of surface unenlivened by a single tree, save what you see at a distance on the edge of the prairie in the centre of which the village stands. This plain is partly enclosed and cultivated, and partly open and grazed by neat cattle and horses. The vegetation of the unenclosed parts has a kind of wild aspect being composed of the original prairie plants which are of strong and rank growth, and some of which produce gaudy flowers. This is not however the flowering season. About a fortnight since they were red with the blossoms of the violet wood sorrel and the *phlox divaricata* the lichnidia of our gardens. They will soon be yellow with other syngenesious plants. I went to look for my brother who lives with old Mr. Wiswall on the edge of the prairie, or close to the timber as they call it here. John was well and appeared glad to see me. I have now established myself with Mr. W. who lives in a two story log house built by his own hands and containing in all three rooms. What do you think of that— you, who with your little family complain of being straitened in a house containing EIGHT apartments besides the hall, the pantry, and the garret of which there are none in this house. Shall I confess the truth to you, and suffer you to judge whether I am not what the French call *un homme à bonnes fortunes* [a lady-killer]? Have I not slept in the same apartment with two young ladies? And am I not according to all present appearances to sleep this night in the same room with another, an accomplished young lady a native of St. Thomas whose native language is French and who keeps the district school? Tomorrow I shall set out on a little journey to the neighbouring counties and perhaps on my return I may tell you of stranger things than these. No room here is furnished unless it has a bed. Many of the houses have but a single room. I have been to look at my brother's farm.[3] There is a log cabin on it built by a squatter, an ingenious fellow I warrant him, and built without a single board or sawed material of any sort. The floors and doors are made of split oak and the bed stead which still remains is composed of sticks framed into the wall, in one corner of the room, and bottomed with split oak the pieces being about the size of staves. The chimney is built of sticks plastered with mud inside. There are two apartments the kitchen and the parlour. The kitchen is without any floor but the bare ground and between that and the parlour there is a passage on the ground roofed over but open on the sides, large enough to drive a waggon through.

June 13th. Today I am to set out with John on horseback on a tour up the Illinois. I carry my plunder in a pair of saddlebags, with an umbrella lashed to the crupper, and for my fare on the road I shall take what Providence pleases to send. The weather although cool before has been hot and sultry since my arrival here— You forgot to put up my roundabout—so I have bought another. It is not likely that I shall proceed as far as the American camp.[4]

I have told you little about the natural productions of the soil and other peculiarities of the country. The forests are of a very large growth and contain a greater variety of trees than are common to the eastward. The soil of the open country is fat and fertile and the growth of all the vegetable tribes is rapid and strong to a degree unknown in your country. There is not a stone or pebble or bit of gravel in all these prairies. A plough lasts a man his life time, a hoe never wears out and the horses go unshod. Wild plums grow in large thickets loaded with a profusion of fruit said to be of excellent flavour. The earth in the woods is covered with May-apples not yet ripe, and in the enclosed prairies with large fine strawberries now in their perfection. Wild gooseberries with smooth fruit are produced in abundance. The prairies and the forest have each a different set of animals. The prairie hen as you walk starts up and whirs away from under your feet, the spotted prairie squirrel hurries through the grass and the prairie hawk balances himself in the air for a long time over the same spot.[5] Here are also the prairie wolf and the prairie fox neither of which I have seen.

Edward appears to be quite contented with the place. I believe it to be salubrious and I am sure it is the most fertile country I ever saw—at the same time I do not think it beautiful. Some of the views however from the highest parts of the prairie are what I have no doubt some would call beautiful in the highest degree; the green heights and hollows and plains blend so softly and gently with each other. Kiss the children for me. My regards to Mr. Sands's family.[6]

Yrs truly

W C BRYANT

MANUSCRIPT: NYPL–GR ADDRESS: Mrs. Frances Bryant / Care of W. C. Bryant Esq. / New York POSTMARK: SPRINGFD. IL. / JUN / 14 POSTAL ANNOTATION: Single / 25 PUBLISHED (in part): Prose, II, 11–16.

1. Similar scenes appear in John J. Egan's moving diorama of the Mississippi Valley (1851?), now in the City Art Museum of Saint Louis. Wolfgang Born, *American Landscape Painting: An Interpretation* (New Haven: Yale University Press, 1948), pp. 91–96, and figs. 59–62; *DAA*, p. 208. Bryant's fidelity in "The Prairies" (1832) to archaeological theory, then current, regarding the Mound-Builders is discussed in Curtis Dahl, "Mound-Builders, Mormons, and William Cullen Bryant," *New England Quarterly*, 34 (June 1961), 178–190. See *Poems* (1876), pp. 184–189. Bryant's description suggests that he must have landed on the *east*, rather than the *west*, shore.

2. Gen. Henry Atkinson (1782–1842) commanded federal forces engaged, together with Illinois militia, in the Black Hawk War. Maginnis is otherwise unidentified.

3. Bryant refers to the farmstead settled in December 1830 by Arthur Bryant, on which John had worked since his arrival at Jacksonville the following spring. See Brown, *John Howard Bryant*, p. 17.

4. American forces were encamped on the Rock River near the site of the present town of Dixon, Illinois.

5. At this point in the selection from this letter printed in *Prose* II, Godwin inadvertently inserted a passage (pp. 15–16) from Bryant's letter to the *EP* from Princeton, Illinois, dated June 21, 1841. Bryant had published that letter in *LT* I, 55–63.

6. The house recently taken by the Bryants at Hoboken was next door to that of Robert Sands and his mother and sister Julia.

246.   *To* Frances F. Bryant

Jacksonville   June 19   1832.

My dear Frances.

I set out as I wrote I should do, from this place on Wednesday the 13th of this month on a little excursion towards the north. John accompanied me. The first day brought us to Springfield the capital of Sangamon County where the land office for this district is kept and where I was desirous of making some inquiries as to the lands in market. Here I put a letter into the post office—the third I have written you since my departure from N. Y. The first I despatched from Cincinnati and the second from St. Louis.[1] Springfield is 35 miles east of Jacksonville. It is situated just on the edge of a large prairie, on ground somewhat more uneven than Jacksonville, but the houses are not so good, a considerable proportion of them being miserable log cabins, and the whole town having an appearance of dirt and discomfort. We passed the night at a filthy tavern and the next morning resumed our journey, turning towards the north. The general aspect of Sangamon County is much like that of Morgan, except that the prairies are more extensive and more level. We passed over large tracts covered with hazel bushes among which grew the red lily and the *painted cup*, a large scarlet flower.[2] We then crossed a region thinly scattered with large trees principally of black or white oak at the extremity of which we descended to the bottom lands of the Sangamon,[3] covered with tall coarse grass. About 7 miles north of Springfield we forded the Sangamon which rolled its transparent waters through a colonnade of huge buttonwood trees and black maples, a variety of the sugar maple. The immediate edge of the river was muddy but the bottom was of solid rock and the water was up to our saddle skirts. We then mounted to the upland by a ravine and proceeding through another tract of scattered oaks came out again on the open prairie. Having crossed a prairie of seven or eight miles in width we came to a little patch of strawberries in the grass, a little way from the edge of the woodland where we alighted to gather them. My horse in attempting to graze twitched the bridle out of my hand and accidentally setting his foot on the rein became very much frightened. I endeavoured to catch him but could not. He reared, and plunged, shook off the saddlebags which contained my clothing and some other articles, kicked the bags to pieces, and getting onto the road by which we came, galloped furiously out of sight towards Springfield. I now thought my expedition at an end, and had the comfortable prospect of returning on foot or of adopting the method called to *ride and tie*.[4] I picked up the saddle bags and their contents and giving them to John, I took charge of the umbrellas which had also fallen off and walked back for two miles under a hot sun when I was met by a man riding a horse which I was very glad to discover was the one who had escaped. A foot passenger who was coming on from Springfield had stopped him after he had galloped about four miles and had taken advantage of the circumstance to treat himself to a ride. I then went back to the strawberries and finished them. As it was now three o'clock we went to a neighbouring house to get something to eat for ourselves and our horses. An old scarlet-faced Virginian gave our horses some corn, and his tall prim looking wife set a table for us with a rasher of bacon, a radish, bread and milk in pewter tumblers; they were methodists, and appeared to live in a comfortable way there being two rooms in their house and in one of them only one bed. A little farther on we forded Salt Creek a beautiful stream perfectly clear and flowing over pebbles and gravel, a rare sight in this country. A small prairie intervenes between this and Sugar Creek which we also forded, but with better success than two travellers who came after us, who attempting to cross it in another place were obliged to swim their horses, and one of them was thrown into the water. At evening we stopped at a log cabin on the edge of a prairie the width of which we were told was fifteen miles and on which there was not a house. The man had nothing for our horses but "a smart chance of pasture" as he called it in a little spot of ground enclosed from the prairie and which appeared when we saw it the next morning to be closely grazed to the very roots of the herbage. The dwelling was of the most wretched description. It consisted of but one room about half of which was taken up with beds and cribs, on one of which lay a man sick with a fever, and on another sprawled two or three children besides several who were asleep on the floor and all of whom were brown with dirt. In an enormous fireplace blazed a huge fire built against an enormous backlog reduced to a glowing coal, and before it the hostess and her daughter were busy in cooking a supper for several travellers who were sitting under a kind of piazza in front of the house or standing in the yard. As it was a great deal too hot in the house and a little too cool and damp in the night air we endeavoured to make the balance even by warming ourselves in the house and cooling ourselves out of doors alternately. About ten o'clock the sweaty hostess gave us our supper consisting of warm cakes, bacon coffee and lettuce with bacon grease poured over it. About eleven preparations were made for repose; the dirty children were picked up from the floor and a featherbed was pulled out of a corner and spread before the great fire for John and myself, but on our intimating that we did not sleep on feathers we had a place assigned to us near the door where we stretched ourselves on our saddle blankets for the night. The rest of the floor was taken up by other travellers with the exception of a small passage left for the sick man to get to the door. The floor of the piazza was also occupied with men wrapped in their blankets. The heat of the fire, the stifling atmosphere, the groans and tossings of the sick man who got up once in fifteen minutes to take medicine or go to the door, the whimperings of the children, and the offensive odours of the place prevented us from sleeping and by four o'clock the next morning we had caught and saddled our horses and were on our journey. We crossed the fifteen mile prairie and nearly three miles beyond came to the Mackinaw a fine clear stream watering Tazewell County which we forded, and about half a mile beyond came to a house where live a Quaker family of the name of Wilson. Here we got a nice breakfast which we enjoyed with great relish and some corn for our horses. Seven or eight miles further brought us to *Pleasant Grove* a fine tract of country and ten miles from Wilson's we came to a Mr. Shurtliff's where we had been advised to stop for the purpose of making some inquiries about the country. Shurtliff lives near the north end of Pleasant Grove and within four miles of the northern limit of the lands in market. The soil is fertile and well watered, the streams being rather more rapid than in Jacksonville and the region more than usually healthy. It is within eight miles of Pekin on the Illinois River, so that it is within convenient distance of a market, there is plenty of stone within a few miles and sawmills have been erected on some of the streams. I am strongly inclined to purchase a quarter section in this place.[5] We were now within two days ride of Dixon's where the American army is to be stationed, but being already much fatigued with our journey, the weather being hot and our horses though young and strong, so very lazy and obstinate as to give us constant employment in whipping them to keep them on a gentle trot on the smoothest road that we concluded to proceed no further. The next morning therefore we set out on our return. I should have mentioned that every few miles on our way we either fell in with bodies of Illinois militia proceeding to the American camp or saw where they had encamped for the night. They generally stationed themselves near a stream or spring on the edge of a wood and turned their horses to graze on the prairie. Their way was marked by trees, barked or girdled, and the road through the uninhabited country was as much beaten and as dusty as the highways on York [Manhattan] Island. Some of the settlers complain that they made war upon the pigs and chickens. They were a hard looking set of men unkempt and unshaved, wearing shirts of dark calico and sometimes calico capotes.[6]

In returning we crossed the large prairie already mentioned by a newer and more direct road to Jacksonville. In this distance we found but one inhabited house and one place about a quarter of a mile from it at which to water our horses. This house was situated in the edge of a small wood on an eminence in the midst of the prairie. An old woman was spinning at the door, and a boy and young woman had just left it with some fire to do the family washing at the watering place I have just mentioned. Two or three miles further on we came to another house in the edge of another grove which appeared to have been built about two years and which with the surrounding inclosures had been abandoned as I afterwards learned on account of sickness and the want of water. We frequently passed the holes of the prairie wolf but saw none of the animals. The green headed prairie fly came around our horses whenever we passed a marshy spot of ground and fastened upon them with the greediness of wolves almost maddening them. A little before sunset we came to a wood of thinly scattered oaks which marks the approach to a river in this country and descending a steep bluff came to the moist and rich bottom lands of the Sangamon. Next we passed through a thick wood of gigantic old elms sycamores mulberries &c and crossed the Sangamon in a ferry boat. We had our horses refreshed at the ferry house and proceeding three miles further knocked up a Kentuckian of the name of Armstrong who we understood had some corn. The man and his wife made no scruple in getting up to accommodate us. Every house on a great road in this country is a public house and nobody hesitates to entertain the traveller or accept his money. The woman who said she was Dutch (High Dutch probably) bestirred herself to get our supper. We told her we wanted nothing but bread and milk, on which she lamented that she had neither buttermilk nor sour milk, but we answered that we were Yankees and liked sweet milk best. She baked some cakes of corn bread and set them before us with a pitcher of milk and two tumblers. In answer to John who said something of the custom of the Yankees to eat the bread cut into the milk she said that she could give us spoons, if we were in *yearnest,* but we answered that they were quite unnecessary. On my saying that I had lived among the Dutch in New York and elsewhere,[7] she remarked that she reckoned that was the reason why I did not talk like a Yankee. I replied that no doubt living among the Dutch had improved my English. We were early on the road next morning and about 10 o'clock came to Cox's Grove a place about 25 miles from Jacksonville. In looking for a place to feed our horses I asked for corn at the cabin of an old settler named Wilson where I saw a fat dusky looking woman barefoot with six children as dirty as pigs and shaggy as bears. She was lousing one of them and cracking the unfortunate insects between her thumbnails. I was very glad when she told me that she had no corn nor oats. At the next house we found corn and seeing a little boy of two years old running about with a clean face I told John that we should get a clean breakfast. I was right. The man whose name was Short had a tall young wife in a clean cotton gown and shoes and stockings. She baked us some cakes fried some bacon and made a cup of coffee which being put on a clean table cloth and recommended by a good appetite was swallowed with some eagerness. Yet the poor woman had no tea spoons in the house and but one spoon for every purpose and this was pewter and had but half the handle. With this implement she dipped up the brown sugar and stirred it in our cups before handing them to us.— Short was also from Kentucky or Ken–tucky as they call it, as indeed was every man whom I saw on my journey except the Virginian, the Quaker family who were from Pennsylvania, and Shurtliff who is from Massachusetts but who has a Kentucky wife. I forgot to tell you that at Armstrong's we were accommodated for the night after the Kentucky fashion with a sheet under our persons and a blanket of cotten and woollen over them. About nine in the evening we reached Wiswall's very glad to repose from a journey which had been performed in exceedingly hot weather, on horses which required constant flogging to keep them awake, and in which we had not slept at the rate of more than three hours a night.

June 20. I went yesterday to make some inquiries as to the time when the stage will take me from Jacksonville. I find that I cannot get to the Illinois river until the 22nd or 23d. I have a strong desire to go to the American camp and if I find a steam boat going up to the rapids where they are stationed I shall probably go there before I return, but I much doubt whether I shall find a boat at this time bound to that place.[8] In the mean time I have seen every thing which this place has to show me and am ready to set out this moment if I had any way of getting on. The mail came in yesterday—it comes but once a week and I was somewhat disappointed in not getting a letter from you— If one should come next Tuesday it will be too late. The papers which have reached me from N. Y. are of the 31st of May. My love to Fanny and a kiss to the little one.

Yrs affectionately

W. C. Bryant.

Manuscript: NYPL–GR address: Mrs. Frances Bryant / Care of W. C. Bryant Esq. / New York postmark: JACKSONVILLE / JE [23?] postal annotation: 25¢ published (*in part*): *Prose*, II, 16–22.

1. Bryant overlooked his first letter, mailed at Maysville, Kentucky, on May 30 (Letter 242).

2. See "The Painted Cup," written on his second visit to Illinois, in 1841, and printed that year in the *EP* and the *Democratic Review*. See *Poems* (1876), pp. 282–283.

3. Bryant refers to the river, throughout this letter, as the "Sangamo," while calling the county "Sangamon." His confusion probably arose from local pronunciation, as well as from the fact that a few months before his visit the name of Springfield's newspaper was changed from the *Sangamon Journal* to the *Sangamo Journal*. See Rusk, *Middle Western Frontier*, II, 152.

4. The country practice called to "ride and tie" was followed by two persons sharing one horse; the first would ride a certain distance, then tie the horse to a tree and walk on, while his companion overtook the horse on foot and rode in his turn. An editorial a few years later illustrated Bryant's happy facility in combining literary allusion with homely experience to enliven political discussion. Noting that Daniel Web

ster and Henry Clay seemed to have borrowed from Henry Fielding's *Joseph Andrews* this custom of sharing one horse in their "pilgrimage" toward the "White House of Loretto," he remarked that Webster would mount first and "skirt through highways and byeways, making speeches, skimming the cream of all taverns by the road side, and eating his way to the White House, like a mouse in a cheese," at the same time permitting his rival "with great magnanimity" to "scour the country" and "reap all the glory left behind by the 'godlike man,'" until "the White House is full in view." *EP*, June 12, 1838.

5. Instead, Bryant bought land near Princeton, Illinois, where his brothers John and Cyrus settled the following fall.

6. No evidence has been found in Bryant's letters or other writings to support Godwin's allegation that he met and was much taken with the "quaint and pleasant talk" of a "raw youth" who led one of these militia companies, and who, he learned later, was Abraham Lincoln. See *Prose*, II, 20; *Life*, I, 283.

7. At Great Barrington, and during summer holidays at Fishkill Landing on the Hudson River.

8. Bryant's urge to visit the American camp was probably in his capacity as a journalist. He did not, however, manage to do so.

247. *To* Frances F. Bryant

Steam Boat Chattahoochee in the River Ohio,
off Mount Vernon, Indiana, June 28th, 1832

My dear Frances.

I am as you will see by the date of my letter on my return. I shall probably arrive at Louisville tomorrow where I shall put this into the Post Office. Instead of proceeding up the river it is my intention, if I can do so conveniently to take the stage for Lexington and thence to Maysville on the Ohio which will take me through one of the finest portions of Kentucky. At Maysville I shall again take the steam boat for Guyandotte; and from Guyandotte I shall go by land across the mountains through the state of Virginia by the Natural Bridge the Sulphur Springs &c. At what time I shall reach home by this route I cannot say, probably in the course of three weeks if not sooner. The road I intend to travel will take me to Fredericksburg in Virginia and thence to Washington. When I found myself obliged to give up the plan of returning by the way of Chicago I thought of going up the river to Pittsburgh and thence to Lake Erie, but Mr. Maginnis whom I mentioned in one of my previous letters has made me such representations of the beauty of the scenery and the *goodness of the accommodations* on the Fredericksburg road that I have concluded to take this opportunity of seeing what I might otherwise never see in my life time.

I was detained in Jacksonville four or five days, waiting for a conveyance to take me to the Illinois river, for Jacksonville like another place we read of though very easy to get into is hard to get out of. There are plenty of horses though the best of them are now like Moll Brook "gone to the wars,"[1] but wheel carriages there are none, or next to none. There is no regular line of coaches running to any place—but whenever a steam boat comes up the river with passengers for Jacksonville a carriage brings them in from Naples and takes back such as may wish to go down to St. Louis. The only incident which signalized the time while I thus loitered at Mr. Wiswall's was the death of a turkey buzzard to which I was in some measure accessary. Somebody had shot a hog in the woods near the house and as soon as the odour gave notice of the fact a flock of these birds gathered about it. I gave notice to a young man living at Mr. Wiswall's who went out and shot one of them for me. It is a kind of Vulture much resembling those figured in books of natural history with a bald wrinkled head and curving bill. The size is apparently equal to that of a middle sized turkey and the plumage is nearly the colour of the darker coloured turkies. The body is however small and light in proportion to its apparent size, but the wings are very long. It is a bird without either strength or fierceness, the talons are small and its only mode of defense, as the people here say is to eject from its stomach upon its enemy the offensive food it has swallowed. As it does nothing but clear the country of the carrion it finds it is not often killed. The quills are sometimes used for writing.

Illinois abounds in game. The plover the killdeer or sand-piper and the marsh quail abound in the prairies, and the common quail in the grounds where there are thickets, or scattered trees. The woods abound with squirrels rabbits pigeons, mourning doves, and the autumn brings the prairie hens and wild turkeys in flocks about the wheat stacks. There is a bird esteemed a great delicacy here called the wood cock, a different bird from that known by the name in the New York markets. It is a large black bird of the wood pecker species.

On Saturday last June 23d I went to the village of Jacksonville early in the morning expecting to find a carriage from Naples to take me to the Illinois. None however had arrived, and I was obliged to stay in that hot dirty place all day. Saturday is an idle day with many of the settlers from Kentucky and the neighbouring states. Accordingly the village was full of them, trading at the shops drinking at the groceries, and swapping horses. In the afternoon many of them were drunk a fight took place, one man was terribly bruised and many jackets were pulled off, but a peace officer having interfered they were put on again. About evening three carriages came in from Naples, in one of them were Peter and his wife who had just arrived from Massachusetts, after a journey of five weeks. They came by the same way which Dr. Jones took, but met with still greater delays. Peter's wife resembles her Mississippi brother.[2] Nothing has been heard of Cyrus since he wrote to Cummington, early in May I believe, expressing his intention to go to Illinois by the way of Chicago. I hope the Indians have not got him.[3]

I set out for Naples early on Sunday morning and got there about nine o'clock. It was not until 3 or 4 in the afternoon that the boat arrived at Naples. The next morning soon after breakfast I was in St. Louis. I called on Mr. Maginnis who received me with great civility and gave me a memorandum for my journey through Virginia.[4] I breakfasted with him the following morning and was introduced to Mrs. Maginnis a New York lady of agreeable manners. I was glad to get a breakfast fit for a Christian in the shape of some griddle cakes of Indian meal instead of those monstrous loads of meat with a small plate of stale sour bread which they give you morning, noon and night on board the steamboats. A western man's notion of living well is to have plenty of meat. The Kentuckian thinks corn bread and bacon the best living in the world. He is right in preferring corn bread to such wheat bread as is to be found here, and I follow his example for the bread made of wheat flour is invariably sour.

On Tuesday morning, June 26 I left St. Louis in this steam boat. I had now an opportunity of seeing a part of the western shore of the Mississippi which on my way up I passed in the night. The mixture of precipices and woods on that side of the river formed a succession of beautiful and striking scenery. Sometimes the rocks flamed with wild roses, for here and in Illinois grows a rose the gayest and most profuse of flowers of any of its tribe. The flowers just opened are of a deep crimson, those which are more unfolded are of all shades between this and a pale damask. I have provided myself with some of the seeds. The Missouri is at this time very high, and is covered with drift wood consisting of dry trunks and fragments of trees of every size. It is a perfect torrent of mud in which the transparent waters of the Mississippi are lost a few rods below their junction. The Missouri water however when suffered to settle is excellent for drinking. The city of St. Louis is entirely supplied with it.

You will not be surprised if at St. Louis I felt a vague desire to wander further. I was on the banks of the longest river in the world. A voyage of five days would take me to New Orleans. To the north west, was the Missouri stretching eighteen hundred miles into the uninhabited interior. Boats ply regularly between St. Louis and Palmyra three hundred miles up the river, and a steam boat called the Yellow Stone sometimes ascends the whole eighteen hundred miles to the United States Military Station at the mouth of the Yellow Stone River. Either course would take me to a new climate and among new people.[5]

The reed cane grows on the banks of this part of the Ohio. I gathered one of the plants this morning. You have seen it often in the shape of fishing poles and walking sticks. At every joint is a stem which branches into a number of smaller ones thickly covered with small lanceolate grass-like leaves having the taste of the sweetest grass and yielding a pasturage of which cattle are very fond.

Among our passengers is a Mr. Burton a slender dark haired sallow faced man of perhaps thirty years of age with plenty of baggage a negro servant an elegant rifle a showy powder flask and a fiddle. When we left

St. Louis the steam boat was uncommonly full of passengers—for you must know that the number, except in the New Orleans boats rarely exceeds a dozen. A grave looking man, very tall with a broad face, hollow cheeks, red whiskers and a huge white hat took passage among the rest. He had a companion in a big white hat also. Yesterday they got Mr. Burton to try his luck at cards and after playing all day and a part of the night they stripped him of all the money he had and all he could borrow. Having squeezed him dry about the middle of the night they took passage for New Orleans in a steamboat which we met on her way from Louisville. This morning the unfortunate gentleman who lost the money was endeavoring to solace himself with playing on the fiddle. He complained that it had but three strings. I told him of Paganini who played better on a single string than any other fiddler on four. He had never heard of Paganini.[6] Since that he has produced a Faro table from his trunk and in playing with another passenger has lost his rifle. His present amusement is brushing his hair with that enormity of nastiness the common brush which in every western steamboat hangs by one of the looking glasses.

Hitherto my journey as it has been the longest so it has been altogether the most delightful I ever took. Had I those with me whom I have left behind I could imagine nothing more pleasant. Travelling to the west had been associated in my mind with the idea of hard[ship]—it is mere pastime.

If you should see Miss R[obbins] tell her that I left Edward [Harte] well and pleased with his new situation. It is not very likely that you will get another letter from me though that will depend on the delays I meet with in my journey. I suppose that by this time you are comfortably settled in your new house— Ah, if you could see the Illinois houses! or what is more to the purpose if you were obliged to sleep in one of them—or live in one of them a week! My love to the children.

Yrs affectionately
W. C. Bryant

June 29. This letter will hardly get at the Louisville Post Office today as we shall not probably arrive until late in the night. I should have mentioned among other things worth seeing on the Mississippi, the Jefferson Barracks, a military station of the United States, on the west bank of the river some forty miles I should think below St. Louis. It is situated in a fine natural park of noble trees principally black oak which extends I am told for some miles back from the shore. The trees are at considerable distances from each other and the tops are spreading and full of foliage. The barracks surround a kind of eminence on which is a level space for military exercises &c.[7] I should take notice also of the floating gristmills turned by the current of the river which go from place to place and grind corn for the neighbourhood where they fix themselves. Storeboats as they are called with little assortments of goods like those in a country store go up and down these rivers and supply the settlers with merchandise apropos of gristmills. I have just passed on[e] at Brandenburg on the Kentucky side where a stream gushes out of the side of a hill a few yards from the Ohio and is made to turn a gristmill before it gets to the river. Talking with some gentlemen at St. Louis of the want of water in Illinois they assured me that the case was formerly the same with Kentucky and that it was feared that portions of it never would be settled for that reason. Since it has been settled and cultivated however springs have appeared and rivulets have been formed where there were none before and the state is now abundantly watered. A stream flows through Lexington where there was none at the time the town was laid out. In Illinois water is found every where near the surface of the ground. In Morgan county it is found impossible to have cellars to the houses on account of their filling with water.

W. C. B.

June 30. We have arrived at Louisville. Soon after writing the above the alarm of fire was given on board our boat. The roof of the upper deck at the stern was discovered to be on fire and the smoke was making its escape in dense volumes. The boat was steered to land and the passengers with their baggage got on shore amidst great confusion. I came in for my share of the accidents having my hat knocked off into the water and my head struck by a plank which a fellow was throwing out so that I was obliged to drop my trunk and save myself by leaping some distance. Luckily however I suffered no material injury—either on head trunk or hat except that my clothes in the trunk were made a little damp. The roofing of the boat was stripped off and the fire got under control in a few minutes, though it seemed at one time as if the boat would be consumed. This was thirty miles below Louisville.

I should think my journey through Virginia might take a fortnight, but I cannot learn any thing very certain of the time it will require. I might come home very soon by the *fast* line which travels night & day but I prefer to sleep nights.— I shall probably stop a day at the Natural Bridge.—8

June 30. We arrived at Louisville last night at half past ten o'clock after an accident which you will find something about in another part of the letter.

MANUSCRIPT: NYPL–GR ADDRESS: Mrs. Frances Bryant / Care of W. C. Bryant Esq. / New York POSTMARK: LOUISVILLE / KY / JUL / 1 POSTAL ANNOTATION: 25.

1. The editors are grateful to Professor Harry Oster for the plausible suggestion that the words "Moll Brook" were associated in popular pronunciation with the subject's name in the French folksong *Malbrough s'en va-t-en guerre,* then well known in this country, and probably sung by Cullen and Frances Bryant and little Fanny in

connection with their study of French. The horses here, of course, have gone to the Black Hawk War.

2. Six weeks earlier Arthur Bryant had married, at Richmond, Massachusetts, Henrietta B. Plummer, sister of his brother Austin's wife Adeline, and of Congressman Franklin E. Plummer of Mississippi. Sarah to Cyrus Bryant, May 8, 1832, BCHS. See 232.12.

3. Cyrus reached Jacksonville on July 6, two weeks after Cullen had left for home. See Letter 248.

4. An undated, unsigned memorandum in NYPL–GR, which is in all likelihood the one referred to, reads: "Mr. Bryant will go to Guyandotte and from there take the stage to Lewisburgh, at Lewisburgh he will leave the main route and take that which goes by Fincastle the Sweetspring and the Natural Bridge. The Natural Bridge is between Fincastle & Lexington about 12 miles from the latter. Mr. Bryant's best plan will be to stop at what is called the Natural Bridge tavern distant one mile & a half from the Bridge the tavern is on the stage road— On the morning that Mr. B. leaves what are called the Falls of the Kenhawa he will enquire from the driver of the stage the exact distance from the 'Falls' to the pass or Cliff on the River. I think it is about 9 miles; the drivers when requested always stop to let passengers visit this fine scene."

5. Although, for the rest of his life, Bryant was an insatiable traveler, he never went farther west than this.

6. The Italian violinist Nicolò Paganini (1782–1840), whose virtuosity was by this time legendary.

7. Near the present Crystal City, in Jefferson County, Missouri.

8. In his haste to rejoin his family after learning of the cholera epidemic in New York, Bryant seems to have by-passed the Natural Bridge. See the accounts of his itinerary in Letters 248 and 249.

248.   *To* Mrs. Sarah S. Bryant

New York   August 23   1832

Dear Mother,

I got back to New York on the 12th of July having been absent on my western journey between seven and eight weeks, nearly three of which were passed in Illinois. I went in the first place to Baltimore, whence I proceeded to Wheeling on the Ohio, travelling for the greater part of the way, through the state of Maryland. At Wheeling I took a steamboat for Cincinnati, where I staid two days. From Cincinnati I went to Louisville in Kentucky and there I took passage for St. Louis in Missouri. At St. Louis I was detained a day and a half. I then went up the Illinois in a steam boat to Naples twenty miles from Jacksonville, whence I was conveyed in a carriage to my place of destination. I found John well. He was at work on Arthur's farm; he had bought a yoke of oxen and various implements for the purpose and had planted a field of corn which like most of the corn planted in Illinois, had not come up very well—about a third of the hills having no plants in them. He planted it over while I was there, but the crows pulled up nearly half of what was planted a second time. The corn is late in all Illinois, but as a great deal of ground is planted with it this year, there will be a large supply provided the frosts do not come unusually early, as they have done for the two last seasons. If they should, the corn will be cut off again. The wheat crop in that state is thin this year. Arthur's field looked better than most—it was thin, but the ears were long. John bought a horse while I was there to plough among the corn—for corn is never hoed there. The farm, concerning which you enquire, and which John thought of purchasing, is contiguous to Arthur's, and like that, is situated in the midst of the prairie on which Jacksonville stands. It is without timber—the land is apparently very good, and there are springs on it—but I think it doubtful whether it is worth while to pay five hundred dollars for an 80 acre lot when there is so much Congress land to be had for $1.25 an acre.[1]

The night before I left Jacksonville, while I was waiting at the Tavern for a conveyance, Arthur arrived with his wife. He had been five weeks on his passage which he described as tedious and uncomfortable— but they both appeared to be well. I think they will have a cold time of it this winter in the little log cabin unless it is much repaired.[2] The doors are composed of small pieces of split wood and are about as serviceable in keeping out the cold as an old flour barrel would be. The stable too lets in the wind as all log stables do, on all sides—and as for privies I do not believe there are a dozen in all Illinois except in the villages. I have had two letters from John since I returned. Before I came away he informed me that he apprehended some difficulty with Arthur about dividing the land, but I told him I did not believe that any could occur; and from a conversation which I had with Arthur the night before I started on my return, I supposed that the matter would be easily arranged. John however informs me that Arthur has proposed to let him have half the farm at the rate he paid for it—but that he must pay him $33\frac{1}{3}$ per cent interest on the purchase money—which would make a difference of sixty dollars or more—I believe.— John has declined doing this, offering to pay 12 per cent. How they will settle this matter I do not know; John has done a good deal of work on the farm and spent a good deal of money in buying seed corn and other things. I should not be surprised, however, if he were to leave the place. If so he will go north, where there are lands not taken up.[3]

I went with him over Sangamon County and through a part of Tazewell. In the latter county I found a lot of 160 acres which I directed John to have entered for me and left him the money. It is a fine country about eight miles from Pekin which lies on the Illinois river. We were gone five days—travelling on horse back and sleeping at night in log cabins where the whole family pigged together in one room.

The country, at least such parts of it as I have seen, is extraordinarily fertile, it is very level however, and some parts of it are destitute of water. I do not believe there is a more productive country on the face of the earth. The soil is a deep rich black, fine mould which when mixed with water makes a composition almost as black as the Extract of Gentian and as sleek looking. It is in short the richest garden soil. I believe the upland prairies to be quite healthy. The general aspect of the country is monotonous,—it wants clear running streams, and has only the beauty which arises from a gently undulating surface and luxuriance of vegetation. It wants turf—the grass grows thin in the fields and prairies, and the sides of the road and the door yards and immediate vicinity of the dwellings are covered with weeds—mostly smartweed and mayweed. The people are principally from Kentucky Tennessee and other slave states. A large proportion of them are ignorant—though often shrewd enough—and are inclined to get drunk and fight on Saturdays. The village of Jacksonville is a remarkably moral place—more so than most villages in New England, and the people seem intelligent. It is a collection of mean little houses about a dirty square, and is one of the ugliest and most unpleasant places I ever saw. It stands in the midst of a prairie and is without a tree, except some very little ones just planted—but these are not on the principal square. The population of Illinois is improving—but they did not seem to me so bad a set as some represent them. I met with nothing but civility and kindness on my journey of a hundred miles in the interior.

On my return to New York I passed through Virginia. I left the Ohio at Guyandot and crossed the state from west to east, passing by the Burning Spring which I stopped to look at, the Cliff at New River, the White Sulphur Springs, the Hot Springs, and the Warm Springs—all of a sulphurous character. I also passed the Virginia University, within sight of Jefferson's seat at Monticello and arrived at Fredericks[burg] on the Rappahannock. A ride of a few miles brought me to the Potowmac where I took a steam boat for Washington.

Cyrus arrived at Jacksonville on the 6th of July after I left the place. I have had a letter from him.[4] He bought a pony for 25 dollars before leaving Michigan, but the animal was taken sick at Niles, a town on the St. Joseph; so he was obliged to leave him behind and proceed with a pack on his back the rest of the journey. From Chicago to Iroquois 75 miles he saw no white person. He passed two nights in the open air— John writes that he camped one night among the Pottawattomies. He went from Chicago to Danville 130 miles and then 170 miles west to Jacksonville. The weather was hot, the pack heavy, no water was to be had except in the creeks, where it was very bad and they were at a great distance from each other so that he suffered trouble with thirst and arrived at Jacksonville almost half dead with fatigue. There were six places where it was 15 miles from one house to another and no water between.

August 24. Today I got your letter of the 21st.[5] What you relate to me of the affairs of John and Peter was not unknown to me, as you will see by what I have already written. I advised John before I came away, to leave the neighbourhood, unless Peter dealt fairly with him, and let him have half the land according to the original conditions; for I was convinced that otherwise this would be the beginning of jealousies and misunderstandings, and that they would live more peaceably apart. I should now advise John not to take the land unless he thinks he is perfectly satisfied that he gets it at the rate at which he was given to understand he should have it when he went out to Illinois,—for if he does I fear there will not be a good agreement between them afterwards. John's last letter was dated the 25th of July. I shall write to him immediately. He must say to Peter as Abraham did to Lot—"Let there be no strife, I pray thee between thee and me. If thou wilt take to the right I will go to the left" &c.[6] Yet Jacksonville is on some accounts a desirable place to live in—the people are more intelligent and orderly and the opportunities of education will be better there than in any other part of the state—for the present at least. There are however other places which present quite as good, and I think better opportunities of enriching one's self by agriculture. As for assisting John in any way myself, I told him when I was there to what extent I could do it. I should think it would be his policy to go to Tazewell County. Cyrus is going to make an exploring excursion as soon as the weather is cool enough.

The cholera is declining here—the alarm is nearly over—the people are returning to their homes and the business of the city begins to revive. At one time so many houses and shops were shut up, and there was such a silence in the streets that every day seemed like Sunday except that you saw no well dressed people going to church. The mortality has been mostly confined to the drunken and the imprudent, though complaints of the stomach, such as diarrhea colic, &c have been common. My wife has been sick abed with complaints of this kind once or twice and I was obliged to keep my bed on one occasion for two days. The disorder occasions extreme weakness. I have never felt myself so soon exhausted by exercise as this summer notwithstanding that I was never so strong as I had been for a year or two previous. The baby has had a great deal of diarrhea. Fanny alone has enjoyed perfect health. She went to Great Barrington in the beginning of June and staid there a fortnight and has been ever since in as complete health as it is possible for a human being to enjoy. We think ourselves as safe here [i.e., at Hoboken] as we should be any where else. My wife sends her love.—My regards to all.

Yr affectionate Son
W   C. BRYANT

As for Miss Robbins we suppose her to be in the country—as she told my wife about the beginning of July that she expected to go, and we have heard nothing of her since. I overtook Edward in going out to Illinois and went with him the rest of the way. He is quite contented with the place.

MANUSCRIPT: BCHS ADDRESS: Mrs. Sarah S. Bryant / Cummington / Massachusetts. POSTMARK: NEW YORK / AUG / 25 POSTAL ANNOTATION: Single paid / PAID 18¾.

1. By the Public Land Act of 1820, the price of government-owned western land was reduced from $2 to $1.25 an acre, and the minimum unit of sale to 80 acres. Morison, *History of the American People*, pp. 403–404.

2. This was the crude squatter's-cabin described in Letter 245. Luckily for Arthur and his bride, who were ill much of the time, the winter in Jacksonville that year was unusually mild. Arthur to Sarah Bryant, April 2, 1833, BCHS.

3. The disputes between the two youngest Bryant brothers were of great concern to the rest of the family. See Letter 260; Sarah to Cyrus Bryant, September 30, 1832, BCHS; John to Sarah Bryant, October 6, 1833, BCHS.

4. Unrecovered.

5. Unrecovered.

6. Cf. Gen. 13:8–9.

249. *To* Richard H. Dana

New York   Oct. 8   1832.

My dear Sir.

I am truly sorry to hear so bad an account as you give of your health.[1] I can only say for your comfort that bilious attacks have been uncommonly violent and dangerous this season. Most of the complaints called here "premonitory symptoms of the cholera" have been, I believe, of the kind, and these have prevailed almost every where. Besides one or two slight attacks, and a general bad state of the bowels which kept me as weak as a cat all summer, I had one which sent me to my bed and kept me there two or three days. I am inclined to think that the severity of the disorder in your case was in a measure owing to the season, and that there is a probability of your suffering less the next time.

You say right we have had a fearful time in New York—the pestilence striking down its victims on the right hand and the left—often at noonday but mostly in darkness, for of the thousands who had the disorder three quarters were attacked at the dead of night. I have been here from the 12th of July when I returned from the westward till the present time, coming every morning from Hoboken to attend to my daily occupation, every morning witnessing the same melancholy spectacle of deserted and silent streets and forsaken dwellings, and every day looking over and sending out to the world the list of the sick and dead.[2] My own health and that of my wife and youngest child in the mean time have been bad, with a state of the stomach like that produced by taking lead or some other mineral poison. Since the second week in September the state of things has changed—and my own health was never better than it is at this moment.

I am much obliged to you for conveying to me the proposal of the booksellers—I forget their names—to print a second edition of my book.[3] There are I believe about a hundred copies of the first on hand and I must see them fairly off before I print again. [Elam] Bliss *sells* as slow as Old Rapid in the play *sleeps*.[4] Any other bookseller would have got off the whole before this time—but he is a good creature and I could not find it in my heart to refuse his instances to be permitted to publish the book. What you say of Blackwood's animadversions about fancy &c is just.[5] I am a little mortified that the transatlantic critics will not look at my "Past" which I think my best thing.[6] You ask who has noticed me abroad. Blackwood you have seen. My book was made the subject of a rather extravagant but brief notice in Campbell's Metropolitan. They say it is also noticed at some length in the last number of the Foreign Quarterly Review which I have not seen. The Atheneum, the Literary Gazette and some of the other weekly literary journals, no great authorities in matters of criticism spoke of the work when it first appeared and made large extracts. I read somewhere that it was reviewed in the Penny Magazine—which though less than a "twopenny affair" (pronounced *tuppeny*) comes out under the auspices of the Society for the Diffusion of Knowledge and has a circulation of I believe 15,000 copies.[7]

I have seen the great west, where I ate corn bread and hominy, & slept in log houses with twenty men women and children in the same room. I went to Baltimore where I took the rail road and crossed the mountains to Wheeling in Virginia. Here I embarked in a steamboat for Cincinnati. From Cincinnati I went to Louisville in Kentucky and then took another steamboat for St. Louis in Missouri. From St. Louis I ascended the Mississippi to its junction with the Illinois, whence I was conveyed in a waggon to Jacksonville where two of my brothers live. At Jacksonville I got on a horse and travelled about a hundred miles to the northward over the immense prairies with scattered settlements on the edges of the groves. These prairies, of a soft fertile garden soil, and a smooth undulating surface, on which you may put a horse to full speed, covered with high thinly growing grass, full of weeds and gaudy flowers, and destitute of bushes or trees, perpetually brought to my mind the idea of their having been once cultivated. They looked to me like the fields of a race which had passed away, whose enclosures and habitations had decayed, but on those vast and rich plains smoothed and levelled by tillage the forest has not yet encroached.[8]

I came back through Virginia, leaving the Ohio at a place called Guyandotte. I visited the Kenha[wa] falls, the cliff on New River, the Burning Springs, saw many fine views from the ridges of the Alleghanies &c &c. At Cloverdale a plantation among the Alleganies I heard that the cholera was in New York—and accordingly I made all haste homewards. The journey was much less fatiguing than I expected to find it. Travelling in the western steam boats is much pleasanter than in the eastern ones. There is not so much hurry, ill manners and confusion—

I hope you have not given up the idea of coming to New York because you could not come this summer.[9] What if you should come in the present month and see how autumn looks in this region? You are a man of leisure and should give a part of your time to your friends.—

I am yrs &c.

W. C BRYANT.

P. S. Dr. [Henry J.] Anderson who has just called tells me that he has no doubt that the notice of my poems in the Foreign Quarterly was written in this country. Their critic's notion of prosody is the same as Dr. Mc-Henry's.[10]

MANUSCRIPT: NYPL–GR ADDRESS: Richard H. Dana Esq / care of William Ellery Esq. / Newport / R. I. POSTMARK: NEW-YORK / OCT / 8 ENDORSED: Wm C. Bryant / Oct 8—1832 / Answered PUBLISHED (in part): Life, I, 285–286.

1. Dana's comments on his health were omitted from that portion of his letter of October 3 published in Life, I, 284–285. The manuscript is unrecovered.

2. This epidemic swept Europe and Great Britain in 1831–1832, and arriving in New York by way of Canada in June, caused more than 3,500 deaths in the city before receding in September. While it still raged, Bryant wrote in the EP on August 20, that, following the exodus of more than 100,000 persons to the suburbs, "so many domestic fires have been put out, and the furnaces of so many manufactories have been extinguished, that the dense cloud of smoke which always lay over the city," as seen from Hoboken, "is now so thin as often to be scarcely discernible, and the buildings of the great metropolis appear with unusual clearness and distinctness." See Hone, Diary, I, 65–74, passim.

3. Dana had apparently proposed that Bryant offer his poems for republication by the Boston firm of Russell, Odiorne, and Company, his own publishers.

4. The source of this allusion has not been identified.

5. See Life, I, 284. A review of Bryant's 1832 Poems by John Wilson in Blackwood's Edinburgh Magazine, 31 (April 1832), 646–664, is reprinted in part in McDowell, Representative Selections, pp. 376–379.

6. "The Past." See Poems (1876), pp. 171–173.

7. The notices to which Bryant refers included those in Metropolitan, 3 (April 1832), 110–114; Foreign Quarterly Review, 10 (August 1832), 121–138; London Literary Gazette, 16 (March 1832), 131–132; and Penny Magazine, 1 (June 30, 1832), 134–135.

8. In "The Prairies," published the following year in the Knickerbocker, Bryant incorporated half a dozen of the ideas and images offered here in prose. See Poems (1876), pp. 184–189.

9. Dana feared to visit New York because of the cholera.

10. See 237.2 and 237.3. A critic in the Foreign Quarterly Review found Bryant possessed of "great descriptive power," but lacking a "good ear for metrical rhythm."

250. [To the Editor of the SACRED OFFERING?][1]

New York Oct. 30 1832.

Dear Sir

I send you a few lines which I wrote for the "Sacred Offering," and which you will forward for publication if you think them worthy—if not dispose of them as you please. I had no verses on hand when I received your note, and the cholera, just then, made us all sadly unpoetical. The little poem is on the other leaf.²

I am Sir
With the highest esteem and respect
Yrs &c
WM. C. BRYANT

MANUSCRIPT: University of Kansas Libraries.

1. Sometime in 1833 a collection of poems taken from *The Sacred Offering: A Poetical Annual* (London, 1831–1834) was apparently published at Boston with the title *Sacred Offering*, by Joseph Dowe. No copy of this work has been found, but in 1838 a second volume, alluding to the first as having appeared several years earlier, was printed with the same title. The editor was not named.

2. This poem, reprinted in the *Sacred Offering* (1838), pp. 15–16, was "The Journey of Life." See *Poems* (1876), pp. 193–194. Although Bryant first collected it in his 1834 *Poems*, his biographer Parke Godwin assigned it to the 1832 collection, then offered the fanciful supposition that it reflected "despondency" over the "failure of the poet's literary schemes after coming to New York in 1825," and dated its composition 1826! *Poetical Works*, I, 346; see also *Life*, I, 228. More plausibly, as this letter indicates, it expressed a natural human reaction to the cholera epidemic, coupled with Bryant's own illness, and that of his wife and baby daughter, with the "premonitory symptoms."

251. *To* Mrs. Sarah S. Bryant

New York   Dec. 17, 1832

Dear Mother.

It is so long since I have heard from Cummington that I begin to feel some curiosity to know what has taken place in the mean time; for so long a period cannot have been entirely barren of events. I take it for granted that you did not go to Illinois last fall, as I have heard nothing of your arrival there from John or Arthur, both of whom have written to me lately. Is there any prospect that Austin will sell his farm? Does he still continue to think of emigrating?¹

John seems to be much pleased with the station which he and Cyrus had selected on the Bureau River, in Putnam County.² He left Cyrus there, and came back to Jacksonville where he took a school. This, however, he was obliged to give up after having kept it about a week, on account of a letter he received from Cyrus, informing him that the person whom John had engaged to assist him in his room, had gone off after working one day, —that there was no other person in the place who could be had, and that John's assistance was indispensably necessary. What Cyrus was doing, and what John was to help him about, is not explained. John, however, is in good spirits, and says that he has now a prospect of getting along in the world. Both he and Cyrus are *squatters* on the land they occupy. John's letter is dated Nov. 21.³

Arthur on the other hand seems to be low spirited. His chronic rheumatism has returned—owing I believe for my part, to living in a cabin which lets in the wind in all directions. Money is scarce with him; he is in debt, and fears that he shall be obliged to part with his farm in order to pay his debts. He complains of the high rate of interest in Illinois, by which a debt once contracted increases with great rapidity.

Cyrus also is in want of money, or is likely to be so next spring, as I learn by a letter received from him not long since.—[4]

As for my own affairs, you may have perceived by the paper, that I have purchased one additional share in the Evening Post and am now the proprietor of one third.— Mr. Gill the Bookkeeper has retired from the firm, though he still continues to act as clerk.[5]

I understand from Frances that you find it difficult, and sometimes even impossible to pay the interest on your note to Dr. Shaw, and that he takes a new note of you when you cannot pay the interest, exacting interest upon interest. Will you do me the favour to let me know what is the amount of the note at present, and at what time in the year the interest falls due—that I may relieve you from the solicitude you must feel at seeing the debt increase from year to year.[6]

What is the state of the ecclesiastical affairs of Cummington? Is Mr. Hawkes still with you? If he is gone, whither? and whom have you in his place?[7]

As to our condition—we are all in good health. Fanny is much better than last winter. She crosses the ferry every day to go to school. Julia is now quite well—better than she has been since we removed to Hoboken. During the greater part of the summer she was ill with teething and a constant diarrhea. At one time she had a violent attack of the dysentery. She is now quite plump and playful. She rides out every clear day in her little waggon and when at home is in continual motion. She does not, however, begin to talk yet.

Mr. Sands died last evening suddenly by an apopleptic stroke. He was my next door neighbour.[8]

Give my regards to the family—

Your affectionate Son
W. C. BRYANT

MANUSCRIPT: BCHS.

1. Austin Bryant had considered following his younger brothers to Illinois, and his mother was eager to go along, feeling no reluctance to leave neighbors not one of whom, she wrote Charity Bryant, "would give nine pence to have us stay" (January 21, 1835, BCHS). But Austin, who managed the homestead for his mother, had recently taken back his own Plainfield farm from a bankrupt purchaser. Sarah to Cyrus Bryant, June 21, 1833, BCHS.

2. Later Bureau County, which John Bryant established with legislative help from Stephen A. Douglas. Brown, *John Howard Bryant*, p. 26.

3. Unrecovered.

4. Unrecovered.

5. Through a complex series of transactions between November 14 and December 1, 1832, Thomas Gill and Hetty Coleman, the founder's widow, retired from ownership in the *EP*, leaving Bryant, Leggett, and Charles Burnham, son of the former business manager, as equal partners. This was effected through a $7,000 loan from Congressman Churchill Cambreleng, which was secured by a mortgage on the paper. See *"Evening Post* Accounts," NYPL–GR.

6. Neither the occasion for, nor the amount of, Mrs. Bryant's debt to her daughter Sally's widower, now remarried, has been determined.

7. Roswell Hawkes (d. 1870) had succeeded the first Cummington minister, James Briggs (1745–1825), and ran a "select school" at Cummington attended in 1826–1827 by John Bryant. Later Hawkes taught at Mount Holyoke Female Seminary after its founding in 1836 by Mary Lyon. See Brown, *John Howard Bryant*, p. 13; *Only One Cummington*, p. 399.

8. Robert Charles Sands (1799–1832, Columbia 1815), Bryant's close friend and collaborator in *The Talisman, Tales of Glauber-Spa*, and the Sketch Club, is reported to have died crying "Oh Bryant, Bryant." *Life*, I, 289. Since he was alone in the house with his mother and sister, with Bryant next door, this seems quite probable.

252. *To* Gulian C. Verplanck

New York   Monday   Dec   17   1832

Dear Sir,

I write in great haste to tell you of the death of our friend Sands. He had been engaged very assiduously on Sunday and the evening previous in preparing an article for Hoffman's Magazine—the Knickerbocker.[1] Between four and five o'clock yesterday afternoon he complained of indisposition, and said he would go up stairs. He rose but soon fell to the floor and being helped to bed shortly fell into a state of stupor from which he did not recover and in about four hours from the attack died without a struggle. His mother and sister are in great grief. The funeral will take place tomorrow.

Yrs truly

W. C. BRYANT

MANUSCRIPT: NYPL–Berg ADDRESS: Hon. Gulian C. Verplanck / Member of Congress / Washington POSTMARK: NEW-YORK / DEC / 19 POSTAL ANNOTATION: FREE DOCKETED: W. C. Bryant.

1. Sands's article "Poetry of the Esquimaux" had been planned to accompany Bryant's poem "The Arctic Lover." See *Poems* (1876), pp. 191–193. These were published with Bryant's "Memoir of Robert C. Sands" in the *Knickerbocker*, 1 (January 1833), 49–59. This was the first of many tributes to writers and artists of his acquaintance which Bryant composed over a period of forty years.

253. *To* Gulian C. Verplanck

New York   Dec   19   1832

My dear Sir

Mr. Garcia has requested me to remind you of his petition about the chain cables. I am sorry to give you the trouble of reading another letter about the business and only do so at his particular request. I suppose he would be very glad to have the question disposed of in some way or other. At present he is, I believe, poor. A lawsuit in which the conduct of his partner in Havana involved him, without however throwing any stain on his individual reputation, has destroyed the credit of the house to which he belonged.—[1]

Yrs truly

W. C. BRYANT

MANUSCRIPT: NYPL–Berg ADDRESS: Hon. G. C. Verplanck / Member of Congress / Washington POSTMARK: NEW-YORK / DEC / 19 DOCKETED: W. C. Bryant.

1. Mr. Garcia is unidentified, but see Letter 235.

254.   To Gulian C. Verplanck

New York   Dec   22   1832.

My dear Sir

As you are at work on the subject of the tariff I take the liberty of inclosing you some observations on the subject of the duty on imported syrup which appears to have been taxed by the tariff of the last session much beyond its real value in comparison with sugar. This disproportionate tax is so much the more objectionable inasmuch as inspissated cane juice is in some respects a raw material and requires a peculiar process for converting it into sugar. The effect of the duty therefore is to throw the concluding process of the manufacture into the hands of the foreigner. Besides it [is] imported in larger quantities as an article of domestic consumption like molasses from the richer and better qualities of which it is difficult if not impossible to distinguish it—a circumstance which will naturally lead to its being introduced under that name in evasion of the law, in spite of any duties that might be imposed.[1]

Yrs truly

W. C. BRYANT

MANUSCRIPT: NYPL–Berg ADDRESS: Hon. G. C. Verplanck / Member of Congress / Washington POSTMARK: NEW-YORK / DEC / 22 DOCKETED: W. C. Bryant.

1. Verplanck, a lame-duck congressman after his defeat for re-election in November, was still chairman of the powerful Committee on Ways and Means of the House. In December 1832 he introduced an administration bill proposing sharp reductions in the tariff. But a compromise bill submitted by Henry Clay was passed the following March, giving a "new lease on life to his reputation as the 'Great Pacificator.'" Van Deusen, *Jacksonian Era*, p. 79. See July, *Essential New Yorker*, pp. 156–162.

255.   To Gulian C. Verplanck

New York   Dec. 24, 1832.

My dear Sir

Mr. Sands's friends are desirous that a collection should be made of such of his works as are most worthy of preservation accompanied with some notice of his life. They know of no person to whom they would so willingly entrust the task of making the selection and writing the memoir as yourself; and none whom, on account of your intimacy with him and your respect for his talents, they could with more propriety solicit to undertake it. Mr. Ward and Dr. Neilson both spoke to me on the subject,[1] and although I have had no conversation with the family about it, yet I understand from Mr. Ward that when the plan of publishing his remains was mentioned to his mother and sister, they both expressed a strong desire that you should be applied to. It is intended to publish the work by subscription for the benefit of the family whom Mr. Sands's death has left in a needy situation. A selection might be made from his works which would do credit to our literature, and accompanied by one of those biographical notices which you so well know how to make it would be a book which every body must have.[2] I have promised to write to you on the subject and request you to undertake the work. You will think with me I doubt not that something should be done for the memory of our friend who during his lifetime was not known as his talents and his writings deserved to make him.

I threw together the other day a few notices of his life for Hoffman's Magazine. Along with what I wrote will be published the fragment of an article which he was composing for the same periodical when he was attacked by the disorder which carried him off. It is a piece of pleasantry an article on Esquimaux literature with translations like Bowring's.[3]

Mr. Sands's death has made a great vacuum in the literary world here, and, numerous as his friends were has occasioned a deeper and more general feeling of regret than you would have imagined.

Will you answer this when you have made up your mind on the question of undertaking to be the editor of such a work as I have mentioned. Think more than once I beg of you before you decline it.[4]

Yours truly
W. C. BRYANT.

MANUSCRIPT: NYPL–Berg ADDRESS: Hon G. C. Verplanck / Member of Congress / Washington / D. C. POSTMARK: NEW-YORK / DEC / 25 POSTAL ANNOTATION: FREE DOCKETED: W. C. Bryant.

1. R. Ray Ward was an active member of the Sketch Club and an intimate friend of Robert Sands's. Callow, *Kindred Spirits*, pp. 18, 27. For Neilson, see 204.1.

2. Some years earlier Verplanck had written a series of eight biographical sketches of famous Americans for the *Analectic Magazine*. See the bibliography of his writings in July, *Essential New Yorker*, p. 291.

3. Sir John Bowring (1792–1872), British editor, diplomat, and extraordinary linguist, translated poems and folksongs from many European and Oriental languages.

4. Verplanck agreed to become nominal editor of *The Writings of Robert C. Sands, in Prose and Verse*, 2 vols. (New York, 1834), and wrote for it a biographical memoir. But, according to Frances Bryant, her husband did most of the work. See Letter 272.

256. *To* Gulian C. Verplanck

[New York, January 7, 1833]

My dear Sir.

I think we must rely upon you at all events to put together the works of Sands with a biographical notice. The plan is to publish them by subscription in two volumes octavo. The execution of the plan will give little trouble; and as nobody can do the life so well as yourself, and as that is incontestably devolving on you, it would be hard not to take your opinion as to the works to which it is to be prefixed.

As to the printing of the laws of the Union I thought we were to have it. I applied for it through Mr. Cambreleng long ago—at the time when Webb turned his somerset—and should take it very hard to be thrust aside by a new claimant. —If we had not made the application so early we should hardly be disposed to contest the matter with Mr. Mumford, but to have one's application lie three months without notice, and then to have another application instantly granted, would be particularly unpleasant.[1] Mr. Cambreleng wrote the letter in the office of the Evening Post—and afterwards informed us that Mr. Livingston[2] was absent at the time it arrived at Washington but the thing would unquestionably be done. If our claims are only *equal* to those of Mr. Mumford which we have the vanity to believe is the case, yet the circumstances under which the application was made ought we think to give us the preference. If the request be not improper, I hope you will make this representation of the case to the department.

Yrs truly

W. C. BRYANT

MANUSCRIPT: NYPL–Berg ADDRESS: Hon G. C. Verplanck / Member of Congress / Washington / D. C. POSTMARK: NEW-YORK / JAN / 7 POSTAL ANNOTATION: FREE.

1. On August 23, 1832, James Watson Webb took his New York *Courier and Enquirer* out of the Jackson party, mainly because of the President's veto of the bill to renew the charter of the Bank of the United States. Hone, *Diary*, I, 72–73. John Mumford edited the Democratic New York *Standard*. See 242.3.

2. Edward Livingston, Secretary of State.

257. *To* Gulian C. Verplanck

New York Jan. 11, 1833.

My dear Sir.

I send you several copies of the proposals for printing Sands's works which were left me [by] Mr. Ward with a request that I would forward them to you, and desire you to dispose of them in such a manner as would be likely to procure most subscribers. The subscription papers have been issued this early in order to take advantage of the feeling of regret produced by Mr. Sands's sudden death, which I assure you is much more general than I had anticipated. I was desirous to wait for your answer to the proposition I laid before you but Mr. Ward was of opinion that any further delay would prejudice the publication, the object of which is to collect something for the family, who will be left in rather a destitute condition. You see we have put a "literary friend" into the proposals. I hope you will not refuse the undertaking as I am convinced that the success of the work will in a good degree depend on it. Indeed we all expect it. If in the execution of it there be any matters of drudgery in which I can relieve you I shall be glad to do so, for I have the thing very much at heart.

The idea takes well here while the people's hearts are soft. Mr. Ward on getting the prospectus went out yesterday morning and in a short time obtained subscribers for 100 copies. The booksellers have suffered the subscription papers to be placed gratuitously in their shops, and several individuals have undertaken to solicit subscriptions. Ward says he will "neither eat nor drink till he has slain Paul"[1] that is until he has obtained 1000 subscriptions in this city.—

Yrs truly
W. C. BRYANT

MANUSCRIPT: NYPL–Berg ADDRESS: Hon   G.   C.   Verplanck / Member   of   Congress / Washington / D.   C. POSTMARK: NEW-YORK / JAN / 11   POSTAL   ANNOTATION: FREE DOCKETED: W. C. Bryant.

1. Cf. Acts 23:14.

258.   *To* Gulian C. Verplanck

New York   Jan   25   1833.

My dear Sir.

My brother Cyrus Bryant who lives at Princeton in Putnam County, Illinois, informs me that he has forwarded to General Duncan[1] a petition from the inhabitants of that County praying for the establishment of a new land district in that region. Of the grounds of this application I know nothing, except the inconvenience of the distance from Springfield the nearest land office which is very considerable. My reason for writing at present, however, is, that I wish to get for my brother, in case the district is established, the place of either Register or Receiver in the land office. Which of these offices is the best I do not know; you perhaps may; of course he would prefer the most lucrative. He has all the qualifications necessary both of character and capacity, and being of a studious turn, would perhaps be allowed leisure for the prosecution of his favorite pursuit, the natural sciences. I need not say how much you would oblige me, by doing what may occur to you as likely to promote his appointment.[2]

The subscription for Mr. Sands's Literary Remains takes wonder-

fully. Mr. Ward will have no difficulty in obtaining his thousand subscribers. A subscription paper is circulating among the ladies with great
success.

yrs truly
Wm. C. Bryant

MANUSCRIPT: NYPL–Berg ADDRESS: To the / Hon   G. C. Verplanck / Member of Congress / Washington / Dist   of   Columbia   POSTMARK: NEW-YORK / JAN / 25
POSTAL ANNOTATION: F[REE?] ENDORSED: W. C. Bryant / The Land District.

1. Probably Joseph Duncan (1794–1844), a member of Congress from Illinois,
1827–1834, and governor of that state from 1834 to 1838.
2. Though Cyrus was apparently not appointed to either of the offices named, he
became the first clerk of the Circuit Court for Bureau County, established with his
brother John's help in 1836–1837. *Bryant Record*, p. 67.

259.   *To* David Hosack and Philip Hone[1]

New York, February 1, 1833.

Gentlemen,

I duly appreciate the compliment contained in your request, that I
should prepare a poetical address to be spoken at Mr. Dunlap's benefit;
and I would do much to serve a man of so much merit, and for whom
I entertain so high a regard.[2]

I find, however, that my engagements will not give me the opportunity of composing any thing with which I should be satisfied, or which
would do credit to the occasion. I must, therefore, beg that you will select
for the purpose, some person of more leisure, and of a happier talent for
occasional compositions.[3]

Gentlemen, with sentiments of high respect,

your obedient servant,
W. C. Bryant.

MANUSCRIPT: Unrecovered TEXT: *Knickerbocker*, 1 (May 1833), 324.

1. Philip Hone (1780–1851), a prosperous auctioneer and former mayor of New
York, was to some degree a patron of the arts, and professed a passion for the theater.
Hone, *Diary*, I, 80. For Dr. David Hosack, see 125.4.
2. William Dunlap (1766–1839), portrait painter and a founder of the National
Academy, playwright, and theater manager, was a central figure in the arts of New
York City. His *History of the American Theatre* (1832) and *History of the Rise and
Progress of the Arts of Design in the United States* (1834) provided essential information about the artistic life of his day. The proposed theatrical benefit in recognition
of his "long and important services rendered to the Drama and to Literature" was an
indication he was already suffering the poverty and ill-health which marked his last
years. See *Knickerbocker*, 1 (May 1833), 324.
3. A few days earlier Fitz-Greene Halleck had declined a similar invitation. The
poetic address was then supplied by George Pope Morris (1802–1864), editor of the
NYM, who is best remembered for his popular poem "Woodman, Spare That Tree!"
Adkins, *Halleck*, p. 258; *Knickerbocker*, 1 (May 1833), 324.

260. *To* Mrs. Sarah S. Bryant

New York   April 25, 1833

Dear Mother,

I this day got your letter by Mr. Albro.[1] I wrote to *you* a day or two since requesting some facts and dates respecting my father's life.[2] I presume you have got the letter and answered it before this time. If not be so good as to write me the very day you receive this giving me the dates of his birth death &c and all the principal events of his life and the time when they occurred. I want them immediately for a biographical work compiling by Col. Saml. L. Knapp.[3]

What you tell me of the discord prevailing among the sons of harmony in Cummington is rather queer. I think that if the people of that place were to spend their long winters in some way that would furnish and improve their minds it would be better for them than to waste it in protracted meetings and quarrels about singing.[4] I have heard today from a young lady of Great Barrington a story about the inhabitants of that place. They had a protracted meeting which lasted fourteen days. A man of the name of Foote was the principal helper of Mr. Burt in the work of endeavouring to get up a revival;[5] but the attempt was unsuccessful, and the meeting was dissolved without the usual ceremony of pronouncing a blessing, on the ground that it would be impious to invoke the blessing of God on such a stiff-necked generation. Immediately after the protracted meeting, the members fell to quarreling among themselves. A part of them who were Antimasons[6] invited a Baptist Antimasonic minister to hold forth on the subject of Antimasonry in the meeting house. The keys of the meeting house being refused they broke open the door and the man preached. The other party stationed a drunken blackguard in the gallery who roared Amen from time to time. The bell was rung before the exercises were over; and at the close the drunken fellow *pretended* to read (for he had never learned to read at all) a kind of oration from a newspaper which he held in his hand. Arrangements were made to prosecute Foote for blasphemy if he had appeared again in Great Barrington.[7] There were other odd proceedings; and the winter appears to have passed no more peaceably than with you. I am afraid that these things are the legitimate consequence of protracted meetings and revivals, which unsettle the mind and make it greedy after excitement of some kind or other. I am sure I never heard of such doings in the quiet, civilized communities of New England until the new fanatical modes of getting up religious excitements were adopted. I think the religious newspapers ought to record these things as they do the revivals. If they do not, they will not give a fair view of the religious state of the community, —they will show only one side. They should call them the Devil's outpourings.

My last letter from Cyrus is dated March 3rd.[8] I presume he related [to you] the 1832[9] story of his operations—how he and John got to Princeton in October, chose the pleasantest of the vacant places though not quite so extensive for two as could have been wished—how they *bought two yoke* of oxen, —how one of the oxen died and another had the horn distemper—how they cut prairie hay to keep them on, which the season being late was wretched fodder wherefore they had to buy the more corn—how they hauled logs and built a cabin, and brought boards from the distance of 8 miles, paying a great price for them—how they had to buy three yoke more of oxen for a prairie team to break up the ground, and drag rails to the place where they were wanted—how they put in some wheat in the fall for a man in the neighbourhood of which they are to have three acres for their share—how they intend to get 40 acres fenced and broken the present season and mostly planted with Indian corn, though they expect but a small crop the first year—how they bought a plough chains and waggon—how Cyrus became ragged—how he bought a pair of cowhide boots and shoes—and a little factory cotton for shirts—how they have worked early and late—how they have been obliged to pay a high price for every thing—how they are out of cash—how they are in trouble for fear the land will come into market and find them unprovided with money to purchase it—how the lots of the new town Princeton will come into market in May, and they would like to purchase some of the lots which will sell from $250 to $5[00]—how they want some stock—cows for milk, hogs, young cattle and perhaps a few sheep—how hogs and young cattle will double in a year with very little care, costing nothing for their keeping in summer, except a little salt for the cattle—and a little corn to be thrown to the hogs occasionally to keep them tame, for there is no such thing as taming a wild hog—all this I presume Cyrus has told you—if not you have it in this letter— John's letter is dated Feb. 2nd.[10] He tells me that for 4 yokes of oxen they paid $160[11]—for a waggon $60—for pork and corn for the cattle $50—for his own horse $65—for Cyrus's horse $50—for boards for house floor $20 —besides which there were rough chains kitchen utensils, provisions and other matters costing he does not say how much. In all their joint expenses for the year will be $700.—

Arthur's letter is dated Feb 6.[12] He writes that he has obtained $200 from Mr. Plummer of Mississippi, with which he paid for his horse, and discharged $130 of John's claims. He owed John still $130—which he intended to pay as soon as he had threshed his wheat. He wanted a waggon but had no money to pay for it—a good one costs from 75 to 100 dollars. He therefore wished me to lend him $100. He was in great indignation at something which he had learned concerning the tenor of John's letters to Cummington.[13]

I sent Arthur 100 dollars according to his request. As Cyrus also wanted to borrow money and as his case seemed even harder than Arthur's I sent him $100 also. This with what I had lent him before makes $300. I have as I suppose you know also advanced to John $200. I have also $300 in Illinois of which $200 are at 25 per cent interest and $100 at 33⅓ per cent. I have written to Cyrus and John to take the interest of this money as it accrues. As for the misunderstanding between Arthur and John I am sorry it should have occurred; but I do not see that any good can come of writing letters about it, which only tend to exasperate. The thing is settled, and it must be left to the deliberate reflections of both parties, to approve or condemn their own conduct. I have written to Arthur giving him my opinion as to what I thought would have been an equitable arrangement between them, but I have been careful in writing to John not to say any thing to increase his dissatisfaction. A writes that he has been trying to get a few dollars in the village this winter by teaching a common school. The rheumatism he says renders labour so irksome that he would gladly find some other employment.

I have now written about every thing that I can tell you about my brothers. I shall doubtless have in a few days a letter from Arthur, and one from Cyrus to acknowledge the receipt of mine with their contents.

As for my own affairs I have little to say. The world goes on with me as formerly. My health has been remarkably regular this winter. I have had no colds nor irregularities of digestion. Frances has also been very well with the exception of a hurt which she received in her knee by falling on the pavement. The injury was severe and the pain great—we sent for a doctor who advised the application of leeches. Sixteen were applied and after them a poultice of tobacco, which allayed the pain. She was confined to her room for a fortnight afterwards. Fanny has been very well and Julia likewise for the greater part of the time—though while in town she was rather cross.[14] My regards to all.—

Yr affectionate son
W   C   BRYANT.

MANUSCRIPT: BCHS ADDRESS: Mrs. Sarah S. Bryant / Cummington / Massachusetts.

1. Probably John Albro, Cummington postmaster between 1827 and 1837. See *Only One Cummington*, p. 305. Mrs. Bryant's letter is unrecovered.

2. Letter unrecovered.

3. On April 27 Sarah Bryant wrote Cullen (NYPL–GR) giving details of her husband's life which apparently provided the basis for an article on Dr. Bryant in Samuel L. Knapp, *American Biography* (New York, 1833). No copy of this work has been found.

4. Earlier Sarah Bryant had recounted to Cyrus the furor raised in Cummington by two factions in the singing school, or church choir, each of which backed its own candidate for choirmaster. See Sarah to Cyrus Bryant, September 30, 1832, BCHS.

5. Sylvester Burt (d. 1836) had succeeded Elijah Wheeler in 1823 as pastor of the Great Barrington Congregational Church. Taylor, *Great Barrington*, p. 343. Foote is unidentified.

6. Antimasonry, a political movement flourishing between 1826 and 1834, while owing its origin to popular suspicion of the secret Masonic order, was essentially a "protest on the part of the common man against the privileges and power enjoyed in government, in business, and in the courts" by members of this exclusive fraternity. The movement stressed morality, temperance, and other causes which "stirred New Englanders and others of Puritan descent." A national Antimasonic ticket opposed Jackson in 1832, but in 1834 its followers entered a new anti-Jackson coalition called the Whig Party. Van Deusen, *Jacksonian Era*, pp. 55–56, 96.

7. An undated list in the Cummington town records, probably made a little earlier, shows that blasphemy was punished there by a fine of one dollar for the first offense and fifty cents for each repetition, plus court costs which often exceeded the fine.

8. Unrecovered.

9. Bryant mistakenly wrote "1833."

10. Unrecovered.

11. Bryant mistakenly wrote "$1.60."

12. Unrecovered.

13. In an undated letter, late in 1832, John told his mother, "I have made a final settlement with Arthur. I think it is the last one I shall ever make with him. . . . My connexion with Arthur was a great injury to me." BCHS. A year later he spoke bitterly of his Illinois brothers: "I have found out by experience that it is best for me to have as little to do with Arthur and Cyrus as possible." But he was grateful to the brother in New York: "William's assistance is all that has held me up." John to Sarah Bryant, December 25, 1833, BCHS.

14. From January to March 1833 the Bryants lodged with a Mr. Crombie on Broadway, returning thereafter to Hoboken. Frances Bryant, "Autobiographical Sketch," NYPL–GR.

261. *To* Gulian C. Verplanck

New York   May 2   1833.

Dear Sir,

Mr. Balestier is desirous of obtaining a permission, from the government, to trade with the Indians in East Florida, from Tampa Bay, southward, on the gulf of Mexico. His wife owns lands in Florida and he is about to go there to settle. I told him that I would speak to you on the subject, as I expected to see you in a day or two, and learn of you the proper mode to make the application, as well as get you to second it if you were so inclined. Not having met with you so soon as I hoped I write this to beg you to tell me how I shall go to work for my friend and whether you can do any thing for him on your part.[1]

Yrs. truly

W. C.   BRYANT

MANUSCRIPT: NYPL–Berg ADDRESS: Hon G. C. Verplanck / 74 Leonard Street DOCKETED: W. C. Bryant.

1. Cullen and Frances Bryant had become acquainted in 1826 with Mr. and Mrs. Joseph Balestier, probably through Eliza Robbins. Mrs. Balestier was a daughter of Paul Revere; her brother Joseph Warren Revere had married Miss Robbins' sister Mary. Joseph Balestier, a Boston merchant who spent several years in business in New

York before going west, later published a brief account of Chicago's early history, *The Annals of Chicago* (Chicago, 1840). See Letter 145; Lesley, *Recollections of My Mother*, pp. 134, 149–150; Rusk, *Middle Western Frontier*, II, 281.

262.   *To* Richard H. Dana

New York   June 21   1833.

My dear Sir

I have called on the only booksellers here who would be likely to undertake the publication of your work. The Carvills declined on account of the "times," observing that they had already on hand some manuscripts which they had paid for a year or two since, and which they had delayed publishing on account of the state of their own affairs and of the book market. They however treated the application very respectfully, and did not decline until they had heard all I had to say, and considered the matter.[1] On going to the Harpers I found that your friend Mr. Wood[2] had *prevented* me as we used to say in the old English dialect[3] which Dr. Webster threatens to reform when he mends the common version of the bible.[4] Mr. Wood appears to have said every thing that could have been said on the subject and to have left the brothers impressed with a high opinion of your talents, but they could not be persuaded that the book would be what they called a *selling book*, at least in such a degree as to induce them to offer any thing for it.

I am sorry to have such an account to give of the success of negociations, but I infer from your letter[5] that you have an offer from some bookseller in your neighbourhood, which you may think it worth your while to accept. You do well in republishing your prose. It will be better received at present than formerly—your poetical reputation will cause it to be sought for and read, and the public can no longer be confined to the cold and artificial style of writing which was then held up as the standard.

Your friend Mr. Wood did not do me the favour to call on me to speak about your works but the Harpers told me that he referred them to Verplanck and myself.

You talked last summer of visiting New York. May I not hope to see you at Hoboken before the leaves fall? I can show you some beautiful walks and rides in the neighbourhood, with our noble bay and river almost always in sight, and the great city in the distance apparently as quiet as if no mischief was brewing there. I shall be absent during the month of July, but after that I shall probably remain here. —My regards to all my friends in Cambridge and particularly to your brother and sisters.

Yrs truly

W. C. BRYANT

MANUSCRIPT: NYPL–GR DOCKETED: W. C. Bryant / June 21—33 PUBLISHED (*in part*): *Life*, I, 294.

1. G. and C. Carvill had been New York publishers of the *USR*, as well as of Bryant's translation of Mignet's *History of the French Revolution* in 1827.

2. Probably Leonard Woods (1807–1878), a Presbyterian clergyman who was then editor of the *Literary and Theological Review* in New York City, and later (1839–1866) president of Bowdoin College. In 1839, again as Dana's agent, he discussed with the Harpers the proposed publication of Richard Henry Dana, Jr.'s *Two Years Before the Mast*. See Bryant to Dana, Sr., June 24, 1839, NYPL–GR; Exman, *Brothers Harper*, pp. 127ff.

3. That is, "came before, made the way easy."

4. Noah Webster (1758–1843), who published his seminal *The American Dictionary of the English Language* in 1828, declared it his aim to "destroy the provincial prejudices that originate in the trifling differences of dialect and produce reciprocal ridicule." But he did not go so far as to retranslate the Bible.

5. Unrecovered.

263. *To* Gulian C. Verplanck

Saturday morning [cJune 22, 1833]

Dear Sir

If you are at leisure will you come over to Hoboken this afternoon. I expect [R. Ray] Ward over—and he has several things to talk about. He has a plan of sending [Samuel] Knapp to Boston to procure subscriptions for Sands's works. —He thinks of going next week himself to Philadelphia. In writing the memoir, recollect that he was born not at New York but at Flatbush during a temporary residence of the family there. He received the second honour in his class the year before he graduated, and when he received his degree pronounced the valedictory.[1]

In haste

W   C. BRYANT

Please answer by the bearer

MANUSCRIPT: NYPL–Berg ADDRESS: Gulian C. Verplanck Esq / 74 Leonard Street.

1. At Columbia College in 1815, at the age of sixteen.

264. *To* Amos Eaton[1]

New York, July 2, 1833.

My dear Sir:

I do not suppose that you intended me to answer the interrogatories in your letter. They were meant, I presume, as a more delicate way of paying a compliment than by direct assertion. I may be permitted to say, however, that few circumstances connected with the history of my writings have given me more pleasure than the approbation you are pleased to express so warmly. To write verses that will please very young men and women, persons of inflammable feelings and imaginations, is no difficult matter; but to obtain the voluntary and even extravagant commendation of a veteran and distinguished votary of Science is a triumph indeed; and I have just put your letter among the few things to which I recur when I wish to refresh my self-complacency. For the guidance in my botanical studies to which you allude, I have ever held myself your debtor; and that you may long live to diffuse a taste for the sciences you pursue with so much ardour and success is the prayer of

Your Sincere friend,
WILLIAM C. BRYANT.

MANUSCRIPT: Unrecovered TEXT: W. M. Smallwood, "Amos Eaton, Naturalist," *New York History*, 18 (April 1937), 187–188.

1. Amos Eaton (1776–1842, Williams 1799), an early popularizer of the natural sciences through his lectures in western Massachusetts and eastern New York from 1817 to 1824 and his *Manual of Botany for the Northern States* (1817), became the first professor of natural history at Rensselaer Polytechnic Institute in 1824. A friend of Dr. Peter Bryant's, whom he called the "most dexterous operator that he had seen handle the surgeon's knife," he later taught Cyrus and John Bryant at Troy, and renewed his acquaintance with Cullen at Great Barrington in 1820. On June 21, 1833, Eaton wrote him, "I read your poems from candle-lighting 'till this time [12:30 A.M.], to my wife, wife's sister, daughter Sarah, and two nieces. My 13 year old William (of whose presence I boast so much) heard me also. Tears fell like showers at some poems, glee [glozed?] at others, love and friendship softened at others. Now Bryant (as you and your wife have been my pupils in Botany, and I have your confidence) do tell me plainly. Do these poems come from your little stooping puny self? Or does some singing, pitying, & fascinating, angel, use you as his vehicle, to relieve cold cloddy man from the harsh tones of hardy science? I am frightened at the thought of having been your teacher in 1820. Had you received your mission then? Did you then know, that you was destined to charm your clamorous coarse old teacher? Did you laugh when I affected to be your superior, because I knew the names of more weeds than you? Had the sacred nine then called on you? Did you then translate, in fancy, my Claytonia, my Anemone, my Solidago, &c. into verse, which you now sing so charmingly? Did you then destine me to early Death, whose terrors you have almost annihilated in your consolating hymn? Did you think of me, when you made your guide-board to the woods? Did Green River (whose banks I trode with you) call up your remembrance of your old School-master? There I showed you the Wind-flower, and traced its tender organs.

"Tell me plainly—is a poet truly a *Vates*? Did you really feel your heavenly birth, when I gave you the name of calyx, corol, and stamen, with loftily affected look?" NYPL–BG. See also *Life*, I, 2.

265. *To* Charity Bryant

Vergennes   July 13   1833.

Dear Aunt

I was this morning with my wife looking for you in Weybridge, but was told by a neighbour of yours who called himself Mr. Howard¹ that you had gone with Miss Drake² to Massachusetts. We were much disappointed at this though we might have saved the trouble of a ride out of our way through Weybridge had I taken the natural precaution to write to you before setting out from home in order to learn whether you would be at home or not. We left our names with Mr. Howard, and proceeded to Vergennes, but being detained here in waiting for the boat from Saturday to Monday, I have found plenty of leisure to write. We left New York on Monday last, the eighth of the month, in the steamboat. At Hudson we took the stage coach for Great Barrington where we left our two children in the care of my wife's sisters. From Great Barrington we went by the stage coach to Pittsfield; from Pittsfield to Bennington, from Bennington to Rutland and from Rutland to Middlebury a very slow and tedious and consequently somewhat expensive journey on account of the very bad arrangement of the stages. The scenery however is uncommonly beautiful and picturesque, and I have no doubt that if a rapid and regular line of stages were established it would become a favorite summer route for those who like good air, and plenty of it (for the valley from Bennington to Rutland is one of the most windy places I was ever in) and beautiful scenery.

We are now going to Montreal and shall take the boat for St. Johns on Monday.[3] It will not be in our power to stop at Weybridge on our return, nor from what Mr. Howard told me should I expect to find you at home. We hope however to have the pleasure of seeing you and Miss Drake in New York, or rather at Hoboken, where my habitation is at present, though my daily business is in New York. I think you would find a passage down the lake the rail road and the river a pleasant one, it would I believe have the attraction of novelty, and would take you but little time.[4] My wife joins me in this invitation, and desires her love. Our best regards to Miss Drake.

> Your affectionate Nephew
> WILLIAM C. BRYANT

MANUSCRIPT: NYPL–Berg ADDRESS: Miss Charity Bryant / Weybridge / Vermont POST-MARK: VERGENNES / VT / JULY / 15 / 1833 POSTAL ANNOTATION: PAID 6 DOCK-ETED: Wm   C. Bryant.

1. Unidentified. Bryant was related, through his grandmother Silence Howard Bryant, to members of her family who had emigrated from Bridgewater, Massachusetts, to Weybridge, Vermont.
2. Sylvia Drake, Charity Bryant's companion. See 58.1.
3. The steamboat ran between Vergennes on Lake Champlain and Saint Jean, Quebec, on the Richelieu River.
4. By 1833 the Saratoga and Schenectady Railroad, chartered two years earlier, offered service twice a day between Saratoga and Albany.

266. *To* Cyrus Bryant

New York   August 15th   1833.

Dear Brother.

I got your letter by Mr. Hartzell[1] yesterday and he has promised to take care of a box directed to you. The two books it contains are for you, as is also the white hat and the things in it, the camlet cloak, the black broadcloth pantaloons, and either the brown coat or the black frock coat as you and John can agree. You may possibly find something worth reading in the loose numbers of the Christian Register on the top.

As for your determination to get married I approve of it highly—provided you find a woman you like—mild tempered, industrious, & frugal with some degree of intelligence—for that is as important a quality as any other. Could you not *lecture* your way to Hartford in the winter? You might I doubt not pick up something by chemical lectures at St. Louis, at Louisville and Cincinnati. But you should write to the lady in the first place, and not come on a fool's errand.[2]

I have lately been to Canada visiting Cummington in my way. For the particulars of my journey I refer you to my letter to John.[3]

The summer with us has been cold and somewhat rainy—the crop of hay has been very large, as has also been that of oats and wheat—the rye has been respectable—but the Indian corn is very late, and the crop will be small. Indeed there are fears that in some parts of the country, Cummington, for example, the corn will not be ripe before the frosts set in. The tassels were just making their appearance there about the latter part of July. In this latitude the weather on account of this unusual coolness has been quite agreeable; the storms have not been of long duration, and we have had but few hot days. It is by far the coolest summer I have known since I came to New York. The city and its neighbourhood have been healthy to an extraordinary degree. It is remarkable that notwithstanding the moisture of the weather the number of mosquitoes is smaller than usual, and though it is so late in the season, we are little annoyed with flies notwithstanding that Hoboken is usually much infested with them.

Along with this I send a letter for Rush,[4] which I wish you would either send by private conveyance or put it in the mail, as is most convenient.

I have concluded to take the two town lots you speak of, as I believe I have already mentioned in a letter to you or John. I have written to John to pay for them out of the money that is to come from Cutler. Since your foolish law limiting the rate of interest to twelve per cent, the effect of which will be to keep money out of your state, I have no doubt that it is better to invest money in land than to lend it. It must be worth 33 or 25 per cent to the settler, or he would not offer it—if so, it must be worth nearly as much to one who employs it in the same way with the settler—that is, who invests it in land. My wife desires to be remembered.

Yrs truly
WM C. BRYANT

P. S. I have a package of plants directed to you from Professor Torrey intended probably for the Lyceum[5] which have been lying at my office for some time. What shall I do with them?

MANUSCRIPT: BCHS PUBLISHED: Helen L. Drew, "Unpublished Letters of William Cullen Bryant," *New England Quarterly*, 10 (June 1937), 346.

1. Unidentified. Cyrus' letter is unrecovered.

2. Cyrus' search for a bride was humorously recounted by his son Cullen many years later: "I suppose he had [concluded that] . . . it was not well for man to be alone, and the apparent object of his journey was, if possible, to persuade some one among his unmarried friends of the other sex to accompany him back to his prairie home. . . . I do not know that he had any particular one in view. . . . I once heard him tell somebody . . . that his 'popping the question' was done by letter and inferred . . . that he made more than one proposal." Failing, in the spring of 1834, to win Elizabeth Putnam of Hartford, Cyrus returned to Illinois with a Worthington bride, Julia Everett (1808–1875), whom he married at Cummington on May 13, 1834. *Bryant Record*, p. 66; John to Sarah Bryant, October 6, 1833, BCHS.

3. Unrecovered.

4. I.e., Peter Rush, now Arthur, Bryant. Letter unrecovered.

5. John Torrey (1796–1873, M.D. College of Physicians and Surgeons 1818) was professor of chemistry at his alma mater, and of chemistry and natural history at Princeton. In 1826 he published *A Compendium of the Flora of the Northern and Middle States*, and in 1838–1843 was joint author with Asa Gray (1810–1888) of *Flora of North America*. Bryant had printed a critical notice of the first of these books in the *USR*. See 160.1.

267. *To* Gulian C. Verplanck

New York   Sept. 10   1833.

Dear Sir,

I am desired, through Miss Sands, by the Miss Stevenses of Hoboken, one of whom travelled 200 miles night and day to hear your Geneva address,[1] to convey to you an invitation from them to drink tea at Col. Stevens's tomorrow (Wednesday).[2] As the young lady took so long and fatiguing a journey on your account, you will not I am sure, refuse to take so short and agreeable a one on hers. Mr. Ward has left town, and has written to Miss Sands to tell me that the Harpers must begin printing, and that he will be answerable for 1250 copies, having ascertained that the subscription list will bear so large an impression. Have you settled in what order the articles are to appear? Which shall be sent to the printers first?

Yrs truly
W. C. BRYANT

MANUSCRIPT: NYPL–Berg ADDRESS: Hon   G. C. Verplanck 74 Leonard Street DOCKETED: W. C. Bryant.

1. *A Discourse Delivered after the Annual Commencement of Geneva College, August 7th, 1833* . . . (New York, 1833).

2. Col. John Stevens (1749–1838, King's [later Columbia] College 1768), pioneer steamboat and railroad builder, lived at Castle Point in Hoboken, where his son Edward A. Stevens later founded the Stevens Institute of Technology.

268. *To* Richard H. Dana

New York   Oct. 2, 1833.

My dear sir.

I had received your volume of poems—for which I thank you much —before writing the notice you speak of, in the Evening Post.[1] It was a hasty article—hasty I mean for a subject to which I was so desirous to do justice; and I saw on reading it over, after it was printed, that I had not been very happy in speaking of the merits of the poem entitled Factitious Life. I had neglected to say any thing of the satire of the piece which was happy and well directed. I have seen the notice of your book in the Christian Register. It was not written by a person capable of judging of your writings, but I thought that the writer meant his article to be a friendly one. By the way, I have to make amends for what I said about a critic of my poems in the Foreign Quarterly Review, before I had seen his article.[2] You may remember what I wrote to you on that subject. Since that time I have seen the review, and have not the slightest doubt that the writer meant to be exceedingly kind, condescending, and patronizing, and all that—the misfortune was that he did not know how to criticize poetry. I have no right to complain, for he wrote in a friendly spirit, and praised me enough I believe, though not in the right places. What is the reason that none of the critics in England or America except Channing, in noticing my things, have said a word about "The Past"?

After all, poetic wares are not in the market of the present day. Poetry may get praised in the newspapers, but no man makes money by it, for the simple reason that nobody cares a fig for it. The taste for it is something old fashioned, the march of the age is in another direction— mankind are occupied with politics, rail roads and steamboats. Hundreds of persons will talk flippantly and volubly about poetry and even write about it, who know no more of the matter and have no more feeling of poetry than the old stump I write this letter with. I see you predict a change for the better in your new preface to the Idle Man. May it come, I say with all my heart, but I do not see the proof of it—or rather if I were called upon to point out any signs of its approach, I could mention no other than the change which criticism has undergone in speaking of your writings. Beyond this I discern no favorable indication.

I believe I have not acknowledged the receipt of your Essay on the Past. I looked for the number of the Quarterly Observer containing it— but the agent here would not sell *single* numbers, and I was not quite ready to subscribe for the work. I liked your article so well that I was sorry not to see it with the other prose pieces in your volume.

I am sorry you could not come on with Mr. Sedgwick,[3] although I fear we could have done nothing for you in the way of providing you with an occupation. I saw Morse the painter, again, yesterday morning. He expressed the highest opinion of your talents, and the greatest desire to see you in his brothers' establishment, if the opportunity of employing you should be afforded, but said that his brother, or brothers—for there are two of them in the Observer—thought that all the departments were full.[4] I saw Mr. Verplanck the other day, when he received the copy of your book. He expressed the kindest remembrance of you, and on my mentioning to him Mr. Sedgwick's plan about the Christian Observer said—what he has several times before remarked—that he thought a professorship in some literary institution, the duties of which were not very laborious, would be the thing for you.[5]

You must not forget your promise to come to New York another year. My wife who desires me to present you her friendly regards, insists on being made a party to the promise and to have a right to require its fulfillment. We shall have you on the hip another year on the score of duty—as you will not pretend that it is a duty to break one's word.

The edition of my poems published by Bliss is all sold but a handful of copies. Bliss is the most unenterprising and unlucky of all publishers —his name is a proverb among the trade for *infelicity* and ill luck in the publishing line. He will sell more books at his counter by retail than most other men—he has sold most of mine that way—but he has the least possible talent at getting them into the hands of other booksellers. All agree that it is the greatest wonder he has done so well with my book. I think of publishing another edition soon, and will get you, when I am ready, to inquire what your booksellers will give for being allowed to publish a thousand copies.

Truly yrs—
WILLIAM C. BRYANT.

MANUSCRIPT: NYPL–GR DOCKETED: W. C. Bryant / Oct 2nd 33 PUBLISHED (*in part*): *Life*, I, 294–295.

1. Dana's *Poems and Prose Writings* (Boston: Russell, Odiorne, and Co., 1833) appeared in two volumes, the first containing his poetry. This apparently reached Bryant before the second, prose volume. His notice was printed in the *EP* for September 28, 1833. Dana's letter is unrecovered.

2. See Letter 249.

3. Probably Robert Sedgwick, whose wife Elizabeth (Ellery) Sedgwick was Dana's cousin.

4. See 194.10.

5. After practicing law briefly, and writing for the *NAR* and *The Idle Man*, Dana had found no regular occupation.

269.   *To* Richard H. Dana

New York   Oct   17, 1833

My dear Sir.

Will you see your booksellers, Russell Odiorne & Co., and see whether they will give me two hundred and fifty dollars for 1000 copies of my book. Mr. Bliss has offered me a check for $200 as soon as I put the work into his hands. If your booksellers do not offer me more I shall let him have it. If they should not care to do any thing about it will you inquire what my volume could be printed for at Cambridge and let me know when you write. I shall probably add to it half a dozen pages—not more.[1] My *manuscript poem* of which you speak was not finished and was not quite good enough to publish.[2] Will you resolve a critical doubt for me. John Wilson finds fault with the passage in the Forest Hymn

> — No silks
> Rustle nor jewels shine nor envious eyes
> Encounter—

as out of place and I am rather inclined to think him right. Shall I leave it out?[3] Will you answer my inquiries about the bargain with the bookseller &c. as soon as your leisure will permit—for Bliss is in haste for my decision.—

I am inclined to think that if Mr. Woods[4] were to write a review of your book Walsh would publish it. He mentioned in his paper the other day that you had published a book and that the poetry it contained has been *printed* in the American Quarterly. Now if he has got a fancy that you have been well spoken of in his Review it is enough—you are down in his books for a great man; for he always makes it a point to stick to the opinions uttered in that work and regularly repels every attack upon its politics, or criticism. I am therefore clean for sending him an article on your work; I will ensure its admission. I forgot to say in my last in answer to your remark on the line—Yonder tall cliff &c—that I agree with you and that I would not have altered it.[5] Your volume of Essays may do by and by—though it would be better to wait until the greater part of the edition of your "poems & prose" is sold off—that readers may not have two of your books to buy at once by which means they might interfere with each other.—[6]

Yrs sincerely

W. C. BRYANT—

MANUSCRIPT: NYPL–GR DOCKETED: W   C. Bryant / Oct   17—33. PUBLISHED (*in part*): *Life*, I, 295–296.

1. The additional poems were "The Prairies," "The Arctic Lover," "The Journey of Life," and "Sonnet, from the Portuguese of Semedo."
2. "The Robber" was published in the *NYM*, 11 (July 6, 1833), 4, and later in

several gift-books, but omitted from Bryant's collected poems at Dana's urging. See McDowell, *Representative Selections*, pp. 356–358, 420.

3. See *ibid.*, p. 400; *Poems* (1876), pp. 112–113. Wilson commented on this in his review of Bryant's *Poems* in *Blackwood's Edinburgh Magazine*, 31 (April 1832), 646–664. Bryant rewrote this passage.

4. Dana's friend Leonard Woods. See 262.2.

5. In Dana's poem, "The Ocean," "How dark and stern upon thy waves looks down / Yonder tall cliff—he with the iron crown."

6. Dana did not publish a collection of essays.

270. *To* Richard H. Dana

New York Nov 2, 1833.

My dear Sir.

I have completed the bargain with Mr. Odiorne, and have given him my book with such corrections and additions as I have been able to make.[1] I shall avail myself of your kindness to look over the proofs. As most of the typesetting is to be done from printed copy, I hope it will not give you much trouble. Should any thing occur to you respecting my book, whether in the way of objection to any parts, or otherwise, you will do me a favour to write to me about it. I need not say how much I am obliged to you for making the bargain with the publishers for me. I have a little piece by me in blank verse entitled "the Prairies" for which I have directed room to be left. It is not yet quite finished—the conclusion gives me some perplexity.[2] The winding up of these things in a satisfactory manner is often you know a great difficulty. I have sometimes kept a poem for weeks before I could do it in a manner with which I was at all pleased. All this is in favour of your advice to write a long poem. I will do it one of these days. I will write a poem as long and as tedious I fear as heart could wish.—

I congratulate you on having become "a centre table poet."[3] Your verses will be repeated by youths and maidens and you will be their poet through life—

Yrs truly

W. C. Bryant

MANUSCRIPT: NYPL–GR PUBLISHED (*in part*): *Life*, I, 296.

1. *Poems by William Cullen Bryant* (Boston: Russell, Odiorne, and Metcalf, 1834).

2. "The Prairies" was first published in the *Knickerbocker*, 1 (December 1833), 410–413. See *Poems* (1876), pp. 184–189.

3. I.e., an established poet whose books are displayed on parlor tables, as much for show as for reading. Note Bryant's comment to Dana in Letter 183: ". . . your poem . . . shall lie in the parlour windows of the rich and fashionable—not the best judges of literary merit to be sure, but the best purchasers of showy books."

271. *To* Richard H. Dana

New York   Nov. 11, 1833.

My dear Sir.

I am much obliged to you certainly for giving yourself so much pains about my verses. Since you think so ill of "the Robber" as to place it below any thing I have written, it shall not go into my book, and I formally authorize you to take the proper measures for excluding it.[1]

The phrase in the Past "wisdom disappeared" I am not quite certain is a defect. I have sometimes thought it was a boldness. Disappeared is used nearly in the sense of *vanished, departed, passed away,* but with more propriety than *vanished,* since that relates to a sudden disappearance. At all events I do not find it easy to alter the stanza without spoiling it.[2]

It was the Edinburgh Review which remarked on the rhyme *boughs* and bows in the Evening Wind. The grammar of the three last lines in that stanza is probably not clear for the critic blundered in copying it, and made nonsense of the passage. Suppose the rhyme and the construction to be amended in this manner

> Go, play beneath the linden that o'erbrows
> The darkling glen where dashing waters pass,
> And stir in all the fields, the fragrant grass.

And let the second line in the same stanza read thus

> Curl the still fountain bright with stars and rouse, &c.[3]

As to the passage in the Forest Hymn, remarked upon by Wilson I see that in attempting to mend it I have marred the unity and effect of the passage. The truth is that an alteration ought never to be made without the mind being filled with the subject. In mending a faulty passage in cold blood we often do more mischief by attending to particulars and neglecting the entire construction and sequence of ideas, than we do good.[4] I think a better alteration than I made would be this

> Communion with his Maker. These dim vaults,
> These winding aisles of human pomp or pride
> Report not. No fantastic carvings show &c &c.[5]

As to the other passage in the same poem, about "Life" and "blooms and smiles," I remember very well when I wrote the word "blooms" that I had a vague idea of its impropriety, but did not know why, until you showed me. I have rung half a dozen changes on the faulty lines—you shall choose—

> —yea, seats himself
> *Upon the tyrant's throne—the sepulchre—*

> *As in defiance, on the sepulchre*
> *In loneliness upon the sepulchre*[6]

The words " that to the gazes seem" in the second line of the Prairies strike me as feeble. I wish the commencement of that poem to stand thus.

> These are the gardens of the desert, these
> The unshorn fields, boundless and beautiful,
> And fresh as the young earth ere man had sinned—
> The prairies, &c. &c.[7]

"To sup upon the dead," I do not like.[8] "Bosom" and "blossom" are in Wordsworth whose rhymes are generally exact

> Fill your lap and fill your bosom
> Only spare the strawberry blossom.[9]

but I will think of it. I have cleared away the rubbish as far as I am able from the first part of the volume at least; and since you have kindly undertaken to read the proofs for me I will give you the trouble to see that the changes noted above are duly made.

Yours truly
W. C. BRYANT

MANUSCRIPT: NYPL–GR DOCKETED: W. C. Bryant / Nov. 11—33. PUBLISHED *(in part)*: *Life*, I, 297–298.

1. See 269.2. Dana's letter commenting on this and other points touched on below is unrecovered.
2. See "The Past," stanza nine, *Poems* (1876), p. 172.
3. Bryant obviously meant to write "[*Blackwood's*] Edinburgh Magazine," as his reference to John Wilson in the next paragraph indicates. His poems were not discussed in the *Edinburgh Review*. Though he later revised these lines in stanza three of "The Evening Wind," Bryant kept the questioned rhyme. See *Poems* (1876), p. 175.
4. More than thirty years later Bryant made this advice, given him as early as 1821 by Dana himself ("I believe that a poet should not be allowed to alter in cold blood—he grows finical"), the theme of "The Poet" (1864). See 74.1; *Poems* (1876), pp. 434–436.
5. This revision was Bryant's final one. See *Poems* (1876), p. 112. The passage originally read: "Here are seen / No traces of man's pomp or pride;—no silks / Rustle, no jewels shine, nor envious eyes / Encounter." *USLG*, 2 (April 1, 1825), 28. Wilson had remarked that these lines "have no business there. . . . Such sarcastic suggestions jar and grate; and it would please us much to see that they were omitted in a new edition." McDowell, *Representative Selections*, p. 400.
6. Dana chose "without hesitation" the first of these lines. Dana to Bryant, December 7, 1833, quoted in *Life*, I, 301. See *Poems* (1876), p. 115.
7. For the didactic third line in this passage, Bryant substituted the superbly appropriate one, "For which the speech of England has no name." See *Poems* (1876), p. 184.
8. Bryant eliminated the offending phrase, making the passage read, "The brown vultures of the wood / Flocked to those vast uncovered sepulchres, / And sat, unscared *and silent, at their feast*." (italics supplied) *Poems* (1876), p. 187.

9. Bryant retained this ryhme, to which Dana had apparently objected, in the second stanza of "I Cannot Forget with what Fervid Devotion." See *Poems* (1876), p. 125. The couplet is quoted from Wordsworth's "To a Butterfly."

272. *To* John Howard Bryant

New York, December 15, 1833

[by Frances Bryant]

Dear Brother

William received your letter yesterday—dated Nov. 18.[1] And as he is a little more hurried, than usual, I take it upon myself to acknowledge the receipt of it. You say that you received the box and all things safe. Ill health prevented me from repairing those articles, as I wished to do; particularly to spare your wife the trouble. I was confined to my bed at the time they were sent.

We are yet at Hoboken and all in good health. William has been living for the last two months on home made, brown bread, milk and baked sweet apples, and I assure you, he is growing fat; he looks quite portly. Would it not be funny, if he should swell up like Doctor Shaw? I think I must soon put a stop to his eating apples and milk. Fanny does not attend school this winter—but studies at home. She goes twice a week to town, to take lessons from Mr. Miller an English landscape painter and drawing master.[2] Her health is very good, she has grown very much since you saw her. Little Julia is the pet of the house; she talks incessantly, but not very plain. —*We think her quite smart.* And now I suppose you would like to know what is going on in the literary world. I will begin at home. Wm. is now writing a review of Mr. Dana's Book of Poems and prose. And as he had before written a review for the North American— it now puzzles him to word *one* differing from that.[3] He wrote a poem a short time since, called the Prairies. It is in blank verse, and is about the length of his Monument Mountain. It was printed the 1st Dec. in the last number of the Knickerbocker. A second edition of his poems will be out soon. It is to be published by Russell, Odiorne, and Co. of Boston. They gave him two hundred and fifty for publishing it. The old edition is sold, there was not much profit. He has heard nothing from the english publication. —Mr. Verplanck is in town. I don't know that he has written anything except a lecture which was delivered before the Mercantile Association; and which I hear is just published. His friends are a little surprised at the stand which he has lately taken in politics.[4] Mr. Halleck I see, and hear, very little of. I think he has written nothing for a long time. —Miss Sedgwick has just returned to the city for the winter. The last thing that I have read, of hers, is the Hunchback in Glauber Spa. —I think that one of her happiest productions. Have you seen the *Glauber Spa?*[5]

We miss poor Sands very much, his works will be published soon. Verplanck undertook to arrange them for the press—but has done but little about it. William has had the greater part of it to do. He was also to write a memoir of him, and the printers are now ready for it. Wm. went to see him the other day, he said that he had not begun it—yet, but thought he should have it ready soon. Mr. Weir took Sands' likeness after his death. Durand is engraving it. It will be placed in the book. We think it a pretty good likeness. Mr. Flint was here last fall, we liked him much, he was full of conversation, and very agreeable. Miss Robbins went to see him—he expressed his astonishment at her powers of Eloquence, and said that she had enough for three pulpits. He has now gone to Cincinnati for his family. You are probably apprised by the papers that he is to edit—The Knickerbocker.[6] We have not received any letters from Cummington for some time, the family were all well then. The rains have done a great deal of damage there this last fall by carrying off their Bridges, fences, etc. etc. —You say that you should like to have mother come out to Illinois. I think that she would be delighted to go. My love to Cyrus, tell him that I should be very glad to see him here, and if I had ten thousand dollars, I would send him enough to bring him here immediately. I wish I could see you for I have a great deal more to tell you (I perceive this is the last page). And the most important thing I should have to talk about is a project of crossing the Atlantic. If we go it will probably be, on the first of June. We think of being absent two or three years, the principal part of the time we intend to spend in France and Italy. Wm. has long been talking about going. I have doubted his accomplishing it, but now I begin to tremble for I believe he is in earnest, not that I should not like to see Europe, but I think it a troublesome undertaking to make a sea voyage with my two children, to say nothing of the land journey, etc. etc. —And now I think you would ask, where is he to get the money for this expedition? Well, in the first place, we have been living as economically as possible, to save something; second Mr. Morris talks of paying him something for writing for his Mirror during his absence.[7] Thirdly, some of his friends say that they will (*if they can*) *git the Gineral* to send by him a few *old newspapers* tied with a *red string*, to France or some other part of Europe, for which he will pay him a little, to help him along. Again, you will ask, how can he leave the Office? Mr. Leggett has promised to supply his place for five hundred dollars a year. I should like to defer this voyage until next fall—and visit you and your wife at Illinois and return by way of Niagara, Bloomfield, Cummington, and Gt. Barrington. Perhaps we shall do so, as Wm. would like to buy a little farm, in order that we may have a place *where on* to rest (if we need one) when we return. I saw Miss Robbins last week she is not very well, but much as usual. I told her that I should write to you soon. She desired to be remembered to you all, and wished Edward [Harte] to be told, that he may look out a farm, as soon as he pleases, and when he has found one that suited him, he must let her know it and she will send him two hundred dollars to pay for it. My respect to Edward, and tell him I am happy to hear that he is contented, for I think he is much better off than he would be here. My best respects to your wife and tell her I hope the time not far distant, when I may have the pleasure of seeing her. Remember me also affectionately to Henrietta.[8] I am now going to stop and let William write.

Yours truly
F. F.

direct your next letter to me.

[by Cullen Bryant]
Dear Brother

Will you tell Arthur to keep the money he owes me until the lands about Princeton come into the market in order that it may be ready to be laid out in land? As for Cutler's note, I find that Doct. Bliss has charged the contents to me on account, and I suppose it will about balance what he owed me for my poem[s]. When you receive the next payment therefore send me your note for all that has been paid. Cannot Cutler give some security so that I shall be certain that it will be paid, before I leave the country? Probably however he would not do this without some extension of the time of payment which I should not like to give him. I do not mean to be responsible to Bliss for the amount in case it should not be collected. I think, as Cyrus wants money as much as you do, that if you let him have half what is collected on the Cutler note, and take the rest yourself, sending me your notes for the amount it will be the extent to which I shall be able to assist you. I mean however that you should take the first payment. As to the money already lent out in Illinois that is, the $300, I wish that that sum together with what I am to receive from Arthur may be invested in land in my name, as soon as it comes into the market. Consult Cyrus, if I do not come out in the spring on the best location. I will write to you again.

Yrs. truly,
W. C. B.

Has Cyrus done anything more about the Register's Office? Is there anything I can do for him? Congress is in session and if there is anything to be done it is well to set about it.

I got the newspaper containing the usury law.

MANUSCRIPT: BCHS ADDRESS: Mr. John H. Bryant / Princeton / Putnam Co. / Illinois
TEXT: Keith Huntress and Fred W. Lorch, "Bryant and Illinois: Further Letters of the Poet's Family," *New England Quarterly*, 16 (December 1943), 637–640.

1. Unrecovered.

2. Undoubtedly George Miller, an English landscapist from Bath who came to New York about 1833, and who exhibited at the National Academy, of which he was an Associate from 1833 to 1838. *DAA*, p. 444.

3. Dana's *Poems and Prose Writings* (1833) was reviewed in the *American Quarterly Observer*, 1 (October 1833), 336–338; *American Monthly Review*, 4 (December

1833), 468–480; and *Christian Examiner and General Review*, 15 (January 1834). The last of these articles has been attributed to Cornelius C. Felton (1807–1862), professor of Greek at Harvard. Bryant may have written one of the first two. Since the book was not noticed in the *NAR*, Frances probably refers to Bryant's 1828 review therein of Dana's *Poems* (1827).

4. A strong Jackson-supporter during most of his eight years in Congress, Gulian Verplanck opposed the President on the issue of rechartering the Bank of the United States, and consequently failed of renomination in 1832. In the fall of 1833 he ran for the New York State Assembly on an avowed anti-administration ticket and was defeated. The following spring he lost a close election as the Whig candidate for mayor of New York. See July, *Essential New Yorker*, pp. 164, 186.

5. [Catharine M. Sedgwick] "Le Bossu," *Tales of Glauber-Spa* (New York, 1832), I, 25–108.

6. Timothy Flint edited the *Knickerbocker* for a brief period in 1833 after the withdrawal of its first editor, Charles Fenno Hoffman. Flint soon resigned in anger at the publisher, whom he called a thorough "scoundrel," and asked Bryant, as one *"sans peur et sans reproche"* (with neither fear nor fault) to settle his affairs with the magazine. See Flint to Bryant, December 28, 1833, NYPL–BG.

7. See Letter 284.

8. Mrs. Arthur Bryant.

273.   *To* Gulian C. Verplanck

[New York?] Thursday morning [December 1833?]

Dear Sir

I wrote you a day or two since respecting the case of Gilbert Kennedy a poor Irishman at Hoboken whose leg is broken in two places and for whom Mrs. Sands is desirous of procuring if your rules will allow it a gratuitous admission into the New York Hospital, as he has not wherewith to pay for medical and other attendance. I presume however my note missed you. Will you be so good as to answer this by the bearer or let me know whether the thing is practicable.—[1]

Yrs. truly

W. C. Bryant

MANUSCRIPT: NYPL–Berg ADDRESS: To the / Hon   G. C Verplanck / 74 Leonard Street DOCKETED: W. C. Bryant.

1. Bryant's first note is unrecovered. Verplanck was a governor of the New York Hospital. July, *Essential New Yorker*, p. 215. Kennedy is unidentified.

274.   *To* Azariah C. Flagg[1]

New York   Jan   6, 1834

Sir

We take the liberty of addressing you confidentially, on a subject, which although it is one of personal interest for us, as proprietors of the Evening Post, concerns also, as we apprehend, the good of the republican party.

Surprise is often expressed at the fact, that while so large a majority of the people of this city are friendly to the National and state administrations, the greater number of the public prints take the other side of the question; and it is asked in what manner these prints are supported. Their advertising columns will, in great part, answer this inquiry. The advertisements of those who hold public offices by the gift of our party are given to the opposition papers. The advertisements of the Custom House are published in the Evening Star and the Journal of Commerce; those of the Post Office appear half the time in the Mercantile Advertiser, and the Courier. The *Masters in Chancery*[2] send their advertisements for the most part to the Commercial Advertiser, the American, the Mercantile, the Daily [Advertiser], the Courier, the Star &c. &c. Thus the business which properly belongs to the journals that steadily support the national and state administrations, goes to encourage and build up those which most violently and scurrilously attack them. The Masters in Chancery in this city are in fact virtually appointed for the benefit of the opposition papers, which not only get the pay for their official advertisements, but the increased circulation which those advertisements occasion. The reasons for their giving this business to the opposition prints are various, —some of them do it because they are actually in the opposition themselves, some because they are acquainted with the opposition editors, some because they are solicited or offered some personal inducements; and thus it happens that scarce a master in chancery in this city, we believe we might say not a single one, publishes his advertisements regularly in the prints of the republican party. It is no wonder therefore, that the opposition journals should be to ours in the proportion of four to one, when they thus contrive to obtain, in addition to the advertising business of their own party, the most profitable part of ours also.

Our object in troubling you with this communication is respectfully to suggest whether the public business does not require that some remedy should be applied to this evil—whether the masters in chancery in the city of New York, and the other legal officers whose advertisements are of any consequence, should not, on receiving their commissions, be informed that it is your indispensable condition that their advertisements shall be sent to the republican prints, designating them by name. Should you think proper to use the influence which your high standing in the party and your situation at Albany give you, to effect this reform, you will confer a personal favor on ourselves, and will also, in our opinion, perform a public service. In case you should need any further information on this subject, or any confirmation of our statement, we beg leave to refer you to Gen. Wetmore the bearer of this letter.[3]

We are sir

with great respect & consideration

yr obt. Servts.

BRYANT LEGGETT & CO

PROPRIETORS OF THE EVENING POST[4]

MANUSCRIPT: NYPL–Flagg.

1. Azariah Cutting Flagg (1790–1873), earlier the editor of the Plattsburgh, New York, *Republican*, became in 1826 Secretary of State for New York, and in 1834 State Controller. A member of the Albany Regency, he is generally considered to have been a statesman of integrity and influence. See Benson, *Jacksonian Democracy*, pp. 68–69; Schlesinger, *Age of Jackson*, p. 178.

2. Officers appointed to assist judges of civil courts by hearing evidence and making reports.

3. Prosper M. Wetmore became a Democratic member of the state legislature in 1834. See 227.1.

4. This letter, in Bryant's handwriting, was almost certainly of his composition.

275. *To* Gulian C. Verplanck

[New York?] Friday morning [*c*January 1834]

My dear Sir

Did you see in the Post of last night an advertisement of a meeting of the Sketch Club at my House at 2 o'clock P. M.? —the mention of the *day* was unfortunately omitted—we meet today—and I hope you will be there—we are to have a long walk and a long talk, and I wish for my part to have a special conversation with you this week about certain matters— Can not you get over [to Hoboken] between 2 & 3?[1]

Yrs truly—

W. C. BRYANT

MANUSCRIPT: NYPL–Berg ADDRESS: Hon. G. C. Verplanck / 74 Leonard Street DOCK-ETED: W. C. Bryant.

1. The Sketch Club met every other Friday evening between November and April at the home of one of its members. Meetings were announced in the *EP* by the cryptic insertion, among the death notices, of the initials "S. C." followed by those of the host, with his address. Callow, *Kindred Spirits*, pp. 16–17.

276. *To* Mrs. Sarah S. Bryant

New York   Feb   3   1834

Dear Mother

Frances, who wrote you some time since, is almost out of patience with waiting for an answer. We have heard nothing of you for four or five months, and do not know whether you and the rest of the family are dead or alive, —to say nothing of our being left in ignorance as to whether the things sent by Mr. Albro reached their destination, and whether the India rubbers fitted you or not. The principal reason for my writing at present is to let you know of a project which I have formed, for visiting Europe, with my family, next summer. If our plan goes into effect we shall be absent a year, and if you do not hear of our return at the expiration of that time, you need not be surprised. I think at present of going to Havre in one of the packets which sail every week from New York for that port; and after visiting Paris, to proceed to Italy, where I shall probably pass the greater part of the time during my absence. I can *live* as cheap abroad as in New York—in Italy I can live cheaper, —and I can be of use to the paper as a foreign correspondent. I shall probably sail about the first of June.

I had intended to send you the money to pay the interest on your note to Shaw, but in consequence of being obliged to make a considerable payment for the share of the Evening Post which we bought of Mr. Gill, I find myself out of funds at present. I hope, however, to visit Cummington with my family before I go, and will then see what can be done.

Austin said something when I was at Cummington, last summer, of coming to New York in the course of the autumn. As he did not find time then, perhaps he may think of visiting us in the Spring, which is not far distant. His wife also might like to see New York and Sarah I am sure would.[1] Will you invite them all here in my wife's name and mine, to come and see us after the river opens. They might come down in the latter part of March, or the fore part of April. During the latter part of April we shall probably be very busy, and our household will be in some confusion, in getting ready for leaving the place, and in disposing of our goods. Whether we go to Europe or not, we shall not remain at Hoboken, and it is even doubtful whether we shall keep house. We are all well and have been so, hitherto in a remarkable degree. Little Julia has grown fat and ruddy and is quite lively and playful. In the beginning of the season she suffered a little indisposition from worms which it cost us much difficulty entirely to expel from her stomach; but I believe she is now wholly rid of them. The winter thus far is very mild. My wife and I have been up the walk a mile or so, almost every day, except when rain or snow was actually falling.[2] There has been however scarcely any snow. A thin sprinkling of it came and remained on the earth three or four days only. I have had another edition of my poems published at Boston.

I judge from a letter which I received from John some time since, that Cyrus intends to *visit* New England next Spring.—[3]

Remember me affectionately to all the family. My wife desires her love. She wishes you to say to Louisa that she is very sorry that she is so burthened with occupation as not to have found time to write to her for many months past.

Your affectionate Son
W. C. BRYANT

MANUSCRIPT: BCHS PUBLISHED: Helen L. Drew, "Unpublished Letters of William Cullen Bryant," *New England Quarterly*, 10 (June 1937), 349–350.

1. Sarah Louisa, eldest of Austin's five children, was then thirteen.

2. This walk along the river bank was described by a local enthusiast in the same year: "The bank of the river is high, and the invigorating sea breeze may be enjoyed

at almost all hours when the sun is above the horizon. In the walks along the river bank, over the ground and in the beautiful fields, studded with clumps of trees, variegated by shady woods, the business worn New Yorker finds a momentary relaxation and enjoyment in Elysian Fields" (the public park laid out by Col. John Stevens on his property at Castle Point). See *History of the Municipalities of Hudson County New Jersey 1630–1923*, ed. Daniel Van Winkle (New York and Chicago: Lewis Historical Publishing Co., 1924), I, 43.

3. Presumably Cyrus, who was to leave Illinois on December 26 in search of a bride, had already reached Cummington. John to Sarah Bryant, December 25, 1833, BCHS.

277. *To* Catharine M. Sedgwick

New York, February 12, 1834.

Dear Friend:

I am sorry to decline any request in which you take an interest, particularly when it is urged with so much delicacy; but I have two good reasons for not undertaking the translation of the ode on the supposed death of Pellico, of which you shall judge.[1] In the first place, I have several things on my hands at present which occupy all my leisure. In the second place, I have looked over the ode, and doubt my ability to produce such a version as would satisfy my friends and myself with anything like a reasonable expenditure of trouble. You know that our English tongue is, of all languages, the most intractable for the purposes of poetic translation, both from the peculiarity of its idioms and the paucity of its rhymes. It is, therefore, a work of vast dexterity and patience—the *ne plus ultra*, I had almost said, of poetic *skill*, though not of poetic genius—to produce a translation in English which shall be a decidedly good poem in itself, animated with the fire and spirit of an original, and at the same time a faithful transfusion of the ideas of its prototype. In the things of the kind which I have executed, I have not kept close to the original, but I should not like to take liberties of the kind with the ode you send me, which is really beautiful and affecting, and deserves to have all its thoughts and images preserved unmarred and unchanged.[2]

I am, very sincerely, yours, etc.,

W. C. BRYANT.

MANUSCRIPT: Unrecovered TEXT: *Life*, I, 293, note.

1. The Italian dramatist Silvio Pellico (1789–1854), best known for his play *Francesca da Rimini* (1815), had published an account of his imprisonment by the Austrians which was translated in 1833 as *My Prisons*. The ode was probably that written by Pellico's prison-companion, Piero Maroncelli, during their confinement at Spielberg from 1822 to 1830. Catharine Sedgwick is said to have been much interested in the recently exiled Italian prisoners of state, among them Maroncelli. *Life*, I, 337–338. See also Adkins, *Halleck*, p. 259.

2. After Bryant declined, Halleck made a translation of Maroncelli's poem which was published together with the original, "Primaverili Aurette," in 1836. When Bryant

sailed for Europe on June 24, 1834, he carried a letter of introduction, dated that day, from Maroncelli to Pellico at Turin. NYPL–GR. Miss Sedgwick's letter requesting the translation of Bryant is unrecovered.

278. *To* John Howard Bryant

New York   Feb   26   1834.

Dear Brother.

When a man pays you a bank note which he tells you some people have supposed to be spurious, and at the same time offers you a large discount from its value if you will take it at your own risk, you may be certain that the note is counterfeit and that he has pretty good reason to believe it so, and the best way in such a case is to return it to him and put yourself to no further trouble about it. Your letter enclosing the $100— note on the South Carolina bank arrived today,[1] and I immediately sent out our clerk to inquire of the brokers as to its genuineness and get me city bills for it if good. He found none of them willing to exchange it, and several of them pronounced it spurious. At S. & M. Alle[n?]'s he was told that a little while since four of these notes of the same denomination had been put off upon the brokers here about the same time, and that upon being sent to Charleston they had been pronounced forgeries. The note you sent me they said was evidently one of the same batch. I therefore send it back to you without delay that you may get the amount of Cutler as soon as possible. I am extremely desirous that you should get the demand in a train to be paid, before I leave the country, if I leave it at all. When you next write let me know what the face of the note is, the date and the indorsements.

I have heard nothing at all of Cyrus, at which I wonder not a little. I wrote more than three weeks since to mother but I have heard nothing from her nor indeed have I had the least intelligence from Cummington since early last fall. You do not inform us in your letter whether the $300— which you lent for me was likely to be paid in season to apply it to the purchase of new lands. Arthur I have not heard from. If he sends me the $100— I do not think I shall send it back to Illinois—but if he does not, I desire that the sum together with the 300 dollars may form a fund for the purchase of lands on my account in the most judicious situation that you and Cyrus may agree upon. I think I wrote to you fully on this subject in my wife's letter.[2] While I am absent I hope you will watch over my interests in Illinois, buy land for me, and see that it is not sold for taxes.

You talk in your letter to my wife of planting an orchard and eating the fruit of it if you live to be old. Why do you not graft your crab apple trees with scions procured from the older settlements in your state? You would then have apples in a very few years. Did you ever think of this? I thought you had already built a house. How comes it that you talk of having a cabin of your own another year? Does the cabin belong to Cyrus?

You speak of Edward—we have heard that he has left Arthur. What is he doing and whom does he live with?

Our winter has been remarkably mild—a season like autumn or spring. We had some cold weather and a little sprinkling of snow in December and the river closed to the north of us—but for several weeks past the temperature has been remarkably high for the season and the river has been open as far as Hudson for several days. The snow went off almost immediately, but a Northampton man told me last week that in that part of the country they had already had sleighing for two months and a half. Remember me to your wife and believe me

Yrs affectionately
W. C. Bryant

[by Frances Bryant]
Dear Brother.

I wish I could tell you that we intend to visit you next summer, for I have a great desire to do so, however I am pretty well satisfied that we shall not have money enough for that, therefore you must not look for us. William seems determined on going to Europe; and I am preparing our clothes as fast as possible, still I think, we *may not go*. I do not intend to be very much disappointed if we should not be able to go in June. What is the difficulty between Arthur and Edward? Do tell me about it. Arthur has written to Miss R[obbins] on the subject; I have not seen the letter. Mr. Sedgwick told William yesterday that he was waiting very impatiently for a letter from you.

Wm's second edition is out, it is very prettily done. Fanny is very well, and desires to be remembered to you. She speaks of you very often. Julia is fat and healthy. Has Henrietta entirely recovered her health?[3] Excuse me for not filling out this sheet, for I have been to town this afternoon and am very tired. Remember me affectionately to your wife & believe me truly yours.

F. F. Bryant

MANUSCRIPT: NYPL–BFP ADDRESS: Mr. John H. Bryant / Princeton / Putnam Co. / Illinois. POSTMARK: NEW-YORK / FEB / 27 POSTAL ANNOTATION: PAID 25.

1. Letter unrecovered.
2. Letter 272.
3. Mrs. Arthur Bryant.

279. *To* Lewis Cass[1]

New York March 19 1834.

Sir.

I have been spoken to by Mr. Robert W. Weir of this city, who desires to obtain the place of Teacher of Drawing at the Military Institution at West Point, and who asks my testimony as to his qualifications. Mr. Weir possesses a high reputation among his brethren of the art, which he has justified by various exquisite productions, in the several departments of portrait landscape and historical painting. He studied, while quite a young man, three years in Italy, during which time he made the proficiency to be expected from fine natural talents, combined with the warmest enthusiasm for the art. I have no doubt of the qualifications of Mr. Weir for the place he asks; though I am sensible that my opinion in relation to such matters is of very little value.[2]

I have the honor to be
with the highest respect &c.
Yr obt Servt—
WM. C. BRYANT

MANUSCRIPT: William L. Clements Library, University of Michigan ADDRESS: To the / Hon Lewis Cass / Secretary of War / Washington / D. C. POSTMARK: NEW-YORK / MAR / 19 DOCKETED: William C. Bryant / March 19th 1834.

1. Lewis Cass had become Secretary of War with the reorganization of Jackson's cabinet in 1831. Bryant had met him at Washington the following year. See Letter 232.

2. On March 22 Cass replied that Weir would be appointed teacher of drawing at West Point if the incumbent, Charles R. Leslie, should decide not to remain. NYPL–BG. Since Leslie resigned soon afterward, Weir was formally appointed on May 8, 1834. See Irene Weir, *Robert W. Weir, Artist* (New York: Field-Doubleday, 1947), pp. 46–47.

280. *To* Cyrus Bryant

New York   Apl. 14   1834.

Dear Brother

I heard of your departure on the 26th of December from Princeton and I afterwards saw an allusion to you in a letter published in a newspaper, the writer of which, a Mr. Hoffman of this city said that he met you at a tavern, a day or two's journey east of Chicago.[1] From not hearing earlier of your arrival at Cummington, I began to fear that you had lost your way, or at least that you had stopped to deliver lectures on chemistry to the backwoodsmen, but as you went so far as to let me know the fact that you are to be married I cannot understand why you keep the name of the lady a secret. You might have told us in perfect confidence that it would go no further. We would have promised not to whisper a syllable of it to the people here.[2]

I should be very glad to see you before you go to the westward, but I do not see that I can come to Cummington, and if you do not come before the first of May we shall have no house to receive you. On the first day of May I shall go with my family to Great Barrington where I expect they will stay a little while.— I shall be there a day or two. If you do not come down before that time could you not contrive to visit Great Barrington on the 1st of May and meet me there?

I suppose you have heard of my intention to visit Europe. I expected to go on the first of June; but circumstances have occurred which will probably oblige me to defer the voyage to a somewhat later period. Mrs. Coleman whom I have more than half paid the note she holds against me for the purchase money of the Evening Post establishment, on being made acquainted with my design to go has demanded of me, in case I should leave the country, two thousand dollars on the principal of the note which is more money than I can raise from my own funds, and there is not much likelihood that I can get it elsewhere. If I cannot I must stay till I earn it; and by sending my family into the country I am making arrangements, by a course of rigid economy to diminish my debts as fast as possible, and to endeavour to get out of the power of these people who want to hamper my movements. Mrs. Coleman is amply secured by a mortgage on the establishment, and during my absence I would have so arranged matters that she should receive regularly her interest and something on the principal, but this does not content her. But even if I should not go I am told that I must pay a thousand dollars this spring. This I shall find it inconvenient to do upon so sudden a demand, having paid out all my surplus funds for the share that I bought of Gill. I have never at any time felt poorer than I do now; and though we have followed a plan of strict economy all winter yet we find it impossible to keep house in this quarter without a considerable outlay, or even to live at board here. Whether therefore our voyage is deferred to late in the summer, to next fall or to next spring, my family stay in the country.

As to the interest on my notes in Illinois, I have already been informed by John that he had received 25 dollars on one note and 50 dollars on another. Of the first sum he said he had paid you half, and was ready to pay you half of the other. He had also he said let you have 30 dollars of a payment which had been made him on Cutler's note. According to this statement there will be $67.50 for you to give your note for, unless you should prefer to give me your note for the $42.50 and wait until you get the $25 before you "promise to pay for value recd." As to the subsequent payments, if there should be any on the notes, including Cutler's I must make you and John agents to receive each others notes as the payments are made. When you divide the money you must give John a note payable to me for your half; and he must give you a note payable to me for his half. This is in case I leave the country; if I do not you can send the notes to me as usual.

We have generally been exceedingly well through the winter, though at present my wife is afflicted with a kind of periodical headache and pains in the limbs arising I believe from a long and very fatiguing walk taken one hot day in March. The weather here this winter has been the mildest and pleasantest I ever knew—scarcely any snow and the ground in a good state for walking except for a few days in February.

Thorburn I have seen, about the English spear grass and Buckthorn. He thinks that his son has not the seeds, as they are not often called for, but he has them himself in New York.³ I think it will be best for me to bring them to Great Barrington. I have some seeds of the *sycamore* the *acer* mentioned in Michaux as growing at Hoboken—the English tree called Sycamore.⁴ I will bring them also that you may, if you please, introduce a new tree into the western plantations. My regards to the family.

Yrs affectionately

W. C. BRYANT

P. S. I have written to every body I knew or thought I could influence at Washington to get the place of Register in the land office for you. I presume that the bill creating new land offices in Illinois has passed the Senate, but I have lost sight of it in the House.⁵

If you should come to N. Y. before the first of May we should be very glad to see you.

W. C. B.

[by Frances Bryant]
Dear Cyrus

You must not go back without letting us see you. I am sorry that you cannot come here; we wish very much to see you, and your *intended* also— Why did you not tell her name? I approve of your manly spirit, in the other affair. We laughed heartily when we read your letter, and thought you did much better, than to sit down, and *sigh* & pout for one unworthy of you, for she must be so, who could serve you such a trick. I really rejoice that you have got a wife, for I am sure you will be much happier with one, than without. You have my sincere wish for your prosperity and happiness, and if it was in my power to do any thing further, I certainly most cheerfully would do it for you. William has been vexed and disappointed in his money matters, and we are now getting ready as fast as possible to go into [the] country, where I hope you will meet us, and we can talk over these affairs freely.

I was sorry that I could not select and repair the articles that William sent you. I was very sick, confined to my bed, at the time, so that I could not even look at the things. He has a *few* on hand now, and they are of very little value. I shall take them to Great Barrington—if you should think them worth taking—you shall have them. I should have written to you, and apologized for not doing it, but I write so bad a letter that it puts William in an agony to read them, therefore out of pu[re] compassion for him, I have given up letter writing. Miss Robbins is here and desires to be remembered to you. It is now past ten—and I must leave this and finish in the morning if possible. If not make my best respects to your lady. My health is poor—and I am quite unfit for the business that I am now obliged to attend to. William goes to Gt. B. with me on purpose to meet you, dont disappoint us. Love to the family, tell L[ouisa] I will answer her letter when I get to Gt. B.

F. F. BRYANT

MANUSCRIPT: BCHS PUBLISHED: Helen L. Drew, "Unpublished Letters of William Cullen Bryant," *New England Quarterly*, 10 (June 1937), 351–352.

1. Probably Charles Fenno Hoffman (1806–1884), first editor of the *Knickerbocker* in 1833, who spent the winter of 1833–1834 traveling in the West and writing letters for the New York *American*, to one of which Bryant refers. He published *A Winter in the West* (New York, 1835).
2. Cyrus' letter is unrecovered.
3. Grant Thorburn (1773–1863), popular Scottish-American florist who had issued the first American seed-catalogue in 1812. A friend of Halleck's and of other literary men, he wrote numerous articles for the newspapers and magazines under the pen name "Lawrie Todd." See Adkins, *Halleck*, p. 301; Hone, *Diary*, I, 325, 397.
4. Both the French botanist André Michaux (1746–1802) and his son François André Michaux (1770–1855) had studied the trees of North America extensively. Probably Bryant refers to François Michaux's *The North American Sylva*, 1817.
5. See Letter 258.

281. *To* Campbell P. White[1]

New York   April 15th, 1834.

Dear Sir

A worthy friend of mine, long a neighbour of yours Mr. Francis Evrard[2] has applied to the Collector of this Port for the place of Custom House Inspector. Swartwout gives him good words; but I hear that several vacancies have been filled by others since he applied; and I suspect that it is intended to adjourn his claim *sine die*. I believe that the appointment would be a useful, as I know it would be a respectable one, which is more than can be said of all Swartwout's appointments.[3] I have suggested to Mr. Evrard the expediency of writing to you who know him very well, and get you to lay his application before the Secretary of the Treasury, who, I am told sometimes directs appointments of this kind to be made. Mr. Evrard being too modest to follow my advice, I take the liberty of making the request myself. Should you think proper to interest yourself in the matter, you will oblige a very honest and industrious man who is in want of occupation. I enclose a copy of the recommendations presented by him to Swartwout the originals of which I have seen.[4] I have the honour to be

With much respect & esteem
Yr obt. Servt
WILLIAM C. BRYANT.

MANUSCRIPT: NYHS ADDRESS: Hon. Campbell P. White / Member of Congress / Wash-
INGTON / D. C. POSTMARK: NEW-YORK / APL / 16.

1. Campbell Patrick White (1787–1859), Irish-born New York merchant, was a
Democratic member of Congress from New York, 1829–1835.

2. Bryant's first landlord in New York. See Letter 127.

3. Samuel Swartwout (1783–1856), once arrested for complicity in Aaron Burr's
treason and later a witness against Burr, served as Collector of the Port of New York
from 1829 to 1838, when he was found to have misappropriated more than $1,000,000
of the funds under his charge. See Hone, *Diary*, I, 356, 375.

4. Bryant forwarded to White copies of two letters signed by nearly two score
business and professional men and firms, recommending Evrard highly.

282. *To* Richard H. Dana

New York   Apl. 22   1834

Dear Sir

It is some time since I went through your book for the purpose of
noting such passages as appeared to me capable of amendment—though
from my delaying to write you might think that I had neglected it. You
shall have my animadversions since you ask for them though I do not
place much stress on them.[1] The line page 33

> I felt its sunny peace come warm and mild
> To my young heart &c—

strikes me as faulty. The epithet *mild* I think tautologous as applied to
peace. It is much like "mild and gentle sympathy" in my Thanatopsis. In
Thoughts on the Soul I am certain I found a bad rhyme when I read the
first edition. I have gone over it two or three times in search of it but
cannot find it. I have marked the line

> "Life in itself, *it life* to all things gives," p. 89.

as a harsh inversion. In the Husband and Wife's Grave the line

> Of uncreated light have visited and lived,

is an Alexandrine which rarely has a good effect in heroic rhyme and is
not used at all in blank verse, and as I think with good reason.

> Page 118   Dear Goddess I *grow* old I trow
> My head is *growing* gray

In this passage the word grow is repeated without any beauty of effect.

> Page 134   Nor live the shame of those *who bore their part* &c

Is not this passage obscure?

> Page 114   Query as to the phrase "*go* with care"

Page 128   "But *fluttered* out its idle hour" Can the word flutter be applied to a flower in this manner?

These are all the verbal faults which I have found in reading over your poems several times. I am sorry I have not a better list to present you, for the sake of gaining credit for my diligence; but we must take things as they are. What a paltry trick was that served you and your friend about the review! I should not have expected it, I should rather have supposed that a man who studies to go with the popular opinion would have thought it good policy to conciliate you but if he had said frankly, at once, "this praise is excessive I cannot put it in my Review" I should have thought much better of him than I now can. The artifice of pretending to like the article and wearing out the patience of the writer by delay until he was induced to withdraw it, is miserable enough.[2] Yet as you say you have been pretty well reviewed, I mean as to the number of notices of your work, and sometimes the notices have come from writers willing to do you justice. I should never have heard of the review of my poems in the Quarterly Observer but for you. I have not seen it yet.[3] Have you seen the article on your own in the U. S. Review?[4]

I am sorry your health continues so bad. My own is much better than usual. I have gradually discontinued the use of coffee and tea, and now I have given them up altogether. I have also by degrees accustomed myself to a diet principally vegetable, a bowl of milk and bread made in my house of unbolted wheat flour, at breakfast, and another at noon, and nothing afterwards. This is not my *uniform* diet—but nearly so. Its effect upon me is so kindly, that while it is in my power to continue it, I do not think I shall ever make any change. All indigestion, costiveness, slight obstructions of bile at one time, and the excessive production of it at another, disagreeable sensations in the head, nervous depression &c. &c. are removed by it, while the capacity for intellectual exertion without fatigue is much increased; in short I do not recollect that I have enjoyed better health or more serene spirits since my childhood, than I have done for more than six months past. I mention these things that you may think of them—though I know it is said that "what is one man's meat is another man's poison."

Do you know that I have a plan of going to Europe? It is therefore that I have been heartily disappointed at your not coming on this Spring. It is not likely that I shall see you before I sail, unless circumstances (which is possible) prevent me from making the voyage until another year. I am sick of the strife of politics—not that I ever liked the quarreling much, though I was always something of a politician—but I have had enough of it, and if I have any talents, they are talents for other things. I do not however give up my connection with the paper for it is my living, my dependence. I hope, however, when less harassed by business, and the multitude of matters that must divide and distract the conductor of a daily paper, to collect my thoughts for some literary enterprise of a kind in which I shall take some satisfaction.

I have seen your daughter whom I was agreeably surprised to find so reposed in person and mind, remembering her as I did only as a little girl. She has the Dana look.[5]

The line you remarked upon as faulty

Kind influences—lo their orbs burn more bright

is not, to my ear unmanageable. I thought I had a parallel for it in Milton, but I do not find it. Some critic, in Buckingham's Magazine,[6] I believe noticed the line as harsh, but I paid no attention to the criticism, being in the habit of disregarding all that is said about my versification. But since it seems faulty to *you* who are quite as great a heretic as I am in this matter I will consider of it and perhaps amend it. It is only leaving out the *S* you know.[7] I thank you for the other passages you have marked and will not fail to profit by your animadversions. I am dear sir

truly yrs

W. C. BRYANT.

May 9th. I had finished a letter, as you see, when I recollected that there were some things in one of your last letters to answer, so I delayed sending it until I should have looked up your letter. This has made more than a fortnights difference in our correspondence as you will see by the dates. Since I wrote the foregoing I have packed up my goods, broken up housekeeping, and accompanied my wife and children to Berkshire where I left them the latter part of last week, and now I am again without a home, ready to wander whithersoever my inclination may lead— provided I can raise the wind.

But I must have a word with you concerning the question you put me anent your versification. In this art I think you have a manly taste and a vigorous and ofttimes a happy execution. In this it appears to me that you have the advantage of most of our writers in verse. The fault that I find with you is that you sometimes adopt a *bad order of the words* for the sake of the measure, or rather you let the bad order stand, for want of diligence to overcome the difficulty. Perhaps, however, you do right; I have sometimes been conscience smitten at wasting so much time in longs and *shorts*—spending so many hours to make a crabbed thought submit to the dimensions of the metre, to frame a couplet or stanza so that the tune of it perfectly pleased my ear at the same time that the expression of the thought was the most perfect that I could command. I fear that this process has been attended with a loss of vigor and freshness in the composition. Your general system of versification pleases me—in that of Mr. Longfellow I see nothing peculiar. So do not let them plague you about your versification.

Yrs truly

W. C. BRYANT

MANUSCRIPT: NYPL–GR ADDRESS: Richard H. Dana Esq / Boston / Mass. POSTMARK: NEW-YORK / MAY / 10 POSTAL ANNOTATION: 18 ENDORSED: Wm. C. Bryant / May 9—34 / Ans. PUBLISHED (in part): Life, I, 303–305.

1. Dana's letter is unrecovered.

2. The parties to this "paltry trick" have not been identified.

3. Bryant probably meant to write "American Quarterly Observer." Dana's book had been reviewed the preceding October in this periodical. See 272.3.

4. There was no publication at that time bearing the title "U. S. Review." Perhaps Bryant intended the *American Monthly Review*, which had carried a notice of Dana's *Poems and Prose Writings* in December 1833. See 272.3.

5. Dana's daughter Charlotte was for many years thereafter a friend and correspondent of Cullen's and Frances'.

6. Joseph T. Buckingham conducted the *New-England Magazine* from 1831 to 1834.

7. Bryant later revised this line in "The Conjunction of Jupiter and Venus" (1826) to read, "Kind influence. Lo! they brighten as we gaze." See *Poems* (1876), p. 157.

283. *To* William Leggett

Great Barrington   Monday   June 2d [1834]

Dear Sir

I thought to have been in New York the beginning of this week but in consequence of Mrs Bryant's not being [rea]dy I am [obliged] to postpone my departure from this place until next Friday or Saturday. I write this to beg you to send me any letters which may come addressed to me at New York from Mr. Cambreleng. You will I suppose receive this tomorrow. The letters immediately put into the post office would reach me on Wednesday. I requested Mr. Cambreleng if he answered my letter within a few days to direct to me at Great Barrington; but I have heard nothing from him. I cannot engage a passage until I hear from him and learn what time the despatches will be ready for me, if I am to have any.[1] If I hear within a day or two I may write to you to trouble you to engage a passage for me. Do not put any thing into the Post Office for me after Thursday.

My wife desires her love to Mrs. Leggett and bids me say that she may expect us there early next week.[2]

Yrs truly

W. C. BRYANT

MANUSCRIPT: William Cullen Bryant II ADDRESS: To / William Leggett Esq. / Office of the Evening Post / New York POSTMARK (in script): Gt Barrington Ms. June 2nd POSTAL ANNOTATION: 12½ DOCKETED: Wm C Bryant / Great Barrington / June 2, 1834.

1. About February 1 Bryant had written asking his friend Congressman Cambreleng (letter unrecovered) to secure for him through Secretary of State Louis McLane official despatches to carry to France, in order to reduce the cost of his passage. On May 26 Cambreleng wrote him, "Mr. McLane tells me that if the French Corvette ar-

rives in time he may have important despatches by the time you propose sailing—in which case he will endeavour to gratify your wishes." NYPL–GR.

2. From about June 9 until they sailed on June 24 the Bryants stayed with the Leggetts in their home on Fourth Street, New York City. Frances Bryant, "Autobiographical Sketch," NYPL–GR.

284. *Memorandum of an Engagement Entered into between George P. Morris and William C. Bryant, Both of the City of New York, on the 10th of June, 1834.*

The said Bryant agrees to furnish twenty poems for the New York Mirror, to be sent to the said Morris from some part of Europe. The said Morris promises to pay for each of the said poems, on delivery, thirty dollars. It is understood that the said Bryant will not, within two years from the present time, furnish any poetical contributions of his own composition, to any other monthly, weekly or daily journal in the United States.—[1]

[signed] WILLIAM C. BRYANT
[signed] GEO. P. MORRIS.

MANUSCRIPT: Saint John's Seminary, Camarillo, California

1. This agreement in Bryant's handwriting resulted in his sending Morris fifteen poems for the *NYM* between March 28, 1835, and April 15, 1837.

285. *To* Andrew Jackson

New York   June 12   1834
Office of the Evening Post.

Sir

I beg leave to lay before you a statement of some circumstances connected with an application of mine to the Department of State which perhaps have not come to your knowledge.

Having formed the design of visiting the continent of Europe with my little family, I requested my friend Mr. Cambreleng to enquire of the Secretary of State whether I could be employed as a messenger of the government, to convey despatches to the Minister of the United States at the Court of France, in such a manner as to obtain a compensation which would lessen the expenses of the voyage. This Mr. Cambreleng readily agreed to do, whenever I should fix upon the time of my departure.[1] Early in February last I wrote to the same gentleman mentioning that I wished to sail in June and requested him to see Mr. McLane in season and get his answer. About the middle of the same month Mr. Cambreleng wrote me that he had mentioned my application to Mr. McLane who said there would be "no difficulty" about it.[2] Knowing that I had to do with a plain dealing administration, I thought myself authorized to rely upon the answer as affirmative, at least, in case the government of the United States should have occasion to send any despatches of importance by a messenger, for I was not by any means guilty of the absurdity of supposing that the occasion would be created on my account. About the middle of last May at a time when our relations with the French government in consequence of the course taken by the Chamber of Deputies rendered it probable that instructions would be speedily despatched to our Minister in France[3] I wrote again to Mr. Cambreleng mentioning my desire to sail in June; and received an answer dated the 26th of May in which he informed me that he had been told by Mr. McLane "that if the French Corvette arrived in time he might have important despatches by the time I proposed sailing, in which case he would endeavor to gratify my wishes—that he would at all events give me official despatches, but, unless of some importance, that would not entitle me to any compensation for the service."[4] The French brig of war arrived shortly after this letter was written, and after waiting a few days I addressed a letter to Mr. McLane alluding to the promise he had made and inquiring when the despatches would be ready, in case any were to be sent.[5] In the mean time I made my arrangements for my departure, with reference to the means I was to derive from my compensation as special messenger. To my utter surprise I have this day received a letter from Mr. Cambreleng informing me that he had got a note from Mr. McLane stating that he had been misunderstood, that he had "avoided constituting me a bearer of despatches properly so called, and entitled to the pay usual in such cases," that for a special messenger he has "been a long time committed with the consent and under an arrangement with the President," but that he would give me despatches *pro forma*.[6] Mr. Cambreleng is positive that he did not misunderstand Mr. McLane, and that in proferring my application he laid a stress upon the compensation. It was indeed the only reason, as he fully understood, and, I think, could not have neglected to state why I asked to be made the bearer of despatches; and Mr. McLane must know that I do not stand in need of the little credit to be obtained by being employed to carry papers of no consequence. —I certainly should both decline giving the government the trouble of preparing them, and myself the trouble of delivering them.

I have proceeded all along upon the ground that I was to be employed as the bearer of despatches to France in case the occasion should arise. I have in fact waited for that occasion, and on its arising have made my pecuniary arrangements with reference to the promise which I understood to be given me, and which from the mode of transacting public business adopted under your administration, I had a right to suppose would be rigidly observed in its *spirit*, and not evaded by a trivial construction. Finding myself in this situation I have thought it my duty frankly to acquaint you with the manner in which I have been treated, relying confidently upon that strict sense of right, which has ever governed your public and private conduct to do me such justice as circumstances may yet allow.[7]

In order to put you more fully in possession of the facts I enclose you Mr. Cambreleng's two last letters relating to my application.[8] The first letter communicating Mr. McLane's answer at the time the application was mentioned to him in February I cannot at present lay my hand on.

I have the honor to be
with the greatest respect and consideration
Your obedient servant
WM. C. BRYANT

MANUSCRIPT: NYPL–GR (draft; final copy unrecovered).

1. Cambreleng had written Bryant six months earlier that he had spoken to Louis McLane, the Secretary of State, who "expressed every intention to gratify you." December 12, 1833, NYPL–BG.

2. Bryant's letter is unrecovered. His recollection of the response was faulty; on February 12 Cambreleng had written, "I had intended speaking to Mr. McLane about your visit abroad—but I have particular reasons for postponing it till it is settled that he remains where he is." NYPL–GR. McLane was then in opposition to the President over the withdrawal of government deposits from the Bank of the United States, and it was thought he might have to resign from the cabinet. See Schlesinger, *Age of Jackson*, p. 101.

3. In April the French parliament had refused to pay damage claims for American merchant ships seized during the Napoleonic wars. Bailey, *Diplomatic History*, p. 195.

4. Cf. MS copy of Cambreleng's letter in Bryant's handwriting, NYPL–GR.

5. Bryant's letter to McLane is unrecovered.

6. MS copy in Bryant's handwriting of a letter from Cambreleng dated June 10, 1834, NYPL–GR.

7. No reply to this letter from President Jackson has been found, nor any evidence that he took action on Bryant's request.

8. These were evidently the original letters from which Bryant made the copies referred to in Notes 4 and 6.

286. *To* John Howard Bryant

New York   June 21   1834.

Dear Brother

I have engaged a passage in the packet ship Poland which sails for Havre on Tuesday. I have visited Cummington and found all our friends quite well. Mother yet talks of going to Illinois; but I found the rest of the family apparently less desirous of a removal than I had expected.[1]

I have your two letters, one written in April and the other in May.[2] I am sorry you have so much trouble about the Cutler note. I supposed you would be compelled to take no more trouble about it than you were willing to take for the sake of the use of the money when collected. I have mentioned your proposition to Bliss about making a deduction, but he does not relish it—so my account with him now remains unsettled till I return. Bliss says you must write to Cutler and tell him that you will sue the note if the agreement he made with you to extinguish it by quarterly payments is not complied with. I asked him directly if he would have it *put in suit*, to which he only answered that you could judge best. At all events he wishes you to write and express his sense of the hard manner at which he has been treated and his surprise that a person so honorable should have failed to meet the engagement which he made with you as the condition of forbearing to sue the note. If however you think yourself pretty certain of collecting it, I say *sue it*.[3]

You ask if 7 per cent can be collected on the note. Seven per cent is our rate of interest, and can be collected in all courts of the United States on notes given here. You speak in one of your letters of lending money in Illinois at 25 per cent and taking land as a pledge. I thought the usury law forbade so high a rate of interest.

I have communicated to Mr. Sedgwick what you say about his business.

I am very glad to hear you are so comfortably established at last and hope to find you on my return still more prosperous. You will not forget to make as good an investment of my money in lands as you can when the lands come into market. I shall write to you on my arrival in Paris and tell you where to direct your letters.

My regards to your wife—

Yrs truly

WM   C. BRYANT

MANUSCRIPT: UVa ADDRESS: Mr. John H. Bryant / Princeton / Putnam Co   / Illinois
POSTMARK: NEW-YORK / JUN / 21 POSTAL ANNOTATION: 25.

1. Sarah Bryant's growing distaste for Cummington was evident in her letters of this time. Since 1831 she had written hopefully of her wish to emigrate; on May 8, 1832, she wrote Cyrus, "Five families go this week from Cummington to Ohio. . . . I desire to leave the place to their own destruction. I wish I was now ready to start for Illi." BCHS. See also 251.1. But Austin Bryant, a busy farmer with 100 acres of land and nearly 100 head of livestock, chairman of the board of selectmen and colonel of the militia regiment, with a large and still growing family, saw the proposed removal as a formidable undertaking.

2. Unrecovered.

3. The involvement of Byrant's publisher Elam Bliss in this situation suggests that Cutler may have been an Illinois bookseller.

287. *To* William Leggett

New York   June 23   1834

Mr. William Leggett

Please deliver to Russell C. Wheeler Esq. a box lying in the office of the Evening Post on which is the following direction:

"For Wm. C. Bryant Esq   To be left at the office of the Evening Post   William Street   N   Y."

WILLIAM C. BRYANT[1]

MANUSCRIPT: NYPL–GR.

1. This letter and an accompanying memorandum, written the day before Bryant sailed for Europe, reveal one of the many important services to friends which led John Bigelow to remark that Bryant "treated every neighbor as if he were an angel in disguise sent to test his loyalty to the golden rule." Bigelow, *Bryant*, pp. 286–287. Sometime in 1833 Bryant had apparently lent money to an American painter, John Rand (see Letter 289), to help him settle in London. At about the same time he had entered suit in North Carolina to recover $5,000 under a forfeited bond for Mrs. Rand, a friend of his aunt Charity Bryant. The box which Bryant instructed Leggett to deliver to Mr. Wheeler, who would collect the recovered funds in his absence, held account books and other records of the case. See Spencer O'Brien to Bryant, November 25, 1833, NYPL–GR; "Memorandum . . . by William C. Bryant agent for Mrs. Lavinia Rand," dated June 23, 1834, NYPL–GR; Callow, *Kindred Spirits*, pp. 71–72; Letter 289.

VII

Proud Old World
1834–1836
(LETTERS 288 TO 314)

> . . . These dim vaults,
> These winding aisles, of human pomp or pride
> Report not.   . . . This mighty oak—
> By whose immovable stem I stand and seem
> Almost annihilated—not a prince,
> In all that proud old world beyond the deep,
> E'er wore his crown as loftily as he. . . .
> —"A Forest Hymn," 1825.

BRYANT'S RELIEF AT SAILING FOR EUROPE in June 1834 was evident in earlier remarks to Dana. "I am sick of the strife of politics," he wrote in April; "If I have any talents, they are talents for other things." He hoped while abroad to tackle "some literary enterprise of a kind in which I shall take some satisfaction." But it was soon apparent that the occasional poems he sent to the *New-York Mirror* could not alone provide such satisfaction. After six months in France and Italy he was still "occupied with nothing of importance," he told Horatio Greenough; he was simply trying "to recover what I nearly unlearned in the course of several years, thinking and writing on political subjects; namely, the modes of thought and mechanism of languages which belong to poetry." He missed the stimulus of his countrymen's applause, and wondered what he was doing so far from home.

Almost the only poems of note Bryant composed in Europe, such as "Seventy-Six," or "Catterskill Falls," embraced American themes or scenes. He tried, with meager success, to versify local legends, as in "The Knight's Epitaph" and "The Strange Lady." The one or two poems with a European coloring to which he managed to give some vitality concerned external nature— "Earth's Children Cleave to Earth" and "Earth." Even here, his thoughts turned homeward:

> . . . Oh thou,
> Who sittest far beyond the Atlantic deep,
> Among the sources of thy glorious streams,
> My native Land of Groves! a newer page
> In the great record of the world is thine,
> Shall it be fairer?

But if the Old World offered little poetic inspiration, it heightened Bryant's awareness of social states, and led him to examine closely the people through whose villages he passed, or in whose cities he settled down. He watched their behavior under their peculiar moral and political imperatives. He saw everywhere the persistence of old customs and the "vestiges of power and magnificence which have passed away." He noted wonders of ancient architecture, just as he did peasant cottages and costumes, patterns of soil culture, and popular amusements. But, viewing the glories of Paris and Rome, the beauties of Pisan churches and Florentine statues, he would not take time, he wrote William Leggett, to "give you a flourish" about them, for such might easily be found in "any book of travels you could lay your hands on."

If Bryant found real satisfaction during his travels in any form of writing, it was in the letters he sent to the *Evening Post* and to a few close friends. His attention was constantly drawn to physical and moral contrasts with his own society. At times his remarks seem those of the artless visitor from a dynamic society who measures the worth of all he sees only by its susceptibility to change. The gay Parisian, surrounded by emblems of ancestral greatness but barred by stern guards from inspecting them closely, turned to fiddling and "jigging," or childish amusements. "Perpetual business, perpetual toil, with intervals of repose," natural for the American, were alien to him; he could hope only for his spot in one of the "great burial places which lie just without the barriers of the City." The degenerate Florentine, whose heritage of literature, science, and art contained "all the apparatus for making great men," seemed as "indolent and effeminate" as his forebears had been "hardy and enterprising." The voluble Venetian, loitering at his coffeehouse in the "most pleasing of Italian cities," gave no thought to its deserted shipyards and decaying wharves. Even the neat, industrious Tyrolese peasant passed his leisure time in docile obedience to the dictates of his parish priest. In the sole instance Bryant reported of open resistance to authority, the young dissenters were quickly banished to a hilltop fortress to strum their guitars in carefree idleness.

Yet there were good things to be learned by the observant democrat. To the Florentine, a work of art was a sacred trust, never, as often in America, to be mutilated or desecrated. In devoutly Catholic Italy, Protestants were "almost everywhere provided with places of worship"—and this at a time when Roman Catholics were mobbed in New York, and one of their convents in Boston burned by Protestant zealots. Sunday, in Italy and Bavaria, was a day not only of rest and worship, but also of harmless amusement at theater, concert hall, park, or beer garden; nowhere did one see the stealthy depravity common in professedly pious American cities. Bryant was much impressed by the public parks at the centers of crowded cities—the Cascine and the Boboli Gardens in Florence, the Villa Borghese at Rome, the English Garden at Munich. These great green spaces in the midst of dense populations became fixed in his memory, as did the innocent and healthful diversions they offered laboring people on Sundays and holidays. A decade later, urging New Yorkers to set aside a large central park, he cited Munich's English Garden, into which "half the population pours itself on summer evenings," as evidence that "among the people of Europe, who are in the habit of assembling in public gardens and other places of light and agreeable entertainment, there are few or no manifestations of the coarseness and violence which is often seen in this country."

Until he met with the "wild splendor" of the "gigantic brotherhood of the Alps," Bryant deplored again and again the wastage of natural beauty he saw everywhere in southern Europe—the lopping of trees, the constriction of winding streams in straight channels, the close cultivation which eroded soil and greenery and left the land hot and dusty. Man's tight rein on nature seemed to symbolize the constraint under which the many labored to enrich the few. Everywhere, idle military forces stood by while women worked in fields divided by ancient hedgerows and overseen by fortress-like châteaux. Bryant was constantly troubled by the begging, the fraud, the extortion, and the thievery to which a traveler was subjected, and by the widespread corruption evident among public officials. These offenses resulted, he thought, from a lack of self-respect induced in the "inferior" classes by their "hopeless dependence and poverty." Repeated observation confirmed his conclusion, soon after starting his journey, that "No American can see how much jealousy and force on the one hand, and necessity and fear on the other, have to do with keeping up the existing governments of Europe, without thanking heaven that such is not the condition of his own country."

Slow to make friends, Bryant found few companions during his travels. There were some exceptions. A stay of two months at Florence brought him often into the company of the young American sculptor Horatio Greenough. Throughout a winter at Pisa he saw much of an English widow, Susan Renner, and an Italian literary scholar at the university, Professor Giacomo (?) Rosini. But the following summer at Munich he found life dull, and confessed to an "intense desire to see the faces and hear the converse of old friends." Not until they got to Heidelberg in October 1835 did the Bryants meet a community of friends much to their liking. Soon after settling there Bryant learned of the sudden illness of his partner, but hearing soon afterward that Leggett was improving and had competent temporary help, he found his family a house for the winter. In December they were joined by Henry Longfellow and his late wife's friend Clara Crowninshield, and for six weeks the older poet and the young Harvard professor of modern languages exchanged frequent visits and rambled together over the hills or along the Neckar River. Longfellow found his companion "pleasant and talkative" and liked him "exceedingly," while Clara felt as though she had always known his wife and daughters.

But by the third week in January Bryant was advised that Leggett was too ill to attend to the *Evening Post*, and that there was need at once for the guidance of its senior editor if the business was to be sustained. So, leaving his family in the care of their new friends, Bryant set out hurriedly for home, only to meet with a series of delays which held up his arrival at New York until nearly the end of March.

288. "Journal &c."[1]

[Paris? *c*July 23, 1834]

June 24th 1834. I left New York in the packet ship Poland bound for Havre. At 3 o'clock in the afternoon we arrived off Staten Island and took our *departure* as it is called for Europe. In conformity with the advice of a medical friend I used the precaution of wearing a tight belt round the stomach to prevent seasickness. In the course of an hour or two however I experienced the uselessness of the experiment, and became as sick as heart could wish.[2]

—25th Still sick.

26th Sea smooth and fair—I was able to walk a little on deck. In the evening I witnessed a most beautiful spectacle the luminous appearance of the sea. The waves broke before the bow of the vessel in sheets of fire; the foam shone on the top of every wave; the ocean seemed full of beacon lights; and in the extreme distance they formed a luminous ring on the edge of the horizon.

I was sea sick until my arrival at Havre and consequently had little disposition to study the characters of my fellow passengers. There was a pretty looking French woman on board a Madam La Laurie, the same who committed such horrible cruelties upon her slaves last winter in New Orleans. Her house took fire and she was unwilling that the firemen should use any means to extinguish it. This led to suspicions that all was not right, and the fire being put out, the house was searched, and an apartment was discovered in which several negroes were confined, some chained in painful postures and others horribly wounded and scarce alive. The populace were so enraged that they would have torn her in pieces had she not made her escape disguised in men's clothes. She took refuge for a time in Mobile and was now returning with her husband to his and her native country. She was specious and polite in her manners, and spoke the Spanish language with fluency, an accomplishment of which she seemed to be rather vain. She seemed much affected with the reserve with which the other ladies on board treated her and was frequently seen in tears; her principal consolation she found in gambling with a Piedmontese woman of equivocal appearance. Her husband Dr. La Laurie was as kind and assiduous as if his wife had been a miracle of female excellence. There was also on board a Mr. Joshua Blake of Boston and his lady. He had formerly been a sea faring man; he had begun the world poor and had grown rich, and being retired from business and having nothing else to do had become for the last half dozen years a dyspeptic and valetudinarian. He breakfasted on coffee and cold mutton; dined heartily on mutton roast or boiled which he always ate without vegetables and washed down with a moderate quantity of sherry; and two or three hours afterwards swallowed several cups of the strongest black tea. In the intervals between his meals he was always chewing slippery elm bark, or eating gum arabic, in order as he said to supply his system with a due proportion of nourishment. Yet with all this care to give his stomach plenty of materials for digesting, it performed its business badly, probably from the very circumstance of having so much work forced upon it; and very little of the nourishment which went down his throat was carried to the account of his system in general. He was one of the thinnest men I ever saw, and had it not been for the folds upon folds of flannel in which he was wrapped I verily believe he would have been blown from the deck in the first fresh gale. He was a kind man, intelligent, and rather interesting in conversation, though inclined to the fault of exaggeration, but the fumes of his indigestion seemed to obscure his judgment and made him always look at the dark side of things. He sat up several nights watching for islands against which the ship was to strike and go down with all its passengers in the middle of the sea, and would often come down from deck looking most dismally and frighten his wife and mine with fearful hints of the danger to which Capt. Anthony was exposing us all by keeping the vessel under such a press of sail. My wife soon found out his infirmity—but his forebodings never made the slightest impression on me. When one is sea sick I believe he never cares for any danger the vessel may be in. Another of our passengers was a young lady from Havana accompanied by her brother the young Marquis Ramos. She was apparently in the last stage of a consumption, and we were all fearful of witnessing a death scene on board, but fortunately it proved otherwise.[3]

MANUSCRIPT: Homestead Collection.

1. Bryant evidently began to keep a journal, on the voyage to Havre, which he soon relinquished to his wife, writing only this fragment himself. It is contained in the first few pages of a letter-book which Frances Bryant kept during their European travels in 1834–1836, and which, with three diaries and another letter-book preserved in NYPL–GR, supplies much homely detail not to be found in the more formal letters written by her husband to his friends and to the EP.

2. Frances Bryant reported that her husband "suffered unmercifully all the way; . . . he was sick during the whole voyage and sat up but little." In almost twenty subsequent ocean voyages over a period of nearly forty years, Bryant seems never to have been wholly free from seasickness.

3. In a letter to one of her sisters from Paris on July 23, Frances names, among other shipboard companions, [Charles Joseph] Latrobe, English nephew of the architect of the Capitol in Washington, who had accompanied Washington Irving on his western tour in 1832, and was now returning to England preparatory to publishing an account of his travels, The Rambler in North America: 1832–1833 (London and New York, 1835), in two volumes.

289. *To* John Rand[1]

Paris   July 20   1834.

My dear sir

You will see by the date of this letter that I am at length arrived in the old world. I left New York in the packet ship Poland on the 24th of

June and landed at Havre on the 15th of July. Before sailing I wrote you a letter which I presume you have received, and therefore I will not trouble you with the recapitulation of its contents.[2] We had a prosperous voyage, but I was made dreadfully sick by it and was kept so from the time we lost sight of the American coast until we got into the British Channel. Mrs. Bryant also suffered considerably, but the children scarcely any, and were in excellent health and spirits during the greater part of the voyage. After being delayed a day in Havre to obtain a passport, after a voyage up the Seine by the steamboat to Rouen where we visited the cathedral and other antiquities, after a journey by daylight of more than a hundred miles in the diligence, by the lower road from Rouen, through a most beautiful and fertile country, and after having been fleeced and sponged at almost every step of the way by a set of people who have learned how to extort money from travellers by practising upon the English, we arrived, night before last, at the city which has been the seat of the greatest empire of modern times, an empire overturned as suddenly as it was erected. I need not describe to you who are an American with what strong feelings of interest I have contemplated the traces of preceding ages which have met me at every step since I entered this country, ancient customs, ancient modes of dress yet preserved among the peasantry, buildings of antique architecture, the ceremonials of an ancient and pompous worship, and the vestiges of power and magnificence which have passed away. There is a period for you. Suffice it to say that we have [been] much pleased with every thing but the trouble of getting a passport, the vexatious examinations of our baggage at every town where we stop, the beggars, and the extortions of hotel keepers and porters, and every body who renders you the most trifling service, and the cheating of the shop keepers. The moment you are detected to be a foreigner by your tongue you become a mark for extortion. Against this however we shall learn to guard in time. At present our plan is to remain about a month in this city and then pass to Italy.

As some time has elapsed since the date of your last letter,[3] I shall expect to hear that you are still making friends among the distinguished circle to which you have been introduced, obtaining new testimonies of approbation from those whose good opinion an artist would desire, and beholding a prospect of fortune and reputation before you.

I believe I did not say in my last how much I was gratified by the good opinion which the author of 'Flirtation' has been pleased to express of my poems as well as by the honour she intends me in sending me a copy of her new work.[4] I am not at all disappointed at the result of the publication of the edition by Andrews—Mr. Irving told me that I would probably get nothing by it.

Write me soon. Direct your letters to the care of Messrs. Welles & Co.

of Paris who are my bankers. Wherever I am they will be sent to me.
—My regards to Mrs. Rand, & believe me

Yours sincerely
WILLIAM C. BRYANT

P. S. My wife and Fanny desire their affectionate remembrances to both
of you. Mrs. Bryant tells me to say that she will write to Mrs. Rand as
soon as she can possibly find leisure.

MANUSCRIPT: Yale University Library.

1. John Goffe Rand (1801–1873) of New Hampshire was a portrait painter who
worked in Boston and Charleston before coming to New York about 1833. That year
he was made an Associate of the National Academy, becoming acquainted with the
Bryants and painting a portrait of the poet, before sailing for London with money
apparently provided by Bryant. The portrait, and letters furnished him by Bryant,
Rand believed, opened for him the doors of fashionable sitters and celebrities, and he
immediately wrote his benefactor of his deep gratitude for "favours received." Rand
to Bryant, January [5/6?], and January 25, 1834, NYPL–BG. See *DAA*, p. 523; Callow,
Kindred Spirits, pp. 71–73.

2. Letter unrecovered.

3. On January 25 Rand had written, "I don't flatter you when I say that your
portrait is universally admired." A Dr. Sleigh who saw it promised the artist letters to
"a *Duke* and several other distinguished characters," and a young lady who was "a real
blue" recited some of Bryant's poems. When Rand presented her with Bryant's auto-
graph clipped from a letter, she promised to introduce the Rands to "a brother of
Miss [Maria] Edgeworth" and other celebrities.

4. Lady Charlotte Bury (1775–1861), author of *Flirtation, Separation, The Di-
vorced*, and other novels, who held an appointment in the household of the Princess
of Wales.

290.   *To* Thatcher T. Payne[1]

[Paris, August 9, 1834]

Dear Payne,

You have heard I presume, from Mr. Leggett of our arrival in France,
of our voyage up the Seine, of our journey from Rouen, and finally of
our anchorage in Paris.[2]

Every step of our journey reminded us that we were in an old country. Almost every thing we saw spoke of the past, of an antiquity without
limit; every where our eyes rested on the handiwork of those who had
been dead for ages and witnessed the customs which they had bequeathed
to their descendants. The churches were so vast, so solid, and so time-
eaten; the dwellings so grey, and of such antique architecture and in the
large towns rose so high along the narrow and cavernous streets; the
thatched cottages were so mossy and their ridges so grown with grass! The
very hills around them looked scarcely so old, for there was something like
youthfulness in their vegetation—their shrubs and flowers. The country

women wore such high caps, such long waists and such short petticoats!
—the fashion of bonnets is an innovation of yesterday, which they have
not yet adopted. We passed females riding on donkeys—the Old Testament beast of burden—with panniers strung on each side—as has been
the custom I dare say ever since the animal submitted to the bridle. We
saw an ancient dame sitting at a door busy with her distaff. She was twist-
ing her thread in the primitive manner, with her thumb and finger. A
flock of sheep was grazing on the slope of a hill—they were attended by a
shepherd and a brace [of] prick-eared dogs which kept them from stray-
ing, as was done thousands of years ago. Speckled birds were hopping
along the side of the road—it was the magpie the bird of ancient fable.
Flocks of what I at first thought the crow of our country were stalking in
the fields or sailing about the old elms—it was the rook, the bird made
classical by Addison. There were old *chateaus* on the hills some of which
were built with an appearance of military strength, telling of feudal times.
The groves by which they were surrounded were often times clipped into
regular walls, pierced with arched passages leading into various directions,
and the single trees were compelled by the shears to take the shape of
obelisks and pyramids. Here and there the lands were divided by an ancient hedgerow which had subsisted perhaps from the time of William the
Conqueror. As we approached Paris we saw the plant which Noah first
committed to the earth after the deluge growing thickly and luxuriantly in
vineyards in the slopes by the side of the road. We observed the tree which
was the subject of the first Christian miracle, the fig,[3] hung with fruit
which had just begun to ripen for the market—and a very insipid fruit
it is, in its fresh state. But when we entered Paris, and passed the Bar-
rière d'Étoile with its lofty triumphal arch, when we swept through the
Avenue de Neuilly and saw the Hôtel des Invalides with the living monuments of so many battles walking or sitting under the elms of its spacious
esplanade, when we beheld the colossal statues of statesmen and warriors
frowning from the bridges over the muddy waves of the little Seine, when
we came in sight of the gray pinnacles of the Tuileries and the Gothic
towers of Notre Dame and the Roman ones of St. Sulpice, and the dome
of the Panthéon, in the vaults under which lies the dust of so many great
men of France, and the column of the Place Vendôme, and the Egyptian
obelisk in the Place Louis Quatorze, the associations with antiquity which
the scene presented from being general, became particular and historical
—they were recollections of ancient power and magnificence—of dynasties
that rose and passed away—of wars and victories which have left no other
fruit than their monuments.

The solemnity of these recollections does not appear to press with
much weight upon the minds of the people. If the French have become
grave as is said what must have been their gaiety a hundred years ago!
To me they seem as merry as light hearted, as easily amused as if they

had done nothing but make love and quiz the priests since the time of Louis XIV—as if their streets had never flowed with French blood shed by Frenchmen, as if they had never won empires at an immense waste of life and lost them again as suddenly as a green horn loses his fortune at a gambling house. The Parisian has his amusements as regularly as his meals. Perpetual business, perpetual toil, with intervals of repose but never of recreation are things he has no idea of—he must play. The theatre, music, the dance, or walks in the Tuileries, sight seeing, a refection at one of the *cafés* whither ladies resort as commonly as the other sex—these are some thing like, these are things which he considers indispensable to existence. I wake in the middle of the night and I hear the fiddle going and feet jigging in some of the dependencies of the huge building near the Tuileries in which I have my lodgings. But to understand how Frenchmen amuse themselves you should have witnessed the . . . celebration of the . . .[4] of people of all ages and some of the most respectable appearance were engaged in what we should call the most childish pastimes.

When a generation of Frenchmen

"Have played and laughed, and danced, and drank their fill"

—when they have seen their predestined number of Vaudevilles, and swallowed their allowance of weak wine and bottled small beer, they are swept off to the Cemetery of Père La Chaise or Montmartre, or some other of the great burial places which lie just without the barriers of the City. I spied the former of these the other day. You are reminded of your approach to it by the shops of stone cutters and sculptors on each side of the street, making the glittering display of polished marble monuments. When you arrive, you find this place of final repose a gayer looking spot than even the haunts of the Parisian in his life time. It is traversed with shady walks of elms and limes, and the dead lie in the midst of thickets of ornamental shrubs and plantations of the gaudiest blossoms, which are carefully tended and kept fresh by watering. Their monuments are often hung with wreaths of artificial flowers, or with those natural ones the beauty of which survives the drying, like the amaranth and the everlasting. Sometimes miniatures of the dead are suspended about, and occasionally ornaments of a more fantastic description from the toy shops. Here and there I saw the inscriptions glittering in gilt letters, on a ground of glazed porcelain, of the most intense purple. Parts of the cemetery seem like a miniature city; the chapels stand close to each other along the path, ornamented frequently with bas relief, and intermingled with statues and busts. If you look into the windows of these showy little buildings you see a silver crucifix, with wax tapers on each side, and stuffed chairs for those who come to pray for the repose of the dead. —In sight of you and below your feet lies the city whose gay multitudes this great burial place is expecting.

Write me a long letter— Make my compliments and those of my wife to Mrs. Payne.

Yrs sincerely
WM C. BRYANT

MANUSCRIPT: UVa (final); NYPL–GR (partial draft) PUBLISHED: *LT* I, pp. 9–14.

1. As with other letters to close friends, such as William Leggett and William Ware, Bryant evidently anticipated that portions of this letter likely to be of general interest might be printed in the *EP*, but that was apparently not done. Bryant revised the letter extensively before publishing it fifteen years later in *LT* I.
2. Bryant's letter to Leggett is unrecovered.
3. Matt. 21:18, 19.
4. Manuscript damaged, making about ten words illegible.

291.   *Contrat fait entre William C. Bryant voyageur, et Leopoldo Ciampolino voiturini, à Gênes, le 8 Septembre 1834.*

Le dit Leopoldo Ciampolino promit et s'oblige à conduire et transporter dans l'espace de quatre jours et demi, le dit William C. Bryant, sa femme, ses deux filles et Mons. William L. Alley[1] avec leur bagage dès la Pension Suisse à Gênes jusques à l'Hôtel de l'Europe à Florence par la voie de Lucque dans une bonne voiture à quatre roues appelée Landau, dont tout l'intérieur sera à leur disposition, et plus, de fournir aux susdites personnes tous les matins pendant le voyage un bon déjeuner à la fourchette, ou bien, du cafe lait pain beurre et oeufs selon leur choix, et de leur donner tous les soirs un bon souper, des chambres convenables de bons lits et des lumières. Le dit Ciampolino, de plus promit de mener les dites personnes à de bonnes auberges, de les conduire avec soin et la dernière attention à leur sureté et celle de leurs effets, et de payer tous les péages et impôts de ponts et barrières sur la route.

Et le dit William C. Bryant promit pour tous ces services et dépenses de payer au dit Ciampolino à la fin du voyage la somme de cent quatre vingt dix francs. Le départ aura lieu le 9 Septembre 1834 à huit heures du matin. Le buonamano sera à la discretion du dit Mons. Bryant.[2]

[signed] ANTONIO CELLI, per CIAMPOLINO

[signed] WILLIAM C. BRYANT.

MANUSCRIPT: NYPL–GR.

1. A youth whom the Bryants conducted from New York to Florence. See Letter 295.
2. "Agreement made between William C. Bryant, traveler, and Leopoldo Ciampolino, carrier, at Genoa, 8 September 1834.

"The said Leopoldo Ciampolino promises and obligates himself to conduct and transport, within a period of four days and a half, the said William C. Bryant, his wife, his two daughters, and Mr. William L. Alley, with their baggage, from the Pension Suisse at Genoa to the Hôtel de l'Europe at Florence via the Lucca highway in a good four-wheeled carriage, called a Landau, of which the whole interior will be at their disposal, and further, to furnish to the aforesaid persons every morning during the journey a good fork lunch, or else, coffee, milk, bread, butter, and eggs, according to their preference, and to give them every evening a good supper, suitable rooms with proper beds and lights. The said Ciampolino further promises to conduct the said persons to good inns, to convey them with care and the utmost attention to their safety and that of their belongings, and to pay all the tolls and duties for bridges and gateways along the way.

"And the said William C. Bryant promises, for all these services and expenditures, to pay the said Ciampolino at the end of the journey the sum of 190 francs. The departure will take place the 9th of September 1834 at eight o'clock in the morning. The gratuity will be at the discretion of the said Mr. Bryant."

Also in NYPL–GR are two other contracts with carriers, in Bryant's handwriting, made during this journey. The first, in French, is dated at Marseilles, August 31, 1834; in this one Charles Martin undertakes to convey the Bryants and William L. Alley from Marseilles to Nice. The second is an agreement, in Italian, by Vincenzo Greco[v?]io, dated at Rome, May 28, 1835, to carry the Bryants and one Adelaide Borghese (unidentified) from Rome to Florence.

292. *To* the EVENING POST

Florence, Sept. 27, 1834.

I have now been in this city a fortnight, and have established myself in a suite of apartments lately occupied, as the landlord told me, in hopes I presume of getting a higher rent, by a Russian prince.[1] The Arno flows, or rather stands still, under my windows, for the water is low, and near the western wall of the city is frugally dammed up to preserve it for the public baths. Beyond, this stream so renowned in history and poetry, is at this season but a feeble rill, almost lost among the pebbles of its bed, and scarcely sufficing to give drink to the pheasants and hares of the Grand Duke's Cascine on its banks. Opposite my lodgings, at the south end of the *Ponte alla Carraia,* is a little oratory, before the door of which every good Catholic who passes takes off his hat with a gesture of homage; and at this moment a swarthy, weasel-faced man, with a tin box in his hand, is gathering contributions to pay for the services of the chapel, rattling his coin to attract the attention of the pedestrians, and calling out to those who seem disposed to pass without paying. To the north and west, the peaks of the Apennines are in full sight, rising over the spires of the city and the groves of the Cascine. Every evening I see them through the soft, delicately-colored haze of an Italian sunset, looking as if they had caught something of the transparency of the sky, and appearing like mountains of fairy-land, instead of the bleak and barren ridges of rock which they really are. The weather since my arival in Tuscany has been continually serene, the sky wholly cloudless, and the temperature uniform—oppressively warm in the streets at noon, delightful at morning and evening, with a long, beautiful, golden twilight, occasioned by the reflection of light from the orange-colored haze which invests the atmosphere. Every night I am reminded that I am in the land of song, for until two o'clock in the morning I hear "all manner of tunes" chanted by people in the streets in all manner of voices.

I believe I have given you no account of our journey from Paris to this place. That part of it which lay between Paris and Chalons, on the Saone, may be described in a very few words. Monotonous plains, covered with vineyards and wheat-fields, with very few trees, and those spoiled by being lopped for fuel—sunburnt women driving carts or at work in the fields—gloomy, cheerless-looking towns, with narrow, filthy streets—troops of beggars surrounding your carriage whenever you stop, or whenever the nature of the roads obliges the horses to walk, and chanting their requests in the most doleful whine imaginable—such are the sights and sounds that meet you for the greater part of two hundred miles. There are, however, some exceptions as to the aspect of the country. Autun, one of the most ancient towns of France, and yet retaining some remains of Roman architecture, lies in a beautiful and picturesque region. A little beyond that town we ascended a hill by a road winding along a glen, the rocky sides of which were clothed with an unpruned wood, and a clear stream ran dashing over the stones, now on one side of the road and then on the other—the first instance of a brook left to follow its natural channel which I had seen in France. Two young Frenchmen, who were our fellow-passengers, were wild with delight at this glimpse of unspoiled nature. They followed the meanderings of the stream, leaping from rock to rock, and shouting till the woods rang again.

Of Chalons I have nothing to tell you. Abelard died there, and his tomb was erected with that of Eloise in the church of St. Marcel; but the church is destroyed, and the monument has been transported to the cemetery of Père la Chaise, and with it all the poetry of the place is vanished. But if you would make yourself supremely uncomfortable, travel as I did in a steamboat down the Saone from Chalons to Lyons, on a rainy day. Crowded into a narrow, dirty cabin, with benches on each side and a long table in the middle, at which a set of Frenchmen with their hats on are playing cards and eating *déjeuners à la fourchette* all day long, and deafening you with their noise, while waiters are running against your legs and treading on your toes every moment, and the water is dropping on your head through the cracks of the deck-floor, you would be forced to admit the superlative misery of such a mode of travelling. The approach to Lyons, however, made some amends for these inconveniences. The shores of the river, hitherto low and level, began to rise into hills, broken with precipices and crowned by castles, some in ruins and others entire, and seemingly a part of the very rocks on which they stood, so old and mossy and strong did they seem. What struck me most in Lyons was the superiority of its people in looks and features to the inhabitants of Paris— the clatter and jar of silk-looms with which its streets resounded—and the picturesque beauty of its situation, placed as it is among steeps and rocks, with the quiet Saone on one side, and the swiftly-running Rhone on the other. In our journey from Lyons to Marseilles we travelled by land instead of taking the steamboat, as is commonly done as far as Avignon. The common books of travels will tell you how numerous are the ruins of feudal times perched upon the heights all along the Rhone, remnants of fortresses and castles, overlooking a vast extent of country and once serving as places of refuge to the cultivators of the soil who dwelt in their vicinity—how frequently also are to be met with the earlier yet scarcely less fresh traces of Roman colonization and dominion, in gateways, triumphal arches, walls, and monuments—how on entering Provence you find yourself among a people of a different physiognomy from those of the northern provinces, speaking a language which rather resembles Italian than French[2]—how the beauty of the women of Avignon still does credit to the taste of the clergy, who made that city for more than half a century the seat of the Papal power—and how, as you approach the shores of the Mediterranean, the mountains which rise from the fruitful valleys shoot up in wilder forms, until their summits become mere pinnacles of rock wholly bare of vegetation.

Marseilles is seated in the midst of a semicircle of mountains of whitish rock, the steep and naked sides of which scarce afford "a footing for the goat." Stretching into the Mediterranean they inclose a commodious harbor, in front of which are two or three rocky islands anchored in a sea of more vivid blue than any water I had ever before seen. The country immediately surrounding the city is an arid and dusty valley, intersected here and there with the bed of a brook or torrent, dry during the summer. It is carefully cultivated, however, and planted with vineyards, and orchards of olive, fig, and pomegranate trees. The trees being small and low, the foliage of the olive thin and pale, the leaves of the fig broad and few, and the soil appearing everywhere at their roots, as well as between the rows of vines, the vegetation, when viewed from a little distance, has a meagre and ragged appearance. The whiteness of the hills, which the eye can hardly bear to rest upon at noon, the intense blue of the sea, the peculiar forms of the foliage, and the deficiency of shade and verdure, made me almost fancy myself in a tropical region.

The Greeks judged well of the commercial advantages of Marseilles when they made it the seat of one of their early colonies. I found its streets animated with a bustle which I had not seen since I left New York, and its port thronged with vessels from all the nations whose coasts border upon the great midland sea of Europe. Marseilles is the most flourishing seaport in France; it has already become to the Mediterranean what New York is to the United States, and its trade is regularly increasing. The old town is ugly, but the lower or new part is nobly built of the light-colored stone so commonly used in France, and so easily wrought—with broad streets and, what is rare in French towns, convenient sidewalks. New streets are laid out, gardens are converted into building-lots, the process of levelling hills and filling up hollows is going on as in New York, the city is extending itself on every side, and large fortunes have been made by the rise in the value of landed property.

In a conversation with an intelligent gentleman resident at Marseilles and largely engaged in commercial and moneyed transactions, the subject of the United States Bank was mentioned. Opinions in France, on this question of our domestic politics, differ according as the opportunities of information possessed by the individual are more or less ample, or as he is more or less in favor of chartered banks. The gentleman remarked that without any reference to the question of the United States Bank, he hoped the day would never come when such an institution would be established in France. The project he said had some advocates, but they had not yet succeeded, and he hoped never would succeed in the introduction of that system of paper currency which prevailed in the United States. He deprecated the dangerous and uncertain facilities of obtaining credit which are the fruit of that system, which produce the most ruinous fluctuations in commerce, encourage speculation and extravagance of all kinds, and involve the prudent and laborious in the ruin which falls upon the rash and reckless. He declared himself satisfied with the state of the currency of France, with which, if fortunes were not suddenly built up they were not suddenly overthrown, and periods of apparent prosperity were not followed by seasons of real distress.

I made the journey from Marseilles to Florence by land. How grand and wild are the mountains that overlook the Mediterranean; how intense was the heat as we wound our way along the galleries of rock cut to form a road; how excellent are the fruits, and how thick the mosquitoes at Nice; how sumptuous are the palaces, how narrow and dark the streets, and how pallid the dames of Genoa; and how beautiful we found our path among the trees overrun with vines as we approached southern Italy, are matters which I will take some other opportunity of relating. On the 12th of September our *vetturino* set us down safe at the *Hôtel de l'Europe* in Florence.

I think I shall return to America even a better patriot than when I left it. A citizen of the United States travelling on the continent of Europe, finds the contrast between a government of power and a government of opinion forced upon him at every step. He finds himself delayed at every large town and at every frontier of a kingdom or principality, to submit to a strict examination of the passport with which the jealousy of the rulers of these countries has compelled him to furnish himself. He sees everywhere guards and sentinels armed to the teeth, stationed in the midst of a population engaged in their ordinary occupations in a time of profound peace; and to supply the place of the young and robust thus withdrawn from the labors of agriculture he beholds women performing the work of the fields. He sees the many retained in a state of hopeless dependence and poverty, the effect of institutions forged by the ruling class to accumulate wealth in their own hands. The want of self-respect in the inferior class engendered by this state of things, shows itself in the acts of rapacity and fraud which the traveller meets with throughout France and Italy, and, worse still, in the shameless corruption of the Italian custom-houses, the officers of which regularly solicit a paltry bribe from every passenger as the consideration of leaving his baggage unexamined. I am told that in this place the custom of giving presents extends even to the courts of justice, the officers of which, from the highest to the lowest, are in the constant practice of receiving them. No American can see how much jealousy and force on on the one hand, and necessity and fear on the other, have to do with keeping up the existing governments of Europe, without thanking heaven that such is not the condition of his own country.

MANUSCRIPT: Unrecovered TEXT: *LT* I, pp. 15–23; first published in *EP* for November 24, 1834.

1. Frances described these lodgings in a letter to her sister on September 24 as consisting of "an antichamber, two parlours, a dining room, three bed rooms and a kitchen, all of them furnished with every article necessary for keeping house." But in the late fall living there became intolerable, she wrote Eliza Robbins, after moving to the more temperate climate of Pisa: "We had our apartments on the south side of the Arno, looking to the North, and exposed to the tramontane winds. . . . The chilly air penetrated our rooms through the crevices of the doors and windows, which were numerous, and we found it impossible to keep ourselves warm." These letters are in Frances' letter-book in the Homestead Collection.

2. An interest in the language and literature of Provence had led Bryant earlier to write two essays, in each of which he translated passages of verse by various Provençal poets. These were "Jehan de Nostre Dame, *Vies des Plus Célèbres et Anciens Poètes Provençaux* . . . ," *NYR*, 1 (July 1825), 104–125; and "Phanette des Gantelmes," *The Talisman for MDCCCXXX*, pp. 238–254. He also wrote a critical notice of J. C. L. Sismonde de Sismondi, *Historical View of the Literature of the South of Europe*, trans. Thomas Roscoe (New York, 1827), for the *USR*, 2 (September 1827), 467–468.

293. *To* William Ware[1]

Florence   Oct. 11   1834.

My dear Sir

Something was said when I saw you last of letters that were to pass between us during my residence abroad. Nearly four months have now elapsed since I left America, and I hear nothing from you—in revenge for which neglect I am going to inflict upon you a long epistle.

I have just returned from a visit to the Museum of Natural History, the finest it is said in the world. Do not be alarmed—I am not going to bore with an account of what you have often seen better described than I could do it. The Professor of Anatomy connected with this institution (I do not now recollect his name) is said to be a man of uncommon talent, particularly as a lecturer. He was obliged to leave Milan on account of his political opinions, a year or two since, and coming to Florence, the professorship of anatomy was bestowed upon him by the Grand Duke of

Tuscany. The lectures are gratuitous, and are attended by the painters and sculptors who come here to study their art. Florence has all the apparatus for making great men—extensive libraries, like the Malbecchian, vast collections of rare manuscripts, like the Laurentian—rich repositories of pictures and works of sculpture, like the Royal Gallery and the rooms of the Pitti Palace, —and this noble cabinet, in which the treasures of the three kingdoms of nature are displayed to the eye of the observer, and eloquently and learnedly illustrated.[2] I am told, however, that few of the Florentines resort to these sources of instruction. They are as indolent and effeminate as their ancestors of the republic were hardy and enterprising —a degeneracy owing, I have no doubt, to the want of political liberty— for say as much as we will of the evils of party spirit and political ambition in a free country, they must be allowed to be powerful quickeners of man's intellect. The despotism of this government appears to be in general mildly administered; prohibited books are sold every where at the stalls and hitherto a disposition has been shown to let off political offenders as lightly as possible—but lately however something of the same jealousy of republicanism has shown itself which has been manifested by the other absolute governments of Europe. A quarterly journal was suppressed a few months since on account of something which gave offense to Austria. This and several other late acts of the Grand Duke have greatly diminished his personal popularity. The rulers of Italy appear to have come to an understanding that it is time to make an example of some of the disaffected. You may recollect that several executions took place last year in Sardinia for alleged conspiracies against the state. The accused were young men, officers of the Sardinian army, among whom the spirit of discontent is general. A few days since several arrests for an offence of the same kind took place at Naples; and at this moment four young men are on trial in Florence for an alleged conspiracy. They are members of a republican association called *Italia giovane* [Young Italy], branches of which are established throughout Italy. Prince Corsini has sent to the judges to say that the court desires them to enforce the law against the accused with as much severity as possible. The trial excites great interest, and the most eminent counsel in Florence are employed on one side or the other.

The annual exhibition of the Royal Academy has taken place since I arrived. I found the spacious apartments crowded with visitors. I thought that this argued a great deal of enthusiasm in favour of the arts, but a friend, to whom I mentioned it, assured me that this was not so much the case as I imagined.[3] The exhibition is gratuitous, and the fashionable throng to it as a convenient morning lounge, to see each other, and to look at some picture or piece of sculpture ordered by some person of their acquaintance. One thing, however, I will say for the Italians—they have not the trick of defacing works of art of which the Americans are guilty.

A work of art is looked upon by all classes here as something sacred—a statue will stand for centuries in a public square within the reach of all the blackguards of the streets and yet receive no injury— The David of Michel Angelo has remained in the Piazza del Granduca ever since the time of the artist, without losing the tip of its little finger—nor do the people merely abstain from wanton mutilation—there is no scratching of the marble with knives, or scribbling upon it with lead pencils. So entire and so general is this respect for such works that the utmost confidence is placed in it. You have here no armed sentinel, with fierce mustachios, posted to keep you from touching the object of your curiosity, as in France. I recollect that in Paris, as I was looking at a colossal plaster cast of Napoleon, a fellow in uniform, as upright and stiff as the musket he carried, gruffly reminded me that I was *too near*. In Florence it is taken for granted that you will do no mischief, and therefore you are not watched. But to return to the exhibition—it contained two or three beautiful little landscapes by young Morghen, son of the celebrated engraver —several pictures by Bezzoli one of the first painters if not the very first in Italy—a statue of Galileo by Costoli which appeared to me to possess much merit—and a group representing Cupid and Psyche marked by much sweetness and simplicity by a very young artist whose name I do not recollect.[4] There was an abundance of portraits, good, bad, and indifferent, and a dozen huge pieces of canvas overlaid with attempts at historical painting. The exhibition is said to be the most indifferent that has taken place for several years past, and certainly, if I may be permitted to judge in such a matter, by no means equal to the average of the exhibitions of the Academy of the Arts of Design in New York.

Talking of pictures reminds me of Cole's fine little landscape taken from the bridge over the Arno close to the lodgings which I occupy. You may recollect seeing it in the exhibition, two years since. It presented a view of the river travelling off towards the west, its banks shaded with trees, with the ridges of the Apennines lying in the distance, and the sky above flushed with the colours of sunset.[5] The same fine hues I witness every evening, in the very quarter and over the very hills where they were seen by the artist when he made them permanent on his canvas. There has been a great deal of prattling about Italian skies—the skies and clouds of Italy do not present such a variety of beautiful appearances as those of the United States—but the *atmosphere* of Italy at least about the time of sunset is more uniformly fine than ours. The mountains then put on a beautiful aerial appearance, as if they belonged to another and fairer world—and a little after the sun has sunk behind them the air is flushed with a radiance that seems reflected upon the earth from every part of the sky. Most of the grand old palaces in Florence are built in a gloomy severe style of architecture, of a dark coloured stone, massive and lofty; and every where the streets are much narrower than with us, so that the city has by no means the cheerful look of an American town. But at the hour of which I am speaking the bright warm light shed upon the earth fills the darkest lanes, streams into the narrowest nook, brightens the sombre structures and altogether transforms the aspect of the place.

It is now nearly the middle of October and there has been no frost in the vale of the Arno. The strong summer heats, which prevailed when I arrived, have gradually, very gradually, subsided into an agreeable autumnal temperature. The trees yet retain their verdure, with a slight tinge of sallow only—but I perceive the foliage growing thinner—and when I walk in the Cascine on the side of the Arno, the rustling of the lizards running over the heaps of crisp leaves, reminds me that winter is approaching; though the ivy which clothes the old ilexes has put on a second and profuse array of blossoms, and the walks murmur with bees like one of our orchards in the spring. As I look up the sides of the Apennines I see the stripes and patches of raw earth, which are every where visible among the olive trees and the well pruned maples which support the vines growing broader every day. Thus far I have been less struck with the beauty of Italian scenery than I expected. The forms of the mountains are more picturesque, their summits more peaked, and their outline more varied than those of the mountains of our own country; and the buildings —of a massive and imposing architecture or venerable from time, seated on the heights, add much to the general effect. But if the hand of man has done something to embellish the scenery, it has done more to deform it. Not a tree is suffered to retain its natural shape, not a brook to flow in its natural channel; an exterminating war is carried on against the natural herbage of the soil, the country is without woods and green fields, and to him who views the vale of the Arno "from the top of Fiesole" or any of the neighbouring heights, grand as he will allow the circle of the mountains to be, and magnificent the edifices with which it is embellished, it will appear a vast dusty gulf, planted with ugly rows of the low pallid and thin-leaved olive and of the still more dwarfish and closely pruned maples on which the vines are trained. The simplicity of natural scenery, so far as can be done, is destroyed; there is no noble sweep of forest, no broad expanse of meadow or pasture ground, no ancient and towering trees clustering with grateful shade round the country seats, no rows of natural shubbery following the courses of the rivers through the vallies. The streams, which are often but mere gravelly beds of torrents, dry during the summer, are kept in straight channels by means of stone walls and embankments; the slopes are broken up and disfigured by terraces, and the trees kept down by constant pruning and lopping, until somewhat more than midway up the Apennines, when the limit of cultivation is reached, and thence to the summits is a barren steep of rock without soil or herbage. The grander features of the landscape, however, are beyond the power of man to injure—the towering mountain summits, the bare walls and peaks of rock piercing the sky, which with the deep irregular vallies, betoken more than any thing I have seen in America an up-heaving and ingulfing of the original crust of the world. I ought in justice to say that I have been told, that in May and June the country is far more beautiful than it has been at any time I have seen it—and that it now appears under particular disadvantages, in consequence of a long drought.

May I ask of you the favour to show this to Mr. Leggett and to ask him to print such parts of it as he pleases. My wife desires her regards, and joins me in asking you to present our best remembrances to Mrs. Ware and our love to the children. Write me as long a letter as I have written you, and direct to the care of Welles & Co., Paris. My wife would have written to Mrs. Ware, but that she like others of her sex, has had "so many other things on her hands" that she has been left little time for writing. She has not however forgotten her promise and means to fulfil it before leaving Florence for Rome, which will be in about . . .[6]

MANUSCRIPT: NYPL–GR (final and draft) ADDRESS: To the Revd. William Ware / New York / United States of America DOCKETED: Bryant. Recd Decr 24–1834.

1. Except for the first and last paragraphs, this letter was printed, after revision and rearrangement, in *LT* I, pp. 24–28. First published in the *EP* for December 27, 1834.
2. Frances Bryant saw these anatomical specimens quite differently. Describing to her sister a visit to the Cabinet of Natural History, she wrote, "I was shocked at the sight of wax human organs, limbs, muscles red & raw, hearts, livers, lungs, and other parts of the body looking as if they had just been torn out. . . . If I ever screamed with fright, I should have screamed then. . . . I have hardly at this moment got over the nervous trembling it produced." September 24, 1834, Letter-book, Homestead Collection.
3. Probably Horatio Greenough. Having met the sculptor in New York in 1828, Bryant renewed their acquaintance at Paris in August, 1834. In Florence they saw much of each other, Bryant sitting to his friend for a portrait bust. See Nathalia Wright, *Horatio Greenough: The First American Sculptor* (Philadelphia: University of Pennsylvania Press [1963]), pp. 51, 101–102; Jonathan Mason, Jr., to Thomas Cole, August 28, 1834, New York State Library; Letter 299.
4. Antonio Morghen (1788–1853), of Florence, was the son of Rafaello Morghen (1758–1833), eminent engraver of works by Leonardo, Raphael, and other Renaissance masters. Giuseppe Bezzuoli (1784–1855), professor at the Academy in Florence, painted a great many portraits and historical pictures. Aristodemo Costoli (1803–1871), another Florentine, was both sculptor and religious painter.
5. Thomas Cole's "View on the Arno," exhibited at the National Academy in 1832, is probably the one now owned by the Montclair Art Museum. Merritt, *Thomas Cole*, p. 33.
6. Conclusion and signature missing.

294. *To* Julia Sands

Florence, October 12, 1834.

. . . I am tempted to ask what I am doing so far from my native country. If one wants to see beautiful or majestic scenery, he needs not go out of the United States; if he is looking for striking and splendid phenomena of climate (I say nothing of uniformity of temperature, for there Europe has the advantage), he needs not leave the United States; if he delights in seeing the great mass intelligent, independent, and happy, he *must* not leave the United States; if he desires to cultivate or gratify his taste by visiting works of art, there are some means of doing so in all the great American cities, and they are all the time increasing. If he wishes to make the comparison between a people circumstanced as are those of a republic and the nations which live under the rickety governments of the Old World—*à la bonne heure* [well and good], as the French say—let him do it, and, after having made the comparison, if he is a just and philanthropic person, who looks to the good of the whole, and not to the gratification of his individual tastes, he will be willing to return and pass the rest of his life at home. If he dislikes being plagued with beggars, if he hates idleness and filth, if he does not like to feel himself in a vast prison wherever he travels in consequence of what is called the passport system, which subjects him to constant examinations and delays in going from one place to another, he must not go to France or Italy; and if he cannot bear being cheated and defrauded by rapacious hotel keepers, servants, and shop-keepers, who are desirous, as the phrase is here, to "profit by circumstances," he must not travel in Europe at all. Do not suppose, however, by this that I have finished my travels, and am coming back. I am only making a plain statement of inconveniences, to which I am willing to submit, temporarily at least, for the sake of gratifying my curiosity. . . .

MANUSCRIPT: Unrecovered TEXT (*partial*): *Life*, I, 310–311.

295.   *To* Saul Alley[1]

Florence   Oct   13   1834.—

My dear Sir

I wrote you a short and hasty letter at Paris respecting your son which I presume you have received long before this.[2] Since that time we have made the journey from Paris to this place and made it without accident or ill luck of any kind. At his urgent request, I consented that he should perform part of the journey alone. An additional motive for this was that as we were going to travel in the diligence we could not all go in that part of the vehicle which is called the *coupé*, and which is the most desirable situation for one who wishes to see the country as he passes. He therefore took a seat in the *coupé* on Monday the 18th of August, and I engaged the whole of the *coupé* for my family for the Thursday following when I left Paris. I rejoined him at Marseilles and engaged a comfortable carriage to bring us to Nice. From Nice to Genoa we all travelled in that part of the diligence called the interior—an experiment of which we were heartily tired before we had proceeded twenty miles. At Genoa we again engaged a carriage to bring us to this place, and performed the rest of the journey in a very pleasant manner. Your son has been engaged since his arrival here in learning the Italian language and in reviewing his mathematics. He appears to have made a good use of his time at school and makes acquirements with great readiness. His curiosity for viewing whatever objects are worth seeing is far stronger than mine, and from his eagerness to examine them I augur that they will make a durable impression on his memory. He gives me even less trouble than I expected. One thing I believe you may be certain of—that he will not spend his money foolishly or suffer himself to be cheated out of it—at least in no greater degree than is the common lot of travellers in this country, where foreigners appear to be marked out for imposition. An experience of three months in the country has enabled us to be on our guard against the rapacity of those who make it a trade to fleece the traveller. Your son's expenses of which I believe he has given you an account are less than I expected, and I think you will find them less than you supposed they would be.

It is my intention to remain in Italy another summer in which case if I return next autumn to the United States I shall proceed immediately by the most direct course to Havre. Should circumstances occur to prolong my stay I shall still make Italy my abode, principally on account of the economy of a residence here. Your son is anxious to see some other parts of Europe—to visit a part of Germany, to see England and Scotland neither of which is it at present my intention to visit. In order to do this it will be necessary that he should leave me early in the spring or the latter part of the winter.[3] Of course he does not think of making the journey alone without your permission. Will you be so good as to write as soon as you receive this, informing me what you think of the project. I think him more capable of travelling alone than any youth of his age I know of— perhaps as much so as any young man of twenty—far more so than many of that age. He has no vicious habits that I know of or any disposition to any—and he is an accurate and careful [calculator?].

[unsigned]

MANUSCRIPT: NYPL–GR (draft) ENDORSED (by Bryant): My letter to / Saul Alley Esq / Oct. 13, 1834.

1. As an accommodation to his friend Saul Alley, a wholesale textile merchant and a leading New York Democrat, Bryant had taken with him to Europe Alley's fifteen-year-old son William, agreeing to see that the boy was tutored in foreign languages. For this, Cullen wrote his brother Austin, "I received a small compensation for the trouble of looking to him, but nothing in comparison with my entire expenses which I bear myself." See Letter 298; Saul Alley to Bryant, July 15, 1834, NYPL–BG; Bryant to George Bancroft, April 19, 1845, MHS.

2. Letter unrecovered.

3. Young Alley stayed with the Bryants in Florence until they moved to Pisa in mid-November, then traveled alone to Sicily and Malta, to Naples for the carnival,

and to Rome, where he awaited the Bryants' arrival in late March. W. L. Alley to Bryant, March 6, 1835, NYPL–GR.

296. *To* the EVENING POST

Pisa, December 11, 1834.

It is gratifying to be able to communicate a piece of political intelligence from so quiet a nook of the world as this. Don Miguel arrived here the other day from Genoa, where you know there was a story that he and the old Duchess of Berri, a hopeful couple, were laying their heads together. He went to pay his respects to the Grand Duke of Tuscany, who is now at Pisa, and it was said by the gossips of the place that he was coldly received, and was given to understand that he could not be allowed to remain in the Tuscan territory. There was probably nothing in all this. Don Miguel has now departed for Rome, and the talk of to-day is that he will return before the end of the winter. He is doubtless wandering about to observe in what manner he is received at the petty courts which are influenced by the Austrian policy, and in the mean time lying in wait for some favorable opportunity of renewing his pretensions to the crown of Spain.[1]

Pisa offers a greater contrast to Florence than I had imagined could exist between two Italian cities. This is the very seat of idleness and slumber; while Florence, from being the residence of the Court, and from the vast number of foreigners who throng to it, presents during several months of the year an appearance of great bustle and animation. Four thousand English, an American friend tells me, visit Florence every winter, to say nothing of the occasional residents from France, Germany, and Russia. The number of visitors from the latter country is every year increasing, and the echoes of the Florence gallery have been taught to repeat the strange accents of the Sclavonic. Let me give you the history of a fine day in October, passed at the window of my lodgings on the Lung' Arno, close to the bridge *Alla Carraja*. Waked by the jangling of all the bells in Florence and by the noise of carriages departing loaded with travellers, for Rome and other places in the south of Italy, I rise, dress myself, and take my place at the window. I see crowds of men and women from the country, the former in brown velvet jackets, and the latter in broad-brimmed straw hats, driving donkeys loaded with panniers or trundling hand-carts before them, heaped with grapes, figs, and all the fruits of the orchard, the garden, and the field. They have hardly passed, when large flocks of sheep and goats make their appearance, attended by shepherds and their families, driven by the approach of winter from the Apennines, and seeking the pastures of the Maremma, a rich, but, in the summer, an unhealthy tract on the coast. The men and boys are dressed in knee-breeches, the women in bodices, and both sexes wear capotes with pointed hoods, and felt hats with conical crowns; they carry long staves in their hands, and their arms are loaded with kids and lambs too young to keep pace with their mothers. After the long procession of sheep and goats and dogs and men and women and children, come horses loaded with cloths and poles for tents, kitchen utensils, and the rest of the younglings of the flock. A little after sunrise I see well-fed donkeys, in coverings of red cloth, driven over the bridge to be milked for invalids. Maid-servants, bareheaded, with huge high carved combs in their hair, waiters of coffee houses carrying the morning cup of coffee or chocolate to their customers, baker's boys with a dozen loaves on a board balanced on their heads, milk-men with rush baskets filled with flasks of milk, are crossing the streets in all directions. A little later the bell of the small chapel opposite to my window rings furiously for a quarter of an hour, and then I hear mass chanted in a deep strong nasal tone. As the day advances, the English, in their white hats and white pantaloons, come out of their lodgings, accompanied sometimes by their hale and square-built spouses, and saunter stiffly along the Arno, or take their way to the public galleries and museums. Their massive, clean, and brightly-polished carriages also begin to rattle through the streets, setting out on excursions to some part of the environs of Florence—to Fiesole, to the Pratolino, to the Bello Sguardo, to the Poggio Imperiale. Sights of a different kind now present themselves. Sometimes it is a troop of stout Franciscan friars, in sandals and brown robes, each carrying his staff and wearing a brown broad-brimmed hat with a hemispherical crown. Sometimes it is a band of young theological students, in purple cassocks with red collars and cuffs, let out on a holiday, attended by their clerical instructors, to ramble in the Cascine. There is a priest coming over the bridge, a man of venerable age and great reputation for sanctity—the common people crowd around him to kiss his hand, and obtain a kind word from him as he passes. But what is that procession of men in black gowns, black gaiters, and black masks, moving swiftly along, and bearing on their shoulders a litter covered with black cloth? These are the *Brethren of Mercy*, who have assembled at the sound of the cathedral bell, and are conveying some sick or wounded person to the hospital. As the day begins to decline, the numbers of carriages in the streets, filled with gaily-dressed people attended by servants in livery, increases. The Grand Duke's equipage, an elegant carriage drawn by six horses, with coachmen, footmen, and outriders in drab-colored livery, comes from the Pitti Palace, and crosses the Arno, either by the bridge close to my lodgings, or by that called the *Alla Santa Trinità*, which is in full sight from the windows. The Florentine nobility, with their families, and the English residents, now throng to the Cascine, to drive at a slow pace through its thickly-planted walks of elms, oaks, and ilexes. As the sun is sinking I perceive the Quay, on the other side of the Arno, filled with a moving crowd of well-dressed people, walking to and fro, and enjoying the beauty of the evening. Travellers now arrive from all quarters, in cabriolets, in calashes, in the shabby *vettura,* and in the elegant private carriage drawn by post-horses, and driven by postillions in the tightest possible deer-skin breeches, the smallest red coats, and the hugest jackboots. The streets about the doors of the hotels resound with the cracking of whips and the stamping of horses, and are encumbered with carriages, heaps of baggage, porters, postillions, couriers, and travellers. Night at length arrives—the time of spectacles and funerals. The carriages rattle towards the opera-houses. Trains of people, sometimes in white robes and sometimes in black, carrying blazing torches and a cross elevated on a high pole before a coffin, pass through the streets chanting the service for the dead. The Brethren of Mercy may also be seen engaged in their office. The rapidity of their pace, the flare of their torches, the gleam of their eyes through their masks, and their sable garb, give them a kind of supernatural appearance. I return to bed, and fall asleep amidst the shouts of people returning from the opera, singing as they go snatches of the music with which they had been entertained during the evening.

Such is a picture of what passes every day at Florence—in Pisa, on the contrary, all is stagnation and repose—even the presence of the sovereign, who usually passes a part of the winter here, is incompetent to give a momentary liveliness to the place. The city is nearly as large as Florence, with not a third of its population; the number of strangers is few; most of them are invalids, and the rest are the quietest people in the world. The rattle of carriages is rarely heard in the streets; in some of which there prevails a stillness so complete that you might imagine them deserted of their inhabitants. I have now been here three weeks, and on one occasion only have I seen the people of the place awakened to something like animation. It was the feast of the Conception of the Blessed Virgin; the Lung' Arno was strewn with boughs of laurel and myrtle, and the Pisan gentry promenaded for an hour under my window.

On my leaving Florence an incident occurred, which will illustrate the manner of doing public business in this country. I had obtained my passport from the Police Office, *viséd* for Pisa. It was then Friday, and I was told that it would answer until ten o'clock on Tuesday morning. Unluckily I did not present myself at the Leghorn gate of Florence until eleven o'clock on that day. A young man in a military hat, sword, and blue uniform, came to the carriage and asked for my passport, which I handed him. In a short time he appeared again and desired me to get out and go with him to the apartment in the side of the gate. I went and saw a middle-aged man dressed in the same manner, sitting at the table with my passport before him. "I am sorry," said he, "to say that your passport is not regular, and that my duty compels me to detain you." "What is the matter with the passport?" "The *visé* is of more than three days standing." I exerted all my eloquence to persuade him that an hour was of no consequence, and that the public welfare would not suffer by letting me pass, but he remained firm. "The law," he said, "is positive; I am compelled to execute it. If I were to suffer you to depart, and my superiors were to know it, I should lose my office and incur the penalty of five days' imprisonment."

I happened to have a few coins in my pocket, and putting in my hand, I caused them to jingle a little against each other. "Your case is a hard one," said the officer, "I suppose you are desirous to get on." "Yes—my preparations are all made, and it will be a great inconvenience for me to remain." "What say you," he called out to his companion who stood at the door looking into the street, "shall we let them pass? They seem to be decent people." The young man mumbled some sort of answer. "Here," said the officer, holding out to me my passport, but still keeping it between his thumb and finger, "I give you back your passport, and consent to your leaving Florence, but I wish you particularly to consider that in so doing, I risk the loss of my place and imprisonment of five days." He then put the paper into my hand, and I put into his the expected gratuity. As I went to the carriage, he followed and begged me to say nothing of the matter to any one. I was admitted into Pisa with less difficulty. It was already dark; I expected that my baggage would undergo a long examination as usual; and I knew that I had some dutiable articles. To my astonishment, however, my trunks were allowed to pass without being opened, or even the payment of the customary gratuity. I was told afterwards that my Italian servant had effected this by telling the custom-house officers some lie about my being the American Minister.

Pisa has a delightful winter climate, though Madame de Staël has left on record a condemnation of it, having passed here a season of unusually bad weather.[2] Orange and lemon trees grow in the open air, and are now loaded with ripe fruit. The fields in the environs are green with grass nourished by abundant rains, and are spotted with daisies in blossom. Crops of flax and various kinds of pulse are showing themselves above the ground, a circumstance sufficient to show that the cultivators expect nothing like what we call winter.

MANUSCRIPT: NYPL–GR (draft) TEXT: LT I, pp. 29–36; first published in EP for January 27, 1835.

1. Miguel (1802–1866), younger son of King John VI of Portugal (1769–1826), succeeded to the Portuguese throne in 1828 under questionable circumstances, and surrendered it under duress in 1834. Bryant wrote "Spain" in error.

2. Bryant probably alludes to her novel *Corinne* (1807), inspired by her earlier visit to Italy.

297. *To* Messrs. Welles & Co.[1]

Pisa   Feb   4   1835

Gentlemen

Will you be so good as to send me, of the papers which may arrive for me from America, only the *New York Evening* Post *for the Country*.

I wrote to New York directing the Country paper only to be sent, but by some mistake, I have received both the Country and the daily paper.[2]

There is another piece of negligence in my American correspondence of more importance—and which gives me greater trouble. More than three months since I wrote to my partners directing them to buy a bill upon you of Welles & Fitch of New York, and to transact the business in such a manner that the amount might be immediately placed to my credit on its arriving at Paris without the trouble and delay of sending it to me for my indorsement; at the same time giving me information of the date amount and terms of the bill. The bill ought to have been sent out to you by the packet of December 8th, or at farthest of the 16th. As I have received no notice of its being sent, I presume that such has not been the case. I wrote again two or three weeks since to remonstrate against the delay if there has been any,[3] but as I am placed in the necessity of making use of the letters of credit with which you have furnished me, while I have no reason to suppose that there are any funds of mine in your hands I am in some perplexity. I beg you will tell me what I shall do. I know from statements that I have received from the establishment that there are funds of mine with which the bill might be bought at any moment with interest on a bill which drawn by me would be paid. —If you advise I will send you immediately a bill for $1000 on Bryant Leggett & Co. or I will leave the matter until the bill on you shall arrive. The bill on B. L. & Co. might be sent to Welles & Fitch with directions not to present it in case a bill on you in my favor had been already purchased.—

Sometime since I had a letter from Mr. John Rand of London informing me that through a Mr. Wiggin he had placed with you to my credit a small sum received for me from a London bookseller.[4] Will you inform me when you answer this whether this has been done?

I am gentlemen
With sentiments of great respect
Yr obt svt
WM   C. BRYANT

I shall leave Pisa for Rome about the 18th of March. I wish papers and letters to be sent to my bankers at Rome that are likely to reach me after that date.

MANUSCRIPT: NYPL–GR (draft).

1. Bankers with Paris offices at the Hotel Meurice, Rue de Rivoli, who commonly handled credit drafts and mail for American travelers on the continent.

2. The country, or semi-weekly edition of the *EP*, published since the paper was founded in 1801, carried news items and editorials from the daily editions. A weekly edition was added in 1841. See Bryant, *Reminiscences of EP*, pp. 337–338.

3. None of the three letters to the *EP*, to which Bryant refers, has been recovered.

4. Although Rand's letter is unrecovered, this sum probably represented royalties

from J. Andrews, London publisher of Bryant's 1832 *Poems*. The London banker Timothy Wiggin transmitted funds to Longfellow during his European travels in 1835–1836. Crowninshield, *Diary*, p. 10.

298. *To* Austin Bryant

Pisa, Tuscany, February 24, 1835.

Dear Brother.

Some letters of mine which have been published in the Evening Post have probably informed you where I am as well as made you acquainted with the principal incidents of my journey. A few days since I received mother's letter of the 3d of January which reached me *in about* six weeks from the date.[1] What it says of the snow and cold weather made me reflect on the difference between this climate and that I have left. We have seen no snow here except on the summits of the Apennines which have several times been seen brilliantly white with it beyond the green fields. The daisy has been in blossom all winter; the flowers of the crocus began to open in January, and about a week since cowslips violets and other flowers began to appear. This week peach and plum trees are in blossom. I have said the fields were green—but it is not with grass, for there is scarce any pasturage here—but with crops of wheat, turnips, cabbages, artichokes, the cauliflower, a kind of bean plant and even flax. These plants, with the exception perhaps of the turnips and cabbages grow very little it is true during the winter, but they keep healthy and advance somewhat, notwithstanding that the night frosts are frequently strong enough to cover still water with a thin crust of ice, which is, however, melted at noon. Orange and lemon trees grow here in the gardens in the open air; they do not blossom during the winter, but they are still hanging with fruit. Notwithstanding this mildness of the climate, the trees of deciduous foliage have remained as bare as in New England, and even now are so torpid to the influence of the sun and genial weather that there is little swelling of the buds to be perceived. There are several kinds of evergreens here, a kind of pine with a top like an umbrella, the ilex which is a species of oak with an abundance of spear-shaped leaves of the size of those of the plum tree, the olive with a grayish green leaf, and the cypress with a spiry growth like that of the Lombardy poplar but foliage like that of the red cedar. Then there are various evergreen shrubs, which are quite common, such as the laurel and the myrtle; even the blackberry bush is an evergreen here. The vines in Italy are trained upon trees which here in Pisa are generally a kind of poplar and in other places are sometimes a species of maple and sometimes the white mulberry and occasionally willow. These trees are all pollards, they have a trunk of about eight or ten feet in height from which half a dozen small branches are suffered to spring, a part of which are annually lopped off as they grow too large, and their places supplied by new shoots. The trees are placed at the distance of about a rod from each other, in rows which inclose long strips of land, covered with various crops. At the root of each tree are planted two or more vines branches of which are strong and fastened from tree to tree in festoons. When the country is viewed from an eminence it appears covered with rows of these cropped trees which with their large knobbed trunks and branches too scanty to cast a shade appear ugly enough.

Pisa is situated in a rich and well cultivated plain on the Arno which flows through the city, between two rows of very massive and lofty houses of stone or of brick covered with stucco having mostly a very ancient and weather stained look. In one of these, in what we should call the second story but which is here called the first, I have my lodgings consisting of seven furnished rooms, besides the kitchen which is also furnished, comprising the entire floor, for which I pay twenty eight crowns a month.[2] We are now in the midst of the carnival, and every afternoon there is a crowd promenading under my window among which are to be seen men women and boys in masks dressed in a variety of odd and fanciful costumes, some endeavouring to divert the rest with their buffooneries and others walking very gravely and quietly up and down the street. On Sundays and holidays the crowd is very great; the country people then flock to the city from the neighbouring farms and villages, and the Pisan nobility drive up and down the Lung' Arno (as the street along the river is called) in their carriages. The shopkeepers and others join the train in hired carriages and this amusement which is called the Corsi, continues until dark. I need not tell you that Pisa has greatly declined from its ancient splendour. The eighteen thousand inhabitants it contains are not a fifth part of its population in the time of its prosperity. Its commerce has been transferred to Leghorn which is so much better situated for that purpose, Pisa being now six miles from the sea—though formerly nearer, as it is said. Its manufactures as is the case with all parts of Tuscany have passed to foreign nations, and it is now only remarkable for its cathedral, baptistry and leaning tower, three remarkable edifices built for religious purposes in its early prosperity, its Campo Santo, or burying ground containing a curious collection of Greek and Roman sarcophagi, and some other remains of ancient sculpture, its University to which about five hundred students annually resort from various parts of Italy and other countries bordering on the Mediterranean to complete their education in law, physic, divinity, and the higher branches of learning, and lastly its fine climate which attracts to it many foreigners to pass the winter. The looks of the Pisans bear testimony to the mildness of the climate, if corpulency be any test—for there is a larger proportion of stout men and women here than I have observed in any place I have seen. The inhabitants are civil to foreigners, but the higher class are not very strict in their morals; married ladies have their *cavaliere servente* ["ladies' man"], and some of

them carry their gallantries to lengths which in any other country would
be deemed extraordinary. The Grand Duke has passed the winter here,
which has made the place much more lively than usual. I went to two of
his *soirées* and to one of them my wife and daughter accompanied me,
and were formally presented to the Grand Duke and Dutchess, the sov-
ereigns of Tuscany.[3]

Mr. Knapp was mistaken as to any person defraying my travelling
expenses.[4] The son of an acquaintance of mine a lad of 15 years of age
went out with me at his father's desire and continued with me till about
the time I left Florence for Pisa which was the nineteenth of November.
I received a small compensation for the trouble of looking to him, but
nothing in comparison with my entire expenses which I bear myself. We
have all been in excellent health, I think better than in America since
we arrived, with the exception of my wife who is I think not so well and
who has grown thin.

Nothing is said in mother's letter as to whether the lands in Illinois
in the neighbourhood of Princeton had come into market or not, and
whether any purchase had been made for me. I cannot help a feeling of
regret at learning that you had parted with the farm in Cummington, but
I have no doubt that the step will be for the advantage of your children.
As to your own individual comfort you will be enabled shortly to judge
whether it has gained by the change.

In about three weeks I shall set out for Rome—from Rome I shall
proceed to Naples and perhaps be in Germany by midsummer. I have
serious thoughts of passing a little time in Germany for the purpose of
learning the language. If you do not get letters from me you will probably learn something of my movements from the Evening Post. When
you remove you had better write to the office to direct whither the paper
is to be sent. —I shall let my wife fill up the remainder of the sheet. My
regards

Yrs truly
W. C. BRYANT.

[by Frances Bryant]

My dear friends Your letter, long and anxiously looked for, for the
days and weeks are long here, when it came gave both pleasure and pain,
the former to learn that you were all well, the latter to be told of your
intended departure. I must confess that I was surprized to hear that you
had sold the farm, and were really going. —I know that you have long
talked of it, yet I could not think that you would go, probably because
I had an interest in hoping that you would not. When we return, should
that time ever arrive, we shall be alone. —Setting aside the idea of home,
and the pleasure of seeing you all again at the old place, we are satisfied

that it is best that you should go, for Cummington is a hard country to get a living in. —I hope you will have as pleasant a time in getting away and arriving at your new place of residence as the circumstances will possibly admit, for I know from experience the delights of moving. William desires me to ask what you are going to do with the books. He says you must not think of selling them or that if you do, you must sell them to him, as he would purchase them himself rather than they should go out of the family. In case you are determined to sell them—if you would pack them up and leave them where he could get them, he would pay for them on his return; provided, he says, that you do not take the best and leave him the books of little value. —I heartily wish that we were there to help pack, and go on with you; it makes me sick to think of your going, before we return.[5]

You ask me how I like this country. The climate during the winter at least is very agreeable. At the coldest period, it has been no colder than bracing October weather, and now the temperature is like that of May or the beginning of June, notwithstanding that the natives complain that it has been [col]der than usual. The figs and grapes in their seasons are [de]licious; the churches are grand and venerable, and the surrounding [moun]tains with their lofty sharp and varied peaks are picturesque to a degree not often seen in the United States. But here ends all that I have to say in praise of the country. —The whole country is made ugly by the mode of cultivation. The trees are all cropped and yield no shade. There are no green meadows, or running brooks, there is scarcely a blade of grass to be seen, the soil is every where dug up by the spade, and in the latter part of summer but the reddish or whitish earth, the fig tree is not so handsome as our oaks which they resemble in foliage, the vineyards are not to be compared in beauty to our cornfields; and the olive trees look like some of our ugly gray-leaved willows. The habitations in the country look comfortless and dirty, the windows are grated with iron like prisons, and the floors paved with stone, never washed and difficult to be swept clean. —When you think of me, do not think of me as one who is without daily vexations, for an American cannot keep house in a foreign country with Italian servants without losing patience almost every hour in the day. I hope you will write to us again as soon at least as you get to Illinois. Write on the thinnest paper that you can find, for that will save postage. —You must all write to me, dont forget us.

Yours affectionately
FRANCES B

MANUSCRIPT: BCHS ADDRESS: To / Col. Austin Bryant / Cummington / Massachusetts / U. S. of America POSTMARK: [NEW-YORK] / SHIP / APR / 9 PUBLISHED: Helen L. Drew, "Unpublished Letters of William Cullen Bryant," *New England Quarterly*, 10 (June 1937), 353.

1. Letter unrecovered.

2. That is, seven English pounds, or about $35 a month. Frances Bryant described these warm and comfortable lodgings at 700 Casa Genoni as close to the house once occupied by Lord Byron. "Autobiographical Sketch," NYPL–GR; letter to Eliza Robbins, December 10, 1834, Letter-book, Homestead Collection. Here at Pisa, in 1821–1822, Byron had finished *Don Juan*.

3. At one of these, a ball given by a Countess [Mastiani?], fourteen-year-old Fanny was "half beside herself at the honor of waltzing with a young nobleman beside the Grand Duke." Frances Bryant to her sister [Mina?], March? 1835, *ibid.*

4. Probably Shepherd Knapp of Cummington, later treasurer of Brooklyn and president of the Mechanics Bank in that city. See S. F. White, "Hampshire County," in *A History of New England*, edd. R. H. Haval and H. E. Crocker (Boston, 1880), p. 186.

5. Late in 1834 Austin Bryant sold the Cummington homestead and farm to one Welcome Tillson. On May 11, 1835, he left with his wife and six children, his mother, and his sister, Louisa, for Princeton, Illinois, by way of the Erie Canal, the Great Lakes, and Chicago. *Bryant Record*, pp. 41, 45; Amanda Matthews, "The Diary of a Poet's Mother," *The Magazine of History*, 2 (September 1905), 208–209; George V. Bohman, "A Poet's Mother . . . ," *Journal of the Illinois State Historical Society*, 33 (June 1940), 172.

299. *To* Horatio Greenough[1]

Pisa   Feb. 27   1835.

My dear Sir.

I am greatly obliged to you for thinking of me, and for stealing time from the labours of your art to write to me. I will endeavour to answer your questions in their order. In the first place, it is my intention to return to Florence, after having seen Rome and Naples, which I shall set out to visit in about three weeks. In the second place, I have passed the winter quite pleasantly. We obtained commodious lodgings on the sunny side of the Arno, where we have made ourselves quite comfortable, and we have not been entirely without acquaintances. In the third place, as to my plans for the summer, I am not quite decided, though it is not improbable that I may cross the Alps in the course of the season, and plant myself in Germany to learn High Dutch. In the fourth place, Mrs. Bryant and the children are quite well. My wife thinks that the air or something else at Pisa agrees with her better than was the case at Florence. The season has been delightfully mild, serene and sunny, with little frost, as it seemed to me, though the people here called it rather colder than usual. The President's message I have seen in the papers forwarded to me regularly by the Havre packets. The Bank is down, as you say, —and the effect has been produced as much by the fortunate mismanagement of those who controlled that institution, as by the good sense of the nation. Had it not been for their purchasing presses and bribing members of Congress by pecuniary assistance, turning the bank into an electioneering engine, attempting to thwart the financial plans of government, setting their creatures to get up a panic and consequent distress, and various other manoevres in which cunning overreached itself, it is not quite certain that the bank would not have been rechartered "with modifications." Their misconduct was perhaps as necessary to its destruction as was the hardness of Pharoah's heart to the deliverance of the Israelites. I hope you will not forget to send me the ode to General Jackson by the author of the "Imaginary Conversations." I am very curious to see how the General looks in verse.[2]

My *labours* as you are pleased to term them are not worth inquiring about. I am occupied with nothing of importance—but I am only trying in my active interests to recover what I nearly unlearned in the course of several years, thinking and writing on political subjects; namely, the modes of thought and mechanism of languages which belong to poetry. I feel sensibly the want of something to stimulate me to exertion, and sometimes fancy that I should find it in my native country, where what I wrote was generally received with exceeding kindness, and created the desire to do better. Of Mr. Fay and his book I have heard nothing since I came to Pisa.[3] From America I have no literary intelligence, except the publication of a History of the United States by Mr. Bancroft of Northampton, an industrious and learned man and a sound republican, who I doubt not has made a good book[4]—and the publication of a novel by a Dr. Bird of Philadelphia, a young man of more than common talent, who carried his work to England with very sanguine hopes of success, and not being able to do any thing with the booksellers there, came back with a flea in his ear and had it printed in America.[5] I am sorry the New York artists obtain no more of the attention of the public. They should recollect that the journals are open, and that well written remarks on the fine arts, particularly new productions of art, would do much to keep the public in mind of the existence of these things. Not that I would expect the artists to write about their own or each other's works, but they have literary friends who ought to do it for them. The poor newspaper editors who have all sorts of subjects to attend to, would be very glad of contributions of this sort.[6]

I am glad to hear that you are so well advanced with your statue. Never mind what Mr. Everett may say of the necessity of sacrificing your taste to what he may suppose to be the taste of the public. If you are to execute the statue, do it according to your own notions of what is true and beautiful, and do not fear that the popularity will not come sooner or later, if the work deserves it. If Mr. Public wants a statue made after his own whims, let him make it himself; but if you undertake it, give us a Greenough. Mr. Everett talks like a politician; but a politician of a bad school— I remember his "consulting the tastes of the people," when he changed his course on the tariff question, and went back from the principles of free trade to the old absurdities about "protecting domestic industry," but I am not aware of any increase of glory which he gained by following his own maxims.[7] I hope to be permitted to see your model when I come to Florence.

I must ask you to congratulate Mr. Mason, in my name, for the agreeable matrimonial adventure which will embellish the journals of his travels in Europe.[8] Present my regards to Mr. Kinlock, and say to him that the letter he was so kind as to procure me has been of the greatest service to me.[9] If you see Mr. [Henry] Miles,[10] remember me to him very cordially. Mrs. Bryant desires her compliments—

I am sir

very truly yrs

WM. C. BRYANT

MANUSCRIPT: UVa (final); NYPL–GR (draft) ADDRESS: Sig. Horatio Greenough / Posta restante / Firenze PUBLISHED (in part, from draft): Life, I, 310.

1. Greenough, who had lived in Florence since 1828, was a warm friend of several New York artists and writers. He roomed with Weir during their study at Rome in 1825, and later associated intimately with Cole and Morse at Florence and Paris. Cooper was his generous patron, commissioning his first notable sculptured group, *Chanting Cherubs*, in 1829. Exhibited at Boston in 1831 and at the National Academy in New York in 1832, it was attacked sharply for its nudity and praised highly for its execution. Reflecting its notoriety, an editorial opponent of Bryant and Leggett dubbed the poet–editors the "Chaunting Cherubs of the Evening Post." Nathalia Wright, *Horatio Greenough: The First American Sculptor* (Philadelphia: University of Pennsylvania Press [1963]), pp. 70–81, *passim*; Nevins, *Evening Post*, p. 139. Firm Jackson-Democrats, Greenough and Bryant were drawn together by their political and social as well as by their aesthetic partialities.

2. Walter Savage Landor (1775–1864), English poet and essayist, had lived for many years in Florence, where he wrote five volumes of his *Imaginary Conversations* (1824–1829). In his February 24 letter (NYPL–GR), Greenough remarked, "Mr. Landor, W. S., was with me a few mornings since—he tells me he has written an ode to Gen. Jackson and has promised to read it to me. I will try to get a copy to send you." In this tribute "To General Andrew Jackson, President of the United States," with which he prefaced the second volume of his *Pericles and Aspasia* (1836), Landor wrote, "How rare the sight, how grand! / Behold the golden scales of Justice stand / Self-balanced in a mailed hand." See Schlesinger, *Age of Jackson*, p. 203. In an undated draft memorandum in NYPL–GR, Bryant described his first meeting with Landor: "In the year 1834 or 5 I was here in Florence. Greenough said to me—Would you like to call on Walter Savage Landor, the author of Imaginary Conversations? I of course said yes, and Greenough after asking Mr. Landor took me to his house. He resided in a pleasant villa on the heights east of the city. I saw a blunt English man before me of middle stature rather square build and with hair touched with grey. The name of Washington was casually mentioned— George Washington said Landor whom I think the greatest man that God ever made." Bryant met Landor again at Florence in 1858. See *Life*, II, 115.

3. Theodore Sedgwick Fay (1807–1898), a New York lawyer, was then traveling in Europe for his health and sending letters home to the *NYM*, of which he was associate editor. In 1835 the Harpers published his first novel, *Norman Leslie*.

4. In September 1834 the first of ten volumes in George Bancroft's *History of the United States from the Discovery of the American Continent* was published at Boston.

5. Robert Montgomery Bird (1806–1854) was already a successful dramatist, sev-

eral of whose plays had been commissioned by Bryant's friend Edwin Forrest, before he published his first novel, *Calavar; or, The Knight of the Conquest: A Romance of Mexico* (Philadelphia, 1834).

6. Greenough relayed to Bryant on February 24 a complaint from the "New York artists as a body" that "business and politics engross the public entirely," adding, "I think that when you return to America we shall have you for an ally. We need a few active friends who have the ear of the public."

7. Greenough was then working intently on a statue of Washington commissioned in 1833 for the National Capitol. He had written Bryant, "I have much advanced my statue and wish heartily you were here that I might have your impressions about it. Mr. [Edward] Everett writes me that it will never be popular—and hints that as I make it for the people I ought perhaps to consult their tastes as much as possible. This is a new view of artistical obligation which I feel a little opposed to."

8. Jonathan Mason, Jr. (c1795–1884), of Boston, a portrait and figure painter then studying in Florence. See *DAA*, p. 428.

9. Francis Kinlock (1798–1840), of South Carolina, studied art in Florence from 1832 until about 1840, the year in which he died at Rome. Meeting Bryant briefly at Paris in the summer of 1834, Greenough had regretted his inability to return to Florence in time to welcome the Bryants in September, and asked Kinlock and Henry Miles (see Note 10) to see them "comfortably settled." *Letters of Horatio Greenough, American Sculptor*, ed. Nathalia Wright (Madison: University of Wisconsin Press [1972]), pp. 113, 178–179.

10. An American banker or merchant in Florence who had been helpful to Greenough as well as to the Bryants. See *ibid.*, p. 113; *Letters of Horatio Greenough to his Brother, Henry Greenough*, ed. Frances Boott Greenough (Boston, 1887), p. 115.

300. *To* Susan Renner[1]

Rome April 7 1835.

We have had rather an agreeable journey to Rome. The first night brought us to Volterra where we remained a day to look at the curiosities of the place. One of the most extraordinary of these is the *Balza* a deep ravine formed by the rains and winter torrents, and terminating near the north wall of the city in a precipice of reddish earth about five hundred feet in height. Every year this frightful chasm approaches nearer the city. The ruins of a convent the inmates of which were removed a few years since to the city for safety stand near the verge—these and some fine pieces of old Etruscan walls must soon fall into the gulf. Next will follow a church not far distant—then another with a monastery—and finally the ravine if not stopped in its progress by artificial means, must undermine and swallow up the walls of Volterra itself with all its monuments of the olden time. I was scarce ever more awe struck than when I stood upon the brink of this precipice and saw the manifest tokens of its gradual approach towards the city. It seemed as if the earth, jealous lest the works of its children should last too long, was preparing to engulf what time had not been able to destroy. —We had a letter to the commandant of the piazza at Volterra who sent his adjutant to shew us the fortress from the top of which is enjoyed a picturesque view extending to a great distance in every direction. Among the mountains to the south was seen the smoke of a lake or pool of hot water highly impregnated with Borax where some Frenchmen have established themselves, and are making their fortunes by obliging the Borax to manufacture itself that is, contriving that the process of extracting the salt shall be effected by the natural temperature of the water, without the aid of artificial heat. The Commandant told me that this pool was always in violent agitation from the gushing of its waters and the escape of the gases and that Dante was said to have visited it to gather images for his *Inferno*.[2]

Turning to the north we beheld a more interesting sight, the roofs of the city we had left the day before clustered on the broad plain of the Val d'Arno, and we thought your house might perhaps be among those on which the eye rested. We saw four well dressed young men on the top of the fortress, with musical instruments in their hands on which they had been playing but stopped as we approached. The officer who accompanied us lifted respectfully his hat to them as he passed. He told us that they were the four persons sentenced last autumn at Florence for political offenses, two of them to three years imprisonment and the other two to four. They were not compelled to labour like the other prisoners, and we were happy to be assured that their personal comfort was provided for. The Commandant who appeared to be somewhat of a liberal afterwards on passing by the fortress pointed to its massive towers and congratulated us that our institutions rendered such engines of government unnecessary in America. I assure you I felt proud of the compliment to my country. In the evening we took tea with the Commandant and his beautiful wife a young Florentine lady. There were two fine ruddy faced children playing in the room of whom the father appeared to be very fond. The cheerful fire, the tea (which however was served in tumblers instead of teacups) the romping children and the handsome mother altogether formed a pretty domestic picture such as I had not before been permitted to witness since I left America. But that you may not complain of my inflicting upon you the entire journal of my travels, suppose us to have arrived at Siena, the aspect of which as that of the inhabitants struck us as more cheerful than that of Pisa. Suppose us to have left Siena with a *Vet*[t]*urino* and on the third day to be traversing a bleak mountain between Bolsena and Ronciglione. Here the transmontane overtook us. The soil was every where covered with a growth of broom, the green and flexible tops of which undulated like a sea in the keen wind blowing from the snowy mountains in sight. A post chaise met us with a figure on one of the outside seats muffled up to the nose—but that nose was too peculiar to be mistaken. My wife knew it to belong to an American acquaintance who had formerly been our family physician.[3] Our carriages were immediately stopped. His lady was with him—and we held a colloquoy of about ten minutes in the most uncomfortable gale I have experienced in Europe. At Ronciglione the wind drove us from the parlour assigned us by rushing down [the] chimney and filling the room with smoke. The host called it *vento di diavolo* [devil's wind], and said that it would blow three days which was literally true, for it blew all the next day which was the last of our journey and two days after our arrival at Rome. Today after an interval of delightful weather it has come again, cold as ever, driving the smoke down the chimney, and compelling me, albeit reluctantly, to extinguish the fire. No wonder the wind is so cold when the mountains in sight of Rome are white with snow. From what I have heard and seen of the climate of Rome I should not think it as equable as that of Pisa. The vegetation when we arrived seemed to us scarcely as advanced as we left it on the Arno. Rome is as you call it a "dirty" city. An American acquaintance who visited it, this winter, spoke of it as clean, but he was just married and probably staid at an Hotel on the *Piazza del Popolo* which is the cleanest part of the city, and was driven rapidly through the other streets in his carriage which prevented his seeing the filth.[4] Fanny has found her tormentors here in abundance.[5] But Rome after all, if dirty, is at least magnificent—magnificent were it only for the Colosseum the noblest of ruins—magnificent were it only for the museum of sculptures in the Vatican—magnificent were it only for the fountains that fill every street with the noise of falling waters—magnificent were it only for the Church of St. Peter's. The other day we went to see the Villa Borghese near the Porta del Popolo. The grounds are laid out in a more natural taste than the Boboli Garden at Florence; and the ground being carpeted with the flowers, the trees populous with buds, and the temperature of the air most genial and delightful we enjoyed our excursion very much. There is a Latin inscription in verse near the entrance inviting the traveller "to repose his weary side on the soft grass," which I took to be a mere flourish, but on entering, I found it was meant to be taken literally, and I sat down on the grass for the first time I believe in Europe.—

W. C. B.

I dare say Mr. Rosini has translated the *Avare* very well.[6] Those who speak of his literary efforts with least commendation admit that he has the merit which they call *stile*, an important quality certain[ly] in a translator. Thank him for retaining so much recollection of me as to put a line or two into your letter,[7] and thank him also for the kind reception his letter has procured me from Sig. Betti the Secretary of the Academy of St. Luke who electrified me by an enthusiastic eulogium upon the republic of the United States.

W. C. B.

MANUSCRIPT: NYPL–GR (draft) ADDRESS: To Mrs Renner Pisa PUBLISHED (*in part*): *LT* I, 436–442. The surviving manuscripts of this letter, and of Letters 305, 306, 307, and 311 are largely in Frances Bryant's handwriting.

1. Susan (Breting) Renner was an Englishwoman of independent means and literary interests whose company Bryant found diverting during his four months' residence at Pisa. The widow of a German physician of Mannheim, she introduced the Bryants to her friends in nearby Heidelberg when they settled there in October 1835.

2. See the description of Malebolge in Cantos 18ff.

3. This American acquaintance has not been identified. The Bryants' family physician at the time they left for Europe was apparently a Dr. Roe.

4. Probably Jonathan Mason, Jr.

5. The fleas with which Rome was "infested." See Letter 301.

6. During his residence in Pisa Bryant had enjoyed a cordial association with Professor G(iacomo?) Rosini of the university there. Rosini was then translating Molière's comedy *L'Avare* into Italian. When Thomas Cole revisited Italy in 1841, he carried Bryant's letter of introduction to Rosini.

7. Unrecovered.

---

301. *To* William Leggett

Rome   April 15   1835

My dear Sir—

The inclosed two poems with those I have previously sent you for Morris's paper make eight which will amount to $240, and as I have no more verses to send at present I give my draft below for the balance of $260 due you for the year about to end.[1] I hope you will receive it early enough to square with your notions of tolerable punctuality.

I wrote you sometime ago requesting you to draw $140 from my share of funds in the office and apply it to paying the interest of the two thousand dollars borrowed by me to buy a part of the share of Mr. Burnham Senr.[2] I presume this has been already attended to. There is also due on the 17th of May next the interest on the note held by Mrs. Coleman against me. This is so clearly to be paid that I presume it will have been paid before you get this without any request or direction from me, but if necessary I hereby give it.

I have been several days in Rome;[3] it is a magnificent old city but terribly infested with fleas. If I had sat down to write a letter for the paper I could give you a flourish about it—but the truth is the subject is trite and almost any book of travels you could lay your hands on would tell you more about it than I could. Mr. Forrest was here when I came but went away in a day or two. He was well and apparently in good spirits.[4] This is Holy Week and all sorts of mummeries are going on.[5] In a few days I go to Naples after visiting which I shall come back and proceed to the northward again— I do not see the E. P. very regularly but I see you have had to pluck a crow with the people that wanted to make more banks— You are clearly in the right to hold the members of the party to the literal fulfillment of their pledge against monopolies, and as honesty is always the best policy, so I hope nothing will be lost by it in the present case notwithstanding you gave battle to the Albany Argus rather roughly at first.[6]

[unsigned]

Messrs Bryant   Leggett & Co.
Gentlemen

Pay to William Leggett Esq. two hundred and sixty dollars and charge the same to my account.
Rome   April 15   1835.

MANUSCRIPT: NYPL–GR (draft) ADDRESS: To William Leggett Esq.

1. Though it is not evident from the *EP* accounts, Bryant seems to have paid Leggett $500 for assuming his share of editorial work during the fiscal year ending May 16, 1835. The manuscripts containing the poems mentioned have not been recovered.
2. Letter unrecovered.
3. Bryant obviously meant to write "several *weeks.*" Frances noted that they reached Rome on March 26, stayed a week at the Hôtel Frantz on the Via Condotta, and then took lodgings at 57 Via Pontifici, Palazzo Corca, where they "kept house as in Florence & Pisa," having their dinners sent in from a *trattoria*, "or cooks shop," for fifty cents a day. Frances Bryant, "Autobiographical Sketch," NYPL–GR; letter to John Bryant, July 23, 1835, Letter-book, Homestead Collection.
4. Earlier, Edwin Forrest had written from Paris, in an undated letter to *NYM*, "I shall probably meet with Bryant in Rome; and, in conversing with him of past scenes and distant friends, shall almost feel myself, for a time, restored to their society." *NYM*, 12 (May 16, 1835), 365.
5. Through the Brazilian minister to the Holy See, Frances and Fanny Bryant were given tickets to the "ceremonies of the Holy Week at the Vatican," where they saw Pope Gregory XVI celebrate High Mass in Saint Peter's. It is not clear, however, whether Cullen accompanied them. See F. Cicognani to Bryant, April 11, 1835, NYPL–GR; Frances to John Bryant, July 23, 1835, Letter-book, Homestead Collection.
6. In November and December of 1834 Leggett had written half a dozen editorials setting forth the *EP*'s firm opposition to monopolistic banking privileges for a favored few, whom he called variously the "scrip nobility," or the "would-be lordlings of the Paper Dynasty." See particularly "The Division of Parties," *EP* for November 4, 1834, and "Rich and Poor," *EP* for December 6, 1834. Both are reprinted in Leggett, *Political Writings*, I, 64–68, 106–110.

302.   *To* William Leggett
Florence   June 12, 1835.
My dear Sir

I received a short time since at Naples your letter inclosing Welles & Fitch's receipt for the second remittance of $500. I thank you for this attention. From Rome some weeks ago I sent you the *eighth* poem for Morris with a draft in your favour on the office for $260, which I hope you have received before this time. Of course when the state of my funds in the concern will admit I should like a further remittance. There is the sum of $1000 to be paid for me to Mrs. Coleman on a bond in which

Mr. Burnham was kind enough to become my security; and that must be looked [to] first. It falls due on the 15th of August. After making due allowance for that if any thing can be spared I should be glad of it. As I have already intimated I have visited Naples since I wrote to you.[1] With my wife and daughter I have strolled through the streets of Pompeii, dived into the darkness of Herculaneum, and climbed to the smoking crater of Vesuvius.[2] We are now about to set out for Venice, whence we shall go to Munich, where I wish to sit down a little while and study German. This rolling about the world with one's family . . .[3]

Night before last, a man-child was born to the Grand Duke of Tuscany, and yesterday was a day of great rejoicing in consequence. The five hundred bells of Florence kept up a horrid ringing through the day, and in the evening the public edifices and many private houses were illuminated. To-day and to-morrow the rejoicings continue, and in the mean time the galleries and museums are closed, lest idle people should amuse themselves rationally. The Tuscans are pleased with the birth of an heir to the Dukedom, first because the succession is likely to be kept in a good sort of a family, and secondly because for want of male children it would have reverted to the House of Austria, and the province would have been governed by a foreigner. I am glad of it, also, for the sake of the poor Tuscans, who are a mild people, and if they must be under a despotism, deserve to live under a good-natured one.[4]

An Austrian Prince, if he were to govern Tuscany as the Emperor governs the Lombardo–Venetian territory, would introduce a more just and efficient system of administering the laws between man and man, but at the same time a more barbarous severity to political offenders. I saw at Volterra, last spring, four persons who were condemned at Florence for an alleged conspiracy against the state. They were walking with instruments of music in their hands, on the top of the fortress, which commands an extensive view of mountain, vale, and sea, including the lower Val d'Arno, and reaching to Leghorn, and even to Corsica. They were well-dressed, and I was assured their personal comfort was attended to. A different treatment is the fate of the state prisoners who languish in the dungeons of Austria. In Tuscany no man's life is taken for any offence whatever, and banishment is a common sentence against those who are deemed dangerous or intractable subjects. In all the other provinces a harsher system prevails. In Sardinia capital executions for political causes are frequent, and long and mysterious detentions are resorted to, as in Lombardy, with a view to strike terror into the minds of a discontented people.

The royal family of Naples kill people by way of amusement. Prince Charles, a brother of the king,[5] sometime in the month of April last, found an old man cutting myrtle twigs on some of the royal hunting-grounds, of which he has the superintendence. He directed his attendants to seize the offender and tie him to a tree, and when they had done this ordered them to shoot him. This they refused, upon which he took a loaded musket from the hands of one of them, and with the greatest deliberation shot him dead upon the spot. His Royal Highness soon after set out for Rome to amuse himself with the ceremonies of the Holy Week, and to figure at the balls given by Torlonia and other Roman nobles, where he signalized himself by his attentions to the English ladies.

Of the truth of the story I have related I have been assured by several respectable persons in Naples. About the middle of May I was at the spot where the murder was said to have been committed. It was on the borders of the lake of Agnano. We reached it by a hollow winding road cut deep through the hills and rocks thousands of years ago. It was a pretty and solitary spot; a neat pavilion of the royal family stood on the shore, and the air was fragrant with the blossoms of the white clover and the innumerable flowers which the soil of Italy, for a short season before the summer heats and drought, pours forth so profusely. The lake is evidently the crater of an old volcano: it lies in a perfect bowl of hills, and the perpetual escape of gas, bubbling up through the water, shows that the process of chemical decomposition in the earth below has not yet ceased. Close by, in the side of the circular hill that surrounds the lake, stands the famous *Grotto del Cane*, closed with a door to enable the keeper to get a little money from the foreigners who come to visit it. You may be sure I was careful not to trim any of the myrtles with my penknife.

But to return to Tuscany—it is after all little better than an Austrian province, like the other countries of Italy. The Grand Duke is a near relative of the Emperor; he has the rank of colonel in the Austrian service, and a treaty of offence and defence obliges him to take part in the wars of Austria to the extent of furnishing ten thousand soldiers. It is well understood that he is watched by the agents of the Austrian Government here, who form a sort of high police, to which he and his cabinet are subject, and that he would not venture upon any measure of national policy, nor even displace or appoint a minister, without the consent of Metternich.

The birth of a son to the Grand Duke has been signalized, I have just learned, by a display of princely munificence. Five thousand crowns have been presented to the Archbishop who performed the ceremony of christening the child; the servants of the ducal household have received two months' wages, in addition to their usual salary; five hundred young women have received marriage portions of thirty crowns each; all the articles of property at the great pawnbroking establishments managed by the government, pledged for a less sum than four livres, have been restored to the owners without payment; and finally, all persons confined for larceny and other offences of a less degree than homicide and other enormous crimes, have been liberated and turned loose upon society again. The Grand Duke can well afford to be generous, for from a million and three hundred thousand people he draws, by taxation, four millions of crowns annually, of which a million only is computed to be expended in the military and civil expenses of his government. The remainder is of course applied to keeping up the state of a prince and to the enriching of his family. He passes, you know, for one of the richest potentates in Europe.

[unsigned]

MANUSCRIPT: NYPL–GR (partial draft) TEXT: from draft manuscript and *LT* I, pp. 37–41.

1. The Bryants left Rome by diligence on April 28, passing through Albano, Velletri, Cisterna, and Terracina, and reaching Naples on May 1. Here they lodged for three weeks at 267 Strada Chiaga. On May 26 they were back in Rome. After a week there and another at Florence, they left for Venice on June 16, spending four days en route through Bologna, Ferrara, and Padua, and on the 20th put up at the Albergo dell'Europa in Venice. Frances Bryant, "Autobiographical Sketch," NYPL–GR; letter to John Bryant, July 23, 1835, Letter-book, Homestead Collection.

2. See the description of this climb in Letter 306.

3. Here the draft manuscript ends, and the rest of the letter is taken from *LT* I, 37–41, there dated May 12 in error.

4. Leopold II (1797–1870) was Grand Duke of Tuscany from 1824 to 1859, when he was forced to abdicate in favor of his son, Ferdinand IV, deposed a year later when Tuscany united with Sardinia.

5. Ferdinand II (1810–1859), King of Naples and Sicily from 1830 until his death, was, throughout most of his reign, an unrestrained tyrant.

303. *To* S[amuel?] D. Bradford[1]

Munich July 13, 1835.

My dear Sir

I got your letter yesterday.[2] We were all glad to hear from you and to learn that you got along with such good fortune—buying elegant carriages for a song, looking at the finest buildings and gazing on the most beautiful scenery of nature at one time and the grandest at another and being whirled over the intermediate distances with a swiftness to your heart's content, and without the nuisance of a travelling companion to interfere either with your tastes or your plans. We are sorry you did not follow your inclination to deviate a little from your course and take Munich in your way, that we might have heard a more particular description of what you have seen from your own mouth. You would have found Munich a pleasant, certainly a very clean and quite a growing city with some galleries of pictures worth seeing. Mr. Stanton came here the day after we did and stayed a week.[3] He had been at the coronation of the Emperor of Austria[4] and was so pleased with the gaieties of Vienna that Munich seemed quite a dull place to him. He said that your arrival was much desired at Vienna, there being an American family there who would have been very glad to have offered you a place in their carriage to

St. Petersburg. So you have escaped not merely one travelling companion, but two of them by not being earlier at Vienna. Mr. Stanton was sighing for Italy and complained of the scarcity and inferiority of the works of art in Germany— He set off a few days since for Baden whence he goes to Switzerland.

For our own part we had as pleasant a time as we could have expected. We went to Innsbruck by way of the new road from Venice opened in 1830. I was astonished at the grandeur of the Alpine scenery— the multitude of sharp needles of rock and rough crags towering in the air—deep gulfs and chasms torrents and waterfalls, to say nothing of the solemn woods of fir and beautiful green vallies which are no less extraordinary a sight. We twice passed the night in two snow storms—one at Venas and the other on the Brenner, and one day after leaving the former of those places we travelled for a considerable distance when the snow was two or three metres deep by the side of the road. We suffered exceedingly from the cold for one or two days and found the German oven beds not uncomfortable. Since our arrival at Munich on the 30th of June we have all been ill with stomach complaints owing I suppose to the extremes of temperature to which we have been exposed— We are now quite well again, and are here at work studying German.

We have apartments in the pleasantest part of the city looking on the garden of the palace and close to the English garden which is the great ornament of the city.[5] It contains a thousand acres or more and is planted with fine trees and shrubs beautifully disposed with openings of green meadows intersected with winding roads for carriages and footpaths for pedestrians, while the Isar divided into a multitude of channels traverses it swiftly in all directions. Here the population of Munich resorts every afternoon in fine weather and more especially on holidays to walk or lie in the shade, to drink beer and suck their pipes at the houses of refreshment, and paddle little barges on the artificial sheets of water. . . .

[unsigned]

MANUSCRIPT: NYPL–GR (incomplete draft).

1. Bradford is identified only as a Bostonian with whom the Bryants traveled at some time during their journey through Italy, and who joined them in their climb up Vesuvius in May 1835. See Letter 306; Frances to John Bryant, July 23, 1835, Letterbook, Homestead Collection.

2. Dated at Innsbruck, Austria, July 10, 1835. NYPL–BG.

3. The Bryants apparently became acquainted with a Mr. Stanton and his family at Florence, saw them again at Rome during Holy Week, and perhaps later at Naples. See W. L. Alley to Bryant, March 6, 1835, NYPL–GR.

4. Ferdinand I (1793–1875), Emperor of Austria from 1835 to 1848.

5. The Bryants lodged with a Signor D. C. Grandi at 31 The Bazaar, from their arrival at Munich on June 30 until they left for Heidelberg on October 2. See Frances Bryant's "Autobiographical Sketch," NYPL–GR.

304. *To* William Leggett

Munich   August 6   1835

My dear Sir.

Since I wrote you last I have received two letters from you giving a statement of the affairs of the office, the manner in which you had arranged the purchase of C[harles] Burnham, the settlement of my account for the half year, and the other dispositions you had made.[1] It is all perfectly satisfactory. I am sure I ought to feel obliged to you for the trouble you have taken and the results you have brought about. Will you be so good as to say to Mr. Hannah that I wish he would mention the gross receipts and expenses of the paper in the semi annual statement he sends me.[2] Now, if you want something for your paper, here it is.[3]

Since my last letter I have visited Venice, a city which realizes the old mythological fable of Beauty born of the sea. I must confess however that my first feeling on entering it was that of disappointment. As we passed in our gondola out of the lagoons, up one of the numerous canals which permeate the city in every direction in such a manner that it seems as if you could only pass your time either within doors or in a boat, the place appeared to me a vast assemblage of prisons surrounded with their moats, and I thought how weary I should soon grow of my confinement and how glad to escape again to terra firma. But this feeling quickly gave way to delight and admiration, when I landed and surveyed the clean though narrow streets, never incommoded by dust nor disturbed by the noise and jostling of carriages and horses, by which you may pass to every part of the city—when I looked again at the rows of superb buildings, with their marble steps ascending out of the water of the canals, in which the gondolas were shooting by each other—when I stood in the immense square of St. Mark, surrounded with palaces resting on arcades under which the shops rival in splendour those of Paris and crowds of the gay inhabitants of both sexes assemble towards the evening and sit in groups before the doors of the coffee houses—and when I gazed on the barbaric magnificence of the church of St. Mark and the Doge's palace surrounded by the old emblems of the power of Venice and overlooking the Adriatic, once the empire of the republic. The architecture of Venice has to my eyes something watery and oceanic in its aspect. Under the hands of Palladio, the Grecian orders seemed to borrow the lightness and airiness of the Gothic.[4] As you look at the numerous windows and the multitude of interposing columns which give a striated appearance to the fronts of the palaces, you think of stalactites and icicles, such as you might imagine to ornament the abodes of the water gods and the sea nymphs. The only thing needed to complete the poetic illusion is transparency or brilliancy of colour, and this is wholly wanting, for at Venice the whitest marble is soon clouded and blackened by the corrosion of the sea air.

It is not my intention, however, to do so hackneyed a thing as to give a description of Venice. One thing, I must confess, seemed to me extraordinary: how this city, deprived as it is of the commerce which built it up from the shallows of the Adriatic and upheld it so long and so proudly, should not have decayed even more rapidly than it has done. Trieste has drawn from it almost all its trade, and flourishes by its decline. I walked through the Arsenal of Venice, which comprehends the Navy Yard, an enormous structure, with ranges of broad lofty roofs supported by massive portions of wall, and spacious dock-yards, the whole large enough to build and fit out a navy for the British empire. The pleasure boats of Napoleon and his empress, and that of the present Viceroy are there, but the ships of war belonging to the republic have mouldered away with the Bucentaur. I saw, however, two Austrian vessels, the same which had conveyed the Polish exiles to New York,[5] lying under shelter in the docks, as if placed there to show who were the present masters of the place. It was melancholy to wander through the vast unoccupied spaces of this noble edifice, and to think what must have been the riches, the power, the prosperity, and the hopes of Venice at the time it was built, and what they are at the present moment. It seems almost impossible that any thing should take place to arrest the ruin which is gradually consuming this renowned city. Some writers have asserted that the lagoons around it are annually growing shallower by the depositions of earth brought down by streams from the land, that they must finally become marshes, and that their consequent insalubrity will drive the inhabitants from Venice. I do not know how this may be; but the other causes I have mentioned seem likely to produce nearly the same effect. I remembered, as these ideas passed through my mind, a passage in which one of the sacred poets foretells the desertion and desolation of Tyre, "the city that made itself glorious in the midst of the seas."

"Thy riches and thy fairs, thy merchandise, thy mariners and thy pilots, thy calkers and the occupiers of thy merchandise, and all thy men of war that are in thee, shall fall into the midst of the seas in the day of thy ruin."[6]

I left this most pleasing of the Italian cities which I had seen on the 24th of June and took the road for the Tyrol. We passed through a level fertile country, formerly the territory of Venice watered by the Piave which ran blood in one of Bonaparte's battles. At evening we arrived at Cenada, where our Italian poet Da Ponte was born,[7] situated just at the base of the Alps the rocky peaks and irregular spurs of which beautifully green with the showery season rose in the background. Cenada seems to have something of German cleanliness about it, and the floors of a very comfortable inn at which we staid were of wood, the first we had seen in Italy, though common throughout the Tyrol and the rest of Germany.

A troop of barelegged boys, just broke loose from school, whooping and swinging their books and slates in the air, passed under my window. Such a sight you will not see in southern Italy. The education of the people is neglected, except in those provinces which are under the government of Austria. It is a government severe and despotic enough in all conscience, but by providing the means of education for all classes, it is doing more than it is aware of to prepare them for the enjoyment of free institutions. In the Lombardo–Venetian kingdom as it is called there are few children who do not attend the public schools.

On leaving Cenada, we entered a pass in the mountains, the gorge of which was occupied by the ancient town of Serravalle resting on arcades the architecture of which denoted that it was built during the middle ages. Near it I remarked an old castle which formerly commanded the pass, one of the finest ruins of the kind I had ever seen. It had a considerable extent of battlemented wall in perfect preservation, and both that and its circular tower were so luxuriantly loaded with ivy that they seemed almost to have been cut out of the living verdure. As we proceeded we became aware how worthy this region was to be the birthplace of a poet. A rapid stream, a branch of the Piave tinged of a light and somewhat turbid blue by the soil of the mountains, came tumbling and roaring down the narrow valley; perpendicular precipices rose on each side, and beyond, the gigantic brotherhood of the Alps in two long files of steep pointed summits divided by deep ravines stretched away in the sunshine to the north east. In the face of one [of] the precipices by the way side a marble slab is fixed, informing the traveller that the road was opened by the late Emperor of Germany in the year 1830. We followed this romantic valley for a considerable distance, passing several little blue lakes lying in their granite basins, one of which was called the *Lago morto* or Dead Lake, from having no outlet for its waters. At length we began to ascend, by a winding road, the steep sides of the Alps—the prospect enlarging as we went, the mountain summits rising to sight around us, one behind another, some of them white with snow over which the wind blew with a wintry keenness—deep valleys opening below us, and gulfs yawning between rocks over which old bridges were thrown, —and solemn fir forest clothing the broad declivities. The farm-houses placed on these heights, —instead of being of brick or stone as in the plains and vallies below, were principally built of wood; the second story, which served for a barn, being encircled with a long gallery and covered by a projecting roof of plank held down with large stones. We stopped at Venas, a wretched place with a wretched inn, the hostess of which showed us a chin garnished with the *goitre* and ushered us into dirty comfortless rooms where we passed the night. When we awoke the rain was beating against the windows, and on looking out, the forests and sides of the neighbouring mountains at a little height above us, appeared hoary with snow. We set out in the rain, but had not proceeded far before we heard the sleet striking against the windows of the carriage, and soon came to where the snow covered the ground to a depth of one or two inches. Continuing to ascend, we passed out of Italy and entered the Tyrol. The storm had ceased before we went through the first Tyrolese village, and we could not help being struck with the change in the appearance of the inhabitants—the different costume, the less erect figures, the awkward gait, the lighter complexions, the neatly kept habitations, and the absence of beggars. As we advanced the clouds began to roll off from the landscape, disclosing here and there, through openings in their broad skirts as they swept along, glimpses of the profound vallies below us and of the white sides and summits of mountains in the mid sky above. At length the sun appeared and revealed a prospect of such wildness grandeur and splendor as I had never before seen. Lofty peaks of the most fantastic shape with deep clefts between sharp needles of rock and overhanging crags, infinite in multitude, shot up every where around us, glistening in the new fallen snow, with thin wreaths of mist creeping along their sides. At intervals swollen torrents, looking at a distance like long trains of foam, came thundering down the mountains, and crossing the road plunged into the verdant vallies which winded beneath. Beside the highway were fields of young grain, pressed to the ground with the snow; and in the meadows, ranunculuses of the size of roses, large yellow violets, and a thousand other Alpine flowers of the most brilliant hues were peeping through their white covering. We stopped to breakfast at a place called Landro, a solitary inn in the midst of this grand scenery with a little chapel beside it. The water from the dissolving snow was dropping merrily from the roof in a bright June sun. We needed not to be told that we were in Germany, for we saw it plainly enough in the nicely-washed floor of the apartment into which we were shown, in the neat cupboard with the old prayerbook lying upon it, and in the general appearance of housewifery, a quality unknown in Italy; to say nothing of the evidence we had in the beer and tobacco smoke of the travellers' room, and the gutteral dialect and quiet tones of the guests. From Landro we descended gradually into the beautiful vallies of the Tyrol, leaving the snow behind, though the white peaks of the mountains were continually in sight. At Bruneck in an inn resplendent with neatness— so at least it seemed to our eyes, accustomed to the negligence and dirt of Italian housekeeping—we had the first specimen of a German bed. It is narrow and short, and is made so high at the head by a number of huge square bolsters and pillows that you rather sit than lie. The principal covering is a bag of down, very properly denominated the upper bed, and between this and the feather-bed below the traveller is expected to pass the night. An asthmatic patient on a cold winter night might perhaps find such a couch tolerably comfortable, if he could prevent the narrow coverings from slipping off on one side or the other. The next day we were afforded an opportunity of observing more closely the inhabitants of this singular region, by a festival or fair of some sort, which brought them into the roads in great numbers, arrayed in their holiday dresses— the men in short jackets and small-clothes, with broad gay-coloured suspenders over their waistcoats, and leathern belts ornamented with gold or silver leaf—the women in short petticoats composed of horizontal bands of different colors—and both sexes for the most part wearing broad-brimmed hats with hemispherical crowns; though there was a sugar loaf variety much affected by the men adorned with a band of lace and sometimes a knot of flowers. They are a robust healthy-looking race, though they have an awkward stoop in the shoulders. But what struck me most forcibly was the devotional habits of the people. The Tyrolese might be cited as an illustration of the remark that mountaineers are more habitually and profoundly religious than others. Persons of all sexes, young and old whom we met in the road were repeating their prayers audibly. We passed a troop of old women all in broad-brimmed hats and short gray petticoats carrying long staves, one of whom held a bead-roll and gave out the prayers to which the others made the responses in chorus. They looked at us so solemnly from under their broad brims, and marched along with so grave and deliberate a pace, that I could hardly help fancying that the wicked Austrians had caught a dozen elders of the respectable society of Friends and put them in petticoats to punish them for their heresy.

We afterwards saw persons going to the labours of the day or returning telling their rosaries and saying their prayers as they went, as if their devotion had been their favorite amusement. At intervals of about half a mile we saw wooden crucifixes erected by the way side covered from the weather by little sheds, bearing the image of the Saviour, crowned with thorns and frightfully dashed with streaks and drops of red paint, to represent the blood that flowed from his wounds. The outer walls of the better kind of houses were ornamented with paintings in fresco and the subjects of these were mostly sacred, such as the Virgin and child, the crucifixion and the Ascension. The number of houses of worship was surprising, I do not mean spacious and stately churches as are met with in Italy but most commonly little chapels disposed so as best to accommodate the population. Of these the smallest neighborhood has one for the morning devotions of its inhabitants, even the solitary inn has its little consecrated building with its miniature spire, for the convenience of the pious wayfarer. At Sterzing a little village beautifully situated at the base of the mountain called the Brenner and containing as I should judge not more than two or three thousand inhabitants, we counted seven churches and chapels within the compass of a square mile. The observances of the Roman Catholic church are nowhere more rigidly complied with than in the Tyrol. When we stopped at Bruneck on Friday evening I happened to drop a word about a little meat for dinner in a conversation with the spruce-looking landlady, who looked so shocked that I gave up the point on the promise of some excellent and remarkably well flavored trout from the stream that flowed through the village—a promise that was honorably and literally fulfilled. At the Post House on the Brenner where we stopped on Saturday evening, we were absolutely refused any thing but soup maigre and fish, the postmaster telling us that the priest had positively forbidden meat to be given to travellers. Think of that! —that we who had eaten wild-boar and pheasants on Good Friday at Rome under the very nostrils of the Pope himself and his whole conclave of Cardinals, should be refused a bit of flesh on an ordinary Saturday, at a tavern on a lonely mountain in the Tyrol by the orders of a parish priest! Before getting our soup maigre, we witnessed another example of Tyrolese devotion. Eight or ten travellers, apparently labouring men took possession of the entrance hall of the inn, and kneeling, poured forth their orisons in the German language for half an hour with no small appearance of fervency. In the morning when we were ready to set out we inquired for our coachman, an Italian, and found that he too although not remarkably religious had caught something of the piety of the region, and was at the *Gotteshaus* as the waiter called the tavern chapel, offering his morning prayers.

We descended the Brenner on the 28th of June in a snow-storm, the wind whirling the light flakes in the air as it does with us in winter. It changed to rain, however as we approached the beautiful and picturesque valley watered by the river Inn, on the banks of which stands the fine old town of Innsbruck the capital of the Tyrol. Here we visited the Church of the Holy Cross in which is the bronze tomb of Maximilian I, and twenty or thirty bronze statues ranged on each side of the nave representing fierce warrior chiefs and gowned prelates and stately dames of the middle ages. These are all curious for the costume, the warriors are cased in various kinds of ancient armor and brandish various ancient weapons and the robes of the females are flowing and by no means ungraceful. Almost every one of the statues has its hands and fingers in a constrained and ungraceful position, as if the artist knew as little what to do with them, as some awkward and bashful people know what to do with theirs. The sight of such a crowd of figures, in that ancient garb occupying the floor in the midst of a living congregation of the present day has an effect which is somewhat startling.

From Innsbruck we climbed and crossed another Alpine ridge scarcely less wild and majestic in its scenery than those we had left behind. On descending we observed that the crucifixes had disappeared from the roads, and the broad brimmed and sugar loaf hats from the heads of the peasantry; the men wore hats contracted in the middle of the crown like an hour glass, and the women caps edged with a broad band of black fur; the fresco[e]s on the outside of the houses became less frequent; in short it was evident that we had entered a different region even if the police and custom house officers had not let us know that we were now in the kingdom of Bavaria. We passed through extensive forests of fir, here and there checkered with farms, and finally came to the broad elevated plain bathed by the Isar, in which Munich is situated. I thought to have given you some account of this city but my sheet is full and I must leave it for another letter.—

WILLIAM C. BRYANT

MANUSCRIPTS: NYPL–GR (complete and partial drafts) ADDRESS: To William Leggett ENDORSED (by Bryant): My letter to/ W. Leggett / Aug. 1835 PUBLISHED: *EP* for September 19, 1835; *LT* I, pp. 42–54.

1. Neither letter has been recovered.

2. Hannah had handled *EP* accounts since Charles Burnham's retirement from the firm the preceding November. Bryant later called him a "drunken and saucy clerk" who kept the books in a "very slovenly manner." See Letter 312; Cullen to Frances Bryant, April 27, 1836, and Bryant to Dana, June 28, 1838, NYPL–GR.

3. The rest of this letter was published with minor changes in the *EP*, and, except for the final sentence, in *LT* I.

4. Although Andrea Palladio (1518–1580) designed only churches, notably San Giorgio Maggiore and Il Redentore, for Venice, his town and country houses in and around nearby Vicenza, with his often republished *I quattro libri dell' architettura* (1570), were greatly influential.

5. In 1834 several hundred refugees from the vain Polish revolt against Russia landed at New York and were later given public lands in Illinois by Congress. This began Polish emigration to this country. Morison, *History of the American People*, p. 480.

6. Ezekiel 27:27.

7. Lorenzo Da Ponte had given Bryant letters to several friends in Italy, calling him therein his "pupil," and "one of my dearest friends." But since the addressees of those letters which have been recovered lived in Milan and Parma, which Bryant did not visit, they were undelivered, and are in NYPL–BG and NYPL–GR. Da Ponte seems to have supplied no introductions to persons at Cenada.

305. *To* Susan Renner

Munich   September 7   1835.

My dear Mrs. Renner.

The first sight of your letter was like meeting with an old friend whom we had not seen for a long time—but the feeling of pleasure was soon changed to regret at the unpleasant news it communicated. —I had already written, nearly three weeks before to your good friend at Heidelberg Madame Barrault de la Gravière to inquire in what part of the world you were, or what could possibly have become of you, but had not yet received an answer, and began to fear that we had lost track of you (is that an American metaphor?) altogether. We are in hopes, however— from what you say that you are in the mending hand, and that we may ere long see you in Germany. —Since we got your letter an answer has arrived from your friend at Heidelberg, who expresses the greatest anxiety to have you with her and who expects you at her house as soon as you are able to resume your journey.[1]

Ah! if my friends would say of me behind my back such fine things as she says of you! —In the mean time take good care of yourself, and get well as fast as you can for the sake of your friends. I see that the cholera has invaded Italy, that it is dreadfully fatal at Genoa, that Milan is thronged with fugitives from that city and that fears are entertained that it may reach Milan itself. Should it come you will doubtless make more haste to leave your present situation, but do not be alarmed beyond reason. I watched the course of the cholera at New York to the end, and know that it borrows a great part of its terrors from the imagination. A quiet mind, regular habits, and the avoidance of all kinds of excess and exposure are preventives next to certain.

Since I wrote to you at Rome we have been to Naples to Florence to Venice and finally came on the new road by Belluno through the Tyrol to Munich where we arrived on the 30th of June weary with seeing sights, and glad to repose in a cool climate with such a place as the English Garden close at hand for our daily walks. How grand we found the Tyrol! —we have no scenery of precisely the same kind in our country— and how cold too! Twice we were overtaken by storms of snow, and one bright morning we travelled for a considerable distance over a country covered with snow. The mountain summits were in all their winter whiteness, and brilliancy, the torrents and cataracts in full rush, the forests in full foliage, and the vallies bright with all their verdure and flowers. I question if the Tyrol was ever seen to greater advantage.

My wife is just recovered from a troublesome illness—a kind of stomach complaint which brought her quite low and obliged us to call in a doctor, an Italian gentleman who seemed quite judicious in his treatment, prescribing in the first place *cose blande calmanti dolcificanti,* as he called them,[2] such as mild emulsions, &c, and finally bringing his prescriptions to the agreeable climax of Old Port. May your doctor order no harsher remedies, and may the result be no less favorable.—

I am now deep in the study of German, which is a crabbed kind of tongue after all, and very obstinately peculiar in prescribing the order of words in a sentence. We have lodgings in a house in the Bazaar, looking on the Hofgarten, and belonging to an Italian family who knew your husband at Mannheim in consequence of one of them having been his patient, and who think they cannot say enough of his good qualities. We are fixed here for the remainder of this month, but at the beginning of the next we intend to go to Heidelberg, where if we find lodgings to our mind, as Madame Barrault de Lagravière supposes we may we shall stay awhile; otherwise we shall proceed to Mannheim. We have now a much stronger inducement for fixing ourselves at Heidelberg, since we have learned it is possible you may come there, which we pray that your health, and the doctors will speedily let you.

Does the state of your health permit you to amuse yourself with new books? Washington Irving has published a "Tour on the Prairies" which I read at Rome.[3] It is a story of a journey made by him in company with a military expedition, into the western wilderness of America, far beyond the settlements of white men. Cooper has published a work, the name of which I do not recollect, but which is said to be a satire, under the disguise of a fictitious narrative on those in America who ape the manners of the English.[4] There is also another work from Irving's pen entitled Abbotsford and Newstead Abbey.[5]

Fanny Kemble Butler has given to the world her journal of a Residence in the United States, which is said to be written with great talent and to be very entertaining. It has had a prodigious run in the United States. I would almost give my ears to see it—but though it has been reprinted as well as the other works I have mentioned, at Paris, it is not to be obtained here.[6]

Adieu. May God send you a speedy recovery. My wife and daughter desire their best love.

Truly Yours
W. C. BRYANT

MANUSCRIPT: NYPL–GR (draft).

1. M. and Mme Barrault de la Gravière, to whom Mrs. Renner recommended the Bryants, were a Parisian couple who ran a school for children. Here little Julia Bryant studied French and German throughout her family's residence of nearly a year in Heidelberg. Neither Mrs. Renner's letter to Bryant from Milan, where she had gone from Pisa for her health, nor those exchanged by Bryant and Mme Barrault, have been recovered.

2. "More or less bland, soothing sweets."

3. A Tour on the Prairies (Philadelphia, 1835).

4. The Monikins (Philadelphia, 1835).

5. Abbotsford and Newstead Abbey (Philadelphia, 1835).

6. Frances Anne Butler, Journal (London, 1835). Bryant's curiosity about this account of an 1832 theatrical tour in the United States by the English actress Fanny Kemble (1809–1893) is understandable, for she had enjoyed the most her association with him and his friends. She found, she wrote, that "they formed a society among themselves, where all those qualities which I had looked for among the self-styled best were to be found. When I name Miss Sedgwick, Halleck, Irving, Bryant, Paulding, and some of less fame, . . . it will no longer appear singular that they should feel too well satisfied with the resources of their own society, either to mingle in that of the vulgar fashionables, or seek with avidity the acquaintance of every stranger that arrives in New York." On the voyage from England she had read through a volume of Bryant's poems lent her by Irving, finding "some of it beautiful, and all of it wholesome," and "the tears rolled down my cheeks more than once as I read." Journal, I, 202–204, 78–79.

306.   *To* Julia Sands

Munich   September 7 [1835]

My dear Miss Sands—

I was sure that you were an age in answering my letter, but I did not know that it had made so slow a voyage to America. Your answer has put to flight all my doubts as to your pretension to the title of a faithful and punctual correspondent—a character which I honour very much in my friends, however far I am from possessing it myself.[1] To receive the letters of a lively and witty correspondent like yourself, at the expected period is one of the greatest of terrestrial enjoyments, and any delay in getting them is, at least, as likely to put one in a bad humour as going without one's daily paper or one's dinner.[2]

Since I wrote you last we have journeyed through several of the Italian states and are now settled for a little while in Germany. Our first move was from Pisa to Volterra, a very ancient city, as you know, one of the strong holds of Etruria when Rome was in its cradle, and even in more modern times large enough to form, in the age of Italian republics, an independent community of considerable importance. It is now a decayed town, containing about four thousand inhabitants, some of whom are families of the poor and proud nobility common enough all over Italy, who quarrel with each other with all the heartiness and zeal of village feuds in our own country; but the Volterra quarrels are the more violent for being hereditary. Poor creatures! too proud to engage in business, too indolent for literature, excluded from political concerns by the nature of the government, there is nothing left for them but to starve intrigue and quarrel. You may judge how miserably poor are the nobility of Volterra when you are told that they cannot even afford to cultivate the favorite art of modern Italy—the art best suited to the genius of an indolent and voluptuous race. There is as I was told but one piano-forte in the whole town, and that is owned by a Florentine lady, a recent resident. No wonder then, said an Italian gentleman to me, that there should be so little harmony in the place.

Just before arriving at Volterra our attention was fixed by the extraordinary aspect of the country through which we passed. The road gradually ascended, and we found ourselves among deep ravines and steep high broken banks principally of a stiff clay, barren and in most places utterly bare of herbage, a scene of complete desolation, were it not for a cottage here and there perched upon the heights, a few sheep attended by a boy and a dog grazing on the brink of one of the precipices, or a solitary patch of bright green wheat in some spot where the rains had not yet carried away the vegetable mould. Imagine to yourself an elevated country like that for example in the western part of Massachusetts—suppose the rocks to be changed to vast beds of clay and then fancy the

whole region to be torn by water spouts and torrents into gullies too profound to be passed with sharp ridges between, —stripped of its trees and
its grass—and you will have some idea of the country near Volterra. I
could not help thinking, as I looked at it, that the earth was growing old
—that the bare heaps of earth [about] me had once been the ribs of rocks
that upheld the mountains—that they had become disintegrated by time
and the elements—and that the rains were sweeping them down to the
Mediterranean, to fill its bed and cause its water to encroach upon the
land. It was impossible for me to prevent the apprehension from passing
through my mind that such must be the fate of other quarters of the globe
in distant ages,—that their rocks must crumble and their mountains be
levelled, until the waters shall again cover the face of the earth, unless
new mountains shall be thrown [up by erup]tions of eternal fire. They
told me at Volterra that this frightful region [had] once been productive
and under cultivation, but that after a plague which had depopulated
the country four or five hundred years since, it was abandoned and neglected and the rains had reduced it to its present state.

In the midst of this desert tract which is however here and there in-
terspersed with fertile spots, rises the moun[tain] on which Volterra is
situated, where the inhabitants breathe a pure and keen atmosphere almost perpetually cool, and only die of fevers and pleurisies; while below
on the banks of the Cecina, which in full sight winds its way to the sea
they die of fevers. One of the ravines of which I have spoken has ploughed
a deep chasm on the north side of this mountain, and is every year rapidly
approaching nearer to the city on the summit. I stood on its edge and
looked down a bank of soft red earth five hundred feet in height. A few
rods in front of me I saw where a road had crossed the very spot now
occupied by the gulf—the tracks of the last years carriages were seen
reaching to the edge on both sides. The ruins of a convent were close at
hand, the inmates of which two or three years since were removed by
government to the town for safety,—these ruins will shortly be under-
mined, together with a fine piece of the old Etruscan wall of the city
built of enormous uncemented parallelograms of stone, and looking as
if it might be the work of the giants who had lived before the flood; a
neighbouring church next will fall into the gulf; and finally if measures
are not taken to prevent its progress the ravine will reach and sap the
walls of the city itself swallowing up what time has so long spared. The
antiquities of Volterra consist of an old Etruscan burial ground, in which
the tombs still remain, pieces of the old Etruscan wall including a far
larger circuit than the present city, two Etruscan gates of immemorial
antiquity—older doubtless than any thing at Rome, —built of massive
stone, one of them serving, even yet, for one of the entrances to the
town, and a multitude of cinerary vessels mostly of alabaster sculptured
with numerous figures in alto relievo. These figures are sometimes alle-

gorical representations, and sometimes embody the fables of the Greek mythology. Among the finest and most gracefully executed are many which represent incidents in the poems of Homer.

We ascended to the top of the Fortress of Volterra—a very ancient-looking and massive stronghold built by the Medici family, the tower of which commands a most extensive prospect. It was the nineteenth day of March, and before us the sides of the mountain scooped into irregular dells were covered with fruit trees just breaking into leaf and blossom. Beyond, stretched the region of barrenness I have already described to the west of which were spread the green pastures of the Maremma where the air in summer is deadly, and still further west lay the waters of the Mediterranean out of which in a clear day may be seen rising the mountains of Corsica. To the north and north east were the Apennines, capped with snow, embosoming the fertile lower valley of the Arno, and the cities of Pisa and Leghorn in sight. To the south we traced the meanderings of the Cecina, and beheld ascending into the air the smoke of a hot water lake agitated perpetually with the escape of gas which we were told was visited by Dante to fill his mind with imagery for the description of Hell, but which is now converted by some Frenchmen into a Borax manufactory—the natural heat of the water serving to extract the salt. The fortress is used as a state prison. We saw on the top of the tower four prisoners of state, well dressed young men with instruments of music in their hands who did not look very miserable. They had been found guilty of a conspiracy against the government. We had letters to the commandant of the Fortress who gave us a very hospitable reception. In showing us the fortress he congratulated us that we needed no such engines of government in America. In the evening we went to his house where we saw his wife, a handsome young lady, the very lady of the piano-forte before mentioned, the mother of two youn[g] children whose ruddy cheeks and chubby figures did credit to the air of Volterra. The commandant made tea for us in tumblers and his lady gave us music.

I have said the more of Volterra because it lies rather out of the usual course of ordinary travellers. After a day passed in this place we proceeded to Siena where we staid three days, to Rome where we staid five weeks and to Naples where we staid three. Of course we visited all the ruins of Rome including the grandest the Coliseum; went down into the catacombs, little Julia with us carrying a wax light part of the way, and saw every thing else which travellers must see, not forgetting St. Peters, my first thought on entering which was that it was as fine as a ball room or a cabin in a new steam boat, and it was only after several visits that my mind was opened to the grandeur and majesty of its proportions. Of course also we made excursions to Tivoli and Terni, and Pozzuoli and Pompeii, and Herculaneum, and Vesuvius. That last was an adventure worth telling of! We set out at midnight on account of the heat, though it was no later than the 17th of May. For four miles or more before arriving at the cone of loose cinders which surround the crater we rode on asses and ponies up a rugged winding road attended by a dozen torch bearers and guides. Two American gentlemen accompanied us.[3] It was quite a grand affair—there was the darkness, and the flare of the torches—and the rocks of ancient lava and the black craggy trains of the lava of last year, and the hollow path and the flapping of the branches of wild fig trees in our faces as we passed, and the half savage looks and strange gibberish of the guides. We stopped to rest at the Hermitage, a house surrounded by vineyards just on the edge of the streams of lava poured forth in the last eruption, and occupied by a friar of some sort or other. Half an hours farther riding brought us to the cone and we climbed up its almost perpendicular sides with extreme toil, wading in the loose volcanic gravel mixed with craggy fragments of lava. My wife and daughter were fairly dragged up by the guides. Of course we were out of breath when we arrived at the summit just as the sun was rising.

We now stood on the edge of a vast hollow within which extended a black crust of irregular surface intersected with fissures which sent up an acrid vapour and insupportable heat. Our station was on the north side of the crater, where the surface for a considerable distance was tolerably level. South of this little plain sank a deep black valley at the further side of which was a profound opening sending up continually huge volumes of reddish looking smoke which rolled over each other down the mountain in a direction opposite to that in which we stood. The edges of the crater except where we came up it, were high sharp, steep and broken, as if the summit of the mountain had suddenly fallen into the gulf below. Nothing could be more beautiful than the green and yellow hues on the western edge—it looked for all the world like a bank of green grass and buttercups. One of the party asked what were the flowers which made so gay an appearance. I told him they were only *flowers* of *sulphur*, which was the literal fact, for it was the sublimated sulphur, deposited on the crags of lava, which gave them this brilliant colouring. Our Cicerone told us alarming stories of the occasional sinking of the crust of the crater on which we stood—how the frightful opening which sent forth the smoke shifted from one side to the other and mountains swelled up within the crater at one time and were suddenly engulfed at another— and talked of the symptoms of an approaching eruption—whether from a desire to impart information or because he wanted to go home for his breakfast I could not judge. I will not undertake to describe what has been described so often—the glorious prospect beheld from the summit of the volcano—the bright blue Mediterranean with its dark shores of rocky mountains—the ancient Parthenope, burial place [of Vergil, pro]bably on the slope of her hills—Pompeii, Herculaneum, Baiae—the towering [is]lands of Capreae [Capri], Procida, and Ischia—the heights gilded and the waters shining in the morning sun. We shot to the bottom of the cone in ten minutes; my wife and daughter gave their boots which were reduced to a most rueful plight to the guides who pocketed them with thanks; we arrived at Naples about ten in the morning and deliberately went to bed.

I have only room to tell you further that Naples is populous, lively, as noisy as New York and inexpressibly dirty—that whoever visits either that place or Rome must lay his account in being eaten up alive by fleas— that the farther you go south of Tuscany the greater cheats you find the people, and that half at least of the pleasure you take in looking at objects of curiosity is counterbalanced by being plagued by swarms of beggars ragamuffins and rogues of all sorts who come upon you at every turn and keep a perpetual din in your ears. The scenery of the bay of Naples is among the most stupendously picturesque I ever looked at but the Lazzaroni I confess disappointed me. They looked altogether too decent, too comfortable, too well clad—they were not half so naked nor half so queer as I had been taught to expect. I had seen quite as shabby looking men and women in other parts of Italy. We were however much amused with Naples and our stay there was rendered more agreeable by the pleasant situation of our apartments looking on the bay and the beautiful public walk called the Chiaja. On our return we passed another week at Rome and another at Florence and then proceeded by way of Bologna to Venice where we arrived in just three months from the time we left Pisa. I have put some of my notes of Venice and of a journey through the Tyrol in a letter to Mr. Leggett which you will see in the Evening Post. I have no room to tell you any thing of Munich and a variety of other matters. My wife has your letter and will answer it ere long. She has been quite ill with a stomach complaint which her doctor *thinks* he cured, but which I *know* I did. Fanny and Julia are quite well—the latter is become a great reader. She has not lost her Italian, and in consequence of speaking the language, is a great favorite of a little circle of Italians here.[4] Pray write again soon, your literary intelligence is really *news* to me.[5] My wife and daughters desire their love.—

Yours truly

W. C. BRYANT

MANUSCRIPT: NYPL–GR (draft) PUBLISHED (*in part*): *LT* I, pp. 436–442; *Prose*, II, 91–98.

1. Miss Sands's letter to Cullen is unrecovered, but that of July 29 to Frances is in NYPL–BG.

2. The portion of this letter published in *LT* I begins here and ends with the Bryants' departure from Volterra; that in *Prose* II continues their journey through the visit to Naples.

3. The two American companions were Bradford (see Letter 303) and a Mr. Crofts of Vermont. Frances to John Bryant, July 23, 1835, Letter-book, Homestead Collection.

4. These Italians were probably Bryant's landlord, Signor Grandi, and his family and friends. Frances wrote John Bryant, "Julia speaks Italian as well as English; she talks to her doll in that language, and when addressed in German answers in Italian." *Ibid.* Note Cullen's comment to William Ware in Letter 307 that little Julia "stoutly denies that she even speaks English, the two languages she uses being according to her account American and Italian, to which she is now adding High Dutch."

5. Julia Sands wrote Frances that Gulian Verplanck had written "beautifully" of Bryant's poems, and wanted their author to see his article in *NYM*, 12 (March 28, 1835), 305–306. She also discussed a volume, *Selections from the American Poets* (Dublin, 1834), in which Bryant was given first place, and of which the *Edinburgh Review* (61, No. 123 [April 1835] 21–40, *passim*) remarked cautiously that, while a "great poet has not *yet* arisen in America," in the meantime "we may be contented with the placid beams of minor stars," among whom Bryant "is likely to be the more general favourite."

307. *To* William Ware

Munich   Sept   14th   1835

My dear Sir.

I did not think when I received your agreeable and very welcome letter that I should answer it from the capital of Bavaria, and at so great a distance of time too.[1] The truth is you allowed me too much latitude, and by giving me an indefinite time to answer your letter have nearly been the cause of my not answering it at all. You see what are the consequences of too great laxity of doctrine. I was charmed with the liberality of your notions on the subject of correspondence and have almost felt disappointed that I did not get another letter from you before I had acknowledged your first. I see however by the length of time which has elapsed that I am not to be so fortunate and therefore to extract another from you I send you this.

You are quite right in your conjecture that a travellers life is not perpetual sunshine even in Italy. The dirty habits of the people, the fleas, the booking up lodgings, getting into them and getting out of them, packing and unpacking, resisting attempts to cheat you, the being inevitably and helplessly cheated by your servants, the looking to your passports and waiting for them after you are ready to set out, making fatiguing excursions in hot weather and standing in cold weather on marble floors till you are chilled to the very marrow of your bones—these and many other little vexations of the same kind compose to[o] large a proportion of such a life to allow me to say that it is without its troubles. I have left out the beggars in this enumeration—How could I?—the noisiest, the most persevering, the most impudent mendicants on the face of the earth. I was glad to get out of Italy—and yet I had a most vehement hankering to stay. Italy is a most beautiful woman no better than she should be, and her suitors must feel the alternate admiration and disgust usual in such cases; until they become accustomed to her failings, and come to like them as some author says, "as well as their own."[2] You are wrong however in supposing that any of us are *yet* spoiled by our residence abroad—indeed we are more zealous Americans than ever, even to little Julia, who takes it quite in dudgeon that she is sometimes mistaken for English; and who stoutly denies that she even speaks English, the two languages she uses being according to her account American and Italian, to which she is now adding High Dutch.

My wife has taken this kind of life more to heart than any of us, her health has been more delicate than in America which has made her easily fatigued with sightseeing, and possessing like most American women something of the housekeeping faculty, she has been daily horrified by the abominations of the Italian domestics, and almost driven to despair by the difficulty of remonstrating with them and setting them right in a language which she was fretting herself to learn in a hurry.[3] She has been more at ease since she has arrived in Germany where every thing is as clean as mops and scrubbing brushes can make it, and where the sound of these instruments is heard almost continually in the houses. Indeed the perpetual washing and scouring of the floors is a serious evil— every day our lodgings are flooded and the air is kept in a constant state of dampness with the evaporations so that we have been obliged to remonstrate with the servant who performs this operation, on the excessive waste of water. Mrs. B. has had a serious attack of illness since she arrived here but is now recovered. The rest of us have been in excellent health and Fanny is quite happy in being allowed to thrum on the piano with a German instructress.

I am not surprised at what you tell me of the advance of luxury in New York. People there seem to think their only way to establish a claim to gentility is by a caricature of English fashionable dissipations. The folly has been gaining ground there for several years, and must flourish I suppose until it is fully blown, and the absurdity of it is apparent. To think of traders and brokers with their wives and daughters trying to ape the mode of life belonging to the most powerful, luxurious and fastidious nobility in the world! I have seen in no part of Europe such extravagance as in New York, no where such an unusual rage for following the fashions, for splendid furniture &c. Am I wrong in supposing that the evil will at length cure itself, and that people of sense, aware of the real purposes and true enjoyments of life, will at length cease to countenance such follies?

I have not been inattentive to the subject of some of the enquiries you put me. As to the present state of religion in Italy, I can answer only in regard to Tuscany, presuming however that what is true of the people of that province, is likely to be true of the rest. I was told that the upper and educated classes were generally sceptical, though they conform extremely to the observances of the Catholic religion, partly from habit and partly from policy. The labouring classes are very superstitious but not very moral. They believe firmly in the efficacy of prayers and penances, and in the intermeddling of the saints in the dispensations of Providence, but are too apt in conduct to copy the bad example of the priests who are for the most part ignorant, lazy and sensual. There are some exceptions to the character of the priests, but I was assured they are rare—however when the priest of a parish is of the right stamp, the difference between his flock and those of the others is very perceptible, —a proof of the docility of the people and the capability of moral education. The priests from their bad conduct and ignorance are held in contempt by the upper class and little reverenced by the lower. There is a strong infusion of low cunning in the Italian character, and I have no doubt that many would think as lightly of getting an absolution by lying a little to a priest, as of cheating an Englishman. A servant in my family who was always declaiming on the strictness of "our laws" as she called the requisitions of the Roman Catholic church and the danger of damnation incurred by a "christian" who should eat meat on Friday used I am fully convinced, secretly to devour meat on that day, but yet had the face on one occasion to come to me for a certificate to the effect that she had regularly observed the fasts of the church, telling me that it was necessary to her obtaining absolution. She used to confess but once a year alleging as a reason for not doing it oftener that a rascally priest had once revealed something disclosed in confession. In the ecclesiastical territories, the dislike of the priests often amounts to hate even amongst the firmest believers. I employed a Vetturino of Foligno, a very obliging and apparently honest fellow to convey me with my family from Rome to Florence. In passing by the Lake of Thrasymenas he showed us a spot near the battle ground of Hannibal and Flaminius, where the year before his carriage had been overturned and precipitated down a bank, and he with his horses his carriage and his passengers had been preserved not only from death, but all injury by the interposition of the Virgin Mary on whom he called for succour. He spoke of various other obligations he was under to the Virgin who according to his account appeared to take a great interest in his concerns. It was natural to suppose that such an undoubting disciple of the church should have some respect for its ministers but the moment he had fairly got out of Romagna into the Tuscan territory he began to revile the priests in the bitterest terms as the curse of the country, a set of tyrants and plunderers who governed in the most oppressive manner and maintained themselves in luxury and splendour by the most intolerable exactions.

In regard to the style of preaching in Italy I do not recollect enough of the article in the Foreign Quarterly to which you refer to say whether the account of it there given is correct. I will give you however what little knowledge I have picked up on this subject. In attempting to listen to the preachers during Lent, for this is the only, or nearly the only time when there is preaching in Italian churches, I was not always able to obtain a position where the speaker could be heard to advantage, a thing the more important on account of the foreign language. I remarked however in every case a sort of monotonous sing-song manner very much resembling that of some of our Baptist preachers, a manner which however, is not inconsistent with considerable effect on the audience. Their discourses turned very much on the peculiar dogmas of the church and very little on subjects of pure morality. A friend of mine, however, at Pisa, a lady assured me that she listened to a very sensible moral discourse in the Cathedral of that place and a very intelligent American at Rome expressed himself delighted with an excellent and animated sermon of the same character pronounced by a Jesuit. I cannot say that I heard any thing of the kind. At Siena I undertook to listen to a person who appeared from his robes to be some dignitary of the church who was holding forth in the Duomo, on the subject of the general judgment. He described the horror and despair of the sinner on that occasion if his conscience convicted him of unrepented sins, of having borne false witness, of having eaten meat on Friday, of having coveted his neighbours goods, and so on, mixing up transgressions against the rules of the church with violations of the decalogue and the precepts of Christian morality. At Viterbo where we arrived on a holiday, we found before the door of one of the churches, a man whose business appeared to be to drum up an audience, and who invited us to enter and hear an excellent discourse. We took him at his word and went in. A tall fresh coloured man had just mounted the pulpit. After a long exordium, he divided his subject into these two propositions. "1st. That the Saviour by becoming the son of the Virgin, lost nothing of his proper deity. —2nd. That the Virgin by becoming the Mother of God lost nothing of her proper humanity." As the manner of the preacher was not particularly attractive, I did not stay to hear how he proved and improved these positions. I heard no written sermons in Italy. Those who held forth had generally loud voices, a qualification for the pulpit common enough in Italy, where almost every body talks twice as loud and ten times as much as an American. There was no want of audiences on these occasions but they appeared to be almost entirely composed of the inferior classes. There are I am told some eloquent men among the persons who preach in the principal churches of the large towns during Lent. When this is the case a general interest pervades the whole population, and those spacious edifices are thronged with listeners of every degree in life.

In speaking of the religious character of the Tuscans I ought not to have omitted to say that there are persons among them who join an implicit belief in the doctrines of their church with a conscientious discharge of moral duties. An American gentleman long settled in Florence who has had occasion to employ considerable numbers of the poorer class, told me that he has met with a few persons of this condition of such constant and inflexible virtue as even to exalt his opinion of human nature. It is the more to be lamented that circumstances should conspire to corrupt and degrade a people among whom such instances exist to show what they would probably become under a better social organization both with respect to government and religion. I do not know that I mentioned in my last that I think very highly of the intellectual capacity of the Italians. They are in this respect a remarkable race, and I only wonder that they are not more debased than they are by the wretched government under which they live.

I found the English protestants in Italy almost every where provided with places of worship. At Florence the service of the English church was performed regularly every Sunday—this was also the case at Pisa, and at Rome there is an English chapel just without the walls.

You inquire whether I see any thing in the mode of observing Sunday in Catholic countries better than in ours. —In France—at least in Paris—I found little difference between Sunday and the other days of the week. The shops were open, labourers were about their daily occupations, and all kinds of secular noises were heard. In Italy on the contrary the shops are shut and manual labour is prohibited on Sundays, and on other holidays of the church, between which and Sundays no distinction is made. After the religious services of the morning are over the inhabitants of the towns proceed to some of the public walks and gardens and amuse themselves by walking about, observing the crowd and greeting their acquaintances. Concerts and philharmonic societies take place on these days; day theatres are open; in the evening balls are sometimes given, and the[y] take care to offer their most attractive representations. Do not, however, connect the idea of debauchery with the theatres in Italy as you naturally do in America. The theatres in Italy have no saloons, no drinking rooms, no places of rendezvous for young men and courtezans, and the audience are as well behaved as at a church. You will see a plainly dressed elderly woman, enter one of these places take her seat in the pit, sit out the representation and go quietly home again. All that meets the eye on these holidays is harmless amusement, there is no quarreling, no rating, no drunkenness. I have seen more disorderly conduct in one Sunday at Hoboken than I have in all the Sundays I was in Italy. Here in Munich the practice is not essentially different. Multitudes walk after service in the English garden, a pleasure ground several thousand acres in extent planted with trees and intersected with rapid currents diverted from the Isar—multitudes resort with their families to the beer gardens, where they are regaled with ill-flavoured bread and a kind of beer somewhat lighter than the strong beer of our country. Many betake themselves to the gardens of the Prater and of the Neuberghausen where there is music and waltzing under pavilions erected for the purpose. For my part I think that the church of Rome with her numerous holidays is quite right in her policy of allowing a part of them to be spent in recreation, for by this means the amusements resorted to are likely to be public and innocent, instead of being stolen and vicious, as Sunday amusements are apt to be in the large towns in America, where there is a good deal of gambling and drinking in obscure corners, and disorderly and infamous houses of every kind expect their greatest gains on Sundays.

I am glad to hear so good an account of what the upper church are doing. Mr. Dewey deserves all that you say of him. With him and Mr. Barlow you will make what they call in New England "a strong team." How does Mr. Arnold get on with his undertaking?[4]

You ask whether I have met with young Flagg in Italy. I heard of him at Florence but it was said that he appeared rather spoiled by the praises he had received, that he was altogether deficient in drawing, and did not seem to be aware of the importance of that branch of his art.[5]

I have little room to speak of Munich. However I am meditating a long letter about it which if it ever has the good or bad luck to be written will appear in the Evening Post. I sent a letter to be published in that paper giving some account of the Tyrol as I saw it on my journey hither. I will only say at present that Munich appears to me a very flourishing city, extremely clean; its inhabitants are industrious and with scarce an exception comfortably and neatly clad, and the ostentation of wealth, so far as I am able to observe is very rare. Perhaps this arises from the fact that the nobility are poor, if so they deserve credit for not being both poor and ostentatious as in Italy. Munich you know is one of the great patronesses of the arts—rivalling in that respect London and Paris— here is an extensive gallery of old paintings, a considerable museum of ancient sculpture and an association at the head of which is the king for purchasing modern pictures of merit and distributing them by lot among the members.[6] There are many fine public buildings and the king is erecting others one after another with a zeal which amounts almost to a mania, and which must require heavy drafts upon the treasury and of consequence upon his people's pockets. The climate of this region is as variable, and in summer even more so than that of New York. I am now sitting by a fire while I write.

I am happy to know that you are so comfortably situated in your new house. I cannot think that the situation is unhealthy. Chambers Street, you know, has always the reputation of being quite healthy and you are precisely in the same region. We often wish we could step into your house from our lodgings in Ludwigstrasse and meet you all in your new parlour. When you go abroad you will understand the intense desire to see the faces and hear the converse of old friends, which is felt I think in a much greater degree in a distant country like this and among people speaking a foreign language than it can be in any part of ones native country.—

Methinks I have written you a very long letter. I shall expect two from you in return. I take you at your word and shall expect you to contribute "of your abundance."

My wife and daughter desire to be remembered. Our best regards to Mrs. Ware. My wife joins me in assuring you of the sincere sympathy we feel on account of the calamity which has befallen your family since you wrote.[7]

Can you tell me what has become of Miss Robbins? We had a letter from her last winter which was duly answered, and we have heard nothing of her since.

Yours truly
W. C BRYANT

MANUSCRIPT: NYPL–GR (draft).

1. Ware's letter, unrecovered, was apparently written before March 1835. See Note 7.

2. Cf. Byron, *The Giaour*, 419.

3. Frances Bryant was of two minds about her household help in Italy. In September 1834 she complained from Florence, "I assure you that I have no small difficulty in keeping house with these dirty miserable servants." But by December, reporting her family "pleasantly situated" at Pisa, she could say with satisfaction, "We have an Italian servant, whom we brought with us from Florence, and whom we find so useful, particularly in protecting us from impositions, which we are subject to every step we take, that I think we shall not be able to do without her while we stay in Italy." Letters to her sister, September 24, and to Eliza Robbins, December 10, 1834, Letter-book, Homestead Collection.

4. Orville Dewey (1794–1882; Williams 1814, Andover 1819, Harvard D.D. 1839) was one of the foremost Unitarian scholars and preachers of his day. Associated for two years with William Ellery Channing at the Federal Street Church in Boston, he had subsequently occupied a Congregational pulpit at New Bedford from 1823 to 1833 before being forced by illness to retire temporarily from the ministry. In November 1835 he was installed as pastor of the Second Unitarian Church in New York. Though Bryant had left Williams College the spring before Dewey entered as a sophomore in the fall of 1811, they are said to have been acquainted "almost from boyhood." Upon Bryant's return in 1836 from Europe they began a warm friendship which endured for the rest of Bryant's life. See Dewey, *Autobiography and Letters*, ed. Mary E. Dewey (Boston, 1884), pp. 53n, 97–98. When William Ware resigned his New York pastorate in 1836, the Bryants became Dewey's parishioners. Barlow and Arnold are unidentified.

5. George Whiting Flagg (1816–1897), a nephew of Washington Allston, was a genre and portrait painter then studying in Europe.

6. This *Kunstverein* ("art union") provided a model for the American Art Union, of which Bryant was a founder, and first president in 1844–1847.

7. In reply, Ware confirmed on October 28 what Bryant had previously heard, that two of his children had died the preceding March. NYPL–GR.

308. *To* William Leggett[1]

Munich Sept 30 1835.

I promised in my last to give you some account of this place. The first thing that strikes a traveller arriving from Italy is the breadth and cleanliness of the streets, the bright exterior of the houses freshly stuccoed or painted, and the clumsy appearance of the steep roofs crowded with dormant windows, particularly in the older parts of the city, where I counted five ranges of dormant windows one above another in the roof of a four story house. If he turns his attent[ion] to the people he perceives that they are generally of a taller stature than those [he has] left, but he misses the intelligent countenances and erect air of the Italians, and begins to inf[er] if he has not already come to the conclusion, that nobody can fully appreciate the symmetry and intelligence of the Italian physiognomy until he has left Italy and begins to compare it with that of other nations. He observes that the women have a less decided taste for brilliant colours which agree so well with an Italian complexion, and that they walk badly. Little ostentation of dress meets his eye—no dandies—and altogether the people have a plain respectable burgess-like appearance. If the time of day be morning he will see numbers of neatly dressed female domestics passing to and from the market place with large baskets on their arms, wearing gloves &c. screening if it be sunny weather their delicate complexions with parasols—their heads bare or if it be a holiday only ornamented with the swallow-tailed Munich headdress of silver lace which covers only the knot of hair on the back of the head. —These women and those of the laboring class from which they are taken are the handsomest in Munich, the beauty of the females being here in inverse proportion to the rank—but they are dissolute to a degree I do not recollect to have heard of elsewhere. This is perhaps partly occasioned by the laws which forbid marriages unless the parties possess the means of supporting a family—and of this certain officers are judges without whose consent no marriages can take place. The consequence is that the foundling hospital is crowded. —The handsomest woman of Munich is the daughter of a woman who sells venison in market, and goes by the name of Die schöne Wildpreterin.[2] She may be seen with her mother at public places in a fine afternoon evidently from her air spoiled by the flatteries she has naturally enough received in a place where female beauty is not a common gift.

But if you would observe the people of Munich more closely you must walk in the English garden and its purlieus— The English garden is a pleasure ground of great extent nearly three miles in length and averaging nearly half a mile in breadth. Nothing can exceed the beauty with which it is laid out. The plantations of trees and shrubs are disposed with the greatest art to produce beautiful views and glimpses of views still more beautiful, varying at every moment, winding walks which keep within the thick shades conduct the pedestrian from one part to another, and carriage roads lead over the open lawns into the forest and out again in various directions. The parts not planted with trees are covered with a turf kept always beautifully verdant by the showery climate. A vast number of shrubs domestic and exotic give to the plantations a variety of foliage and shades of colour which is not commonly found in European forests. —Canals from the Isar the banks of which are so contrived that they seem like natural brooks flow with a rapid current in almost as many directions as the paths which traverse the garden. They are crossed by numerous bridges which are contrived so as to produce picturesque effects, and are sometimes broken by artific[ial cas]cades and in one place the waters are collected in a little lake spotted with [smal]l islands and with trees dipping their pendant branches into the water—. . . .

[unsigned]

MANUSCRIPT: NYPL–GR (incomplete draft) ADDRESS: To Mr. Leggett.

1. Intended by Bryant for publication in the *EP*, this letter was evidently not printed because Leggett had fallen seriously ill before it reached New York. See 311.2.
2. "The lovely venison-seller"; dialect.

309. *To* Susan Renner

Heidelberg – Oct. 11 1835.

My dear Mrs. Renner.

You cannot judge of the degree of our disappointment on being informed yesterday by M. Barrault that you had relinquished the idea of coming to Heidelberg this winter. When we arrived we were told that you were expected with the utmost confide[nce] and it was one of the principal inducements for our fixing ourselves h[ere] for the winter that we were to have the pleasure of your society.[1] I had been for several days l[ook]ing out for a house—and had just with some difficulty, for the place is full of English a[nd] other foreigners, found a house that pleased me not far from Mrs. B's and engaged it for six months, when I learned that you were not to come. Your friends the Barrault family were much afflicted by the intelligence—Madame in particular who had felt quite certain that you wou[ld] shortly arrive. My wife was frightened away from the [Köln House?] because she was told that you would not come to see her [so often as you otherwise would?] on account of its distance from Mme Barrault's where you were to stay. I can easily conceive that at this season the passage of the mountains, which I found so uncomfortable even at the end of June, might be dangerous for persons of weak lungs. Your friend[s] here I thought appeared to be much alarmed at the account you gave of your health and the post[pone]ment of a journey which you had expressed your determination to make, but we all hope that the change in your plans is not so much owing to any unfavourable turn in your complaint as from the advice of physicians who understood the clim[ate] of the country through which you were to pass in your way to Heidelberg.

You spoke in your last of passing the winter at Munich. I do not think it would have suited you. The climate is exceedingly inconstant passing frequently from extreme degrees of cold to extreme degrees of heat. The morning will perhaps rise warm in general, and bef[ore] noon you will be chilled with the keen and piercing air of the Alps. The alternations of temperature are quite as great and I am sure they succeed each other more rapid[ly] than any part of the United States I have lived in. I was told that complaints of the lungs are frequent, and the cause of much mortality. Then, as to the *resources* of Munich with the exception of galleries of painting and sculpture, and its theatre, I did not find them very great. I could [not] see the English literary journals nor get any English books to read—nothing but the petty gazet[te] of Galignani, which is so full of scandal about America and who treats our country as a backbiting gossip treats a neighbour against whom he has a spite.[2] —I had no acquaintances in Munich and therefore found a long residence in it quite dull. I judge from your letter that in Milan you have far greater opportunities of knowing what is going on in the literature of the English language than one could possibly have at Munich.—

Your friends here received us with the utmost kindness and have been exceedingly useful to us. They appear to me amiable intelligent, and deserving of your esteem which they return in a very high degree. I am much pleased with the picturesque environs and the woody solitudes of the surrounding mountains which however owing to the bad weather I have as yet trodden but little. I shall become acquainted with them as soon as the weather gets clear.—

The article in the "Atheneum" which you mention the biographical part at least, was probably written by Mr. Willis a young American, a poet, who I understand is now engaged in that journal.[3]

I do not think we shall be unpleasantly situated—There is something to be said in favour of a residence in small towns as well as of large cities— If large towns are the gayest small towns offer the best [ex]amples of national character. Large towns are too much alike in modes of life and manners; small ones preserve what is peculiar to the country. In large towns you study human nature more in masses—in small you analyze the individual—with much more that an ingenious person might I suppose say on the subject.—

My *numerous* family are all in excellent health.[4] My wife who had become terribly thin is picking up again—her stomach has wonderfully enlarged its [functions?] of reception and digestion within a short time past and I expect to present her to you in the [spr]ing when you come hence in better case than you have seen her. —In the mean time I [ho]pe it is unnecessary to repeat my injunctions that you should get [we]ll as soon as possible. There is the book on America yet to be written and that is no light matter. —The Atlantic is to be crossed and an extensive country to be explored "many cities and many men" to be visited and a lively and witty and withal a full true and impartial account of America and the Americans [to] be given.

Bry.—

MANUSCRIPT: NYPL–GR (draft) ADDRESS: To Mrs. Renner / Hotel de la [Ville?] / Milan. ENDORSED (by Bryant): My Letter to / Mrs. Renner / Oct. 11, 1835—.

1. The Bryants left Munich on October 2 and, passing through Ulm, Stuttgart, and Karlsruhe, reached Heidelberg October 6. Here they stayed at the King of Portugal Hotel until November 1, and then began housekeeping at 266 Friedrichstrasse. Frances Bryant, "Autobiographical Sketch," NYPL–GR.

2. *Galignani's Messenger*, published in English at Paris. See Letter 310.

3. Nathaniel P. Willis, associate editor with George Pope Morris of the *NYM*, was then a roving reporter for the paper with headquarters in England, where he also wrote for several British publications. Bryant refers to an article, possibly by Willis, called "Literature of the Nineteenth Century. America," in *The Athenaeum*, No. 377 (January 17, 1835), pp. 52–55, in which his poetry and that of James G. Percival were discussed at some length.

4. An allusion to a comment in the *Athenaeum* article that Bryant was a poet who had found the law uncongenial, and, "with a large family growing on his hands," turned to political journalism.

310.   *To* the EVENING POST

Heidelberg, December 9, 1835.

It is a source of constant vexation to Americans residing in Europe, to see in the publick prints, and hear reported in conversation, exaggerated stories of riots, Lynch trials, and violence of various kinds committed in the United States. The same story is often given in half a dozen shapes, and it is dressed up by the fancy of different journalists, accompanied with malignant comments, so that it passes for so many different outbreaks of popular government. The London journals have been quite diligent in this dirty business; the Tories had a political object; they wanted to show that liberal institutions are unfavourable to social order, and therefore seized with eagerness on every thing which gave a pretext for saying that violence has taken place of law in America; and latterly, the Whig journals, fearing that the radicals would attack the Peerage, have followed the example of the Tories, and have clubbed their wits to show that America is in a bad way, owing to the want of an aristocracy. It is droll enough sometimes to see what trash the Morning Herald, for example, rakes together for this purpose. "All is fish that comes to their net," from an assault and battery in the back-woods to a brawl amongst sailors in a fishing town. The American papers are searched and turned inside out for "horrid outrages." The French gazettes, the ministerial and Carlist particularly, translate a part of these precious collections; but the wretched jumble of paragraphs, which goes under the name of Galignani's Messenger, copies them with the utmost fidelity, giving its readers one or two daily, that they may last the longer and make the stronger impression. Sometimes the lesson for the day is a duel on the Mississippi, sometimes a riot, sometimes a Lynch case, sometimes a bloody murder, sometimes a simple horse-whipping; and, when nothing better is at hand, a diatribe against the government of the United States for not preventing its citizens from going to the Texas, where Austin's Colony is quarreling with the Mexicans, or a stale joke against the Yankees from the John Bull or the Age. Galignani's paper is almost the only one in the English language to be found in the greater number of the reading-rooms on the Continent; and nobody who looks at it daily, and takes its testimony for true, can believe that America is any thing but the seat of general anarchy, a place where no man's life is safe and no man's property secure; where an unpopular opinion cannot be uttered, except under the penalty of tar and feathers; where people prate about the liberty of the press, and pull down the printing offices of those who publish things which are not pleasant to them. The creature, whoever it may be, that holds the scissors for Galignani's paper, if without talent, is not without malignity; for while all this stuff appears in the columns of the Messenger, there is nothing of a contrary tenour; not a friendly or candid paragraph towards America, such as sometimes makes its appearance in some of the English prints, finds admittance. John Bull, on the continent, is greatly edified with this kind of reading, and gravely makes up his mind that "the Americans are unfit for a republican government." Upon my word, I heard one of them say so. The same stories, in their different shapes, find their way into the German gazettes, which are controlled by the friends of absolute government, and a prejudice is raised against our country and its institutions. We are supposed to be a nation of rowdies, gougers, and Lynchers, and a professor of law in the University of Heidelberg, the other day, in the course of a lecture, alluded to the United States as a country where fist-law, *Faust-recht*, took the place of common law and statute. Some honest people there are, who suspect that all this is not right, that there is exaggeration some where, and that those who collect all these stories are only striving to make out a case against republican institutions; but in the meantime the injury to the American character abroad, and to the cause of freedom in general, is great. The misfortune is, that a part of what is laid to our charge is true, and that disorders have been perpetrated in America, which can neither be denied nor excused; but our accusers will not allow that they are the result of a temporary excitement—a diseased state of feeling which cannot last; they will not consider the long period which has passed under our institutions, when such excesses were never heard of, nor seen; that they are no more the result of our form of government, than a scuffle between schoolboys is the result of our form of government.[1] Nothing can exceed the glee of the partizans of despotism at finding this "hole in our coat." An American gentleman at Munich, told me, that he never took up an European newspaper without fear and trambling, lest his countrymen had given some new occasion for scandal, and scarcely ever laid it down without a sense of indignation at the exaggeration and unfairness of the journalists, whenever the affairs of our country are in question. We are all looking with patience for the time, when the fever at home will be over, and our country will recover its former reputation for being that in which individual rights are most sacredly respected.

MANUSCRIPT: Unrecovered TEXT: *EP* for January 26, 1836.

1. Bryant alludes here to the disorders caused by anti-Negro and anti-Catholic mobs in New York and other eastern cities in 1834–1835. Leggett repeatedly excoriated in *EP* editorials those responsible for these riots, whom he called "a motley assemblage of infuriated and besotted ruffians, animated with a hellish spirit," to whom "the cabin of the poor negro, and the temples dedicated to the service of the living God, are alike the objects of their blind fury." *EP*, July 12, 1834. See also "The O'Connell Guards," *EP*, June 25, 1835.

311. *To* Susan Renner

Heidelberg Jan 25.—1836.

My dear Mrs. Renner

I hope the languor and apathy of which you speak is only a season of repose which Nature has prudently allowed herself in order to recover from the exhaustion of sickness, and that by and by you will feel the advantage of this, in finding yourself restored to all that cheerfulness and vivacity of spirits which you had in your happiest days. Pisa is not certainly an ill chosen place for this slumber of the intellect, —if yours does indeed slumber, of which I see no evidence in your letter.[1] The quiet of the place, and the drowsy effect of its atmosphere are recommendations to invalids of a too excitable temperament.

I am obliged to leave Europe very unexpectedly on account of the illness of a friend who had the management of my affairs, and of whose death I shall probably hear before I arrive at Havre.[2] I set out tomorrow, much to my regret, for I had hoped to pass this and the next winter in Europe. Whether I shall ever return is problematical. My wife and "numerous family" remain behind until Spring—perhaps they will even pass the summer in Europe.[3] If I can so arrange my affairs as to return I shall do so, but this is extremely doubtful. I hope however still to be allowed the pleasure of your correspondence. A letter sent to Leghorn would reach me in New York, though it would have a quicker passage from one of the French ports particularly Havre. I shall look with extreme interest for tidings of your welfare, and it will be a cause of the greatest satisfaction if I am permitted to believe that a friendly remembrance of me remains among richly endowed minds in a distant hemisphere.—

The winter of Heidelberg has been uncommonly rigorous so say the *Einwohner* [inhabitants], and it is perhaps fortunate that you did not execute your plan of coming here in the autumn. The season is beginning to grow milder and I had promised myself much pleasure in watching the progress of spring among these mountains and glens. I had Mannheim to see, and a visit to make to Erbach, and I had thought of crossing the Swiss Alps in the course of the summer and seeing Turin Milan and the Lake of Como all of which I left out of my first journey in Italy. If you had not previously gone to the northward we should have met you on the borders of this lake. I must now give up all these and return to occupations somewhat ungrateful—the common lot.

I am glad you like Brown.[4] He is original and very fine in his way. I suppose you only jest, when you talk of going to America, yet I should not be much afraid of the effect of our institutions and modes of life on a mind like yours. You would pardon some things which you might not like, for the sake of others which you would consider of the highest value. Minds of the common European stamp I believe are not apt to like our country.

I leave this letter to be finished and forwarded by my wife[5]—and bid you farewell with the most cordial wishes for the recovery of your health and cheerfulness.

Yours sincerely
W. C. BRYANT.

MANUSCRIPT: NYPL–GR (draft).

1. Unrecovered.

2. About October 15, 1835, William Leggett developed a "bilious fever of a high grade" from which it was feared he would not recover. This was reported to Bryant by Michael Burnham, Jr., then acting in his father's former capacity as business manager of the *EP*, in a letter dated November 6 which Bryant endorsed as received at Heidelberg on December 8. In Leggett's absence, Burnham wrote, Theodore Sedgwick III agreed to provide leading editorials, and Henry Anderson, Bryant's former associate in the *NYR*, would "furnish something every day on political economy." NYPL–BG. Bryant was seemingly reassured at first that the paper would not suffer immediately, for there is no evidence of his alarm before January 18, when he told Clara Crowninshield that "he had received bad news, that his partner was very sick and that he expected to be obliged to go home immediately." Henry Longfellow spent that evening at the Bryants', noting later that Bryant had "received several letters from America, with news, which require his immediate return." Crowninshield, *Diary*, p. 220; Longfellow, manuscript "Journal, May 21, 1835—July 17, 1836," LH. The letters Longfellow mentions are unrecovered, but one may suppose they reported the setback suffered

by Leggett after an earlier partial recovery. See Henry J. Anderson to Bryant, January 22 [1836], NYPL–BG.

3. On December 11, 1835, Longfellow had arrived at Heidelberg, less than two weeks after the death at Rotterdam of his young wife, Mary Potter Longfellow, during what had been planned as a study tour of Europe to last a year and a half. With Longfellow was his wife's companion on that journey, Clara Crowninshield (1811–1907). Hearing the Bryants were in Heidelberg for the winter, she and Henry sought them out at once, found them companionable, and for six weeks were much in their company. Bryant and Longfellow took long walks together over the hills, and Longfellow liked the older poet "exceedingly"; Clara found herself drawn toward the Bryant family "more and more," and felt as if she had "always known them." When she learned that Bryant must go home, perhaps taking his family, she shed "bitter tears." But within two days it was decided that Frances and her daughters would remain at Heidelberg, and Clara began happily to "lay plans about going together." Crowninshield, *Diary*, pp. 199–222, *passim*; Longfellow, "Journal, May 21, 1835—July 17, 1836," LH. Bryant left Heidelberg on January 25, the day this letter was written to Mrs. Renner.

4. Lacking Mrs. Renner's letter, one may assume that she had been reading the writings of Charles Brockden Brown (1771–1810), the American author of *Wieland* (1798) and other novels.

5. This letter is entirely in Frances Bryant's handwriting.

312. *To* Frances F. Bryant

Paris Jan 30 1836.

My dear Frances,

I arrived here last evening and took lodging at the Hotel des Etrangers in the Rue Vivienne, a comfortable and rather well conducted public house and not very dear. You see that I was five days in arriving. At Carlsruhe I found my travelling companion waiting for me with his father and brother and sister, with whom I breakfasted, and who commended him very earnestly to my charge.[1] He is not a bad looking man at first sight, though with quite a Jewish cast of countenance; indeed you are struck with the blackness of his hair and eyes—quite blue-black—as somebody once expressed it in speaking of the people of southern Italy—and his very clear brown complection, but when you look at him more closely you perceive a kind of imbecile hanging of the under lip and a wandering of the eyes, as if he was looking about him for help or advice, or as if he turned them upon you in dread of reproof. I found him utterly irresolute and destitute of decision in almost every possible circumstance, perfectly infantine in all his transactions with men, and needing as much looking after as a boy of five years old. He speaks a little Italian French and English but it is difficult to make him comprehend any thing in either of these languages; so that I am frequently put to my bad German —this however may be owing to want of practice on his part as he has learnt these languages only from books. I saw nothing remarkable in the country between Heidelberg and Strasbourg. Of Carlsruhe I only remarked that the streets were wider and more regular than in most German towns. We passed the Rhine in the night, and arrived at Strasbourg at eleven o'clock. The *Malleposte* [mail-coach] was just going out, and we accordingly lost the opportunity of going to Paris by that vehicle— but Mr. Ratisbonne[2] had taken seats for us in the diligence which was to go at nine o'clock the next morning. We set out in a thick fog which hindered us from seeing any thing of Strasbourg—even the outside of the famous Cathedral. We travelled all day and all night, and the next day about eleven in the morning we found ourselves at Metz, an old German town where traces of the language are still preserved, though I am told they are gradually disappearing. Take the map and cast your eye over the road running from Strasbourg to Metz to the south of Nancy, and you overlook a tract in which the language principally spoken by the peasantry is a dialect of the German. When you go, however, take the road through Nancy, it is more direct. We were told that we must wait at Metz until four in the afternoon for the arrival of the Nancy diligence. I spent this time in looking at the town and the Cathedral a building the style of whose interior reminds you somewhat of that of Rouen, but the outside is disfigured by a front of Grecian architecture, and the figure of the building wants regularity. I should have mentioned that our road to Metz passed through the province of Alsace and through German Lorraine. Alsace has a rich soil, and is finely cultivated, and in the neighbourhood of Saverne is highly picturesque with hills and rocks and forests and plantations of fruit trees, and streams and old castles on the heights. When we got into [the] diligence a second time our party in the interior was composed of an elderly German who had lived thirty years in St. Petersburg, very noisy and with the spirits of a boy, a young French officer very civil but fond of wagging, a big blowzy cross Lorraine cook maid, a young Lorraine mechanic red haired and choleric, and our two selves. The old [German] kept up a terrible uproar, crowed like a cock, barked, imitated the sound of a trumpet, cracked his jokes on poor Zimmern, got him into a quarrel with the cook maid, quarreled himself with the cook maid, and then with the red haired Lorrainer, and finally made us laugh till we were tired, and so the farce went on till we arrived at Paris. At Verdun where we stopped in the middle of the night we found a confectioner's shop open in order to sell sugar plums to the passengers—the best in the world are made here. We passed through Ste. Mén[ehould] in Champagne the environs of which are one vast orchard of Apple trees and the villages the dirtiest I have seen though the peasantry are said to be the most wealthy in France—through Châlons badly built with many wooden houses but very neat for a French town, and embellished with a fine old Cathedral of the outside of which we had but a distant glimpse—through a part of Champagne, Pouilleuse, wide, arid barren plains, —through Ep[ernay?] a village remarkable for its Gothic church of the florid architecture which marked the decline of the order, and through Meaux where in the old Cathedral we saw the monument and statue of Bossuet.[3] In the course of our journey we had a glass of champagne on the soil where it is made. The roads were in the worst possible condition and we arrived at Paris a day later than if they had been as good as usual. Poor Zimmern was almost frightened out of his wits by the rocking of the carriage. I was not in the least fatigued by the journey. I have made my arrangements for setting out tomorrow at 5 o'clock in the afternoon for Havre, whence the packet sails on Tuesday.

I have a letter from Oakley of the 2nd of January, in which he says that Mr. Leggett is apparently a little better but that it must be long before he recovers if at all, that Charles Mason a young man author of the articles signed A New Yorker in the Evening Post is engaged to conduct the paper until my return, and that five hundred dollars is all that can be remitted to me at present.[4] In the letter is a kind of brief statement of my account in Hannah's handwriting from which it appears that on the eighteenth of November there was paid Mr. Leggett 220 dollars of my money, which is 110 dollars more than he was entitled to for the half year, and that there is still due me after remitting the $500, the sum of $249 on the last half years dividend. Why this was not remitted also no explanation is given but Mr. Hanna[h] adds a note in which he says that a letter giving an account of the transactions of the Evening Post goes out by the same packet that brings me Mr. Oakley's letter. My banker does not find any such letter among those which have arrived. The affair has been managed in a very slovenly manner. My share of the last half years dividend was $1490. The remittance sent me falls short by a thousand franks of the sum for which I have drawn on Welles & Co. I shall immediately send over to Welles & Co. 2500 franks which will leave 1500 subject to your order. If you have occasion for money I think you may as well take of Messrs. Zimmern to the extent of what you want until you arrive at Paris. I shall give directions when I send it over to have it applied as you direct. I find by Welles' account that Mr. Rand paid the money and it is set to my credit. I have written to him.[5]

When you see Mr. Zimmern tell him that his brother bore the journey very well. I fancy from something that he said to me that he supposes the dollars of America to be the same thing with the 5 franc pieces of France. Our dollars are the Spanish dollars and are divided into a hundred parts called cents. The five frank piece passes current in America for about 93 cents and the Spanish dollar sells in France for about 106 sous. I shall pay Mr. Philip Zimmern in American or Spanish dollars which are the currency of our country unless I am otherwise directed. Will you say this to Mr. L. Zimmern?

When you come to Paris I think that Meurice's will be pleasanter than the Hotel des Etrangers, being near the Thuilleries. Will you ask Teres[e/a?] for the Tailors Bill which she paid and keep it for me? If you do not intend to pay at the Museum after this month I suppose you must give notice that I am gone. Forrest is here, he has travelled through Greece visited Constantinople and traversed Russia; he has left off shaving and wears a beard like the Grand Turk. He was much surprised to hear of Leggett's case—he thought him recovering.[6] Tell Mr. Longfellow that I cannot remember the names of the Bostonians here. There was nobody I knew. Mr. Pierpont is travelling in Europe—but he is not now here.[7] I shall finish at Havre.

CARA GIULINA MIA. SII BUONA, ED UBBIDIENTE ALLA MADRE, ED AMABILE CON TUTTI. SPERO CHE TUA MADRE ME DIRA BUONE COSE DE TE NELLE SUE LETTERE.[8]

Havre   Feb 1, 1836. —We have arrived safe, and sail tomorrow, if the wind which is now contrary should become good. I was rewarded for an overland drive from Rouen hither by the odd look of the hamlets situated among their tall trees. —I have no further space nor time— Good bye—write to me often—give my regards to the Barraults, Mr. Stewart[9] and all our American friends—Love to F. and J.—

Affectionately

W C. BRYANT

MANUSCRIPT: NYPL–GR ADDRESS: Madame Bryant / No. 266 / Friedrichstrasse / Heidelberg / Gr. Duché de Bade POSTMARK: LE HAVRE / 1 / FEVR / 1836 / (74) POSTAL ANNOTATION: C–F–4–R / 23.

1. Bryant escorted to New York Philip Zimmern, son of a Heidelberg banker, August Zimmern, and brother of the Louis Zimmern referred to later in this letter. The Bryants had apparently seen the Zimmerns socially at Heidelberg. See Crowninshield, *Diary*, p. 248; Longfellow, *Letters*, I, 559, 562.

2. Unidentified.

3. Jacques Bénigne Bossuet (1627–1704), Bishop of Meaux, eminent orator, and controversialist over church doctrine.

4. This letter from Oakley, apparently an employee of the *EP*, is unrecovered. Charles Mason (1804–1882) graduated from the United States Military Academy in 1829 as top man in his class, and taught engineering there until 1831. Thereafter he was admitted to the New York bar. Practicing law in New York City from 1834 to 1836, he wrote articles for the *EP*, then served as its acting editor from early January to late March 1836, when Bryant returned to New York. Mason left the *EP* at the end of May, and soon afterward emigrated to Iowa Territory, where he was Chief Justice of the Supreme Court from 1838 to 1847, and subsequently had a distinguished legal and business career. See George W. Cullum, *Biographical Register of the Officers and Graduates of the U. S. Military Academy, at West Point, N. Y.*, 3d ed. (Cambridge, 1891), I, 419–420; Willard Irving, *Biography of an Iowa Businessman: Charles Mason, 1804–1882* (Iowa City: University of Iowa, 1963), pp. 1–9; Cullen to Frances Bryant, June 11, 1836, NYPL–GR.

5. Letter unrecovered. The payment referred to was probably the one from a London publisher mentioned in 297.4.

6. Edwin Forrest and Leggett were close personal friends; during Leggett's first illness and afterward Forrest gave him continuing financial assistance. See James Rees, *Life of Forrest* (Philadelphia, 1874), p. 148; W. R. Alger, *Life of Edwin Forrest* (Philadelphia, 1877), I, 373; Proctor, *Leggett*, pp. 243–244.

7. In 1835–1836 the poet John Pierpont was visiting Europe in the hope of improving his health.

8. "My dear little Julia. Be good, and obedient to your mother, and agreeable with everybody. I hope that your mother will tell me good things of you in her letters."

9. Identified in Crowninshield, *Diary*, p. 223*n*, as "an Englishman living in Heidelberg with his wife and daughters." Here he is called "Dr. Stuart," perhaps in confusion with the name of Dr. G. Verryn Stuart, who treated Mary Longfellow at Amsterdam. See *ibid.*, p. 135.

313.   *To* Frances F. Bryant

New York   April 1   1836

My dear Frances.

I have made it my first duty on my arrival here to make arrangements for your comfort in Europe. I find that $500— had been remitted to Welles & Co. while I was on my way to America. This with the $500 which I now send by the first packet that sails since my arrival will give you a balance of four thousand francs, that is, nearly eight hundred dollars and not far short of two thousand florins, subject to your disposition. I have written to Messrs. Welles & Co. to honour any drafts which you might make payable to the brothers Zimmern, and to pay you the balance on your arrival at Paris.[1] If you should want letters of credit on any place to which you may go—write them to that effect. Cut off the receipt above and preserve it with the other which you have.[2] In case of any mistake it may be necessary to show it to Welles & Co.—

I arrived here on the evening of the 26th of March after a passage of 50 days. I was detained five days at Havre waiting for a fair wind. We got out of the harbour at last but the wind which at first was favorable soon chopped about and blew in our faces for five days more, when, the gale increasing, the Captain ran into Plymouth Harbour. The entrance of this harbour is quite narrow and it is impossible to get out of it without a very favorable wind which did not arrive until seven days afterwards. I went on shore twice. Plymouth, Stonehouse and Devonport, three towns lying close to each other and containing about a hundred thousand inhabitants, are beautifully situated at the mouths of the rivers Plym and Tamar. The shores are bold and varied. Mount Edgecombe a nobleman's seat covered with fine trees, overlooks the water and a beautiful [basin] beside the Navy Yard at Devonport at the mouth of the river Tamar is filled with vessels of the British navy. Plymouth is talked of for its handsome women, but I saw nothing remarkable in the way of female beauty —I only took notice that all the women walked with remarkably swift and long strides and that many of them had red noses. From Plymouth to New York we had a rough passage during which I was sick the greater part of the time. I found myself the better however for keeping as much as possible on deck, and eating as much as I was able at dinner. In this way I kept up my strength and did not become much thinner on the voyage.

It was between eight and nine in the evening when I landed. I had my baggage taken to the American Hotel and set out immediately for Mr. Burnham's to enquire whether Mr. Leggett was dead or alive. I was much shocked to find Mr. Burnham gone.[3] They told me however that Mr. Leggett was recovering. I saw him the next morning; he is much changed in his personal appearance, sallow, dark emaciated with an expression of pain and anxiety in his countenance. He is getting well slowly however, very slowly, and thinks it doubtful whether he will ever regain his original vigor of constitution. I must therefore remain in America for the present and assume the management of the paper. I find the concerns in as good a condition as I expected, though a part of my money had been paid for Mr. Leggett's debts, which was the reason that no greater remittance was made me on the 2nd of January. I am now putting things into a better train and do not apprehend that any thing has occurred to make the paper less productive than formerly. I do not learn that the number of subscribers has diminished or that the amount of advertising is lessened. Mr. Leggett's reputation and standing in the community are much raised.

I found Mr. Sherwood grown rich and retired from his old occupation. He told me that your sisters and their families at Great Barrington were all well. Mr. Burt is dead. F. Rogers has been scalded to death by the bursting of the boiler of a steamboat at Charleston. He was about to be married. Mr. Ware and his wife are very well. I saw Miss Sands at R. Sedgwicks on Sunday and had the honor of a kiss on the right cheek. Mrs. Sedgwick is in bad health. The rest of your friends here are also I believe well. I hear that Mrs. Johnson mother of our friend Margaret who married a Mr. Twining is dead. Margaret has two fine children. She is gone or is going with her husband to Illinois where he is appointed professor in some institution.[4] The winter has been horribly cold here. The people have been smoking and drying themselves before anthracite fires and look quite sallow. Miss Robbins is in Philadelphia. I have seen Miss Martineau. She talks agreeably and with considerable sprightliness.[5] What do you say to returning by the way of England? The passage would be a little cheaper, for you could make an arrangement to pay only for the wine you drank instead of paying twenty dollars for wine as I was obliged to do at Havre. You might write to Mr. Rand, to give him notice and go to his house on your arrival at London. He could make all the necessary arrangements for your passage which might perhaps give you some trouble if you were alone at Havre. As I probably shall not cross the ocean again I am anxious that you should make use of this opportunity for seeing England—but I wish you to be governed entirely by your own desire in this respect. I am very anxious to hear from you and the children and impatient for your return. I do not regret however that you did not come with me. The bad roads, the rainy weather, the delay at Havre,

the long and stormy passage would have worn you all out. —My love to
Fanny and Julia and many kisses to Jule. Give my best regards to Mr.
Longfellow and Miss Crowninshield and to Mr. Barrault and his family.
Remember me also to Mr. Stuart if he is still in Heidelberg. But perhaps
this letter may reach you in Paris. Adieu—write often—and let me see
you as soon as you have finished your visit.—

Yrs affectionately

WM C. BRYANT

MANUSCRIPT: NYPL–GR ADDRESS: Madame F. F. Bryant / aux soins de Messrs   Welles
& Co   / Banquiers / Paris POSTMARK: BUREAU MARITIME (HAVRE) / 27 /
AVRIL / 1836 POSTAL ANNOTATIONS: 28 / AVRIL / 1836 / PAYS D'OUTREMER /
PAR LE HAVRE ENDORSED: (by Cullen Bryant) Messrs   Welles & Co. will / oblige
W. C. Bryant by / forwarding this to Mrs   B. / at Heidelberg unless she has /
given notice of her departure; (by Frances Bryant) date April 1st received May
6th.

1. Letter unrecovered.
2. At the top of this sheet is the following addition: "Duplicate / Recd   from
Messrs. Bryant & Leggett the equivalent in dollars of two thousand five hundred &
ninety eight 75/100 francs, which am't   we request Messrs. Welles & Co   of Paris to
hold subject to the order of Wm. C. Bryant Esqr—

New York 31 March 1836—

$2598.75.   Gracie & Sargent."

3. Addressing Bryant at Heidelberg on January 22 (NYPL–BG), Henry Anderson
had reported the death two days earlier of Michael Burnham, Sr., former business
manager of the *EP* and Bryant partner. Not having seen this letter, Bryant was of
course startled, but since he was aware that Frances would have read the news, he said
no more of it here.
4. William Sherwood owned the building at 385 Fourth Street in which Bryant
took lodgings two months after his return to New York. Rev. Sylvester Burt had been
Congregational minister at Great Barrington since 1823. Frank Rogers was a son of
Dr. Benjamin Rogers, Bryant's one-time office-mate at Great Barrington. Margaret
Johnson and her mother had been fellow-boarders with the Bryants in 1827.
5. Harriett Martineau (1802–1876), English journalist and economist, spent the
period 1834–1836 in the United States. She published her observations in *Society in
America*, 2 vols. (New York and London, 1837), and *In Retrospect of Western Travel*,
3 vols. (London, 1838).

314.   *To* Messrs. C. W. Lawrence and Others[1]

New York   April 2   1836.

Gentlemen.

It is unnecessary for me to say how much the honour you have done
me has increased the pleasure of my return to my native land, and how
high a value I place on such a testimony of kindness from hands like
yours. I cannot but feel, however, that although it might have been worth-
ily conferred upon one whose literary labours abroad had contributed to
raise the reputation of his country, yet that I, who have passed the period
of my absence only in observation and study have done nothing to merit

such a distinction. This alone would be a sufficient motive with me, even
if there were not others which I might mention, to decline your flattering
invitation.[2]

I am Gentlemen

With the highest regard and consideration

Yr obt. Servt.

W. C. BRYANT

MANUSCRIPT: Columbia University Libraries ADDRESS: To Messrs   C. W. Lawrence &
others. PUBLISHED: *Life*, I, 313 (with changes).

1. Within a week of his return from Europe Bryant was asked by two dozen fellow
New Yorkers to meet them at a dinner designed to express their "high sense" of his
"literary merits and estimable character." Among the signers of the letter of invitation
were his close friends Henry Anderson, Asher Durand, Fitz-Greene Halleck, Henry
Inman, Samuel Morse, James Kirke Paulding, Thatcher Payne, Robert Sedgwick, Prosper Wetmore, and Gulian Verplanck; others of prominence included Dr. John W.
Francis, Charles Fenno Hoffman, Washington Irving, George Pope Morris, and John
Howard Payne. Letter dated March 31, 1835, quoted in *Life*, I, 312. Bryant's reply was
addressed to Mayor Cornelius W. Lawrence, one of the signers.

2. Bryant's refusal is laid by Godwin to modesty *(Life*, I, 313), and by Bigelow to
a reluctance to appear, as had Washington Irving on a like occasion in 1832, as one
who had enhanced his country's reputation abroad *(Bryant*, p. 217). But Bryant suggests here other motives "which I might mention," and, reporting the invitation later
to his wife, he was terse and equally cryptic: "Of course I declined" (Letter dated at
New York, April 14, 1836, in NYPL–GR). One may, rather, suppose him mindful of
Fenimore Cooper's refusal of a similar invitation in 1833, when, as Bryant put it long
afterward, the novelist returned to find a chilly welcome in the American press for his
supposed criticism of American society while in Europe. See Bryant, "Cooper," p. 69.
Though Bryant had been absent from the *EP*'s editorial chair for nearly two years,
he did not disavow Leggett's furious attacks on monopoly, political corruption and
favoritism, financial speculation, suppression of free speech and assembly, and the
persecution of blacks, abolitionists, and foreigners—for all of which Leggett had been
pilloried in administration and opposition press alike as "impious," a "knave," an
"anarchist," and a "madman," and the *EP* officially "read out" of the Democratic
party. On the contrary, Bryant had endorsed his partner's policies while in Europe,
and written sharply to the *EP* of his shame at the excesses of the "genteel mobs" at
home (Letter 310). Now, returning to his editorial desk, he made Leggett's strictures
his own—in substance and vigor, if not in phraseology. It seems likely that a reluctance
to expose his friends to the opprobrium which was sure to follow was an important
consideration in his declining to let them honor him. See Leggett, *Political Writings*,
I, x–xiv; Nevins, *Evening Post*, pp. 145–153, 164–165; Schlesinger, *Age of Jackson*,
pp. 187–191; Bryant, *Reminiscences of EP*, pp. 329–332, and "William Leggett,"
Democratic Review, 6 (July 1839), 17–28.

Abbreviations and Short Titles

Adkins, *Halleck*. Adkins, Nelson Frederick. *Fitz-Greene Halleck: An Early Knicker-bocker Wit and Poet*. New Haven: Yale University Press, 1930.

"Autobiography." "An Autobiography of Mr. Bryant's Early Life," in Godwin, Parke, *A Biography of William Cullen Bryant, With Extracts from His Private Correspondence* (New York, 1883), I, 1–37.

Bailey, *Diplomatic History*. Bailey, Thomas A. *A Diplomatic History of the American People*. 6th Ed. New York: Appleton–Century–Crofts [1958].

BDAC. *Biographical Dictionary of the American Congress, 1774–1961*. Washington: United States Government Printing Office, 1961.

[Beers] *Berkshire County*. *History of Berkshire County*. 2 vols. New York: J. B. Beers, 1885.

Benson, *Jacksonian Democracy*. Benson, Lee. *The Concept of Jacksonian Democracy: New York as a Test Case*. New York: Atheneum, 1964.

Bigelow, *Bryant*. Bigelow, John. *William Cullen Bryant*. ("American Men of Letters.") Boston and New York: Houghton–Mifflin, 1897.

Birdsall, *Berkshire County*. Birdsall, Richard D. *Berkshire County: A Cultural History*. New Haven: Yale University Press, 1959.

Brown, *John Howard Bryant*. Brown, Elmer R. *Life and Poems of John Howard Bryant* [Elmwood, Illinois, 1894].

Bryant, Frances, "Autobiographical Sketch." Manuscript "Fragment of 'An Autobiographical Sketch' by Mrs. W. C. Bryant," Goddard–Roslyn Collection, New York Public Library.

Bryant, Sarah Snell, "Diary." From 1793 until shortly before her death in 1847 Cullen Bryant's mother kept a daily diary. Manuscript portions of this are in the Bureau County Historical Society at Princeton, Illinois; published selections have appeared in Amanda Mathews, "The Diary of a Poet's Mother," *The Magazine of History*, 2 (September 1905), 206–209, and in George V. Bohman, "A Poet's Mother: Sarah Snell Bryant in Illinois," *Journal of the Illinois State Historical Society*, 33 (June 1940), 166–189. A manuscript memorandum, by Arthur Bryant, of important events recorded in this diary before 1820 is in the Bureau County Historical Society.

Bryant, "Cooper." Bryant, William Cullen. "James Fenimore Cooper, A Discourse on His Life, Genius and Writings, Delivered at Metropolitan Hall, New York, February 25, 1852," in *Orations and Addresses by William Cullen Bryant* (New York, 1873), pp. 45–91.

Bryant, *Reminiscences of EP*. Bryant, William Cullen. *Reminiscences of the Evening Post: Extracted from the Evening Post of November 15, 1851. With Additions and Corrections by the Writer*. New York: Wm. C. Bryant & Co., Printers, 1851. Reprinted in Bigelow, *Bryant*, pp. 312–342.

Bryant, "Verplanck." Bryant, William Cullen. "Gulian Crommelin Verplanck, A Discourse on His Life, Character and Writings, Delivered Before the New York Historical Society, May 17, 1870," in *Orations and Addresses by William Cullen Bryant* (New York, 1873), pp. 197–258.

Bryant II, "The Middle Years." Bryant, William Cullen II. "Bryant: The Middle Years; A Study in Cultural Fellowship." Unpublished Ph.D. diss., Columbia University, 1954.

Bryant II, "Poetry and Painting." Bryant, William Cullen II, "Poetry and Painting: A Love Affair of Long Ago," *American Quarterly*, 22 (Winter 1970), 859–882.

Bryant II, "Thanatopsis." Bryant, William Cullen II, "The Genesis of 'Thanatopsis,'" *New England Quarterly*, 21 (June 1948), 163–184.

Bryant Record. The *Bryant Record for 1895–96–97–98: Being the Proceedings of the Bryant Association, at its First Four Annual Reunions, Held at Princeton, Illinois.* Princeton, Illinois, 1898.

Callow, *Kindred Spirits.* Callow, James T. *Kindred Spirits: Knickerbocker Writers and American Artists 1807–1855.* Chapel Hill: University of North Carolina Press, 1967.

Crowninshield, *Diary.* The *Diary of Clara Crowninshield: A European Tour with Longfellow 1835–1836.* Ed. Andrew Hilen. Seattle: University of Washington Press, 1956.

DAA. Groce, George C., and Wallace, David H. *The New-York Historical Society's Dictionary of Artists in America 1564–1860.* New Haven and London: Yale University Press [1957].

Dexter, *Graduates of Yale.* Dexter, Franklin Bowditch. *Biographical Sketches of the Graduates of Yale College, with Annals of the College History.* 6 vols. and suppl. New York and New Haven: Yale University, 1885–1912, 1913.

Drake, *Dictionary of American Biography.* Drake, Francis S. *Dictionary of American Biography Including Men of the Time.* Boston, 1872.

EP. New York *Evening Post.*

"*Evening Post* Accounts." Manuscript record of semi-annual dividends of the New York *Evening Post,* 1828–1849, with a record of shareholders and stock transfers, in the Goddard–Roslyn Collection, New York Public Library.

Exman, *Brothers Harper.* Exman, Eugene. *The Brothers Harper: A Unique Publishing Partnership and Its Impact Upon the Cultural Life of America from 1817 to 1853.* New York: Harper & Row [1965].

Fitzlyon, *Libertine Librettist.* Fitzlyon, April. *The Libertine Librettist: A Biography of Mozart's Librettist Lorenzo da Ponte.* New York: Abelard–Schuman, 1957.

Gardner and Feld, *American Paintings* I. Gardner, Albert Ten Eyck, and Feld, Stuart P. *American Paintings: A Catalogue of the Collection of the Metropolitan Museum of Art.* I. *Painters Born by 1815.* New York: The Metropolitan Museum of Art [1965].

Hone, *Diary.* The *Diary of Philip Hone, 1828–1851.* Ed. Allan Nevins. 2 vols. New York: Dodd, Mead, 1927.

July, *Essential New Yorker.* July, Robert W. *The Essential New Yorker: Gulian Crommelin Verplanck.* Durham, North Carolina: Duke University Press, 1951.

Leggett, *Political Writings.* A *Collection of the Political Writings of William Leggett,* Selected and Arranged, with a Preface, by Theodore Sedgwick, Jr. 2 vols. New York, 1840.

Lesley, *Recollections of My Mother.* Lesley, Susan I. *Recollections of My Mother, Mrs. Anne Jean Lyman of Northampton: Being a Picture of Domestic and Social Life in New England in the First Half of the Nineteenth Century.* Boston and New York: Houghton–Mifflin, 1899.

Life. Godwin, Parke. A *Biography of William Cullen Bryant, With Extracts from His Private Correspondence.* 2 vols. New York: D. Appleton, 1883.

Longfellow, *Letters.* The *Letters of Henry Wadsworth Longfellow.* I. *1814–1836.* Ed. Andrew Hilen. Cambridge: The Belknap Press of Harvard University Press, 1966.

LT I. *Letters of a Traveller; or, Notes of Things Seen in Europe and America.* By William Cullen Bryant. New York: Putnam, 1850.

McDowell, *Representative Selections.* McDowell, Tremaine. *William Cullen Bryant: Representative Selections, With Introduction, Bibliography, and Notes.* New York: American Book Company [1935].

Merritt, *Thomas Cole.* Merritt, Howard S. *Thomas Cole: Introduction and Catalogue,* Exhibition of the Memorial Art Gallery of the University of Rochester. [Rochester: Memorial Art Gallery, 1969].

Morison, *History of the American People.* Morison, Samuel Eliot. *The Oxford History of the American People.* New York: Oxford University Press, 1965.

Mott, *American Journalism*. Mott, Frank Luther. *American Journalism: A History of Newspapers in the United States Through 250 Years 1690 to 1940*. New York: Macmillan, 1941.

NAR. North American Review.

Nevins, *Evening Post*. Nevins, Allan. *The Evening Post: A Century of Journalism*. New York: Boni & Liveright [1922].

NYM. New-York Mirror.

NYR. New-York Review and Atheneum Magazine.

Only One Cummington. Foster, Helen H., and Streeter, William W. *Only One Cummington: A Book in Two Parts*. Cummington, Massachusetts: Cummington Historical Commission, 1974.

Poems (1876). *Poems by William Cullen Bryant*. Collected and Arranged by the Author. Illustrated by One Hundred Engravings from Drawings by Birket Foster, Harry Fenn, Alfred Fredericks, and Others. New York: D. Appleton [1876].

Poetical Works. The Poetical Works of William Cullen Bryant. Ed. Parke Godwin. 2 vols. New York: D. Appleton, 1883.

Proctor, "Leggett." Proctor, Page S., "William Leggett (1801–1839): Journalist and Literator," *The Papers of The Bibliographical Society of America*, 44 (Third Quarter 1950), 239–253.

Prose. Prose Writings of William Cullen Bryant. Ed. Parke Godwin. 2 vols. New York: D. Appleton, 1884.

Rusk, *Emerson*. Rusk, Ralph Leslie. *The Life of Ralph Waldo Emerson*. New York: Scribner, 1949.

Rusk, *Middle Western Frontier*. Rusk, Ralph Leslie. *The Literature of the Middle Western Frontier*. 2 vols. New York: Columbia University Press, 1925.

Schlesinger, *Age of Jackson*. Schlesinger, Arthur M., Jr. *The Age of Jackson*. Boston and Toronto: Little, Brown [1945].

Sedgwick, *Life and Letters. The Life and Letters of Catharine M. Sedgwick*. Ed. Mary E. Dewey. New York: Harper, 1871.

Smith, *Pittsfield*. Smith, J. E. A. *History of Pittsfield, Massachusetts from the Year 1800 to the Year 1876*. 2 vols. Boston, 1876.

Taft, *Minor Knickerbockers*. Taft, Kendall B. *Minor Knickerbockers: Representative Selections, With Introduction, Bibliography, and Notes*. New York: American Book Company [1947].

Taylor, *Great Barrington*. Taylor, Charles J. *History of Great Barrington*. New Edition. Great Barrington, Massachusetts: Published by the Town of Great Barrington, 1928.

Thompson, *American Literary Annuals*. Thompson, Ralph. *American Literary Annuals and Gift Books 1825–1865*. New York: Wilson, 1936.

USLG. United States Literary Gazette.

USR. United States Review and Literary Gazette.

Vail, *Knickerbocker Birthday*. Vail, R. W. G. *Knickerbocker Birthday: A Sesqui-Centennial History of the New-York Historical Society 1804–1954*. New York: The New-York Historical Society, 1954.

Van Deusen, *Jacksonian Era*. Van Deusen, Glyndon G. *The Jacksonian Era: 1828–1848*. New York: Harper & Row, 1959.

Williams, *Spanish Background*. Williams, Stanley T. *The Spanish Background of American Literature*. 2 vols. New Haven: Yale University Press, 1955.

Wright, *American Fiction 1774–1850*. Wright, Lyle H. *American Fiction 1774–1850: A Contribution Toward a Bibliography*. Revised edition. San Marino, California: Huntington Library, 1948.

"Youth." McDowell, George Tremaine. "The Youth of Bryant: An Account of the Life and Poetry of William Cullen Bryant from 1794 to 1821." Unpublished Ph.D. diss., Yale University, 1928.

Index

The numbers refer to pages.

Numbers in **bold face** denote the opening page of a letter addressed to the person listed in the entry.

A number in parentheses indicates more than one letter to the same person on the same page.

An asterisk marks a page containing principal biographical data not readily found in the standard works of reference.